DATE DUE

			PRINTED IN U.S.A.

Children's
Literature
Review

Guide to Gale Literary Criticism Series

For criticism on	You need these Gale series
Authors now living or who died after December 31, 1959	*CONTEMPORARY LITERARY CRITICISM (CLC)*
Authors who died between 1900 and 1959	*TWENTIETH-CENTURY LITERARY CRITICISM (TCLC)*
Authors who died between 1800 and 1899	*NINETEENTH-CENTURY LITERATURE CRITICISM (NCLC)*
Authors who died between 1400 and 1799	*LITERATURE CRITICISM FROM 1400 TO 1800 (LC)* *SHAKESPEAREAN CRITICISM (SC)*
Authors who died before 1400	*CLASSICAL AND MEDIEVAL LITERATURE CRITICISM (CMLC)*
Authors of books for children and young adults	*CHILDREN'S LITERATURE REVIEW (CLR)*
Black writers of the past two hundred years	*BLACK LITERATURE CRITICISM (BLC)*
Short story writers	*SHORT STORY CRITICISM (SSC)*
Poets	*POETRY CRITICISM (PC)*
Dramatists	*DRAMA CRITICISM (DC)*
Major authors from the Renaissance to the present	*WORLD LITERATURE CRITICISM, 1500 TO THE PRESENT (WLC)*

For criticism on visual artists since 1850, see

MODERN ARTS CRITICISM (MAC)

ISSN 0362-4145

R

volume 31

Children's Literature Review

Excerpts from Reviews,
Criticism, and Commentary
on Books for Children
and Young People

Gerard J. Senick
Editor

Sharon R. Gunton
Alan Hedblad
Associate Editors

 **Gale Research Inc.** • *DETROIT* • *WASHINGTON, D.C.* • *LONDON*

STAFF

Gerard J. Senick, *Editor*

Sharon R. Gunton, Alan Hedblad, *Associate Editors*

James A. Edwards, Michael Magoulias, Brian J. St. Germain, *Assistant Editors*

Jeanne A. Gough, *Permissions & Production Manager*
Linda M. Pugliese, *Production Supervisor*
Donna Craft, Paul Lewon, Maureen Puhl, Camille P. Robinson, Sheila Walencewicz, *Editorial Associates*
Elizabeth Anne Valliere, *Editorial Assistant*

Sandra C. Davis, *Permissions Supervisor (Text)*
Maria L. Franklin, Josephine M. Keene, Michele M. Lonoconus, Shalice Shah, Denise Singleton, Kimberly F. Smilay,
Permissions Associates
Jennifer A. Arnold, Brandy C. Merritt, *Permissions Assistants*

Margaret A. Chamberlain, *Permissions Supervisor (Pictures)*
Pamela A. Hayes, Keith Reed, *Permissions Associates*
Susan Brohman, Arlene Johnson, Barbara A. Wallace, *Permissions Assistants*

Victoria B. Cariappa, *Research Manager*
Maureen Richards, *Research Supervisor*
Robert S. Lazich, Mary Beth McElmeel, Donna Melnychenko, Tamara C. Nott, *Editorial Associates*
Karen Farrelly, Kelly Hill, Julie Leonard, Stefanie Scarlett, *Editorial Assistants*

Mary Beth Trimper, *Production Director*
Catherine Kemp, *Production Assistant*

Cynthia Baldwin, *Art Director*
C. J. Jonik, *Desktop Publisher*
Willie Mathis, *Camera Operator*

Library of Congress Catalog Card Number 86-645085
ISBN 0-8103-5704-6
ISSN 0362-4145

Printed in the United States of America
Published simultaneously in the United Kingdom
by Gale Research International Limited
(An affiliated company of Gale Research Inc.)
10 9 8 7 6 5 4 3 2 1

The trademark **ITP** is used under license.

Contents

Preface

Literature for children and young adults has evolved into both a respected branch of creative writing and a successful industry. Currently, books for young readers are considered the most popular segment of publishing, while criticism of juvenile literature is instrumental in recording the literary or artistic development of the creators of children's books as well as the trends and controversies that result from changing values or attitudes about young people and their literature. Designed to provide a permanent, accessible record of this ongoing scholarship, *Children's Literature Review (CLR)* presents parents, teachers, and librarians—those responsible for bringing together children and books—with the opportunity to make informed choices when selecting reading materials for the young. In addition, *CLR* provides researchers of children's literature with easy access to a wide variety of critical information from English-language sources in the field. Users will find balanced overviews of the careers of the authors and illustrators of the books that children and young adults are reading; these entries, which contain excerpts from published criticism in books and periodicals, assist users by sparking ideas for papers and assignments and suggesting supplementary and classroom reading. Ann L. Kalkhoff, president and editor of *Children's Book Review Service Inc.,* writes that "*CLR* has filled a gap in the field of children's books, and it is one series that will never lose its validity or importance."

Scope of the Series

Each volume of *CLR* profiles the careers of a selection of authors and illustrators of books for children and young adults from preschool through high school. Author lists in each volume reflect these elements:

- an international scope.

- approximately fifteen authors of all eras.

- the variety of genres covered by children's and/or YA literature: picture books, fiction, nonfiction, poetry, folklore, and drama.

Although earlier volumes of *CLR* emphasized critical material published after 1960, successive volumes have expanded their coverage to encompass important criticism written before 1960. Since many of the authors included in *CLR* are living and continue to write, their entries are updated periodically. Future volumes will supplement the entries of selected authors covered in earlier volumes and will include criticism on the works of authors new to the series.

Organization of This Book

An author section consists of the following elements: author heading, author portrait, author introduction, excerpts of criticism (each followed by a bibliographical citation), and illustrations, when available.

- The **Author Heading** consists of the author's name followed by birth and death dates. The portion of the name outside the parentheses denotes the form under which the author is most frequently published. If the majority of the author's works for children were written under a pseudonym, the pseudonym will be listed in the author heading and the real name given on the first line of the author introduction. Also located at the beginning of the introduction are any other pseudonyms used by the author in writing for children and any name variations, including transliterated forms for authors whose languages use nonroman alphabets. Uncertainty as to a birth or death date is indicated by question marks.

- An **Author Portrait** is included when available.

- The **Author Introduction** contains information designed to introduce an author to *CLR* users by presenting an overview of the author's themes and styles, occasional biographical facts that relate to the author's literary career or critical responses to the author's works, and information about major awards and prizes the author has received. Introductions also list a group of representative titles for which the author or illustrator being profiled is best known; this section, which begins with the words "major works include," follows the genre line of the introduction. Where applicable, introductions conclude with references to additional entries in biographical and critical reference series published by Gale Research Inc. These sources include past volumes of *CLR* as well *Authors & Artists for Young Adults, Classical and Medieval Literature Criticism, Contemporary Authors, Contemporary Authors Autobiography Series, Contemporary Authors Bibliographical Series, Contemporary Literary Criticism, Dictionary of Literary Biography, Drama Criticism, Nineteenth-Century Literature Criticism, Poetry Criticism, Short Story Criticism, Something about the Author, Something about the Author Autobiography Series, Twentieth-Century Literary Criticism, and Yesterday's Authors of Books for Children.*

- **Criticism** is located in three sections: **Author's Commentary** (when available), **General Commentary** (when available), and **Title Commentary** (in which commentary on specific titles appears). Centered headings introduce each section, in which criticism is arranged chronologically. Titles by authors being profiled are highlighted in boldface type within the text for easier access by readers.

- The **Author's Commentary** presents background material written by the author or by an interviewer. This commentary may cover a specific work or several works. Author's commentary on more than one work appears after the author introduction, while commentary on an individual book follows the title entry heading.

- The **General Commentary** consists of critical excerpts that consider more than one work by the author or illustrator being profiled. General commentary is preceded by the critic's name in boldface type or, in the case of unsigned criticism, by the title of the journal. Occasionally, *CLR* features entries that emphasize general criticism on the overall career of an author or illustrator. When appropriate, a selection of reviews is included to supplement the general commentary.

- The **Title Commentary** begins with the title entry headings, which precede the criticism on a title and cite publication information on the work being reviewed. Title headings list the title of the work as it appeared in its first English-language edition. The first English-language publication date of each work is listed in parentheses following the title. Differing U. S. and British titles follow the publication date within the parentheses.

  Entries in each title commentary section consist of critical excerpts on the author's individual works, arranged chronologically by publication date. The entries generally contain two to six reviews per title, depending on the stature of the book and the amount of criticism it has generated. The editors select titles that reflect the entire scope of the author's literary contribution, covering each genre and subject. An effort is made to reprint criticism that represents the full range of each title's reception, from the year of its initial publication to current assessments. Thus, the reader is provided with a record of the author's critical history. Publication information (such as publisher names and book prices) and parenthetical numerical references (such as footnotes or page and line references to specific editions of works) have been deleted at the editor's discretion to provide smother reading of the text.

- Selected excerpted are preceded by **Explanatory Notes,** which provide information of the critic or work of criticism to enhance the reader's understanding of the excerpt.

- A complete **Bibliographical Citation** designed to facilitate the location of the original book or article follows each piece of criticism.

- Numerous **Illustrations** are featured in *CLR*. For entries on illustrators, an effort has been made to include illustrations that reflect the characteristics discussed in the criticism. Entries on major authors who do not illustrate their own works may also include photographs and other illustrative material pertinent to the authors' careers.

Special Features

Entries on authors who are also illustrators will occasionally feature commentary on selected works illustrated but not written by the author being profiled. These works are strongly associated with the illustrator and have received critical acclaim for their art. By including critical comment on works of this type, the editors wish to provide a more complete representation of the author's total career. Criticism on these works has been chosen to stress artistic, rather than literary, contributions. Title entry headings for works illustrated by the author being profiled are arranged chronologically within the entry by date of publication and include notes identifying the author of the illustrated work. In order to provide easier access for users, all titles illustrated by the subject of the entry will be boldfaced.

CLR also includes entries on prominent illustrators who have contributed to the field of children's literature. These entries are designed to represent the development of the illustrator as an artist rather than as a literary stylist. The illustrator's section is organized like that of an author, with two exceptions: the introduction presents an overview of the illustrator's styles and techniques rather than outlining his or her literary background, and the commentary written by the illustrator on his or her works is called "illustrator's commentary" rather than "author's commentary." Title entry headings are followed by explanatory notes identifying the author of the illustrated work. All titles of books containing illustrations by the artist being profiled as well as individual illustrations from these books are highlighted in boldface type.

Other Features

- The **Acknowledgments,** which immediately follow the preface, list the sources from which material has been reprinted in the volume. It does not, however, list every book or periodical consulted for the volume.

- The **Cumulative Index to Authors** lists all of the authors who have appeared in *CLR* with cross-references to the various literary criticism series and the biographical and autobiographical series published by Gale Research Inc. A full listing of the series titles appears on the first page of the indexes of this volume.

- The **Cumulative Nationality Index** lists authors alphabetically under their respective nationalities. Author names are followed by the volume number(s) in which they appear. Authors who have changed citizenship or whose current citizenship is not reflected in biographical sources appear under both their original nationality and that of their current residence.

- The **Cumulative Title Index** lists titles covered in *CLR* followed by the volume and page number where criticism begins.

A Note to the Reader

CLR is one of several critical references sources in the Literature Criticism Series published by Gale Research Inc. When writing papers, students who quote directly from any volume in the Literature Criticism Series may use the following general forms to footnote reprinted criticism. The first example pertains to material drawn from periodicals, the second to material reprinted from books.

[1]T. S. Eliot, "John Donne," *The Nation and the Athenaeum,* 33 (9 June 1923), 321-32; excerpted and reprinted in *Literature Criticism from 1400 to 1800,* Vol. 10, ed. James E. Person, Jr. (Detroit: Gale Research, 1989), pp. 28-9.

[1]Henry Brooke, *Leslie Brooke and Johnny Crow* (Frederick Warne, 1982); excerpted and reprinted in *Children's Literature Review,* Vol. 20, ed. Gerard J. Senick (Detroit: Gale Research, 1990), p. 47.

Suggestions Are Welcome

In response to various suggestions, several features have been added to *CLR* since the series began, including author entries on retellers of traditional literature as well as those who have been the first to record oral tales and other folklore; entries on prominent illustrators featuring commentary on their styles and techniques; entries on authors whose works are considered controversial; occasional entries devoted to criticism on a single work or a series of works; sections in author introductions that list major works by the author or illustrator being profiled; explanatory notes that provide information on the critic or work of criticism to enhance the usefulness of the excerpt; more extensive illustrative material, such as holographs of manuscript pages and photographs of people and places pertinent to the authors' careers; a cumulative nationality index for easy access to authors by nationality; and occasional guest essays written specifically for *CLR* by prominent critics on subjects of their choice.

Readers who wish to suggest authors to appear in future volumes, or who have other suggestions, are cordially invited to write the editor.

Acknowledgements

The editors wish to thank the copyright holders of the excerpted criticism included in this volume, the permissions managers of many book and magazine publishing companies for assisting us in securing reprint rights, and Anthony Bogucki for assistance with copyright research. We are also grateful to the staffs of the Detroit Public Library, the Library of Congress, the University of Detroit Library, Wayne State University Purdy/Kresge Library Complex, and the University of Michigan Libraries for making their resources available to us. Following is a list of the copyright holders who have granted us permission to reprint material in this volume of *CLR*. Every effort has been made to trace copyright, but if omissions have been made, please let us know.

COPYRIGHTED EXCERPTS IN *CLR*, VOLUME 31, WERE REPRINTED FROM THE FOLLOWING PERIODICALS:

Best Sellers, v. 44, September, 1984. Copyright 1984, by the University of Scranton. Reprinted by permission of the publisher.—*Book Week,* v. 2, August 22, 1965. Reprinted by permission of the publisher.—*Book Window,* v. 7, Spring, 1980 for a review of "Mister Magnolia" by Margaret Walker; v. 7, Summer, 1980 for a review of "The Ghost and Bertie Boggin" by Eileen A. Archer. © 1980 S.C.B.A. and contributors. Both reprinted by permission of the publisher.—*Book World—The Washington Post,* May 12, 1991. © 1991, *The Washington Post.* Reprinted by permission of the publisher.—*Booklist,* v. 74, April 15, 1978; v. 75, March 15, 1979; v. 76, October 15, 1979; v, 77, April 1, 1981; v. 78, May 15, 1982; v. 80, November 1, 1983; v. 80, August, 1984; v. 81, February 15, 1985; v. 81, April 1, 1985; v. 82, January 1, 1986; v. 82, April 1, 1986; v. 83, February 15, 1987; v. 83, March 1, 1987; v. 85, January 15, 1989; v. 86, September 1, 1989; v. 86, November 1, 1989; v. 86, April 15, 1990; v. 87, February 1, 1991; v. 87, April 15, 1991; v. 88, October 1, 1991; v. 89, September 1, 1992. Copyright © 1978, 1979, 1981,1982, 1983, 1984, 1985, 1986, 1987, 1989, 1990, 1991, 1992 by the American Library Association. All reprinted by permission of the publisher.—*The Booklist,* v. 70, March 15, 1974. Copyright © 1974 by the American Library Association. Reprinted by permission of the publisher.—*The Booklist and Subscription Books Bulletin,* v. 64, May 15, 1968. Copyright © 1968 by the American Library Association. Reprinted by permission of the publisher.—*Books for Keeps,* n. 30, January, 1985; n. 39, July, 1986; n. 41, November, 1986; n. 45, July, 1987; n. 48, January, 1988; n. 49, March, 1988; n. 50, May, 1988; n. 51, July, 1988; n. 53, November, 1988; n. 56, May, 1989; n. 58, September, 1989; n. 59, November, 1989; n. 62, May, 1990; n. 65, November, 1990; n. 68, May, 1991; n. 75, July, 1992. © School Bookshop Association 1985, 1986, 1987, 1988, 1989, 1990, 1991. All reprinted by permission of the publisher.—*Books for Your Children,* v. 18, Autumn-Winter, 1983; v. 19, Autumn-Winter, 1984; v. 20, Spring, 1985; v. 20, Autumn-Winter, 1985; v. 24, Summer, 1989; v. 25, Autumn-Winter, 1990; v. 26, Spring, 1991; v. 26, Summer, 1991; v. 27, Autumn-Winter, 1992. © *Books for Your Children* 1983, 1984, 1985, 1989, 1990, 1991, 1992. All reprinted by permission of the publisher.—*British Book News,* Children's Supplement, Autumn, 1981. © *British Book News,* 1981. Courtesy of *British Book News.*—*British Book News Children's Books,* September, 1986; March, 1987; December, 1987; March, 1988; June, 1988. © The British Council, 1986, 1987, 1988. All reprinted by permission of the publisher.—*Bulletin of the Center for Children's Books,* v. 20, November, 1966; v. 21, October, 1967; v. 27, June, 1974; v. 30, September, 1976; v. 31, September, 1977; v. 32, May, 1979; v. 33, December, 1979; v. 33, January, 1980; v. 34, April, 1981; v. 37, October, 1983; v. 37, June, 1984; v. 39, November, 1985; v. 39; February, 1986; v. 40, December, 1986; v. 40, May, 1987; v. 40, June, 1987; v. 41, May, 1988; v. 41, July-August, 1988; v. 42, January, 1989; v. 42, March, 1989; v. 42, May, 1989; v. 43, September, 1989; v. 43, November, 1989; v. 44, March, 1991; v. 44, May, 1991; v. 45, April, 1992. Copyright © 1966, 1967, 1974, 1976, 1977, 1979, 1980, 1981, 1983, 1984, 1985, 1986, 1987, 1988, 1989, 1991, 1992 by The University of Chicago. All reprinted by permission of The University of Chicago Press./ v. XVIII, September, 1964. Copyright © 1964, renewed 1982 by The University of Chicago. Reprinted by permission of The University of Chicago Press.—*Canadian Children's Literature,* n. 2, 1975; n. 11, 1978; ns. 31-32, 1983; n 51, 1988. Copyright © 1975, 1978, 1983, 1988. All reprinted by permission of the

A Criticial Guide to Canadian Children's Literature in English. Oxford University Press, Canadian Branch, 1975. © Oxford University Press (Canadian Branch) 1975. Reprinted by permission of the publisher.—Hildick, Wallace. From *Children & Fiction: A Critical Study in Depth of the Artistic and Psychological Factors Involved in Writing Fiction for and about Children.* Evans Brothers, 1970. Copyright © by E. W. Hildick. Reprinted by permission of the author.—Inglis, Fred. From *The Promise of Happiness: Value and Meaning in Children's Fiction.* Cambridge University Press, 1981. © Cambridge University Press 1981. Reprinted with permission of the publisher and the author.—Martin, Douglas. From *The Telling Line: Essays on Fifteen Contemporary Book Illustrators.* Julia MacRae Books, 1989. Text © 1989 Douglas Martin. All rights reserved. Reprinted by permission of Walker Books Ltd.—Moss, Elaine. From *Picture Books for Young People.* Revised edition, The Thimble Press, 1985. Copyright © 1981, 1985 Elaine Moss. Reprinted by permission of the publisher.—Ray, Shelia G. From *The Blyton Phenomenon: The Controversy Surrounding the World's Most Successful Children's Writer.* Andre Deutsch, 1982. Copyright © 1982 by Shelia Ray. All rights reserved. Reprinted by permission of Andre Deutsch Ltd.—Sebesta, Sam Leaton and William J. Iverson. From *Literature for Thursday's Child.* Science Research Associates, 1975. © 1975, Science Research Associates, Inc. All rights reserved. Reprinted by permission of the authors.—Solt, Marilyn Leathers. From "The Newbery Medal and Honor Books, 1922-1981: 'The Egypt Game'," in *Newbery and Caldecott Medal and Honor Books: An Annotated Bibliography.* By Linda Kauffman Peterson and Marilyn Leathers Solt. G. K. Hall & Co., 1982. Copyright © 1982 by Marilyn Solt and Linda Peterson. Reprinted by permission of Marilyn Leathers Solt.—Snyder, Zilpha Keatley. From "Alternate Worlds," in *Innocence & Experience: Essays & Conversations on Children's Literature.* Edited by Barbara Harrison and Gregory Maguire. Lothrop, Lee & Shepard Books, 1987. Copyright © 1984 by Barbara Harrison and Gregory Maguire. All rights reserved. Reprinted by permission of Lothrop, Lee & Shepard Books, a division of William Morrow and Company, Inc.—Stoney, Barbara. From *Enid Blyton: A Biography.* Hodder and Stoughton, 1974. Copyright © 1974 by Gillan Baverstock. All rights reserved. Reprinted by permission of the publisher.—Trease, Geoffrey. From *Tales out of School.* Second edition. Heinemann Educational Books Ltd., 1964. Second edition © Geoffrey Trease 1964, renewed 1982. Reprinted by permission of the author.—Woods, Michael. From "The Blyton Line, " in *Enid Blyton: A Biography.* By Barbara Stoney. Hodder and Stoughton, 1974. Copyright © 1974 by Gillan Baverstock. All rights reserved.

PERMISSION TO REPRODUCE ILLUSTRATIONS APPEARING IN *CLR*, VOLUME 31, WAS RECEIVED FROM THE FOLLOWING SOURCES:

Illustrations by Jill Barklem from her *The High Hills*. Philomel Books, 1986. Text and illustrations copyright © 1986 by Jill Barklem. Reprinted by permission of Collins, an imprint of HarperCollins Publishers Limited./Illustration by Quentin Blake from his *Snuff*. J.B. Lippincott, 1973. Text and illustrations © 1973 by Quentin Blake. Reprinted by permission of HarperCollins Publishers, Inc./Illustration by Quentin Blake from *How Tom Beat Captain Najork and his Hired Sportsmen*, by Russell Hoban. Atheneum, 1974. Text copyright © 1974 by Yankee Rover, Inc. Illustrations copyright © 1974 by Quentin Blake. Reprinted by permission of Harold Ober Associates Inc./Illustration by Quentin Blake from *The Wild Washerwomen*, by John Yeoman. Text copyright © 1979 by John Yeoman. Illustrations copyright © 1979 by Quentin Blake. Reprinted by permission of A.P. Watt Ltd./Illustration by Quentin Blake from *The Improbable Book of Records*, compiled by Quentin Blake and John Yeoman. Text copyright © 1975 by Quentin Blake and John Yeoman. Illustrations copyright © 1975 by Quentin Blake. American edition text copyright © 1976 by Quentin Blake and John Yeoman. Reprinted by permission of A.P. Watt Ltd./Illustration by Quentin Blake from his *The Story of the Dancing Frog*. Alfred A. Knopf, 1985. Copyright © 1984 by Quentin Blake. Reprinted in the United States by permission of Alfred A. Knopf, Inc. Reprinted in the British Commonwealth and Canada by permission of Random Century Group Ltd./Illustration by Quentin Blake from his *All Join In*. Copyright © 1990 by Quentin Blake. Reprinted by permission of Little, Brown and Company./Illustration by Bob Graham from his *The Wild*. Copyright © 1986 The Ninety-Seventh Chariot Pty. Ltd. Reprinted by permission of Peter Bedrick Books./Illustration by Bob Graham from his *The Adventures of Charlotte and Henry*. Copyright © 1987 by Bob Graham. Used by permission of Viking Penguin, a division of Penguin Books USA Inc./Illustration by Bob Graham from his *Crusher Is Coming!* Copyright © 1987 by Black Bird

Children's Literature Review

Jill Barklem

1951-

(Also writes as Gillian Gaze) English author and illustrator of picture books.

Major works include *The Big Book of Brambly Hedge* (1981), *The Four Seasons of Brambly Hedge* (1988), *The Brambly Hedge Treasury* (1992).

Barklem is the author and illustrator of the "Brambly Hedge" stories, an immensely popular series of picture books for primary school children that features a society of anthropomorphic mice living in tree homes in rural England. Evoking the Victorian and Edwardian eras in her texts and pictures, Barklem presents her audience with a nostalgic and idyllic picture of country life. She also imbues her works with rural English tradition and family warmth and security, as each of her characters maintains an important role in the daily functionings and social well-being of the community. Many critics have noted the resemblance between Barklem's stories and those of Beatrix Potter; most of these commentators contend, however, that while Potter remained true to animal nature when humanizing the actions of her characters, Barklem has created a world of children masquerading as mice. Further comparison between the two authors has prompted criticism for what has been described as the excessive wordiness of Barklem's text and the cluttered detail of her illustrations. Others, while praising Potter's wit, have denigrated Barklem's text as dry and her characterization as shallow. Despite these comments, Barklem has garnered considerable praise from numerous reviewers who approve of the careful detail of her pictures. Crafting her illustrations with sepia ink and watercolor, Barklem is commended for offering much for young readers to discover through the patterned china, wallpaper, and fabrics, as well as the floral arrangements and other such features, with which she invests her work. Similarly, Barklem is noted for her realistic sense of scale—for example, small blossoms make large floral arrangements for the mice—and for the authenticity of her settings. Representative of these more positive responses to Barklem's "Brambly Hedge" series is Margaret Adamson's assertion that the author has created a "delightfully intricate little world" with "charming" stories and illustrations that are "perfectly detailed representations of community living at its best, filled with colour, warmth and busyness."

Barklem began her career in 1974 by writing and illustrating books under her maiden name, Gillian Gaze; she also provided pictures for works such as the "Haffertee Hamster" books by Janet and John Perkins and a series of collections of prayers and graces. During this period, Barklem also researched English customs, flora, and other geographical and cultural details for her "Brambly Hedge" stories. Her first four books, *Spring Story, Summer Story, Autumn Story,* and *Winter Story,* were published simultaneously in 1980 as individual volumes in a "miniature"

format. *Spring Story* introduces the field mice who comprise the community of Brambly Hedge, centering on the picnic celebration of young mouse Wilfred Toadflax's birthday. *Summer Story* features a wedding; *Autumn Story,* the search for young Primrose Woodmouse, who is lost and frightened; and *Winter Story* the festivities surrounding the Snow Ball at the Ice Hall. These four works were collected in the omnibus volume *The Four Seasons of Brambly Hedge.* Barklem is also the creator of two other "Brambly Hedge" stories, *The Secret Staircase* (1983) and *The High Hills* (1986) which were published as full-size volumes. The former involves the intrigue and excitement of a secret staircase and a hidden treasure discovered during preparations for the annual mid-winter celebration, while the latter is an exploration adventure in which Wilfred, in hopes of finding gold, accompanies elderly Mr. Apple on a mission of charity to deliver blankets to the voles in the High Hills of Brambly Hedge. These two works have also been published together as *The Brambly Hedge Treasury.* Barklem's series has sold millions of copies in England, and her creations have been marketed on china, greeting cards, and other products both there and in the United States.

GENERAL COMMENTARY

Margaret Adamson

The secret staircase is set against the mice's preparations for a midwinter's Eve celebration. Primrose and Wilfred look for a quiet spot to practise a recitation and find a hidden door opening on to a secret dusty staircase. Nervously, the two little mice climb the stairs and make an amazing discovery, which ensures a very successful Midwinter's Eve.

In *The high hills* Wilfred accompanies a party of mice taking blankets to the voles in the High Hills, who live under harsh conditions. Wilfred is convinced that there is gold to be found in the hills, and his attempts to find it lead them into danger in the unfamiliar mountainous terrain.

These are quality books, from the excellence of the illustrations, to the physical characteristics of the books themselves. The stories are charming, and the illustrations are perfectly detailed representations of community living at its best, filled with colour, warmth and busyness. The fact that the plants and animals belong to the northern hemisphere does not detract at all from the works or from the enjoyment of this delightfully intricate little world.

> *Margaret Adamson, in a review of "The Secret Staircase" and "The High Hills," in* Reading Time, *Vol. 34, No. 2, 1990, p. 8.*

TITLE COMMENTARY

Spring Story; Summer Story; Autumn Story; Winter Story (Brambly Hedge Books) **(1980)**

[*The following excerpt is from an essay in which critic Margery Fisher compares the Brambly Hedge Books with Jenny Partridge's Oakapple Wood stories, noting that both Barklem and Partridge were much influenced by Beatrix Potter.*]

The Brambly Hedge books are a tastefully produced series which recall the Little Grey Rabbit titles but as if they had been redesigned for the 1980s by Tricia Guild. The stories centre on a collection of mice and the pleasant world they inhabit "on the other side of the stream, across the field". Their neat country cottages are full of pretty fittings and furnishings—patchwork quilts, long, circular tablecloths and rows of pots with frilled covers—while the Store Stump, a tree stump where all the food for Brambly Hedge is kept, is stuffed with enough nuts, honey, jams and pickles to do credit to Arabella Boxer.

The Spring Story is devoted to Wilfred Toadflax's birthday and largely concerns a picnic which is secretly prepared for him. One of the many strengths of Jill Barklem's illustrations is the beautifully detailed flower drawings appropriate to each season which decorate the outdoor scenes: violets, primroses, apple blossom and blue bells for spring, honeysuckle, kingcups and buttercups, wild roses and forget-me-nots in high summer, hawthorn and crab apples, hips and blackberries for autumn. To any child close enough to the hedgerows to be able to spot the real thing, these books can provide good lessons in natural history.

The characterization of the mice is simple and not troubled by any real problems. There is a passing reference to Wilfred's naughtiness with acorn missiles. Primrose Woodmouse, the subject of the Autumn Story only has time to worry fleetingly when she is lost about the weasels before being found by loving parents and neighbours. It is a nostalgic picture of a rural idyll. The old order is preserved with Lord Woodmouse in his ancestral home (though it is a relief to note he is not above taking mint tea with the cook and that his wife Daisy is distinctly bourgeoise, being the daughter of homely Mr and Mrs Apple). Old Oak Palace itself is an intricate warren of staircases in an oak tree, leading to high ceilinged bedrooms with four-posters. Yet it is still sufficiently countrified to have stencilled borders on the walls, bunches of dried flowers suspended from the beams and a suspicion of Laura Ashley in the closet. In the kitchens the food has a pleasingly simple chic: these mice seem to enjoy French cheese; Provençal crockery adorns the Welsh dressers.

The encroaching autumn and winter prevents the illustrations from becoming too coated in sugary pastels. The darkness of the night among the brambles and toadstools and the slightly haunting shadows as the mice search for Primrose introduce a darker note. The wide sweep of the snow-covered fields in the Winter Story, contrasting with the warm firesides, toast and soup inside are very appealing. The series is to be recommended but parents should not be surprised if walks are delayed while every hedgerow is searched for signs of these delightful inhabitants.

> *Celina Fox, "In among the Hedgerows," in* The Times Literary Supplement, *No. 4042, September 19, 1980, p. 1029.*

C. S. Lewis's test of a literary theory of general application was whether it would cover *The Tale of Peter Rabbit.* It is unlikely that anyone would use a Brambly Hedge book for such a criterion. Many of Jill Barklem's pictures of hedgerow mice are very beguiling, particularly when seen by natural light. There is a meticulous sense of scale: a crabapple takes up as much room in a mouse's Welsh dresser as a pumpkin would in yours or mine. Primroses make an imposing hydrangea-sized flower arrangement. The thick, creamy paper which Collins have used makes the ***Autumn Story,*** with its reddening leaves, rose hips and blackberries especially sumptuous.

But some of the illustrations overwhelm with detail; the profusion is almost suffocating, particularly in the transverse sections of mouse-households. Can that be a mouse-loo with acorn for pull? Would that Heath Robinson cheesemaking contraption work? The eye, trapped in these tiny mazes, would like to get out and stretch, preferably by looking at a barren moor in the far distance.

Four at a time is no way to take these books. One Brambly Hedge per month or even per season, as appropriate, is probably the right dosage. These small masterpieces of book production should be savoured slowly, not swallowed whole after the manner of reviewers.

From The High Hills, *written and illustrated by Jill Barklem.*

But, oh that Jill Barklem had illustrated someone else's texts! Churlish of me, when she has been so prodigal of her talent, but it needs careful pruning if it is not to run rampant and use up all its early vigour. It is in the writing that one misses the salt of Potter or the spark of the present fablemaster Arnold Lobel, whose Toad says "Wake me up at about half past May".

The clue to the construction of a Brambly Hedge story lies in the little motifs above the title on each cover—a birthday cake, a strawberry-topped cream confection, a steaming pie, a cloth-wrapped pudding in a blue and white striped basin. Mrs Barklem is offering us the gastronomic delights of a sort of Platonic nursery childhood. Characters are introduced by the quality of their kitchens. Mrs Apple "was a very kindly mouse and a wonderful cook. The cottage always smelled of newly-made bread, fresh cakes and blackberry puddings". Each of the stories, apart from the autumn one, culminates in a huge feast and even the exception, in which a young mouse gets lost, ends with the safely-tucked-up Primrose being sung a lullaby in which "pies and puddings fill the stories". It is as if the young Keble Martin had doodled all over the margins of his mother's Mrs Beeton.

The naturalism is lovely, the food is lovely, the anthropomorphism is tolerable and every illustration would make Jill Barklem's fortune in birthday cards. But someone, somewhere should have remembered that brambles do scratch.

> *Mary Hoffman, "Rats and Mice and Such*

Small Deer," in The Times Educational Supplement, *No. 3360, November 14, 1980, p. 25.*

Barklem has aptly captured the flavor and color of each season in these homey chronicles of hedgerow life. The little creatures who populate Brambly Hedge are charming, whimsical, and folksy, reminiscent of Beatrix Potter's characters. There is a sense of family and country tradition, of warmth and security. The delicate pastels and rich details are picture perfect and utterly satisfying. The only problem is excessive verbiage, but children will enjoy listening to brief stretches read aloud.

> *Barbara S. Worth, in a review of "Autumn Story" and others, in* Children's Book Review Service, *Vol. 9, No. 5, January, 1981, p. 34.*

'Comparisons are odious', but the resemblances to Beatrix Potter's books, I would even say the relationships, of these small-format illustrated tales are so obvious that comparisons do become inevitable. Both Jill Barklem and Jenny Partridge depict, for the nursery years, small hedgerow and woodland animals whose adventures seem at first sight much like those of Mrs. Tittlemouse or Jeremy Fisher, in fact, resemblances come to seem less important than differences. There is, first, the way the animals have been humanised. Beatrix Potter's matching of character to circumstances was always exact. Foxes and badgers do sometimes indulge in territorial skirmishes; rabbits do invade kitchen gardens and fall prey to foxes; pigs are sent to market and ducks lay away from the farmyard. To come within stricter limits (since all Jill Barklem's characters and some of Jenny Partridge's are mice), Mrs. Tittlemouse's unwanted guests and the escapade of Tom Thumb and Hunca Munca are authentic, while the less literal adventures of Town and Country Mouse and the Tailor of Gloucester's secret helpers have the authority of tradition behind them. Jill Barklem's mice live in a natural habitat but their activities—a birthday picnic, a lost child, a wedding and an Ice Ball—could be used in relation to other animals with little alteration except in scale. Similarly, Jenny Partridge chooses a field mouse for a newspaper round, involves a vole in a culinary disaster and makes a mole into a cobbler; here, there is no essential reason for the choice of characters. Like most of Beatrix Potter's successors, the two authors reviewed here are writing not only *for* children but also *about* children (and a few grown-ups) disguised as animals, whereas Beatrix Potter had her eye firmly set on the animals themselves (the depicting of Mr. John Taylor, the Sawrey grocer, as 'Mr. John Dormouse', in *Ginger and Pickles,* was a rare private joke).

The short texts of Jill Barklem and Jenny Partridge at first sight resemble Beatrix Potter's in style, but neither can match the spare, selective quality of her prose. Compare her description of Jeremy Fisher's dinner-party:

> He put some sticking plaster on his fingers, and his friends both came to dinner. He could not offer them fish, but he had something else in his larder.

> Sir Isaac Newton wore his black and gold waistcoat.

And Mr. Alderman Ptolemy Tortoise brought a salad with him in a string bag.

And instead of a nice dish of minnows—they had a roasted grasshopper with lady-bird sauce; which frogs consider a beautiful treat; but *I* think it must have been nasty!"

with the description of fieldmouse Primrose's visit to the harvest mice, in Jill Barklem's *Autumn Story:*

> Primrose found the tiny front door, and went inside. It was very cosy. There was a thistledown carpet on the floor, and the neatly woven grass walls were covered with books and pictures. The two elderly harvest mice who lived in the house were very glad to have a visitor. They set Primrose down, gave her a slice of cake, and handed her their album of family portraits to look at.

Certainly Beatrix Potter had the advantage of writing about the world she lived in. Chairs and dishes, jackets and tools were chosen, for the most part, from things in daily use and so was the etiquette of social gatherings: no nostalgia interfered with the purity, the homogeneity of her style. There is no reason, of course, to criticise Jill Barklem and Jenny Partridge for allowing themselves the pleasure of nostalgia in evoking a rustic past, but the enterprise is a dangerous one. There is more than a touch of vulgarity in Jill Barklem's *Summer Story* in the description of the wedding of Poppy Eyebright from the dairy and the miller Dusty Dogwood, when Mr. Apple proposes a toast:

> "To the bride and groom! May their tails grow long, and their eyes be bright, and all their squeaks be little ones.". . .

Beatrix Potter's approach to children was sensible and totally uncondescending. She enjoyed watching small animals—at times, actually enjoyed their company—and invited children to do the same on equal terms with her. By comparison, both Jenny Partridge and Jill Barklem seem to be trying too hard to accommodate themselves to their readers: the gap between old and young seems at times very wide indeed.

The gap is least noticeable in Jill Barklem's illustrations, for where her text is rather laboriously devised and her plots selected 'for children', her pictures are, or so it would seem, initially made to please herself. There can be no doubt of the loving attention to detail, the evidence of long research, in the minutiae of her interiors, in particular—in pie dishes and casseroles, curtained beds and bowfronted grates, and still more noticeably in the mob caps and tail coats worn by her mice (though there is little precision and individuality in her depiction of mouse faces and forms. We have only to compare Lord Woodmouse or Mrs. Apple with Johnny Townmouse or Hunca Munca, for example, to see the difference). Jill Barklem's pictures are dainty, their colours beguiling and their atmosphere playful, but in her anxiety to get every last dish and candlestick into them she has lost, in many cases, the functional simplicity which makes Beatrix Potter's interiors such a joy. The full-page illustrations of *Spring Story* and the others are too crowded for ocular comfort. It is only in the small marginal pictures (for instance, in a vignette of Mrs. Toad-

flax toasting bread in *Winter Story* or pushing her exhausted son Wilfred home in a barrow from his birthday spring picnic) that the artist is forced to be selective, so that her artwork stands up far better to comparison with her predecessor. (pp. 3803-05)

Children will enjoy both [the Brambly Hedge and the Oakapple Wood stories]—I have no doubt of that. I would only suggest that they are in no way *alternatives* to the essential, classic works of their distinguished ancestor. (p. 3806)

Margery Fisher, in a review of "Spring Story" and others, in Growing Point, *Vol. 19, No. 5, January, 1981, pp. 3803-06.*

Collins [Barklem's English publisher] may have a money-spinner here. Jill Barklem's four little books of the seasons seem to be just what doting aunts are looking for at Christmas or birthday times: lots of colour, pretty draughtsmanship, and, as books go, cheap.

Each book takes a look at Brambly Hedge in one season of the year. Spring celebrates a birthday, Summer a wedding, Autumn the harvest and Winter a Snow Ball. The same mice characters appear in each and are portrayed, prettily dressed, with considerable skill. The drawing of wild flowers is also admirable, and Miss Barklem is particularly ingenious in dissecting trees in order to reveal the domestic economy of each mouse establishment.

With all this there is a marked lack of individuality. The stories, if it is not too much to describe them as such, are told in a very flat style, and the scenes, well drawn as they are, are conventional in their charm. There is an absence of true creativity, a lack of personality. Racey Helps, one might say, rather than Beatrix Potter or even Alison Uttley.

Still, it does not much matter what the critics say. These books will sell on sight, if not like hot cakes, at least like lukewarm pies. (pp. 9-10)

M. Crouch, in a review of "Spring Story" and others, in The Junior Bookshelf, *Vol. 45, No. 1, February, 1981, pp. 9-10.*

The Brambly Hedge books depict the seasonal activities of a community of humanized mice. Each story focuses on an event that involves the entire community: finding a lost child (*Autumn . . .*); festivities after a heavy snowfall (*Winter . . .*); a surprise birthday party for a child (*Spring . . .*); a wedding (*Summer . . .*). Whether working or celebrating, the characters form a harmonious community in which each has an important role. Although the books are small, the attractive illustrations, which portray all important actions and settings, are remarkable for their colorful and meticulous detail—down to the patterns on china or curtains. Outdoor scenes show colorful, carefully differentiated flowers and plants. The texts, while satisfactory, sometimes lack the attention to detail that distinguishes the pictures. *Summer Story,* for example, provides top-to-bottom views of a dairy and a flour mill, but a bit more explanation would help to answer possible inquiries on how things work. However, the everyday adventures of the mice, portrayed in typical childhood situations, should provide both entertainment and reassurance (kindly adults provide security) to young children, and the exceptional illustrations should give many hours of pleasure.

> *Anita C. Wilson, in a review of "Autumn Story" and others, in* School Library Journal, *Vol. 27, No. 7, March, 1981, p. 128.*

The Big Book of Brambly Hedge (1981)

Children who expect fantasy to be as precise as scenes from real life (and that is most children) will appreciate the map in *The Big Book of Brambly Hedge* which identifies the scenes of the mouse-adventures in the four Brambly Hedge books—Old Oak Palace, for instance, seat of Lord and Lady Woodmouse, or the Flour Mill and the Dairy Stump where Poppy Eyebright makes cheeses. Just as useful and enjoyable is a picture showing the various mouse characters picking blackberries, with a key to their identities. The blow-up of nine pictures from the original miniature books is less consistent. In the most crowded scenes (like the larder where Mr. Apple looks for sugared violets for small Wilfred Toadflax or the same Mr. Apple explains plans for the Snow Ball from the Store Stump) the enlargement is far more comfortable to the eye than the original illustrations and details which seemed too numerous now fall into place in the whole composition; in the Store Stump scene there are depths and inner rooms which for the first time take their proper place in the design. Other less crowded pictures (a scene from the Snow

From The High Hills, *written and illustrated by Jill Barklem.*

Ball, the Toadflax family's tree open to view, another interior of the Flour Mill) enlarge less well; colours have become blurred and outlines look haphazard and careless. All the same, the idea was a good one and the exercise in scale may perhaps suggest to the artist that at least in the miniature format she could do with greater selection of detail. (pp. 3960-61)

> *Margery Fisher, in a review of "The Big Book of Brambly Hedge," in* Growing Point, *Vol. 20, No. 4, November, 1981, pp. 3960-61.*

The British author-artist created four enticing fantasies about the tiny anthropomorphs of Brambly Hedge, books entitled *Spring Story, Summer Story, Autumn Story* and *Winter Story.* Now the publishers present a lovely collection of scenes depicting the activities in the magic forest in an outsized softcover with charming notes about Dusty Dogwood's flour mill, Lord and Lady Woodmouse's hospitality, et al. The text, however, is almost an incidental attraction. What children will want are the 12 big paintings that can be neatly removed and hung on a wall as posters, in full color and jampacked with delicious details.

> *A review of "The Big Book of Brambly Hedge," in* Publishers Weekly, *Vol. 221, No. 5, January 29, 1982, p. 67.*

The Secret Staircase (1983)

Jill Barklem's first four volumes of the mice of Brambly Hedge were greeted with somewhat faint praise in our pages although the reviewer did opine that despite such criticism they would probably sell very well. As indeed they have: to the tune of over a million copies and eleven re-prints.

This recent book retains the same formula. The pictures show the prettily dressed mice in their overcrowded rooms which fill so cleverly the tree trunk they inhabit. The story is of the finding of a secret staircase and a successful Midwinter party. There is of course a new Royal Doulton addition to their Four Seasons Brambly Hedge Plates Collection to match the new book.

Readers will welcome the larger style of presentation if not the increased price. Perhaps it presages the spread of Brambly Hedge into other areas of childhood interest.

> *D. A. Young, in a review of "The Secret Staircase," in* The Junior Bookshelf, *Vol. 47, No. 5, October, 1983, p. 204.*

Why can I, who grew up in the country and now teach country children, not 'respond to the gentle rural life of the mice of Brambly Hedge'? The latest in the saga concerns the Christmas festivities at Old Oak Palace—carefully secularised into 'mid-winter celebrations'—and is a predictable mish-mash of blazing fires, good old country cooking at its best, children dressing up, and a dollop of Enid Blytonish adventure. It is, I suppose, just conceivable that a few privately-educated girls in the lusher parts of Surrey might identify with Lord and Lady Woodmouse and their tiresome brood; everyone else would do better to hang on to their £3.95 and wait for spring.

> *Sue May, in a review of "The Secret Staircase," in* The School Librarian, *Vol. 31, No. 4, December, 1983, p. 348.*

With this book Jill Barklem's Brambly Hedge people come of age. It is a longer story set at Christmas time and has all the fairy tale magic of a Beatrix Potter like miniature world of mice who live in the depths of a tree. Lady Woodmouse is busy making carraway biscuits in the kitchen and the rest of the family are preparing the great feast for the traditional midwinter celebrations. A grand entertainment has been planned and Primrose and Wilfred chosen to give a recitation. Their search for costumes leads them to the discovery of the secret room packed full of treasures. Wonderful opportunity for Jill Barklem's exquisite detailed drawings—a magical book to give at Christmas time.

> *Anne Wood, in a review of "The Secret Staircase," in* Books for Your Children, *Vol. 18, No. 3, Autumn-Winter, 1983, p. 3.*

Holly, ivy, mistletoe, trays of food and a celebration by a fire conjure up a pagan midwinter festival in Britain. . . . This charming evocation of a midwinter festival (shorn of Christmas meaning) and of anthropomorphic mice living an elegant human-like existence in English hedges and an old oak tree will keep children spellbound. A mild element of mystery (a secret staircase and a myriad of snug rooms) keeps the story moving. The watercolor illustrations, soft, muted and reminiscent of Beatrix Potter, are done in such fascinating detail that children will pore over them again and again. There is a quality of believable fantasy about the drawings which enhance the equally believable fantasy of the text. A merry and pleasant tale with a reassuring picture of young life in Mouseland.

> *Hope Bridgewater, in a review of "The Secret Staircase," in* School Library Journal, *Vol. 30, No. 7, March, 1984, p. 138.*

The High Hills   (1986)

When mice Lily, Flax, and Mr. Apple set out for the High Hills of Brambly Hedge to deliver needed blankets to the voles, young Wilfred mouse begs to accompany them in the hope of finding the gold described in an exciting history book he has just read. The romantic adventure Wilfred anticipates becomes a fearsome reality, however, when he and Mr. Apple are trapped on fog-enshrouded peaks. But toting all of the gear suggested in the early explorer's tome and armed with his own resourcefulness, spunky little Wilfred leads his injured, elderly companion home to safety. Youngsters, particularly those fond of previous Brambly Hedge episodes, will delight in the mouse-child protagonist's saving the day and in the affectionately detailed illustrations that transport readers from the weaver's tidy shop to the mountain ledge, where Wilfred and Mr. Apple cozily spend the night, and back to the security of the little hero's warmly lit home.

> *Ellen Mandel, in a review of "The High Hills," in* Booklist, *Vol. 83, No. 13, March 1, 1987, p. 1011.*

Detailed watercolor illustrations beautifully underscore the story of Wilfred, a mouse who becomes inspired by reading an adventure book.

While on a short journey to a neighboring village, Wilfred gets a chance to save the day by using the exploring skills and "essential gear" he gleaned from reading his explorer's tale. . . .

The lesson is a gentle one: persistence pays off. Wilfred's insistence on bringing along his elaborate supplies is rewarded, and even the dust he mistakes for gold turns out to be a rare lichen that the villagers need. Young readers will enjoy this lovely tale and the illustrations, which are reminiscent of Beatrix Potter's style.

> *Nita Kurmins Gilson, "Mice Are Nice— Especially in Tales Like These," in* The Christian Science Monitor, *April 17, 1987, p. 26.*

The Four Seasons of Brambly Hedge   (1988)

> [The Four Seasons of Brambly Hedge *is an omnibus volume which contains* Spring Story, Summer Story, Autumn Story, *and* Winter Story.]

This wonderful volume . . . is full of nostalgia and an age that never really was. The anthromorphic creatures of the English countryside are vaguely reminiscent of Beatrix Potter but the illustrations are vastly more detailed and less aggressive than Potter's.

The key figures are a family of mice who are industrious, funloving and solid citizens of rural England. They capture the enchanted spirit of the late Victorian or Edwardian eras when God was in heaven and all was well with the world. As such there is nothing to frighten or threaten the young reader and Barklem's skill as a storyteller makes the stories very suitable for children up to middle or late primary school.

Parents and teachers who have not come across **Brambly Hedge** before will be as equally enchanted as the young readers. This book is a real feast both visually and aurally and will be treasured particularly on private shelves.

> *Howard George, in a review of "The Four Seasons of Brambly Hedge," in* Reading Time, *Vol. 34, No. 2, 1990, p. 14.*

The Brambly Hedge Treasury   (1992)

> [The Brambly Hedge Treasury *is an omnibus volume which contains* The Secret Staircase *and* The High Hills.]

Don't expect the mouse-characters to resemble Beatrix Potter's bad mice in temperament but accept a faint resemblance to Hunca Munca and his wife by virtue of the dolls' house background. The Brambly Hedge setting is carefully chosen as a suitable habitat, with oak, hornbeam and crabapple trees and plenty of collectable provisions like elder and blackberries, suggesting that the tales could be read as celebrations of the countryside, but the main impression is one of a dolls' house existence. However precisely Lord Oakapple's mansion and the stump where Poppy Eyebright makes her cheeses are described, the minutiae in pictures of food, platters, chairs and tables, clothes and toys suggest that loving manipulation of toy accessories that belongs to childhood. In this edition the two stories, prefaced by character-studies and explanation of the dwellings of the Woodmouse, Toadflax, Dogwood and other families, follow small adventures backed by immensely detailed woodland scenes. In the first, rustic Primrose and homely Wilfred, looking for costumes for their Midwinter play, find a secret apartment full of delectable antique playthings. In the second, adventurous Wilfred, inspired by tales of bygone explorers, is allowed to accompany a party taking blankets to the needy voles in the desolate hills; the lad is unexpectedly resourceful when mist traps the travellers. The plots are staples of junior adventures, used with a light tone, and the packed scenes have the perennial charm of the miniature. (pp. 5632-33)

Margery Fisher, in a review of "The Brambly Hedge Treasury," in Growing Point, *Vol. 30, No. 5, January, 1992, pp. 5632-33.*

Quentin Blake

1932-

English author and illustrator of picture books and fiction.

Major works include *How Tom Beat Captain Najork and His Hired Sportsmen* (written by Russell Hoban, 1974), *The Wild Washerwomen* (written by John Yeoman, 1979), *Mister Magnolia* (1980), *The Story of the Dancing Frog* (1984), *All Join In* (1990).

Blake uses familiar motifs—the folktale, the cumulative tale, the alphabet book, the counting book, and the nursery rhyme—to provide young readers with picture books that are considered original, imaginative, charming, and delightful. Lauded as a gifted humorist and storyteller whose books are both genuinely funny and keenly observant of human nature, he is also celebrated as a brilliant artist and craftsman whose deceptively simple illustrations in pen and ink and watercolor create character and mood with a minimum of line. Blake invests his works with a strong theatricality and fills them with zest and movement. Including elements of fantasy in most of his books, which he writes in both prose and verse, Blake often uses historical settings such as the Middle Ages and the eighteenth and nineteenth centuries to introduce elements of social history along with his broadly comic characterizations. Although he specializes in nonsense, Blake underscores many of his works with sensitive and often poignant aspects of the human condition. *The Story of the Dancing Frog,* one of his most well-received books, demonstrates this quality: recounted as family history by a mother to her small daughter, the tale describes how Great Aunt Gertrude, who has recently been widowed, is prevented from drowning herself by the sight of a frog dancing on a lilypad. Gertrude and the frog, whom she names George, become increasingly successful on the strength of George's talent and travel the world before retiring together to the south of France. At the end of the story, the child asks, "Are they dead now, then?," and her mother, whom Blake implies is herself widowed, answers, "That was a long time age, so I suppose they must be." Blending the fantastic with the realities of loneliness and loss, *The Story of the Dancing Frog* is noted as an especially resonant and touching story about friendship. loyalty, and love.

Blake began drawing as a small boy—"I wasn't especially encouraged by anyone," he says—and submitted cartoons to his grammar school magazine. His Latin teacher took an interest in his work and introduced him to her husband, *Punch* cartoonist Alfred Jackson, when Blake was fifteen; two years later, Blake became a regular contributor to *Punch.* He studied English at Cambridge, deciding against art school because of his desire to receive an education in literature. After three years at Cambridge, Blake received a year of teacher training before attending the Chelsea College of Art for eighteen months; during this period, he became a freelance illustrator, contributing cartoons to

Punch and the *Spectator* on a regular basis. At the age of twenty, he created his first children's book, *Patrick,* which was not published until 1968, and began to illustrate the works of other authors. Blake has provided the pictures for over two hundred books by such writers as Lewis Carroll, Sylvia Plath, Evelyn Waugh, Rudyard Kipling, and Dr. Seuss; he is especially well known for his illustrations for the children's books of Joan Aiken, Michael Rosen, Patrick Campbell, J. P. Martin, and Nils-Olof Franzen. His greatest success as an illustrator is perhaps reserved for the works of Roald Dahl, Russell Hoban, and John Yeoman, the latter a friend with whom Blake attended Cambridge and with whom he has cowritten some texts. As a collaborator, Blake is usually considered an equal with the author due to his ability to capture the nuances of their texts in his illustrations. Influenced by theater and film as well as by such artists as Daumier, Picasso, Degas, and Ronald Searle, Blake has developed a recognizable style which is characterized by its sketchy, dashing lines and glowing color washes. Praised for its fluidity and confidence as well as for its exaggeration, energy, detail, and quirkiness, his art reflects Blake's concentration on both the drama of illustration and portrayal of character. Critics are usually receptive to Blake as both artist and author:

John Mole dubs him "our street-wise Ardizzone," while Elaine Moss calls him "the genius who turns a difficult manuscript into a thoroughly acceptable and beckoning book." Naomi Lewis adds, "Any book which has Quentin Blake as an illustrator is in luck, for who can match his zany wit and euphoria, his engaging charm, his wild assurance of line?"

In addition to his books for children, Blake has written and illustrated a picture book for adults and has created dust jackets for adult novels. He also teaches illustration at the School of Graphic Design at the Royal College of Art in London, where he served as head of the illustration department from 1978 through 1986 and where he was later appointed Senior Fellow. In 1981, he was elected a Royal Designer for Industry and received an Order of the British Empire in 1988. Blake has been the recipient of several awards for the books he has written and illustrated: in 1980, he received the Greenaway Medal for *Mister Magnolia,* a work that was also placed on the International Board on Books for Young People (IBBY) honour list for illustration in 1982; *All Join In* won the Emil/Kurt Maschler Award in 1991, and *The Story of the Dancing Frog* was a runner-up for this award in 1985. Blake has also won several prizes for his collaborations: *How Tom Beat Captain Najork and His Hired Sportsmen* was placed on the IBBY honour list for illustration in 1976, while *The Wild Washerwomen* was highly commended for the Greenaway Medal in 1979. *Rumbelow's Dance,* another collaboration with John Yeoman, was a runner-up for the Emil/Kurt Maschler Award in 1980, while *The Giraffe and the Pelly and Me,* a work written by Roald Dahl, and *The Rain Door,* a book written by Russell Hoban, received the same status in 1985 and 1986 respectively. Blake was also the recipient of Holland's Silver Pencil in 1986 and has won several child-selected awards.

(See also *Something about the Author,* Vols. 8, 52; *Major Authors and Illustrators for Children and Young People; Contemporary Authors New Revision Series,* Vols. 11, 37; and *Contemporary Authors,* Vols. 25-28, rev. ed.)

ILLUSTRATOR COMMENTARY

It was a bit over twenty years ago, when I was already working free-lance as a cartoonist and illustrator for *Punch* and *The Spectator,* that I first began to think that it might be interesting to illustrate books for children. As I didn't really know how to set about finding this kind of job, I asked John Yeoman, who was a friend from Cambridge days, to write something for me to illustrate. The book was a little collection of stories called **A Drink of Water.** It's now out of print, although one of the stories lives on in a somewhat altered form in the picture book **Beatrice and Vanessa.** At about the same time, as it happened, the art director of Abelard Schuman asked me to illustrate another book for children; and I was embarked on an activity that gradually expanded, so that now, a hundred and fifty books later, it occupies the large majority of my free-lance time.

As well as illustrating books by a variety of authors, I've done a number of picture-storybooks of my own. In one

way they represent a different kind of activity, and I'll come back to them later. I'm certainly not one of those children's illustrators who like to illustrate only their own ideas, and one of the aspects of the job in which my interest has developed and continues to develop is that of working not so much with authors as with their manuscripts. John Arden, the playwright, called a collection of essays about his craft *To Present the Pretence;* and I can't help feeling that what I do in relation to a text may be something like the directing and acting of a play.

Certainly the urge to act a text is a strong one. Once or twice people have expressed surprise to discover that I'm capable of straightforward drawing from life. The fact is that a great deal of naturalistic knowledge is subsumed in drawings that try to express movement rather than substance. My drawings are in fact very carefully planned, but at every stage they are drawn quite swiftly and spontaneously because they reflect me trying to be *that* person performing *that* action or gesture. What the mime on stage does is not exactly life, but he signals it to the audience. The observation of life partly comes out of your own body.

So there is the urge to act the story. A good deal depends, consequently, on my first instinctive reactions to a text. For a picture-storybook I read the manuscript several times and then do a set of roughs to the appropriate format pretty continuously over a day or so, in a kind of intensive gallop. It's an attempt to get down my feelings about the gestures and reactions of the characters and to begin to organize them as a sequence of pages. I think that to me the unit is not the individual picture but the whole book, as it works from beginning to end. Obviously this isn't the same for every illustrator.

No two books are quite the same, but **How Tom Beat Captain Najork and His Hired Sportsmen** makes a useful example—not least because I think Russell Hoban is one of the best writers writing for children, one with an intimate sense of the sound and the shape of language, about whose work I have a great deal more thoughts and enthusiasm in me than there is room for here. At any rate, it will be understood that to have the few typewritten sheets of the original manuscript arrive in my hands felt like the glint of gold in the pan. As ours would be a new author-artist relationship, I was asked to provide one or two sample drawings. This request was reasonable enough—it's better to get things straight and understood before getting in too deep—but at the same time it's difficult to do a satisfactory finished drawing without going through the process of digesting the book. So I found myself doing, speculatively, the whole sequence of roughs for the story, to find out how those people looked and walked and reacted to each other. Tom—relaxed, poised, private; the Captain—angular, commanding, uncertain; Aunt Fidget—armor-plated, unembraceable, basilisk-eyed. I've written these few words to characterize them; but my hope is, of course, that with luck there might be something about them expressed in the pictures that couldn't be got into words.

It took another set of roughs—and more—(when Russell Hoban had expressed *his* agreement to the project) to get the pages into a varied and expressive sequence; for instance, Tom's fooling around experiences come in half a dozen small framed drawings opening into a larger un-framed one for his wobbling and teetering exploits; and there are open double-page spreads for the extraordinary games and a narrow-framed drawing across two pages for the long gloom of Aunt Fidget's dining table. The division of the text into pages was all the trickier because any Hoban sentence is carefully patterned and shaped, so that you can't break it in half or trail it on to the next page. You have to keep it together. Fortunately it's the kind of re-striction that squeezes new answers out of you.

At the time of illustrating the first Captain Najork book I was offered the opportunity of meeting Russell Hoban—an opportunity which I declined, then, and took up only subsequently, simply because I seemed to be getting such clear messages from the text itself. Collaborations call for a varying degree of discussion; but often it's sufficient to have an author who has the instinct and experience to offer visual opportunities, and it's these opportunities that you see rising to the surface as you read the story.

In Roald Dahl's **The Enormous Crocodile** there were the opportunities of disguising the crocodile (as the palm tree, the seat, the seesaw, and so on) and also of, as it were, *being* the crocodile. Both author and illustrator then have their own contribution to make to the book. I tried to let the nature of the story influence the way it was drawn, too; the crocodile obviously isn't a real crocodile or even a sim-ple storybook crocodile. He's a sort of energetic demon, like Richard III or Punch in the Punch-and-Judy show. I drew him deliberately in a rather simple way, like the Punch-and-Judy crocodile, and he has two straight rows of teeth for biting people with. Crocodiles' teeth are noth-ing like that, really.

As I've said, collaborations don't necessarily demand a lot of active collaboration, and this is true of the books I've done with John Yeoman. We don't actually talk about the books a great deal (though we talk a lot about other things), and often I don't see the manuscript until it's ab-solutely finished. But he knows that I'm the person who is going to do the drawings, and he writes with a shrewd awareness of visual possibilities and puts in things he knows I'll enjoy. In **Mouse Trouble** I had the pleasure of being both a dopey cat and a lot of lively mice. I even had to be mice *pretending* to be frightened, and the ingenious author put in a little sequence of the cat *practicing* mouse-catching on a screwdriver and *practicing* being praised by the crotchety miller. I think it's that kind of idea that helps to give the book feeling as well as simple narrative.

The Wild Washerwomen is also, of course, full of pretexts for running about and fooling around, like the dash through the market square; and it was after it was pub-lished that John Yeoman reminded me of the advantage of still pictures: the fact that you can have the pleasure of all the activities before you at once—catastrophe in con-templation. As it happened, the same book provided an example of the fact that the illustrator can and should make his own contribution to the text. One London re-viewer, after giving a brief account of the plot, noticed that everyone ended up living happily ever after "with the woodcutters woodcutting and the washerwomen wash-ing." Which emphasizes the fact that you have to look carefully at the pictures in picture books because the at-tentive spectator will notice a lot of redistribution of roles; and although the narrative closes at that point, our hope was that the last picture would remain open with things to talk about and speculate on.

Perhaps at this stage, having commented on a few individ-ual books, I should put in a note or two both about the way I draw and how I feel about the way children's books ought to be illustrated. I've already suggested that the more I can get the whole sequence of pictures working to-gether, the better I like it; not that this is a prescription—because I can see that a perfectly uniform set of pictures (like, say, Nicola Bayley's in *The Tyger Voyage*) has its own validity—but a way that seems to suit my fluid narra-tive feeling. Another general consideration that concerns me—from the point of view of drawings and of humor—is the idea that things shouldn't be over-emphasized. I don't really like humor that nudges you or hits you over the head. I don't mean that there can't be wild happenings; but they shouldn't be played for more than they are worth, and the spectator should be left with something to contrib-ute. In the same way I'm quite happy with very detailed drawings, but I don't really like drawings with a lot of fancy technique buttered on to them; that seems to belong rather to an adolescent world of teenagers and young par-ents who are impressed by display.

My own way of drawing is, I'm told, very recognizable (it's hard to know that sort of thing from the inside) and has once or twice been described as "deceptively slap-dash." Thank God for that "deceptively," because it's hard to think of something that calls for constant attention as slapdash. Although I sometimes look back at the draw-ing with an element of shock, it seems to me at the time a perfectly natural way of expressing myself; and I sup-pose it has the character of a sort of handwriting.

If this underlying handwriting is always present, part of the attraction of working for different authors—and in-deed different publishers, who have different expectations of your work—is to edge the way of drawing this way and that, appropriate to the needs of the text.

While I say "attraction," it has to be admitted that the edging process itself can be a fairly painful procedure, with a good deal of preliminary small-scale agonizing about this ink? that paper? and so on. It's only when you seem to have discovered the happy compromise that it becomes all right. For instance, a book of British fables (commis-sioned by a Japanese publisher) seemed to call for an ap-proach slightly more naturalistic than usual, with a good deal of scratchy shading, simply because it had to accom-modate both "The Three Bears" and "The Well at the World's End" in addition to stories with darker incidents, such as "Mr. Fox." This approach took some time to find. By contrast **Custard and Company,** which was an attempt to present Ogden Nash's verse to its youngest possible readers, required, with all those dotty animals, a more car-toonlike approach.

An element of fantasy is present in most of the books I have illustrated. It's not absent from two books of verse by Michael Rosen—**Mind Your Own Business** and

Snuff was Sir Thomas Magpie's page. A page is a
boy who goes to live with a knight as his servant and
also to learn how to be a knight himself when he
grows up. Snuff very much wanted to be a knight but,
unfortunately, although he tried his best, he didn't
always get things right.
    Snuff was sitting on the roof in the sunshine,
feeding the pigeons. As he scattered the crumbs his
mind was far away, imagining what it was like to be a
knight and have all kinds of adventures.

From Snuff, *written and illustrated by Quentin Blake.*

Wouldn't You Like to Know; but they are essentially
about the everyday life of children, especially boys, and illustrating them presented a cluster of interesting problems. The solution to one of them involved drawing with
a soft nylon or fiber-tipped pen, so that the pictures,
though still drawn out of my head, had just a little more
suggestion that they might have been drawn from life. Another problem was that very few people, apparently, are
enthusiastic about buying a book of poems, apart from
nursery rhymes at the appropriate level. So it was interesting to me to suggest a broader page format; settle the
poems down on the bottom margin, instead of hanging
them from a title at the top, and have some pages with
drawings but no verses—in a general attempt to present
a book that was a mixture of words and pictures rather
than formally a book of verses.

Of course, none of this would have been in order if Michael Rosen's poems hadn't already had the sort of infor-
mality of approach that rendered it appropriate. And
poems they indeed are, so that there was the other little
problem basic to illustration of deciding what *not* to illustrate. The way I approached it was to try and decide which
poems worked best on their own and to avoid them—the
more atmospheric or intimate in mood would only be im-
paired by the attempt to match them in pictures. As our
tactic was to play up the accessibility of the verses, I illustrated the more obviously amusing and active ones, and
Michael Rosen supplied me with other childhood reminis-
cences that he hadn't used in his writing. We were, so to

speak, illustrating poems that weren't there, and in that
way, I hope, built up an interplay of words and pictures,
the main purpose of which was to help the reader towards
the central matter of the book, the verses themselves.

A similar approach, but with a shift of emphasis, is apparent, I think, in my third collaboration with Michael
Rosen: *You Can't Catch Me.* This offers some of the
poems from the two previous books, together with new
poems, to a younger audience in the form of a full-color
picture book. There is an even balance here between the
author and the artist, and many of the poems have been
chosen because they give opportunity for illustration. Michael Rosen is a skilled presenter and dramatizer of his
own work; with a group of children he can bring out wonderfully its meaning and possibilities. And in the absence
of author-as-presenter I think the illustrator has the function of *assisting* the young reader to the poem. First of all,
by quite simply giving the circumstances of the poem so
that the reader doesn't have to guess—for instance, in a
dialogue, *who* is talking—and, more important, to push
the reader toward some of the implications of the poem,
to help it unfold in his or her mind.

A good deal of what I've written so far has been about illustration relating to and ministering to the text; but by
way of conclusion I'd like to add one or two notes on the
books which I have written and illustrated myself. They
comprise five picture-storybooks, all published by Jonathan Cape: the first, *Patrick,* in 1969; the most recent, *Mr.*

Magnolia, in 1980; and two picture books and a collection of stories about a creature called Lester, springing out of a series of television programs for the BBC.

The point to be made, as far as I am concerned, is that these books were originally thought of as pictures and sequences of pictures. They started with some image—a tree of food, a tightrope walker—that I fancied in my mind's eye and grew from that. The words were an addition to the pictures. I was once asked—by an educationist or a librarian, as I remember it—"How do you justify pictures in children's books?" Of course, pictures have, as I've suggested, their ways of serving the text, and there are also times and places when they aren't required; but they don't need justifying. They can be good on their own terms and with their own intrinsic values—ones which, alas, far too few adults feel at home with.

So I embrace the simplicity of both the story and the pictures, in which there may not seem to be, for the grownup, much to talk about. To ease that frustration, it would be quite possible for me to invoke a range of stylistic references—I have extensive knowledge of my drawing's genealogy—but at the present moment I would rather invite the spectator of whatever age to believe that I have never spoken in any other language and that these pictures are simply happening. (pp. 505-13)

> Quentin Blake, "Wild Washerwoman, Hired Sportsmen, and Enormous Crocodiles," in The Horn Book Magazine, *Vol. LVII, No. 5, October, 1981, pp. 505-13.*

GENERAL COMMENTARY

Elaine Moss

When I suggested to Quentin Blake that the purpose of my visiting him in his large, rambling, book-filled flat off the Old Brompton Road in London was to discuss the serious contribution of the humorist to children's illustration, he laughed, kindly: and the glint in his eye told me that a cartoon was bubbling up inside him. For the absurdity of sitting down to discuss such a topic with straight faces instead of feasting merrily on Quentin's books and drawings which were playing hide-and-seek with one another on the shelves and stacked against the walls, was instantly apparent to us both.

But Quentin Blake is gentle, unassuming and accommodating. So he sat and talked politely and seriously about humour, his brown eyes alight with intelligence, his small white hands—deprived of pencil and paper for once—constantly moving to help him express his ideas in words instead of, as is more natural to him, in line.

Ever since he was a schoolboy in suburban Sidcup (he grew up with the suburb in the thirties, the school being for him a cultural oasis in a philistine desert) he had wanted to draw. His career as a cartoonist began, indeed, on the backs of exercise books. But the cartoons soon took a balletic leap straight into the pages of *Punch,* which was paying Quentin seven pounds each for illustrated jokes before he was out of the sixth form. Didn't this make him

something of a hero? He shrugs off the idea. Did it bring his parents round to support his leanings towards a career in humorous art? No, because, quite understandably, they wanted security for him, "something like banking or teaching".

For Quentin shone in other ways, though he is rather careful not to say this. He suggests, modestly, that it was the good teaching of his English master, J. H. Walsh (of *Roundabout by the Sea* fame) that "got him in" to Downing College, Cambridge, where he took an English degree, going on to the Institute of Education in London for a year's teacher training. Then, fully fledged as a graduate English teacher, he decided *not* to teach. "If I start doing it I might like it, I thought"—so at last he turned his attention, seriously, to humorous art.

If you think making cartoons for *Punch* is a light-hearted, easy occupation for an artist, Quentin will quickly disabuse you of the notion. He discovered, when he began to indulge in this passion full time, that "you spend hours thinking up jokes with great labour; so many ideas are funny but not visual. It's a gruelling business and most of the while you are not drawing, which was what I really wanted to be doing."

So, still maintaining the *Punch* contact, he decided he "should get a bit of art training". He sought out Brian Robb, painter, illustrator, cartoonist and lecturer at Chelsea, who advised him on what part-time courses to take. "Don't come to mine on illustration!", he said. Thus began a lifelong friendship and professional association, for Quentin now teaches in Brian Robb's illustration department at the Royal College of Art.

Strangely enough, it was Quentin Blake's covers for the *Spectator*—"it was like being in repertory, playing a different role each week"—that finally brought him into the children's book field. John Ryder, collecting material about children's book illustrators for *Artists of a Certain Line* in the early sixties, asked Quentin for a contribution, having seen his cover illustration for a *Spectator* children's book number. Quentin, with characteristic honesty, said he "wasn't a children's book illustrator but would very much like to be". And quickly he set about becoming one by providing a set of line illustrations to a book of stories called **A Drink of Water** by his friend John Yeoman. (pp. 33-5)

Quentin Blake is sometimes author as well as artist, producing the texts for his own picture books, but he insists that he is not essentially a writer and that **Patrick, Jack and Nancy, Angelo** and **Snuff** were thought of first in terms of pictures "with bits written in underneath afterwards". He starts with a notion of the kind of pictures he'd like to make—music's visual kaleidoscope (**Patrick**), a tight-rope and some *commedia dell' arte* characters (**Angelo**)—and then extends them gradually to make a story. He is delighted that Weston Woods has produced an animated film of **Patrick** with no words—just a violin accompaniment.

Quentin Blake enjoys making picture books on his own, but he also finds it stimulating to collaborate with an author, whose text must be matched, in its humour, by his illustrations. Almost always the text comes first, presenting to Quentin the problems he enjoys solving. For he believes that these invoke his ingenuity and stretch his powers so that the resulting piece of illustration is altogether better than it would have been, had the problems inherent in the text not existed.

When John Yeoman showed him the text for *Sixes and Sevens,* for instance, Quentin recognized it at once as an ingenious counting book, potentially full of interest. But how could he turn a deliberately repetitive text—about a boy poling a raft up river "from here to Limber Lea" and picking up 1 kitten, 2 mice, 3 school-mistresses, etc., at successive landing stages—into a picture book in which each opening challenged the eye and mind? Anyone who knows the book . . . will remember with joy Quentin's triumph. The scene changes, the weather changes, and each new addition to the raft's steadily increasing load causes its own special chaos. Although Quentin Blake speaks with mild affront at an author's temerity in writing about "hundreds" of mice—John Yeoman's *Mouse Trouble*—one feels that he was secretly delighted at the prospect of having to draw them. Indeed, one of his most inspired illustrations is a double page showing "hundreds of mice" in the old mill having a marvellous time "using the great millstone as a roundabout . . . balancing on the turning beams . . . and sliding down the grain chutes".

These books are pure fun. *Captain Najork* is an altogether more sophisticated collaboration between an established fantasist, Russell Hoban, and perhaps the only illustrator who could have given visual form to his text without underplaying or overplaying the absurdity. When Cape sent Quentin the manuscript of this story, along with two others, he instantly chose *Captain Najork* and couldn't wait to get his hands on it. Instead of the sample drawing the publisher asked for, he supplied quick, rough sketches for the whole book, developing the characters as he went along. "Russell Hoban apparently said 'O.K., let him do it' and I did it in a way I've never worked before: I didn't show the book to anyone till it was finished. The story is so positive and complete and structured that a meeting with Russell Hoban would have been irrelevant. The vibrations were so strong that I needed nothing more. So I worked and worked and then turned up at Cape saying, 'Here it is!' "

The text of *Captain Najork* is comparatively long for a picture book, and it was Quentin's admiration for it as a distinguished piece of humorous literature, his sensitivity as a reader, that enabled him to match it with his illustrations. In discussing the problems it threw in his path his whole philosophy of illustration became manifest. The story is about a "fooling-around" boy, Tom, whose aunt, Aunt Fidget Wonkham-Strong, sends for the disciplinarian Captain Najork and his four hired red-striped sportsmen to beat the "sportive infant" at what turn out to be merely complicated variations of Tom's personal "fooling-around" games. So Tom, of course, manages to out-womble, out-muck and out-sneedball the lot of them. "The games had to look plausible," says Quentin, "without me trying to show exactly how they worked. Sneedball sounds terribly convincing—a marvellous word. So you

mustn't ruin the author's joke by making the illustration too specific. You leave a bit to the reader's imagination, the least you can do that enables them to see the joke the better. Then there was the weight and balance of every sentence and paragraph of Hoban's: you could only break the text at certain points without damaging this, but accepting the challenge, which meant rearranging the design of the pages very often, is an example of how overcoming difficulties can actually improve illustration."

Quentin Blake is not only a picture-book artist. His line drawings enliven the text of many a novel for children, notably the *Agaton Sax* detective stories and the *Uncle* saga. "Illustrating someone else's novel is like acting in a play—or producing it," he says. "You give visual form to a host of characters." Certainly the huge cast of the *Uncle* books owes an enormous debt to this illustrator; so does many an author whose novel has been given the humorous trademark of a Blake jacket.

Just occasionally, as with *Mind Your Own Business,* Michael Rosen's profile of a boy in a series of poems, one feels that Quentin Blake is more than an illustrator: he is the genius who turns a difficult manuscript into a thoroughly acceptable and beckoning book. "Some of the poems were light and amusing, some more serious, some quite complicated. Where pictures would have interfered with the effect of the poems, I kept off illustrating altogether. *Illustrating, as an activity distinct from drawing, demands a sense of what you simply mustn't do.*"

Quentin Blake was by now being very serious indeed about humorous drawing, about the way he solves layout problems and shape problems before doing the finished black and white sketches of the people who skip and prance and almost fly sometimes across the pages of, say, *The Armada Lion Book of Verse* or *The Puffin Joke Book*—just two of the many anthologies he has enlivened. It is this implied sense of movement in his drawings (he admires inordinately the serial drawings of Caran d'Ache, who could imply a train passing a field by making four consecutive drawings of a cow with her head and eyes moving to follow its imaginary passage) that makes him wary of embarking on cartoon film. For in cartoon film you make movement *actually* happen, so movement by *implication* loses its power. Blake's stills (if one can call anything he draws a "still") for Jackanory's presentation of Rosemary Manning's *Dragon in Danger* and Joan Aiken's *Tales of Arabel's Raven* seemed to me far more effective than any cartoon film could have been.

But Quentin is interested in film, particularly in the work of Jacques Tati, whose humour depends so often on a way of looking at otherwise quite ordinary things in special juxtaposition. "Many people who in Renaissance times would have been painters are today working in theatre or films."

Illustration pulls influences in from the general art world—from drama as well as from painting. Quentin Blake admires those painters of the past (it's going out of fashion now) whose pictures were almost one-act plays. He speaks with warmth about Tintoretto and Goya and with passion about Daumier who, through his sense of form and the strength of his line, can emphasize the relationships between the people he draws. "The captions were often written by other people. The jokes in themselves might be feeble, but the humour and drama were there in the pictures."

It is the abundant humour and light drama in Quentin Blake's pictures that children instantly respond to. Though professing to know very little about children ("I haven't got any, you know," he says cheerfully) one has only to see him submerged by the clamouring young when he agrees to draw for them at a book exhibition to know that his rapport with them is natural. "I never think of myself as an adult and ask 'what do *they* want?' It's more a feeling of being a child with them." (pp. 35-9)

Elaine Moss, "Quentin Blake," in Signal, *No. 16, January, 1975, pp. 33-9.*

Lindsay Duguid

Quentin Blake's work is unmistakable: gob-struck youths and gormless maidens, wicked small boys and batty old ladies, desperate desperadoes, parrots, monkeys, cats, mice and frogs, all rendered in a characteristically insouciant squiggly line, heightened with colour. His creations are always full of life and movement. They appear to dance round the page and form sudden tableaux of considerable comic force. Who could resist Potiphar's wife in *Joseph and the Amazing Technicolor Dreamcoat* (1982), gazing pop-eyed and lascivious at the golden-haired Joseph; or the solemn farmer applying undue pressure to pig-tailed Betsy Baker in *Quentin Blake's Nursery Rhyme Book* or the determined females going to work on their menfolk in *The Wild Washerwomen;* or Red Riding Hood in her slinky wolfskin coat in *Roald Dahl's Revolting Rhymes* (1982)? All is not simple hilarity, however. Pathos, uncertainty and a sort of melancholy are (perhaps increasingly) apparent in books such as *The Story of the Dancing Frog, The Marzipan Pig* (1986) and *The BFG* (1982), whose gentleness and good intentions are remarkably evoked by the tremulous contours of his enormous ears. But even Blake's most lyrical moments—in *Patrick, Mister Magnolia* and *Angelo*—share a certainty of purpose with his depiction of Michael Rosen's more down-to-earth inventions in *Don't Put Mustard in the Custard* (1985) *Smelly Jelly Smelly Fish* (1986) and *Hard-Boiled Legs* (1987).

Quentin Blake works in a room which looks as though it might come from a particularly jokey cartoon depicting an illustrator's life. On the shelves are copies of nearly every book he has illustrated, more books than a strictly representational drawing could dare attempt to show. Horizontal piles of paper, pots of different pens, pencils and brushes, sketch-pads, proofs lie everywhere, seemingly at random. Yet Blake knows where things are and can bring out the roughs for two of next year's projects, a bound proof copy and a set of preparatory drawings for his latest book, *Quentin Blake's ABC,* all evidence of the controlled creativity that working on many different titles requires. There is a balance between chaos and discipline; a casual manner is achieved by taking pains. Blake works in a methodical way from an original sketch, through stages of drawing using a lightbox to preserve the original image while re-working it through several stages. Early versions of his *ABC,* for example, show an apparently finished drawing; attendant children are added, then taken away, characters move into the foreground, change costume and expression, a parrot flutters in. A recent critic referred to Blake as a member of the "scrawl and scribble school". The *ABC* shows how far this is from the truth. Its classically simple form, the elegance of his line and the beautifully composed lay-outs all demonstrate that his effects are hard won. In an age of board books and pop-ups, his work has always been in the purest picturebook form.

Blake started as a children's book illustrator in the 1960s (*A Drink of Water and Other Stories* by John Yeoman, 1960 was one of his first commissions; his first solo venture was *Patrick* in 1968). It was a time when the picture book was starting to come into its own: artists such as John Burningham and Brian Wildsmith were trying new informal ways of working and colour was becoming an important factor. A looseness of form seemed to go with contemporary assaults on repression and convention and with celebrations of freedom. Blake himself claims that the genesis of his own books was almost accidental: he did *Patrick* because he wanted to use colour, *Dancing Frog* because he used a drawing of an idealized frog to show some teachers the difference between his drawing and a natural history study; *Mister Magnolia* is really a counting book. Yet these books are informed by free-flowing movement and a spirit of liberation. *Angelo,* for example, a charming, gentle story which has also seen life as a puppet play in the Little Angel Marionette Theatre in Islington, is about the power of the theatre (which also features in *Dancing Frog* and John Yeoman's *The Young Performing Horse,* 1977) and more generally about escape and fulfilment. One of his own favourites, *How Tom Beat Captain Najork and His Hired Sportsmen,* tells how a child overcomes the forces of righteousness as exemplified by Aunt Fidget Wonkham-Strong. Blake praises the strength of Russell Hoban's text but also provides several heart-warming pictures of Tom fooling his way out of trouble. Quentin Blake is definitely on the side of children. Unlike many writers for the young, he has no axe to grind: "What is important for me is what it *feels* like to be a child and this is what I'm really trying to do in my drawings—capture what it feels like to be that particular child doing that action, squelching through mud or climbing a fence". He sees his books as communicating directly with an individual. This ability to live in the present is something he has in common with Roald Dahl—along with a shared desire to envisage such things as a lavatory thrown from an upper window or a plate of spaghetti made of worms. (Some of his drawings really have to be termed Hogarthian if you are going to feel better about the pig-like nostrils, hairy arms and gaping teeth.)

Collaboration is clearly something Blake excels at. He is a modest, amiable man, well-suited to the give and take, freely acknowledging the illustrator's secondary role—he interprets the author's intentions—likening it to that of an accompanist and relishing the variety of challenges he is offered. "I don't think I would want to illustrate *Pride and Prejudice,* but it would be very interesting to try. Even

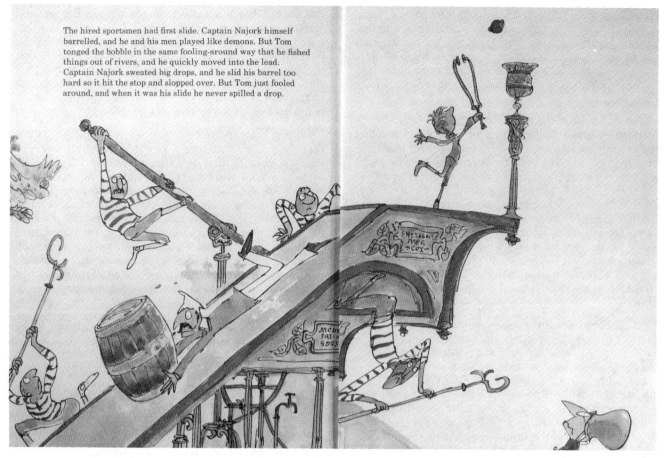

The hired sportsmen had first slide. Captain Najork himself barrelled, and he and his men played like demons. But Tom tonged the bobble in the same fooling-around way that he fished things out of rivers, and he quickly moved into the lead. Captain Najork sweated big drops, and he slid his barrel too hard so it hit the stop and slopped over. But Tom just fooled around, and when it was his slide he never spilled a drop.

From How Tom Beat Captain Najork and His Hired Sportsmen, *by Russell Hoban. Illustrated by Quentin Blake.*

though the pictures might not be very satisfactory I would get something out of it. It's getting the idea of how to draw something that I like, when I know what I'm going to do . . . After that it's plain sailing." In the recently published ***Our Village*** (1988), his traditional landscapes of penny-farthings, scarecrows, village school and skating pond, seen throughout the day and the passing seasons, beautifully complement John Yeoman's gentle text. Yeoman renders the lives of mute inglorious Miltons in verse which has echoes of Stevenson, Kipling and Betjeman.

Before his early retirement in 1986, Blake was head of illustration at the Royal College of Art, where his students must have regarded him as not only a teacher but an object-lesson in professionalism. His personal pantheon contains—along with Bonnard, Picasso, Degas—Honoré Daumier, an artist who for most of his adult life did drawings for newspapers several times a week, drawing straight on the printer's lithographic stone; Daumier found the technique which suited him and produced thousands of drawings, each of them an original work of art.

But as well as being the consummate professional (Douglas Martin's forthcoming *The Telling Line: Essays on fifteen contemporary book illustrators* . . . contains an invaluable bibliography listing nearly 200 titles—"roughly six a year for 30 years" says Blake), Blake is a storyteller and a communicator. The frontispiece to his ***ABC*** con-

tains a wry self-portrait, the slightly scruffy enchanter-figure with his scarf and espadrilles is wearing a magic robe of coloured letters and inspiring an audience of six small children, a teddy and a dog, exhorting them to look and learn. One of Blake's most popular and endearing works, ***Mister Magnolia,*** won the Kate Greenaway medal in 1980 and he has a scrapbook containing comments on his book by various children. Some obligingly point out to him particular things which they have noticed such as the purple dinosaur and the single boot, some tell the story, some put the work in context—"I can say it with Miss Jenkins"—some indulge in literary criticism—"I like it because it's bumpy to say". All these elements are part of the picture-book experience and their testimony is a tribute to a skilled practitioner of the picture-book art.

Lindsay Duguid, "Artist Enchanter," in The Times Educational Supplement, *No. 3806, June 9, 1989, p. B9.*

Douglas Martin

In common with so many book artists, Blake draws analogies between the theatre and illustration as interpretative arts, but he places the emphasis not on direction or set design or ensemble as others have done, but on acting as being the more direct comparison. The text is the starting point to be studied closely in order to generate an individual performance; similarly his drawing aims to be dynamic and gestural in response to the unfolding action—in contrast to other, equally valid types of illustration which may be more passive or contemplative in intent. This view may serve to lead into a consideration of some of his best successes as well as to explain his yearning for some of the roles that have so far eluded him.

A glance at a list of the titles which Quentin Blake has illustrated reveals a further aspect of what Pevsner called 'the Englishness of English art' (or literature for that matter); that is to say, the currents of observation which can be traced from the margins of illuminated manuscripts, and from Hogarth, as they flow into the mainstreams of later English satire, humour and eccentricity. The course of satirical caricature from Gillray to Gerald Scarfe and Ralph Steadman has frequently been plotted, but there is also a gentler stream which links Rowlandson to such present-day artists as Quentin Blake and John Lawrence and which is concerned with the observation of character without recourse to the cutting edge of the caricaturist school.

Blake's apolitical nature makes him a natural running mate for those whose patron saints are Lear and Carroll, the writers of humorous sense and nonsense at all levels, and the greatest number of the books which he has illustrated fall into this loosely defined category. There is an affinity between the drawings of Edward Lear and those of Quentin Blake which falls outside the accustomed pattern of stylistic similarities or influences; it is more that they share a sense of the absurd and an instinct for timing and, above all, that an equivalent mastery underlies the spontaneity and sparkle of their respective line techniques.

Quentin Blake has said that the selection of incidents and what he calls confrontations—the points at which illustrations should occur—is largely subjective and instinctive, and it can be shown that his procedures differ from those of most narrative illustrators by virtue of his stylistic individuality and creative intention. He has the quickest of minds and the readiest stylistic attack and so can go into action in situations which those with a more deliberate technique do well to avoid. It appears that he selects an instant in a developing situation and records it not as an arrested frame but in a way that engages the viewer in projecting the movement forwards in time; in a sense the focal point is frequently a little ahead of the drawing. All non-essentials are excised in the interests of making the situation plain and packing energy and movement into the figure drawing.

His first commission from the Folio Society was for *The Hunting of the Snark* in 1976, and the volume which resulted is quintessential Blake. The Society's books frequently offer their illustrators a chance to stand aside a little from received commercial criteria, and this delightful book works because Blake's innately sophisticated approach to design is allowed to follow its course. 'It is the book as a whole which is the illustrator's canvas, and the placing on the page is as vital as timing is to verbal delivery.' The visual entrances and exits through printed binding cloth, preliminary and end pages, are superbly managed, as is the positioning of individual drawings in rela-

tion to text. The anticipatory reference to the Butcher and Beaver on the left page of the spread disguises the fact that text and illustration will terminate to great effect in the couplet which resolves 'Fit the First'. Blake believes that he has gained in insight through gradually changing his stance from one of initial willingness to leave the layout to the book designer to one of needing to control the detailed *mise-en-page* personally. (pp. 248-51)

The penalty for stylistic distinctiveness is sometimes to be thought guilty of sameness, but the assembled evidence does not point in that direction in Quentin Blake's case. Wit and invention are always sparklingly fresh, style of interpretation modulates from one author to the next, and his use of media is constantly varied to produce a range of line qualities and freely handled line and wash or watercolour effects. There are a number of repeated mannerisms or trademarks of a kind which follow from adopting such an autographic and quirky mode of address, and which will be noticed in any comparative review of the books, but these are not of a kind to obtrude in normal conditions of use.

As the number of volumes illustrated by Quentin Blake rapidly nears the 200 mark, it is surprising to reflect that this output has been achieved against a background of teaching, administrative and other outside commitments which frequently left only half the week free for drawing. With so many titles it helps to be able to trace a pattern of long-standing partnerships, where only the conjoint activity of author and artist allows characters and situations to enjoy a full existence. Everyone will have their favourites from among the *Agaton Sax, Arabel* and *Uncle* series, and the many titles produced in collaboration with such writers as Patrick Campbell, Roald Dahl, Michael Rosen and—over the longest time of all—with John Yeoman. . . .

An illustrator frequently has to adapt to a pre-existing text and Blake finds it challenging to locate the optimum wavelengths for writers as individualistic as Dahl, Russell Hoban, and Rosen; and this he did nowhere more triumphantly for this particular trio than in Dahl's *The Giraffe and the Pelly and Me,* Hoban's *How Tom Beat Captain Najork and His Hired Sportsmen,* and Rosen's *Mind Your Own Business.* In contrast the books produced with John Yeoman seem to be based on a closer affinity of style and intention. *Rumbelow's Dance* is a cumulative story delivered at Quentin Blake's pace and angled to his particular strengths and here, as in the felicitous *Mouse Trouble,* John Yeoman has provided splendidly crafted picture book texts. (p. 252)

Quentin Blake is oddly diffident about the books for which he has supplied his own texts, although these clearly demanded a lot of careful work. Most began with an idea that generated a visual narrative to which he later added words. He was pleased that the pictorial structure of his first book, *Patrick,* proved so sound that when it came to making an animated film it was possible to leave out the words and use a violin accompaniment as soundtrack.

The Kate Greenaway Medal awarded to *Mister Magnolia* in 1980 recognised Blake's distinctive contribution through his own picture books, and the three titles he has since published show an augmentation of his inventiveness in developing stories in a way that is only possible given an integrated starting point—where words and images can play leapfrog in a fertile mind. The visual pace and energy in the earlier books lead the reader's attention forward from beginning to end, at times with such momentum that they carry the words along with them like a string of railway coaches. This provides a marvellous inducement to read or listen to the stories, as well as for the storyteller to make adventurous use of subject-matter and its presentation; but there is the attendant danger—which is fundamental to the case-bound picture book format—that everything may be over too quickly in terms of apparent length. There are a number of ways around this problem and the one which Blake chooses is the masterly control of pace. In *The Story of the Dancing Frog,* the central character can leap, almost literally, from page to page for sure-fire continuity, whereas the unnamed mother can recall episodes at a more leisurely tempo as flashbacks; pictures and words can be made to freeze-frame, leaving the development in time, back and forth from a set tableau, to the child's imaginings. This is storytelling and illustrative book designing at its most accomplished: the observer's eye follows as bidden, oblivious to the means deployed.

Mrs Armitage on Wheels uses the time-honoured device of cumulative additions to punctuate the progress of the scatty lady, her bike and her dog, which (after the fashion of 'This is the House that Jack Built'), lets the reader move back and forth between what is happening at each stage and what has gone before: the way the book ends by starting afresh (this time with roller skates) poises the reader on the edge of yet a further cycle of development, another movement, this time into the future.

The most recent of this group of picture books, *Our Village,* is one of the most interesting yet, since it lets us see the development of the structure beneath the surface. A bird's eye plan of the village and where its inhabitants live appears on the front endpapers, and again as the back endpapers—but this time at night. This simple device frames the story, which in pictures and John Yeoman's verses moves at a gentle pace, with occasional bursts of excitement, from dawn to dusk and from spring to winter.

Although all Quentin Blake's illustration is characterised by an abundance of humour and vitality, lightness of handling should not be equated with slightness in substance. His technical means are always adequate for what he has to say, and however much this may astonish us in terms of range, dexterity and unpredictability, it is invariably pertinent to the text. It must have taken initial courage to decide to draw in so direct a manner—where in a sense there is nothing to hide behind if inspiration flags—and to seek for applications in areas of publishing where on the face of it the chances of success looked the most precarious. As he stated in an earlier interview: 'If they like it, I'll do it. If they don't, I'll give up.' Needless to say, they did. His inimitable style qualifies this widely gifted artist to illuminate fresh aspects of adult literature and the classics in the future as well as continuing to delight children

of all ages with the witty and sparkling line which he has made his own. (pp. 253-54)

> *Douglas Martin, "Quentin Blake," in his* The Telling Line: Essays on Fifteen Contemporary Book Illustrators, *Julia MacRae Books, 1989, pp. 243-63.*

Kate Kellaway

Quentin Blake compares the actual creation of a children's book to acting. As he draws, he says, he often pulls faces (as certain musicians do when they are concentrating hard). He has a frolicking imagination. His work has not aged over the years. His illustrations give a sense of speed, as if all the characters were drawn in an inspired hurry by a dancing hand. It's 'like handwriting', he says. He enjoys the spontaneity but explains that it can be difficult and gives a surprising example.

In *All Join In,* two children are looking round a study door. The text reads: 'When William's in his study / and his thoughts are very deep / We come and help him concentrate . . . '. It was dicey getting *exactly* the right look on the children's faces. He did not want them to look too naughty. He has succeeded in making them appear perky, curious and far brighter than poor William whose hair stands on end, whose glasses have slid half-way down his nose and who is stroking his cheek ponderously, trying to work.

Disturbed or disturbing, adults in children's books reveal much about their creators. . . . Quentin Blake has no children of his own and his drawings tend not to show conventional families. His adults tend, he admits, to be more out of control than the children. He goes in for wild, extended gaggles of people though it is, he agrees, sometimes possible to identify a Mum (the pale disconsolate woman with spiky yellow hair in *All Join In*).

I reprove him for always drawing such fat grannies. His grannies are forever swooning under the weight of vast bellies covered in floral print. He recalls: 'My grannies *were* fat'.

Aware that picture books are read repeatedly, Quentin Blake, to limit the potential monotony, [pops] divertingly superfluous details into [his] illustrations. Blake points out the baby on the title page of *All Join In.* The baby is oblivious, reclining on a cushion with no intention of joining in. Elsewhere his babies are cheerful maniacs, pouring yellow tea everywhere.

He says that pictures usually come before the words. But his writing has rhythm and verve and a great sense of dramatic timing; he knows exactly how to exploit the gap between one page and the next.

In his new book *Cockatoos* the birds are in flight from an old fool called Professor Dupont. On every page *we* can see the cockatoos, but the professor can't. Blake says that, in a sense, the cockatoos are children outwitting a teacher. And there's a perceptible intake of breath as the page turns and the reader descends on a perfectly judged last line.

> *Kate Kellaway, "The Darkness All Around Us,*

and the Warm Light Inside," in The Observer, *July 5, 1992, p. 62.*

TITLE COMMENTARY

Patrick   (1968)

Quentin Blake, in *Patrick,* has a nice idea and exploits it with gentle humour and matches it, moreover, with a technique which is simple and effective. Patrick buys a second-hand violin and discovers that it has unsuspected qualities. Fiddling his way through Ireland he makes the pleasantest kind of havoc of the not-ordinarily-normal everyday life of that delectable land. The country has become colourful and exhilarating to the limit, and beyond, by the time his fiddle has done its best. A highly enjoyable light-weight book.

> *A review of "Patrick," in* The Junior Bookshelf, *Vol. 32, No. 6, December, 1968, p. 352.*

Quentin Blake's eye-catching, lively, full color pictures carry his slight story about a young man and his marvelous violin. When Patrick plays the instrument, fish, birds, and cows turn into brightly colored, plumed, or decorated creatures. Patrick's music causes a whiskery tramp's pipe to suddenly give off showers of fireworks, and transforms a lowly peasant cart into a gaily designed thing of beauty. Finally, Patrick, the animals, the peasant, and two little children encountered along the way form a procession, "And they all got back to the town before dark." Seven- and eight-year-olds can read the text—harder words are repeated at least once—but the book's also good for read-alouds, even though the music is in the pictures rather than in the words.

> *Muriel Koth, in a review of "Patrick," in* School Library Journal, *Vol. 16, No. 4, December, 1969, p. 39.*

In *Patrick* Quentin Blake breaks new ground by writing his own text for a delectable picture-story book for four- to eight-year-olds. The exquisitely matched fantasy of words and pictures and their highly satisfactory arrangement on well-designed pages make this an exceptionally

attractive book to read and look at. . . . A gay procession of dancing, star-studded cows, flying fish and multi-coloured birds meets a melancholy tinker and his wife, who grow merrier and fatter as they listen and eventually lead the whole procession back to town with a decorated horse and cart. An enchanting book in every respect.

> *J. S. Jenkins, in a review of "Patrick," in* Children's Book News, *Toronto, Vol. 3, No. 6, November-December, 1988, p. 309.*

Jack and Nancy   (1969)

Another sprightly fantasy from Quentin Blake: a boy and girl on a picnic ("many years ago") are suddenly blown to a jungle isle, where they have a happy time among the parrots and tropical fish until they are rescued by a passing ship. Jolly pictures of Jack Tars in Treasure Island rig, happily reminiscent of the Darwins' *Mr. Tootleoo and Co.* Elegantly produced.

> *A review of "Jack and Nancy," in* The Times Literary Supplement, *No. 3529, October 16, 1969, p. 1201.*

Jack and Nancy is a desert island story with an 18th-century nautical background, full of parrots, white bell-bottomed trousers and a big green umbrella which carries the children away in a storm. Blake's work has a glowing liquid sketchiness that seems effortless, and is what they call 'enchanting' without being cute. (p. 628)

> *John Fuller, "Jacqueline & Co./Infants," in* New Statesman, *Vol. 78, No. 2016, October 31, 1969, pp. 626-28.*

Angelo   (1970)

Quentin Blake is a genuinely funny artist. His *Angelo* is high romance, maiden in distress, elopement and all, but the drama is played against a comic backcloth. There are no cheap laughs in this story of a family of travelling entertainers, but it leaves the reader with a warm, satisfying

Self-portrait. From The Improbable Book of Records, *compiled by Quentin Blake and John Yeoman. Illustrated by Quentin Blake.*

glow. The artist handles his brief text well, and twines around it a string of brilliantly simple drawings.

> *A review of "Angelo," in* The Junior Bookshelf, *Vol. 34, No. 6, December, 1970, p. 345.*

Snuff (1973)

Snuff is a page to Sir Thomas, who despairs of making the awkward boy a knight until, on a visit to the bootmaker, they foil four boot thieves thanks to Snuff's quick thinking: the plan is to march sixteen of the craftsman's boots past the cellar window when the robbers are inside, shouting "where are those boot thieves," "let me at them," etc., until the culprits, believing themselves out-numbered, flee screaming to the woods. Blake's sportive sketches keep the whole thing marching briskly to the end though of course the jaunt is far from necessary.

> *A review of "Snuff," in* Kirkus Reviews, *Vol. XLI, No. 21, November 1, 1973, p. 1195.*

Sir Thomas Magpie takes very seriously the job of training his page, Snuff, to be a knight. But money is very short, they have to share one skinny horse between them and Snuff himself seems better adapted to dreaming than to doing. However, when their friend the Bootmaker is threatened by four horrible Boot Thieves, Snuff defeats the felons with ingenuity and strategic skill that a general might envy. Snuff's reward is a horse of his own, free boots for life and the assurance that knightly qualities are his after all. Quentin Blake's vivid paintings underline with a cartoonist's vigour the humour of the story and the amiability of his characters.

> *A review of "Snuff," in* The Times Literary Supplement, *No. 3742, November 23, 1973, p. 1431.*

The mice have been at Sir Thomas Magpie's boots. The knight and his squire Snuff reach the bootmaker's shop just in time to see half the stock vanishing in the arms of robbers; Snuff's awkwardness with armour and deportment is excused when he devises a clever plan to put the robbers to flight and recapture their loot. A pleasantly satirical use of medieval accoutrements, with surely a backward glance at Tenniel; colour brilliantly used for humour and for decoration; a suspicion of melancholy and moral underneath.

> *Margery Fisher, in a review of "Snuff," in* Growing Point, *Vol. 12, No. 6, December, 1973, p. 2299.*

How Tom Beat Captain Najork and His Hired Sportsmen (1974)

[How Tom Beat Captain Najork and His Hired Sportsmen *is written by Russell Hoban.*]

ILLUSTRATOR'S COMMENTARY

[*The following excerpt is from an interview by Aidan Chambers.*]

Aidan Chambers: Picture books used to be thought of as books for toddlers to cut their literary teeth on. But in the last few years, writers and illustrators have found a new lease of life in making picture story books which are more suitable for the over-sevens because of the sophistication of their texts and pictures. One book, above all, typifies for me this new kind of picture book. It is the hilarious *How Tom Beat Captain Najork and His Hired Sportsmen*, written by Russell Hoban. Tom is an unfazable ten-year-old, whose superlative skill is playing silly, time-wasting games. His guardian, Aunt Fidget Wonkham-Strong, a lady of terrifying presence, decides to put an end to such accomplished malingering, and calls to her aid the athletic Captain Najork and his muscled sportsmen to take on Tom at his own games. The illustrations were drawn by Quentin Blake. Where, I asked him, did he begin, when an author's typescript landed on his desk?

Quentin Blake: The first thing I do is a series of rough drawings of the whole book, so that I can work out how it's going to fall on the pages—how it's going to be divided up, and what the scenes are going to be.

[Chambers:] That sounds awfully simple as you say it, but, in fact, the questions involved there seem to me to be quite awful ones. I wouldn't know where to begin.

[Blake:] May I just read the little bit of text that comes on the first page? 'Tom lived with his maiden aunt, Miss Fidget Wonkham-Strong. She wore an iron hat and took no nonsense from anyone. Where she walked the flowers drooped and when she sang the trees all shivered.'

[Chambers:] Now, it was your decision to take those three sentences and put them on the first page with a picture which takes up three-quarters of it. How did you decide that?

[Blake:] Well, this is the introduction of the two most important characters, and the good thing about this text is that Russell Hoban gives you significant details, but not an excess of details.

[Chambers:] Give us an idea of that.

[Blake:] Well, the iron hat. That's a marvellous imaginative leap, isn't it? And once you know that, you know almost all you need to know. I had a vision of what she looked like, and so I had to draw this Victorian-looking lady, because she is repressive in a Victorian sort of way. She has a bustle, so that she looks as though she hasn't got a normal human anatomy.

[Chambers:] It is quite an extraordinary behind! It grows up into the air . . .

[Blake:] The front isn't that much better, either, because it's got things stuck into it. Various sorts of pins and things which make her definitely unembraceable. And then she has a sharp nose, a tight mouth and an eye that looks like—I don't know . . . I think I had a pterodactyl or something like that in mind!

[Chambers:] I was going to say a chameleon's.

[Blake:] That's right. At the same time, one's got to make her so that although she's repressive, she's not boring—she's got to have a sort of evil vitality of her own.

[Chambers:] What is a surprise to me is the other significant character, Tom himself, and the way you have drawn him. Perhaps you'd describe him.

[Blake:] Well, he's walking along in a relaxed sort of way just behind the great bustle of Aunt Fidget, and he's looking at us. He's pretty relaxed, he's got his hands in his pockets because he's actually able to deal with this frightful woman, and also, later on, we discover that his skill in fooling around and messing about is a real skill.

[Chambers:] You're signalling all kinds of clues about Tom and his relationship to his aunt and the rest of the book in that one drawing.

[Blake:] Absolutely, yes. One of the most interesting things about illustrating someone's text is that you are using this sequence of signals. It's like producing a play, in fact, in that each of these people is not just doing natural things—they are actually giving signs about their character and how they're reacting, at each step.

[Chambers:] The whole book seems to me to have been conceived as a great piece of theatre, probably a kind of comic ballet. Do you see it as theatre in your head?

[Blake:] I do, actually.

[Chambers:] But not as film?

[Blake:] No. My publisher said to me at one stage, 'Couldn't we have a close-up here?' and I had to say: 'No, this isn't a film, it is theatre.'

> *Quentin Blake and Aidan Chambers, in an interview, in* The Listener, *Vol. 96, No. 2483, November 11, 1976, p. 622.*

How Tom Beat Captain Najork and His Hired Sportsmen is a romp, a tongue-in-cheek saga of juvenile triumph in the face of adult oppression. Not that Tom, the hero, ever seems particularly oppressed. Although he has to live with his aunt, Miss Fidget Wonkham-Strong, who wears an iron hat and causes flowers to droop when she passes by and trees to shiver when she sings, and although his meals consist of such choice items as greasy bloaters and cabbage-and-potato sog, Tom is a buoyant character, whose irrepressible passion for fooling around stands him in good stead when Captain Najork and his sportsmen turn up to teach him a lesson. Tom vanquishes these dedicated professionals at their chosen sports of sneedball, womble and muck, and finishes up with a delightful new aunt called Bundlejoy Cosysweet, while Captain Najork and Aunt Fidget marry and live happily ever after. Quentin Blake has a lot of fun interpreting into visual terms the mad, incomprehensible jargon of Captain Najork's games, and he produces a splendidly zany set of illustrations. (p. 718)

> *"Violence, Ararchy or Just Good Clean Fun," in* The Times Literary Supplement, *No. 3774, July 5, 1974, pp. 718-19.*

Russell Hoban's *How Tom Beat Captain Najork and His Hired Sportsmen* must surely be the funniest, whackiest,

most satisfying book published this year for the five-to-nines.

Tom, who has a lamentable tendency to fool around, lives with his Aunt Fidget Wonkham-Strong, a formidable lady who is without malice but is, like her hat, made of iron. The tale of how he acquires instead a new aunt suitably named Bundlejoy Cosysweet is highly complicated, highly moral and hilarious.

Quentin Blake's drawings, every line deliciously eloquent, form the other half of a perfect marriage between illustration and text. A splendid book to set a child giggling, if you can bear to let go of it yourself.

> *Susan Cooper, in a review of "How Tom Beat Captain Najork and His Hired Sportsmen," in* The Christian Science Monitor, *November 6, 1974, p. 11.*

[*How Tom Beat Captain Najork and His Hired Sportsmen*] embodies almost every single virtue of British storytelling. The characters are strongly presented: "Tom lived with his maiden aunt, Miss Fidget Wonkham-Strong. She wore an iron hat and took no nonsense from anyone." The diction is crisp and the rhythms delightful. The Briticisms roll nicely off the tongue: "Eat your mutton and your cabbage and your potato sog." And the unfamiliar terms certainly seem manageable: "The Captain's side raked first. Tom staked. The hired sportsmen played so hard that they wombled too fast. . . . " Our young hero measures up, but that is the giveaway. *How Tom Beat Captain Najork and His Hired Sportsmen* is Russell Hoban's lovingly exaggerated imitation of an English story, illustrated by Quentin Blake whose loony, pop-eyed characters enliven some of the best current English books. Hoban, creator of all those absolutely American stories about Frances, has written a book more English than an English one—up to a point. Young Tom talks with Captain Najork as with an equal, extending a challenge of his own with no self-protective posture of humility, and although he measures up, it is to his own standards, not those imposed upon him. Now what do you suppose the British reviewers made of that?

> *Mary Nickerson, in a review of "How Tom Beat Captain Najork and His Hired Sportsmen," in* School Library Journal, *Vol. 27, No. 2, October, 1980, p. 119.*

Lester and the Unusual Pet; Lester at the Seaside (1975)

Lester at the Seaside and *Lester and the unusual pet* celebrate the doings of a strange, stick-like dragonesque creature who wanders about with his ally Otto, who is something like a frog and something like a teapot. These engaging animals, happily like the spontaneous creations of children, enjoy fun on the beach with the trumpet fish ("Toot! Toot!") and, in the second book, avenge themselves on a tiresome dwarf called Nose with the help of a still more peculiar creature with a round head and two small feet and, in between, yards of string. The end of this second book, "And they sat round the gramophone and played "Happy Feet" seven times straight off ", may conveniently demonstrate the mood of these brief bits of nonsense, in which Quentin Blake as always makes simple line do exactly what he wants it to do and adds his typically casual-seeming and carefully disposed colour.

> *Margery Fisher, in a review of "Lester at the Seaside" and "Lester and the Unusual Pet," in* Growing Point, *Vol. 14, No. 4, October, 1975, p. 2714.*

Quentin Blake's **Lester at the Seaside** takes place in bright sunlight. Lester and his friends Otto and flap-eared Lorna are wildly eccentric-looking monsters with quite conventional tastes, and their day out combines the ordinary pleasures of sea and sand with the author's own brand of dotty invention. These stories appeal to a surprisingly large age range. The confident freedom that characterizes Quentin Blake's text and drawings creates an effect of consistent, if illogical, comic fantasy which looks easy to achieve but is fraught with pitfalls for an inexperienced writer.

> *Julia Briggs, "Available and Expendable," in* The Times Literary Supplement, *No. 3864, April 2, 1976, p. 395.*

The Puffin Book of Improbable Records (with John Yeoman, 1975; U.S. edition as The Improbable Book of Records)

We're skeptical of the authors' claim that this book . . . will be issued to all US Marines for the nutritional content of its paper and ink. We ourselves didn't find items about "a potato bearing a striking resemblance to Queen Victoria" or "the largest quantity of carrot wine ever to be made in a New York basement flat" very filling. But we concede that the cumulative effect of Pythonesque proper names (Mr. Alfred Bight . . . Mrs. Nora Kneewind of Swampscott) and Blake's scribbled nuttiness is a state of droll satiety. Particularly worthy of note are Mr. Origen Pest of Kanab who modeled "83 life-size effigies of himself out of

candle ends" and the record for the "largest number of hedgehogs to do a perfect forward roll in succession"—as is the expression on the face of Mr. Lemuel Potter's Caspian perch, caught in the midst of its 42nd "partially successful" escape attempt. Lenny Zork and Frieda von der Piffle of Wry, Nottingham found this "pretty dumb but we laughed a lot anyway" . . . and that's for the record.

> *A review of "The Improbable Book of Records," in* Kirkus Reviews, *Vol. XLIV, No. 13, July 1, 1976, p. 734.*

This spoof on the *Guiness Book of World Records* requires no familiarity with the original; it should amuse even the uninitiated. From the first piece of information—that the book "is the only one to be issued to all the U. S. Marines as part of their survival kit on account of the high nutritional value of its paper and printing ink"—and from the accompanying illustration of the compilers measuring an octopus's tentacle, it becomes clear that the author-artist team has produced another zany creation. The inventiveness of the records is almost less brilliant than the way they are visually depicted; the artist has worked out all the intricacies of a man balancing twenty-eight bananas on his nose and the subtle qualities of a potato bearing a striking resemblance to Queen Victoria. (Incidentally, the authors inform us that this tuber "stood in for Her Majesty at a number of rather boring royal functions.") Every improbable record is wonderfully absurd; each picture, even more madcap; and the entire creation, delightful. (pp. 489-90)

> *Anita Silvey, in a review of "The Improbable Book of Records," in* The Horn Book Magazine, *Vol. LII, No. 5, October, 1976, pp. 489-90.*

For addicts of Guinness and Ripley—a witty spoof that attempts to appeal to both sides of the Atlantic but is really weighted on the side of the British. Americans will miss the humor of "the longest football fan's scarf " (over 7.2 miles and begun as a sock) or the sausage served for school dinner 8,947 times and returned uneaten, and few

From The Wild Washerwomen: A New Folk Tale, *written by John Yeoman. Illustrated by Quentin Blake.*

will even know what a "conker" is. Blake's colorful drawings are deliciously demented, and the combined wit of Blake and Yeoman is most marvelously evident in inventive names for their record holders (Eliza Widdershins, Adam Senilitude). But, like Hoban's *How Tom Beat Captain Najork and His Hired Sportsmen,* also illustrated by Blake, the humor is so parochial that the audience for this will be very, very limited. The picture-book set or even those in the lower elementary grades will not find this their cup of tea.

Marjorie Lewis, in a review of "The Improbable Book of Records," in School Library Journal, *Vol. 23, No. 2, October, 1976, p. 104.*

The Adventures of Lester (1978)

Devotees of Jackanory will relish a permanent record of the adventures of Lester, Otto and Flap-eared Lorna. They live by the Boots-and-Shoe tree and their television is badly in need of maintenance. They organise their own Olympic Games which include cake-weight guessing and throwing the Welly. I suppose it is a teeny-bopper's Monty Python. Anything illustrated by Quentin Blake delights me and I am sure will delight countless numbers of children.

D. A. Young, in a review of "The Adventures of Lester," in The Junior Bookshelf, *Vol. 42, No. 3, June, 1978, p. 139.*

The Wild Washerwomen: A New Folk Tale (1979)

[The Wild Washerwomen *is written by John Yeoman.*]

Told in the manner of a folk tale, the story tells how seven washerwomen—Dottie, Lottie, Molly, Dolly, Winnie, Minnie, and Ernestine—worked hard washing mountains of dirty laundry in the river. Finally, disgruntled with their job, they went berserk, splashing passers-by with muddy water, raising havoc in the marketplace, stealing fruit in orchards, and generally making themselves the terror of neighboring villages. But meeting their match in seven woodcutters who lived in the forest, they all married and settled down to a happy life of clothes-washing and woodcutting. The preposterous, joyful narrative and the expressive caricaturing of the slapdash line drawings washed with color are perfectly balanced; story and pictures move from page to page in a hilarious progress, the illustrations continuously echoing and expanding the often understated humor of the text. (pp. 50-1)

Paul Heins, in a review of "The Wild Washerwomen: A New Folk Tale," in The Horn Book Magazine, *Vol. LVI, No. 1, February, 1980, pp. 50-1.*

The team of John Yeoman and Quentin Blake is way out on its own, far ahead of the field. This is the rare matching of kindred spirits, a harmony of humour.

The seven washerwomen, so exquisitely differentiated in Quentin Blake's drawings, are put upon, victimised and hard done-by their ruthless Victorian-type laundry-master Mr. Balthazar Tight. One day he pushes them too far, and then they do their share of pushing, burying him under a mountain of very dirty, very smelly laundry. Not since Falstaff went out for foul linen has there been such a splendid moment in laundry literature. Having broken with tyranny the washerwomen become wild indeed, running amok and terrorising the neighbourhood. Seven woodcutters try to subdue them by adopting a terrifying disguise, but the washerwomen see in their blackened faces and grimy bodies only a challenge to their own professionalism. By the time the woodcutters have been well and truly scrubbed, rinsed and laid out to dry, a strong feeling has sprung up between them and their conquerors. A happy ending indeed, with one of the most idyllic of Mr. Blake's double-spreads.

This is genuine, all-pervading humour, untouched with satire but firmly based in real values. Let us stop laughing for a moment to thank two masters for a joyous and universally acceptable offering.

M. Crouch, in a review of "The Wild Washerwomen," in The Junior Bookshelf, *Vol. 44, No. 1, February, 1980, p. 19.*

Good grief, are we still having to deal with this sort of thing? Seven washerwomen rebel against their employer, make off with a goat cart, and rampage through the countryside, overturning market stalls, stealing food, ringing churchbells. (A dissatisfied, assertive woman will go out of control.) There are several jaunty illustrations of the women beating up men, bending their rifles, dunking them in rain barrels. Eventually seven burly woodcutters hear about the women and, after dirtying themselves to look as frightening as possible, encounter them on a woodland path. One of the women cries, "Come on girls, remember you're washerwomen!" and the men are washed and wooed. (All those women really wanted was. . . .) The last picture is of the men, women, and their babies all sharing tasks together—a sop to liberation and a patently illogical one at that. Alas, the story is happily illustrated with giddy and well-designed watercolors, so children might be attracted to it, and artfully paced so they might remember it. Let's hope this talented English team will thump a different drum next time around.

Mary B. Nickerson, in a review of "The Wild Washerwomen," in School Library Journal, *Vol. 26, No. 7, March, 1980, p. 127.*

All conservatives and all men be warned that this book is both subversive and Militant Lib. As soon as it is placed in a library it will provoke a queue of eager readers. How could anyone resist a fairy tale about seven washerwomen, called Dottie, Lottie, Molly, Dolly, Winnie, Minnie and Ernestine, who take up the cudgels against the exploitation of the laundry owner, Mr. Balthazar Tight? Having found freedom, they go on the rampage in the local town and behave in the most reprehensible way, to the consternation of the local population. All ends happily, with seven weddings and a 'Seven brides for seven brothers' romp. A most exhilarating book. The pace is fast and furious, the pictures crammed with Mr Blake's spiky-fingered females and unkempt dogs. I loved every moment.

Gabrielle Maunder, in a review of "The Wild Washerwomen," in The School Librarian, *Vol. 28, No. 2, June, 1980, p. 143.*

Mister Magnolia   (1980)

Mr Magnolia is the sort of person you cannot help liking on sight; he is cheerful, agile, and alive with energy, and Quentin Blake's witty and graceful drawings establish him as a character very rapidly in this short book. Unlike most of Quentin Blake's other books this is a story which is suitable for quite young children. Mr Magnolia has almost everything he needs in life except another boot—he has only one. The book is just long enough to demonstrate Mr Magnolia's accomplishments, introduce his friends, and explain his dilemma before someone turns up with the present that will complete his happiness. It will be a pity if this book has no sequel—it is an excellent introduction to Mr Magnolia and his friends, who are obviously only just launched on their adventures.

Myra Barrs, "For Young Abecedarians," in The Times Educational Supplement, *No. 3329, March 28, 1980, p. 28.*

Quentin Blake has excelled himself with this book whose hero has only one boot. It is a lively attractive book, full of the most marvellous drawings of mice, owls, children and lots of other characters. It is a wonderful collection, on a bright, happy, vibrating kind of book and it must surely be Quentin Blake's best to date. Do buy it.

Margaret Walker, in a review of "Mister Magnolia," in Book Window, *Vol. 7, No. 2, Spring, 1980, p. 12.*

'Mr Magnolia has only one boot'—a promising start for a rhyming nonsense-tale in which flute, newt, suit, scoot and other words dictate the action. The rhythm and cumulation invite participation from small listeners, who can also watch the adventures of the dashing hero and see how the characters he meets (dinosaur, lady musicians, children, mice and others) gather at the end to see him open a parcel with predictable contents. Quentin Blake's typically active line and emphatic colour and his comic detail have never been put to better use.

Margery Fisher, in a review of "Mr. Magnolia," in Growing Point, *Vol. 19, No. 1, May, 1980, p. 3708.*

Very brief, very silly, very jolly, this nonsense story will be fun to read aloud. Poor Mr. Magnolia has all sorts of interesting treasures and attributes but, alas, only one boot. He doesn't let that stop him from making friends, going places, and at last, a kind little girl presents him with an oddly shaped parcel. He unwraps and unwraps, and a beautiful blue boot with a gold star emerges. Like all good nonsense verse, this one has a compelling rhythm; once you start, you'll read right on, and it will only take about three minutes flat.

Joan McGrath, in a review of "Mister Magnolia," in School Library Journal, *Vol. 26, No. 10, August, 1980, p. 46.*

Rumbelow's Dance   (1982)

[Rumbelow's Dance *is written by John Yeoman.*]

Any book which has Quentin Blake as illustrator is in luck, for who can match his zany wit and euphoria, his engaging charm, his wild assurance of line? In John Yeoman's **Rumbelow's Dance,** a boy is sent to visit his lonely grandparents. He dances along (that's his way) and inspires a host of lagging travellers to do likewise. (But why *should* the "lazy" pig want to get to market?) Finally the old grandparents do a graceful dance on their own. A dazzling display of Blakerie—but possibly, when the effervescence has died down, it is hard to say what remains.

Naomi Lewis "Once upon a Line," in The Times Educational Supplement, *No. 3464, November 19, 1982, p. 32.*

As the Pied Piper piped his way out of town in the 1880s with the lavish illustrations of Kate Greenaway, so Rumbelow dances his way back in again in the 1980s in a far more nonchalant manner, depicted by Quentin Blake. The children of Hamelin "Tripping and skipping, ran merrily after the Wonderful music with shouting and laughter", while Rumbelow's crowd have let their hair down a little and enjoy their instructions to "Smile with the day, Tripping along, singing a song, Waving your stockings and socks on the way."

Kate Greenaway and Quentin Blake were and are leaders in their field. Mr Blake has illustrated a hundred and fifty books, is Head of Illustration in the School of Graphic Arts at the Royal College of Art, and in 1980 won the Kate Greenaway Prize for his book **Mr Magnolia,** though it was really also in recognition of his great contribution to children's literature.

Considering that the innocent hearts and souls of the little people for whom they are illustrating have not changed at all, the difference between these two artists is astonishing. Miss Greenaway's style is elegant and meticulous, Mr Blake's is sketchy and shambolic. But they both enchant. Perhaps it is the detail which Miss Greenaway chooses to include, and the detail which Mr Blake chooses to leave out which is the peculiar secret of each of them. Mr Blake, for example, doesn't need eyebrows on his characters, he just uses tiny dots for eyes and creates the most extraordinarily humorous expressions in an instant.

As for the text of **Rumbelow's Dance,** it is the sort of thing young children love to hear and old parents get bored with reading. Like the woman who can't get her pig home from market, Rumbelow performs in reverse. A repetitive verse grows longer and longer with each page as Rumbelow collects a wild and motley crew along his way through water colour woods until he has a mad procession dancing and prancing behind him into town. They all tumble in a gaggle of arms and legs onto the door-step of Rumbelow's grandparents and end up dancing market day away. It is the perfect medium for Mr Blake to display his range of rural lads, lasses and animals and a happy one for John Yeoman, who once he's written the first verse, is away.

For four to seven year olds I would recommend it because

it is light and merry and happy and, perhaps best of all, has no hidden political message. The illustrations are superbly funny though the text is less so. My four year old son should, in the end, be the ultimate judge, and he, when I'd finished reading it to him said, "That was good that."

Candida Lycett Green, "Prancing Along," in The Times Literary Supplement, No. 4156, November 26, 1982, p. 1306.

It would be absurd to offer any criticism of **Rumbelow's Dance.** There is no better partnership today than Yeoman and Blake. Word and drawing seem to have come about through a single creative act. The story is a memorable variant on the cumulative folk-tale. . . . Most attention will inevitably be directed to the pictures, which show Quentin Blake at his inventive best, but do look closely at the words. John Yeoman applies the repetitive formula—repetition with variation—with the greatest skill and gusto. There is not a syllable too many nor a word out of tune. How good to see such fun and unaffected popular appeal coming out of a work based firmly on fine craftmanship and sound observation.

M. Crouch, in a review of "Rumbelow's Dance," in The Junior Bookshelf, Vol. 47, No. 1, February, 1983, p. 10.

Quentin Blake's Nursery Rhyme Book (1983)

Quentin Blake's Nursery Rhyme Book contains, as you might expect, a selection of more or less unfamiliar (but still chantable) nursery rhymes and a number of lively drawings where a few confident lines and some splashes of colour evoke the highly characteristic features of Mr Punchinello, Jack Sprat and any number of attendant children, cats, dogs and bosomy ladies. Quentin Blake's illustrations are unusual for a book of this kind in that they manage not to dominate the page while remaining rewarding in themselves. Here Blake seems to be working on a Chagall-like theme of flight—Jack-a-Dandy hops higher than the houses; Jumping Joan bounds into the air far above the heads of her family and friends; the Man in Brown is depicted achieving a graceful trajectroy in pursuit of the Pig. A small doubt remains over whether the rhymes and pictures may not have gone a little too far in their pursuit of originality. A greater doubt concerns the wisdom of publishing a moderately expensive book containing sixteen not terribly memorable rhymes for a market which has already been supplied with the works of Provensen, Bayley and Briggs.

Elizabeth Barry, "In Brief," in The Times Literary Supplement, No. 4208, November 25, 1983, p. 1312.

Quentin Blake has gone to some of the less familiar pages of the Opies' books for the material for his new and outstandingly brilliant picture-book. In two respects this is quite different from any other collection of nursery rhymes. First, he makes out of each set of inconsequential verses a complete drama, expressed sometimes in a single picture, sometimes in half a dozen or so laid cunningly across the page in apparent spontaneity. Next, he makes

an entity of these unrelated pieces, not only by the use of a unifying style, but by introducing recurrent characters. They all come joyously together in the last pair of pages, when the forward young woman of 'Ickle ockle' brings her formerly reluctant bridegroom to the wedding accompanied by a rumbustious gaggle of guests gathered from other pages. It is all done with Mr. Blake's characteristically fluid line and in delicate colour, with rich humour and keen observation informing every image. Lucky children, and parents, who are privileged to share this vision of a cheerful, brutal and totally unpredictable world.

M. Crouch, in a review of "Nursery Rhyme Book," in The Junior Bookshelf, Vol. 48, No. 1, February, 1984, p. 11.

A small group of rather eccentric, unfamiliar nursery rhymes taken from the collections of Peter and Iona Opie is illustrated in the artist's energetic, quirky style. Most of the nursery rhymes and their pictures are engaging; for example, "Pussy Cat ate the dumplings / Pussy Cat ate the dumplings / Mama stood by, / And cried, Oh, fie! / Why did you eat the dumplings?" shows a rapidly expanding cat and a hapless mama. But "Goosey, goosey gander, / Who stands yonder? / Little Betsy Baker; / Take her up and shake her," is somewhat ambiguous, as a sporting-looking gent roughly shakes a little girl and departs with a pleased look on his face. Nearly all the characters reappear in a grand finale in the last illustration. The very peculiarities of the rhymes are matched and even emphasized by the illustrations; it is astonishing what a variety of expressions and characterizations can be achieved by a few scratchy lines. Not a standard Mother Goose collection—but fresh and funny.

From The Story of the Dancing Frog, *written and illustrated by Quentin Blake.*

Ann A. Flowers, in a review of "Quentin Blake's Nursery Rhyme Book," in The Horn Book Magazine, *Vol. LX, No. 2, April, 1984, p. 180.*

The Story of the Dancing Frog   (1984)

Quentin Blake seems to be on hand wherever you turn, and his instantly recognizable combination of sprightly pen and watery brush is a guarantee of frequent delight. He is our street-wise Ardizzone, often doodling at the edge of whimsy and never one to miss the opportunity for a marginal joke. His pictures are improvisational, curiously featherweight, and full of a witty pathos spiced with mischief. Whereas for a more meticulous narrative illustrator like Maurice Sendak there is a dark, haunted magic in the web of his cross-hatching, for Quentin Blake the most sombre mood is grey or sepia wash, and even though his lines can droop with melancholy they soon pick up again. However strongly he hints at a deeper sadness, there's always animation to keep your spirits up, a busy optimism, a relish of the bizarre, even a silliness of invention, and above all the kind of adaptability which ensures popular success.

These observations, which apply generally to Blake's output, are prompted by his latest picture book for which he has also written the text. *The Story of the Dancing Frog* is told, at the end of the day, by a tired mother to her small child. There is an air of loneliness and loss from the outset (no colour until the story itself begins) for which imagination must compensate. Father is not around and is referred to, only once, in the past tense. Aunt Gertrude too—the story's heroine—suffers the loss of her husband after a brief spell of romantic happiness and is prevented from drowning herself, in the nick of time, by the sight of the eponymous frog dancing on a lilypad. There's a moment—and a sequence of pictures—of great tenderness as Gertrude walks into the water, picks up the frog, and carries it home to set in motion a series of delightful events in which she and her new friend, bound together as Good Companions, tour the world. George the Frog, an absolute natural, dances with a Russian ballet company with a Parisian showgirl dressed in feathers, and with Fred You-know-who in a smash-hit Broadway musical. Gertrude suffers hardship to keep the show on the road, and even turns down an offer of marriage out of loyalty (and, yes, love) for George. They spend their retirement in the south of France where Gertrude sorts out their press cuttings and, in warm weather—in two marvellously sunny pictures—gives George a shower with the watering can.

"And are they dead now, then?" "Well, that was a long time ago, so I suppose they must be." Back to the present and the child taking the cocoa and sandwiches back to the kitchen. *The Story of the Dancing Frog* is an affectionate book; gentle, wise, poignant and comic.

John Mole, "Space to Dance," in The Times Literary Supplement, *No. 4258, November 9, 1984, p. 1294.*

Quentin Blake performs here a very neat trick indeed and makes the reader part of the dialogue between storyteller and listener. All the questions asked by young Jo are precisely the questions the reader will ask, and the colloquial style of the storyteller seems to include the reader in the intimate circle. The story itself is one of Blake's exotic romps. This time the protagonists are Gertrude, the sorrowing widow of a gallant sailor, and her dancing frog, George.

> 'Was that his name, then?'
> 'I don't know. Maybe it was just his stage-name.'

From being a comfort to Gertrude in her grief, George leads them on to fame and fortune and becomes an international celebrity, reclining in glasses of champagne and partnering a girl dressed in bananas in Paris. It's exactly the book to give to 'reluctant' readers—witty, fast-moving, ingenious—and is a gem to read aloud.

Gabrielle Maunder, in a review of "The Story of the Dancing Frog," in The School Librarian, *Vol. 32, No. 4, December, 1984, p. 347.*

Blake's whimsical, entertaining story also has a slim thread of pathos, which gives the tale some unexpected resonance. Almost a story within a story, this unfolds in the guise of a mother recounting a piece of family history to her daughter. The general absence of dramatic tension would seem to be a flaw but for the tale's convincing aura of reality. The matter-of-fact tone in the telling provides a veneer of truth that carries the reader easily along. Not to be missed, of course, are Blake's illustrations, which, in their wacky way, portray events just as seriously as the narrative implies. The touching relationship blossoms surely in the thorough cartoon scenes, which hold many chuckling asides but which also accent an underlying affection for this unlikely pair.

Denise M. Wilms, in a review of "The Story of the Dancing Frog," in Booklist, *Vol. 81, No. 15, April 1, 1985, p. 1117.*

[*The Story of the Dancing Frog* is] a 'more or less' true story, a tale within a tale, told to a child at bedtime by her weary mum. Colour is used emotively; the world of the teller and listener is merely sepia. Then, when Gertrude's adventures begin, Blake splashes in the tints of froggy green, fluid blues and a range of subtle greys—ash, smoke, violet, rose, ivory, buff. His line is quirky, agile and sure as George's gifted feet. The light touch with pen and paint catches the humour and hints at the sadness of this enigmatic tale of courage, loss, imagination, fortitude, loyalty, friendship and luck. It is Blake at his best. (p. 8)

Jane Doonan, in a review of "The Story of the Dancing Frog," in The Signal Selection of Children's Books, *1984, pp. 7-8.*

The Giraffe and the Pelly and Me   (1985)

[*The Giraffe and the Pelly and Me is written by Raold Dahl.*]

Blake's frenetic watercolors are quite appealing, but they do not redeem this slight story. A little boy wandering by a deserted old grubber (sweet shop) notices some movement within and meets the owners of the Ladderless Window-Cleaning Co. The building's new tenants—a giraffe, a pelican and a monkey—have hardly introduced themselves to the lad when a chauffeur-driven limousine arrives to invite the glass-shining team to clean the 677 windows of the Duke's house. After demonstrating their cleaning finesse (and catching a burglar in the process), the three are rewarded with edible gifts and an invitation to live with the Duke. Young Billy receives the renovated sweet shop stocked with candies of the world, which Dahl describes in detail. The charming illustrations surrounding the verse beg to climb off of the oversize pages. Perhaps the effect would be smashing as an animated cartoon, but the minimal plot development makes this an extremely weak book. (pp. 69-70)

> *Susan Scheps, in a review of "The Giraffe & the Pelly & Me," in* School Library Journal, *Vol. 32, No. 4, December, 1985, pp. 69-70.*

Roald Dahl's outrageous sense of humor has come to the fore again in a tall tale about a boy who joins forces with a window-cleaning company composed of a giraffe, a pelican, and a monkey. . . . Reminding one of *Charlie and the Chocolate Factory,* the book shows the boy being given the best sweet-shop in the world, deliciously filled with such glorious sweets as "Mint Jujubes that will give the boy next door green teeth for a month," "Stickjaw for talkative parents," and Scarlet Scorchdroppers, guaranteed to keep a person warm. Quentin Blake's illustrations are an integral part of the story; it is hard to imagine it without his choleric Duke, cheerful pelican, and scruffy little boy. Not one of Dahl's major efforts, but a captivating story and a wonderful read-aloud. (pp. 46-7)

> *Ann A. Flowers, in a review of "The Giraffe and the Pelly and Me," in* The Horn Book Magazine, *Vol. LXII, No. 1, January-February, 1986, pp. 46-7.*

The boy narrator—delightfully evoked in Quentin Blake's drawings—who acts as business manager to the firm is given a special reward for his part in the enterprise, because the Duke sets him up in his own sweetshop, a typical Dahl notion thought out with mouth-watering and jaw-sticking detail.

Despite the picture-book format and an abundance of characteristic drawings in Mr. Blake's exuberant manner, this is not really a book for the smallest. The text is very long, and among the genuine wit and high spirits there is rather too much of the mock naivety of which Mr. Dahl is sometimes guilty. Do children really like to be condescended to in this way? Visually the book is irresistible, and the basic idea is as funny and original as one could wish.

> *M. Crouch, in a review of "The Giraffe and the Pelly and Me," in* The Junior Bookshelf, *Vol. 50, No. 1, February, 1986, p. 14.*

Roald Dahl's new picture story book, illustrated with Quentin Blake's usual brilliant ability to capture the feel of a text rather than merely to describe its events, is about three friends who form a co-operative called 'The Ladderless Window-Cleaning Co.' (which is where the giraffe comes in . . .). Reading it, I can understand the endless

appeal this writer has for young readers. This book is exactly the kind of story they themselves write—full of more and more exaggerated occurrences—with a plot which gallops along leaving the path behind littered with holes and inconsistencies (not that anyone ever bothers to look). Adjective piles on adjective, adverb on adverb. I must admit to finding it a little frenetic, but that only goes to show how *old* I am.

> *Gabrielle Maunder, in a review of "The Giraffe and the Pelly and Me," in* The School Librarian, *Vol. 34, No. 2, June, 1986, p. 139.*

The Rain Door (1986)

[*The Rain Door is written by Russell Hoban.*]

It may be unfair to approach a children's book with adult expectations, but the combination of Russell Hoban and Quentin Blake makes it unavoidable. Perhaps the disappointment is unavoidable too. But the story of Harry and his translation to a magic world beyond the sky, where rain is made, somehow fails to deliver. There is ingenuity in the concept of a rag-and-bone man whose cart of junk contains the wherewithal of piping water down from the sky; the materialization of an enchanted door has a resonance which goes back through C. S. Lewis to Lewis Carroll; and the finale, where Harry drives a thundering cart through the sky, pursued by a roaring lion, and creates a rainstorm over London, should carry a Wagnerian exhilaration.

But there is too much contrivance, and too little exposition; resourceful as he is, Harry never claims the attention he should. The atmosphere of a fantastical world which lies behind the rain may remind adult readers of Francis Ford Coppola's film *The Rain People,* or even Ray Bradbury, but children are more likely to wonder about the likelihood of horse-drawn rag-and-bone carts, and to miss the play on words like thunder and lightning. Quentin Blake's whimsical illustrations are effective, sketchy lines drawn against vivid colour-washes; the rain door itself is brilliantly suggested. But Hoban does not convey that peculiar and intense vision epitomized in his earlier masterpieces like *The Mouse and His Child* and *Riddley Walker.* The charm is there, but it fails to carry the performance.

> *Roy Foster, "In Brief," in* The Times Literary Supplement, *No. 4346, July 18, 1986, p. 798.*

With most of his authors—Roald Dahl, John Yeoman—Quentin Blake operates on equal terms. Russell Hoban is clearly in charge in this extraordinary and joyous book. Mr. Hoban knows how to find magic in the most commonplace of subjects and situations. Here he evokes the very smell of a hot dry day with its shimmering light and the passing of a melancholy rag-and-bone man, and with them he opens the rain door into a characteristically fantastic world. Harry, who is rash enough to follow the rag-and-bone man and finds a door with no knocker or handle but a key-hole, is one of Quentin Blake's typical little boys, self-contained, persistent. Stepping out of a sun-drenched London street Harry finds himself in a desert littered with the rag-and-bone man's junk. In the distance he hears a lion threatening the rag-and-bone man's horse. Out of the bones and bolts and springs that lie scattered on the desert floor he builds a passable dinosaur that winds up—a nice Hoban touch—and goes lumbering over the desert with its horn going GAHOOGA. Despite the need to wind up frequently Harry arrives on the scene to find the rag-and-bone man fighting off the lion with a bit of iron piping. The dinosaur does the trick. Harry takes the reins while the rag-and-bone man rigs up his hose and sprinkler, and the rain falls. The lion provides the thunder, and the horse—named Lightning—flashes across the sky. There are magnificent scenes of London domes and towers under rain. Back on earth Harry returns to his world and the rag-and-bone man drives off, shouting 'Any old thunder!' A book only Russell Hoban could have conceived, and he executes it with the surest of touches. Every turn of his wit and wisdom is matched with a vivid swift image from Quentin Blake. What was it all about? We may not be able to answer, but we are surely privileged to have been there and to have shared in the fantasy and the fun.

> *M. Crouch, in a review of "The Rain Door," in* The Junior Bookshelf, *Vol. 50, No. 6, December, 1986, p. 217.*

Despite the light tone and lively style of the writing and the comic flair of the equally lively paintings, this doesn't come off as successfully as previous books by Hoban and Blake. First published in Great Britain, this picture book fantasy is weak in plot and development: a boy thinks he hears a rag-and-bone man calling "Rainy numbers up," and follows him into the aqueous blur down the road to begin a series of improbable (and, alas, not very plausible, even within the parameters of the fantasy) events.

> *Zena Sutherland, in a review of "The Rain Door," in* Bulletin of the Center for Children's Books, *Vol. 40, No. 10, June, 1987, p. 189.*

A wonderfully inventive, offbeat fantasy tells how a crashing thunderstorm is created one stifling summer day. In narrative concept and in page design the text and the line-and-watercolor illustrations are inseparable; all of the author's energy, ingenuity, word play, onomatopoeia, and untrammeled imagination are beautifully realized by the artist. Beginning in the languid heat of the day, words and pictures rush headlong to a hyperbolic climax and come to an end in an atmosphere of refreshed, water-soaked quietude.

> *Ethel L. Heins, in a review of "The Rain Door," in* The Horn Book Magazine, *Vol. LXIII, No. 4, July-August, 1987, p. 453.*

Mrs. Armitage on Wheels (1987)

Blake relies upon a jaggedy, straggly line to build a sense of character in visual rather than verbal terms. He creates a lean, bespectacled heroine who has uncanny mechanical aptitude and an open, inquiring face. His narrative is a simple chain of parallel segments. He equips Mrs. A's bicycle with a tool kit, towel and soap rack, picnic basket, cassette player, dog seat, umbrella, and sail-like thingamajig. The latter sends the bike into a crashing tailspin and

Mrs. A scraps the whole mess and switches to skates. (pp. 82-3)

> *Donnarae MacCann and Olga Richard, in a review of "Mrs. Armitage on Wheels," in* Wilson Library Bulletin, *Vol. 63, No. 7, March, 1989, p. 82-3.*

When a normally quiet, self-contained child in one's class sits holding her toes and squeals "Oh, no no no it's too much—she's not to fall!' you feel you're on to a winner.

When the rest of the children join her, then you know that Quentin Blake has them hooked yet again! Mrs Armitage's inimitable personality, her amazing additions to her bicycle and the delightfully idiosyncratic twist at the end of the story must make it a new classic! (pp. 8-9)

> *Judith Sharwood, in a review of "Mrs. Armitage on Wheels," in* Books for Keeps, *No. 65, November, 1990, pp. 8-9.*

Quentin Blake's ABC (1989)

Unshaven and balding, the genial man in pink striped pyjamas shoots past on roller-boots. Sporting an outsize scarf emblazoned with the multicoloured letters of the alphabet, as well as a green umbrella and a cat clinging to his tattered coat, he is a mischievous figure. Children skate alongside him dressed in cowboy hats and paper crowns; all seem eager to find out what lies inside the book-cover they embellish.

The answer is **Quentin Blake's ABC,** each page drawn with the scratchy pen lines and loosely brushed washes of colour which identify their maker at once. Blake's acrobatic zest is established straight away with the letter A. An elderly gent in morning dress casts his top hat aside and, with consummate poise, juggles six red and green apples in the air. Children react delightedly, just as they do on the next page where B is celebrated with a splendidly messy breakfast in bed. While a mountainous mother aims toast at her expectant mouth, an anarchic gaggle of kids,

But the very best of all is when we ALL JOIN IN

From All Join In, *written and illustrated by Quentin Blake.*

toy animals and a very lively monkey snuggle beside her among the crumbs and jam. Blakeland is an unpredictable place, where people are often ambushed by sudden, exclamatory surprises. C stands for Cockatoos, "learning to scream", and they dismay the family with their raucous eruptions. The only person to relish their din is Granny, who raises her ear-trumpet towards them as if relieved to find a noise capable of penetrating her deafness at last.

In the past, Blake has perhaps been best known for his Roald Dahl illustrations, many of them displaying a gift for satanic distortion. Glimpses of it are found in the *ABC*, most notably with "I is for Illness / (which *nobody* likes)". An entire family is afflicted with unspecified ailments, and while one child rests in bed everyone else stands around clutching medicine bottles, pills, hot-water-bottles and a hand-mirror—used by a small boy who sticks out a monstrous green tongue in front of the glass. Another note of alarm is sounded further on, when V turns out to be a Vet pressing his stethoscope to the stomach of a pet dragon whose tail lies forlornly on the floor. On the whole, though, Blake maintains a beneficent disposition in this light-hearted book. When he draws the wonderfully wobbly contours of a woman, upside-down in a stream with her legs projecting from the water, no hint of tragedy disturbs the scene. Instead, she smiles as two ducks dive down to befriend the welcome intruder. On another page, the kittens gleefully engaged in scratching an armchair are in little danger of retribution from the gentle old lady who discovers them.

Joie de vivre is paramount most of the time. Whether gazing in awe at a spectacularly splashy firework display, leaping on to a muddy beach or going for a ride on an ostrich, the children in this ABC are motivated above all by the pleasure principle. P is for Parcel, held by a tousled mother who examines its elongated, lumpy shape with fascination. Festooned with labels and airmail stickers, it has clearly come a long way. The caption invites us to "guess what's inside", and it's tempting to imagine a body inside the brown paper. But if I'm right, there's nothing sinister about the package. Once unwrapped, the figure is bound to leap out and beguile everyone with a display of high spirits in Blake's most irrepressible manner; as his namesake William once wrote, Energy is Eternal Delight.

> *Richard Cork, "J for Joy," in* The Times Literary Supplement, *No. 4501, July 7, 1989, p. 757.*

Big pages, big print. Upper and lower case letters. Plenty of white space to set off the letters and the rhyming text at the foot of each page. Funny, lively, inventive pictures that also have the small-child appeals of exaggeration and incongruity. Line-and-wash drawings accompanying the text for "Q is for Queen with a cloak and a crown" and "R is for roller skates—watch us fall down!" show, for example, scruffy looking parents (Blake's line does wonders) participating amicably with duster/fans and towel/trains in the cortege of their wee daughter, who is proud and beaming and wearing her mother's shoes. Roller skaters, all falling down, come in all sizes on the facing page.

> *Zena Sutherland, in a review of "Quentin Blake's A B C," in* Bulletin of the Center for

Children's Books, *Vol. 43, No. 1, September, 1989, p. 4.*

With its rhyming text and hilarious watercolors, this oversized alphabet book is sure to charm the socks off young children. "A is for Apples, some green and some red/ B is for Breakfast we're having in bed." This rhythmic movement flows throughout the text, with the rhymes creating scenes of great fun, such as "L is for Legs that we wave in the the air," with an illustration of an adult and three children all standing on their heads. Every letter offers a good chuckle, some even an outburst of laughter, as Blake invites his readers to giggle over his crazy characters and detailed artwork, splashed on the page in his usual lighthearted manner. A sure delight for all young children, and an important addition to the concept book arena.

> *Leslie Barban, in a review of "Quentin Blake's ABC," in* School Library Journal, *Vol. 36, No. 2, February, 1990, p. 80.*

All Join In (1990)

The seven snatches of doggerel offered here are designed to persuade small children to participate either in mime and action or, more often, in enjoying onomatopoeic sounds. For example, "Sorting out the kitchen pans" evokes Ding Dong Bang, Bing Bong Clang, Ting Bong Dong, Clang Ding Bong, exercising listening ears with a teasingly uneven sequence, and similar effects help in brisk accounts of children interrupting their elders, a cat chorus at bedtime and a spring-cleaning romp. Sprawling all over the pages, spidery wash and line pictures give a robust expression to moods and actions, mainly and congenially subversive.

> *Margery Fisher, in a review of "All Join In," in* Growing Point, *Vol 29, No. 5, January, 1991, p. 5461.*

British illustrator Quentin Blake's latest picture book presents six short poems, as bouncy and boisterous as school bus songs and illustrated with equally high spirits. Parents and teachers will easily spot the book's central theme—the joys of cooperation—but what will endear the book to children is the ongoing idea that lots of kids making lots of noise can have lots of fun. Cheerful kids, depicted in humorous pen drawings with watercolor washes, romp through the pages with a fine, Blakean sense of merriment. Each poem has a refrain; the book's title echoes the refrains of the first and last selections. The verses beg to be read aloud or, better still, sung to story hour or classroom kids. Chances are, they'll all join in.

> *Carolyn Phelan, in a review of "All Join In," in* Booklist, *Vol. 87, No. 16, April 15, 1991, p. 1647.*

These verses may be as unsubstantial as meringue, but they're just as tasty. Frenzied action and cheerful noise are the focus of each of six poems that share the ebullient quality of Blake's dashing line and humorous approach in illustration. One poem begins, for example, with "When William's in his study / and his thoughts are very deep /

We come and help him concentrate— / We go BEEP-BEEP BEEP-BEEP." The audience will relish the noise, the rhyme, the rhythm, the "join in" refrain—and the delightful idea of disrupting the pursuits of adults.

Zena Sutherland, in a review of "All Join In," in Bulletin of the Center for Children's Books, *Vol. 44, No. 9, May, 1991, p. 211.*

Blake's frolicsome illustrations wrap around six rambunctious participation poems, the first and last of which all but demand that audiences "all join in." Tucked between are gleeful noisemakers, dapper ducks, exhilarating slides, musical kettles, and cacophonous cats, all captured in their comic quintessence by Blake's colorful pen-and-watercolor drawings. Each poem offers a subtle invitation for added verses. At times the illustrations surpass their text or vice versa, but overall they are splendid. The poems are rousing good fun, and when they are at their best the book becomes like a well-loved coat one wishes to toss aside to better enjoy a romp. The creative writing potential, the printed poems to refer to if they slip from memory, and the joyful cartoons guarantee repeated delight.

Jody McCoy, in a review of "All Join In," in School Library Journal, *Vol. 37, No. 7, July, 1991, p. 54.*

[In these poems Blake] highlights the personalities of ordinary folk. *All Join In* must really be seen to be appreciated, given its great array of scruffy characters:

When Sandra plays the trumpet
    it makes a lovely sound
And Mervyn on his drum-kit
    can be heard for miles around
Stephanie is brilliant
    when she plays the violin
But the very best of all is when
    we ALL JOIN IN . . .

Poems that follow are splendid blends of wit, logic, and commotion.

Blake's cartoon artistry brings depth and empathy to all these ruckus makers. Embedded in the lines are little outbursts of excitement, small blobs of thicker ink that make the contours jaggedy. Colors add unconventional patterns to the garments, and white spaces move in and around the spots of color in ways that keep the whole image animated. The result is vibrant, comic, folksy.

Donnarae MacCann and Olga Richard, in a review of "All Join In," in Wilson Library Bulletin, *Vol. 66, No. 2, October, 1991, p. 106.*

Cockatoos (1992)

Quentin Blake in top form is unbeatable, and he is certainly at his inimitable best in **Cockatoos:** exquisite drawing, a strong theme, his brand of logical nonsense. Professor Dupont, a creature of habit, has ten cockatoos who, after the nth repetition of his morning ritual, decide to revolt. Their ingenuity ought to have had its reward, but, as Mr. Blake observes sadly, 'some people never learn'. A final wordless picture shows the cockatoos swinging into action, this, one feels, for the last time. An observant child will quickly realize that this is, among other things, a counting-book. A steadily increasing number of birds, from one to ten, appear in the pictures, unseen by the learned but not very bright professor. The whole joke is carried off with appropriate sobriety.

M. Crouch, in a review of "Cockatoos," in The Junior Bookshelf, *Vol. 56, No. 4, August, 1992, p. 141.*

A new Quentin Blake is always a joyous event, and this is an enchanting puzzle picture book, in which a platitudinous professor hunts frantically through a traditional French house for his ten missing cockatoos. It is a counting book also in the sense that a sequence of ten pictures reveals first one, then two, and so on, up to the full ten cockatoos hiding in different parts of the house, but, since the numbers are not written anywhere, its chief educational value will lie in encouraging attention to detail and the separation of figure from ground. It may also give some lessons in social history, through the wonderful clutter in attic and cellar, and the furnishings of the other rooms. Even this, however, will not be its greatest value: that comes in the sheer pleasure of the professor's absurdity, the cockatoos' ingenuity, and Quentin Blake's masterfully casual lines.

Audrey Laski, in a review of "Cockatoos," in The School Librarian, *Vol. 40, No. 3, August, 1992, p. 93.*

Cockatoos is about human idiosyncrasy more than it is about cockatoos. Professor Dupont is a creature of unswerving routine and the cockatoos in his conservatory become sick to death of it. So they take matters into their own hands and leave. The joy of the book is in finding the parrots in each of the pictures that trace the Professor's search for his birds, and in their response to his persistent behaviour, depicted without words on the last page.

The pen and watercolour sketches capture the moods and attitudes of the characters with a dot and a stroke of the pen in the care-free style that has made Blake's illustrations so popular, together with his portrayal of human idiosyncrasy. There is much to be looked at and looked for and laughed at in the pictures that complement, so completely and so effectively, the simple but maturely expressed text.

Philip S. Kidner, in a review of "Cockatoos," in Reading Time, *Vol. XXXVI, No. IV, 1992, p. 14.*

Enid Blyton

1897-1968

(Also wrote as Mary Pollock) English author of fiction, nonfiction, picture books, plays, and retellings; journalist, and editor.

Major works include *The Enchanted Wood* (1939), *Five on a Treasure Island* (1942), *The Castle of Adventure* (1946), *Little Noddy Goes to Toyland* (1949), *The Secret Seven* (1949), *Six Bad Boys* (1951).

The following entry emphasizes general criticism of Blyton's career. It also includes a selection of reviews to supplement the general criticism.

The author of approximately six hundred books for children and young people, Blyton is perhaps the most successful and controversial English writer in the field of juvenile literature. She is considered a literary phenomenon, an author whose sales at one time rivaled those of the Bible and Shakespeare, and is often lauded for her part in developing what critics refer to as the "Blyton industry," which includes toys, films, magazines and other spinoffs in addition to her books. Blyton wrote in every genre and for every age group: in the area of fiction, her works encompass school stories, adventure stories, mystery stories, and circus stories as well as the realistic novel. She is also the author of informational books that blend fact and fiction, verse, picture books, plays, and retellings of Bible stories and traditional tales as well as adaptations of works ranging from Aesop and Homer to Joel Chandler Harris and Jean de Brunhoff. Often utilizing motifs such as desert islands, kidnapped princes, and foreign kingdoms, Blyton wrote many series and is especially well known as an author of formula fiction. She is perhaps most recognized as the creator of Little Noddy, a wooden elf who constantly nods his head due to the spring in his neck and who is the hero of over fifty fantasies, and the stories for middle graders detailing the exploits of the Famous Five and the Secret Seven, siblings and cousins who solve mysteries on their school holidays that involve smugglers, spies, and robbers; replete with clandestine meeting places and secret passages, these books are often called the most widely read series in children's literature. Praised for her narrative skill, Blyton is often considered a masterful storyteller whose works reflect her youthful perspective, understanding of children and their needs, and aptitude for creating in a variety of genres; several of her books are also credited with transcending their formulas. Beloved by the young for creating simple, accessible stories that emphasize action while providing humor, ritual, and reassurance, she wrote her books in a chatty but direct style that characteristically eschews large words and long descriptions. Blyton is also acknowledged for the popularity of her works with beginning and reluctant readers, and she is usually considered a premier example of a purely escapist writer. Sheila G. Ray notes, "No other writer has succeeded to the same extent in meeting the evident need which there

is amongst children for books of this kind," and adds that Blyton "possessed skills which have not been combined so successfully by any other writer."

Born with a photographic memory, Blyton began to write stories and poems as a small child. A tomboy, she became head girl and captain of games at school, and based one of her most popular creations, George (Georgina) of the Famous Five, on herself as a young girl. Blyton's father left the family when she was twelve, an event that effected her deeply; she later dramatized it in her problem novel *Six Bad Boys*. At the age of fourteen, she published her first poem in a children's magazine. Originally planning to become a concert pianist, Blyton became interested in teaching kindergarten, studying the Froebel and Montessori methods that later influenced her writing for children. She began her professional career by contributing a special page for children to the magazine *Teacher's World,* an addition that brought her instant popularity. As a writer, Blyton usually produced between six and ten thousand words per day; beginning in 1922 with the publication of her poetry collection *Child Whispers,* she increased her production with each decade. Her amazing literary output—for example, thirty-two titles appeared in 1950, her most prolific year—led to the suggestion that she employed a team of ghost writers. Her popularity escalated to the point where Blyton became a household name: Bob Dixon notes that "If a parent knows the name of only one author of children's books, it is hers." Mystery and adventure series figure prominently in Blyton's oeuvre. The circus is one of her favored backgrounds, often providing the setting for unusual characters, adventures, and close contact with animals, themes Blyton recognized as popular with children. Unlike her mystery and adventure novels, Blyton's school stories—set in progressive educational academies—are more concerned with behavior than plot, exploring idiosyncracies in a humorous fashion. Although Blyton has been criticized for her unrealistic depiction of society, in *Six Bad Boys* she attempts to account for the delinquent behavior of six youngsters as the result of poor parenting on the part of their working mothers. Blyton is also the author of pure fantasies, such as the series which began with *The Adventures of the Wishing Chair* (1937) and *The Enchanted Wood* respectively; derived from Norse legends, these humorous works are set in fantastic lands of Blyton's own invention. Blyton received her greatest commercial success with the Noddy series, which she created with Dutch painter Harmsen Van Der Beek, the first illustrator of the stories. Tracing the adventures of the elf and his friends Big Ears, a hundred-year-old brownie, and the policeman Mr. Plod, the stories usually involve the rescuing of polite but naive Noddy by his more worldly friends, all of whom reside in Toyland Village. Noddy became a manufacturing commodity: Noddy dolls, pajamas, and toothpaste flooded the marketplace, leading many to question Blyton's incipient objective in creating the character. In addition to her books, Blyton is the editor of several story collections and nature books. She also edited several popular magazines for children which prompted her audience to organize and support various charities, and she served as the editor of books on teaching methods for adults.

Initially, reactions to Blyton's works were comparatively docile. Although some critics complained about the volume of the books and the lack of believability of her concepts, most observers were favorably disposed toward the author. Beginning in the late 1940s, she increasingly came under attack from educators and librarians, who dismissed her works as undemanding reading and pointed to their weak characterizations, mediocre plots, and impoverished vocabulary, especially in the Noddy books; during this period, librarians also began to ban Blyton from their institutions. During the 1960s, Blyton, who claimed that her books contained absolutely sound moral principles, was censured as racist and sexist for writing odious stereotypic descriptions of minorities and women in regard to dress, occupation, and lifestyle. Still others decried her snobbish preoccupation with middle-class attitudes and suburban family life. In addition, reviewers began to dismiss Blyton as a bad writer, a hack whose arch tone, inconsistency, and literary tricks did nothing to enrich the experience of childhood reading. Despite this intense opposition, she remained immensely popular with children, to whose tastes the author admittedly catered. Blyton's merits are currently being reassessed: several commentators acknowledge that her values represent a bygone era

and are not consciously exploitive, while others commend her effort to make reading enjoyable for children. Recently, there has also been a resurgence of critical interest in the author as one of children's literature's most distinctive—and interesting—cases.

(See also *Something about the Author,* Vol. 25; *Major Authors and Illustrators for Children and Young Adults; Contemporary Authors,* Vols. 25-28 and 77-80; and *Contemporary Authors New Revision Series,* Vol. 33.)

AUTHOR'S COMMENTARY

[*The following excerpt is from* The Story of My Life, *Blyton's autobiography for young readers.*]

[How] do I write my books? How do I think of my stories? I will tell you from the beginning, and try to explain clearly.

First of all, I must tell you that there are two distinct ways of writing a book.

Some authors like to think out the whole story or plot carefully, and make notes of it—a kind of short summary. They think out their characters, and note them down—names, characteristics, colour of eyes, hair, and so on. They think out the setting for their story and may make a plan of the house or garden or countryside they are going to write about. They may even write out a list of the chapters and what they are going to put into them.

Other authors make out no list at all, nor do they make any notes. They invent nothing beforehand. They could not possibly tell you what was going to happen in their books. They draw their story completely from their imagination. It may come out with ease or with difficulty, but it comes, not from the author's conscious mind or deliberate invention, but from his imagination, or, as some people put it, from his subconscious, his 'under-mind', the place where his dreams come from.

Now, as a rule you can tell, when you read a book, whether the author is of the first or second kind. Children can usually tell at once, and I have found that most children as a rule prefer those authors who depend on their imagination rather than on their invention. I think this is why such books as *Alice in Wonderland* are successful. There is something natural and spontaneous and convincing about that kind of book that no amount of conscious and careful invention could produce. It is, as someone once said, 'utterly readable'.

I don't think it really matters much which kind of author one is. Both kinds produce good books, but perhaps those who depend solely on their imaginative powers have more verve and liveliness in their stories, and it is often impossible to put down their books until we have finished them. But anyway, if one is an author, one cannot help being born as one kind or the other! It is something that the writer himself cannot alter.

As most of you know, I am the second kind. I could not possibly *invent* a plot or characters and write them down before I began a book. As for planning out my chapters, that would be impossible too—I don't even know what the book will be about till I begin it!

Now let me try to tell you how I set to work. You will remember that I told you about my night-time 'thoughts'—and how these strange 'thoughts', as I used to call them, came flowing into my mind, weaving themselves into stories of all kinds. All I had to do was to lie still with my eyes closed and let the stories come. I saw them all in my mind's eye as they unfolded.

I do not *think* these stories, as we think out a problem, or ponder over something. They came all ready made, as it were, pouring out complete. Whatever characters there were in the story I could see clearly in my mind's eye and, for the time being, the story was real to me. I was pleased or sad, afraid or delighted, as the story unfolded in my mind.

And it is in exactly the same way that I find my stories now. If I sit in my chair and shut my eyes for a minute or two, in comes the story I am waiting for, all ready and complete in my imagination.

I sit in my chair and think, 'Now today I am going to begin a new book. What shall it be? Adventure? Circus? Nature? Fairy-tale? Mystery? I think it is time for a fairy-tale! A fairy-tale it shall be!'

I have to find two things when I write a book. I have to find my characters, of course, and the setting for the story—the place where everything happens. So I shut my eyes, and I look into my mind's eye.

You know what that is, don't you? We all have one. When I talk to children in public, I show them each their mind's eye. I say: 'Now—shut your eyes for a minute—keep them shut. Now, while they are shut, think of Father Christmas! Think of him—now open your eyes.'

The children all open their eyes and look at me. Then I say: 'Now, when I said to you, "Think of Father Christmas," you saw him, didn't you? You saw him clearly—red suit, red hood, round red jolly face, white beard and all. Well, you used your *mind's eye* to see him. He's not really here, but you saw him for that minute!'

Now, I use my mind's eye the whole time when I write a story. It is almost as if I am looking out of a window, or at a private cinema screen inside my head, and see my characters there—and what I see, I write down. (pp. 85-8)

Where *do* I get all the adventure from? I don't know. I don't know any more than you do. That is the strange part, the part I can't really explain, the part that seems almost like magic. I don't know what the adventures are going to be! And yet, day after day, my fingers fly over my typewriter, and I fill the pages with queer, exciting or comical adventures without ceasing.

The only way I can partly explain it is by using the 'private cinema screen' idea I spoke of a few pages back. It is as if I were watching a story being unfolded on a bright screen. Characters come and go, talk and laugh, things happen to them. . . . [the] whole story sparkles on my private 'screen' inside my head, and I simply put down what I see and hear.

The story comes out complete and whole from beginning to end. I do not have to stop and think for one moment. If I tried to think out or invent the whole book, as some writers do, I could not do it. For one thing it would bore me, and for another it would lack the vigour and the extraordinary touches and surprising ideas that flood out from my imagination. People in my books make jokes I could never have thought of myself. I am merely a sightseer, a reporter, an interpreter, whatever you like to call me.

The only thing that is mine where the book is concerned, is that it is *my* imagination that has supplied every word. Although it is something beyond myself, bigger than I am, it is still mine. I cannot alter it in any way, but I *can* supply it with more and more facts to feed on; I *can* make the road to it easy to travel, so that at any moment I can open the way from my imagination to my conscious mind, and can put into written words the stories and fantasies that come flooding out when I fling wide the gates.

It is open to all writers to enrich their imagination and to make it easy of access. The more one observes and hears and learns, the more one reads (and that is very important), the more one ponders and muses *consciously* on this, that and the other, the richer the imagination becomes. Can you understand that? I hope so, because I am not only writing this particular chapter for you *now,* but so that you may remember it when you are grown-up, and need a mind packed full of good things.

Some writers find it difficult to open the gates to their imagination. You know how I do it—by shutting my eyes, letting my mind go blank, and then looking in my mind's eye for what I am seeking. I find it easy because the gates were open from my earliest childhood, and much practice has meant that they can be swung open now at my slightest touch.

Some writers, particularly those that have to *invent* their stories instead of leaving them to the imagination, work very slowly. A book may take them six months or a year. Those who use their imagination are much quicker than those who have to invent, but even so some imaginative writers are much quicker at their work than others.

I am very lucky. I have such easy access to my imagination, and the flood of ideas pours out so fast and so furiously that it is all I can do to type quickly enough to keep up with them. It is a help, of course, to be able to handle words with pleasure and ease, and to know exactly what words to use. But the *speed* of a writer's work depends entirely on the force, vigour and swiftness of his imagination.

He has to work at the pace of his imagination. If it is a powerful one he is impelled to work quickly. He cannot do otherwise. If his imagination is not so easy to get at, and ideas merely trickle out, then he will write slowly. You can see this happening when your teacher sets your class a story to write, or asks you to describe something that happened in your holiday.

Some children write a few words and stop. Their minds' eyes are completely blank. Their imagination, their memory, cannot supply them quickly with what they want. But other children will speed along, their pens hardly able to keep up with what they are thinking.

As a rule, children who read a lot can write more easily and better than children who read little. They know how to handle words, and their minds are well supplied with facts and fancies because of what they have read. Also, observant children find it easier to write than unobservant ones—they can usually find plenty to say. I wonder which kind of child *you* are!

The luckiest authors are those who have been gifted with an imagination that is easy to get at, and one that is powerful and fertile. There is little hard labour attached to their work. Indeed, it can hardly be called work. It is a delight and a pleasure, and these writers are not happy unless they can work at their books whenever they want to.

I could write a whole book at one sitting if only I didn't have to eat or sleep. When I begin a book, I know it is complete and whole in my imagination, that every detail will be there, and that beginning, middle and end are already prepared, so that the story moves off swiftly, grows and develops, and will round itself off satisfactorily at the end. The exciting thing to me is the development of the story. As I don't know myself what will be in the book I am in the happy position of writing and reading a new story at one and the same time!

It is easy for a writer with a powerful and practised imagination to write ten or twelve thousand words in a day. I could write much more if only my arms didn't get tired of being poised over my typewriter.

If you could lock me up into a room for two, three or four days, with just my typewriter and paper, some food and a bed to sleep in when I was tired, I could come out from that room with a book finished and complete, a book of, say, sixty thousand words. I would not be tired at the end of it because I should have used my imagination, as distinct from my brain. Brain work *is* tiring. Using one's imagination is not.

A book like this one I am writing for you now does not come from my imagination, of course, but from my conscious mind. I think of what I write. I have deliberately planned this book for you. Therefore I am writing it slowly, because *I* am in command, and not my imagination. A nature book is much the same. It is mainly composed of facts, and these cannot be left to the imagination. So some of my books, those that are not 'stories', are written just as you, for instance, would write an essay on something you had learnt in your geography lesson. You would use your brain and your memory, not your imagination. (pp. 95-9)

I have really written [these last chapters] for two kinds of children—those who long to write themselves, and have probably begun already—and those who ask me insistently, whenever they see me: 'Miss Blyton, *how* do you write your books?'

Well, now you know! (p. 99)

> *Enid Blyton, in her* The Story of My Life, *1952. Reprint by Grafton Books, 1986, 126 p.*

E. H. Colwell

[*The following excerpt is a review of* The Sea of Adventure *by English librarian Eileen H. Colwell. Her comment "But what hope has a band of desperate men against four children?" is often quoted by critics noting the unreality of Blyton's works.*]

[*The Sea of Adventure* is the] fourth of this author's series of stories about four children and a parrot. The children's friend Bill, who is something mysterious to do with Scotland Yard, is in danger from a gang of criminals. He "disappears" with the children to some lonely islands, inhabited only by sea-birds. Strangely enough, the gang has chosen this very spot for their headquarters. They kidnap Bill immediately and the children are left marooned with only a puffin for company. But what hope has a band of desperate men against four children? Bill is soon rescued, and the children reveal the gang's hidden store of arms at the bottom of a lagoon.

This is the usual type of adventure story produced by this terrifying writer; exciting but devoid of atmosphere and with the human characters having little to distinguish one from another. The best character studies are the puffins who provide light relief that helps to cover the weak spots in the plot.

The Sea of Adventure will be welcomed by the children who "simply must" read the "latest Blyton," and then never read it again.

> *E. H. Colwell, in a review of "The Sea of Adventure," in* The Junior Bookshelf, *Vol. 12, No. 2, July, 1948, p. 75.*

Colin Welch

[*The following excerpt by critic Colin Welch is often considered a major catalyst for the beginning of the Blyton backlash. In her biography* Enid Blyton, *Barbara Stoney calls it "widely quoted, particularly by those who wished to impose sanctions on Blyton's works."*]

If you have small children and they don't like Noddy, you are very lucky. I have; they do; I am not. This insipid wooden doll, with its nodding head crowned with cap and bell, with its taxi and its friend Big Ears, has opened a rift between parents and children which time alone may heal. They love it; we don't. And we can't agree to differ, live and let live, because we parents have to sit and read the stuff to them.

The Noddy business has by now taken its place among Britain's major non-warlike industries, along with sauce-bottling, the pools, cheesecake photography and the manufacture of ice-lollies, righteous indignation, and plastic pixies. The business is founded on the mass-production of Noddy books, of which 12 million had been sold two years ago: 12 titles, that is to say, and about a million sold of each. The export branch produces Noddy books in countless foreign languages, including Tamil, Hebrew, and Swahili. By-products, controlled by five separate companies, include Noddy soap and Noddy chocolates, Noddy pyjamas and nighties, Noddy painting books, jig-saws, Christmas annuals, cut-outs on cereal packets and models

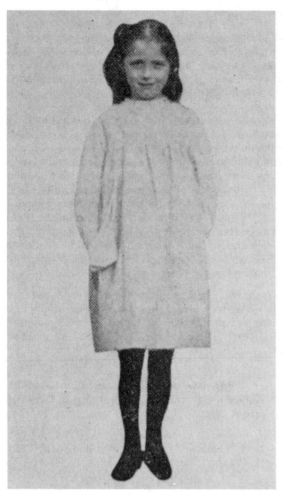

Blyton at the age of seven.

("smashing fun modelling Noddy and his friends: all easily made from Sculptorcraft Rubber Moulds"). Noddy has also appeared on television and the West End stage, though not yet at the Royal Court.

Noddy's onlie begetter is a former schoolmistress called Enid Blyton. She has been described by William Hickey as "a sweet-looking woman in her middle years. The outstanding thing about her is her eyes. They are deep and kind." The really outstanding thing about her is her industry. In the five years 1948-52 inclusive, she managed to fill nearly four close-printed columns of Whitaker's Cumulative Book List—261 titles by my count. In 1955, she clocked up 59 titles, more than a book a week (not all of them about Noddy, of course). Last year, flagging slightly, she only managed 28. She also produces a fortnightly magazine ("the only magazine I write"), runs four children's clubs (the Famous Five Club, the Busy Bees, the Sunbeam Society, and the Magazine Club), and personally answers a thousand or more fan-letters a week.

The scale of her activities has naturally aroused suspicion that she must be a corporate entity like Dumas et Cie, or even some sort of electronic brain. These allegations she indignantly denies: it is all her own work, all done by

hand. "Once I get started," she has said, "I've just got to go on and on. Oh, I love it. . . . Stories flow from my imagination like cotton from a reel." According to her husband, "It has been a constant battle to restrain her from working. The sheer effort of turning out 10,000 words daily—sometimes 14,000—has resulted in heart-strain. She never lets up. . . . She is a remarkable woman, but now she must rest." 14,000 words daily—if we assume a seven-hour writing day—means 2,000 words an hour, about 33 words a minute, a word every two seconds. Miss Blyton's style may be flat, her material banal, her method unreflective; written at such a lick it is astonishing that her works make as much sense as they do. Measured beside this literary Stakhanovite, such prodigies of productivity as Trollope, Zola, and Balzac shrink to mere idle dilettantes.

Miss Blyton is, by Johnson's definition, no blockhead. Even two years ago, the royalties on Noddy alone totalled £400,000. With an income estimated at £50,000 a year, she must be about the highest paid woman in the British Isles. It would be quite wrong, however, to assume that she writes only for money. She writes not merely to amuse, but to edify. Her art is not for art's sake. She is committed: she has A Message.

"Into my books," she says, "I pack ethical and moral teaching. . . . I do not write merely to entertain. My public, bless them, find in my books a sense of security, an anchor, a sure sense that right is always right and that such things as courage and kindliness deserve to be emulated." Thus does she range herself firmly with Dr. F. R. Leavis against Lord David Cecil's hedonistic æstheticism.

If not "merely" entertaining, however, the Noddy books undoubtedly do entertain the people they are meant to entertain. The sales are unanswerable—the more so, since the books could not possibly entertain anyone else. Noddy books are not enjoyed by grown-ups and forced upon children: they are enjoyed by children and forced upon grown-ups. The story behind practically every copy sold is of a delighted child and an adult's dead body.

The essence of a children's classic—perhaps of any classic—is that it can be enjoyed at a number of different levels. The adventures of *Alice in Wonderland* and *Through the Looking-glass* the tales of Grimm and Andersen; the wistful nonsense of Edward Lear; Beatrix Potter's strange stories, in which the matter-of-fact surface half conceals a sort of mysterious poetry; *The Wind in the Willows, Doctor Dolittle* and *Winnie the Pooh*—all these books have delighted generations of children. They have also delighted generations of grown-ups. And when parents read them to their children, it is to experience a complex harmony of pleasures: they find delight in the book itself; they recapture the delight it once brought them as children; and they see awakened that same delight in a new generation. These books thus form a most precious link between the generations, binding them together, part of the family, forever part of the life of each member of it.

To compare, say, Winnie the Pooh with Noddy is not really unfair. Both appeal primarily to the same age group, both with complete success. In other respects, the difference is startling. The Pooh stories are written with wit, taste and economy of means, and an almost magical felicity of form. For sheer craftsmanship take the story "in which Pooh and Piglet go hunting and nearly catch a woozle." The mounting suspense as these two enchanting fools plod round and round the tree in the snow, tracking first one woozle, then two, three, and four, and the effortless way in which the illusion is finally pricked, make this in miniature a perfect short story. Compared with such happy mastery, Noddy is mere drooling, shapeless meandering—"cotton from a reel."

If children enjoy Noddy, is that all that matters? Miss Blyton, of course, wouldn't think so; neither would I. By writing ruthlessly *down* to children, she does not merely bore and antagonise grown-ups. Her Noddy books also fail to stretch the imagination of children, to enlarge their experience, to kindle wonder in them or awaken their delight in words. They contain nothing incomprehensible even to the dimmest child, nothing mysterious or stimulating. They have no "contact with nescience"; they never suggest new and exciting fields to conquer. By putting everything within reach of the child mind, they enervate and cripple it. "Those children," says Miss Blyton, "who find exams easier to pass and scholarships easier to win, are nearly always those who have been much read to in their earlier years." It is hard to see how a diet of Miss Blyton could help with the 11-plus or even with the Cambridge English Tripos. It certainly did not help poor Christopher Craig, of whom, at his trial for murder, it was stated that "the only books he knows anything about are the books of Enid Blyton, which he gets other people to read for him."

The idea that children should have special books is a fairly modern one. Until Victorian days, children by and large read grown-up books or none. In Noddy, "the book for children" is carried logically *ad absurdum*. Victorian children's books often involve long words and quite complex intellectual and moral problems. Since then children's books (not excluding *Winnie the Pooh* of course, in which "writing down" is used half-ironically) have been more and more closely geared to the supposed intellectual powers of their public. Enid Blyton is perhaps the first successful writer of children's books to write actually *below* her audience. "Only not-so-bright children like Enid Blyton," was the acid comment of a town librarian. "My books," replied Miss Blyton, somewhat irrelevantly, "are read in palaces as well as in working-class homes. They are suitable for every child's mentality." In fact, her appeal is not only to the not-so-bright. Her books seem to possess a mysterious fascination for all children, bright and not-so-bright alike.

To what ends, then, does Miss Blyton use her influence over children? It is not easy to say. For all her protestations of lofty purpose, there is little explicit moralising in the Noddy books. One can only go by the characters Miss Blyton appears to find sympathetic. Of these the chief is Noddy himself.

Noddy is not perhaps intended to be admirable. According to his creator, he "is like the children themselves, but more naïve and stupid. Children like that—it makes them feel superior. He is the helpless little man who gets into trouble and invites sympathy—a children's version of the early Charlie Chaplin." But he is undoubtedly intended to be attractive and influential. He is always "dear little Noddy"; he is "always so friendly and polite that everyone likes him"; "he is quite the nicest person in Toy Village"; he cleans his teeth, brushes his hair, polishes his shoes, drinks his milk, eats his bread; he can make children respect policemen, tidy their rooms, eat up their porridge; echoing his creator, he thinks it "good to work hard and earn lots of money"; he is also an artist who composes (or rather "feels coming," like Elgar) songs which, sung by the composer, are invariably received with rapturous enthusiasm. Mr. and Mrs. Tubby Bear like to hear one every morning; "Isn't he clever?" says Miss Rabbit; "How *does* Noddy think of his songs?" asks Miss Blyton: "no wonder everyone is clapping him and calling for more." Several critics have thought Wagner rash actually to incorporate in *Die Meistersinger* a melody, the Prize Song, which he himself declared to be of transcendent beauty, a masterpiece: wiser perhaps, to have flunked the challenge and left it to the imagination. Miss Blyton is equally intrepid. Her pages are lavishly enriched with the fruits of Noddy's genius, of which the following—greeted as usual with universal applause and cheers—is a fair sample:

> I'm only little Noddy
> Who's got a song to sing,
> And a little car to ride in,
> And a bell to jingle-jing.
> I've a little house to live in
> And a little garage too.
> But I've something BIG inside me,
> And that's my love for YOU—
> My love for ALL of you!

The "little-man" sentimentality and crooner's clichés of this declaration are in fact redolent less of "the early Charlie Chaplin" than of the mature Norman Wisdom—to whom in other respects Noddy bears a certain resemblance.

His poetic gifts apart, to call Noddy "more naïve and stupid" than any normal child is a gross understatement. His imbecility is almost indecent. It is somehow symbolised by the ceaseless nodding of his head, a movement—presumably involuntary—upon which great emphasis is placed. The clinical explanation of this palsy or St. Vitus's dance is that the victim's head is supported by a spring. Yet, in the light of Noddy's manifest feeble-mindedness, it is bound to acquire a deeper and more sinister significance. One recalls Zinsser's description of St. John's Evil, a mediæval scourge in which whole villages, driven mad by want and misery, went about shaking and nodding. As characters in Dickens and Wagner have their own catchphrases or themes, so Noddy nods—or "nid-nods." "There goes the little nodding man," cries everyone in Toyland. "Look at his head nid-nodding as he drives." Noddy himself seems to regard his affliction with pride; it also appears to give pleasure to others. Noddy's milkman is paid in nods: "He tapped Noddy's head again as soon as it began to stop nodding and made it nod again, up and down, up and down. 'Payment for *two* bottles,' he said."

More striking even than Noddy's imbecility is his timidity, which again borders on the pathological. Courage may be "a thing to be emulated"; it is not emulated by Noddy. He is terrified of everything. His friend, Big Ears, a 100-year-old Brownie who acts as a sort of father- or male-nurse symbol, knocks at the door: " 'Rat-a-tat-a-tat.' Little Noddy woke up in a hurry and almost fell out of bed in fright. His little wooden head began to nod madly." Bouncing balls scare him so much that he wants to get down a rabbit-hole. He is terrified by the sea ("It's too big. Let's go and find a dear little sea. This one's too big and it keeps moving") and by holidays: " 'They sound sort of prickly,' said Noddy. Big Ears laughed and laughed. 'Not *holly*-days made of prickly *holly*!' he said" (Big Ears' laughter is timely: this is about as near a joke as Miss Blyton gets). When four golliwogs steal his taxi and all his clothes (including "his dear little trousers and shoes"), "Noddy couldn't move an inch. He was so full of alarm that he couldn't say a word. . . . He wriggled and shouted and wailed 'You bad, wicked golliwogs'. . . . Noddy was all alone in the dark wood. 'Help!' he called. 'Oh, help, help, HELP! I'm little Noddy and I'm all alone and LOST.' " He is overwhelmed by self-pity. "He stumbled along through the trees, tears running down his cheeks.

> 'I've lost my hat,
> I've lost my car;
> I simply don't know
> Where they are!
> I'm all alone;
> Won't ANYBODY
> Come to help
> Poor little Noddy?'

Help, of course, is soon forthcoming, in the shape of Big Ears and Mr. Plod the policeman, who arrest the golliwogs and restore Noddy's possessions to him. Though utterly resourceless himself, Noddy is never in trouble for long. There is always somebody to run to, someone to whine and wail at. The machinery of benevolent authority (Big Ears) or of the state (Mr. Plod) can always be invoked to redress the balance between cowardice, weakness, and insanity on the one hand, and vigour, strength, and resource on the other. In some respects, the Noddy books give the impression of being an unintentional yet not wholly inaccurate satire on—or parody of—the welfare state and its attendant attitudes of mind.

If Noddy is "like the children themselves," it is the most unpleasant child that he most resembles. He is querulous, irritable, and humourless. " 'Whoo-ooo-ooo!' said the wind at the top of its voice, and blew some flowers out of a jug on Noddy's table. 'Don't,' said Noddy. 'Now look at the mess you've made! It's my busy morning, too!' " A clockwork clown turns somersaults in Noddy's garden. "Do stop, Clown," Noddy frets, "you always make me feel so dizzy. . . . Oh, don't start going head-over-heels again. Look, you've squashed one of my plants." He is unnaturally priggish. "I would rather like to see you knock a lamp-post down," says the clown: "BANG! What a noise it would make." "Now you're being silly," is Noddy's sanctimonious reply. He is also a sneak. An elephant from Mr. Noah's Ark wants Noddy to drive it to the wood, so that it can knock down trees: "that's what real elephants

do," it explains. Noddy, of course, is "alarmed." "That's silly and dangerous . . . you're a very bad elephant. I shall tell Mr. Noah of you." The elephant struggles into the taxi. " 'Please get out,' begged little Noddy"—all to no avail. Off they go, Noddy's head nodding sadly ("Whatever was he to do?") and the elephant thoroughly enjoying itself, blowing the horn and making everyone jump "dreadfully." Soon the elephant goes to sleep. Noddy's head nods "madly"; he smiles to himself: "he knows what to do." "What to do" is, of course, to drive the elephant to Mr. Noah's Ark, report it, and request that it be smacked. "Certainly, certainly, certainly," says Mr. Noah.

In this witless, spiritless, snivelling, sneaking doll the children of England are expected to find themselves reflected. From it they are to derive "ethical and moral" edification. But Noddy is not merely an example: he is a symbol. Noddy, according to Miss Blyton, "is completely English, and stands for the English way of life. He's very popular in Germany. It's interesting to think that a generation of young Germans is absorbing English standards and English morals." The Russians, it seems, have pirated some of Miss Blyton's books, but not yet Noddy. "I wish they would," says Miss Blyton. "I don't care about the royalties—I should like the Russian children to read English stories. It might help them to understand our way of life." It is disquieting to reflect that they might indeed.

It remains only to add that Miss Blyton was a strong supporter of Suez. So, I bet, was Noddy: indeed, circumstantial evidence might suggest that he was the moving spirit behind the whole enterprise. (pp. 18-22)

> *Colin Welch, " 'Dear Little Noddy': A Parent's Lament," in* Encounter, *Vol. X, No. 1, January, 1958, pp. 18-22.*

Janice Dohm

English children can be singularly fortunate in their reading, for most of the best children's authors of the past and present have been English. Much of their work has been shared by children in America, and I am only one of countless Americans who feel grateful to England for some of the most rewarding reading experiences of childhood, from our first introduction to Beatrix Potter to our graduation, via Arthur Ransome, to adult literature. (p. 99)

It was something of a shock to come to England and find that many children saw less of that heritage than we had at home, and that few of our finest books were imported in comparison with many imports which fell well below our library standards. There was obviously enough of good, high and highest quality to exhaust the funds of any school or public library, yet these seemed to be represented in only a haphazard fashion, most selectors relying heavily on the mediocre and rather bad.

Of course every nation has its share of third- and fourth-rate entertainment, banal films, music, radio shows or books, whose producers justify their work by pointing out their popularity, or the popularity of similar material. Hundreds of books exploiting the same routines with varying degrees of slickness are published each year for every dozen of higher quality. Like all mass-produced material these appeal to the mass-instincts in the audience, and it was not surprising to find that many parents and children were clamouring for more, especially since many were covering their ignorance of all other books by clinging noisily to the names of the one or two authors whose names they knew. But I was surprised, being biased in favour of anything English, to find how little such books had to offer. In the place of the books written because their authors had something to say, and said it with an individual voice, was it essential for children to have these undistinguished, indistinguishable juvenile versions of sixpenny thrillers and romances, with their repetition of old slogans and wish-fulfilments, unreal excitement, empty heroics and commonplace humour and philosophy? I could see a parent, unsure of children's books, being caught by the jacket promising childish pleasures and by the easy-looking text, full of exclamation marks; but teachers and librarians surely looked further, however pressed for time and lacking in interest?

Of course books of distinction and individuality take time, thought and trouble to discover and promote, and some institutions find it simpler to fill in space with books written to a routine formula which make it so easy to fill a request for 'another book just like this', a request which can be very awkward if 'this' is a book like *A Bow in the Cloud* or *The Ark*. Through lack of time or background, through indifference or ignorance, such selectors underestimate the scope and strength of children's literature and rely on a 'popular' author's reputation. Since Enid Blyton is the obvious choice of the present generation, it should not seem unfair to consider her work as a representative example of this whole level of production.

Miss Blyton is a useful example because she has expressed her views and explained her methods fairly often, and because she helped make her own reputation by sheer numbers (some 300 books in something like fifteen years) and by identifying herself in the public mind with children's books, writing letters to the Press, issuing statements in articles and advertisements, and proclaiming her variety, wide appeal and morality on every occasion. Photographs in the autobiography she has written for children [**The Story of My Life**] show her to be a pleasant-looking woman with an attractive family, and the text describes her home, garden, pets and busy life and repeats her assertions of love and understanding of children (qualifications shared by millions, including non-authors and anti-Blytonists, but seldom claimed by any author capable of expressing his affection for children in and through his work). She gives only the briefest information about her childhood (perhaps she found it dull), but reveals that she had a photographic memory for all she read and also the ability to 'see' whole stories unfold in her mind. (pp. 99-101)

Miss Blyton's feelings may be intense but she is incapable of communicating them adequately and does not seem to realize that children are capable of responding to someone who can. She has several times decried the 'classics', admitting the virtues of only a few, and it seems likely that though she read widely as a child she did not feel very deeply what she read. Perhaps the photographic memory accounts for that, recording without feeling; it undoubtedly accounts, with her 'private cinema', for her present fluency. She states with a strange pride that her conscious mind could never pour out all the funny, amazing, exciting, fantastic and generally wonderful ideas that her subconscious so easily rattles off. There is no denying that all this makes easy reading—the reader need use no intelligence or vocabulary, can even skip whole sentences and passages without losing his way, and simply sits back and watches the film unroll.

In spite of her obviously good intentions and her glowing testimonials it is hard to find much to praise in her work. She deserves credit for working very hard to establish herself; she has read advice on writing for children and applies most of the standard formulas; her little verses scan better than most at this level, and she is less liberal with current slang, preferring 'gosh' to the dateable 'smashing'. She provides the sort of artificial stimuli which provoke a clamorous demand, and consequently feels she is satisfying a real need. She is convinced that her own kind of work contains everything any normal child can want, and is quick in self-justification. (Her angry retort to Mrs. Mitchison's dismissal of all such work as tosh, in 1951, was that half the attacks made on her work by librarians came from jealousy, the other half coming from 'stupid people who don't know what they're talking about because they've never read any of my 270 books'.)

Her name seems to have been established first among teachers, who saw her work in *Teachers World* and in textbooks (though it is hard to see any teacher enjoying her science stories, which often muddle Nature and fairy doings in the most outmoded fashion). But on the whole her texts, Nature books, strip-picture books, plays, annuals and retellings of Biblical and traditional stories have little effect aside from making her name more widely known, for when children ask for a Blyton they mean a collection of nursery stories or an adventure book, usually the latter.

Some of the nursery stories, especially in the earlier collections, are quite pleasant, in the manner of Rose Fyleman and Agnes Grozier Herbertson. But the adult reader becomes increasingly conscious (and the child reader presumably increasingly unconscious) of the repetition, inconsistencies, tricks and triviality. The listener is perpetually being asked questions, exclamation marks pepper the pages and the tone is too often that of a superior adult exaggerating horror at nursery vices or an arch adult pretending to believe in fairies. Fairyland, that country of infinite possibilities, is usually reduced to a mere miniature suburbia—these fairies go a-marketing for cigarettes and hair-curlers and have cinemas, dance-bands and wireless. They sometimes reward good children by becoming visible on toadstools pantomime-fashion, but their magical powers are more often used to teach the naughty an unimaginative lesson and otherwise seem confined to playing silly or spiteful tricks on their neighbours.

In both these little stories and the books for older children, all is reported to be harmony and pleasantness, but what is felt is smallness and superficiality, and the general atmosphere (especially after reading several dozen Blytons in a row) seems pervaded by pettiness. There are feuds, jealousies, misunderstandings, grievances, mean triumphs and revenges, idle ridicule and name-calling, people 'paid out' and 'shown up' and 'served right'. There is the kind of morality invoked in schoolroom (or office) bickerings, or in a badly conducted classroom where the teacher shows her 'understanding of children' by pointing out the faults of a pupil in a way which gives the class a chance to indulge in mockery and self-righteousness. Any reader fortunate enough to know Mrs. Ewing's story *Snap-Dragons* will know what is meant when I say that the Blyton children, whether 'good' or 'bad', operate on the level of the little Skradtjes. But Mrs. Ewing, being a true moralist, left her readers feeling they did not want to use or read such conversation again, whereas Miss Blyton gives the impression that it is a necessary part of childhood. The realism she imparts to some of her heroines' hurt feelings and spitefulness suggests that either she is still immature enough to be nursing early grudges, or believes that all children inhabit only this world of self-absorption and are incapable of understanding any other.

This is the cumulative effect on an adult, however, and the children, though doubtless gratified by anything which feeds their ego in this way, usually read the books for the excitement of the adventures. Most of the adventure tales run in series, like the Secret Seven, who will stop at little to be 'one-up' on a group of copy-cat contemporaries who have the nerve to try to solve 'their' mysteries. There are the Famous Five identified by George, who is one of the readers' favourites, perhaps because she is most easily recognizable. Her origins are obvious: she thrives on the common ambition of all girls to be boys and most children to own dogs, by being insulted if anyone takes her for a girl (though she is now in her teens), and disliking almost everything but her dog Timmy. Many children feel they have 'difficult' fathers, so George has one who matches her for unpleasantness. He is excused because he is a scientist and all scientists (or geniuses of any kind) are peculiar; George is excused because she is said to be honest and loyal. As she automatically hates anyone who does not take to Timmy at once and resents anyone to whom Timmy takes, she is raging and sulking most of the time and her loyalty is apt to be muddled. But she is the one allowed to find most clues or unmask the criminals, sometimes because she has disobeyed orders and gone to the secret passage or cave or turret at the crucial moment. In

Blyton with her first pupils when she was governess and teacher at Southerhay, Surbiton. In a letter to one of the children, Brian Thompson, in 1962, Blyton wrote that "it was one of the happiest times of my life when I had that little 'school'. . . . I think it was the foundation of all my success, for I 'practised' on you, you know . . ."

the *Four Find-Outers* a gentle younger girl finds the clues (because her brother is always calling her a silly baby) and the balance might seem redressed, except that the series is made objectionable by the feud with Mr. Goon the local policeman. Since he is made an unsympathetic character, fat and disliking children, the Four may speak to him as offensively as they please—cheekiness seems oftener encouraged than discouraged in all the books—and be as underhand as they like in dealing with him. They make some dutiful speeches about respecting the law, but are quite capable of withholding evidence from Goon or waylaying him in what is, after all, his job, even if they do see it as interference with 'their' mystery. Once or twice they even manage to put him in trouble with his supervisor, a great triumph, and all done to give little readers a good giggle.

In one of the Adventure series (identified by Kiki, the parrot, and two children who have frequent battles, slapping and screaming at each other, usually because the brother has tricked his sister into contact with some small animal which she hates to a pathological degree), the children are hosts to a Ruritanian princeling, and ridicule his accent, his hair-cut, 'fancy' manners and babyish ways in the crudest fashion. They finally decide their treatment has made him 'almost' as good as an English boy, though of course none of these foreigners can comprehend the English code of honour. (This is the only set of Blytons we have in America and I have often wondered what the children think of such statements; perhaps they are too busy reading our own mediocrities to notice?) This point is repeated in the circus and school books, where foreign artistes, pupils and language mistresses all wonder at this Honour, while their own lack of it makes much action and humour possible. (Besides foreign pupils the schools usually have their quota of the wealthy, beautiful or gifted, who are either proved to be unhappy and inferior in some way or revealed as geniuses, and so either comic or peculiar and obviously above all laws.) In any case Honour seems to consist of framing promises which can be broken in spirit while obeyed in word, just as almost the only resourcefulness displayed is in calling other children names and in evading their parents. This convention, like the overworked one of commenting on the stupidity of adults, is found in children's books at most levels, but unless given really sound interpretation is merely pandering to the public.

But Miss Blyton is not the only provider of this sort of thing, for there are always dozens of well-meaning people with a knack for writing quick-moving prose who make a regular living by writing a book or two a year, and as many more again who write only one or two in a lifetime, all using the same material and the same approach. It is impossible to blame any of them for satisfying an undoubted demand for superficial, ephemeral material, any more than we can blame the people who make formula films or music or anything else which will fool 'most of the people most of the time'. Most of them honestly enjoy the same type of entertainment themselves, and enjoy reproducing it for others. But there is no denying that the world they present is very small and trivial; for all its undersea passages, jungle adventures and trips to Neptune, it never

leaves the most underprivileged child's mental environment, and it usually suggests that any book which does so is probably difficult and dull, for prigs and intellectuals only. Yet even the most under-privileged child can enjoy books of the order of *Johnny Crow* and the *Jungle Books,* and no one who has known or seen the difference between a child's shining response to them and the empty clamour (like teen-agers' for a crooner) accorded the formula book can doubt which is really 'just what the children want'. (pp. 101-06)

> *Janice Dohm, "The Work of Enid Blyton," in* Young Writers, Young Readers: An Anthology of Children's Reading and Writing, *edited by Boris Ford, revised edition, Hutchinson & Co. (Publishers) Ltd., 1963, pp. 99-106.*

Geoffrey Trease

'Children's writers have definite responsibilities towards their young public,' Enid Blyton told me. 'For this reason they should be certain always that their stories have sound morals—children *like* them. Right should always be right, and wrong should be wrong, the hero should be rewarded, the villain punished.' Most really competent observers seem agreed that children like morals if they are artistically woven into the fabric of the story, and not pinned on. It is only the adult who fights shy of them. The important thing is that the moral should be concerned with the problems of the child's own life, or at least within its normal range of observation. No one, incidentally, should be misled by title of Miss Blyton's book, *Five get into Trouble.* (p. 116)

For an example of Miss Blyton's school fiction at its best, take *The Naughtiest Girl in the School.* The theme is the first term of a spoilt little girl at a progressive co-educational boarding-school—a most unusual setting, at the time, for juvenile fiction is conspicuously insensible to the changes of the last few decades. Desmond Coke, himself a notable writer of school stories, remarked in his preface to *The Worm* in 1927: 'Education is, in these days, so vital that every serious school story must of necessity have theories below it: to underline them is bad art.' Thomas Hughes would have agreed with the first part if not the second. Yet, though Arnold's revolution at Rugby quickly produced the classic *Tom Brown,* the other outstanding changes in education during the past hundred years find no notable reflection in stories, and (wrote Anthony Buckeridge in *The Author* in 1958) 'the result is the creation of an unrealistic type of school which the reader rejects because it is outside his experience'. It is more remarkable that *The Naughtiest Girl in the School*—which gives a convincing picture of a 'progressive' institution reminiscent in some respects of Curry's Dartington—is the work of a writer generally thought of as prolific rather than original.

It is difficult to estimate Enid Blyton's influence; her two hundred-odd books, of course, cover not only school stories but adventures, religion and Nature Study. Her sales and popularity with younger children are immense. If that is the only criterion (as Captain Johns has maintained) I suppose her books are the best children's books in Britain, if not the world. Few people over ten would seriously suggest that they were. There, is on the contrary, a widespread tendency to dismiss them in educational and library circles. One children's librarian spoke to me, with feeling, of their 'intense mediocrity', and Dorothy Neal White, in her otherwise excellent survey, ignores their existence. Other children's writers are loth to criticize. If there are any of us so unworldly as to feel no pangs of envy (and who would not like to know that even in the height of the paper shortage one of his sixteen publishers had allotted sufficient for 250,000 copies of a single title?), at least there is none of us who could hope to escape the suspicion of that human weakness.

The Blyton school stories entertain, but except occasionally, as in **The Naughtiest Girl,** they can hardly be said to go far in depicting reality, stimulating the imagination or educating the emotions. Their style, drained of all difficulty until it achieves a kind of aesthetic anaemia, is the outstanding example of the trend towards semi-basic. . . . The exclamation-marks, which often splash across the page like raindrops, suggest the kindergarten teacher telling the story 'with expression'. We can almost hear the voice raised or arrested so as to draw the maximum response from the little listeners. Someone said to me the other day, 'these books are ideal for children—before they can read', and a teacher remarked that their simplicity of style, combined with their entertainment value, made them useful in the early stages of reading, because they broke down the child's resistance to print. Froebelized fiction is a sad symptom of our times, when some children 'resist' that literacy which their grandparents regarded as a prize to be struggled for. If children go on reading such stories long after the age at which they should be getting their teeth into something more nutritious, it is pointless to disparage the author who produces them. It would be more profitable if other authors would set to work and write equally popular books with themes and vocabulary more stimulating to the mental growth of the reader; and if those teachers who seem to imagine that Latin can be learnt by drawing pictures of a trireme could get back to the old-fashioned idea that effort is still, even in modern life, occasionally inescapable. (pp. 117-18)

> *Geoffrey Trease, "Midnight in the Dorm," in his* Tales out of School, *second edition, Heinemann Educational Books Ltd., 1964, pp. 107-23.*

Michael Woods

[The following excerpt is from an essay originally published in the Autumn, 1969 issue of Lines.]

Imagine an author with an output of over two hundred books, loved by millions, not only in this country but in most of the English speaking world and the continent of Europe. Suppose, too, that this author not only ran a twice-monthly magazine and contributed to many famous journals, but also wrote many songs, plays and poems. Surely nobody could but admire and respect such phenomenal success—such variety and such creativity? Yes of course, but not if it belongs to a children's author called Enid Blyton.

Enid Blyton was probably one of the most successful writers of children's books this country has known. A visit to any public library will make this clear; usually every one of Enid Blyton's books the library possesses is out on loan! But what of the writer herself? What information will we find about her? Surely such a large stone in the pond of children's books must have created some ripples in the adult section. But not Enid Blyton. She has remained virtually ignored, even by those adults who are most concerned with children and children's books. Even comics have fared better, and have been taken seriously as phenomena of our times by sociologists and others. It is virtually impossible to find any information about Enid Blyton, apart from a few lines in *Who's Who 1969,* which forgot to include her age and the fact that she died in November 1968.

If one draws a dividing line at puberty, the reactions on either side to the name Enid Blyton will be vastly different. One might almost use it as a test to determine whether a young person is mature enough to be admitted into a cinema to see an 'X' film. Amongst her vast public of children, just a whisper of her name conjures up feelings of excitement and anticipation; amongst adults reactions range from derision to nausea. What is it about Enid Blyton's works that causes such strong feelings? Such admiration on the one side, and anger on the other? Can it be jealousy on the part of the adults at her fantastic success through doing something that appears so obvious and simple? Perhaps it is, but my feelings are that the answer lies deeper than that. Adults may crave background details as necessary for realism and atmosphere in a story, but to a child, however, they are just an irritation that gets in the way of the main action. It is action they want, and with Enid Blyton it is action they get.

The same is true for characterisation. Invariably the main characters are groups of four or five children, usually siblings and their cousins, ranging in age from about seven to fourteen, roughly the age boundaries of Blyton readers. Groups this size are usually safe because of their numbers. They are not so large as to be unwieldy. One may suppose they reflect, perhaps, the nuclear family, and offer far less opportunities for tension within the group than, say, units of three—the eternal triangle. It seems a deliberate policy on Enid Blyton's part to define the characters in her books only in the haziest terms. It is very difficult to tell children apart, especially in a series like the 'Secret Seven'. Those children who do stand out are complete oddities; George, the girl who tries to be a boy in the 'Five' series, and Philip, the boy who talks to animals in the 'Adventure' series. Elaborate characterisation may be necessary in an adult novel, but in children's fiction it is probably a waste of time at best. Children's imaginations readily supply characters to suit their own needs, and Enid Blyton's policy of being vague about her characters enables the young reader to identify more easily with them.

Another inescapable point about Enid Blyton's writing is its strong upper-middle-class bias. Vague mention is made of 'Cook', the children are shown in one drawing arriving in a chauffeur-driven car, and other minions are always at hand to arrange things for them, without any hint of worldly remuneration. The children adopt a superior attitude, not only to the crooks, but also to the cooks of the world, and Enid Blyton tosses this off casually as though it is the only right and natural order of things.

Apart from its convenience in so many ways, for instance, being on hobnobbing terms with police inspectors and being able to conjure up impossible things like horse-drawn caravans and helicopters, this superior setting carries much weight with the young readers, in rather the same way that having army officers drawn from the upper echelons of society is supposed to inspire confidence in the troops. It does so by subtly adding to the fantasy element of the story, and with a few deft strokes places it well and truly beyond the experience of the majority of her readers.

Enid Blyton encourages the judgement of others by super-ficialities. Everybody is most clearly labelled 'good' or 'bad', 'us' or 'them' in the author's own old-fashioned ste-reotype. Crooks always have rough voices, and are hu-mourless and incredibly stupid. The children are always polite and nice to each other, they are always laughing—especially at others less fortunate than themselves. In the *Mountain of Adventure* which is set in Wales, the local people seem to say nothing else but 'Look you, whateffer' and nearly choke themselves on food. In *The Six Bad Boys* which is a rare and unsuccessful attempt at social re-alism, Enid's own obvious middle-class prejudices are even more in evidence:

Bob, a middle-class boy from a broken home, meets up with a delinquent gang of working-class boys. 'None of the boys was very clever,' she writes. 'Patrick [introduced as 'a wild Irish boy'] had a streak of cunning that the gang found useful' . . . When Bob met the gang their leader Fred . . . rose to the occasion. He had sized up Bob at once—a boy a bit above them in station . . . (and later) 'All four boys admired Bob and liked him, and because he was better dressed than they were and came from a better home they were proud to have him share their cellar.'

Another primary attraction is the inevitable inclusion of a strong animal interest. Of course the animals are usually dogs, and, in fact, one of the 'Famous Five' in the series of that name is actually 'Timmy', George's dog. Like all Blyton animals he always appears to know exactly what is going on and 'woofs' in the appropriate places. Even more fantastic is 'Kiki', a parrot in the 'Adventure' series, who comments on and takes part in everything that hap-pens. This imputation of human attributes to animals ap-peals to children, because it is something that they secretly believe to be true anyway. For adults though, this is one of the most infuriating aspects of Enid Blyton's writing, not merely because it is patronising, but because it seems a deliberate attempt on the author's part to cash in on chil-dren's gullibility, and perpetuate a lie.

We have now established some of the ingredients of the successful 'Blyton' formula: superior social status, the ab-sence of anything that smacks of the work-a-day world, the high fantasy level and the strong animal interest. These factors have played a large part in establishing Enid Blyton's success but they would hardly be enough without a very good and usually well-written story. There are nat-urally enough a few rough corners and hurriedly patched up endings, the suspense though is admirably controlled and is exciting often at times even at an adult level.

Some critics observed, not without justification consider-ing Enid Blyton's phenomenal output and variety of styles, that the books were written by a syndicate follow-ing a formula much as we have described above. This may be true, but it does not really help with an explanation. Each Blyton book carries the inimitable 'Blyton' stamp just as it bears her babyish signature with those coy dots beneath. For me Enid Blyton is a real person. No syndi-cate would allow itself to exhibit such foibles. The secret of success lies not in calculated exploitation by a cynical adult or adults of a vast number of gullible children. I do not honestly believe she was clever enough for that. She was, I am sure, really a child at heart, a person who never developed emotionally beyond the basic infantile level.

'Mother, Mother!', the typical Enid Blyton adventure story is rarely without this familiar evocation in its first few lines, and of course there is dear old Mummy (never 'Mum' you may observe) ready at hand to offer succour and attention in abundance. Often the request is for food and Mother chides goodnaturedly but abundantly, 'Dar-ling, you have only just had your breakfast.' Mother is suitably faceless and universal. The food is more reminis-cent of an orgy in an Edwardian emporium than a modern child's idea of a good 'blow-out'. Enid Blyton writes of tongues, ham, pies, lemonade and ginger-beer. This is not just food it is archetypal feasting, the author's longing for the palmy days of her own childhood.

It is in these opening lines that the author catches the child's imagination to prepare it for the adventure ahead. Once a firm home base is established, once the young read-er sees that the writer has her priorities right, he can fol-low her through the most improbable hair-raising deeds. It parallels the young child's need to cling to its mother in a strange environment, emerging only gradually to ex-plore its new surroundings and fleeing back to its mother at the first sign of danger. But Enid Blyton never goes too far, the children are wrapped in a cocoon of middle-class niceness which demands respect from even the beastliest villain. There is never any real threat to the children, no upsetting fears or panicky terrors; it is all so nicely under control.

Another interesting feature of these opening chapters is that Enid Blyton often has the father killed off or maimed in some way before the book opens; those who survive the massacre are inevitably amiable, pipe-smoking buffoons, as harmless as toothless tigers. An exception is George's father, 'Uncle Quentin', who is a rather irritable scientist, but he is never very much in evidence. When it is neces-sary to introduce a man, he is typically a walking compen-dium of everything within, but in all other ways a com-plete goon.

Bill Cunningham of the 'Adventure' series is a good exam-ple. He is actually a policeman, not your ordinary 'copper' of course, but something referred to mysteriously as 'high-up'. In another series, 'The Secret Seven', the children's mentor is also a policeman; this time an Inspector. Such characters help the plot along by enabling the author to cut corners and get crooks arrested and jailed in a paragraph. The policeman of course also symbolises super-authority and one word of praise for the children is enough: ('Well done you kids, we have had half the police force in the country looking for this little lot.') Care is taken however to keep this potentially threatening authority figure well into the background for most of the time and he is usually shown as tolerant and thoroughly non-threatening: one of Enid Blyton's most obvious failings is that she cannot handle men. (pp. 216-20)

For most adults who write children's books, once the communication barrier has been largely overcome, the main problem is to write what children want to read and yet remain intellectually honest to themselves in presenting the world as it really is. For Enid Blyton it seems unlikely that any such dilemma raised its head: she was a child, she thought as a child, and she wrote as a child; of course the craft of an extremely competent adult writer is there, but the basic feeling is essentially pre-adolescent. Piaget has shown us that children tend to make moral judgement purely in terms of good and bad and that it is only with the advent of adolescence that the individual is able to accept different levels of goodness and to judge the actions of others according to the circumstances. Enid Blyton has no moral dilemmas and her books satisfy children because they present things clearly in black and white with no confusing intermediate shades of grey. For the adult of course this is what makes life interesting; for the child ambiguity is untenable. The reason Enid Blyton was able to write so much (most of her books appeared in the ten-year period, 1945-1955) was because she did not have to make any effort to think herself back into childhood or wrestle with her conscience about the falsity of what she wrote.

Gossip about the famous naturally feeds on public doubts as to the validity of the eminent personages' adopted pose. Clerics become debauchers; politicians, embezzlers and generals, cowards. Inevitably Enid Blyton was labelled by rumour as a child-hater. If true, such a fact should come as no surprise to us, for as a child herself all other children can be nothing but rivals to her. Perhaps this is why she so constantly put her bold adventurers in dark tunnels and on lonely islands, while canny adults like Bill Cunningham, Mrs. Mannering and Uncle Quentin remained behind, enjoying holidays as they ought to be enjoyed, without children or animals to bother them! (p. 220)

> *Michael Woods, "The Blyton Line," in* Enid Blyton: A Biography *by Barbara Stoney, Hodder and Stoughton, 1974, pp. 216-20.*

Wallace Hildick

At the most obvious levels [*Five Run Away Together*] is fully in line with a number of the strongest requirements of readers of the eight-to-twelve age-group. It is a long story—a children's novel—running to some 190 pages, thus satisfying the demand for more prolonged immersion or escape, the antithesis to which produces the grumble, increasingly heard from children at this stage, that "I don't like short stories because they end just when you're getting into them." Then it carries exploration of the familiar to the running away, fending for oneself stage, as the title proclaims. And, at a period—the pre-pubertial—

when the clean-limbed sexless outlook reaches its snowiest peak, the readers are presented with paragons of such an outlook in the four leading characters—with a girl, Georgina, dressing like a boy and being called George, and frequent references to the smelliness and pimpliness of their adversaries.

A critical reading of the book discloses other features that are equally attractive to the intended readership and some that are not to be underestimated by the most discriminating adult. For example, Enid Blyton never loses sight of the fact that she is unfolding a tale: hardly a page passes without the dramatic insertion of a piece of necessary information or the sounding of a bugle note of alarm. The basic situation is exquisitely prickly: Georgina's mother's illness and her being rushed with her husband to the hospital miles away, shortly after the girl's three cousins arrive for the holidays, leaving them for over a week in the company of the unpleasant Mrs. Stick and her equally unpleasant husband, son and dog. The timing here is, as in most parts of the book, excellent, the reader being given just enough time before the bombshell of the parents' departure to begin intensely to dislike the Sticks, and the child characters equal time to show their dislike and so lay themselves more fully open to retributive unpleasantness. Collectively, the characterization of the Four (the Five includes George's dog) is quite brilliant. Here we have fully portrayed the nasty, snobby, cruel selfishness that most children are capable of when they go around in packs of this sort—a dark side to childhood that very, very few children's authors ever touch on, and then usually only in their hero's and heroine's adversaries.

Enid Blyton can also be quite perceptive about some of her characters' less unpleasant foibles. George's father, the Uncle Quentin of the story, has an uncertain temper:

Blyton at her home, Old Thatch, Bourne End, with Bobs the dog, who figured prominently in her columns for children.

The three children did not very much like George's father, because he could get into very fierce tempers, and although he welcomed the three cousins to his house, he did not really care for children. So they always felt a little awkward with him, and were glad when he was not there.

This is refreshingly unusual enough, in a field where the heroes' and heroines' fathers are usually stereotyped as bluff hearties or mild eccentrics. But the author goes on to explore Uncle Quentin's character a little further, a little deeper, with commendable precision, uncovering the vein of remorse that so often lurks under the surface of such personalities:

"What are you going to do today?" asked Uncle Quentin, towards the end of breakfast. He was feeling a little better by that time, and didn't like to see such subdued faces round him.

A vein that is, as I say, often there—but rarely noticed by most children's authors—just as the following shrewd observation can't often have been made in this field:

". . . Let's do it each night if we stay a week on the island. George, did you ask your mother?"

"Oh yes," said George. "She said she thought we might, but she would see."

"I don't like it when grown-ups say they'll see," said Anne. "It so often means they won't let you do something after all, but they don't like to tell you at the time."

—a comment worthy of Ivy Compton-Burnett herself.

Pockets of shrewdness, then, an awareness of the elementary needs of children of this age in the way of length and subject-matter, and a remarkable, probably quite unconscious knack of identifying with them in some of their more primitive if least pleasant urges—these are the qualities we are bound to respect in such books. But their deficiencies are equally considerable. They lack density. There is no fixing in time or space, no richness of circumstantiality. The sea could be any sea, or no sea at all. The Five could be anywhere, or nowhere. Even worse, apart from the *collective* personality, the pack personality . . . , the children are characterless, the only real differentiation made between them being in size or age or sex (and hardly that in George/Georgina's case). (pp. 90-2)

Unevenness, lack of balance, the failure of an author to follow through artistically and logically: these are so often at the root of what is potentially harmful in children's (to say nothing of adults') fiction. So far we have been discussing this in relation to physically dangerous activities and violence, but perhaps the most important of the three major problem areas is the one involving the sort of deep-seated anti-social behavior that manifests itself in indiscriminate contempt for or hatred of whole classes of people—because it is the most insidious in its growth and widespread in its effects. At one end of the scale we have social snobbery and cliquishness, at the other we have nationalist hysteria, class and race hatred, ghettoes and gas chambers.

That is why I am now bound to criticize strongly Enid Blyton's *Five Run Away Together*. As already mentioned . . . the author makes no bones about portraying the darker side of childhood in her heroes' and heroines' ganging-up against the intruding Stick family. Here, for instance, is George putting the verbal knife into Edgar Stick—and twisting it—as the Five set out on a picnic:

On the way they met Edgar, looking as stupid and sly as usual. "Why don't you let me come along with you?" he said. "Let's go to the island. I know a lot about it, I do."

"No, you don't," said George, in a flash. "You don't know anything about it. And I'd never take *you*. It's *my* island, see? Well, *ours*. It belongs to all four of us and Timmy, too. We should never allow you to go."

" 'Tisn't your island," said Edgar. "That's a lie, that is!"

"You don't know what you're talking about," said George, scornfully. "Come on, you others! We can't waste time talking to Edgar."

There, in its nakedness, is all the moral brutality of a certain almost universally experienced phase of childhood. And it is all the more convincing because the writer—probably unconsciously—shows approval of the brutality. Note the authentic ring of merciless, petulant, childish viciousness in the authorial ". . . Edgar, looking as stupid and sly as usual." So characters, readers and author become one in their pack-hunting, and if it is somewhat nauseating it must also be allowed that it is absolutely true, far truer to human nature than the work that would present Edgar as the normal child hero and the spiteful ones as his abnormal antagonists, or the Four as normal "nice" children, with Edgar as the spiteful outsider, as might have happened in a Bobbsey Twins book (where the bully, Danny Rugg, plays just this kind of role).

The same note also occurs in the exchanges that Julian, the older boy, has with the Sticks from time to time, with the additional spice of class warfare. . . . [Here] he is, putting the whole family in its place:

"Good riddance to bad rubbish," murmured Edgar to himself. He was lying sprawled on the sofa, reading some kind of highly-coloured comic paper.

"If you've anything to say to me, Edgar, come outside and say it," said Julian, dangerously.

"You leave Edgar alone," said Mrs. Stick, at once.

"There's nothing I should like better," said Julian, scornfully. "Who wants to be with him? Cowardly little spotty-face!"

"I don't want to look at you," said Julian at once.

"Now, now, look 'ere!" began Mr. Stick, from his corner.

"Now, look 'ere," said Mr. Stick, angrily, standing up.

"I've told you I don't want to," said Julian. "You're not a pleasant sight."

"Insolence!" said Mrs. Stick . . .

And so, one is tempted to add, say all of us. For Julian *is* an insolent brat, and none the less so for the author's approval. But insolent brats abound, alas, and she must be congratulated for providing such an accurate, chillingly convincing picture—as accurate and chilling and convincing as Robert Liddell's in his acid, perceptive novel of prep-school life, *The Deep End.* (pp. 147-49)

Perhaps one reason for the inordinate venom with which Enid Blyton's name is mentioned by many librarians and teachers in Britain is the discomforting accuracy with which she reflects some of the nastier traits of children of the middle classes, to which they themselves belong.

But having said that children do tend to be cliquish, spiteful, and intolerant, and having granted that insofar as the author presented them in this light she was doing a good job—a much better job in fact than many a more highly-praised children's author is capable of—one must roundly condemn her failure to make it clear that such behavior as George's toward Edgar and Julian's toward Mr. and Mrs. Stick was as irrational at first as it was reprehensible at any time, that spite and contempt may come easily to children but are none the less unpleasant for that. Where she aggravated her failure was in giving this behavior her positive approval, in such passages as the one quoted on page 147, and in the obvious relish with which she has the children bandy about such names as "Spottyface" for Edgar and "Stinkerdog" for the Sticks' dog. Here indeed, in the matter of the dog, Enid Blyton touches the very core of childish malicious irrationality, pursuing it, as author, with the same derogatory nicknames, and all the time stacking the emotional scales against it in all comparisons with George's dog, Timmy, who is presented throughout as a brave, lovable, faithful, clever animal.

This indeed is what sickens one: the gleeful *totality* of the children's hatred of the Sticks, and the way the readers are encouraged not only to approve of this but to participate in it through the author. And what surprises and disappoints one is the fact that this author could, as has been suggested several times, have made a much better job of the narrative. She had the sharpness of observation, the timing faculty and a sense of responsibility that were sufficiently well developed in other matters. Safety considerations are always very carefully taken into account, and generally raised through the medium of Julian (who lays down the law about how to behave near the edge of cliffs as conscientiously as any officer anxious for the well-being of his men), while in some matters of child psychology Enid Blyton was as clinically considerate as any other trained teacher. . . .

But in the one supremely important area of human relationships—between people of different upbringing, habits and outlook—the author seemed to be blind to the consequences of her attitudes, seemed in fact to be herself as irrational and as abandoned in her irrationality as a child, and this probably accounts for much of her enormous popularity with children. That is why I have spent so much time on this particular book, for it highlights a type of irresponsibility that by no means died out with the jingoistic anti-foreigner fiction that Orwell wrote about. Reading it, I was put in mind time and again of another children-on-an-island story: a story in which the quality of the writing is much higher but many of the attitudes portrayed are just as primitive. The only difference in this last connection is that in *Lord of the Flies* William Golding did not present the gleeful witch-hunts and elated self-righteous viciousness of the children in a favorable light, with his full approval, and for the approval of child readers. (pp. 149-51)

> *Wallace Hildick, "Variations in Technique and Content" and "Adult Responsibility: Authors' and Critics',"* *in his* Children & Fiction: A Critical Study in depth of the Artistic and Psychological Factors Involved in Writing Fiction for and about Children, *1970. Reprint by The World Publishing Company, 1971, pp. 79-124, 125-55.*

Gillian Tindall

[The following excerpt is from a review of Enid Blyton: A Biography *by Barbara Stoney.]*

The growing feeling against the world of Blyton has, I believe, little to do with any particular book or character, and everything to do with the passing of the social era which she represented. Whatever her assailants have claimed, it is not really Little Noddy, or Big Ears or the Famous Five or the Secret Seven or any other specific incarnation of the Blyton moral system that grates on us today but, rather, an outdated concept of childhood. We do not now want our children to be as Enid Blyton wanted them to be; we do not, indeed, believe that they are as she said they were. We are as sickened by her consistent picture of jolly, priggish, snobbish, sexless mini-folk as the parents of the 1930s, who so readily bought her 'nice, unalarming modern stories' for their own children, were sickened by the sin-and-death obsessed protagonists of many Victorian tales for children. There are fashions in children as in everything else. It therefore seems to me not beyond the bounds of possibility—no, scrub that, it seems to me a virtually certain bet—that some future revolution of sociological thought will bring about the partial rehabilitation of the Blyton *oeuvre*, particularly some of the most imaginative and least derivative stories such as *The Faraway Tree.*

But not, by definition, in our time. While there are large numbers of us, not only alive but still relatively young and vociferous, who can remember just how stultifying, patronising, authoritarian and reality-denying were the favoured middle-class attitudes to children big and small up to the 1950s, Enid Blyton will continue to be hated. What sort of literary figure was this, we inquire with outrage, who believed her pap-like stuff to be ideal reading matter for children (children?) of 'up to 15'—who called her modern villa 'Elfin Cottage'—who, on the outbreak of war in 1939, encouraged her young daughters to refer to the Anderson shelter as the 'Bunny Burrow'?

The answer, however, is that the responsibility for this miasma of whimsical dishonesty does not really lie with Miss Blyton herself. It was not her fault that she had the mental outlook and tastes of a particularly unsophisticated nursery governess—as well as some of the abilities. . . . The fault really lies with the era. What sort of period was it that not only encouraged such a writer but treated her as if she were E. Nesbit and J. M. Barrie rolled into one? What sort of period indeed was it that produced virtually no other children's writer of any standing (with the questionable exception of Arthur Ransome) against whom the ubiquitous Blyton could be measured? It was almost inevitable that among the sludge of Thirties and Forties books, all called *Yet Another Pony for Gillian* (more or less), Blyton's very versatility, her ability to turn her hand convincingly to almost any type of story for any age-group, should make her outstanding.

The corollary is obvious; an author can be so versatile only if she has, in fact, no professional integrity, no original vision of her own. Enid Blyton was a superb hack, an utterly dedicated book-maker, a tireless borrower of other people's visions. And this, in fact, is the true charge against her—not an ideological one at all, nor even a more general social one, but a literary one: she tried her hand at almost every classic type of children's literature—School Story, Adventure Story, Fairy Story, Tales of Naughty Children—and produced an easy-to-assimilate, softened and synthetic version of every one of them. She even stole *The Pilgrim's Progress* and turned it into a smug yarn of her own. Her biographer appears to believe entirely Enid Blyton's own tale that she 'saw' her stories projected as on a cinema screen. Possibly. But this was by no means their only source.

Gillian Tindall, "Something Nasty in the Burrow," in New Statesman, Vol. 88, No. 2271, September 27, 1974, p. 434.

Edward Blishen

[*The following excerpt is from a review of* Enid Blyton: A Biography *by Barbara Stoney.*]

Enid Blyton's "secret lay", [Barbara Stoney concludes in her biography *Enid Blyton*] "in her very ability to look with childlike wonder on to a world of constant enchantment and surprise, putting aside those things which were unpleasant and keeping only her dreams of life as she would like it to be".

Nearly every word in that verdict is ambiguous. For "enchantment and surprise" it is possible to read "whimsicality and banality". It is not difficult to argue that what is truly unpleasant is the avoidance of the "unpleasant", and that to feed children with evasion is no less undesirable because children are ready to embrace what appeals—without hesitation or shame to their immaturity. Though it must be said that part of the reason for the gigantic success was, clearly enough a pure gift for marketing—with immense thrust and industry driving the product on its way. . . .

At the end, distress of mind overwhelmed Enid Blyton. All the realities she'd suppressed—it's Mrs Stoney's guess—rose to the surface. "She was forced into an unhappy introspection of herself " and "perhaps she did not like

what she saw". A wretched story, that one doesn't want to be raking over. But if it had to be told, it should have been in the light of a firm attempt at judgment. And surely it had to be told: because behind it lies the phenomenon, still puzzling, that someone who almost never displayed verbal originality, who falsified the moral texture of things and seems certainly to have written out of an arrested and evasive imagination, should have claimed a larger and more devoted audience than almost any other writer who has ever lived.

Edward Blishen, "Life at Elfin Cottage," in The Times Educational Supplement, No. 3096, September 27, 1974, p. 27.

Barbara Stoney

Following the success of her first full-length children's adventure story—*The Secret Island*—in 1938, Enid had written a second book involving the same characters: 'Jack', 'Mike', 'Peggy', 'Nora' and little 'Prince Paul', and this proved as popular as its predecessor. She had by this time realised from her readers' letters that these fast-moving, exciting tales, woven around familiar characters with whom the children could identify, had a far wider appeal than she first supposed and she set about writing other full-length stories on similar lines. These proved so successful that each developed into series, whose followers were soon demanding that she should produce annually fresh 'adventures' or 'mysteries' for one or another of their favourite characters. Among those destined to remain most popular were *The Famous Five* (Hodder and Stoughton); *The Secret Seven* (Brockhampton Press); the *Adventure* series (Macmillan); the *Mystery* series (Methuen) and the *'Barney' Mystery* books (Collins). All these consistently sold many thousands each year, both at home and overseas, and went into several reprints, including paperback editions, and some of the characters were taken up by commercial concerns to market toys, games and stationery.

By far the most successful of all the 'family adventure' books were the twenty-one stories Enid was eventually to write about 'Julian', 'Dick', 'Anne', 'George' and the dog 'Timmy'—*The Famous Five*. When she began this series in 1942 with *Five on a Treasure Island,* she only meant to write six books, but her readers had pleaded with her to increase this to twelve. Even this number, however, did not appear to satisfy the children and they wrote in their hundreds clamouring for more. By the time she had written the last book in the series—twenty-one years after the first—close on six million *Fives* books had been sold and this figure continued to grow with each year that passed, as a fresh generation of children began following the adventures. (pp. 151-52)

Enid always acknowledged that 'George', the main character in this series, was based on a 'real person, now grown up', but only once did she reveal the true identity of this girl 'who so badly wanted to be a boy and acted as if she were'. The 'real' George, she wrote in *The Story of My Life,* had been 'short-haired, freckled, sturdy and snub-nosed . . . bold and daring, hot-tempered and loyal'—and, like her counterpart, had also been sulky on occasions. At the head of the same page in the autobiography appears a clue to the true origin of George, though the description of her physical appearance would seem to belie it. Beside a photograph of Enid with her spaniel, Laddie (also portrayed as 'Loony' in another series), is a similarly posed drawing of George with her dog, Timmy. Was this a wry joke on Enid's part—or was she unaware of this photographic implication? No one knows. But it was only in an unguarded moment, many years later, while discussing the *Fives'* popularity in France, that she eventually confessed to Rosica Colin, her foreign agent, that George was, in fact, based upon herself.

She did not always draw her characters or situations from life, but would sometimes find, after she had completed her story, that her 'undermind' (as she termed it) had unearthed long-forgotten memories of people and places, or she would recognise someone she knew in a character she thought she alone had created. Bill Cunningham (or 'Smugs' as he preferred to call himself), who appeared in all eight books of the *Adventure* series, was one example of this. She had met the original at an hotel in Swanage the summer before her marriage to Kenneth [Darrell Waters, her second husband], and had found him amusing company. She had laughed when he jokingly suggested that she put him into one of her books—just as he was, 'bald head and all'—and call him 'Bill Smugs of the Secret Service'. But when she came to write the first of a new series for Macmillan—*The Island of Adventure*—she found, to her surprise, that this engaging man had somehow appeared in her plot, along with four children—Jack, Philip, Dinah and Lucy-Ann—and Kiki, a talking parrot she also recognised from her childhood. She never saw the real Bill Cunningham again, but the fictional version became an important character throughout this popular series.

A jovial Police Inspector—Stephen Jennings—who first came into contact with Hugh [Pollock, her first husband] during the organisation of the Beaconsfield Home Guard, little guessed when he was introduced to Enid that he, too, would soon become well known to millions of her readers as Inspector Jenks of the *Mystery* books. After meeting him she had, from time to time, sought his advice on plots which involved police procedure and when she began writing *The Mystery of the Burnt Cottage* in the late autumn of 1942, she asked if he would mind being brought into the story as the kindly, shrewd Inspector, who was a friend to the five main child characters. He had cheerfully agreed and from then on appeared in every one of the fifteen books that made up the series. He was amused to discover that when he was promoted, first to Chief Inspector and then to Superintendent, Enid saw to it that his fictional counterpart was similarly elevated. His only criticism to her of the stories was that he felt she had rather 'overdone' her portrayal of the other, entirely fictitious, policeman involved—the rather pompous and stupid Mr. Goon—all too often outwitted and sneered at by the 'Five Findouters': Fatty, Larry, Daisy, Pip and Bets.

Enid's ideas for stories came from countless sources, but a great many were undoubtedly sparked off by hearing of the exploits of real children—either from themselves or their parents. Ewart Wharmby, of Brockhampton Press, happened to mention to her, soon after their meeting in 1949, that his four children had just formed a 'secret' society, with very firm rules and a password designed to keep intruders from their ramshackle 'headquarters'—a shed at the bottom of the garden. She was greatly amused by his story and was quick to follow it up by a letter to his eldest son asking for further details, which he duly supplied. With her usual intuitive skill over the handling of such matters, she enclosed money along with her letter of thanks—'to defray expenses'—and was delighted to hear later that this had been spent on a feast of 'jelly and chips' for the Wharmby secret society. But the rewards for Enid and Brockhampton Press were far more substantial, for out of this idea was created the first of the fifteen *Secret Seven* books, woven around the adventures of seven children and their dog, whose popularity both at home and overseas has only been surpassed by that of the *Famous Five.* (pp. 152-54)

In an article for *The Author* in 1958, Enid wrote that there were a 'dozen or more different types of stories for children—including adventure, mystery, fairy, school, nature, religious, pony and family' and she had tried them all, but her favourites were those centred around a family which, 'if told in the right way, would always sell as fast as any adventure . . . ' But this could equally well have been said of anything she cared to tackle during those golden days of the 'forties and 'fifties. Her stories for young children, particularly those told in strip form like **Mary Mouse** and **Bom the Drummer,** were just as popular with the under-sevens as most of Enid's tales written for their older brothers and sisters. But topping the popularity poll among all her characters for the younger age group, from the moment he first made his appearance, was a friendly little fellow with a nodding head, whose name and Toyland adventures were to bring not only further fame and fortune to his creator, but a storm of criticism and controversy.

Early in 1949, David White of Sampson Low, Marston and Company Ltd., the publisher of Enid's successful *Holiday Books,* was hoping to interest her in another series recently launched by his company. These books were dependent upon strong, central characters of a 'Disney-like' type, and David White was searching for an artist of sufficient calibre to carry such a series through with Enid. He happened to be looking through a batch of sample drawings, submitted to him by an agent, when he came across a sheet of what he later described as 'fantastically lively little people, beside tiny houses in the lee of bluebells as proportionately big as trees'. On making further enquiries, he discovered that not only had the drawings been submitted entirely by mistake, but they were already being used to illustrate booklets given away by a jam manufacturer, and were the work of a Dutchman—Harmsen Van Der Beek. Undeterred, and convinced of the potential of this artist, whose unique style had so impressed him, David White lost no time in summoning him from Holland and arranging a meeting with Enid.

From this first encounter, it was obvious to everyone present that the proposed collaboration was destined for success. Through an interpreter, for Van Der Beek's English was not good, David White explained that he would like to use the artist's unusual, continental-style toys and small people, with their distinctive houses and shops, as a visual background for a new series to be written by Enid—and from that moment writer and artist took over.

The first sight of Van Der Beek's drawings had excited Enid immensely. This tall, thin, rather mournful-looking man seemed to understand her own pictorial imagination and his vivid expressive illustrations both captivated and inspired her. She immediately described the central character she had 'seen' emerging from a background that she felt '*must* be Toyland' and the Dutchman, with a curious, palm-uppermost style of drawing, sketched in pencil a quaint, toy figure with long ball-topped hat over tousled head—exactly, Enid claimed, as she had visualised. Enthralled, she suggested other characters which were taken up by an enthusiastic Van Der Beek and by the time the meeting came to an end, both had a clear idea of the form the new series would take. On Monday, March 21st, 1949—four days later—a small package arrived on the publisher's desk with the following letter:

> . . . I have finished the first two Little Noddy Books, and here they are. I have written them with a view to giving Van Beek all the scope possible for his particular genius—toys, pixies, goblins, Toyland, brick-houses, dolls houses, toadstool houses, market-places—he'll really enjoy himself! . . .

The first story—**Little Noddy Goes to Toyland**—was published later the same year and its sales exceeded all expectations. Children were instantly attracted to Van Der Beek's distinctive drawings and seemed to identify themselves with Noddy—the little toy man who always meant well, but invariably ended up in trouble of one kind or another and had to seek help from his Toyland friends. Other *Noddy* books of various sizes and types followed in rapid succession and Enid also contracted to write a daily strip series for the London *Evening Standard*—all of which Van Der Beek insisted on illustrating. . . . He died suddenly in Holland in 1953, but his characters lived on as he created them. By that time they were so well established, other artists were able to perpetuate their appeal—with the aid of a special pictorial 'Noddy dictionary', prepared by Sampson Low. This carried details of all the Toyland characters and a map of the village, which marked the houses, shops and 'places of interest' mentioned in Enid's stories.

The 'dictionary' also served as an aid for the many British manufacturers who had been quick to realise Noddy's potential selling power and were already using 'this best-loved children's character'—as one described him—in a variety of ways. By the middle 'fifties, the range of 'Noddy' products had become so wide that a walk through any large store at this time would have revealed one or another of the Toyland characters displayed in almost every department. There were 'Noddy' toys and games of every description, toothbrushes, soap, stationery, chocolate, clothing, cutlery, pottery and furnishings. During the Christmas season, large Noddy replicas, with 'bobbing' heads, were used as part of the decorations or as a means of collecting for the four main Enid Blyton charities. Meanwhile, the book sales alone were enough to keep Noddy before the public eye, for by 1956 these had already reached almost unprecedented figures. By the end of the decade with the character's regular appearances on stage and television screen, well over twenty million copies of his books had been sold in England alone. (pp. 156-60)

Noddy's impact generally—whether in book, film, play or television puppet form—was phenomenal. He became the subject of music hall jokes and sketches, pet rabbits were named after his pixie friend 'Big Ears' and many a British policeman was referred to—a shade derogatorily—as 'Mr. Plod'. Before the decade was over 'Enid Blyton' and 'Noddy' had become household names—and to many the two were synonymous, despite the continued popularity of her other series. (p. 163)

Enid always found it difficult to understand those who criticised her work. She sincerely believed that she was providing her young readers with enjoyable, exciting—but never frightening—stories, that at the same time laid down certain moral codes of behaviour. Librarians and educationalists did not always agree. They questioned her involvement in the actions of some of her main characters who, they felt, too often displayed petty, spiteful, vindictive—even cruel—behaviour towards their adversaries,

Blyton at work with her daughters, Gillian (left) and Imogen.

who were usually of a different nationality or social back-ground to her predominantly middle-class English heroes or heroines. They disliked her style with its limited vocabulary 'drained of all difficulty until it achieved a kind of aesthetic anaemia' as one critic put it. Others considered her work 'too mediocre' to even give it mention and ignored her very existence.

Her reply to them all was that she took no note of critics over twelve years of age and that no one could deny her immense, universal appeal among the children themselves. Half the attacks made on her work she claimed came from jealousy and the other half 'from stupid people who don't know what they're talking about because they've never read any of my books . . .' Her stories were read 'in palaces as well as in working-class homes' and 'whatever the child's mental capacity' were equally well enjoyed. Reluctant readers found her books easy to read and this gave them an incentive to experiment further, while other children, who required more mental stimulus, 'took hold' of her stories and set their own imaginations to work over the characters and the settings.

But the main target for the anti-Blytons throughout the 'fifties and early 'sixties was undoubtedly Noddy—'the most egocentric, joyless, snivelling and pious anti-hero in the history of British fiction', according to one critic of the time. Colin Welch, in a five-page feature in the January 1958 edition of *Encounter,* went further: 'If Noddy is "like the children themselves" [*Enid's own description*] it is the most unpleasant child that he most resembles'. (pp. 164-65)

Mr. Welch's article, 'Dear Little Noddy—A Parent's Lament', was well received and widely quoted, particularly by those who wished to impose sanctions on Enid's works. Several librarians had already removed her books from their shelves completely, giving a variety of reasons for so doing. The main complaint against her stories appeared to be that with such a prolific output (still increasing at the rate of a dozen or more each year) it was quite possible for children to be introduced to one or another of Enid's books at the age of two or three and read no other author until they progressed 'if ever, on such a spoon-fed diet' to adult literature. Stories of greater depth and characterisation, of which there was now a wide range, were thus being ignored.

The anti-Blyton—and, more particularly, anti-Noddy—campaign gathered momentum and by the end of the 'fifties scarcely a day passed without one newspaper or another giving publicity to the banning of Enid's books by librarians—not only in Britain, but in New Zealand, Australia and elsewhere. 'Murky undertones' were claimed to have been found in some of Noddy's adventures: his relationship with Big Ears was 'suspect' and Enid's 'racial discrimination' was shown by her use of black golliwogs as the villains in one of the Toyland tales. She countered the latter by saying that she had written far more *good* golliwogs into her stories than bad and gave, as an example, **The Three Golliwogs** in which they appeared as the 'heroes' throughout:

> Golliwogs are merely lovable black toys, *not* Negroes. Teddy bears are also toys, but if there hap-

pens to be a naughty one in my books for younger children, this does not mean that I hate bears!

Whatever the action of the librarians, Noddy's popularity continued and his stories, along with her other books, were taken up and read as fast as they appeared on the market. Far from reducing the numbers of her young readers, the disappearance of her books from library shelves resulted in increased sales, particularly when the first of her cheap, paperback editions were brought out in the early 'sixties. Children could now afford to buy the books for themselves and a certain one-upmanship developed, in some quarters, over the collection of complete 'sets' of her series. (pp. 165-67)

Several years after her death, despite her critics being as fierce as ever in the condemnation of her work, her stories continue to be bought and enjoyed by children the world over. To them—and to hundreds of her former readers—she remains the spinner of magical tales, almost without equal. (p. 179)

Barbara Stoney, in her Enid Blyton: A Biography, *Hodder and Stoughton, 1974, 252 p.*

Blyton standing by a portion of the bookcase where she kept the books she had written.

Nicholas Tucker

> A wretched story, that one doesn't want to be raking over. But if it had to be told, it should have been in the light of a firm attempt at judgment. And surely it had to be told: because behind it lies the phenomonon, still puzzling, that someone who almost never displayed verbal originality, who falsified the moral texture of things and seems certainly to have written out of an arrested and evasive imagination, should have claimed a larger and more devoted audience than almost any other writer who has ever lived.

So writes Edward Blishen, reviewing in the *Times Educational Supplement* Barbara Stoney's recent, unflattering biography, *Enid Blyton*. Discussion of children's literature in general rarely has any particular impact, but the mere mention of Enid Blyton is nearly always enough to release a flood of interest. People everywhere seized on Barbara Stoney's book, many with their own decided views on the central enigma mentioned by Blishen: why should such a bad writer have fascinated so many of us when young, and continue to hold some—if not all—of the same attraction for children today?

Taken together, the reviews in themselves make interesting reading. Here, after all, was a good, newsy story (Enid Blyton divorced one husband in dubious circumstances, and treated her own mother heartlessly—a darker side to **Sunny Stories** indeed.) Yet trying to understand the Blyton literary phenomenon in most cases requires more general expertise than the mere accident of having once been an addict oneself, or perhaps some experience of one family's reading taste today. So who should review the book? In fact, whilst there were still odd examples of the resident funny man or special friend of the literary editor being invited to have a go at something they obviously knew little about, most reviews were informed and to the point. Whatever detractors may sometimes say, on this showing the whole topic of children's literature is probably better served critically today, at least in major newspapers and magazines, than ever before.

When it came to assessing Enid Blyton's almost infamous appeal, many reviewers followed a line first mentioned by a psychologist, Michael Woods, and also by E W Hildick in his lively book *Children and Fiction*. This is that Enid Blyton appealed to children because she remained a child herself; if children could write, the argument goes, they would write like Enid Blyton. She is therefore detested by many librarians and teachers because, in Hildick's words, 'of the discomforting accuracy with which she reflects some of the nastier traits of children of the middle class'.

Michael Woods, in an article "Blyton Revisited", spells out this explanation in more detail. Characters in the adventure stories are oversimplified stereotypes, especially when it comes to the good and the bad. Animal pets behave with adult understanding, there are endless descriptions of food and physical difficulties disappear as if by magic. In all these ways, Enid Blyton 'thought as a child, and she wrote as a child'. No wonder she was so popular

with young people, presented with something that simply entertained them at their own, unexalted level.

This argument, although attractive, seems to me to rest upon a *non sequitur*: why *should* children particularly like someone who thinks and feels as they do? There are many other childish books in existence that make no special appeal to anyone. When children have their own stories published, it is often those most typically childish elements in their prose that prove most captivating to adults, but which elude other readers of the same age, as in Daisy Ashford's *The Young Visiters*. Besides, it is a tautology to say that children like books because they appeal to children. *Treasure Island, The Secret Garden, Black Beauty* are also still very popular, and whilst they also incorporate some fantasies that could be described as childish, it does not follow that their authors too 'thought as children', although obviously some element of sympathy must be there. It could also be argued, though, that some of their attraction lay in the distinctly adult way in which a childish fantasy is then developed and sophisticated. The view that children must like something simply because it always remains childish is inaccurate and needlessly depressed, ignoring better and quite different writers who have also been popular during the short time widespread book reading by children has been at all common. For example, Naomi Lewis states [in *The Observer*, 1974]: 'Her readers, at least, were given what they believed they wanted. Well, the most popular bread is the white sliced loaf. The most popular newspaper is——. You begin to wonder—what kind of tune did the pied piper really play?' But the answer, surely, is many different tunes, from fairy stories and nursery rhymes through to comics and popular classics, both good and bad.

The whole notion of Enid Blyton's mysterious transmutation into a child when writing for children, although encouraged by her own published speculations, has surely been exaggerated. Her writing is altogether too professionally competent to support this exclusive explanation of her gifts. Even the famed 'limited vocabulary' of her books has been overstressed. Looking through the last ten pages of **The Mystery of the Spiteful Letters,** I find 'righteous', 'mystification', 'reprimanded', 'courteous', 'anonymous', 'deduction' and 'conclusions'. True, some of these words are repeated more than once, but this is neither the language of child nor ur-child.

Another possible explanation for her success, adopted by critics, lies in the supposed 'fit' between Enid Blyton's values and those of the suburban prewar middle classes for whom she wrote. Here, the argument goes, was an author who herself reacted against Victorian gloom and virtuosity in books, and produced comfortable, undemanding characters, ideal for parents who wanted, according to Gillian Tindall [in *New Statesman*, 1974], 'nice unalarming modern stories for their children'. These days, Miss Tindall continues, we are properly 'sickened by her consistent picture of jolly, priggish, snobbish, sexless mini-folk', which to us now, represent 'an outdated concept of childhood'. Yet the real fault lies in the era in which Enid Blyton wrote: 'What sort of period indeed was it that produced virtually no other children's writer of any standing (with the questionable exception of Arthur Ransome)?'

There are odd points of reasoning in this thesis, not least its ignorance of literary history. The reaction against Victorian 'sin and death obsessed protagonist took place in late Victorian and Edwardian England, in writers like E. Nesbit, Kenneth Grahame and Rudyard Kipling, who were producing books before Enid Blyton was born and when she was a child. Amidst 'the sludge of thirties and forties books' (Miss Tindall is at least good as a phrase-maker) there were in fact works by Tolkien, Walter de la Mare, John Masefield, T. H. White, and Hugh Lofting—quite a rich sludge, surely, even without the addition of Arthur Ransome, questionably or not?

Neither can this argument explain Enid Blyton's continuing popularity today. True, there is not quite the same addiction as before, but sales remain high, and Thames Television is reported to be planning films about The Famous Five and The Secret Seven. Certainly she was a woman of her time; her behaviour to domestic staff was harsh by any standards, and her attitudes to social issues such as capital punishment and juvenile delinquency predictably reactionary. Yet other writers have also been in tune with their own backgrounds, but this on its own has never been seen as an adequate explanation for their popularity at the time, and certainly not thirty years after such typically period pieces were written.

A more realistic answer could lie in the accessibility and marketing of her books. As [Bob Leeson in] the *Morning Star* [1974] put it, 'she was a worker, and a hard worker'. With so many books under production, copies were bound to find their ways into bookshop, Christmas stocking and eventually jumble sale. Children who finished one book could then turn immediately to another: with a different author, there might be a waiting period of one year. Meanwhile, there were fortnightly magazines to buy, clubs to join with their own badge and secret sign, all helping to keep her name in front of her growing public. Less prolific authors could compete in terms of neither production nor self-advertisement. Geoffrey Trease describes in his autobiography [*A Whiff of Burnt Boats*] how rare it was for any new author's work to get public notice at this time. With few bookshops specializing in children's books, no cheap paperbacks to give other new authors any quick, widespread popularity, and little attention to good children's literature in its own right, no wonder she had it so much her own way. To make matters worse for her fellow writers, despite rationed newsprint and a general shortage of paper in wartime, Enid Blyton almost alone was allowed to sail on unaffected, publishing no less than eleven books in 1940. Her publishers had confidence in her, and to an extent they were right. Come a new social problem, such as the evacuation, and Enid Blyton was at hand to write something interesting for young children experiencing the countryside for the first time and not sure what to look out for. (Would any writer, good or bad, act with such despatch over an equivalent social challenge today?) Indeed, at a time of change it must have been comforting to go on receiving more of the same thing in this way, a form of continuity with the past and reassurance for the future.

Obviously extraordinary productivity and aggressive marketing cannot be the complete answer to Enid Blyton's triumph, although she was a very able businesswoman who in one letter to her publishers foresaw the whole progress of the Noddy series even before it had been launched. But commercial success must be based upon an appeal that endures, and there can be no complete answer as to exactly what this was. We don't even know how many children Enid Blyton really did appeal to. Was it a majority amongst all children, or all literate children, or all book-reading children, or only a minority of all these groups, large in itself, but not the massive nationwide readership so often claimed? On the other hand, some children may have detested her; a reading survey I was once involved with showed her as least favourite for some, as well as top for a great many more. But given she had a large following, it is almost certain that her ultimate appeal was multi-fold, very much depending upon the personality of each young reader, and impossible to subsume in any one hasty hypothesis. Accessibility, childish appeal, social convention and undemanding all-action writing obviously had some importance, and there were other attractions, all playing their part in the eventual complex interaction between book and individual child.

For example, her writing was almost always unfailingly positive. This quality of hectic cheerfulness obviously irritated, perhaps even unsettled, some of her critics, making them even quicker to seize on the psychological denial operating in her own life, and the final vulnerable and depressed old age. But for young readers, this type of optimism had its attractions. For a teacher, and especially one who so often boasted of her qualifications, Enid Blyton rarely tried to improve or educate her readers in her fiction. Rather, she constantly presented children with a flattering and jolly picture of themselves in stories where they regularly outwit adults, prove competent beyond their years, and in short have it nearly all their own way. Buying a Blyton book, in this sense, was buying a good image of oneself and the world, where exciting things could happen almost to order, and where nasty repercussions could be kept well under control.

Other writers might shudder at this type of deception, preferring their characters to come across adventure unwillingly and by accident, or even experience non-adventures leaving everyone wiser in the end. With Enid Blyton's adventure stories, there was no such holding back. A good mystery was well and truly broached by the end of the first few chapters, and the author herself would make it clear that things were going to get a lot more exciting yet. In Hildick's words, hardly a page would pass without some 'bugle note of alarm'—your money's worth, indeed. When day was done, with the child characters carrying off the honours, glowing with congratulations from mother, Chief Inspector or local squire, there would always be another story to turn to bearing the same seductive fantasy of a world where children had all the fun and knew most of the answers.

Real children, on the other hand, are small, inexperienced and to a certain extent vulnerable to an adult world that generally renders them ineffective. But here was an author who gave them a quite different picture of themselves, and who insisted that she loved and valued them into the bargain (and also that children everywhere returned the feeling). If a child wrote to her, back would come an affectionate letter; her correspondence must have been greater than any other writer, living or dead. The good image children received need not necessarily stop at reading her stories. As Bob Leeson wrote in the *Morning Star,* in one of the most perceptive reviews of Barbara Stoney's book, 'Long before *Blue Peter* and TV were heard of, she organized blanket collections, silver paper collections, etc., for charities. She encouraged children in the countryside to write to children in the towns telling about nature'.

Some of the work done and causes supported in this way seem as admirable now as they must once have appeared to the thousands of children who worked for them. The one critic who found something shameful in organizing children to support charity, thus perpetuating 'society as it is', seems to assume that children who do nothing have a better chance of becoming class-conscious revolutionaries. Just as likely, they continue to do nothing, but thinking less of themselves and possibly of others too. But for the Busy Bee (Enid Blyton the Queen Bee, of course), Pug Pup (Pick up glass, Pick up paper society), Famous Five or Sunbeam Society club member, here was a chance to discover that the real world could also be like something out of a Blyton novel. Given the word, children *did* cheerfully set to work, money *did* flow in, and good results *did* materialize. Never mind that the real picture was more complex; for the moment the Blyton activist could justifiably feel pleased both with himself and with the whole race of children who had clubbed together in this way.

One of A S Neill's favourite ideas, taken from his own mentor, the American educationist Homer Lane, was that an adult should be 'on the child's side'. In a sense, could this also be true of Enid Blyton? Not that she would have approved of Neill, or that she was particularly good with children face to face (although a popular storyteller in school or library, her own offspring, who also enjoyed her company, were only allowed into it for short periods). Yet in her own way, she believed in children just as strongly as Neill himself and carried some of this belief to both her readers and their teachers; her many articles on infant education written for *Teacher's World* were often progressive, and some still read well today. Above all, her books were child-centered rather in the same way as comics or annuals—literature without interest for adults, but where the child could reign, unfettered and supreme. Of course this is a false image, yet children may always have known this, choosing a Blyton book as they choose their own daydreams, simply *because* of the blissful escapism that followed. There were always other authors, and indeed the rest of life itself, to provide the necessarily more realistic picture.

This fantasy content, however pleasing to the young, would have meant little if Enid Blyton had not also mastered her craft as a novelist too. Whether we like them or not, her books are technically adept, the work of a skilled writer. Her plots forge ahead almost in an ecstasy of action. It is untrue to imagine they were always easily pre-

dictable; the excitement and happy ending may have been, but not the details in between, and to that extent she can keep even the most skeptical adult reader uncertain until the last few pages.

Finally, how she worked! Barbara Stoney's biography makes clear that writing became a necessity for her, indeed almost a disease. Without it, she once confided in one of her daughters, she found her thoughts 'closing in' on her. But it would be a misuse of psychology to think this necessarily explains away all the toil she put into writing and working for young people, an effort surely unprecedented in the world of children's literature. To finish with the admirable Bob Leeson again: 'What can one say to such a fantastic output? Are we glad that there was only one Enid Blyton? Or do we perhaps wish that those who consider their approach superior could match her energy and single-mindedness?' (pp. 191-97)

> *Nicholas Tucker, "The Blyton Enigma," in* Children's literature in education, *No. 19, Winter, 1975, pp. 191-97.*

Mary Cadogan and Patricia Craig

It is possible to trace a decline in the adventure story which culminates in the books of Enid Blyton; possibly these have been the most widely read children's books of the twentieth century. She pushed the "mystery" theme

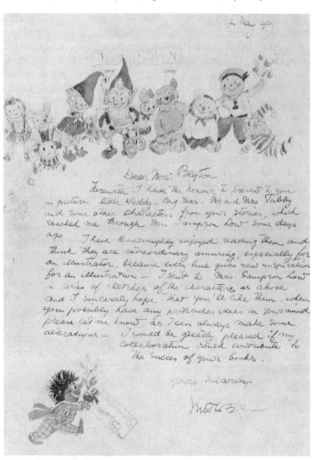

Letter to Blyton from Harmsen Van Der Beek with his first detailed sketches of Noddy and his friends.

as far as it could go in one direction: that of simplification of style and crude dramatization of content. Her approach has been almost precisely the obverse of Arthur Ransome's. His effect in one sense is to bring out the significance of commonplace childhood experiences; hers to present a string of "significant" occurrences in a way which is totally commonplace. She is consistently trite. She "writes down". She introduces herself coyly into the stories in the form of a disembodied benevolence: "What fun they were going to have!" "They certainly would have fun!" Yet few children seem to resent this approach; the Enid Blyton combination of cosiness and excitement has proved almost irresistible, and parental disapproval and library bans have actually helped to keep her books in circulation. Their popularity has never waned. They have been criticized for shoddiness of style, for a too-conscious play on the child's gullibility, for a specious jollity; with less justification, perhaps, for colour prejudice and for their promotion of a "middle-class ethic". None of these has affected the books' appeal, which is located centrally in the characters' enthusiasm, their constant sense of being "on holiday" and "in the thick of things". Enid Blyton's objective has been essentially philistine, her method simply to shear off layers of meaning or ambiguity, so that only the most superficial expression of "involvement" or "enjoyment" remains. She has made sure of the reader's support by a number of obvious devices. Natural, but slightly anti-social, qualities of children—greed, for example, intellectual laziness and conservatism—are presented in such a way that they appear wholly justifiable, even attractive. Readers are told at once of each character's particular foible, so that this will raise a laugh when it is next referred to—and references to it thereafter are constant and plain. An artificial limit is set to everything else in the books, including the author's vocabulary. Writing, for Enid Blyton, became so mechanical that she could complete an 80,000-word book (*The River of Adventure*) in five days: she began it on Monday and finished it on Friday of the same week. She was unforgivably careless, and many of her inconsistencies, surprisingly, have not been picked up by editors or proof-readers. In one book there is a cat which is referred to as "he" and "she" indiscriminately; its name is changed gratuitously in the following book of the series. A character who has been described as someone's sister suddenly becomes the same person's niece. This disorder implies a kind of arrogance in the author which contradicts the image of a thoughtful and reasonable older friend which she tried to project; it is backed up, however, by her assertion that she took no notice of critics over the age of twelve. The order in the books is of another, quite unrealistic, sort. The impetus of each story is towards a nursery-world tidiness; criminals are tidied away in gaols, unruly or selfish children have these traits straightened out of them, and this is effected with a disingenuous ease.

The Enid Blyton "adventure" and "mystery" stories involve five main sets of characters: the "Famous Five", the "Adventurers", the "Find-Outers", the "Rockingdown—Rat-a-Tat" group, and the "Secret Seven". *Five on a Treasure Island* was published in 1942, and its impact was immediate. It contains one fairly strong character, and it is this girl, George, who has carried the series; the other three children are as unmemorable as the author can make

them. Of Dick we are told only that he has a large appetite; Julian, the oldest, has a sense of responsibility and a smooth approach. Anne, as a foil to George, is the archetypal "feminine" girl, fond of dolls and cooking and "playing house". She is "babyish" to begin with, but becomes less so. In George, on the other hand, there is something for the reader to come to grips with: fierceness, resentment, the wish to have been born a boy. George is always in a false position; like all tomboys she can be "as good as", but this implies a basic deficiency. She never can be the genuine article. Anne, in an unusual moment of spite, points out " 'They're *real* boys, not pretend boys, like you' " and this crucial deadlock has a force which transcends even the author's bland treatment of it. For Enid Blyton the whole complex business of social rôles and attitudes is thoroughly simple, on the surface. George wants to be a boy and behaves as if she were one, and that is the end of the matter. This is George's "character", and to go deeper into it would be to impede the flow of events in the stories. Character is the least of Enid Blyton's concerns; the lightest indications of one tendency or another are enough to fit in with the lines of the plot. One child is fond of animals, another of birds; one girl is meek, another hot-tempered; one boy is a scamp, another fat and brainy. In the "Secret Seven" books, which are intended for younger readers, the author has hardly bothered to provide the seven with distinguishing marks more interesting than their names. It is the plots which are important, and these all move towards the point at which the children's effectiveness can be manifested, when the criminals are recognized and outwitted. These wrongdoers metaphorically wear striped jerseys and eye-patches; invariably they lock the children up in some uncomfortable place, usually underground, and make the usual threatening gestures, but the reader has to make a mental effort to be taken in by these. When the sense of adventure has to be expressed by a child it becomes inarticulate in a way that is meant to be touching:

> "Oh, George, don't be silly," said Julian. " . . . Anyone would think we were in the middle of a big adventure!"
>
> "Well, I think we are," said George unexpectedly, and she looked rather solemn. "I sort of feel it all around me—a Big Adventure!"

This is the extent of the children's emotional reactions to danger and intrigue: they sort of feel it all around them.

It was probably the author's pursuit of the highest common factor, in a social sense, which led her to locate her characters firmly in the middle class; this represents an aspect of the "normality" which her books are constantly striving to express. Her moral sense is entirely simplistic: she is on the side of law and order, and is at pains to uphold all the conventions and traditions which these can involve. She depicted a world in which social boundaries *are* clearly marked; her books are full of urchins who know their place, whom the principal characters befriend. These have names like Sniffer, Nobby, Tassie, and Ginger, and express themselves in a series of expletives: "Cor!" "Lova-duck!" "Coo!" They are not naturally as brave or resourceful as the middle-class children. If they stay to tea they eat in the kitchen; they are cheeky, shrewd and reluctant to wash. The latter trait is also foisted on to foreigners in general, even if they belong to the upper class:

> "All his clothes of the Very Very Best, even his pyjamas—but did he wash? Not he! And if you said you'd pop him into the river he'd run a mile, wah-wahing!"

> "Lots of foreigners are like that," said the third boy, munching away. "We've got two at our school. One never cleans his teeth, and the other howls if he gets a kick at football."

This is a type of smutty, chauvinistic humour which children enjoy, and incidentally it sums up two objectives of British education: to instil an acute sense of cleanliness and to teach the pupils to take their punishment like a man. The former may be still socially valid but the latter has a jingoistic connotation which has very little relevance at the present time. There is no sense that Enid Blyton has dissociated herself from the more vulgar or untenable opinions of her characters; her own viewpoint, her teacher's ethic, is everywhere conveyed. Her morals may not be pointed, in the sense of sharp, but they *are* pointed. In general they may be related to the seventh commandment of the Christian Church, though it is simply convenient that this ties up with the usual ending of the adventure story. Thieves cannot prosper, but neither can people who are selfish, thoughtless, slovenly or lazy. It is plain that Enid Blyton was conscientiously aware of a responsibility to her readers. Beyond a belief that childhood ought to be a time for "having fun", however, she had few liberal or progressive opinions. It is because of her way of expressing this "fun", a jokey, chatty, reassuring tone, that her books have thrived. Most children will respond, at least for a time, to the undemanding jolliness of her style. Children who read nothing else quite often will read Enid Blyton.

Her conventionality is nowhere more clearly apparent than in the distinctions which she makes in her treatment of boy and girl characters. Her boys are consistently "chivalrous" in the most rigid way . . . (pp. 336-40)

Only in George are the girl's instinct for self-assertion and her demand for equality adumbrated. The author has withheld complete approval from George, and for this reason George is one of her most interesting creations. It is the characters of whom she approves most who are the nonentities—Julian, Dick, Jack, Larry, Roger, Peter. George is not quite fairly treated: there is no suggestion that her fantasy of being a boy is just as "normal" as Anne's acceptance of a "housewifely" rôle. Her cousins go along with George's eccentric behaviour for the sake of peace, and because they like her: along with the "masculine" qualities of recklessness and aggression she has cultivated those of loyalty, courage (" 'You're the bravest girl I know' ") and truthfulness. In *Five Go To Mystery Moor* George is brought face to face with another girl who behaves as she does; for comic effect the author has to make them dislike one another on sight:

> " . . . That awful girl Henrietta too. Why do we have to put up with her?"

> "Oh—Henry!" said Anne, with a laugh. "I

should have thought you'd find a lot in common with another girl like yourself, who would rather be a boy, and tries to act like one!"

George and Henry react to one another "like a couple of idiotic school*girls*", and this makes George's well-adjusted cousins laugh. It also underlines the fact that they are *not* boys, and Henry herself is forced in the end to accept this fact, with its more hateful implications. When she is at a loss to know what to do, she thinks, " . . . there's no grown-up here tonight except Mrs Johnson. . . . I'm going to dress, and then get William. He's only eleven, I know, but he's very sensible, and he's a boy. He'll know what to do. I only *pretend* to be a boy." This, one feels, is the author's view of girls who "pretend to be boys": that they are pretentious and silly. They will "grow out" of it; the growing out is a process of adjustment. "Real" boys who are forced to take notice of the trait are inclined to sound dismissive, smug and obtuse: this is in spite of the author who plainly felt that she was giving the reasonable, balanced view: " 'Hold your horses, George, old thing,' said Julian, surprised. 'After all, you've often been pleased when people have taken *you* for a boy, though goodness knows why. I thought you'd grown out of it a bit. . . .' "

George is "difficult", but her quirks, her originality, are excusable because of her age. Grown-up female characters in the books who do not conform to the traditional, cosy image of "a mother" are made out to be utterly shallow and worthless. The two types—maternal and worldly— are contrasted most explicitly in *Six Cousins at Mistletoe Farm*: the "hardworking, cheerful, sensible" farmer's wife, and the spoilt, high-heeled, whining, vanity-ridden "Aunt Rose". Aunt Rose is "brought to her senses" only when she is faced with the prospect of losing her husband and children; she resolves to subjugate her own interests and inclinations to theirs, thereby fitting in with a pattern of self-effacing domesticity which the author considered admirable.

Her recurrent use of the "happy family" as a fictional motif has a direct relation to her own experience. Her adolescence was insecure; she disliked her mother, whom she saw for the last time in the 1920s (Mrs Theresa Blyton died in 1950). The author's father walked out on his wife and children in 1912; the episode was re-created nearly 40 years later, in *Six Bad Boys.* This is perhaps Enid Blyton's nastiest story; she has taken, unusually, a "topical" theme and sentimentalized it, bringing to the problem of juvenile delinquency an attitude dispiritingly retrogressive. Of the six boys, four are unredeemably lower class, outside the author's pale; the two whose "downfall" is related have problem families, we are told that they are good boys at heart but emotionally deprived. The father of one has deserted his family, driven away by his wife's querulousness; the other boy's mother wilfully creates the vacuum in her son's conscience by her decision to *go out to work.* At the time, in the early '50s, there was a great deal of public concern about latchkey children and the morally deteriorating effect on a child of coming into an empty house. A mother's place quite literally was in the home; she could leave it only at the expense of her children's ethical well-being. Of course Enid Blyton's own childhood experiences had predisposed her to accept this debatable view; it is stated over and over again in **Six Bad Boys.** Having got hold of what she believed to be a serious, psychological truth the author could not leave it alone. The pathetic "bad boys" find a way into the cellar of an empty house; they try to manufacture in this dismal setting a measure of the home comforts which they all lack. By this simple device the author emphasizes the nature of their moral deficiencies. Of course they have to steal money to "furnish" the place. They are caught, brought up in court, and some are sent to approved schools. Enid Blyton's ultimate remedies, however, are as weak, exasperating and implausible as her causes: " 'Coo—I shan't be bad again, now I've got a proper home!' " The diminishment of "badness", the banality, the whole cotton-wool lack of sharpness or insight are typical of the author at her worst. Here, she has subordinated characterization entirely to an endorsement of her own point of view. The book is an addition to the antifeminist propaganda of the time. This was compounded largely of the findings of popularized anthropological and psychological studies. Women's "natural" functions naturally were stressed, and the gloss was in the lipstick, shining kitchen equipment, the bright magazines whose golden girl typically renounced her birthright for a home in the suburbs.

The guilt which society imposed on working mothers is likely to have had an effect more psychologically damaging to their children than the mere fact of a temporarily empty house. The "villain" of **Six Bad Boys** is Bob's widowed mother, who insists on her right to work: 12-year-old Bob, however, expects her to sit at home all day keeping the house warm for him:

> "I think I shall soon find a job to do," said his mother. "I'm bored now. And I want a bit more money."
>
> "Don't do that," said Bob, suddenly filled with panic, though he didn't know why. "I like to think of you at home all day. I don't want to think of an empty house—and no fire—and no kettle boiling. Don't you get a job, Mum. . . ."

Enid Blyton's poor, ill-treated Bob in fact is self-pitying, destructive, a thoroughly unsympathetic emotional blackmailer. His whining has a solid, socially-approved backing, however: " 'He is your only child,' [said the magistrate] 'Don't you think you could give up your work and care for him again?' " Few mothers in that situation would have the gumption to answer No, as Bob's mother does; this is presented as the final evidence of the unfortunate woman's hardheartedness. The story has a happy ending, of course: Bob is adopted by the "proper" family next door: " 'I used to envy them because I hadn't a family too,' he thought. 'But now it's *my* family. . . . I belong! Here I go walking in, to join my family!' "

It is odd that the need to be employed, usually so serious, dignified or forceful a topic, should be made here to seem frivolous, indicating in its subject a flighty nature. But it is not grim financial necessity which drives Bob's mother out of the house but boredom: the point seems to be that it is morally justifiable for mothers to be employed only if they would *prefer* to be at home. However it is looked at, the tedious, restrictive concept of "women's work" was always basically illogical.

When character is made the focus of interest in an Enid Blyton book the author's dormant sentimentality is given a free rein. In the adventure stories there is a certain coarse exploitation of the sense of danger, the *frisson* of a mock Gothic thrill. The castles, lighthouses, rocky islands, underground caverns, waterfalls, deserted valleys, cliff-top buildings, secret passages, Elizabethan manors, lonely farmhouses, have a significance for the reader which the author does not need to analyse. They work their own effect, which is to involve the reader in an uncritical response to the situation. Of course Enid Blyton cannot avoid the attenuation of everything which comes within her compass: nothing is allowed to retain an element of the sinister, tragic or unexplainable. Her colours are taken straight from the nursery paint-box; it can only be within the context of the nursery itself that she has cultivated an awful habit of speaking to her characters: "Good night, Ern and Bingo! You're quite safe, though Somebody has peeped in at the window, and knows you are there! Don't worry, it was only the black cat next door—and she fled as soon as she saw Bingo! Sleep tight!" Structurally, her most successful books are those which involve the five "Find-Outers"; the series began with a number of stories which imitate a detective-story pattern, with "clues", a list of suspects, the step-by-step elimination of all but the culprit. The children's detecting efforts are obstructed by the preposterous Mr Goon, a comic-strip policeman of heavily drawn irritability. The "Find-Outers' " baiting of Mr Goon often verges on the spiteful; the children are not altogether pleasant, they are obsessively inquisitive in a way which is "not British": they simply cannot mind their own business. They do not "fall into" an adventure, they poke one out. This of course involves an unseemly kind of prying into the "suspects' " lives. The central figure in the books is "Fatty"—Frederick Algernon Trotteville—a plump boy who is boastful, self-assertive, clever, but essentially truthful and kind-hearted. Again, it is the author's reservations about Fatty's personal qualities which have made him notable; but he stands out at the expense of at least three of his friends. These are totally recessive, merged with the village background. The fourth, Bets, occasionally is allowed a measure of limelight: she is the "baby" whose innocent observations often put Fatty on the right track. Fatty is what the servants call a "caution"; he thinks too much of himself, but always with reason. The author's precarious hold on plausibility, however, slips altogether when it comes to the presentation of Fatty's relation to "Inspector Jenks"—a "high up" policeman who is in every way the antithesis of Mr Goon. She may have uncovered the common children's fantasy of being accepted on equal terms by elders whom they wish to impress, but to present this as if it were feasible instead of containing it within a *Billy Liar* situation is to have an effect precisely contrary to the one which is intended. By going all out for the reader's gratification, as it were, the author has underlined her own tongue-in-cheek condescension:

> " . . . What a fathead that fellow Goon is, isn't he? [said Inspector Jenks] Still, I'm glad I came

over here. I'd like you to take a hand now, in this mystery, Frederick."

"Oh—thank you very much, sir," said Fatty, thrilled.

"I'm not telling Goon this, because he's such a blunderer," said the Chief, "but I have a distinct feeling that the Lorenzos are back in Peterswood for some reason or other. . . ."

This is going too far, even for the most rabidly self-confident or unimaginative reader. However, the early stories do have an inventiveness, an intelligent extension of the basic motif—the burnt cottage, spiteful letters or whatever—into a well-reasoned plot which is deadened only slightly by the ponderous or self-conscious quality of the humour.

The final "mystery" in this series, however, is wholly nonsensical. In ***The Mystery of Banshee Towers*** all the weakest elements of the earlier stories are thrown together. The author's tendency to moralize is everywhere indulged. The age of her audience appears to have dropped by several years, moreover, perhaps because her own powers were in a state of decline: "Ern stared at Fatty. What queer things Fatty sometimes said—but they were worth remembering. Ern thought, 'Nothing like trust in a family.' That meant trusting one another. There was quite a lot in that idea. Ern decided to think about it when he was in bed." A softening, a deflation, has overtaken Fatty, Ern, Mr Goon, even Buster the dog. The dialogue is depressingly silly: " 'Real or unreal, that banshee is MOST mysterious' ". The tone of fey mock solemnity which the author usually reserved for her own intrusions is extended here to the characters: the effect is one of slackness and affectation: " 'Do begin the Meeting, Fatty,' she said. "We're LONGING to hear about this new Mystery. Is it *really* one?' " This puts the characters, and the readers, inescapably in their place. (pp. 336-47)

> *Mary Cadogan and Patricia Craig, "Swallows and Ponies," in their* You're a Brick, Angela! A New Look at Girls' Fiction from 1839-1975, *Victor Gollancz Ltd., 1976, pp. 333-54.*

Bob Dixon

Blyton is less a writer than a whole industry, a phenomenon in the world of children's literature. (p. 56)

Attempts to evaluate Blyton's work have, so far, and mostly, not gone much beyond the level of criticism of language and structure in the stories. Certainly, a study of these is very revealing but here I wish to concentrate mainly on attitudes and values in the content of this writer's work.

Unlike most of her adult supporters, Blyton, like W. E. Johns, had no doubt about whether she wielded any influence in her work. In her foreword to a complete list of those of her books which had been published up to about the end of 1950, she makes her views quite plain:

> I do not write merely to entertain, as most writers for adults can quite legitimately do. My public do not possess matured minds—what is said to them in books they are apt to believe and fol-

low, for they are credulous and immature. Therefore I am also a teacher and a guide (I hope) as well as an entertainer and bringer of pleasure. A best-selling writer for children (particularly the younger ages) wields an enormous influence. I am a mother, and I intend to use that influence wisely, no matter if I am, at times, labelled 'moralist' or even 'preacher'. And my public, bless them, feel in my books a sense of security, an anchor, a sure knowledge that right is always right, and that such things as courage and kindness deserve to be emulated. Naturally, the morals or ethics are *intrinsic* to the story—and therein lies their true power.

In her own comments upon her work, Blyton repeatedly assures us that she loves children. It follows, she's asserted more than once and perhaps rather defensively, that she must therefore write for every age group and write every type of book. So, there are books, if not series of books, in every conventional category: adventure, school stories, mysteries, circus tales, nursery stories and so on. The fact that the stories can be categorised in such a way, however, tends to suggest that the superficial and trivial elements are uppermost. It's worth noting here that Blyton didn't believe in including material in her stories which would, in her estimation, be painful or disturbing to children.

In her autobiography written for children and published around 1952 . . . Blyton tells us more about her aims and objectives:

> all the Christian teaching I had, in church or Sunday-school or in my reading, has coloured every book I have written for you . . . most of you could write down perfectly correctly all the things that I believe in and stand for—you have found them in my books, and a writer's books are always a faithful reflection of himself.

At the end of this book, she feels able to state: 'I am sure that you know exactly what I stand for, and the things I believe in, without any doubt at all.'

To complete the picture of Blyton's aims and intentions in her work we have to look again at her preface to the list of books already referred to. Here, she sees herself as having a mission to spread the word abroad on an altogether grander scale. . . .

> Quite apart from my millions of English-speaking readers, I have to consider entirely different children—children of many other races who have my books in their own language. I am, perforce, bringing to them the ideas and ideals of a race of children alien to them, the British. I am the purveyor of those ideals all over the world, and am perhaps planting a few seeds here and there that may bear good fruit; in particular, I hope, with the German children, who, oddly enough, are perhaps more taken with my books than any other foreign race (and this applies to the German adults too!). These things, of course, are the real reward of any children's writer, not the illusions of fame, or name or money.
>
> (pp. 56-8)

[It] isn't perhaps too difficult to see why Blyton has been taken up in former British colonies where the ideology is, broadly, the same as in Britain itself, even though it's one that has been imposed and indoctrinated through the administrative structure and through the education system. With other countries, Blyton's success is more difficult to understand though it rather depends upon which of her books have been translated into the languages in question. It's certainly difficult to imagine how the *Famous Five* books, for instance, would come across to a Russian or, say, a Japanese reader.

This series is, in fact, typical of Blyton's writing for older children and it'll repay us to consider it in some detail. There are 22 *Famous Five* adventures and all the stories have the same basic characters. ***Five Fall into Adventure*** . . . was the ninth in the series and was first published in 1950. Along with all the others, it's still in print, after numerous editions and impressions. The 'Five' are: Julian, aged 12; Dick, his brother, aged 11; Anne, their sister, aged 10; Georgina, aged 11, who is cousin to the other three and who only answers to 'George' as she insists on being thought of as a boy; and Timmy, George's dog.

In this particular story, 'the Five' are drawn into an adventure when some unspecified 'papers' are stolen from George's father's study. He's a famous scientist, though

we never find out exactly what his line is. It turns out that Jo, a circus- or gypsy-girl (we are given to understand that they are more or less the same) whom 'the Five' meet on the beach was used by her brutal and unlovable father in this robbery. Later, she's used in a successful attempt to kidnap George and Timmy. Jo's father is in league with various unspecified foreign agents who have names such as Markhoff and Red. However, motivated by love for Dick, Jo helps 'the Five' and is (almost) accepted by them after she's been given a good scrubbing by Joan, the cook, and is wearing some of George's old (but clean) clothes. It's largely through Jo's agency that the gang, including her father, is rounded up and carried off by the police. At the end of the story, she's to be adopted by the cook's cousin and is to see 'the Five' sometimes, if she's a good girl. (pp. 58-9)

'The Five' never change, in any of the stories in which they appear, in any respect worth considering. In this particular story, it's Jo who makes the superficial change to enter *their* world. Readers are expected to align themselves with 'the Five' and with the values which they represent. . . . Here, Jo moves from being a 'dirty little ragamuffin' to becoming a 'forlorn little waif', motivated largely, we're given to understand, by affection for Dick. She's also deserted by her father and thus gives 'the Five' an opportuni-

Blyton at a party for the 100,000th member of the Enid Blyton Magazine Club, 1957.

ty to exercise their superiority and charity upon her. The scrubbing administered by the cook and Jo's dressing in George's old (but clean) clothes is an initiation into the world of 'the Five' on a symbolic level. . . . It's very interesting to note that precisely the same ritual is enacted in Blyton's earlier story, *The Castle of Adventure.* Here, Tassie, a 'gypsy girl' who's dirty and smells is given a good scrubbing in the bath and then an 'old cotton frock of Dinah's'. (Dinah and Philip, in this story, and their three associates are the social equivalents of 'the Five'.) Tassie takes a liking to Philip and follows him 'like Philip's dog'. We are told, 'She was more like a very intelligent animal than a little girl,' and that she can climb 'like a monkey'. Jo, too, is constantly compared to an animal—a squirrel, a monkey, a cat and a weasel—and it scarcely seems possible to explain this entirely in terms of her agility. She's 'gypsy-like' we are told, and Julian, on one occasion, 'wondered if she was Welsh'. At any rate, it's clear that she deviates from the norm of middle-class, English humankind. Where some degree of affection is shown towards her it's such as we might feel for a pet animal. (pp. 65-6)

For the most part, 'the Five' are scarcely distinguished as separate beings, certainly as far as their social views are concerned. Timmy's usually recognisable as a dog but his outlook on life is very similar to that of the other four. Amongst the others, the only distinguishing feature is one of culturally-conditioned 'masculine' and 'feminine' roles, but here, as we'll see, there's a certain amount of confusion in the case of George. The boys, Dick and Julian, are scarcely nonentities—it's a single nonentity split into two. They have a prep school background and are jolly plucky. They know right from wrong and their literary destiny is, clearly, to figure in the stories of *Woman's Own.* Anne is quite insignificant but George, whom Blyton based upon herself, is perhaps (unless we exclude Noddy) Blyton's most fortunate, or fortune-making, invention. She's a very bad case of what Freud saw as a castration complex, and her success with readers rests almost entirely upon the fact that, in our society, and for what seem very obvious reasons, small girls frequently wish they were boys. (pp. 66-7)

The *Famous Five* stories illustrate very clearly Blyton's method of work. She's described this at considerable length in her autobiography: 'It is as if I were watching a story being unfolded on a bright screen . . . I simply put down what I see and hear . . . I do not have to stop and think for one moment.' Later, she refers to 'the extraordinary touches and surprising ideas that flood out from [her] imagination' and states that she uses 'imagination, as distinct from [her] brain'. This explains a lot. In *Five Fall into Adventure,* flaws occur at almost every turn in the story. For instance, twice when people are locked up, the keys are left in the locks on the outside so that the prisoners can be easily released by others. If a wall has to be scaled ivy happens to be growing conveniently on it. Again, George, who's eventually kept prisoner in a fort-like place on the coast, is conveniently seen at a window; then, it's assumed that there's a room next to the one in which George is held; Jo assumes, further, that if she can get into the assumed room she can set George free (assuming that she can unlock the door). All of these assumptions, piled one on top of another, turn out to be correct.

In this story, too, as already mentioned, George and Jo look alike and can be mistaken for one another.

This is the kind of thing that goes on all the time in Blyton's work. It's a pity she never felt it necessary to plan or prepare her stories. Almost the least a writer can do is to take care of elementary details of structure and children have as much right to expect this as anyone else. To give them less is to treat them with something approaching contempt. The point needn't be laboured here as I'm not mainly concerned with questions of structure and probability. It should be noted, however, that such aspects of a writer's work also carry implicit attitudes and values.

Language, of course, even more obviously and not only as regards meaning, also carries values. In Blyton, the language we are invited to identify with is, sociologically, middle-class based. It's colourless, dead and totally undemanding. A consideration of a list of names even, might make anybody wonder where the much-vaunted imagination can be: Appletree Farm, Buttercup Farm, Redroofs, Sunny Stories, Chirpy and Twitters (sparrows), Prickles (a hedgehog) and Bobtail (a rabbit). I thought 'the sea shone as blue as cornflowers' in *Five Fall into Adventure* was a welcome touch, all things considered but, thirteen years and twelve books in the series later, it was still shining 'as blue as cornflowers'. Compare this, for instance, with the image in [Leila Berg's] *The Hidden Road* . . . when Nicola pulls the wellingtons out of the mud—'they made a squelching sound, like jelly cut with a spoon.' It's a vivid image and one perfectly appropriate to a story for children.

What overwhelmingly pervades every aspect of Blyton's work, both fiction and non-fiction, is the insistence on conformity—and conformity to the most narrow, establishment-type beliefs, practices and values. She never seems to have been troubled by any doubt and would not have appreciated that creative doubt is the necessary precursor to change—but then, she was not interested in any kind of change. We've seen, through 'the Five', the insistence, at a social level, on English middle-class attitudes, by means ranging from outright instruction to others more subtle, if less conscious. It's time to consider a wider context now and to look into the broader implications of a conformism that amounts to reaction.

Naturally, the stress on the middle-class English (perhaps I should even say upper-middle-class English, judging by the number of servants of all kinds, even governesses) implies its opposite, which is that other people will be held in contempt, despised or hated to the degree that they deviate from this assumed norm. Thus the English working classes, when they appear at all, are figures of fun, if submissive to their natural masters, and only disliked and portrayed as rather stupid if they are rebellious. Gypsies and circus people, and even the Welsh, represent greater degrees of deviation while foreigners are, simply, criminals. They are all rather less than human, as we saw in the case of Jo. We are not usually told which countries, precisely, the foreigners come from in Blyton's stories. Specific details of all kinds are almost entirely avoided, probably because their inclusion would make writing too much like hard work. However, the names of the foreigners are often

German or Russian. These, though, are white and racially-related to the English. It's in the case of black people that the greatest degree of deviation possible is reached. (pp. 67-9)

The conformity I'm talking about has to do mainly with ideas, of course. However, the visual aspects already touched upon . . . have symbolic value. The half-conscious belief that the more closely people resemble one another, the more they'll think alike, is partly true, especially when we take dress and appearance, as well as racial features, into account—even though such a belief isn't very useful in a practical, day-to-day sense. However, a similarity of outlook has to be related, in the first place, to economic considerations. Moral attitudes can only be related to basic economic circumstances, though not in the simple and superficial sense we find in Blyton's work, where the implication is that greater wealth and status mean greater 'goodness'. Although there are certainly exceptions, it's easy to see that the opposite is probably nearer the truth. The trouble is that children, in their reading, are almost never invited to consider this.

The common factor, underlying all questions of conformity, is a strong sense of hierarchy. With this in mind, we can see that the class allegiance, jingoism and racism noted above are merely stops on the same line. What's fundamental is the sense of hierarchy. Further, underlying this strong hierarchical sense is fear, which is the emotional mainspring.

What strikes me, in considering this mental outlook, is, notwithstanding what Blyton has said, the desperate lack of imagination—in human terms the sheer lack of that feeling for others on which all really civilised manners and values are founded. This lack is bound up with fear, which is the fundamental factor in the whole ideological complex—a fear of what is different or unusual, a fear of the non-conformist and the unconventional, a fear of anything that's new and threatens change.

The 'badness' of those who deviate and therefore menace the world of Blyton is usually signalled in some obvious way as though we have to be advised that they are evil. Thus, they are often deformed or crippled . . . In *The Castle of Adventure,* we have 'a very dangerous spy' called Mannheim or Scar-Neck and 'badness' can be signalled by still more superficial nonconformity in appearance. As the illustrations to the stories often show, people of evil intent tend to be bearded or ill-shaven. We may note the 'straggly moustache and mean, clever little eyes' of Jo's father in the extract quoted and which Dick, incidentally, seems to notice from an extraordinary distance. Smell . . . also acts as a signal.

Certain of Blyton's stories are even more specifically about conformity. In *First Term at Malory Towers,* Gwendoline, a 'spoilt' new girl at public school, is gradually broken in and made to conform through a series of petty and spiteful episodes. In one of these, hair, as usual in schools, takes on a symbolic role and Gwendoline is forced to plait hers. *The Naughtiest Girl in the School* has precisely the same theme. In seeing schools as institutions with a principal aim of enforcing conformity, Blyton isn't, perhaps,

very far wrong. In seeing mindless conformity as a good in itself, however, and conformity, moreover, to the kind of ideology we now begin to distinguish, we may be unable to agree with her. In Blyton's work, nonconformity in younger children is virtually the same as naughtiness and the usual remedy is 'spanking', especially in a school setting. The title of a picture book for younger children, *Dame Slap and her School,* as well as the contents, give a very clear indication of Blyton's attitudes.

The non-fiction work of this writer is not my special concern here but it's worth remarking that in it we find represented those attitudes with which we are now familiar but in a rather more open, if perhaps less powerful, form. Her fawning book, *The Story of Our Queen* and the extremely conventional *A Story Book of Jesus* show how the land lies.

In a wider social context, it's perhaps only fair to mention a story which seems to me to represent the most advanced stage Blyton achieved in her writing, even though it's a stage which most writers with a reasonable degree of social awareness might well start from. It's entitled *The Six Bad Boys* and shows a recognition, albeit in a rather mechanical way, of the connections between some crime and social circumstances such as broken homes and overcrowded living conditions. This in itself represents a considerable advance but, even so, there's no idea of seeing crime in a wider economic and ideological context. Many of the usual prejudices are still found in the story. For instance, Patrick 'a wild Irish boy' is the one who incites the others to crime and who informs on the rest of the gang when questioned by the police. Interestingly, however, he's not the leader of the gang. Here, very likely, Blyton found herself in two minds. The leader would normally initiate action but it wasn't really possible to have an Irish boy as leader; nor was it possible to have an English boy begin the move to deliberate crime and inform on the others later. Of the six boys, Bob and Tom are (lower) middle-class and, although it's clear that their family circumstances were to blame in the first place, they are represented largely as being led into crime by the boys 'down in the town', especially Patrick. These boys meet in a cellar and we are told that Bob is 'a bit above them in station. All four boys admired him and liked him, and because he was better-dressed than they were and came from a better home they were proud to have him share their cellar.' The boys are variously dealt with by the juvenile court and in the last chapter, which is one year later, we have reports on how they are getting along. The two middle-class boys are getting along well and it seems fairly likely that three of the other four will be redeemed. However, there doesn't seem much hope for Patrick.

Throughout Blyton's work, the attitude to the police is interesting and here again we find some conflict of values. Conformity to law and order, understood in a purely conventional way, is strongly underlined but, cutting across this, is the powerful sense of class allegiance. As the latter is uppermost, it follows that ordinary policemen, who are working-class, are neither feared nor respected and are often held in contempt by children who either go to public schools or are even provided with governesses. Normally, these policemen are respectful, addressing the children as 'Missy' or 'Sir', and they appear conveniently at the ends of the stories to carry off the criminals who have been tracked down by 'the Five', 'the Five Find-Outers and Dog' or any of the other self-appointed junior vigilante groups which figure in the stories. Sometimes, however, as Mr Goon does in the series of stories featuring the last-named group, ordinary policemen fall foul of the children. Here, Goon comes in for some contempt from 'the Five Find-Outers and Dog' seemingly because, in solving 'mysteries', they do his job better than he does. It's perhaps understandable that he's not very deferential towards them. In *The Mystery of the Spiteful Letters,* the fourth book of the series in question, we find that it is, however, a very different matter where *Inspector* Jenks is concerned. The children get on very well with him and he rather sides with them against the wretched Goon.

Enough has been said now, I feel, to establish the ideological framework of Blyton's writings. Further reference to her vast output, particularly as she wrote to very few, and very simple, basic formulas, only confirms the main thesis outlined here. As already stated, Blyton is not only a literary phenomenon but a whole industry. She not only marketed her name in the publishing field but lent it to all kinds of products, such as 'Noddy' soap, toothbrushes and records and Blyton diaries. These, and sometimes the books, give information about the Blyton clubs. Originally, there seemed to be four of these, all with a charitable bent and, for the most part, providing membership and badges for a subscription, but in the 1972 diary only three are mentioned: the Busy Bees Club, or in other words, the youth section of the People's Dispensary for Sick Animals, of which Blyton was 'Queen Bee' and which, at one time, had a stated membership of 300,000; the Sunbeam Society, a support group to the Sunshine Fund for Blind Babies and Young Children, with a stated membership (1972) of 35,000; and, related more directly to the literary front, the Famous Five Club, which provided funds 'to help sick children' and which had, in 1972, 183,000 members 'in every part of the world'. In 1974, the membership of this club was approaching 220,000 and still rising at the rate of about 6,000 a year. To many people, even if it isn't consciously acknowledged, charity is a substitute for justice, as, for them, privileges are preferable to rights. To take the almost spontaneous kindliness of children and channel it off in this way is a serious matter.

Blyton has done her work well. If a parent knows the name of only one author of children's books, it's hers. If a shop sells books for children at all, it'll probably have ten times as many Blyton titles as those of any other author. There always seems to be a demand for stories written to a formula, stories which are totally undemanding and conventional, but while children undoubtedly feel a need for security and reassurance there's no need to suppose that it has to be provided in this way. (pp. 69-73)

> *Bob Dixon, "Enid Blyton and Her Sunny Stories," in his* Catching Them Young: Political Ideas in Children's Fiction, Vol. 2, *Pluto Press, 1977, pp. 56-73.*

Cedric Cullingford

Enid Blyton's books are still overwhelmingly popular. There can be few children in Great Britain who are unfamiliar with at least some of them. Their popularity holds up in the face of virulent criticism. They are banned from many libraries, and in some countries banned altogether. Enid Blyton has been accused of being racialist, class-conscious and dominated by the ethics of materialism. Those teachers who think we live in a golden age of children's literature seem to feel the most threatened by her books. It is as if Enid Blyton were corrupting what would otherwise be children's purer, more astringent tastes.

Her books are very easy to attack. Their innocence of tone leads them straight into the delighted satire of critics. Examples of her stereotyped views of foreigners, gypsies and the working class crowd every book. We find naive attitudes that smack of rank prejudice. (p. 290)

But Enid Blyton is not making any *conscious* gestures towards exploiting racialist attitudes in her young readers. You might as soon expect her to be writing a satire herself. Clearly, the attitudes she expresses come as naturally as leaves to a tree.

Many commentators have remarked on the ease with which she wrote, as if this meant that she was writing *like* a child. In her recent biography, Barbara Stoney seemed to imply that Enid Blyton thought as a child. I doubt if this is so. But there is no doubting her appeal. One librarian in Cumbria, with the agreement of all the local schools, banned Enid Blyton completely. Instead the shelves in the county and school libraries were stocked with more favoured authors, like Rosemary Sutcliff. Despite this, by far the most popular author with the children was Enid Blyton. They found their own means to gratify their own tastes. It reveals something about the strength of their tastes—as well as the fruit of such opposition—that they were determined to fulfil them.

Why is she so popular? It is obviously no answer to say she is popular *because* she had immoral views, or was childish, or wrote badly. The way to an answer is to analyse both her technique and the attitudes of children. Her books closely fit particular needs in children, a need that they also satisfy by watching TV and reading comics.

The technique of *The Three Golliwogs* with one idea repeated in a number of different circumstances, is standard. Constant repetition of the same sentence in a story is a favourite device for young children. To use the same plot in different forms gives a similar pleasure to older children. There is a security in the structure.

In many of her books, Enid Blyton creates a sense of possible adventure without having to make anything actually happen. In *The Castle of Adventure* or *Five go to Demon's Rock* it is only halfway through that we find any suggestion of action. Instead, the reader is kept in a state of comfortable expectation that depends on knowing that something *will* happen in the end.

This sense of anticipation is balanced by the reassurance of the utterly familiar. If Enid Blyton makes a joke, then it will be used as often as possible; it creates a repetitive momentum of its own. Thus, if one child has a mouthful of toffee, to the detriment of his speech, then he will *always* be unable to talk for toffee. (This is the case with Sid, in *The Mystery of the Vanished Prince,* 1951.)

Security always has the edge over excitement in Enid Blyton. In her archetypal scene, the Famous Five are exploring a tunnel of a cave. They go in further than any child dare go—but never *too* far before finding a light switch, or steps. The young reader is not kept in too much suspense.

Enid Blyton herself stressed the importance of reassurance: "My public, bless them, feel in my books a sense of security, an anchor, a sure knowledge that right is right"; or "It always amazes me when people deride books for being what they call 'escapist'. . . . All adventure stories are 'escapist' . . . mine among them. I cannot think why some people use this adjective in a derogative sense—such stories fulfil a very real need."

To her, an adventure is essentially something which children *want* to have. We often come across the phrase, "Let's have an adventure." Adventures are so unfrightening that the author has to resort to pointing out the putative excitement: "It was very unpleasant *indeed.*" We find a character saying "This is most exciting!" in case we hadn't noticed.

There is not so much a sense of a happy ending as the reminder, throughout her books, that all does not have to be taken too seriously. As in Bond films, the sense of ritual and humour removes any threat.

There is no exploration of the real world. The attraction of her world is that it is as far removed from "real" as Hollywood's. Even on a lighthouse out at sea, the milkman still delivers milk every morning, and there happens to be a tunnel heading straight down to the treasure.

Amid this feeling of security . . . , the author can afford to sit back and talk to the readers direct. When a character remarks that "there aren't any adventures to be found *there*," the author replies: "Ah—you wait and see . . . you don't know the Five! If there's any adventures about, they're bound to be right in the middle of it!"

The fact that she reveals prejudices against certain characters is not as important as the fact that her readers know exactly what to think about them. As in a western, the bad are obviously bad; the foolish are obviously foolish, like Mr Goon the policeman. Or take this, from *Claudine at St Clare's*: "This matron was thin and sour-looking. She had very thin lips that met together in a straight line. She smiled at the girls, but her smile stayed at her mouth and did not reach her eyes." She's sure to turn out a villain, and be punished.

Everyone is clearly portrayed, and fits naturally into the simplified chauvinism of children, with their exaggerated responses to good and bad. Enid Blyton's famous gift of "picturing" a scene, and then writing the required 40,000 words straight out, sprang from this simplified vision. She naturally turned to castles, caves and islands for inspiration.

As with the mass media, it is the very lack of demands that appeals. Many people know that children watch a great deal of television. It is not so generally known that children's taste in television is for thrillers, for the popular "adult" programmes on prime time. (pp. 290-91)

Like Enid Blyton, television thrillers give a sense of security . . . plus a slight sense of titillation.

Enid Blyton's popularity reveals something about the natural taste of children. If we are not surprised by the fact that children prefer the same programmes as the majority; and if we are not surprised at their taste for comics and magazines—then we should not be surprised at their love of Enid Blyton. We may not approve of such a taste, but we should try to understand it. To analyse Enid Blyton in adult terms—calling her a snobby racialist—is to miss the point. All right: a gypsy is "more like a very intelligent animal than a little girl" (*The Castle of Adventure,*) or two foreigners are referred to as "One never cleans his teeth and the other howls if he gets a kick at football" (*The Mystery of the Vanished Prince*). These are innocent gestures; children are unaffected by them. They are not conscious of the implications.

Children are not easily affected by the opinions they read. They are imbibing entertainment in the way they will continue to expect from the mass media. If anyone thinks of banning Enid Blyton's books, he should also ban television, radio, magazines and comics. The satisfactions offered are the same. (p. 291)

Cedric Cullingford, "Why Children Like Enid Blyton," in New Society, Vol. 49, No. 879, August 9, 1979, pp. 290-91.

Fred Inglis

[No] book which aims to deal ambitiously with children's reading can simply condemn the novels of Enid Blyton, and have done with her. She raises in a specially piercing way questions as to what popularity really is, how it is won and whether it matters. . . . She stands as a supreme example of the twistpoint between manipulation and expression. . . . (pp. 186-87)

She is ostentatiously 'a case'. For the details of her life make clear that she stood at no remove at all from the moral and emotional world of which she wrote; at the end, as Barbara Stoney delicately tells us, her control over both mind and body was distressingly intermittent, and she sought to hide herself from the reality of her illness and approaching end by living in the world she had created in 200-odd children's novels. Brian Jackson, in a striking article on Enid Blyton [in *Use of English* 26, No. 3 (1975)], wrote that

Enid Blyton reads like one of her own children: in her twenties she embarrasses her friends by calling herself 'Richard' or 'Cabin Boy', and whistling hands-in-pockets like a young jack tar from some Victorian boys' yarn. In her forties, she is playing conkers with her husband and confiding to her diary that she's 'got an eighter'.

And he goes on, 'The fantasies she focuses into childish fiction protect her from the emotional realities', and this

Blyton considering book illustrations at her last home, Green Hedges, Beaconsfield.

is no doubt a substantial part of her own psychological story. Indeed when she is obviously living in the real world, she does so with a disagreeable selfishness—offhand, cruel indifference and vengefulness towards her mother, her first husband, her friends and her servants—which emphasizes the rightness of Jackson's judgement. But the self-protectiveness of her psychology is the high degree of her involvement in the fantasies, together with her keen, energetic sense of how to make a fortune out of them.

The components which Jackson mentions as typifying her successful recipe, 'the grafting of the saccharine remains of old Bavarian toyland culture onto the world-wide hunger for miniature Disneyland', are certainly part of the instant mixture of her stories; just as solid and regular are the doses of high Beaconsfield snobbery, the picture-postcard nursery ruralism of Mistletoe Farm, the childish frame of legalism and retribution which shapes all the stories and gives the policemen such prominence.

Any success in popular culture will draw out a mixture of ready-to-hand substitute foods, brightly coloured, fatty, sweet; and bad for you. But it is not enough to rest on the solidarity of the educated, and to wait for laughs. It is

clear that Enid Blyton calculated her successes shrewdly, and became with increasing experience a very able businesswoman—able, according to the best tenets of marketing, to manipulate her customers, to catch and feed that strange but surprisingly stable monster, popular taste. She sensed with 'an instinctive creativity [which is] simultaneously naive and masterful' (Jackson's words) the conservatism of children, and built for it an enclave whose geography was drawn from the rich residues of a popular culture where the scenery is always and by definition behind the times. To say this, however, is to do no more than describe her recipe book. . . . Enid Blyton's unique achievement is to have made of her mixture an entirely flat geography, but to have written so much and so repetitively that this one-dimensional world becomes to its tourists as familiar and as easily traversed as the world of the *Beano, Krazy* and *Whizzer and Chips.*

Its lack, when compared with the comics, is to have none of their lurid cheerfulness, their noisy irreverence and barmy characters. The similarity is the entire safety of both worlds. Enid Blyton invites children to hold her hand on a walk through an adventure recounted with such flatness both of diction and of representation that any reader could be sure that no threat either to experience or to technique lurked in any sentence. Jackson mentions the safety which she offers to children whose grip on reading is perhaps premature and often uncertain:

> Possibly the explanation lies nearer sociology than either personal psychology or literature. I suspect it begins with the determination of advanced economies that children should be taught to read at seven. Few of us ever master so difficult an intellectual art as literacy ever again in life; and perhaps millions of us, during those titanic years, need to enjoy our new-found gains not tautly, as in school, but in regressive comfort. The bright and beautiful and private world of Enid Blyton met that desire.

Reading by its very nature rebuts the separation between skilfulness and cognition. You can't just learn to read without taking in what you are reading. Reading Enid Blyton is technically easy, but it is also emotionally and cognitively easy. In a useful note which Barbara Stoney reprints in the biography, Michael Woods guesses that Enid Blyton can never have been troubled by the tension felt by the adult writer for children between the world as it is and the vision he presents to children of the better place he would wish them to make it. 'She was a child, she thought as a child, and she wrote as a child . . . the basic feeling is essentially pre-adolescent . . . Enid Blyton has no moral dilemmas . . . Inevitably Enid Blyton was labelled by rumour a child-hater. If true, such a fact should come as no surprise to us, for as a child herself all other children can be nothing but rivals to her.'

That last remark compresses psychological explanation into a *very* narrow morality. Children do not merely hate their rivals, and both the life and writing of Enid Blyton evidences the extent to which she cherished the devotion and admiration of children. But like all of a certain class of really gigantic bestsellers—like Edgar Rice Burroughs, creator of Tarzan, like Luke Short and Ian Fleming, like Jean Plaidy and Mary Stewart—Enid Blyton gives all her enormous energy for work and her powerful belief in what she creates to representing the crude moral diagrams and garish fantasies of a readership which needs its authors far less than they, the authors, need the readers. Enid Blyton, like, so far as one can tell, Ian Fleming, precisely occupied the frame of moral reference of her own books. The lack of reality in both authors . . . is in some sense quite intentional. To push the prose into the depths of experience is to put yourself in danger. The point is rather to present a one-dimensional reflection in which a few, very simple, flat cues are enough to release a fantasy which never gets out of hand. An analogy with violence in certain TV serials is helpful. For it seems that in watching television, children are made anxious and distressed—or, indeed prompted to imitative action—only insofar as the violence breaks the convention of harmlessness. The conventional death by clutch-and-crumple in cowboy movies is, as we would all guess, entirely untroubling. There are hazards in saying so, because it's hard to tell what children are really watching for: plenty of girls, apparently, remain unmoved by the simple bullet holes in shoulder or chest, but become most anxious for the welfare of the cowboys' horses as they are tumbled over in a cloud of prairie dust.

But the general and familiar point stands. A high degree of conventionality permits reader and watcher to organize and manipulate their own fantasy. So with Enid Blyton, the one-dimensionality of the reflection guarantees a happily and safely unimaginative world where there is neither thought nor action but only the representation of an image with which you can do what you like. It is a paradoxical way to put the point, but I would say that children read Enid Blyton in order to *avoid* 'using their imaginations', and that this would be true even for the most backward and reluctant reader. Hence the great happiness she undoubtedly brings. This happiness is completely of a piece with Enid Blyton's urgent need to pretend that the world is the world of 'Green Hedges' and 'Elfin Cottage' and 'Old Thatch'. Her particular 'promise of happiness' *cannot* be kept. That is perhaps why so many teachers and parents of earnest persuasion (and who would not think it important to be earnest for his or her children?) become so angry with Enid Blyton. She promises that the falsehoods in which she herself strenuously wished to believe will come true. And her falsehoods are in no way related to the ordinary, necessary fictions of the imagination, precisely because although they can't be taken back to the world, they can only make it uninhabitable. If a child were to try to live Enid Blyton's narrow snobberies and vengefulness, her pitiful fancies of secret seven and famous five, in the real world, he or she would only come to disaster. But no normal child does. The imaginative charge simply isn't strong enough. So the pleasure of reading her on such a scale is like that of tirelessly bouncing a ball against a wall. It is contented and tranquil. In the strict sense, it is marginal; the pleasure of such privacy is only possible in its own little enclave. The novels transform time into a safe anaesthetic. (pp. 187-91)

> *Fred Inglis, "Cult and Culture: A Political-Psychological Excursus," in his* The Promise of Happiness: Value and Meaning in Children's Fiction, *Cambridge University Press, 1981, pp. 182-212.*

Sheila G. Ray

When the decision of certain library authorities not to buy the works of Enid Blyton was questioned, it was necessary to provide reasons for this decision. The reasons fell into two categories—those linked to literary quality and those linked to the values and attitudes reflected in her work. As far as the latter are concerned, they are essentially the values of the middle class prevalent in the 1930s; some are still relevant today (for example, the insistence on not leaving litter around the countryside), while others are quite inappropriate to a multi-cultural society and a society that we like to think is committed to equality of opportunity. The same criticism, however, might be made about writers of accepted literary quality.

Most of the criticisms that relate to literary quality also relate to Enid Blyton's simplicity. Her books are simple even when compared with many of the other books written for children, and read by them at about the same age that they are reading Enid Blyton. Her plots are well constructed and undoubtedly exciting, but the simplicity of the writing and of the characterization lays them open to criticism because, to an adult reader, they are often incredible.

Although the characterization is described as poor, this is an oversimplification of the matter. In creating characters, Enid Blyton tells her reader everything that it is necessary to know and tends to make the characters wholly good or wholly bad, or to give them, and to emphasize continually, one outstanding feature. This works well for the most part, but it must be admitted that sometimes what is said about a character contradicts the evidence provided by what that character says or how that character behaves. This is most likely to happen in the case of minor characters, such as Susie in **The Secret Seven** or Mafumu, the little native boy, in **The Secret Mountain.** Similarly Enid Blyton is careful to inform the reader that something is good, exciting, queer, creepy or horrid, instead of letting events speak for themselves.

There is a lack of depth in Enid Blyton's work which to some extent arises from the way in which she wrote, which did not allow for any research or checking of facts. She made some use of her own experiences, but for the most part she was content to invent, whether it was the name of a government department or some proprietary or technical name, in a way which convinces the more immature reader, but fails to satisfy at a more sophisticated level.

The strongest criticism which can be made of Enid Blyton, however, relates to her vocabulary. She makes use of a very limited number of words and seems at times to have an almost pathological fear of using a word which might not be understood by all her readers. Words such as lovely, nice, dear, little, cosy, peculiar, horrid, dreadful and, most unfortunate of all, queer, fill her pages. There is little use of metaphor or simile, and exclamation marks are constantly used to lend emphasis to comments and remarks. Thus a circle is created: her very simplicity is a major attraction as far as children are concerned, but it is the simplicity which condemns it in the eyes of many adults.

No one can deny that there was and still is a market for Enid Blyton's work. She was well aware of this market and of the needs of the various age groups for which she wrote. In this sense her writing can be seen as a commercial operation, catering for a clearly defined market, a fact which caused the Schools Council Research Project team to categorize all her work as 'non-quality'. However, she was also very sincere in her writing, evidently liking what she wrote because her only concern was to write the kind of story which she believed, quite accurately, children wanted. In view of the enthusiasm and affection with which adults frequently recall their childhood reading of Enid Blyton, she perhaps cannot be regarded as 'wholly bad', even in the literary sense.

No other writer has succeeded to the same extent in meeting the evident need which there is amongst children for books of this kind. As Elaine Moss wrote [in *Signal* 14] in 1974:

> . . . children could do with more new straight undemanding adventure stories properly written—books that would oust forever the Blyton series now being reissued, which Margery Fish-

er, in a recent number of *Growing Point,* condemned as 'slow poison'. Enid Blyton demonstrated that children are so hungry for *stories* that they will read the same story over and over, slightly disguised.

However, this is more easily said than done. Enid Blyton almost certainly had an advantage in embarking on her career as a children's writer when she did but she also possessed skills which have not been combined so successfully by any other writer. She varied her plots so that although the outcome might be predictable, there were plenty of elements to hold the reader's attention.

Enid Blyton's work caters for two kinds of children's needs. There are those children who, as Joyce Stranger pointed out [in *The Author* 86, 1975], may 'never gravitate beyond Blyton' and there are those who will, but who need plenty of practice in order to acquire fluency. Joyce Stranger again [in *Books for Children* 10, 1975]:

> Reading is an adventure, not a chore to be fostered as a sort of daily do your stint. What if children do move from Blyton to comics to books that you perhaps consider also rans? Do you always read for the good of your soul?

Even her sternest critics admit that Enid Blyton provides children with easy and enjoyable reading material at a time when they need plenty of practice in order to become fluent readers: by her keenest defenders, this is seen as the main justification for her work. It is interesting to observe that in recent years, in order to encourage Welsh children to read Welsh language books, a series of stories called 'Cyfres y Llewod' ('Lions Series') has been modelled on the 'Famous Five'. (pp. 201-04)

The fear is expressed that the reading of too much Enid Blyton may make a child reader lazy. Is it not possible that for some, perhaps most, children, it provides preparation for more demanding and more enriching literary experiences? There is much in Enid Blyton's work which could be usefully exploited in the development of an appreciation of literature.

The majority of children grow out of Enid Blyton naturally and the very fact that her work caters so well for the immature is a contributory factor in this. Although examples can be found of young people who are mentally retarded or who fail to develop emotionally, continuing to read Enid Blyton's books in their middle and late teens, there is nothing to suggest that they would fare any better if her work did not exist.

Adverse or favourable comments are made by those who care, but does it really matter what children read? Just as we know little about the way in which individual children respond to fiction, we know little about the long-term effects of poorly written, boring, immoral or frightening books, although it is generally agreed that some of those stories that we read and hear as children do stay with us and in some way furnish our minds. Books, however, are only one of many influences which affect children's attitudes and behaviour, and it is impossible to isolate cause and effect.

There seems little doubt that enjoyment of Enid Blyton's

books encourages the reading habit and the research which I carried out amongst students in higher education showed that those who had, as children, read a lot of Enid Blyton had also read a lot of other authors as well, and that reading and enjoying her when young is not a handicap to academic achievement.

The attitudes of adults towards Enid Blyton are influenced by the circumstances in which they are involved with children's reading. Publishers and booksellers are likely to be affected by commercial pressures, teachers and parents by their concern that children should acquire the reading habit and critics by the convention that literature which they consider to have little merit is not worthy of their attention. What attitude should librarians adopt? It is hoped that this examination of the more popular series and titles will help librarians to become more aware of the issues involved but . . . it may well be that the Blyton phenomenon, although a continuing one, has ceased to be a problem for librarians. (pp. 204-05)

> *Sheila G. Ray, in her* The Blyton Phenomenon: The Controversy Surrounding the World's Most Successful Children's Writer, *Andre Deutsch Limited, 1982, 246 p.*

Petronella Breinburg

1927-

(Also writes as Bella Ashey and Mary Totham) South American-born English author of picture books, fiction, and plays, and reteller.

Major works include *Legends of Suriname* (1971), *My Brother Sean* (1973; U. S. edition as *Shawn Goes to School*), *Sally-Ann's Umbrella* (1975), *Us Boys of Westcroft* (1975), *Brinsly's Dream* (1977).

Breinburg is recognized as one of the first English writers for young people to create books with black children as protagonists. Best known for her series of picture books about the West Indian children Sean and Sally-Ann, she is credited with writing stories for and about children who have emigrated into the United Kingdom that are both authentic and universal. Describing the daily experiences of her characters in a direct but sympathetic manner, Breinburg is often praised for the strength of her characterizations and her understanding both of childhood and the multiracial urban communities in which she sets her works. The themes of her picture books focus on determination, self-reliance, overcoming anxiety, and the relationships of the main characters with their siblings and friends. In *My Brother Sean,* for example, small Sean, terrified on his first day of school, is helped to adjust by his teacher, mother, and older sister, who tells the story in retrospect. *Sean's Red Bike* (1975; U. S. edition as *Shawn's Red Bike*) shows Sean, now a bit older than in the first book, saving for, and receiving, a new bicycle; although his first attempts to ride are awkward, he confidently assures his audience of neighborhood children that he will do better next time. Sean is considered a particularly engaging character: his popularity with the students of a South London school, who requested a companion for him, led Breinburg to create the lively Sally-Ann. In the second book of the "Sally-Ann" series, *Sally-Ann in the Snow* (1977), Breinburg shows her protagonist being laughed at by the older children in her neighborhood because she is afraid to go down a snowy hill in her friend's box; while the other children are away, she triumphantly slides down the hill. Of the "Sally-Ann" books, Eileen Colwell writes that the series "fills a gap in providing easily read stories of an integrated community in which there is no racial prejudice."

Born in Suriname, South America, Breinburg began writing for children after moving to England. As a London primary school teacher, she told stories of her homeland to her pupils; inspired by these children, who wanted to read the stories but could not find published versions, she wrote her first book, the folktale collection *Legends of Suriname.* She was prompted to create the character of Sean by a small boy to whom she used to tell stories to keep out of mischief and who wanted badly to go to school. Although Breinburg wrote *My Brother Sean* in 1969, she was unable to have the book published until 1973 due to what

Elaine Moss calls "an apartheid approach to children's books." Breinburg and illustrator Errol Lloyd, who was born in Jamaica and provided the pictures for the "Sean" books, refused to appear on a BBC television program for being what Breinburg calls "the first author and artist to make books about black children *for* black children" due to their belief that there should not be a segregated approach to children's literature. A part-time secondary school English teacher since 1974, Breinburg is also the author of *Us Boys of Westcroft,* a young adult novel that provides a realistic portrayal of a London high school. As opposed to her picture books, Breinburg clearly depicts prejudice in *Us Boys of Westcroft,* which is acknowledged for containing a gripping narrative and well-portrayed characters. Breinburg is also the author of a story for older primary graders, *Brinsly's Dream,* which describes how a Guyan boy, a talented goalie who wants to be a famous footballer, is kidnapped at the beginning of an important match. As with her picture books, *Brinsly's Dream* stresses initiative and determination as the reasons for the ultimate success of her character. Breinburg is also a playwright for both children and adults as well as a storyteller and lecturer on creative writing at various universities.

She received the Suriname Linguistic Bureau "honorary place" award for *Legends of Suriname* in 1972.

(See also *Something about the Author,* Vol. 11, *Contemporary Authors New Revision Series,* Vol. 4, and *Contemporary Authors,* Vols. 53-56.)

GENERAL COMMENTARY

Elaine Moss

The desperate need for picture books with black or Asian children in them is evident every minute of the day. Britain has been very slow off the mark in this respect. . . . (p. 113)

Petronella Breinburg, a black woman who was born in multi-racial Suriname, and Errol Lloyd, a Jamaican, have recently collaborated on two British picture books centering on a black child, Sean. The books, *My Brother Sean* and *Doctor Sean,* are not yet available in paperback; when they are they will surely attract the Jamaican community in the market the way the [Ezra Jack] Keats books now do. But Petronella Breinburg and Errol Lloyd strongly and rightly resented the suggestion (made by a minion of the BBC who was attempting to charm them on to a programme) that the two of them were "interesting because they are the first author and artist in Britain to make books *about* black children *for* black children". They stress that their books are for *all* children: by publishing them as front-ranking picture books The Bodley Head has not only flown in the face of other publishers' rejection of the stories (on the absurd grounds that "Jamaicans don't buy books"—as though the books weren't for a white readership as well as for an avid black one) but has demonstrated the belief that a flood of second-rate material to fill the gap that at last is seen to exist would be a disaster. The political and social consequences of an apartheid approach to children's books is very apparent to Petronella; she put forward her views on books for *all* children at a Women's Lib meeting recently and reports, sadly, that she was howled down by those who fail to think their tailor-made philosophies through. Errol Lloyd, who has just taken his bar finals and will soon have to decide between a pin-striped suit and his present relaxed appearance as an artist, says mildly that publishers are in business and by and large feel under no obligation to venture into series which fill a sociological need.

How important it is for white children that the gap should be filled was then demonstrated by Petronella, who is a teacher in a secondary school in Sidcup. She told of a fourteen-year-old boy who was resistant to being taught English by a Negro. "What do you expect, Miss?" he said. "Negroes are not teachers. They're bus conductors and they work in hospitals." Far from being appalled by this, Petronella sympathized with her pupil. "On TV and in books that is what he sees. Naturally the child says, 'What is going on?'" What, indeed. (pp. 114-15)

> *Elaine Moss, "A Mirror in the Market Place,"*
> *in Signal, No. 15, September, 1974, pp. 113-16.*

TITLE COMMENTARY

My Brother Sean (1973; U.S. edition as *Shawn Goes to School*)

[Children] reach an age when constant proximity to their mothers ceases to be the answer to all their needs. For all that, the first separation can be painful if the ground has not been well laid, and stories about play-group, nursery or school can be helpful in letting the child know what to expect. *My Brother Sean,* Petronella Breinburg's terse, simple story about a small boy's first day at nursery, pulls no punches. Although Sean has always wanted to go to school he is bewildered and tearful in the new situation, and when his mother and sister want to leave him he cries again. Finally, he is happy to be left, and there the story ends. (pp. 1437)

> *"Grandmother's Footsteps and Some More Progressive Games," in* The Times Literary Supplement, *No. 3742, November 23, 1973, pp. 1436-37.*

In spite of the large numbers of West Indian immigrants in some of our bigger towns and cities, few children's picture books have emerged which have either reflected this aspect, or have catered for this section of our community. A small redressing of the balance is made with this story. . . . The illustrations by a young Jamaican [Errol Lloyd] are dramatic and highly colourful, the heads are over emphasised and the bodies often out of proportion, but nevertheless, the faces have an intensity which makes the book come to life. The text by a teacher from Suriname, is brief, basic and concise, making it an ideal early reading book. The fact that Sean is a young West Indian boy at school for the first time is, however, incidental. Any child starting school would be able to identify with him on that first exciting step from babyhood into childhood.

> *Pat Garrett, in a review of "My Brother Sean,"*
> *in* Children's Book Review, *Vol. 111, No. 6, December, 1973, p. 170.*

It's not often that a book written to fill a specific purpose succeeds on any but a functional level; however, here is one that speaks to a problem artistically. The subject is a child's fear of school, and the young protagonist is Shawn, who has always wanted to go to school but when the big day comes, panics at the brink of his new experience. Shawn cries, but comfort and support from a kind teacher, his mother, and older sister ease his fears until finally he smiles a "teeny weeny smile" and his mother and sister leave. The loving sympathy of the text is magnified in the rich, warm oil paintings [by Errol Lloyd] of children in their nursery school setting. For preschoolers, an attractive, soothing look at a child on his own for the first time. (pp. 817-18)

> *A review of "Shawn Goes to School," in* The Booklist, *Vol. 70, No. 14, March 15, 1974, pp. 817-18.*

[This] describes a child's first day at school—as told by his older sister. The style is very simple and direct, the pictures bold but also simple, with vigorous use of color. Shawn cried, a full-throated roar of dismay. But the kind, smiling teacher said there were "lots of nice kids," and Mom pointed out the toys, Shawn's sister the swing, and a friendly classmate the donkey, a real one, for riding. The story ends, "Shawn smiled a teeny weeny smile." But the smile tells all. This is the sort of book we need more of, the light, firm treatment of a universal experience in a story with minority group protagonists. (pp. 153-54)

> *Zena Sutherland, in a review of "Shawn Goes to School," in* Bulletin of the Center for Children's Books, *Vol. 27, No. 10, June, 1974, pp. 153-54.*

Doctor Sean   (1974; U.S. edition as *Doctor Shawn*)

[**Doctor Sean**] has a minimal thread of anecdote about a group of negro children playing hospitals, a game which must stop when dinner is served. It is not informative, perhaps it is not meant to be, but neither is it original nor interesting as a story. . . . In this book the stethoscope is not named, but inadequately described as 'that thing doctors use to listen to people's chests,' and this characterises the whole approach of the book; one which arouses interest but does nothing at all to satisfy it.

> *John A. Cunliffe, in a review of "Doctor Sean," in* Children's Book Review, *Vol. IV, No. 3, Autumn, 1974, p. 97.*

This book is most welcome. The author presents a warm and loving Black family with a mother who understands that play can't always be done neatly! Many Black parents must leave their children home unattended for lack of babysitting money, requiring the children to develop self-reliance at an early age. The book shows that "problem" in a positive light. Another good feature of the book is that both Shawn and his sister, in their conversation, express awareness of the fact that the roles of doctor and nurse have nothing to do with being male or female.

> *Ed Celina Marcus Snowden, in a review of "Doctor Shawn," in* Interracial Books for Children Bulletin, *Vol. 6, No. 1, 1975, p. 4.*

"A bandage for you, sir?" asks pretend Doctor Shawn while his sister, playing nurse, says to younger Josephine, "Let me comb your hair while you wait for the doctor." Playing doctor gets a little messy, with the cat knocking over the doll's crib and Shawn dispensing sliced banana pills, but then Mom comes home from shopping and serves lunch—so that even though Shawn's sister has mentioned that she was doctor last time, what you see here (in Lloyd's paintings of shiny brown faces against outlined slabs of chalky bright color) is females playing their traditional helping roles. And there's not much else to see at any level, which only confirms our belief . . . in the overwhelming superiority of American picture book illustration.

> *A review of "Doctor Shawn," in* Kirkus Reviews, *Vol. XLIII, No. 3, February 1, 1975, p. 120.*

Sally-Ann's Umbrella   (1975)

Specially written for the pupils of a school in South-East London who had requested a companion for the popular small boy Sean, this is a warm-hearted, direct anecdote about a little West Indian girl who is at first too bashful to show her school friends the bright patterned umbrella her aunt has given her; when she does open it the wind carries it on to the roof and the caretaker has to retrieve it. Crayon pictures [by Ossie Murray], vivid and descriptive, underline mood and event very pleasantly and with something of the simple, strong vision of a child.

> *Margery Fisher, in a review of "Sally-Ann's Umbrella," in* Growing Point, *Vol. 15, No. 2, July, 1976, p. 2921.*

Sean's Red Bike   (1975; U.S. edition as *Shawn's Red Bike*)

Shawn (**Doctor Shawn, Shawn Goes to School**) is now old enough for a two-wheeler, and his heart is set on a bike he sees in the store. He saves his allowance, does chores, and finally get the bike. His first attempt at riding is not wholly successful, but he will do better next time, he confidently assures an audience of neighborhood children. . . . The story is slight, although it demonstrates industry and persistence as well as Shawn's cheerful acceptance of the fact that it takes time to learn a new skill. (pp. 3-4)

> *Zena Sutherland, in a review of "Shawn's Red Bike," in* Bulletin of the Center for Children's Books, *Vol. 30, No. 1, September, 1976, pp. 3-4.*

Further exploits of Shawn, an engagingly straightforward Black child, who is shown a little older here. Shawn wants a red two-wheeler "with a shiny new bell" and gets one after saving his pocket money, gifts, baby sitting earnings, etc. The fact that Shawn doesn't know how to ride his brand new bike doesn't deter him, and despite repeated crashes, the story ends with Shawn vowing to make it "around the corner" the next day. A simple pleasant story about determination. . . .

> *Melinda Schroeder, in a review of "Shawn's Red Bike," in* School Library Journal, *Vol. 23, No. 1, September, 1976, p. 96.*

Us Boys of Westcroft   (1975)

A realistic inside view of the last year at a London secondary school, where tensions build up to disaster. Walter is 15 and black, looking back on that year, trying to pick up the pieces of his life, wondering what went wrong. Taut, colloquial, topical, the story welds together the frustrated confusion of the boys and the wary authoritativeness of the teachers into a gripping narrative, and allows knowable personalities to emerge through a net of social and educational prejudice.

> *Stuart Hannabus, in a review of "Us Boys of*

Westcroft," in Children's literature in education, *No. 2, Summer, 1982, p. 63.*

What Happened at Rita's Party   (1976)

What happened at Rita's party was just what happens at any nice little girl's party and the fact that Rita was black didn't make any difference at all. They almost didn't let Ella come in because she was wearing jeans and the cake was late but it turned up in the end. This book is racially integrated and socially respectable but not particularly interesting.

> *Dorothy Nimmo, in a review of "What Happened at Rita's Party" in* The School Librarian, *Vol. 25, No. 1, March, 1977, p. 35.*

Brinsly's Dream   (1977)

Brinsley's Dream is to be a famous footballer but when a local team is started the Guyanan boy is soon tired of theory and elementary practice and annoyed at being treated like a child by the Popapulos brothers, enthusiasts who have the kind of talent Brinsley covets. Another of his dreams, of being kidnapped, does oddly come true when supporters of a rival team snatch this promising goalie at the outset of a vital match. Lively, natural and authentic in atmosphere, this tale for the times reflects the varying interests and problems of a mixed urban community with evident knowledge.

> *Margery Fisher, in a review of "Brinsly's Dream," in* Growing Point, *Vol. 15, No. 8, March, 1977, p. 3060.*

I am sure this is a true world, authentic in rhythms of speech and details of life-style; I believe it all, but I still find it rather small, flat and a bit boring. Brinsly is alive and well and living in an inner London suburb but we remain outside his dream. The book is very well made but not, somehow, created.

> *Dorothy Nimmo, in a review of "Brinsly's Dream," in* The School Librarian, *Vol. 25, No. 1, March, 1977, p. 35.*

No doubt it could be argued that fiction has a duty to explore racial tensions which surround young readers, and I would not argue with that. But it seems to be the *predominant* issue of contemporary, multicultural fiction, and that cannot be healthy. We need more stories for juvenile readers which have positive heroes and heroines, which *celebrate* cultural diversity, which are so well written that no matter what the cultural origins of the characters all readers can identify with them.

Of course, there are such positive stories about, many of

them written, significantly, by authors whose cultural roots are not British: the insider's story is perhaps the most authentic. But it's not all plain-sailing even here. Petronella Breinburg's . . . **Brinsly's Dream,** for example, set in contemporary Britain, will appeal to all football enthusiasts as well as having a special appeal to readers of West Indian origin, yet while being positive in showing the success of a coloured boy through his own initiative and determination, the book is embarassingly sexist. Mothers and daughters do little but bake, nag, and talk babies: the fair sex are unfairly presented.

> *Richard Brown, in a review of, "Brinsly's Dream," in* The Times Educational Supplement, *No. 3493, June 10, 1983, p. 22.*

Sally-Ann in the Snow   (1977)

[Breinburg and illustrator Ossie Murray have] produced a second picture book for our multiracial society: Sally-Ann is evidently West Indian, but the colour differences between the children tobogganing in the park are there only by inference from the illustrations. Sally-Ann is laughed at by the older children for her fear of going down the snow-covered slope in her friend Sandra's box, but while the others are engaged in a snowball fight, triumphantly she overcomes her fears. The pastel texture of the bluey sky and snow-covered skylines, the pale impression of the city and the houses behind the firmly outlined children in the park, are most attractive. (pp. 274-75)

> *M. Hobbs, in a review of "Sally-Ann in the Snow," in* The Junior Bookshelf, *Vol. 41, No. 5, October, 1977, pp. 274-75.*

Sally-Ann's Skateboard   (1979)

There have been several picture books already about Sally-Ann, the lively coloured child. Here she acquires a fibreglass skateboard and all the protective clothing necessary. She has promised not to skate on the street but an older boy 'borrows' her new board, and in pursuing him they both come to disaster.

[Illustrator Ossie Murray] has produced attractive and gaily-coloured pastel illustrations. Occasionally the background of the pages is too obtrusive and obscures the print. This series fills a gap in providing easily read stories of an integrated community in which there is no racial prejudice.

> *E. Colwell, in a review of "Sally-Ann's Skateboard," in* The Junior Bookshelf, *Vol. 43, No. 5, October, 1979, p. 265.*

Jane Louise Curry

1932-

American author of fiction and retellings.

Major works include *Beneath the Hill* (1967); *The Sleepers* (1968); *The Daybreakers* (1970); *Poor Tom's Ghost* (1977); *The Bassumtyte Treasure* (1978).

Considered one of the most prominent American fantasists in juvenile literature, Curry is the author of fantasies, mysteries, and retellings for readers in the middle grades through high school. She incorporates history and myth into virtually all of her writings, which have been celebrated for their success in making history meaningful and relevant to children. Her stories, which reflect the careful scholarship for which she is praised, feature settings in America and the British Isles and use both historical and contemporary time periods and cultures; the works draw on familiar sources—such as the Arthurian Legend—while focusing thematically on the nature of time and the atemporal and universal struggle between good and evil. In her novels, Curry endeavors to demonstrate the power that past actions and choices wield over the present: "My fictional world," she has written, "reflects my understanding of the workings of the real one—complex, organic, and dynamic—in which all human relationships, deep or casual, present or past, can touch or turn, blight or enrich us." Critic Marcus Crouch calls Curry "one of the most promising new voices from America," adding that "she blends the most convincing naturalistic presentation of modern society with the supernatural in masterly fashion."

Curry is best known for her eight-volume series of fantasies about the history of Abáloc, considered a unique mythical version of pre-Columbian America that effectively blends Welsh and United States history. Lauded as thought-provoking and ambitious, the series—which includes *Beneath the Hill, The Change-Child* (1969), *The Daybreakers, Over the Sea's Edge* (1971), *The Watchers* (1975), *The Birdstones* (1977), *The Wolves of Aam* (1981), and *Shadow Dancers* (1983)—describes how a group of inquisitive young people discover Abáloc, an ancient and magical precursor of the West Virginia mining community in which they live, and other places and events of the past through a series of time-travel adventures. Curry uses these "time slips" in many of her novels; through this device, her characters assist others while themselves maturing through their experiences. In addition, these novels demonstrate that a young person's search for identity necessarily entails an examination of both family and cultural history. Curry has written several acclaimed ghost stories which feature mystery, suspense, and intricate plotting in addition to the time travel motif. She is also the author of fantasies depicting—with dry humor—the misadventures of children who have been shrunk in a reducing machine. Although some commentators find the plots of her novels convoluted, most praise Curry's graceful, evocative style as well as her lively characters and ingenious mixture of

history and fantasy; in addition, reviewers often note that her works provide children with a sense of continuity between time past and time present. Curry is also commended for imparting useful and interesting information in her works, many of which feature real people, places, and events, such as the Johnstown Flood of 1889 in *The Great Flood Mystery* (1985) and book pirating involving Charles Dickens in *What the Dickens!* (1991).

Born in Ohio, Curry was raised there and in Pennsylvania, states which serve as backdrops for many of her novels. After studying art and art education, she accepted a position as an art teacher in Los Angeles, where she became familiar with Native American culture and legend. After moving to England to study medieval and Elizabethan literature, she wrote her first book *Down from the Lonely Mountain: California Indian Tales,* a collection of twelve Native American stories which she retold; Curry is also the author of a second collection, *Back in the Beforetime; Tales of the California Indians* (1987). She then began to create her Abáloc novels: set in the small, contemporary mining community of Apple Lock, the series chronicles how several of the town's children discover that the artifacts they find buried in a mound date back to the Ice Age, a time when their neighborhood was known as Abáloc and was populated with giants, fairies, and a variety of magical creatures. When unregulated strip-mining threatens the economic security of the town, the young people deduce that the hardship of the community stems from the land's residual evil. The series also includes *The Sleepers,* a novel that is generally considered Curry's best: the story concerns two archaeologists and four children who, after stumbling upon an underground cave where King Arthur and his band sleep with twelve of their thirteen treasures, are transported back in time to assist Arthur in his quest for the missing valuable. Considered a masterful blending of history and fantasy, the Abáloc novels have been hailed by critics as a poignant warning to children not to ignore the past. Many of Curry's ghost stories also explore the redemptive might of history and its powerful influence on the present. In *Poor Tom's Ghost,* for example, a twentieth-century English boy returns to seventeenth-century London in order to alter the destiny of an Elizabethan actor who haunts both the boy's father and the dilapidated home he has recently inherited. Noted for its convincing characters and dialogue, *Poor Tom's Ghost* is often considered a fantasy *tour de force.* Curry received the Edgar Allan Poe Award for *Poor Tom's Ghost* in 1977 and *The Bassumtyte Treasure* in 1979; both novels were runners-up for the prize. She also received the Children's Literature Award from the Southern California Council on Literature for Children and Young People in 1979 for her body of work.

(See also *Something about the Author,* Vols. 1, 52;' *Something about the Author Autobiography Series,* Vol. 6; *Major Authors and Illustrators for Children and Young Adults; Contemporary Authors,* Vols. 17-20; *Contemporary Authors New Revision Series,* Vol. 7.)

TITLE COMMENTARY

Down from the Lonely Mountain: California Indian Tales (1965)

This is a collection of California Indian animal myths with stories centering on the origin of the land, the theft of fire and light and the misadventures which arise from certain personality traits attributed to the various animals. Storytellers should be alert to the mildly stylized pattern of speech which is usually successful in suggesting Indian dignity and economy of words, although read all at one sitting it can begin to wear. The author commands her subject best in the last stories of the book and it is in these that a sense of humor and drama come through. The most memorable animal character is Coyote, who appears throughout, always consistently motivated by egotism and alive with foolery. [Illustrator] Enrico Arno's black and white drawings are well designed and, like the text, speak best in conjunction with the more amusing stories. This should have the usual strong regional market but offers some possibilities for storytellers anywhere.

A review of "Down from the Lonely Mountain," in Virginia Kirkus' Service, Vol. XXXIII, No. 4, February 14, 1965, p. 170.

A dozen tales, told of the world when it was new and of animals that helped to shape it, present American Indian legends with unusual charm and liveliness. . . . Filled with humor and drama, told with economy, color, and an easy flow, all the stories will serve the storyteller well and will be enjoyed for reading aloud. An excellent companion to Anne B. Fisher's *Stories California Indians Told,* which contains different stories of the same type.

Virginia Haviland, in a review of "Down from the Lonely Mountain: California Indian Tales," in The Horn Book Magazine, Vol. XLI, No. 4, August, 1965, p. 390.

"Far to the south, in the seasons before there was this world where animal folk and Indians dwell, there was a Lonely Mountain." Mysteriously and musically a new storyteller begins her collection of 12 tales about an early world in which only animals dwell—Eagle, Wus the fox, Kaai the Crow, mole, coyote, cottontail. These animals behave like Indians with magical powers, creating the world to suit their taste. Eagle was their chieftain who called councils to decide difficult problems. Bravely coyote secured light, fire was acquired, and blue jay sent to bring home the dawn so the transition from light to day would not be abrupt. Their efforts were not always successful, for there were still Witsduks in the world, creatures named for the Snow-the-Wind-Blows-and-Drifts who delighted in making animals shiver. But the animals got along, even cottontail and foolish little blue bird chicks, for though they teased and sometimes hurt each other, there was always some creature to lend a helping hand.

Enrico Arno has made perfectly delightful drawings, humorous and dignified, with the animals arrayed in full Indian regalia. This book will give pleasure in homes as well as in schools and libraries for its simple, charming handling of these legends, though we regret the absence of notes to explain which printed sources were used and which elements combined to create the stories.

Margaret Sherwood Libby, in a review of "Down from the Lonely Mountain: California Indian Tales," in Book Week—The Sunday Herald Tribune, August 22, 1965, p. 17.

Beneath the Hill (1967)

[In *Beneath the Hill*] Miggle's well-planned treasure hunt develops into more than she anticipates. The key she has found becomes a symbol of the quest she and her cousins are unwittingly drawn into, in this perfect fantasy about the past and the present, about good and evil. . . . The pleasures of a good story are supplemented by the author's consistent inventiveness in character and detail, her harking back to Welsh legend, her restrained and careful writing.

Helen B. Crawshaw, in a review of "Beneath the Hill," in The Horn Book Magazine, Vol. XLIII, No. 4, August, 1967, p. 461.

From the author of *Down From the Lonely Mountain,* a fine collection of Indian tales, comes a fantasy rooted in the quixotic to contemplative nature of children and the concerns of Celtic-Arthurian legend. It begins, personally, circumstantially, with a trick treasure hunt, and mounts to a harrowing confrontation of good and evil, as the make-believe treasure becomes more-than-real, as the Bane, a scar on the mountainside created by strip-mining, becomes not only a threat to the landscape but also a threat to the existence of the Fair Folk of the Dark Wood (y Tylwyth Teg) who dwell within the mountain. Who are these folk, stranded so strangely somewhere in the Alleghenies? They set sail from Wales many years earlier from their mystical homeland of Tir na'nOg and found themselves, accidentally, in America, where they set up housekeeping in the caverns of a mountain previously inhabited by the Avenaki Indians. In the struggle to contain the evil which the Bane is unloosing, three very individual children find themselves the allies—sometimes wonderstruck, sometimes uneasy—of the Fair Folk. Before a way is found, Miggle, Arthur (Dub), and Stevie learn much about their own character from their farseeing friends. And in the end: "The Bane grew green. The . . . spring overflowed even in the drought of August. And the folk came at last to Tir na'nOg." Despite the stilted medieval speech of the Fair Folk, this will hold conviction for the imaginative child; in the words of Maclin, "A keen ear and a keen heart that holds nothing impossible sees much." It has elements of Green Knowe and *Wrinkle in Time*—fine company for any fantasy to keep.

> *A review of "Beneath the Hill," in* Kirkus Service, *Vol. XXV, No. 2, January 15, 1967, p. 61.*

A quite successful blending of realism and fantasy, with a group of children (cousins) encountering a small colony of people who dwell within the mountain. . . . The realistic elements are excellent, with good characterization and dialogue; the fanciful aspects seem rather complicated and elaborate, but they are faithful to the genre, being tied to Celtic legend, and the relationship between the two groups of characters is both sympathetic and a deft solution to the puzzle of the book: the purpose of the strange key that one of the children has found. (pp. 25-6)

> *Zena Sutherland, in a review of "Beneath the Hill," in* Bulletin of the Center for Children's Books, *Vol. 21, No. 2, October, 1967, pp. 25-6.*

Beneath the Hill is a blissfully enjoyable book for any child of ten or upwards with imagination who also enjoys adventure. The children, Miggle, Arthur, Stevie, Trish and Kit are a splendidly real bunch and their excursion into the world of faery is so strange and yet inevitable that it carries the reader along in unquestioning suspension of disbelief to the end.

> *"Kingdoms of the Mind," in* The Times Literary Supplement, *No. 3475, October 3, 1968, p. 1113.*

The Sleepers   (1968)

First Garner, then Mayne (in *Earthfasts*) probed the conjunction between "now and the time that waits below now," but the phrase is Jane Curry's and hers is a different, more domestic dig. Two boys and two girls, presumably in their mid-teens, inadvertently discover—in the course of their elders' archaeological surveying—the entrance to a tunnel into the Scottish Eildon Hills, legendary Roman-British site. Or is it inadvertent? Jennifer was earlier approached by a boy on Battersea Bridge with a cryptic message for her brother; he looked ordinary enough, but when she painted him, he came out in a garment of skins with a Celtic spear and brooch. And then there is the bronze bell buried at the entrance to the passageway and the accompanying instructions which the children decipher (in the course of two funny sorties into London libraries): "When Britain the king needs / Ring me to wake him." The king is Arthur, sleeping with his men in the chamber at the end of the tunnel—not the Knights of the Round Table but an earlier, truer breed, "kind of tired and dirty and sad." How Gillian and H. P., Jennifer's brother, retrieve the bell from the British Museum (in a sequence reminiscent of the *Mixed-Up Files* [by E. L. Konigsburg]); rouse Arthur so that he can wrest the missing Thirteenth Treasure from Margana (in the guise of the Morgan Sand and Gravel Company); and arrange for Arthur and his men to sail away with the Treasures (in a houseboat) and so fulfill prophecy makes a climax as packed as this recap, with a neat balance of amusing reality and sensitive projection. Not as stirring or original as the author's **Beneath the Hill,** but potentially involving for children who'd be overwhelmed by Garner or Mayne.

> *A review of "The Sleepers," in* Kirkus Service, *Vol. XXXVI, No. 8, April 15, 1968, p. 459.*

The new fantasy by the author of **Beneath the Hill** is similar in structure to the earlier book; again the interweaving of the past with the present shows evidence of careful scholarship. But the characters are delineated more sharply and the complex elements of the plot more clearly presented. In this original treatment of a well-worn theme, several children and adults discover the cave where King Arthur sleeps with his companions until Britain shall have need of him again. To save the Sleepers and twelve of the Thirteen Treasures of Britain from the quarrying of the Morgan Sand and Gravel Company (really Fata Morgana, evil sister of the King, who plots his destruction) entails a series of lively and sometimes humorous adventures: the unraveling of a five-hundred-year-old prophecy of Thomas the Rhymer; the unsaying of the spell that imprisons Myrddin (Merlin) in a hawthorn tree; the theft from the British Museum of the bronze bell that will awaken the Sleepers; a swift midnight ride to London with the Treasures to put them safely aboard a houseboat, on which the Sleepers sail away to "beyond the North." The adults play credible roles in the story and participate in the magic to a varying extent—to the degree to which each is able to suspend his disbelief. A rewarding fantasy.

> *Diane Farrell, in a review of "The Sleepers," in* The Horn Book Magazine, *Vol. XLIV, No. 4, August, 1968, p. 427.*

You can manipulate the King Arthur myth to fit any here and now, which is its strength and fascination. Here in **The Sleepers,** the King sleeps and waits in a story about archaeology. Two honest archaeologists helped by four children discover in a semi-private search (by means of the new machine which traces different kinds of rock formations on a dial) the cave where Artair and his band sleep, with twelve of their thirteen treasures. An "official" archaeological dig, employing the Morgan Sand & Gravel Co., turns out to be concealing the old enemy, Fata Morgana, Morgan Le Fay (quite properly reclining on white velvet in a de luxe caravan), intent upon drilling through to the cave, capturing the treasures, killing the sleepers and so getting an evil hold upon Britain. In order to wake Artair to the danger there is need that the bronze bell, found by the children at the cave entrance near the roots of the ancient Eildon Tree, be rung. But this has already gone up to the B. M., with consequences which may be imagined. Merlin, white-bearded and querulous, directs operations, at first appearing among the roots of the tree: and although one wonders why he is given eighteenth-century archaic to talk, this is not a bad Merlin, if a little uncertain (why does he understand about wire fences, alarums and drilling machines, but not, apparently about trains?).

The treatment of Arthur is interesting in that Jane Louise Curry really has it both ways fairly successfully. There is a realistic, uncomfortable, severely practical discovery of the sleepers, snoring gently in their cave, properly ragged Romano-Britains after battle; and a little less convincing when they start to talk and plan. But for the last battle with Morgan the author retreats to a distance, giving us sword, lance and pealing horn under a summer night sky, apocalyptic and undetailed. While for the last vision of all, when the King and his band reach London victorious and appear through a sudden mist swirling over an Embankment which is "then" and not "now", to bear away the Treasures in the houseboat Lucy (one of the little ships of Dunkirk, appropriately enough), she has gone completely "Idyllic", and very movingly so. The early part of this story, the search with the new machine, is slow and over-detailed for any but the "archaeological" reader, for the technical interest has taken first place and makes the characters difficult to distinguish and the geography tortured. Once over this, it is an exciting, varied, fast-moving fantasy with its heart in the right place, and shows some skill in the full use of a big bunch of characters, young and older, second-sighted and down-to-earth, all delineated with zest and some conviction.

> "Crusaders, Monks and Britons," in The Times Literary Supplement, No. 3501, April 3, 1969, p. 351.

Because of her love of British earth, of the Celtic past and all things Arthurian, what Jane Louise Curry has done in **The Sleepers** is reminiscent in both material and spirit of the altogether more abundant examples of time fantasy that have come out of the British Isles, but imprinted throughout with her own reflections, her private vision. In relation to the private vision: when she was halfway through her writing of **The Sleepers,** she happened upon William Mayne's Earthfasts, which is also built around that part of the Arthurian legend which claims that Arthur and his knights are even now sleeping timelessly in some underground cavern. "It was so perfect, so enviable," she says, that she stopped work in despair and could only go on with her book when she was persuaded to real-

ize that "the difference in vision would eliminate any sense of 'trespass.' " Again and again the turns of the plot—a firmly woven structure concerned with the awakening and release of Arthur and his men and the rescue of their treasures, the Thirteen Treasures of Prydain, from the grasp of a still living Fata Morgana and Medraut—bring to light Miss Curry's own illuminations about truth, about time, about magic and what one can bear to know of the interrelationships of the past and the present.

Her book rises out of the legend of the Sleepers, but in another way out of one of the children's, Jennifer's, sensitivity to what can be sensed rather than seen, which in its turn is closely related to the child's sensitivity as an artist. She is able to put herself entirely out of mind, to make herself open, uncluttered, expectant, ready to receive. And it is Jennifer, when the children venture through the long dark underground passage, with their little flashlight, toward the Sleepers' cavern, who is aware of

> a growing sense of space and lightness within the close darkness, a feeling that the others, though close enough to hold, were ages distant. The world drained away, pouring over the edges of her vision into the dark. She knew, from having watched with patient eyes the play of light on the river, and of leaves against the sky, that it was a way of seeing with a sense beyond sight; a way that could be taken at will. Yet this was different. It could not be turned off. It was the only way, in the darkness of the hill, that her eyes would let her see. Blinking, shutting them: nothing helped. Something was there, ahead, for which the whole of the world might slide away—if she let it slip. Or time might open out like a flower and be still.

At this point, when the children finally behold Arthur and his men asleep among their treasures, Miss Curry gives us two illuminations about the material of the story, one concerning the real Arthur and the real men who loved him and fought at his side—fleshly, suffering human beings—and the other about the confrontation of twentieth-century children with what is outside of time as we know it. The Arthur, the Cai, Peredur, Geraint, Gwalchmai, Bedwyr of Rosemary Sutcliff's Sword at Sunset, even, are men such as the men of our day, of our own height, and Arthur himself is a giant, as legend tells. In Mayne's Earthfasts . . . they are removed, formalized, felt rather than clearly discerned, not human beings so much as forces, brief impingements on a time not yet ready for them. For Miss Curry they are anything but this: the children can scarcely believe what they see after all they have read, for these are little men hardly taller than themselves, dirty and worn and shabby, wearing chain mail that might have been picked up at a rummage counter. They are infinitely vulnerable, therefore poignant somehow in the defenselessness of their ancient sleep. Jennifer's reaction to this incredible meeting (and we desire always that the author shall sense to the full, and be capable of making us sense, precisely what is felt by some one protagonist in any extraordinary situation) is that

> she had become aware of a horror mingled with the beauty of the world they had stumbled into. The sad men; time's standing still; existence reft

Curry (center) at age eleven, with her mother, father, sister Mary An, and brother Billy.

from action; being held apart from doing. It was neither wrong nor evil, exactly, but alien. Somehow there was in it a deeper horror than H. P. 's practical fears of theft and embarrassment. She stared at the treasures, saw and listened to them. Did they glow and pulse with some power of their own?

In the wake of Jennifer, the other children see as she sees, though they do not "feel" the Thirteen Treasures of Prydain as she feels them, nor the pull of Time as she feels it. But what of the adults? In such fantasies as this, what children are experiencing in their freshness of vision, their uninhibited state of awareness, adults, enmeshed in their own facts and preoccupations, their vision dimmed, are usually shut away from. But one of them, Mrs. Lewis, is not, and sees and talks to Merlin when he emerges into our time, possibly because she so firmly believes that "naught's impossible that is imaginable." Finally, however, she cannot go into the hill and behold Arthur and the Treasures. "In the end I felt too old to see and touch the hereness of things I've imagined or believed in—without being . . . lost. The children still have the resilience to come and go between then and now and the time that waits below now. . . . I thought that if I saw the whole of it, I could never again prune a rosebush or make a pot of coffee with the same contentment." But the elderly Scottish duke in whose land the cavern lies, does behold the King and talks to him—to Artair—and here we touch upon that which is central about Time and the British Isles: "But then . . . our families have been here in the north for perhaps two thousand years. The idea of all this

is not so strange for us." Nor strange for Jennifer, who understands now how "Time inside [the cavern] must have stood almost still until the Sleepers were stirred by the bell's ringing. Even now it moved only slowly, like molasses, while the hours ran like water down the hillside out under the stars." Released at last, the weary men on their little horses, the fell ponies, ride through the mist with Merlin (Myrddin) walking at Arthur's side, and the children, standing on a gray-green riverbank somewhere outside the walls of Londinium, watch the wide low boat unfurl a blue sail and move soundlessly away with the Treasures and Arthur and his men aboard. Both reader and children are left with the paradox that "time past has become now, and today has restored tomorrow," a paradox explainable only in an awareness of Time as a Globe. (pp. 100-03)

The best English fantasists seem to be masters of a subtlety of effect and of conviction which the Americans have not yet discovered or are perhaps incapable of. . . . [As] a matter of fact none of the time tales written by Americans, except for *The Sleepers,* can compare with the English when it comes to memorable characterization, to the creation of place, wider implications and vibrancy of tone. If Jane Louise Curry's book is not on the same level as Boston's, Pearce's, or Mayne's, it is still far ahead of the American time fantasies when it comes to communication of feeling for the past and for Time as a globe. (pp. 132-33)

Eleanor Cameron, "Fantasy," in her The Green and Burning Tree: On the Writing Enjoyment of Children's Books, *Atlantic-Little, Brown,* 1969, pp. 3-136.

The Change-Child   (1969)

More rumbles in Middle Earth but they come late, and Eilian puzzles long about why she is "lame and . . . different" in a Welsh limbo undated (Elizabeth's reign) until halfway through and undefined (as to its connection with the Fairy Folk) until almost the end. The reader is adrift altogether, more even than Eilian whose only clue is a false one, her resemblance to Mamga, her grandmother, the reputed Queen of the Red Fairies. But the Red Fairies, as Eilian discovers during her stay on the rim of the Great Dark Wood, are common thieves cloaked in illusion and Eilian's disenchantment turns to dismay when Mamga treacherously promises her to the (ig)noble Rastells in hopes of protecting her own people. (Simon Rastell seeks to marry Eilian to regain Plaseirian, a rich property newly claimed by Eilian's father—but that is almost literally another story.) Always hovering on the edges is young Goronwy, vaguely different also, and eventually the portal to the Fairy Folk: he is a change-child, being part human, and so-less so—is Eilian, for she is of the blood of the ancient Singer who wed Ywen of the Fairy Folk. Her difference and her gift for singing understood, Eilian can return in inner peace to Plaseirian. And in outer peace the Rastells, in fury at the death of Simon, have set fire to the Great Wood and departed. Driven out, the Fairy Folk depart too, for Tir 'na 'nOg, but Goronwy remains with Eilian and her song, "Yesterday, today, tomorrow—Joy is bloom to time and sorrow." What is well-ended . . . is raggedly begun, and altogether this not inconsiderable book fails to take hold like some of its fellows in Welsh fantasy. (pp. 439-40)

> *A review of "The Change-Child," in* Kirkus Reviews, *Vol. XXXVII, No. 8, April 15, 1969, p. 439.*

This poetically-written fantasy set in Wales during the reign of Elizabeth I concerns a young girl, Eilian, whom people call a changeling. Eilian yearns to be a poetess and to live with the Fair Folk, to whom she feels she probably belongs. Interwoven is an intrigue to force her into marriage with the son of the local squire who wants to gain possession of a farm she's likely to inherit; to escape this fate Eilian flees with her grandmother to the wood, where she encounters a band of vagabonds whom she initially believes are magical Fair Folk. Later, she meets some of the genuine Folk, one of whom, loving her, chooses humanity and thus mortality for her sake. The plot is occasionally rambling, and the widespread use of unexplained Welsh words is frustrating. Still, this is acceptable romantic reading, though not in the Garner/Mayne class.

> *Frances Green, in a review "The Change-Child," in* School Library Journal, *Vol. 15, No. 9, May, 1969, p. 84.*

The grace and the imaginative niceties of the surface [of **The Change Child**] cover a basic narrative uncertainty as to what the book is really about. . . .

We are back in Celtic myth here, but myth romantic, elegiac, somewhat in the Victorian tradition if less verbose. Miss Curry catches some of the melancholy, but misses the underlying power of the originals. And if her Eilian is a not uninteresting, even subtle creation, by blurring the divisions between the two worlds she explores, the real and the fairy, she effectively de-fuses them, makes both less credible.

> *"Mythical Countries," in* The Times Literary Supplement, *No. 3589, December 11, 1970, p. 1449.*

The Daybreakers   (1970)

Confoundment, confusion, explanation; confoundment, confusion, explanation: what would be a fantasy of past wrongs and present rightings shapes up primarily as The Mystery of the Indian Mound. Black Callie opens contact by impulsively(?) building seven snowmen, sniveling little "drippy" Tapp wantonly(?) sacrifices a rabbit, and his cousin Melissa, Callie's classmate, discovers with Callie the long snow-free hillock, the hole that becomes a "treasure" chamber, and the Edge as it once was, grassy and tree-ringed, before despoliation. Seized by brown strangers, the girls and Callie's twin Harry, who's followed them, become pawns in the struggle of Abalok against the powerful seven cities of Cibotlan; later they will return to Abalok with new knowledge and several classmates to intervene actively. But most of the action occurs in *now*-troubled Apple Lock, West Virginia—strip-mined, polluted, on half sessions because the school budget's been defeated; and among the polyglot youngsters in Class 206 who build the findings into a joint project, a historical museum of the area. Their delving and decoding is intriguing though the dialogue is strained—a stab at the casual slang of kids that doesn't come off. Meanwhile their discoveries make archaeological history (not that they get much credit), help shore up the school system and maybe "stop all the uglification." An echo of **Beneath the Hill** but a far cry from it.

> *A review of "The Daybreakers," in* Kirkus Reviews, *Vol. XXXVIII, No. 8, April 15, 1970, p. 452.*

The gift for fantasy and the superb craftsmanship that marked Jane Louise Curry's earlier books are richly manifest in this engrossing, intricately wrought story. Harry and Callie are black twins living in the ugly and backward West Virginia mill town of Apple Lock. An odd compulsion to explore the deserted wood on a high ridge above town leads Callie, her white friend Liss, and Harry one snowy day into an underground cave. From there they emerge into an ancient, beautiful world and are caught up in the life-and-death struggle between the gentle people of Abáloc and their powerful enemies of Cibotlán. In a moment of crisis a small blue stone provides the magic that restores the children to their own time and later, as they are needed, returns them to the past.

The children's efforts to understand and to help their friends of Abáloc by deciphering their alphabet and their discovery that the perilous past and the problem-filled present are indissolubly linked, for both good and evil, are superbly handled. The writing is vivid, the ideas challenging, the children fresh and alive. Their adventures make rewarding reading.

> *Polly Goodwin, in a review of "The Day-breakers," in* Children's Book World, *May 17, 1970, p. 5.*

In *The Daybreakers* Callie and her friends—black and white—break through the thin crust dividing modern Pennsylvania from pre-Columbian America, to tilt the balance of history in favour of justice and enlightenment. They also, to the distress of the adults in the story and that of some readers too, rob an ancient burial mound of its treasure for their own "museum". Miss Curry is at her considerable best in the scenes of the past, in which she captures both the pageantry and the brutality.

> *"Modern Magic and Ancient Sorcery," in* The Times Literary Supplement, *No. 3583, October 30, 1970, p. 1251.*

Mindy's Mysterious Miniature   (1970; British edition as The Housenapper)

Mindy bought a dollhouse at an auction for sixty-eight cents and twelve lemon soda bottles, and underneath layers of grime discovered exquisite furnishings in perfect scale. It was almost as if a real house had been shrunk. In fact, that had happened fifty-five years before. A mad inventor with a machine called the Reducer reduced the town of Dopple to Lilliputian-size and turned it into a museum exhibit operated now by the inventor's nephew Willie Kurtz. Mindy's house was somehow separated from the exhibit and lost; but Willie Kurtz wanted it back. He managed to expand the house to normal size and reshrink it with Mindy and a neighbor, Mrs. Bright, inside. The house was transported to the museum where Mindy and Mrs. Bright met eight miniature inhabitants of Dopple who had guarded the secret of their existence for more than half a century. Mrs. Bright and Mindy devised a scheme to escape unshrunk, a scheme which ensured the happiest of endings. Stories of "little people" have an indigenous charm, but it is difficult to feel much sympathy for the cowering citizens of Dopple who have given up all thought of escape. The most engaging character in the book is Mrs. Bright, a cheerful grandmotherly sort who makes the best of every situation. There is enough suspense to warrant calling the book a mystery; actually, it is entertaining farce. However, readers who expect the complexity and substance of *The Sleepers* and *The Daybreakers* will be disappointed.

> *Diane Farrell, in a review of "Mindy's Mysterious Miniature," in* The Horn Book Magazine, *Vol. XLVI, No. 6, December, 1970, p. 616.*

[*The Housenapper*] is a wonderful story, filled with all the right ingredients. The excitement mounts from the beginning when Mindy first finds the marvellous doll's house, so perfectly filled with everything to fit. It is no surprise to find that this is not in fact a doll's house, but a real house considerably reduced in size by the wicked and vin-

dictive Willie Kurtz. The best thing about the story is the way in which the author has visualised how it would be if one were only five inches high: the way voices would sound, the great obstacles to be overcome when descending from a table, the terrifying gust of wind caused by a passing car; all are well-imagined and used to give a true sense of a small world among the monsters we know.

Jane Curry's portrayal is fascinating and, as the story progresses, deeper and more subtle relationships appear. The way in which Mindy and the old lady, her friend, react to the other old people they find, who have been hidden in their shrunken homes for nearly fifty years, and fire them with a desire to escape and live in the world again, has a nice logic.

The illustrations, diagrams and maps fit and it is altogether an admirable book to read aloud to seven or eight-year-olds. Nine to twelve-year-olds will enjoy reading it themselves.

> *Sylvia Mogg, in a review of "The Housenapper," in* Children's Book Review, *Vol. I, No. 3, June, 1971, p. 86.*

[*Mindy's Mysterious Miniature*] begins with a realistic and sustained scene at a farm auction, the discovery of a strange dollhouse, a visit from a mysterious man who seems to want the dollhouse, and a collection of family incidents. We are nearly a third of the way through the book before it springs into fantasy: Mindy and her companion become miniature occupants of the dollhouse. The fantastic idea is appealing, but pace has by this time dampened our enthusiasm.

> *Sam Leaton Sebesta and William J. Iverson, "Literary Elements," in their* Literature for Thursday's Child, *Science Research Associates, Inc., 1975, p. 81.*

Over the Sea's Edge   (1971)

Based on the mythical westward voyage that the Welsh Prince Madoc was supposed to have made in the 12th Century, this fantasy provides a fascinating, though unsubstantiated, theory of what might have been 300 years before Columbus. Davy Reese finds an ancient medallion in an Ohio river cave, and finds himself transported from the 20th Century back through time to change places with Dewi ap Ithil, a 12th-Century Welsh boy with visions of the future and a thirst for education. Davy (now Dewi) is instrumental in helping to rescue the famous Prince Maduac from maiming and death, and in 1170 he sails with him to find the legendary seven cities of Antillia. Landing in what is now Alabama or Mississippi, the small band of Welshmen travel north in hopes of finding great wealth. During their journey, they meet Coala, the priestess of the Serpent oracle, who believes Maduac to be a god, and promises, for her own reasons, to lead them to Abáloc (or Avalon) where they will find gold. On the way, they confront and skirmish with soldiers of Cibotlán. The Seven Kings of Cibotlán wish to conquer Abáloc and Dewi is captured by Prince Lincoas of Abáloc and his followers. Because of a prophecy he had heard in Wales (which is also known to Lincoas), Dewi comes to feel that there is a common bond between Wales and Abáloc. Lincoas, with the help of Maduac, Coala and Dewi, is able to save his people, defeat the evil wise man, Neolin, and unravel the prophecy. Davy and Dewi remain where time has transferred them and each finds fulfillment in his new life. The fast-paced story is supported with excellent characterizations; philosophical ideas are present but not imposed on those readers who want to enjoy action alone. Though a guide to Welsh pronunciation is an unfortunate omission, the rhythmic prose is splendid.

> *Nancy Berkowitz, in a review of "Over the Seas's Edge," in* School Library Journal, *Vol. 18, No. 2, October, 1971, p. 118.*

Although she begins with the familiar time-shift, Jane Curry has developed her book in an individual way. It will not please every English reader that an American boy of today changes places unwillingly (and permanently) with a Welsh boy of 800 years ago. Nor will all be pleased to see Avalon turning up so far across the Atlantic; in this the author is drawing upon two main traditions: that the Isles of the Blest lie in the western seas and that there was a tribe of American Indians who spoke Welsh.

In this sort of time switch, the author's difficulty is to make the reader aware of what it feels like suddenly to wake up as another person in another age. Here a short-sighted boy in his new identity has good vision, and thereby the differences between the old life and the new are heightened. Generally speaking Jane Curry takes trouble to get her details right, though Coala learns Welsh as rapidly as any hero in Edgar Rice Burroughs beats the language barrier. The pace of the story slows in the central section, but increases again at the end.

The blurb reminds us that this is, like *The Daybreakers,* an exploration of pre-Columbian America. While both books are complete in themselves, those who read both of them and the earlier *Beneath the Hill* will find that they all throw light on each other. The reader who likes to watch problems being unravelled will find *The Daybreakers* most to his taste. *Over the Sea's Edge* offers less complexity in the telling.

> *Maureen F. Crago, in a review of "Over the Sea's Edge," in* Children's Book Review, *Vol. I, No. 6, December, 1971, p. 193.*

A complementary narrative rather than a sequel to *The Daybreakers,* . . . [*Over the Sea's Edge*] explores the idea of time as circular rather than as linear so that movement in and out of centuries is less a journey than a merging of past and future. . . . The introduction of characters from the earlier book—Prince Lincoas, Queen Erilla, the wise Ayacas—as well as references to previous events not fully explained within the context of the story, suggest that the two books should be read sequentially. More complex than *The Daybreakers,* possibly because the theme is more convoluted and the action more past than present, the narrative at times seems amorphous. The style, lacking the practical observations of the very contemporary children in the earlier book, is more philosophical in tone. Yet, the whole is a fascinating and daring exploration of the meaning of identity and the quest for personal realization within the limiting circle of time.

> *Mary M. Burns, in a review of "Over the Sea's Edge," in* The Horn Book Magazine, *Vol. XLVII, No. 6, December, 1971, p. 610.*

In the twelfth century a Welsh Prince Madoc, escaping from the treachery and internecine warfare of the royal houses, sailed west over the sea's edge with a party of companions in search of a land of gold and silver and rivers of pearls. Saint Brendan had gone that way before, and there might be Welsh-speaking brethren to greet them.

Jane Louise Curry makes this familiar legend the starting point of her remarkable novel, linking it with the results of pre-Columbian archaeology in America. Her story starts today in Ohio, where David Reece—his name suggests a Celtic origin—has been dreaming. But the boy who haunts his dream world begins to appear in daytime and to dog him like a doppelgänger. The word is his father's and it is more apt than he knew, because Dave confronts the boy at last and faces himself. The other self has come out of the past and Dave takes his place, becoming Dewi, the dogsbody of Dolwydlan Castle.

A problem of these time-switch stories is how to deal with transferred knowledge. Does the twentieth-century boy retain his memory of his own time and its technology, and does he know what his alter ego did about the environment he has unwillingly acquired? Miss Curry manages a most acceptable compromise. Dewi half remembers his past, but the memory gets fainter as his involvement in the twelfth-century present grows; similarly, at first he is confused over the complexities of Welsh castle domestic economy, but he learns quickly.

Chance, or an esoteric design, makes Dewi one of Madauc's companions and so a member of the crew of Gwennan Gorn, the fifty-foot ship in which they sail beyond the Isles of the Moon to the Fortunate Isles. Here, briefly, Dewi finds his doppelgänger again, sleep-walking in his pyjamas beside the great river. But the other David escapes and Dewi goes on to the Island of the Apple Trees to play his part in the conquest of the seven kingdoms.

It is a strange story, bitter rather than heroic. There is much interest in the portrait of Madauc who comes near to being corrupted by responsibility and ambition. Madauc is a medieval adventurer, greedy for gold more than power or fame, but he is also a Celt, a visionary and at times a poet.

The story ends, as it began, with Dave Reece in twentieth-century America. Packed off for a holiday with Aunt Milly, he potters about by the river, discovering a cave and in it a manuscript account of the voyage of Madauc, written in the twelfth-century by Dewi ab Ithil. The river may be "murky with swirls of detergent suds . . . and a faint, unpleasant smell of sewage", but the Island of the Apple Trees is still there and the river still flows down to the ocean where Madoc sailed.

For all the violence of the story one's final impression is of reflection rather than action, and the conclusion is that

Curry, third from left, onstage at the Mountain Playhouse in Jennerstown, Pennsylvania, c. 1951. She writes, "I am the ingenue in (to the best of my recollection) George Washington Slept Here . . . (and then again, it may have been Wallflower) . . ."

"dreams hold their share of truth. And that the deepest wisdom of dreams is that waking joys are deeper yet."

> *"Voyage to the Sunset," in* The Times Literary Supplement, *No. 3640, December 3, 1971, p. 1510.*

The Ice Ghosts Mystery (1972)

The mystery is threefold. First, Mrs. Bird and her three children attempt to learn whether Professor Bird, a California seismologist, is missing or dead after his disappearance during a ski trip in Austria. Secondly, they try to find an explanation for the ghosts who keep superstitious people away from a vast mountain cave. Finally, they ferret out the origin of elusive, illegal underground detonations that cause earthquakes and avalanches. The complex plot is ingeniously woven and sustained in a beautifully vivid setting. The characterization, however, is less strong, for as in many tales of adventure and mystery, the individuals are superficially treated. The children behave believably, but the reader is not drawn impellingly to any one of them.

> *Virginia Haviland, in a review of "The Ice*

Ghosts Mystery," *in* The Horn Book Magazine, *Vol. XLVIII, No. 5, October, 1972, p. 467.*

The Ice Ghosts Mystery is for older, more sophisticated readers [than Wendy Robertson's *Theft*]. It is a complex adventure, preposterous but entertaining. The American author, Jane Curry, has a no-holds-barred attitude to writing for children. At times her book is reminiscent of Peter Dickinson's *Emma Tupper's Diary*, an equally unconventional mystery. The seismologist Professor Bird has disappeared while skiing in the Austrian mountains. It hardly seems fair to reveal just why or what the unpleasant Pfnürs have to do with the curious series of earthquakes, avalanches and floods which are bringing welcome business to the Fairweather Insurance Group. Is there really a scientific explanation for both Perry Bird's toothache and the unsatisfactory milk yield in Riesenmoos? One does not have to understand transistor micro-circuits or be interested in pagan spring rituals to enjoy this book—but it would help.

> *"Returning to the Scene," in* The Times Literary Supplement, *No. 3709, April 6, 1973, p. 383.*

Jane Curry has left the realms of pure fantasy to produce a straightforward, but well done, mystery of the James Bond 'Scientist disappears while skiing in Switzerland' variety. . . .

This yarn is a cut above the usual mystery story. Told with humour, even the broken German of the villain with his fiendish master plan has a touch of class. A creditable piece of work for teenagers to enjoy.

> *Jessica Kemball-Cook, in a review of "The Ice-Ghosts Mystery," in* Children's Book Review, *Vol. III, No. 4, September, 1973, p. 112.*

The Lost Farm (1974)

"Imagine you were only five inches high. What would the world seem like to you? What dangers would you encounter?" A favourite topic for school essays since the publication of *Gulliver's Travels.* It's a good exercise in imaginative thinking and a popular subject for children's stories: Jane Curry's **The Lost Farm** tackles the problems convincingly.

Petey, his useless drunken father and tough grandmother are "reduced", and find themselves and their farm left as miniatures in a full-scale 1922 American world. Attempts to seek help fail, and the difficulties of survival are both fearful and funny: sheep are killed by bees, starlings gobble up the apples and rain threatens to wash the entire farm away. As the years slip by, Petey learns the art of survival, using acorns for flour and manure for heat. . . . Totally unsentimental about her little people, Jane Curry writes with a refreshingly dry wit. Mentioning, for example, the terrible life Petey's mother had had with his father, she comments: "When Maybelle saw how sick she was, she took her chance and died on it." Petey, however, takes his chance and lives. At the end of the story, a lonely old man, he is finally magnified again. But the reader leaves that strange little farm with regret.

> *"Fearful and Funny," in* The Times Literary Supplement, *No. 3760, March 29, 1974, p. 332.*

Jane Louise Curry is a highly professional weaver with a scholarly knack for varying her background colors from Celtic to Elizabethan to California Indian. In **The Lost Farm** she adapts herself easily to a down-home style: "Shrunk? The whole dad-burned farm?" Her Petey and Granny are plucky and likable, and the problems they face in the new wilderness around their miniaturized farm are fascinating. But as a handmade design this book seems patched together with yarn left over from the author's earlier **Mindy's Mysterious Miniature,** a charming tale in which an entire town was reduced to dollhouse size by a mean man with a magical reducing machine. here the machine never really ticks and shakes, and, crammed in at the end of the rug, it makes a knobby lump.

And there is another flaw. The whole point of a fantasy is the total and giddy control of the artificer over the canceled laws of nature. The author has only to say masterfully, *This* is the new logic, *I declare* this to be the pattern for this carpet, up, up and away! Roll, pitch, yaw!" But

this nice rug of Jane Curry's keeps wobbling and grazing the floor because the wincing reader can't help wondering (*kabump!*) why the shrunken people don't just go out to the road and flag down a passing neighbor, instead of trying and failing for 50 years to get to town.

> *Jane Langton, "Carpets and Doormats," in* The New York Times Book Review, *March 31, 1974, p. 8.*

Those who remember **The Housenapper** with pleasure will be delighted at the prospect of a sequel. **The Housenapper** features Willie Kurtz, a paranoiac inventor who, in a fit of pique, reduced the town of Dopple and eight of its inhabitants to Toytown dimensions. **The Lost Farm** also employs Kurtz, now under the alias 'Professor Lilliput', as its *deus ex machina*. Pete MacCubbins's father 'Dustbin' (nicknamed after his business in old magazines and bottles) gets on the wrong side of the Professor by 'collecting' a birthday present for his son from Lilliput's travelling exhibition. True to form, the Professor points his Reducer at Dustbin and he, Granny, Pete, the animals and the farm and outbuildings are immediately miniaturised.

The author proves, once again, her ability to rationalise the fantasy element in a workaday world, but it is difficult to believe that the local people thought that the McCubbins family had left the neighbourhood—with a farm and outbuildings? This is carping, perhaps, in view of the enjoyment I got from the story itself and the detailed accounts of farming problems when one is in 'reduced' circumstances.

> *Margot Petts, in a review of "The Lost Farm," in* Children's Book Review, *Vol. IV, No. 2, Summer, 1974, p. 64.*

Parsley Sage, Rosemary and Time (1975)

Young Rosemary finds that the word "Time" engraved on a stone in an old herb garden is not misspelled. She picks a sprig of "thyme" and is instantly transported back to 18th century New England. With another time traveler, a girl named Baba, Rosemary is found in the company of old Goody Cakebread. The dear old lady has recourse to a magic cupboard when she learns she is about to be accused of witchcraft. She tries to join her friends, the Indians, but is caught by officials and jailed, along with the two girls. Magic is called for again to save all concerned and to get the two girls back into the 20th century. Ms. Curry has woven a most entertaining fantasy and [illustrator] Charles Robinson's pictures add to the charm of a special book.

> *A review of "Parsley Sage, Rosemary and Time," in* Publishers Weekly, *Vol. 207, No. 6, February 10, 1975, p. 57.*

While visiting her freewheeling Aunt Sibby in Maine, Rosemary follows Sibby's cat Parsley Sage into a walled garden where mossy letters spell out on stones the four words of the title, and all living things except herself are suspended in mid-gesture when she touches the leaves of the thyme/time plant. But the implications of this marvelous opportunity are never pursued; instead Rosemary swallows a pinch of the herb and steps into colonial times, finding herself and another younger, modern day girl jailed as imps of the devil with sympathetic Goody Cakebread who is "accused for a witch." Rosemary returns (with the aid of Goody Cakebread's magic cupboard) to discover not only that a younger Aunt Sibby was her small companion on the journey but also that the diapered baby who was also along is now the handsome young man who arrives to buy back his ancestral home from Aunt Sibby and will no doubt stay on to share it. All of which is milder and less exotic than we might have expected even considering the poor pun it is based on—but Rosemary's garden shimmers invitingly and the friends she makes from Parsley Sage on are uniformly welcoming.

A review of "Parsley Sage, Rosemary and Time," in Kirkus Reviews, *Vol. XLIII, No. 6, March 15, 1975, p. 306.*

Parsley Sage, Rosemary & Time . . . is about a girl who discovers, in a secret, overgrown herb garden (the power of the weed . . . ?), the "center of time," and is forthwith plunged into early 18th-century New England—preachers, Indians, slaves, witches, the lot. The idea may be fertile, but the plot is so densely tangled with implausible incidents and coincidence that no amount of raking and hoeing can make it intelligible (too much Looking Glass and not enough Alice).

Alix Nelson, "Gather, Ye Witches and Warlocks," in The New York Times Book Review, *May 4, 1975, p. 26.*

The Watchers (1975)

His reputation as a troublemaker and his father's remarriage result in 13-year-old Ray Siler's being sent to Twillys' Green, West Virginia to live with his dead mother's mountain kin. Entering the mountain culture is, in itself, a great shock, but, in addition, the young boy finds himself dealing not only with his present problems but also with the past and future. The traditions of the ancient folk from "Up Top" of the hollow intrude first into his dreams, and then into his life, while an impending scheme to mine coal from the Clewarks' land threatens to destroy the future. As in Curry's **The Ice Ghosts Mystery** an intense feeling of the culture and the people pervades, and atmosphere and plot dominate at the expense of characterization. However, Ray does emerge as a full character, and the plot moves quickly although the many details and intricate turns may create some fuzziness.

Carolyn Johnson, in a review of "The Watchers," in School Library Journal, *Vol. 22, No. 3, November, 1975, p. 73.*

This is the old Pendragon legend deftly transported to the West Virginia hills and interpreted as a struggle against an evil, insatiable hunger. Ms. Curry relates this hunger to the destruction of the land. She leisurely sets the mood in the first two chapters, and some readers may find this pace too slow. However, fantasy readers will find this very satisfying indeed.

Nelda Mohr, in a review of "The Watchers,"

in Children's Book Review Service, *Vol. 4, No. 5, January, 1976, p. 44.*

Before I had even finished reading **The Watchers** I had rushed off to the library and ordered the author's other books, so constrained was I at having missed so outstanding a writer before. Although Jane Curry is now living in England this book is essentially about her American homeland. It tells of the strange people living at Twilly's Green, a hollow in the Virginian mountains. To this strange settlement comes Ray, a distant nephew sent back to his dead mother's people when his father remarries. The past is very near to the surface in the Hollow, and the twentieth century American way of life seems hardly to have touched the Clewarek family. One is having to remind oneself constantly that this is not a time fantasy book but about today—or is it, are The Watchers still there, what is the meaning of the strange runic letters and has the Gare always stood 'Up Top' as it does today. It is impossible to do justice to the book in a brief review, it is one which should be read and enjoyed by children of 10 up, especially those whose impression of America is gleaned from watching too much television. (pp. 223-24)

J. Russell, in a review of "The Watchers," in The Junior Bookshelf, *Vol. 40, No. 4, August, 1976, pp. 223-24.*

If you liked *Elidor, The Owl Service* and *Red Shift,* you'll probably like this book as it falls into the same genre of history-mystery-fantasy, but Jane Curry's scene is West Virginia and its hills and hollows. Ray Siler, a thirteen-year-old motherless boy, is sent to Twilly's Green by his father to live with his mother's kin, the Clewareks. The village, which is more an extended family, everyone intermarried until they all look alike, keep themselves to themselves and have managed to keep the coal under their hill intact. They have also vaguely maintained the tradition of 'the watcher' who must guard against some kind of evil threat. Ray soon finds himself inside the skin of Ruan, a slaveboy in an undetermined pre-Columbian kingdom who, betraying his master, has helped to open the powerful Shrine of Darkness symbolised by a hooped snake. The theme of the story, to put it seriously, is temporal and spiritual power; Arbie Moar, the local bigwig, is fascinated by irrational sources of power and tries to get the image of the snake for his own by swindling Twilly's Green out of its coal rights. Tül Isgrun, the original name of the place, is characterised as this bottomless hunger of greed which involves manipulation and waste. Ray comes to Twilly's Green greedy and resentful, but as his bitterness is overcome with the love his relatives have for each other and him, he comes out of the dark to protect Twilly's Green from destruction. A serious book, the delight being in the names and speech and down-homisms of a traditional community. A book which finds something to say about good and evil without further bankrupting of the concepts. Worth every penny.

Nancy Telford, in a review of "The Watchers," in Children's Book Review, *Vol. VI, October, 1976, p. 15.*

The Birdstones (1977)

What starts out as a prank, when six sixth-grade girls register an imaginary classmate in their overcrowded school, becomes a mystery to them when a real Dayla Jones starts showing up at school. It turns out that the newcomer is a visitor from the pre-Columbian past the same children brushed with in *The Daybreakers;* she's disguised as a contemporary to mislead a strange, sinister group of loiterers who, in turn, are really enemies of Dayla's people and have followed her through the same chink in time. Exactly what they are up to isn't clear—and Curry's seeming lack of interest in their story considerably undercuts the urgency attached to a climactic, stagey Halloween party that the children plan as a cover for Dayla's safe return to her proper period. In truth, the sober, italicized hints of ancient mystery read almost like a parody of such fantasy, and don't mix with the old-fashioned "six chums at school" narration or the self-consciously contemporary slang and multi-ethnic casting. Like *The Daybreakers,* it rings false.

A review of "The Birdstones," in Kirkus Reviews, *Vol. XLV, No. 14, July 15, 1977, p. 728.*

The Birdstones continues Jane Curry's attempt to evoke an ancient American past, transporting pre-Columbian

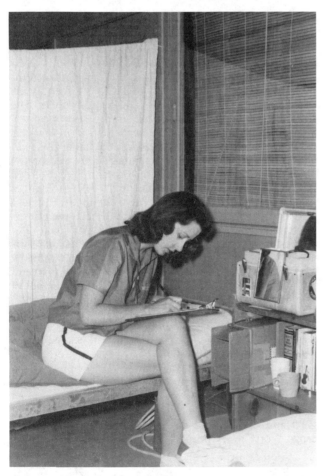

Curry as a counselor at Girl Scout Camp Osito, Big Bear, California, c. 1959.

pursuers and pursued into the modern West Virginian town of Apple Lock. To anyone who has not read **The Daybreakers** the large—and cursorily introduced—cast may bewilder. But just as the book is about to disappear completely behind an unusually impenetrable hedge of American slang and school jargon, twin plots emerge—and when we are not watching Ms Curry work them out, good plots they are. How to return Dalea and the others to the sub-Tolkien-speaking past civilization of Abáloc is a problem which becomes mixed up with the schoolgirls' creation of a fictitious classmate, and in the background, casual details bring the town and the school to life. Yet we have chapter headings like "The Plot Thickens", an abundance of "he froze in his tracks", unoriginality, and, worse, a somewhat disingenuous fumbling at key points in the plot.

Peter Hunt, "Designs from the Past," in The Times Literary Supplement, *December 1, 1978, p. 1396.*

Jane Curry's latest book confirms the impression that here is one of the most promising new voices from America. She blends the most convincing naturalistic presentation of modern society with the supernatural in masterly fashion.

As in **The Daybreakers,** we are in the small community of Apple Lock. The boys and girls, and their elders, go about their daily business, working, quarrelling, having fun. After their success in the water parade—they played the young ladies of Miss Pinckney's Academy swept away by the floods of 1878, with Teeny starring as a great blue heron pathetically calling "Frahnk, Frawnk!"—the girls have to think up something new to make the daily round of school amusing. They come up with Dayla Jones, an imaginary new girl who has a desk, a locker, books and homework but no physical existence. It becomes rather a chore to keep up with her essays and arithmetic, but the girls get away with it for a long time. Then things go wrong; Dayla Jones materialises. Inconspicuous, elusive, Dayla is unquestionably real, poor on spelling but imaginative. Where has she come from? The answer, convincing enough for those who have read Miss Curry's earlier book, is the past.

Co-existent with modern Apple Lock is Abaloc, the pre-Columbian Indian village. Dalea and her grandfather are the guardians of the old traditions in the face of invasion, and the crisis sends Dalea, and her enemies, right into the twentieth century. The sinister queen possesses the somewhat improbable body of Mrs. Buttery, deputy librarian and bore. There is a splendid climax complete with fireworks, and the story retains one final kick for the very last words.

Abaloc and the magic from the past would be quite unacceptable, however well presented, if it were not for the sparkling reality of Apple Lock and its community. Miss Curry is most successful in showing a happily integrated school and town with sharply individualised personalities, black, white and all shades between. Pooch, Teeny, Callie, even bossy Angela, all come right out of the page and live their own independent lives. It is all beautifully done.

M. Crouch, in a review of "The Birdstones," in The Junior Bookshelf, *Vol. 43, No. 1, February, 1979, p. 48.*

Poor Tom's Ghost (1977)

The haunted house in **Poor Tom's Ghost** is a monstrous Victorian folly, complete with crumbling crenellated parapet, which a newly formed, footloose theatrical family, the Nicholases, hope to make their first permanent home. The ugly hulk conceals a second, more gracious mansion from Elizabethan times, as the Nicholases are delighted to discover, but their intrusion revives an ancient tragedy.

Eerie sobbing in an empty, moonlit room and illusions which flicker darkly even in the daylight hours lead inexorably to the possession of Tony Nicholas by the ghost of a fellow actor, from Shakespeare's stage. His thirteen-year-old son Roger steps back into the past to free him, and is almost marooned in plague-ridden London.

This is a superbly atmospheric story, full of suspense and chilling moments. If anything, the past is even more believable than the present, the Elizabethan dialogue being a good deal more convincing than the forced theatrical banter of Nicholas and his wife. At least Roger, with his chronic anxiety and camouflage charm, is genuine and moving, a sensitively observed child of our times. The break-up of his newly acquired family and banishment to boarding-school are to be dreaded more than spectres, and any home, however haunted, is better than no home at all. . . .

[**Poor Tom's ghost**] leaves its reader pleasantly haunted—and how else should a ghost story succeed?

Juliet Page, "Childhood Haunts," in The Times Literary Supplement, *No. 3931, July 15, 1977, p. 864.*

After a long succession of fantasies which have always revealed her varied writing talents but which have often fallen short of being wholly successful (always excepting her shorter novels for younger readers), Jane Louise Curry has created a *tour de force* in **Poor Tom's Ghost.** For those who recall Antonia Barber's *The Ghosts,* an immense favorite with children who discovered it, the plot of **Poor Tom's Ghost** is even more fascinating in its manipulation of "time-hops".

The story's setting is a pretentious, Victorian horror of a house which conceals some intriguing human and architectural secrets. The new owners of the house, the Nicholas family, have been leading the wandering life of a theatrical family. Tensions are already appearing in the mother-father relations and son Roger is delighted by the prospect of a permanent home but is not quite prepared for the delapidated monstrosity with which he is now confronted. However, in order to save the family, Roger is determined that they should remain there. Unknown to the Nicholases the house is really a solid, late Elizabethan manor with its curious story of love and tragedy involving the family of the first owner, the Elizabethan actor Tom Garland. As the twentieth century family uncovers the original house so Garland's spirit starts to merge with and con-

trol the personality of Roger's father, himself a Shakespearian actor.

It is therefore not without some surprize that a sophisticated contemporary London theatre audience is confronted with an early 1600's rendition of *Hamlet.* Eventually Roger is drawn into the original Elizabethan story as Tom's brother, Jack Garland. By sifting through some historical data about Tom's life and half-remembering Jack's thoughts, Roger is precipitated into early seventeenth century London as he attempts to lay poor Tom's ghost and free his father. The manner in which he accomplishes this is breath-taking and the final time-twist to the story, intriguing.

Each tiny piece of this complex mosaic is exactly right. The parents' dialogue of veiled, sarcastic *double-entendres* is as artificial as the pasteboard walls which surround them and the fragile family relationships are similar to those of the earlier family. Unlike the overwhelming majority of children's fantasies (including those by E. Nesbit), there are no awkward ploys to exclude the adults from the action. **Poor Tom's Ghost** is a triumph for Jane Louise Curry and a challenging read for the older child who has a taste for time-fantasy. (pp. 22-3)

Patrick Verriour, in a review of "Poor Tom's Ghost," in The World of Children's Books, *Vol. II, No. 2, 1977, pp. 22-3.*

In a time-shift story set in and near London, thirteen-year-old Roger Nicholas is enthralled when his father inherits an old, dilapidated house. His father, Tony, is an actor: his stepmother is an American actress. Tony is playing Hamlet at the time, and through the uncovering of evidence that the house is of Elizabethan vintage, father and son slip back to the seventeenth century, where Roger is Jack, the evil younger brother of Tom Garland (Tony), a Shakespearian actor. Roger knows he is both Roger and Jack, but Tony doesn't know all the adventures and difficulties experienced by Tom. All through a week of time-shift, two friends of the family are helping strip the house; one of them suspects that something supernatural is going on. Roger manages—as Jack—to help poor Tom out of the troubles he's in. At the end of the week, a real-life scene repeats itself and Roger realizes that the frenzied week never occurred at all. This last episode undermines the credibility of the fantasy, since there is an uneasy conflict between the time-shift participants and the realistic, practical involvement of the two friends. The story is further weakened by a rather self-conscious presentation of research, almost as though the sources for a dissertation had been used for the book. However, the writing style is nicely honed, the characters and dialogue convincing, and the relationships effective; it is pleasant, too, to encounter a second-marriage family with no adjustment problems.

Zena Sutherland, in a review of "Poor Tom's Ghost," in Bulletin of the Center for Children's Books, *Vol. 31, No. 1, September, 1977, p. 12.*

Jane Curry tells her sad story with tremendous power, compelling the reader to total surrender. Her rich imagination is supported by scholarship, and for her, as for the reader, the two Elizabethan ages are equally clear and real. Masterly as the ghost story is, the effect of the book is strengthened and deepened by its picture of human relationships. The Nicholas family, oddly assorted and confused by dedication to the stage, is shown in all its complexity. None of the cosy security of family life here, but the sparks struck by strong and abrasive personalities provide occasional brilliance of illumination.

This is not a book to be fitted neatly into a predetermined classification. It is difficult, deeply disturbing, calling for many re-readings and new assessments. The one conviction coming from a first reading is that here is a book which approaches greatness, one in which past and present, people and setting, are fused under enormous pressure.

> *M. Crouch, in a review of "Poor Tom's Ghost,"*
> *in* The Junior Bookshelf, *Vol. 41, No. 6, De-*
> *cember, 1977, p. 349.*

The Bassumtyte Treasure   (1978)

Back home in New Hampshire 10-year-old Tommy's grandfather had often entertained him with stories about their English ancestral home, Boxleton House, counseling him to remember a cryptic riddle that had been passed down through the family. When Tommy arrives and finds the 400-year-old manor house and garden in need of repair and his financially strapped guardian-cousin fearful of losing the estate, he determines to locate a legendary treasure. Clues slowly emerge through carvings found in a secret room, some long-forgotten tapestries, and the ghostly nudgings of Lady Margaret, a sixteenth-century mistress of Boxleton House; but the mystery seems inextricably linked to two old portraits and an ancient medallion passed down to Tommy by his grandfather. Only when the treasure is found does the true significance of the riddle come to light and the long-rumored connection to Mary, Queen of Scots, prove valid. In contrast to some of Curry's past books that have suffered from convoluted plots, this adroitly conceived mystery—with only a touch of (perhaps unnecessary) time fantasy—has a strong, readable line, with time for the characters and a clever integration of historical incident.

> *Barbara Elleman, in a review of "The Bassum-*
> *tyte Treasure," in* Booklist, *Vol. 74, No. 6,*
> *April 15, 1978, p. 1347.*

[*The Bassumtyte Treasure* is] a workmanlike book. . . . Boxleton House is threatened with sale (to an Arab millionaire, this being 1978) and Tommy, arrived from America bearing the family riddle, passed down from Mary Stuart's time, sets out to save the day. And so off through puns and mazes, secret rooms, windfalls, decent adults, whimsical vicars, and touches of *Tom's Midnight Garden.* Jane Curry just—but only just—avoids the touristy; it is almost as if she had found a charming Gloucestershire house, with charming people, and charming plot-ends lying around, and this is the result. If all this sounds condemnatory, let it not be thought that this book (and *The Birdstones*) is not energetic and interesting and, on occa-

Cold Springs Farm, near Johnstown, Pennsylvania, where Curry and her family moved when she was in junior high. Curry wrote Poor Tom's Ghost *here, and the farm appears in her books* Beneath the Hill, Mindy's Mysterious Miniature, *and* The Lost Farm.

sion, gripping. It is merely that well-meaning recycling of material cannot earn a whole-hearted recommendation.

> *Peter Hunt, "Designs from the Past," in* The
> Times Literary Supplement, *No. 4000, De-*
> *cember 1, 1978, p. 1396.*

When Tommy Bassumtyte reverses his great-grandparents' journey from Gloucestershire to New Hampshire he provides the key to a four-hundred-year-old riddle. Tommy quickly immerses himself in the Old World, epitomised in a gabled Elizabethan house with a secret. The traditional writer's props of hidden rooms, ghosts and a lost treasure are finely reworked and enlivened by a precise historical knowledge to make a tense and fast-moving story. The characterisation is careful and the language evocative. The maze is both an element in the story and an emblem of the way it unfolds. Those who appreciate puzzles and riddles will delight in this book.

> *Chas White, in a review of "The Bassumtyte*
> *Treasure," in* The School Librarian, *Vol. 27,*
> *No. 1, March, 1979, p. 53.*

The past evoked by Jane Curry is richly romantic and the elaborate decorative details and lush emotional tone which pervade **The Bassumtyte Treasure,** a tale of an old secret uncovered, demand a particular mood in the reader. A certain Thomas Bassumtyte of Tudor times, involved in an unexpected and intriguing way with Mary Queen of Scots, has passed on certain physical traits (and perhaps others as well) to a young descendant, another Thomas, who comes from America to live with his uncle, who is deeply concerned with his family's past and with the fate of the Cotswold manor which he can no longer afford to keep up. Predictably, the family treasure of priceless embroidery is discovered and the museum specialist who identified small Thomas's finds provides a pleasant touch of romance to round off the story. It is only too easy to sentimentalise over Cotswold Tudor and this book is so tightly crammed with knot gardens and mazes, tapestries and ciphers, that for all its ingenuity it provoked in me a reaction towards the more robust time-slip of Alison Uttley in *A Traveller in Time.*

> *Margery Fisher, in a review of "The Bassum-tyte Treasure," in* Growing Point, *Vol. 18, No. 1, May, 1979, p. 3516.*

Ghost Lane   (1979)

During a summer in a small English village, 11-year-old Richard Morgan becomes puzzled over some mysterious robberies in a nearby manor house. Accompanied by pert Francesca and her younger brother Nolly, who never talks, Richard makes friends with owner Mr. Drew and attempts to track down the thieves. Strange lights at midnight, the discovery of a secret passageway, and a kidnapped Nolly add to the intrigue. Each of the children plays a crucial role, but it is when Nolly's desire to communicate finally overpowers his locked-in fears that the mystery is solved. Curry expands her story, set against the background of the Glyndebourne Festival Opera, with sensitive interrelationships among characters. The climax lacks the fulfillment promised in the plot but is nevertheless better controlled than in some of her past books and moves along at a lively pace.

> *Barbara Elleman, in a review of "Ghost Lane," in* Booklist, *Vol. 75, No. 14, March 15, 1979, p. 1154.*

An excellent mystery-adventure story gives evidence of Curry's maturity as a writer, for here she combines strong characters, good dialogue, an intriguing setting, and a well-constructed story-line. . . . Everything works out logically in a solution that is not too pat, and the story moves at a brisk, but not relentless, pace.

> *Zena Sutherland, in a review of "Ghost Lane," in* Bulletin of the Center for Children's Books, *Vol. 33, No. 5, January, 1980, p. 91.*

Equally adept in both the fantasy and mystery forms, Jane Curry for her most recent novel has chosen the latter. Although not as weighty, demanding, and ambitious as her five-volume series about Abaloc and **The Sleepers, Ghost Lane** is a briskly moving, effortlessly told story of eleven-year-old Richard Morgan. His playing at detection turns serious when he finds himself enveloped in a real mystery involving possible appearances of ghosts and perplexing burglaries around Glyndebourne, scene of the popular opera festival. The story also features likeable characters, especially Nolly, the strange little boy who can't or won't talk, and engaging descriptions of some of the preparations for the opening performances at the Glyndebourne Festival. As a mystery, **Ghost Lane** is quite satisfying because clues are sufficient and helpfully placed. The atmosphere appropriate to an old, fine, and ghost-ridden house is convincingly built up. A final fillip is the occasional hint that ghosts have been sent by at least two of the characters. Thus, Curry has added to the mystery a touch of the ghost story; and all in all, she plays fair with the reader.

Young readers should find the story quick and diverting reading.

> *Francis J. Molson, in a review of "Ghost Lane," in* The World of Children's Books, *Vol. VI, 1981, p. 53.*

The Wolves of Aam   (1981)

There is a certain freshness about the heroic fantasy, the first of a projected pair about Astarlind—a land with a long and curious history built from legends of time long past. Various peoples have inhabited the land, among them the Silvrin, who are elves; the Tiddi, small, pointy-eared, long-toed hunters of horses; and the Men, neither reliable nor well-liked. The Tiddi have all but died out, and the story centers on Runner, a Tiddi who cannot remember his past, and his friends Cat and Fith. In the course of his adventures, Runner makes many friends: the conjuror Lek; the talking wolves of Aam—beautiful, loyal, and brave; and the large and shaggy Icelings, who are brusque but kind and live with their kin on the great Ice. In addition he meets assorted baleful beasts and maleficent men and giants. The complex tale concerns Runner's vaguely remembered past and his ownership of the Moonstone, one of twelve great stones. The convoluted twists and turns of the plot are brisk and riveting, the Tiddi are endearing and well characterized, and especially awe-inspiring are the great wolves of Aam. Although the similarities to Tolkien are glaringly obvious, there are, nonetheless, many original touches, and its comparatively short length makes the book more accessible to children. (pp. 196-97)

> *Ann A. Flowers, in a review of "The Wolves of Aam," in* The Horn Book Magazine, *Vol. LVII, No. 2, April, 1981, pp. 196-97.*

Set in the fictional land of Astarlind, this evocative tale spins out the story of the Tiddi—a small, shy group of people who are older than the race of man. One of their members, an orphan called Runner, loses his lucky dreamstone that the conjurer Lek declares is one of the ancient sky-stones of unknown powers. In this first of two tales about Tiddi, Runner, his friends Cat and Fith, the magical wolves of Aam, and two giant Icelings bravely journey north to retrieve the precious stone. Numerous places and names are confusing with no glossary provided, and the long descriptions and plot complexities relegate this to high-fantasy devotees. A reader who pursues it, however, will find the story rich in imagination and will strive with the unusual and fascinating characters as they valiantly penetrate the brooding mountain citadel of Gzel. (pp. 1097-98)

> *Barbara Elleman, in a review of "The Wolves of Aam," in* Booklist, *Vol. 77, No. 15, April 1, 1981, pp. 1097-98.*

This first of "two tales of the Tiddi and the ancient secret that lies at the heart of the Opal Mountain" presents a high fantasy world of exotic beasts and birds that converse in Old English, and men both evil and noble. In ideas, characterization, blending of disparate elements, ability to engage the emotions, and sheer creativity, **Wolves** simply does not measure up. Dyed-in-the-wool fantasy fans, however, will surely enjoy the adventures of Runner and his friends with their echoes of Norse mythology, Tolkien, and Le Guin.

> *Althea K. Helbig, in a review of "The Wolves of Aam," in* Children's Book Review Service, *Vol. 9, No. 14, August, 1981, p. 127.*

Shadow Dancers   (1983)

Lek, the young conjurer who appeared in **The Wolves of Aam,** is still attempting to prove his innocence in connection with the disappearance of Nirim, a sacred stone. He is joined in his quest by Findral, one of the wolves of Aam, and by Fith, Cat, and Arl—all of whom belong to a race of small people known as the Tiddi. Their search takes them to the ancient city of Avel Timrel and to a heretofore unknown tribe of Tiddi who have been coerced into working the honeycomb of mines for the evil Lord Naghar. Of course, the five find the magic stone, defeat Lord Naghar, and liberate the Tiddi; Lek redeems his good name, and Cat and Arl incidentally discover their real heritage. Easier to follow than its predecessor, the new book, too, is reminiscent of Tolkein in its small people and its carefully devised setting. Plotting her territory with considerable imagination, the author has enriched it with an elaborate—and occasionally confusing—mythology. The characters have an appealing liveliness, while Lord Naghar and his sinister henchmen exude enough menace to sustain the suspense right through the closing chapters.

> *Ethel R. Twichell, in a review of "Shadow Dancers," in* The Horn Book Magazine, *Vol. LIX, No. 5, October, 1983, p. 580.*

Curry vividly etches a magical land of high mountains and mysterious caverns and peoples it with an array of diversified and imaginative characters. A tendency to overdo, however, clouds her plot line, and only high-fantasy readers who became involved with the world of Astarlind in the first volume will follow the story through to its complicated but dramatic conclusion.

> *Barbara Elleman, in a review of "Shadow Dancers," in* Booklist, *Vol. 80, No. 5, November 1, 1983, p. 406.*

This sequel to her 1981 **The Wolves of Aam** brings back most of the characters of that mythopeic fantasy in a continuation of the adventures of Lek the Conjuror and his Tiddi companions, Cat and Fith.

While the plot is interesting enough, and some of the characters show originality, the secondary world Curry creates is highly derivative. She has taken a large portion of Tolkien, leavened it with a dash of Le Guin, and come up with a half-baked world that is both predictable and boring, at least to the adult reader. Imitation may be a sincere form of flattery, but it does not make for exciting reading.

Anyone who enjoyed **The Wolves of Aam** will probably also like **Shadow Dancers,** and juvenile readers will probably not be bothered by the derivative nature of the book,

but few adult readers of modern fantasy will want to bother with it.

> *David Stevens, "Derivative Fantasy in a Half-Baked World," in* Fantasy Review, *Vol. 7, No. 7, August, 1984, p. 46.*

The Great Flood Mystery   (1985)

This has many elements of the standard middle-grades mystery story: an indefatigable and perspicacious child detective and his pals, a doubting adult, and a not inconsiderate proportion of contrivance. On the other hand, there's plenty of action, a bit of danger, some suspense to give the story appeal, and some local history to give it substance. A mysterious burglar seems to be interested only in historical records, but Gordy, whose family is staying with an elderly relative while they rent their house to a professor, discovers, with help from some older residents, that a missing street map may lead to treasure buried at the time of the Johnstown Flood. It will probably surprise few mystery story addicts that the burglar is unmasked and the treasure found. Characterization is shallow, the writing style animated.

> *A review of "The Great Flood Mystery," in* Bulletin of the Center for Children's Books, *Vol. 39, No. 6, February, 1986, p. 105.*

Treasure hidden during the Great Johnstown Flood is the focus of this Saturday matinee-style adventure. . . . All of the ingredients are here: hidden clues, a disguised villain and a trio of young sleuths who operate with little adult interference. While the resolution depends heavily on coincidence, and there is only minimal character development, this mystery, like the old matinee adventures, provides satisfying, if undemanding, entertainment.

> *Elaine E. Knight, in a review of "The Great Flood Mystery," in* School Library Journal, *Vol. 32, No. 7, March, 1986, p. 158.*

Gordon Hartz, a "boy who called wolf", makes a startling discovery, but is not believed by his parents due to past behavior. Joining forces with two friends, he begins to uncover surprising facts concerning a hidden treasure. Excitement, adventure and mystery prevail in this story that will totally capture the attentions of young readers. The Pennsylvania setting will be an added attraction to those familiar with Johnstown.

> *Becky C. Stiffler, in a review of "The Great Flood Mystery," in* Children's Book Review Service, *Vol. 14, No. 9, April, 1986, p. 101.*

The Lotus Cup   (1986)

A painfully shy teen realizes her extraordinary talent for pottery-making and becomes more socially adept as a result in this well-written if slightly specialized novel.

During a class trip to a local ceramics museum, Cordelia (Corry) Tipson views some Lotus Ware pottery made by her great-grandfather Lucas Tipson's now-defunct company and sees a young woman in a photo whom she

Curry in her studio.

strongly resembles. Corry knows little about her family's past, and the museum visit sparks her interest. Later, Tip, an attractive new boy in school, reveals that he and Corry are half-cousins, sharing the same great-grandfather. The girl in the photo is Corry's great-grandmother, Cordelia; Tip is descended from Lucas' second wife. Tip has run away from his latest boarding school and is living alone in his great-grandmother's house. He shows Corry some Tipson family memorabilia, including a smashed Lotus Ware cup. Corry, who has become intensely involved in pottery-making, tries (unsuccessfully) to restore the cup. She receives an assist with her work from Tip and her old friend, Don, and is dismayed when both boys fall in love with her. At first, shy Corry avoids the two completely, but as her confidence grows through artistic self-expression, she is finally able to tell them she just wants to be friends. By novel's end, some family mysteries are solved and Corry fires a successful replica of the Lotus Cup.

Interested readers will learn a great deal about pottery-making here; those not into the subject may simply skip over the craft detail. However, both will enjoy the novel's likable characters and well-conceived plot, and will also get a good sense of what it takes to be an artist.

A review of "The Lotus Cup," in Kirkus Reviews, *Vol. LIV, No. 5, March 1, 1986, p. 390.*

[In ***The Lotus Cup***], Corry conquers her shyness and learns that people can't know what you're feeling unless you tell them. Curry has written an absorbing, refreshingly unsentimental tale of the simultaneous joys of artistic creativity and self-discovery.

A review of "The Lotus Cup," in Publishers Weekly, *Vol. 229, No. 17, April 25, 1986, p. 82.*

Information on the art of making procelain is deftly interwoven into a story of romance and mystery. . . .

With the encouragement and help of some old, former potters, Corry becomes determined to reproduce a Lotus Cup, such as the one her great-grandfather had given her great-grandmother. The steps she follows to turn clay into exquisite china is accurately and technically detailed—perhaps too technically for some readers. But they will be carried along by their interest in Corry as she grows in confidence when dealing with her mother, the two boys who show an interest in her and her plans for the future.

Curry has written a book that reflects her love of ceramics and her love for all of her well-drawn characters. (p. 101)

Lucy V. Hawley, in a review of "The Lotus Cup," in School Library Journal, *Vol. 32, No. 9, May, 1986, pp. 100-01.*

Back in the Beforetime: Tales of the California Indians (1987)

A fine collection of creation myths and *pourquoi* tales from a variety of tribes. The stories are entertaining, with the wit and humor one expects from a great storyteller.

The first story tells "How Old Man Above Created the World" before retreating to the big white tepee, Mt. Shasta. The rest of the tales are about animals: why mole has squinty eyes, why yellow jackets have stripes, etc. Trickster Coyote is central to most of the tales. It is he who decides to create man, only to have his creation usurp him, as the "beforetime" ends and man's world begins.

It is a shame that the tribal origins of each tale are not given. An afterword explains that some of the tales are composite versions, but only the rough geographic grouping by state is explained. [Illustrator] James Watts' black-and-white drawings match the literary style by striking a nice balance between Amerindian detail and modern humor. Storytellers, social-studies teachers and librarians should all find this book very useful, as well as highly enjoyable.

A review of "Back in the Beforetime: Tales of the California Indians," in Kirkus Reviews, *Vol. LV, No. 3, February 1, 1987, p. 219.*

Drawing from lore of various California Indian tribes, Curry arranges 22 stories into a cycle of creation myths featuring Coyote, the trickster who contrived that "the animal people had sunshine by day and the moon at night, fire to warm them and to cook with, and salmon and pine nuts in season." His last venture, making a man, begins the period of Aftertime, when, as Old Man Above warns, "no longer will your folk be both animals and people, with the powers of both. No longer will any among you be shape-shifters and workers of magic. You will be animals only, and only Man will have the powers of speech and spirit." These stories of Beforetime, meanwhile, are alive with the mischief, malice, and magic that allowed the clever to survive. Coyote is, as often as not, defeated by his own wiles, as when he tries to fool Badger out of a deer and ends up eating acorns for dinner. Yet by hook or crook, he does manage to win his way, as in his recruiting the animals to steal pine nuts from the Mountain Bluebirds. Like Moses' Israelites, the animal people complain and sometimes despise Coyote, but he is indominable even to the day of his last tricks on Dog. Curry's words are well-turned, the stories brief and often humorous; this is a cohesive, readable collection for introducing young readers to Native American mythology.

Betsy Hearne, in a review of "Back in the Beforetime: Tales of the California Indians," in Bulletin of the Center for Children's Books, *Vol. 40, No. 9, May, 1987, p. 165.*

An important feature of North American Indian mythology is the primitive culture hero in animal form, especially the trickster-hero like Coyote or Raven. Such a figure often displays mischievous or disagreeable characteristics but may also act with compassion, wisdom, and strength as a kind of intermediary between the earth's creatures and a supreme being. Opening with the creation of the world in the "Beforetime," the book deals with a full company of the " 'Animal People' " and, presaging the "Aftertime," closes with the establishment of the first men and women. The legends—many of them etiological stories—are not random selections but are unified by ethnic atmosphere, characters, and incidents. Familiar Indian motifs appear in the explanations of natural phenomena and in the origins of the behavior and appearance of common birds and beasts. Frequently cast as a boastful, foolish nuisance who is sometimes deceived and outwitted, Coyote is also shown as omniscient and magnanimous. So abundant are Indian stories about Coyote that in Jane Curry's new work there is thematic similarity to, but no actual repetition of, the material found in her out-of-print volume *Down from the Lonely Mountain.* Although the reteller states that she is "a storyteller rather than a folklorist," one would have hoped, nevertheless, to find documentation of her sources. On the other hand, her narrative style is thoroughly beguiling: "Back in the Beforetime, when the World was new as new and flat as flat, Old Man Above, who had made it, sat above the sky and puzzled what to do with it. The World floated far below, wrapped up in the deep dark, for it was so new that the stars were still unlit."

Ethel L. Heins, in a review of "Back in the Beforetime: Tales of the California Indians," in The Horn Book Magazine, *Vol. LXIII, No. 5, September-October, 1987, p. 622.*

Me, Myself, and I: A Tale of Time Travel (1987)

To forestall the theft of his most promising work, computer whiz J. J. borrows his mentor's closely guarded time-machine and travels into the past, where he tries to foil the thief without destroying his own future.

At 16, J. J. is a successful inventor, for two years a graduate student of Professor Poplov's (an authority on holography) and the complacent boyfriend of lovely Polly Ambruster. Telling his own story, J. J. also reveals himself as a garrulous nerd. But when he discovers that Max Sharp is horning in on Polly, as well as coming up with electronic moneymakers remarkably like his, he reasons his way into Poplov's "Pandora's Box" and, miscalculating, ends up four years back. He meets himself (Jacko) at age 12, is appalled (reciprocally) at his own pomposity, and finds computer-tapping well under way. He and Jacko go back another four years (now they are three), and there's some frantic negotiations with Poplov, who wonders whether the trouble-making time machine should ever be built—a logic-spinning riddle.

Though characterization is minimal, Curry makes the most of her intriguing idea, getting her three main characters back to the present as one plausibly integrated personality in spite of the paradoxes she raises. Comedy grows naturally out of the situation of self confronting self; there's a satisfying degree of suspense and some nifty twists and insights. Good fun.

> *A review of "Me, Myself, and I: A Tale of Time Travel," in* Kirkus Reviews, *Vol. LV, No. 18, September 15, 1987, p. 1391.*

All this book has to offer is silly characters in a lightweight story combined with a difficult concept. . . . While the characterization is on the level of a '50s sci-fi movie, as is the scientific gadgetry, the plot, with its back-and-forth shifts in time, is intricate and fairly difficult to follow. The preoccupation with avoiding the paradox of changing one's past from a future dependent on that past gets in the way of the mystery and adventure. The exploration of the paradox pushes the readership up to junior high where the story and characters will seem awfully juvenile. The jacket illustration fits the older group but only a few of them will stick with the story.

> *Carolyn Caywood, in a review of "Me, Myself, and I: A Tale of Time Travel," in* School Library Journal, *Vol. 34, No. 3, November, 1987, p. 114.*

Although the idea of using the same character at three different ages is interesting. Curry's explanations of time travel are confusing. The writing style is choppy with lots of exclamations and incomplete sentences (not a good example for middle schoolers), and too much teenage jargon, as in "You'll strip your gears if you try to figure out the Great Fred Flap all at one go." The cover art looks more appropriate for an occult novel than a science fiction book. The book might interest talented and gifted students since the main character is one. Otherwise, an optional purchase.

> *Lucinda Deatsman, in a review of "Me, Myself and I," in* Voice of Youth Advocates, *Vol. 10, No. 5, December, 1987, p. 243.*

The Big Smith Snatch   (1989)

Four children are seized by a pair of modern-day Fagins—in a taut, sinister, but nonviolent page-turner.

Mr. Smith has found a job in Philadelphia, but just as his wife and five children are about to set off cross-country from L.A. to join him, Mrs. Smith collapses and is hospitalized. Boo, at 12 the eldest, is off on an errand; by the time she returns, a social worker has whisked away the younger four—into the clutches of J.D. and Peachie, bogus foster parents. As Boo searches desperately for them, her brothers and sisters are getting royal treatment in a big, old house with seven other children, while they learn exciting games like "snatch" and "seek." Soon they're playing these games in other people's houses, in the dead of night. Though the young Smiths' suspicions dawn into certainty, Peachie and J.D. have a tight set-up that seems impossible to escape.

While the Smiths aren't take-charge types . . . , they're solidly individual, and Curry supplies a rich assortment of background characters. The bad guy's *modus operandi* is all too plausible. The story does depend on coincidence: J.D. and Peachie's house happens to be near the Smiths' old neighborhood, and their van is distinctive enough to be traceable. In the end, the police descend and the Smiths are reunited; readers will exit with a smile. Fine suspense.

> *A review of "The Big Smith Snatch," in* Kirkus Reviews, *Vol. LVII, No. 14, July 15, 1989, p. 1073.*

Children will find Curry's plot especially fascinating; a fairy-tale motif of malevolent figures tempting children with all manner of goodies is woven through the story, allowing readers to sense the unknown evil that lurks about the Smiths. Like fairy-tale heroes who triumph, the Smith kids persevere, effectively scheming to save themselves, although the police beat them to it. Highly entertaining, this also carries an underlying message about how easy it is to become homeless and how economic adversity can tear families apart.

> *Denise Wilms, in a review of "The Big Smith Snatch," in* Booklist, *Vol. 86, No. 1, September 1, 1989, p. 68.*

A smooth, fast-paced adventure that's rather old-fashioned in spite of the presence of a bag lady and current street scenes in L.A. . . . Each child's personality is briefly but clearly delineated, with Boo's in greater depth. The tension builds quickly, and the ending, although abrupt, satisfies by bringing the family back together. In fact, much of this tale's delight comes from the large family with its poverty, warmth, and loyalty, as well as children's fascination with sudden emergencies and the need for resourcefulness. A good, involving story. (pp. 116-17)

> *Sara Miller, in a review of "The Big Smith Snatch," in* School Library Journal, *Vol. 35, No. 14, October, 1989, pp. 116-17.*

Little Little Sister   (1989)

In a graceful, well-honed style that recalls folk literature, the story of a Thumbelina-sized girl.

Though the farmer and his wife have given up wishing for a daughter, their son yearns for a little sister. All three are enchanted, then, when one springs from an apple seed, but they're also overprotective: they bell the cat and keep Little Sister safe indoors. Undaunted, Little Sister quietly makes friends with the cat and escapes the house, following her brother on errands; the third time, hiding in his pocket, she helps him get a good price for the heifer he's selling, serves as his conscience when he dawdles too long in town, gets him home in time to rescue their animals from a sudden flood, and proves that, as their father says, "the wide world may be no place for either of you alone . . . but together you do very well."

[Illustrator Erik] Blegvad's realistically detailed, finely crosshatched, delicately tinted illustrations and the book's small, square format are just right for this charming modern fable about a sensible, assertive character earning her right to freedom and responsibility.

A review of "Little Little Sister," in Kirkus Reviews, *Vol. LVII, No. 19, October 1, 1989, p. 1472.*

A well-written tale with motifs similar to Tom Thumb's. . . . The narrative is rhythmically patterned in both the words and in the action that Blegvad's precise pen-and-wash art reflects with verve. It's refreshing to find an adventurous, clever female in context of substantial storytelling with picture-book appeal.

Betsy Hearne, in a review of "Little Little Sister," in Bulletin of the Center for Children's Books, *Vol. 43, No. 3, November, 1989, p. 53.*

Stories about miniature beings have a particular, quasi-visual appeal, aesthetic perhaps for adults but for the very young especially attractive because such beings operate to some extent at their own level of height. A familiar folk-tale motif is used for a fanciful comment on a family problem of adjustment in **The Little, Little Sister.** When a tiny child is born from an apple-seed to a farmer and his wife their normally-sized son is delighted and uses his talent for woodwork to make suitable furniture for Little Sister but her energetic sense of adventure worries him. When she stows away in his basket and enjoys her own kind of fun at the local market her parents are anxious for her safety and her brother, led astray by a cake-seller and the blacksmith's cider, feels responsible even before her quiet voice in his ear reproves him but still claims her freedom. Because she can overhear financial discussions she wins the right to go to the market regularly as her heedless brother's advisor and her delight is shown very clearly in smooth wash and line pictures which make the most of the humour in differential sizes, showing also a range of expressions from exasperation to tenderness which brings the picture-book into close relation with family patterns everywhere. (pp. 5386-87)

Margery Fisher, in a review of "The Little, Little Sister," in Growing Point, *Vol. 29, NO. 3, September, 1990, pp. 5386-87.*

What the Dickens! (1991)

If you're in the market for a good read-aloud with plenty of action, a plucky heroine, an unusual historical setting, *and* comical bad guys, this is it. Set on the Juniata Canal in Pennsylvania in 1842, Curry's entertaining story follows the adventures and misadventures of 11-year-old Cherry Dobbs and her twin brother, Sam, as they chase Charles Dickens up and down the Juniata trying to recover a stolen manuscript. Cherry is a delight. She's smart, action-oriented, a great admirer of Charles Dickens, and a writer herself. As she and her brother trail Mr. Dickens, alternately losing and rescuing his journal, they encounter a variety of folks who, like their own family, make a living traveling the canals. By the end of the book, readers will have painlessly acquired a surprising amount of information about life on a canal boat, the entertainments of the time, and copyright laws. Librarians be warned: you may need to dust off your copies of Dickens' works when the kids finish reading this adventure. (p. 327)

Chris Sherman, in a review of "What the Dickens!" in Booklist, *Vol. 88, No. 3, October 1, 1991, pp. 326-27.*

A book rich with historical accuracy and enticing readers to enjoy the works of Dickens is bound to win the favor of librarians. However, it is the rip-snorting adventure of saving the manuscript from two nasty villains that will capture the young reader. Some of the connections that allow the adventure to flow seem a bit unlikely but lives do have their unlikely passages. A grand adventure with a literary/historical bonus. (pp. 308-09)

Jody McCoy, in a review of "What the Dickens!" in Voice of Youth Advocates, *Vol. 14, No. 5, December, 1991, pp. 308-09.*

What the Dickens! is the perfect book for all book lovers who also love mysteries. They will delight in reading about the Dobbs twins' ordeal while retrieving one of the famous Charles Dickens or Mr. Boz manuscripts from book thieves. Not only will readers experience a taste of life along the Pennsylvania canals, but they will also be caught up in Cherry and Sam's terror of being captured and thrown off by the thieves. Both entertaining and educational—a must for all young readers.

Maxine Kamin, in a review of "What the Dickens!" in Children's Book Review Service, *Vol. 20, No. 7, February, 1992, p. 80.*

Bob Graham

1942-

Australian author and illustrator of picture books.

Major works include *First There Was Frances* (1985), *The Wild* (1987), *Crusher Is Coming!* (1987), *Grandad's Magic* (1989), *Greetings from Sandy Beach* (1990).

The creator of books for preschoolers and readers in the early grades, Graham is recognized as one of Australia's most popular author/illustrators. Acclaimed for the imagination, humor, warmth, and authenticity of his works as well as for his vivid depictions of experiences commonly shared by children, he is considered an especially insightful observer of the thoughts and feelings of the young. Graham is also praised for the dry, understated wit of his texts and illustrations, a quality that strongly appeals to adult readers. According to critics Donnarae Mac-Cann and Olga Richard, Graham's "low-keyed family dramas are continually enhancing the art of the picture book. . . . Few authors are so independent in their approach, so free from the need to borrow from earlier books." Graham's simple texts relate episodes of daily family life in a manner consistent with the realistic occurences that he presents. Addressing themes that center on the relationships of children with each other, their families, and their pets, he often challenges stereotypes in his books by demonstrating that appearances can be deceiving. For instance, *Crusher Is Coming!* relates the anxiety of young protagonist Peter over the impending visit to his home of tough-guy classmate Crusher, whom Peter is sure will ridicule him if he is kissed by his mother or shown affection by his baby sister Claire. Crusher, however, delights in the attention he receives from Peter's mother and spends most of the afternoon playing with Claire. Discussing the work, which is considered one of Graham's finest, *Publishers Weekly* praised as "ingeniously conveyed" the author's "empathy for family workings and understanding of the way a child struggles with typical domestic situations." Graham's illustrations have also garnered much positive commentary; frequently citing the exuberance of his line drawings and the bright, cheerful quality of his color washes, many reviewers have compared him favorably with such celebrated illustrators as James Stevenson and John Burningham. Working in a cartoonlike style and with a variety of sketch sizes, Graham expands upon his often deadpan texts with his pictures, which are noted for evoking character and action with a minimum of lines.

Graham graduated from the Julian Ashton Art School of Sydney in 1968, and was subsequently employed as an artist, resource designer, and illustrator for various governmental and private enterprises. The inspiration for his first children's book, *Pete and Roland* (1981), had, according to Graham, "presented itself" when his son Pete "wandered in early one morning with a small parakeet that he had found in the garden." The story of a young boy who cares for an ailing bird until it returns to the wild, the book

was commended for its understated humor and whimsical tone. *Where is Sarah?* (1985), the fourth of a quartet of books—including *Here Comes Theo* (1983), *Here Comes John* (1983), and *Bath Time for John* (1985)—featuring two small siblings and their affectionate dog Theo, has been lauded by commentators for its insightful portrayal of the behavior of children. Hiding uncomfortably in the weeds, older sister Sarah is briefly sought by Theo and her infant brother John, both of whom are quickly sidetracked into other more interesting pursuits. Such wry commentary on a child's disposition also informs Graham's *First There Was Frances.* This work, in which the title character moves into a small home, marries, and soon welcomes a host of others, including relatives with pets, has been described as lively and boisterous. Liz Waterland has written: "What appealed to me most was the total lack of any plot, motivation or explanation for any of the happenings in the book. It reads just like a young child's story . . . 'and then, and then, and then.' " Graham has also written several concept books for young readers, which he has grouped into the series "I Can, Science Early Learners," and "Busy Day Board Books." *Frances* received a Picture Book of the Year commendation at the Children's Book of the Year Awards in Australia in 1986, and also earned Graham the Certificate of Honour for Illustration from the International Board on Books for Young People (IBBY) in 1988. *Crusher Is Coming!* and *Greetings from Sandy Beach,* the latter a comic vignette capturing a child's view of family vacation, were Picture Book of the Year winners in 1988 and 1991, respectively; *Grandad's Magic* was a runner-up for this award in 1990.

(See also *Something About the Author,* Vol. 63.)

GENERAL COMMENTARY

Tony Bradman

[*The following excerpt is from an interview by Tony Bradman.*]

Theo is a small black dog of indeterminate breed. Theo lives with Sarah and her little baby brother, John.

Theo is very playful.

In Bob Graham's *Here Comes Theo,* in fact, this particular canine is so playful and friendly that he knocks Sarah over to give her 'the licking treatment'. Dog owners, especially owners of small, black and over-affectionate mongrel dogs will know exactly what the licking treatment consists of: a warm, rasping, red tongue slopping all over your face at a high rate of knots.

Such seemingly minor details form an essential part of the appeal of Bob Graham's work. It's the sort of closely observed, everyday part of life in a family house which draws young children in—and makes them laugh. In *Here Comes John,* a companion volume to the book which features the licking treatment, baby John crawls along the garden path and meets . . . a snail. He's saved from a fate worse than yeucch! by Sarah's well timed intervention, and there will be many older brothers and sisters among the book's readers who will have had the same experience of stopping baby siblings from eating something nasty they've just found. Put this together with the sort of combination of words and pictures that make these books ideal for early reading and you've found a name well worth recommending.

Bob Graham is a softly spoken Australian who once lived in Manchester for a while. 'That was just after I got married. My wife Carolyn comes from London originally, and her parents still live in England.' Their first child, Naomi, was born while the couple were living in Manchester, and although both of them wanted to try and make a go of life in the old country, harsh economic reality forced a return to the Antipodes. 'It just wasn't much fun living in a small flat without enough coins for the meter. But I do love the English countryside, and I'd really like to come and settle here.'

Down under, Bob and Carolyn have moved house 12 times in 14 years, finally settling in a house on top of a hill in the middle of a rain forest near Melbourne. Daughter Naomi is now 16 and her brother Peter 14. All of which may explain why Bob Graham's first large format picture book, *Pearl's Place,* was about moving house. Arthur, the hero of the story, lives in a block of flats with his mum

where he's not allowed to keep pets. Then he discovers Pearl, who lives in an old rambling house which contains hundreds of budgerigars.

A budgerigar also features in the book which first brought Bob Graham's work to my attention [*Pete and Roland*]. . . . This touching little story of how Pete finds and looks after budgerigar Roland until the day Roland flies away comes, says Bob Graham, from an experience in his own family. *Jenny's Baby Brother* . . . has the same ring of truth about it. Jenny isn't very keen on her new baby brother until he does something remarkable—like splatting her in the eye with a perfectly aimed shot from his highchair.

Re-settled in Australia Bob Graham put his art school training to use and worked for a while for the government printing office in Sydney where he did what he describes as 'educational artwork'. 'But I had always been interested in children's books, and one day when I was at home from work with an illness I decided to start one. That book eventually became *Pete and Roland.'* From there he went from strength to strength. Several of his books have had foreign editions, most notably in countries such as France, Germany, Norway, Finland and America. In this country he is now published in hardback by Blackie and by Hamish Hamilton, for whom he did the Theo, John and Sarah books. There are now two more of those titles forthcoming: *Where is Sarah?* and *Bath Time for John.* In both of these the irrepressible Theo causes all sorts of havoc with a game of hide and seek, a toy frog who ends up missing a leg and Sarah's face—which gets the licking treatment once again.

Apart from appearing to be a little bemused at the success of his creations, Bob Graham looks like a very happy man indeed. Perhaps that's got something to do with the fact that he's always liked children's books—to the extent that they've come before other things in the Graham household.

'My wife works in a bookshop, and we're lucky to have lots of books stacked up all around the house. Children's books, I think, are most important. Our kids at any rate always had books—they even had books before we had the telly! In fact they've even had books sometimes instead of, or before, other things.'

Family input still plays a large part in Bob's work even though his children are now well past the picture book stage. 'My kids are a captive audience, but they do give me a lot of constructive criticism. I show them my books and get lots of ideas from them. In fact Pete's very good on artwork—he draws very well himself, and I'm a great fan of his work. I try not to push him too much, just encourage him.'

That warm family feeling, and knowledge of the way children are, based on real parental experience, informs his latest picture book for Blackie, *Libby, Oscar and Me,* to be published in February. It's a dressing up story, again based on family experience, this time of daughter Naomi's dressing up games in the past. He's also working on a new picture book called *First There was Frances,* the story of

The Duck needs more space, it needs The Wild,   and *that* starts at the garden fence.

From The Wild, *written and illustrated by Bob Graham.*

a lady who collects animals—which again is based on someone he knows.

A growing reputation has led to lots of commissions and projects. 'I've got so much to do that it'll be no telly for me for a while', he said.

With books like Bob Graham's to share more adults and young children might feel like turning the set off for a while themselves.

> *Tony Bradman, "Bob Graham," in* Books for Keeps, *No. 30, January, 1985, p. 17.*

Jill Bennett

Bob Graham has a special talent for showing what it is like to be a child: he writes about ordinary things with perception, affection and humour, qualities which he underlines and expands in his charming illustrations. . . .

> *Jill Bennett, in a review of "Libby, Oscar & Me," in* Books for Keeps, *No. 39, July, 1986, p. 15.*

Books

Anyone who hasn't discovered Bob Graham has been missing some great books, and is in for a real treat when they get round to rectifying their mistake. He has a talent for making both grown-up *and* child laugh—not just gig-

gle, but seriously fall about. He also specialises in great surprise endings.

> *A review of "The Wild," in* Chicago Tribune— Books, *May, 1987, p. 31.*

Lee Galda and Barbara Tobin

Bob Graham books for . . . [preschool and early primary school children] reflect a theme of warm family security, together with the gentle humor of the small joys and perils of everyday family life. His deceptively simple, spare yet expressive pen and wash drawings often reveal a delightful surprise of detail, like characters from another story roaming in the background. The universal appeal of his earlier books, such as **First There Was Frances, The Red Woolen Blanket, Charlotte and Henry,** and **Here Comes Theo,** have made Graham an international success. Subsequently he has won the Australian Picture Book of the Year award for both **Crusher Is Coming!** and **Greetings from Sandy Beach. Grandad's Magic,** a runner-up in this award, shows the chaos caused at Sunday lunch by Grandad's attempts to outdo young Alison's juggling tricks with his former magic specialty of whipping the tablecloth out from under all the plates.

Crusher Is Coming! is a tenderly funny story of Peter's attempts to impress Crusher, the school football hero, when he comes home to play one day after school. Peter's efforts to project a macho image, including hiding all his stuffed animals, go unnoticed when Crusher is captivated by Peter's baby sister Claire. Young readers will be bound to notice the change in Peter's attitude toward Claire as a result of Crusher's visit.

Graham's sense of humor prevails again in his latest release, **Greetings from Sandy Beach.** The family's seaside camping trip is filled with familiar small disasters, like uncooperative tents and beach bullies, in this case, the Disciples of Death. Adults will enjoy this as much as their small charges and will surely hope that even as Graham's own children grow up, he will continue to draw on his family memories and observations of other people's children to keep producing these endearingly funny, joyful stories of ordinary family happenings. (pp. 148-49)

> *Lee Galda and Barbara Tobin, "Dreamtime Downunder: Exploring Australian Books," in* The Reading Teacher, *Vol. 46, No. 2, October, 1992, pp. 146-56.*

TITLE COMMENTARY

Pete and Roland   (1981)

In the garden early one morning, "a fat and rather tired parakeet" waddled up to Pete and fell asleep in his hand. The boy named the bird Roland and let him fly inside the house where he "looped the loop, and sat puffing on the picture rail, and the lamp, and did little messes on the drawing table." Although Pete's family resurrected a cage, Pete suspected the bird didn't like it and would leave the door open. But one day Roland disappeared. While he never returned, Pete was cheered because he was "almost sure that he saw Roland with a whole flock of old racing pigeons, and he seemed to be getting along very well." The small, bittersweet story, told in well-chosen words, suggests that love and possession are not inextricably linked. Informal drawings, washed in pale watercolor, reinforce the story's implication that delight can come from brief, casual encounters. (pp. 44-5)

> *Nancy C. Hammond, in a review of "Pete and Roland," in* The Horn Book Magazine, *Vol. LXI, No. 1, January-February, 1985, pp. 44-5.*

This simple tale tells the story of young Pete, who finds a rather fat and tired parakeet in his backyard. Pete decides to name him Roland and keep him in the old bird cage from the basement. Roland is not all that happy with the cage, however, and Pete chooses to leave the door open so that Roland won't have to stay inside. This works well initially, but one day Pete comes home from school and Roland is gone. Does he ever see his parakeet again? Well, Pete thinks he does—flying through the air with a flock of racing pigeons, and he seems to be getting on quite nicely. This British import shows something of the dry humor associated with that country. There are fine, understated cartoon scenes of Roland nibbling the wallpaper, pecking Pete's aunt, and making little messes on the dresser. There is also something of the famous British reserve in Pete's reaction to his loss. Though he does make every effort to locate the bird, he is not in the least devastated about its

departure. The spare telling and clean but colorful cartoons have a certain adult feeling that may make this more appropriate to a slightly older group than the regular picture-book set. (pp. 843-44)

> *Ilene Cooper, in a review of "Pete and Roland," in* Booklist, *Vol. 81, No. 10, February 15, 1985, pp. 843-44.*

This Australian import is a simple, low-key story about a young boy who finds a distressed bird and cares for it—until it flies away. . . . The simple text and numerous, charming illustrations (reminiscent of Quentin Blake) should appeal to young readers, although a few Briticisms may be troublesome. Children who are not aware that parakeets exist in the wild in Australia may assume that Roland is someone's escaped pet and will find his joining a flock of pigeons very unlikely. While there are other books about the loss of a domesticated wild animal or a pet, they are longer and more serious. This one is appealing due to its light and cheerful tone.

> *Deborah Vose, in a review of "Pete and Roland," in* School Library Journal, *Vol. 31, No. 7, March, 1985, p. 150.*

Pearl's Place   (1983)

Arthur turns happily from the angularity of a tenement-block to the untidy house where huge, sloppy Pearl and her small daughter enjoy a cosy conglomeration of dust and dogs (with one room given over to free-flying budgerigars). We are not told whether the boy and his mother take up Pearl's offer of an empty flat in her house instead of the 'shadow of their building'; the object of the book is to enforce visually, in scribble pictures slashed with colour, the contrast between space and construction, free movement and claustrophobia.

> *Margery Fisher, in a review of "Pearl's Place," in* Growing Point, *Vol. 22, No. 5, January, 1984, p. 4201.*

Outstanding picture book by a comparatively new Australian author/artist. Arthur lives in a big block of flats with his Mum (no Dad) and his life at home is rather arid due to regulations in their flats. All that is changed when he and his Mum meet Pearl:

"We've got three dogs, two cats, three hundred budgies, and you can throw water bombs off the roof" Pearl said, and put a large packet of chocolate biscuits into her trolley."

Vitality and fun is what Pearl is all about—Bob Graham too.

> *A review of "Pearl's Place," in* Books for Your Children, *Vol. 19, No. 3, Autumn-Winter, 1984, p. 19.*

Here Comes John   (1983); Here Comes Theo   (1983); Bath Time for John   (1985); Where Is Sarah?   (1985)

Bob Graham has pitched these books [**Here Comes John** and **Here Comes Theo**] exactly right, avoiding tweeness and condescension. To respect a snail, as a child might, isn't easy, but on its own scale the adventures of the gasteropod featured in **Here Comes John** are as important as those of many a romantic hero. It negotiates an open box labelled "Get rid of unsightly snails" and a row of eager-beaked birds, escapes being stamped on by Theo the dog and is finally snatched from death in the jaws of baby John by bossy older Sarah. The book's title suggests that it will be about John, but the children are kept to the edges of both stories: Sarah is introduced by her feet and legs.

The dangers the snail overcomes are illustrated in witty cartoons seen from ground level. At the climax ("it's heading straight for John's mouth") the tiny creature sits precariously in the baby's fingers, just between his open lips and the inquiring nose of the dog. Two birds are perched on the fence and a large purposeful Sarah approaches from the opposite page. In **Here Comes Theo** the snail is relegated to its natural place while Theo charges about, knocking down almost everything in sight including Sarah and John, though not the snail. John's taking of his first step, a major event from an adult point of view, is a mere incident here, even at first a puzzling one ("but where *is* the step?", I was asked). Indeed the existence of adults goes almost unacknowledged in these two books. It is just hinted at in a glimpse of a trowel and some half-planted tomatoes and by the fact that Sarah calls Theodore by his full name when she is angry.

Graham's narrative is short and plain; as important for what it doesn't say as for what it does. The snail's protective shell is mentioned but its two friends, an ant and what looks like a lizard, have no such shells and do not appear when the beaky birds are sitting on the fence. Graham's use of repetition makes it possible for a small child to "read" the books himself after only one adult reading. And, like that of fairy tales and unlike that in books written purposely for "easy reading", the repetition relates to the development of the story. These books are fun, with bright pictures and bright jackets. And yet useful lessons emerge: "You *don't* put snails in your mouth, do you?" and "He *shouldn't* take his socks off"—morals that are undoubtedly more significant to a three-year-old than information on how to lay tables or behave at the dentist's.

Paula Neuss, in a review of "Here Comes John" and "Here Comes Theo," in The Times Literary Supplement, *No. 4226, March 30, 1984, p. 338.*

These two small books [**Bath Time for John** and **Where Is Sarah?**] from a collection of four have simply drawn and coloured pictures with just enough detail to engage a young child's attention while also making the characters seem real people.

Bath time for John is an absolute winner. Sarah takes baby brother for his bath, accompanied by a wind-up frog and Theo, the wayward dog. Feeling excluded from the bath-time games, Theo runs off with the frog, followed in wild pursuit by Sarah and of course 'skidding, crawling' wet baby John. They eventually return to the bathroom and the 'cold grey bath', but not before John 'has leaves and dirt sticking to him' and Theo has made 'tooth marks in the plastic frog'. The absence of any parents in the scenario make it even more enchanting.

The story-line of **Where is Sarah?** is less immediately attractive. It will, however, appeal particularly to children who have tried to play hide-and-seek with a toddler only to find that once they have hidden themselves, the toddler has forgotten what the game was all about. This time John has a rubber crocodile which 'he feeds with soggy crisps' while poor Sarah ends up 'hot and itchy with insects biting her'. Her only compensation is that she gets the 'licking treatment' from Theo—depicted in two pictures not to be missed.

Monica Hughes, in a review of "Bath Time for John" and "Where Is Sarah?" in The School Librarian, *Vol. 33, No. 3, September, 1985, p. 231.*

This series is absolutely wonderful! Bob Graham books have always been favourites with the children I teach, but these eclipse the lot. The adventures of two young children and their dog, in everyday situations, are beautifully portrayed: poor Sarah hiding in the long grass, long forgotten by her seekers; Theo the dog who always greets the children with a flying leap and the licking treatment; and John who can't walk . . . or can he? The most popular has to be **Here comes John**. . . .

J. S., in a review of "Here Comes John" and others, in Books for Keeps, *No. 51, July, 1988, p. 7.*

[This] quartet speaks directly to a young audience with language that is disarmingly simple but ingeniously able to portray situations that appeal immensely to the self-interest of young children. Featured are a baby named John, his older sister, Sarah, and their dog, Theo. In **Bath Time,** Theo runs off with John's toy frog. Sarah tries to re-

From The Adventures of Charlotte and Henry, *written and illustrated by Bob Graham.*

trieve it and John follows; Theo bites off a leg, but John doesn't really mind, for now the wind-up frog swims in a circle. *Here Comes John* chronicles baby John's encounter with a snail—from the snail's perspective. "Look out, snail!" begins the story, for it's dangerous for the little creature to cross the garden path. Theo and Sarah both avoid stepping on the snail, and John, crawling along on his hands and knees, picks up the snail and nearly eats it. In *Here Comes Theo,* the family's exuberant little terrier enjoys leaping at the children and giving them "the licking treatment." When John takes his first step, he is rewarded with a flying leap from Theo. *Where Is Sarah* is perhaps the most effective in capturing quintessentially childlike behavior. Sarah is hiding in the weeds, and John and Theo are looking for her. Both dog and baby get sidetracked, leaving Sarah to sit, hot and itchy, in her weedy hideout. The language is understated and witty: "Sarah is finished with this game," observes the unseen narrator, who leaves the reader with a view of John poking grass into his toy crocodile's mouth. Graham's stories are illustrated with quick line-and-wash drawings. The cartooned faces and simple compositions cater to toddler comprehension capabilities, while adults sharing the books with children will enjoy the dry humor that permeates the scenarios.

Denise M. Wilms, in a review of "Bath Time for John" and others, in Booklist, *Vol. 85, No. 10, January 15, 1989, p. 870.*

When authors create stories about life in and around the playpen, what kind of audience do they have in mind? Clearly, the tales' barely perambulating babes are on a different level from that of potential child readers and listeners. It takes people old enough to be self-reflective to enjoy an occasional backward glance, a reminder of what experience must have been like at the beginning. But irrespective of audience, a rendering of life in the playpen soon becomes monotonous. Authors need ingenuity to turn newborns and toddlers into central characters. . . .

Bob Graham's approach is deceptively simple. John and Sarah are independent, self-directed children in *Here Comes John, Bath Time for John, Where Is Sarah?,* and *Here Comes Theo.* Theo is the mischief-making family dog. Sarah is about eight years old and is very earnest about her role as big sister. John changes gradually from the crawling to the toddling stage. He crawls along the garden path and nearly swallows a snail (one of the typical, minor adventures of this affectionately conceived threesome).

In *Here Comes John,* Graham absorbs what he sees and replays it with no extraneous diversions. His children are drawn with a thin, wobbly line that is as free of pretense as the kids. Each picture captures the essence of the actors, giving us the impression that the feelings of the youngsters, as well as their appearances, are understood and accepted. We know how it must feel for Sarah to lift John. To make it work, her legs are parted and her spine is a bit out of whack. She looks off-balance. John, in contrast, is still a rubbery infant. As for the endangered snail, we know before the author tells us that John will try to eat it. The whole scenario is so natural and simple that there is something also magical about it.

When Graham draws Theo like a dark, textured mop, or a group of crows watching the action from a nearby fence, he uses the same sketchy, loose manner. He adds light washes of soft color but leaves enough white space to create an unfinished, fluid look to the composition.

Similarly, this author/artist makes no attempt at sharp definitions in *Bath Time for John.* He keeps his focus on John's wind-up frog, the mad dash by Sarah on the trail of Theo (who has snatched the frog from the tub), and the nude, dirt-spattered John who joins the chase.

Comic situations in *Where Is Sarah?* are as uncontrived and fleeting as the episode about the bath. There is no psychological hype about sibling rivalry or injured egos. Personality is on display here, but it is seen in relation to how children, without forethought or concern, let one activity be preempted by another. Searching for Sarah (who is hiding in tall grass) is the main plot thread, but we forget about it just as the protagonists become preoccupied with other matters. Sarah squirms in her insect-infested hideaway, John stuffs "chips" into the gaping mouth of his toy crocodile, and Theo bounces about in the grass in pure doggish ecstasy.

Theo is a shaggy, nervous mass as he awaits his "targets" in *Here Comes Theo.* Graham renders him as a mere streak, a low, diagonal form without defined legs or body. But the animal is well understood by his illustrator. Graham is again giving us the essence of action and character in simplified form (in this case, a pet quivering with excitement as he prepares to bestow the "licking treatment"). Sarah is a stocky little person, the ultimate sister/mother/nurturer. She is patient, wary, and a bit weary as she keeps a watchful eye on her baggy-diapered, unpredictable brother.

In all these books Graham gives the narrative the same unlabored movement from page to page that one would find in a good filmstrip. And it works so well because he withholds all but the essential visual notation. He knows that what he has left out is unimportant to the urgency of the image.

Donnarae MacCann and Olga Richard, in a review of "Here Comes John" and others, in Wilson Library Bulletin, *Vol. 64, No. 5, January, 1990, p. 93.*

Libby, Oscar and Me (1984)

Emily is a little girl who enjoys dressing up. Master of disguises, she is equally a master of the art of living. Whether playing with her cat Libby or her dog Oscar, sitting musing, or trundling her toys to the park, everything is transformed by her wild imagination. Emily is to be found in Bob Graham's *Libby, Oscar and Me.* A sense of association with a child's experience, wit, and a command of the picture-book form has produced a genuinely funny picture book. Its humour stems from the disjunction between what Emily tells us about her life, and the visual narrative of the same material. It is inspired irony which every child, as well as adult, will recognize. Emily, Libby and Oscar look as if they are so charged by Graham's lively line, that they can barely allow him the time to scribble in some crayon and splash on some paint before they disappear over the page. The low eye-level, and large forms balanced by small details—an apple-core, some cigarette ends by the back door, a bird pecking crumbs—reinforce the child's world view. The rhythms of the story are matched by the shape and size of illustration, and both build to a climax when Libby puts a pack of dogs to flight in a double-page visual maelstrom.

> *Jane Doonan, "Amiable Beginnings: Picture Books," in* The Times Literary Supplement, *No. 4278, March 29, 1985, p. 351.*

Graham favors parents who will not mind reading his story again and again, as tots will beg them to. As recited by Emily, a venturesome child, the adventures are hilarious and illustrated in brightly colored pictures that do full justice to unfolding developments.

> *A review of "Libby, Oscar & Me," in* Publishers Weekly, *Vol. 227, No. 24, June 14, 1985, p. 72.*

This picture story book aimed at the pre-school child has as its theme the dressing-up box, key to flights of fancy and innovation. This box has above average contents including a wide selection of hats, a mask and snorkel, a witch's broomstick, and a splendid plastic nose. The illustrations, showing Libby's many disguises, are full of movement, but the text is somewhat fragmented and there is a lack of the cohesion needed to make the idea work.

> *Maisie Roberts, in a review of "Libby, Oscar and Me," in* The School Librarian, *Vol. 33, No. 3, September, 1985, p. 220.*

First There Was Frances (1985)

An amusing, appealing look at the way the formation of a family can bring a boisterous joy to life. First, there is Frances, a woman living alone outside the city. She is joined by Graham, a bearded fellow who becomes her husband. A dog and babies are not far behind, and then Grandma comes to complete the family circle. Well, it's not quite complete. Katy the goat shows up and of course the guinea pigs, Errol and Berryl, Grandma's canary, and a tabby cat. When the fierce and smelly billy goat Nugget arrives, followed by his and Katy's baby goats, and more baby guinea pigs, plus a few horses—whew, then it's time to move to the country. A fast-paced, furious story needs exuberant pictures, and this book surely has them. With a style that somewhat resembles James Stevenson's, Graham offers scrawly, colorful cartoons that catch every delicious morsel of the fun.

> *Ilene Cooper, in a review of "First There Was Frances," in* Booklist, *Vol. 82, No. 15, April 1, 1986, p. 1140.*

First There Was Frances is . . . short on text, but vivid and innovative as graphic art. . . . Bob Graham creates ultrasimple, parallel narrative sequences:

> First there was Frances. Frances lived alone.
> There was a long wooden fence near her house,
> and over the fence was the city. *Then* came. . . .

At this point we meet Graham and a dog, Teak, and we have a glimpse of their lives before they join up with Fran-

ces. Then come two babies, Grandma, cats and kittens, guinea pigs and piglets, and goats. A mature viewer sees the satirical treatment of this melange, while a toddler delights in the visual detail, in the slapstick, and perhaps at an unconscious level, in the positive, penetrating observations of the artist.

Household trappings are designed so that the very texture of domesticity—the messy, happy ambiguity of middle-class life—shows up dramatically. It is a heterogeneous group (Frances has a bike, Graham a motorcycle, Grandma a van, and the youngsters a menagerie), but the illustrator unifies them as alert, self-actualizing individuals. He organizes the hodge-podge so that the viewer feels he or she is applying the "less-is-more" principle. Lines and colors are handled loosely to fit the scramble of activity; the sketchiness suggests buoyancy. Yet Bob Graham's drawing skills are precise when the effect calls for this quality (as in a strikingly convincing birdcage), and there is clear evidence of judicious preplanning throughout. (pp. 62-3)

> *Donnarae MacCann and Olga Richard, in a review of "First There Was Frances," in* Wilson Library Bulletin, *Vol. 61, No. 1, September, 1986, pp. 62-3.*

A comic, cumulative effect is created by both story and pictures in a book about a patient, generous-hearted woman, who extends her hospitality to ludicrous limits. . . . Scraggly, breezy drawings, their firm lines enclosing droll portrayals of animals and people, fill the pages with cheerful color and suggest the boisterous energy and gusto of Quentin Blake, John Burningham, and James Stevenson. And the amiable nonsense is carried through in the names bestowed on the creatures: Errol and Berryl, the guinea pigs; Triller, the canary; Toyful, the alley cat; Nosy, the ferret; Nugget, the fierce billy goat; the baby goats, Ruby, Earl, and Curl.

> *Ethel L. Heins, in a review of "First There Was Frances," in* The Horn Book Magazine, *Vol. LXII, No. 5, September-October, 1986, p. 580.*

A jolly book this, about a very '*Guardian*' readers' sort of family—all bearded dad, jeans-wearing mum and children called Marisol and Fraser. It has a sort of *House That Jack Built* feel about it; starting with Frances on her own and gradually building up an entire family with dozens of pets and a very laid back life-style.

What appealed to me most was the total lack of any plot, motivation or explanation for any of the happenings in the book. It reads just like a young child's story . . . 'and then, and then, and then' . . . a long list of events that happen—but who knows why? (Just like real life, in fact!) Where did Katy the goat come from? And why did she live in the laundry? We shall never know.

> *Liz Waterland, in a review of "First There Was Frances," in* Books for Keeps, *No. 49, March, 1988, p. 18.*

"Science Early Learners" series: Heat; Moving; Push; Senses; Sound; Water; Wheels (1985-86)

The continuing emphasis by the DES on the scientific education of young children, and the response of publishers to that emphasis are to be welcomed, for the roots of an ability to explore the world with interest and meaning grow in the infant school. However, getting children to develop inquiring minds and a scientific approach to things is hard work, so how much do "science early learners" help? There are six, 16-page storybooks in full colour for infant and early junior readers. . . .

The authors are sound in their stated reasons for teaching science and set about implementing these reasons through six standard science topics, water, heat, senses, wheels, moving and sound. . . . Scientific concepts form the main content of the storybooks, for example the one on water is mainly concerned with the concept of volume, and the storybook on sound with the fact that sounds are caused by vibrations. These gave me pause for thought. Does reading about Harry, in and out of his bath either on his own or together with his dog Albert, even though the illustrations show the resultant changes in water level, give children any understanding of volume? I'm sure the authors intend lots of practical experience to back each story up. . . . I also wondered if it was necessary, or even provident, with infants to say that "a sound . . . makes waves which spread out in the air. You can't see these waves." Surely the experience of gathering sounds, and feeling where vibrations occur is enough.

The few suggestions for practical activities that occurred on the last page of each storybook were valuable, but it is a matter for regret that the illustrations in these children's books, even though in cartoon style, do not reflect the multi-ethnic society around us. . . .

Overall, a straightforward, if unexciting attempt to bring help to the cause of infant science.

Roy Richards, "Early Warning," in The Times Educational Supplement, *No. 3666, October 3, 1986, p. 31.*

The Wild (1986)

The most attractive book [of those reviewed, which also include *Unlucky Wally* by Raymond Briggs, *The Old Joke Book* by Janet and Allan Ahlberg, and *Stone Soup* by Tony Ross] is *The Wild.* Bob Graham proceeds from an element of experience untainted by the need to nag us with it. A house set in the country is a picture of safe domesticity. Outside is the Wild, to which various family pets are drawn, and into which they disappear. The child and his simple parents are set in the soft dark-green vastnesses of a hill and wood. There is a primitive magic here which does not smack of opportunism or cynicism, but which both assures and confronts a child with the otherness of the non-human world. It is lightly done and unpretentious. It is a real book.

George Szirtes, "A Need-to-Nag Basis," in The Times Literary Supplement, *No. 4383, April 3, 1987, p. 357.*

An Australian with two other successful picture books to his credit presents an ebullient exploration of the differences between domestic, tame, and wild.

Russell, little sister Mary, their parents and an assortment

of pets live in a cozy house on the edge of The Wild. The night Russell reads about a lion from a zoo returning to the African plain, his pet rabbit and frog escape and also return to the wild. The family searches for them in vain, though helped by their two thoroughly domesticated dogs, placid Rosy and bouncy Molly, who tends to behave as if she is herding sheep. Everyone is playful in this family, but the duck plays too rough, pecking red patches on Dad's bald pate; since her wings have been clipped, they decide to take her to the half-wild park.

Graham's green watercolor world provides a lush background for his skillfully drafted comic figures, with such delightful details as little Mary seating her teddy bear firmly across Dad's nose as she rides on his shoulders, and an occasional, not-too-ominous fox making the other side of the fence truly wild. A concept book that provides chuckles and a few pleasant shivers along with its lesson.

A review of "The Wild," in Kirkus Reviews, *Vol. LV, No. 11, June 1, 1987, p. 857.*

I've always been a fan of Bob Graham but I have to say that I found this book rather disappointing. At first sight it looks like a winner with varied picture sequences, some in comic strip format, others being single or double page spreads, and the characters appear to have Graham's usual humorous appeal; but the story itself is rambling and disjointed. Told in the present tense, it lacks pace and, in places, textual cohesion. Indeed some of the spreads can be read in more than one sequence without much altering the flow. Its theme however is thought-provoking and worthy of discussion but this is certainly not a book for those still needing contextual support from the illustrations.

Jill Bennett, in a review of "The Wild," in Books for Keeps, *No. 58, September, 1989, p. 9.*

The Adventures of Charlotte and Henry (1987)

Cartoon panels and numbered captions tell the story of the friendship between happy-go-lucky, impetuous Charlotte and thoughtful, worried Henry. Their contrasting personalities complement each other nicely throughout a series of short chapters. Charlotte's frantic antics worry Henry, but he is always there to dust her off and patch things up, and he never says, "I told you so," which endears him to his more rambunctious pal. Cheery crayon and watercolor panels are captioned by short, choppy phrases; the vocabulary is suitable for early readers, but most of the spirit and action is derived from the subtly-humored illustrations. The format renders this difficult to share with a group, but independent readers will enjoy the warm, albeit slight, stories, and most will recognize the schemes and skirmishes of these two friends.

Kathleen Brachmann, in a review of "The Adventures of Charlotte and Henry," in School Library Journal, *Vol. 34, No. 6, February, 1988, p. 60.*

In *The Adventures of Charlotte and Henry* Bob Graham has experimented with a quasi-comic-strip layout for five stories about two friends—Henry who worries and Charlotte who is wild. Graham's drawings are amusing and vivacious (in an earlier book, *Pearl's Place,* they matched a rather odd little story perfectly); and the five tales, of high jinks of one sort or another, are quite jolly. But the layout is tricky for young children to follow, and the stories end with more of a whimper than a bang.

Lindsay Mackie, "Heading Back to Home," in
The Times Literary Supplement, *No. 4458, September 9, 1988, p. 1000.*

Originally published in France, these five amusing stories will be the cause of much merriment. Each story epitomizes the flavour of true friendship. Charlotte and Henry could not be more unalike. Charlotte is bigger than Henry. She is a boisterous, exuberant, inventive, fun-loving gogetter; Henry is an introspective, cautious, anxious, non-assertive worrier. Each is a perfect foil for the other. The strength of their friendship lies in their warm-hearted caring attitudes towards each other and their recognition of each other's needs.

The stories themselves are short and simple. The realistic plots depict: Charlotte rolling down a hill in a tyre; Charlotte and Henry contriving to skip with a rope; Charlotte alleviating her boredom with Henry's toys; Charlotte mending one of Henry's toys; and Charlotte demonstrat-

ing her grand jetté ballet leap to Henry. There is nothing contrived or stilted here. Graham's wonderful perceptions of human behaviour are portrayed with wit and accuracy. Each subtle nuance is captured and recorded. Readers will delight in discovering new details each time they explore these tales.

The stories are presented in pseudo comic-strip format. Each page is divided into small, informal illustrative blocks. Cartoon-style Charlotte and Henry, rendered in watercolour and crayon, are typical of all Graham's characters. How does he manage to convey such mood and expression with two dots for eyes and an almost non-existent mouth? Short, numbered, one-to-two sentence commentaries under most pictures and the use of natural dialogue demonstrate Graham's skill at perfect picture-word combinations.

B. S., in a review of "The Adventures of Charlotte and Henry," in Magpies, *Vol. 3, No. 5, November, 1988, p. 27.*

Crusher Is Coming! (1987)

Pete warns his mother not to kiss him after school, be-

"Would you like some tea and fairy cakes, Basher?" says Peter's mom.

"*Crusher*, Mom, and I don't think he would."

"Yes please," says Crusher.

From Crusher Is Coming !, *written and illustrated by Bob Graham.*

cause he is bringing home a football hero named Crusher for a visit. And he doesn't want baby sister Claire to intrude, either. But Crusher is a sweet-natured lug, and Claire beguiles him. Pete watches helplessly while his friend gives the baby horseback rides, joins in a tea party and reads Claire a book. Graham's new slant on sibling rivalry is droll and replete with funny moments: " 'Would you like some tea and fairy cakes, Basher?' says Peter's mom." This matter-of-fact tone cleverly underscores the humor of the situation: the author's empathy for family workings and understanding of the way a child struggles with typical domestic situations are ingeniously conveyed.

> *A review of "Crusher Is Coming!" in* Publishers Weekly, *Vol. 233, No. 17, April 29, 1988, p. 74.*

A deft hand and a sense of humor make Graham's lively line and wash drawings enjoyable in themselves and a fine foil for the deliberate blandness of a story told entirely in dialogue. The set-up: a boy is pleased but nervous at the impending visit by his school's football hero. Pete reminds his mother to call the visitor "Crusher," not to give him a kiss when he and Crusher come home, and above all to keep baby sister Claire out of his room. The development: Crusher, although politely responsive to doing whatever Pete suggests, is obviously smitten by the baby and happily plays with her. The denouement: after Crusher leaves, Pete gives Claire a piggyback ride just as his hero did. Clever, funny, and touching without being saccharine.

> *Zena Sutherland, in a review of "Crusher Is Coming!" in* Bulletin of the Center for Children's Books, *Vol. 41, No. 11, July-August, 1988, p. 229.*

[*Crusher Is Coming!* is an] amusing picture book . . . What is left unsaid in the dialogue is shown in the illustrations. The full-color pictures are full of movement and humor; they are done with watercolor and ink, with a bit of crayon for texture and emphasis. Their sketchy liveliness is reminiscent of James Stevenson's work. This book is an artful combination of text and illustration. There is a slight discrepancy between the format and the audience, though. Independent readers in the first or second grade—children old enough to understand the social life of the classroom—would enjoy the book much more than preschoolers would; but this book looks like a read aloud for a younger child. Librarians will have to put this book in the right hands.

> *Lauralyn Persson, in a review of "Crusher Is Coming!" in* School Library Journal, *Vol. 35, No. 1, September, 1988, p. 160.*

[*In the following excerpt, Michael Rosen responds to a* Books for Keeps *survey asking selected authors and illustrators which books they would give to their "favorite toddler, in-between and teenager" as holiday gifts. Rosen indicates that his choice for infants would be Graham's* Crusher Is Coming!]

This is a brand new delight and so shunts out of the limelight some of my old favourites like David McKee and Anthony Browne. Peter tells Mum that Crusher is coming home for tea, so he doesn't want to be kissed and he

doesn't want toddler Claire hanging around. He clears out all his little soft animals. When Crusher arrives, football boots round his neck and plaster on his forehead, it's baby Claire he's more interested in mucking in with. People think that non-sexist books means books about girls; this is a non-sexist book about boys.

> *Michael Rosen, in a review of "Crusher Is Coming," in* Books for Keeps, *No. 53, November, 1988, p. 29.*

Bob Graham lives up to his reputation—another excellent read. He gently mocks the frailty of human nature and leaves us wryly recollecting similar personal experiences. Peter's preparations for the visit of his friend Crusher are elaborate. He reorganises his room and places the family on their best behaviour—particularly his toddler sister who is banished for the duration! Crusher confounds all expectations by thoroughly enjoying himself doing all the things Peter had been embarrassed about and, in particular, delighting in the company of Peter's baby sister!

> *Judith Sharman, in a review of "Crusher Is Coming!" in* Books for Keeps, *No. 65, November, 1990, p. 8.*

The Red Woollen Blanket (U.S. edition as *The Red Woolen Blanket*) (1987)

The new baby's bright red blanket is treasured, first by her parents and then by Julia herself. She and her blanket become inseparable. "Julia got bigger. Her blanket got smaller." Pieces disappear under lawn mowers, inside her dog and the vacuum cleaner—until that fateful day, Julia's first at school, when the remaining blanket fragment disappears for good. The natural progression of events leading to Julia's maturing and acceptance of her loss will be reassuring to young blanket lovers and their parents. Sharp-eyed youngsters will know where the blanket has gone and just who needs its comfort now. Simple, colorful illustrations humorously depict Julia's world as it expands and the blanket contracts.

> *Elizabeth S. Watson, in a review of "The Red Woolen Blanket," in* The Horn Book Magazine, *Vol. LXIV, No. 3, May-June, 1988, p. 341.*

A light hearted look at a small girl's security blanket from the time it is new and clean until, greatly reduced in size, it disappears forever on her first day at school. This warm hearted domestic tale will reassure small children. Pen and wash drawings show some nice touches of domesticity.

> *Mandy Cheetham, in a review of "The Red Woollen Blanket," in* Magpies, *Vol. 3, No. 3, July, 1988, p. 26.*

In this delightful Burningham-like picture book, full-page pictures vary with two smaller paintings per page as simple, comic bright watercolors follow Julia and her blanket from her birth through her first day at school. She loses little threads of the blanket all the way, but because she is growing up, she hardly misses the last threads. Mother and father are as funny (through somewhat adult lines) as Julia and her dog's antics. The picture of a new-born arriving home from the hospital, sitting up with her head unsupported, is not possible, and some of the British terminology will be unfamiliar to young children ("She slept in her special cot wrapped tight as a parcel"). However, there is enough action to move readers along through seasons and early childhood. This may work for very small group story times, but it is more suited for family enjoyment.

> *Susannah Price, in a review of "The Red Woolen Blanket," in* School Library Journal, *Vol. 34, No. 11, August, 1988, p. 81.*

Has Anyone Here Seen William? (1988)

Here we have another typical Bob Graham family, complete with dog. This time the focus is two year old William who wanders off together with his small wind-up bear. Small pictures show each situation building up until William's absence is noted, then in a double-page spread William is found. Wonderful observation of people and animals, gentle humour and a delightful warmth combine to make another gem of a book. Don't miss the endpapers.

> *Jo Goodman, in a review of "Has Anyone Here Seen William?" in* Magpies, *Vol. 3, No. 4, September, 1988, p. 25.*

Mixed media illustrations that have action, humor, and a raffish use of flyaway line provide most of the impact in a picture book with a direct text that serves as foil to the pictured excesses of a child's second year. His parents and three siblings repeatedly sound the alarm with the title question; William, increasingly mobile, staggers about getting into minor—usually messy—difficulties. The book ends with William, at the end of a hard day of birthday celebration, hunted yet again and found by his patient parents, curled up asleep in the dog's basket in the kitchen. The catalogue of antics should please the read-aloud audience, who will no doubt sympathize with William's ability to get into trouble with no deliberate intent and no real harm to anyone.

> *Zena Sutherland, in a review of "Has Anyone Here Seen William?" in* Bulletin of the Center for Children's Books, *Vol. 42, No. 9, May, 1989, p. 224.*

Although the plots in Bob Graham's books tend to be fairly tame, any excursion into one of his delightful picture book worlds inevitably leaves readers feeling rather windblown, for the subtle entropy of family life takes over. From the moment, for example, that little William takes his first wobbly step, his two parents and three siblings have no peace. "Wind him up and off he would go. Nothing stopped him until his energy ran out." The frequent apprehensively posed query "Has anyone here seen William?" usually precedes a loud crash. Bedrooms are transformed into chaos; refrigerator contents serve as a midnight snack for William and the family dog; and similar mishaps abound. The familiar pursuit of a dogged toddler becomes even more amusing in the droll, colorful illustrations depicting William on the go in various unlikely situations. Even children without younger, active siblings should thoroughly enjoy the antics. (pp. 356-57)

> *Karen Jameyson, in a review of "Has Anyone Here Seen William?" in* The Horn Book Magazine, *Vol. LXV, No. 3, May-June, 1989, pp. 356-57.*

Grandad's Magic (1989)

In his latest work, Graham has created a magic of his own through sprightly watercolors and the enchantment of a story of family tradition and old age warmly told. Sunday lunch always includes Grandma and Grandad, Grandad's tricks, and Mom's precious china dogs, down from the mantle to protect the fruit on the lunch table—until Grandad attempts his former "best trick" of pulling the tablecloth out from under everything on the table—including the china dogs. All ends well, but from then on, lunch is served on plastic plates on place mats, while the precious china dogs remain on the mantle. Despite the changes, the aura of magic and the caring familial bonds remain, as does Grandad's mischievous spirit. This gentle tale of age and family, affectionately and humorously expressed, is sure to amuse children. Although some of the pictures are small, the flow of both text and art will make this a charmer for story hours.

> *Cathy Woodward, in a review of "Grandad's Magic," in* School Library Journal, *Vol. 35, No. 15, November, 1989, p. 82.*

Family warmth and security always characterize Bob Graham's work and **Grandad's Magic** has all those deft Graham touches—the miscellany of chairs at the family dinner table, the thin long-suffering smile of Mum's face as her precious ornaments descend floorwards, and the ubiquitous, but convenient dog, for whom virtue isn't enough reward. Grandad's magic tricks are very trying and daughter's emulation looks like testing family solidarity in the future, but the love across generations and the acceptance of people, foibles and all, lingers satisfyingly.

> *Jenni Connor, in a review of "Grandad's Magic," in* Magpies, *Vol. 5, No. 2, May, 1990, p. 22.*

Bob Graham's Grandad reminds me of Margaret Mahy's Great-Uncle Magnus, and adults whose fun-loving antics incur parental disapproval are always popular with children. The comic plot of this highly enjoyable story is enhanced by Graham's tongue-in-cheek style and use of understatement. Don't miss the subtle characterization of Rupert the dog.

> *V. Taylor, in a review of "Grandad's Magic," in* Books for Your Children, *Vol. 25, No. 3, Autumn-Winter, 1990, p. 11.*

[Bob Graham's] low-keyed family dramas are continually enhancing the art of the picture book. In **Grandad's Magic** Graham turns an ordinary domestic chronicle into a story that captures the pleasant, unpredictable minutiae of everyday life. Few authors are so independent in their approach, so free from the need to borrow from earlier books.

The principal actors are Grandad (who is teaching Allie to juggle), Allie (his young granddaughter), Allie's mother (who decorates her Sunday dinner table with two cher-

From Has Anyone Here Seen William?, *written and illustrated by Bob Graham.*

ished figurines), and Rupert (the dog who is so attached to his overstuffed chair that he leaves it only for dinner and trips to the toilet). When Allie begins to master her juggling trick, Grandad is prompted to display a long-dormant skill: removing the tablecloth without removing the dishes. His performance is a near-success, but he sends an orange careening into a figurine and the figurine bouncing onto Rupert's broad back. This episode is really an excuse for filling the book's pages with subtle truths about families.

Graham's linear style looks hesitant, unsure, but is really conceived with unmistakable certainty. In fact his line "talks" to us. About Rupert and his chair it says: "These forms are frumpy, but I need to define that frumpiness—frumpy Rupert as distinct from frumpy chair. So I'll doodle and diddle a little around Rupert's ear and tail but keep the frowziness of the chair smoother—a little more even and continuous but never so slick that it looks new or foam-filled." The whole book has this capacity to express Graham's keen interest in what he is defining. Parents, grandparents, children—they are all drawn with a tender, tenuous line that acknowledges the differences in things. And there is so much hard-to-describe affection, whether Allie rushes to greet new arrivals, or a towel is placed under little brother's chair, or Dad accidentally places his coffee spoon in his slipper. Such details match the story and extend it.

> *Donnarae MacCann and Olga Richard, in a review of "Grandad's Magic," in* Wilson Li-

brary Bulletin, *Vol. 65, No. 4, December, 1990, p. 121.*

Greetings from Sandy Beach (1990)

Bob Graham is a past master at the portrayal of warm, family relationships shown with a clear-sighted fondness. The qualities for which his books have been valued in the past are shown in abundance in *Greetings from Sandy Beach.* This is a wonderful story of a family holiday which begins with tears all round (and they are only going away for a weekend!) and ends with development having taken place in each of the characters. Written in the first person with an absolutely sure touch, the words capture with complete authenticity the way a child thinks, speaks and observes. The text works beautifully alone but is enhanced by the vitality and fun of the illustrations, which are understated yet expressive, packed with detail but not too busy or cluttered. It is through these that the reader receives a great deal of the story. Graham makes extensive use of humour which is directed at both adult and child readers, but which is never condescending or patronising.

This is a book which works well on a number of levels, has a great deal of social comment, a theme of the importance of the development of community spirit and a clear message of not judging people by appearances. It is a book to reflect on, and to return to, time and again.

> *A review of "Greetings from Sandy Beach," in* Reading Time, *Vol. XXXV, No. III, 1991, p. 4.*

A delightful tale of one family's camping holiday at the beach, a beach they share with a bus load of school children and a motorcycle gang, the Disciples of Death.

Told through the eyes of a child, this book should be enjoyed by children of many ages. Young children will relate to the holiday itself, from the tearful farewells and the never-ending trip to the arrival at the beach. Older children will empathise with the embarrassment felt by the main character when she is seen with her parents by other school children.

The illustrations should also draw a chuckle or two, particularly the girl changing her clothes in a tent while being unknowingly watched by other school children.

An enjoyable book, deserving of its "shortlist" status. Recommended for 5-8 year olds.

Renya Spratt, in a review of "Greetings from Sandy Beach," in Magpies, *Vol. 6, No. 3, July, 1991, p. 28.*

A seemingly doomed camping trip at the seashore turns into a sunny vacation in this wacky picture book by the creator of **Crusher Is Coming!** and **The Red Woolen Blanket.** When a family reaches its campsite only to find a gang of motorbikers called the Disciples of Death, Dad thinks things look bleak—"Don't go near them," he warns. But outward appearances prove misleading as the "bikies" help Dad set up the tent, play in the sand and pass out raspberry popsicles. Graham's matter-of-fact text, peppered with the daughter's flavorful observations, reads much like a long, comical postcard. The full-color paintings feature crayon accents that impart a breezy, slightly slapdash air. Black dot eyes and bulbous noses go a long way to enhance the cast of innocent and congenial characters. But most pleasing of all, the book's child protagonist—unburdened by any preconceived notions—never sees the Disciples as a threat, and eventually Dad learns this valuable lesson, too.

A review of "Greetings from Sandy Beach," in Publishers Weekly, *Vol. 239, No. 7, February 3, 1992, p. 80.*

The Children's Book Council of Australia's "Picture Book of the Year" (1990) is a delightfully offbeat portrayal of a family of four at the beach for the weekend, with details that are perfectly plausible yet unlike the usual clichés. At the campsite, the neighbors on one side are the "Disciples of Death," a booted, unwholesome-looking trio with a small dog in goggles and a blanket draped over their motorcycles in lieu of a tent. "Stay away," warn the parents—but the Disciples are the first to pitch in when help is needed, and by the second night they're all chatting companionably together. Meanwhile, the adults have genially joined in the children's imaginative play and the narrator has also made friends with the most truculent of a busload of schoolchildren, camping with their teacher. With his own unique style, Graham rivals James Stevenson in his ability to conjure a scene or a character in a few deft, relaxed lines. A worthwhile message presented in a comically realistic vignette with lots of child appeal.

A review of "Greetings from Sandy Beach," in

Kirkus Reviews, *Vol. LX, No. 4, February 15, 1992, p. 254.*

Rose Meets Mr. Wintergarten (1992)

The familiar scenario of rapprochement with an elderly curmudgeon gets a new spin: The Summers fill their garden with flowers; children Rose, Faith, and Baby Blossom join their parents each day to enjoy the sunrise from the roof. Meanwhile, under the gray clouds next door, Mr. Wintergarten's creepy home lurks behind barbed wire. Despite her friends' scary stories, Rose braves the forbidding mansion to request a lost ball, taking along flowers and cookies. Softened in spite of himself, the old man begins to engage in a bit of ballplaying over the fence.

The exaggerations, especially as extended in Graham's illustrations, move the story into myth: Rose/Persephone, confronting the dour Wintergarten against a bleak sweep of gray, recalls John Burningham's splendid visualizations of his mythic stories; the deft pen and watercolor sketches here are also notable for their gentle, winsome humor. Another imaginative contribution from this fine Australian artist.

A review of "Rose Meets Mr. Wintergarten," in Kirkus Reviews, *Vol. LX, No. 19, May 15, 1992, p. 669.*

With humor and insight, Graham's text authentically conveys the language and emotions of childhood. Without being heavy-handed, Rose challenges some confining stereotypes in the name of humanity. Graham's bright ink-and-watercolor illustrations portray the Summers family as a likable hippie brood—Mom wears a Gandhi-like robe with sandals and a headband; the children are named Rose, Faith and Blossom—and Rose's dot-eyed innocence speaks volumes.

A review of "Rose Meets Mr. Wintergarten," in Publishers Weekly, *Vol. 239, No. 26, June 8, 1992, p. 62.*

Graham's characters are, in one sense, overly familiar, but in some details quite original. His Rose is like countless literary cherubs who have won over the hearts of Scrooge and other curmudgeons. She loses her ball in the neighbor's tangled shrubbery and fears an encounter unless her mother watches from the gate. Mr. Wintergarten, as it turns out, is thoroughly redeemable—hardly a devourer of children, as rumor has it.

But while Rose's adventure reads like a rehash, still this child has no affinity with the boring pages of "Dick and Jane." Graham juxtaposes the chilly life-style of Wintergarten (dark house, chained dog, disgusting lunch) with the positive, creative behavior of the Summers family (generous gift-giving, elaborate garden-planning, unique ritual-making, as in the gatherings on the rooftop at sunrise). Nonconformity is suggested by father's enormous beard, mother's jazzy headband, and the ram and chicken that serve as pets.

Pictorially Graham reiterates his concern with the quality of life. Color is used for a sparkling, brilliant effect. Raw colors are played off muted greens and ochers to produce a jewellike aura, and thin, squiggly lines are used for carefree outlines and accents. Portraits are handled with simplicity, but little mannerisms come through, as when the children clasp their hands together in anxiety. Mr. Wintergarten sometimes resembles his growling dog and is sometimes depicted as a continuous black shape, including a long shadow in the same color. The portraits are persuasive and prepare us for the grand transformation from haunted house to spacious playground. Mr. W. uproots his cacti and barbed wire and plays soccer with the best.

Graham always offers his readers an innocent, appealing population, people anyone would welcome as next-door neighbors.

> *Donnarae MacCann and Olga Richard, in a review of "Rose Meets Mr. Wintergarten," in* Wilson Library Bulletin, *Vol. 67, No. 1, September, 1992, p. 91.*

Roderick Haig-Brown

1908-1976

English-born Canadian author of fiction.

Major works include *Silver: The Life Story of an Atlantic Salmon* (1931), *Panther* (1934; U.S. edition as *Ki-yu: A Story of Panthers*), *Starbuck Valley Winter* (1943), *Saltwater Summer* (1948), *The Whale People* (1963).

The following entry presents general criticism of Haig-Brown's career. It also includes a selection of reviews to supplement the general criticism.

Regarded as one of the finest prose stylists in Canadian literature, Haig-Brown wrote several acclaimed novels for adolescent readers that have led to his recognition as a pioneer in the development of juvenile literature in Canada. These writings, which include and often interweave animal biographies, adventure stories, and historical fiction, are noted for their authentic depictions of the Canadian wilderness and its wildlife. An avid hunter, fisherman, and conservationist, Haig-Brown drew upon his familiarity with the woods and rivers of Canada's Pacific coast to create stories that, according to Ruth Osler, "show by influence and direct telling the results of a long, deliberate and intelligent observation of the natural world and a deep respect for its laws and customs." The author's two animal biographies, *Silver: The Life Story of an Atlantic Salmon* and *Ki-yu: A Story of Panthers,* are imbued with his love of nature and appreciation for the beauty of the western Canadian landscape. Commentators note that these works contain enough factual information to be of interest to adults, yet captivate young people, who respond to their engaging adventure scenes. Haig-Brown also wrote coming-of-age stories, *Starbuck Valley Winter* prominent among them, that reveal his widely praised insight into adolescent thought and emotion. W. J. Keith notes that most of Haig-Brown's juvenile fiction features "boy-heroes [who] embark upon personal voyages of discovery," adding that themes of exploration and self-discovery are common elements in the author's works. In the wilderness adventures of his young protagonists, Haig-Brown explores themes of friendship, courage, integrity, and strength among characters who largely reflect his own love and respect for the land. Although some critics have objected to what they view as the author's excessively graphic depiction of the bloodshed caused by predatory animals in such works as *Ki-yu,* and others have lamented the glaring lack of noteworthy female characters in his fiction, most commentators commend Haig-Brown for his unsentimental and realistic portrayal of the harshness of life in the wild. Describing Haig-Brown as "an undisputed giant of Canadian children's literature," Jon C. Stott maintains that the author's adolescent novels are "important treatments of a significant aspect of the Canadian experience: the human encounter with the grandeur and danger of the natural environment."

Haig-Brown was born in England, where his uncles intro-

duced him to hunting, sparking his lifelong interest in wildlife. At the age of eighteen he traveled to Canada's Pacific coast region, working in a logging camp and as a trapper and guide for the next three years. At twenty-one Haig-Brown returned to England, where he wrote his first book, *Silver,* for a young acquaintance to whom the story is dedicated and narrated. The book depicts a salmon's life cycle and the events in its annual journey upriver to spawn. Two years later, Haig-Brown's homesickness for the Canadian northwest led him to move to Vancouver Island, which he made his permanent home and where he served as a Provincial Magistrate and Judge in Children's and Family Court from 1941-1975. In Canada, Haig-Brown continued to write and publish. His second book, like *Silver,* is an animal biography: *Ki-yu* follows the lives of a Vancouver Island panther and the bounty hunter who stalks him. Haig-Brown defended the novel against charges that its depiction of the violence in nature is too graphic, arguing that children should not be misled about the reality of life-and-death struggles in nature. In *Starbuck Valley Winter* Haig-Brown is praised for convincingly depicting a young man's struggle to accept the responsibilities of adulthood. The story involves sixteen-year-old Don Morgan's efforts to earn money for a fishing boat by spending a summer trapping martens in the woods of British Columbia. Similarly, in *The Whale People,* one of Haig-Brown's most widely praised works, Atlin, son of the chief of a pre-Columbian tribe of whale hunters, assumes the leadership of his people after his father dies during a whale hunt; the novel traces his growth as he develops the leadership abilities he needs in his new role as chief. *The Whale People* has been praised for its carefully researched portrayal of the region's tribal life, and is particularly commended for examining the connection between the tribe's physical dependence on the whales that they hunt and their spiritual relationship to all of nature. Haig-Brown also wrote several acclaimed works of fiction and nonfiction for adults on similar subjects and themes. He received the Canadian Library Association Award for best juvenile fiction for *Starbuck Valley Winter* in 1947 and for *The Whale People* in 1964, the Governor General's Award for best juvenile fiction for *Saltwater Summer* in 1948, and the Canadian Authors Association's Vicky Metcalf Award for his body of juvenile fiction in 1965.

(See also *Contemporary Literary Criticism,* Vol. 21; *Something about the Author,* Vol. 12; *Major Authors and Illustrators for Children and Young Adults; Contemporary Authors,* Vols. 5-8, 69-72; *Contemporary Authors New Revision Series,* Vols. 4, 38; and *Dictionary of Literary Biography,* Vol. 88.)

AUTHOR'S COMMENTARY

[The following excerpt is from an interview by Glenys Stow.]

STOW: W. O. Mitchell has suggested that a man can only write with validity about the terrain and experiences of his childhood. It seems to me that you have proved him to be wrong. Do you think that your long training as a naturalist and a quiet, perceptive observer has given you, though an adult, an ability to feel for a new landscape in a way that normally only a child can do in his native environment?

HAIG-BROWN: W. O. Mitchell is right of course, as he usually is, and I do very often feel a sadness that I didn't experience a childhood in the country of my adoption. But when I came [to Canada] first, I was still pretty young and I had some intensely happy years without any serious responsibility. I worked when I felt like working and for the rest, I enjoyed the country; I went out to hunt and fish and try this and that and the other thing with no great sense that I had to make some life work of it; simply that all was experiment and was new experience. This, I suspect, is something very like a childhood in that the senses, accepting newness, are very acute.

I had, in a sense, been reborn and I was learning very, very fast so that I could adapt to all the newness and find my way among it with confidence and certainty. In order to feel at home I had to learn as rapidly as possible something about the trees, plant life, the birds and fish and wildlife and all the other natural things about me. This sort of need inevitably sharpens observation.

STOW: A child's eye for the truth of his surroundings

takes him beyond surface detail, doesn't it? In your preface to *Panther* you state your conviction that

> nothing in nature, so long as it is honestly observed and honestly described, can harm the mind of a child. Almost all the ills of the human race may be traced to the fact that it has strayed too much from nature and knows too little of the natural order of things. Conceal from children, if you will, the baseness of man. But let them read and understand the ways of animals and birds, of water and wind and earth; for these things are pure and true and unspoiled.

Your books for children are entertaining, by your own definition of that word; they contain sustenance for the mind. But don't you also write in the hope of showing adults and children an older way of life which is more basic, more traditional, more spiritual than their own?

HAIG-BROWN: I do, most intensely, want to let people know, whether they are adults or children, something of the way the life of the world, apart from humans, is. I don't think that it is necessarily true that natural life, wildlife or human life lived close to it is more basic or more traditional than civilised human life of cities. It has its own values and its own messages, its own lessons. But enormous numbers of people do live in cities, remote from most forms of natural life. They go out into the countryside at certain times of the year, on holiday, and see various things that have meaning or value for them, but one wonders and is concerned as to how deeply they see into the meaning of those lives about them, whether they are lives of trees and plants, or lives of animals or lives of fish. I would like all people to see and understand more because there is both pleasure and fulfillment in seeing and understanding, and because the only hope of preserving the natural world is in the deep understanding of people. What I would like most of all is for the city people to be observant of the very large areas of natural life that exist in cities. Opportunities for observation are frequent, almost constant and I think are largely unused and thereby much pleasure and much satisfaction is lost and wasted. Yet I cannot say that I have, or would want to have any aim as positive as this. I want to describe what I have seen and felt myself, in such a way that the sensations and values are fully conveyed. If this is done in any significant degree at all, the writer's mission is essentially fulfilled. What people do with it from there is beyond his control and so it should be because the purpose is to reveal, stimulate, excite, develop and share, not to dictate or control.

STOW: Your descriptions of fish and animal life certainly give the reader vicarious opportunities to observe in a breadth and detail that most of us have neither the skill nor the chance to practise. You also make the natural cycle so engrossing that we can sense the drama in life-death pattern of a salmon's journey, for example, or of a panther's struggle for survival. Your first children's book, *Silver: The Story of an Atlantic Salmon* (1931) which is structurally based on this cycle, has both qualities, observation and drama, as has your book on a similar topic written ten years later, *Return to the River* (1941). Could you give us some ideas on what makes one a story for children and the other an adult book? Or would you say that the dividing line between the two is in fact rather nebulous?

HAIG-BROWN: As the dedication explains, *Silver* was written deliberately as a child's story. *Return to the River* was not. *Silver* was my first book and, while I was extremely anxious to get away from anthropomorphism, I was still far too much influenced by writers like Fortescu who wrote *The Story of a Red Deer* and Charles Kingsley's *Water Babies* and so on. The book, I think, is somewhat too cute. In spite of this, it has been, over a long period of time, quite consistently popular with both adults and children; except for a brief period during the War when no paper was available, it has never been out of print.

Return to The River was an all-out attempt to tell an animal story as it should be told with as much reference as possible to the real way of life of the animal and as little as possible to human comparisons. There are no concessions to simplicity, concreteness, or anything else that I would normally consider desirable in writing for children. The result, of course, is a book that children can appreciate just as well as adults because children, like adults, become interested in a subject very much in proportion to the intensity with which it is examined and discussed. I think it is right to say that the dividing line between the two books is somewhat nebulous, if only because so many adults read and enjoy *Silver*. *Return To The River* is simply a much stronger and more firmly thought out book than *Silver* and the research behind it was far better informed. The subject, though complex, is not difficult, and I would assume that *Return* would appeal to somewhat older children than *Silver.*

STOW: Does the fact that *Silver* is set in Britain and *Return to The River* in Canada affect anything more than the landscape and natural life described? Does it make a difference to the mood of the story, or the conclusions drawn?

HAIG-BROWN: I would think that the difference in my own age and stage of maturity made more and greater difference between *Silver* and *Return* than the difference in setting. At the same time I was aware that the setting of *Return* had a certain grandeur and the fish themselves, in their massive abundance, were an altogether bigger and more impressive story than the smaller run of the smaller river in Great Britain. So, I would say the mood is substantially different and I would suspect that the conclusions left to the reader would be somewhat different too since I had, in *Return,* a more sophisticated concept of salmon as a massive and important resource.

STOW: Of your second children's book, *Ki-yu: A Story of Panthers* (1934) you note a critic as objecting to the number of killings involved in the tale. Violence appears often in your stories, especially in those which focus on hunting by animal or human predators. In view of the concern which is often voiced about the effect of T.V. violence on children, what are your feelings about death and injury as topics in juvenile fiction, and what are some of the problems facing a writer who handles these experiences?

HAIG-BROWN: *Ki-yu (Panther)* was not written for children, though it does seem to have been adopted by children and for children. It was intended to be a realistic tale of a wild animal and it was intended again to get away from the cuteness and anthropomorphism that has, in the past, been too much associated with animal stories. The violence in this and, I hope in my other stories too, is incidental to the story itself and to conceal it or play it down would probably be both dishonest and unsatisfying. T.V. violence is an abomination, played purely for its own sake, its own kicks and thrills and it is essentially false 90% of the time. This is evil in itself and I have no doubt that its effects are evil. Death and injury, which are things incidental to life, so long as they are shown as incidental to life, are topics of great importance for children as well as for anybody else. Honesty, I think, is the key word here. If you are using violence as a showpiece to attract readers, it has to be wrong. If you are using it in the attempt to show something as it really is, then your problem is to handle it realistically, without making it too offensive. The impact of the printed word is extremely heavy; heavier than a passing picture and altogether heavier than reality itself where there are always many trivialities that distract. A writer must balance all these considerations with care and adjust his descriptions to give what he feels to be the proper weight and value. To deny death, which is often beautiful, to children, is an offense. To conceal injury and pain is an offense. To exploit either or both is the worst offense of all.

STOW: *Ki-yu* follows the cycle of a panther's life from his conception and the subsequent death of his father at a hunter's hands, through the year and nine months during which his mother cares and hunts for him and his sisters until they too are killed, through his developing maturity, his mating and the battles with other predators, to the inevitable end in aging, sickness, and final destruction by a pack of wolves. During this sequence you describe Ki-yu with knowledge and sympathy, but never become anthropomorphic; and you convey with equal understanding the feelings and experiences of the human hunter who pursues the panther throughout his life. Children's books so often present conflicts in black and white terms. How have you been able to avoid this trap?

HAIG-BROWN: I think the simple answer to the avoidance of black and white thinking is sympathy for both sides. In this particular instance, my first interest is in the wild animal Ki-yu so, clearly, I have the strongest kind of sympathy for him and his doings. But, at the same time, I have personal experience as a hunter and of the hunter's very deep respect and appreciation for his quarry. It seems to me that this is pretty much what life is all about. The hunter has his function although it may be misconceived by some standards. The animal has its indisputable function which it performs inevitably. One does not have to arrive at judgments in such situations as this. It is only necessary to lay them out honestly and sympathetically so that the reader can understand and reach his or her judgment.

STOW: In this book you describe the panthers of Vancouver Island as being relentlessly hunted. Does this still occur today, and is there any danger of their becoming extinct?

HAIG-BROWN: Panthers are not hunted relentlessly any more, in fact they are protected and are recognised as a game animal with a special permit and restricted limits. I don't think they will ever become extinct on Vancouver Island, certainly not by hunting, though the removal of the forests and encroaching civilisation will make things increasingly difficult for them. Fortunately there are always mountains and I don't suppose the encroachment will move very rapidly into them. I discussed this a little in the foreword to the latest edition of *Panther* (Houghton-Mifflin, New York 1973).

STOW: In *Starbuck Valley Winter* (1943) and its sequel *Saltwater Summer* (1948) you describe the adventures of a boy of sixteen who goes, sometimes alone, sometimes with a friend, to manage a trapline in the B.C. mountains and then to skipper a fishing boat along the coast. Returning to my question about the distinction between a child's book and an adult's, aren't you chiefly concerned with mature and independent experience? These novels are exciting to me as a reader because, as well as learning a great deal about the wildlife of B.C., I can identify with someone who is learning to operate as an adult in a dramatic and challenging environment. It seems to me that your children's books are, like those of a number of other excellent writers, really on the borderline of the teenager's world. They are about his becoming a man.

HAIG-BROWN: A child's novel and an adult novel are essentially the same except that in the novel for a child, one tends to emphasise action and concrete situations rather than depending on introspection and complex thought. So, the dividing line really is very slight. In writing *Starbuck Valley Winter* and *Saltwater Summer,* I was looking towards the teen-age market because I had been told that there was a great and serious lack of "good stories" for young people in this age group. For some years I deliberately planned that one book in every three I wrote would be directed to children and I felt this as being something of a responsibility. Young people—let's say between the ages of 12 and 20—are always struggling and striving towards self-realisation in some form or another, so I suspect they are always looking slightly ahead to the next stage of development and wondering about it. I suppose this is why one tends to emphasise the theme of growing up and developing from fairly childish things. This is a struggle that everyone faces and so should have universal appeal.

STOW: You spoke earlier about sensations and values which you hope that readers will experience through your writing. Could you talk more about some of these? Don Morgan certainly has new experiences and acquires new values when he moves from the city to his uncle's farm, and more still when he becomes a hunter and fisherman. Some of these you discuss openly (as in the courtroom episode in *Saltwater Summer,* for example); many more, both sensory and ethical, are implied.

HAIG-BROWN: I find myself wondering, in answering these questions, if I am not doing a little too much rationalisation and self-justification. I have never made it a practise to think about past books; in fact, I have never read a book of mine through once it has been printed and

bound. I refer to them only as my attention is drawn to them by others, then perhaps read a chapter or an essay and leave it at that, once I have determined what the question in the reader's mind is all about. So, we could say that I am not competently self-critical but you, to some extent, are forcing me into it and what I say may not be all that sound. The sort of values one wants to pass on to readers are often more vividly expressed as fresh or first experiences. A child or young adult is always moving into fresh experience and so these things are often best shown through a child's eye. Move a child from the city to the country, or vice versa, and immediately the newness is enhanced and the challenge increased. In writing for children, I would guess that sensory values can be described, but ethical values are much better implied. In fiction writing of any kind, it is always better to show something rather than expound upon it. The perceptive mind of a child facing new experiences is therefore a good means of justifying the description of sensations.

STOW: Friendship, communication, mutual trust, and the responsibilities of one human being towards another seem to me to be very important in your books. In *Starbuck Valley Winter* a hostile and lonely man, Lee Jetson, is brought back to the human community through his association with Don and his friend Tubby. Similar situations are often handled by lesser writers in a stereotyped way ("noble teenagers win the heart of crusty old hermit"), but are you able by the gradual exploration of Jetson's background and actions, and by the balancing weaknesses shown in the boys, to make the result psychologically in writing, or is it simply a pleasant by-product?

HAIG-BROWN: I have always been convinced that it is impossible to hate anyone if you know them really well. I have also had the opportunity of observing quite a number of old trappers and prospectors who had spent a lifetime in the woods and were, shall we say, quite idiosyncratic. All these men had their own stories and their own particular prejudices that one had to respect if there was to be communication. I think I am trying to say that first judgments are by no means always sound and that sympathy, understanding and tolerance can usefully be extended to almost everyone. In a sense, one is describing a relationship between human and human that is somewhat similar to the relationship between human and creature that we discussed earlier. The difference is that here we can come at a happy conclusion, because the humans can communicate effectively.

STOW: Sheila Egoff comments that *Mounted Police Patrol* (1954) is made less compelling than your earlier books by an "overtly moral tone." Could you tell us how this story set in Alberta came to be written? It is an exciting tale, certainly different from your previous ones, and it seems to concern the hunting of men rather than of animals. What do you think of Sheila Egoff's remark about it?

HAIG-BROWN: I was not particularly anxious to write this book but my publishers knew that I had been on loan from the Army to the Mounted Police for a period during the War, and were anxious for me to do something with it. I could not find any really good reason for not doing

Haig-Brown at the age of four.

it and my mind, of course, began to work on details of plot and character and I thought that I could make an interesting book. It may have been unwise to choose a city kid with a chip on his shoulder, but I suppose this comes out of spending so much time on the bench and naturally wondering what would become of an association such as the one examined in the book. The contrast between the values of the policeman and the values of the boy inevitably lead to too much moralising, and I wouldn't question that Sheila Egoff is right in her assessment. My purpose was not to moralise but to demonstrate the life of an R.C.M.P. constable in a small rural detachment. By centering the interest in the boy, possibly I overbalanced this somewhat but the essential theme still remains and I do feel a considerable resentment at the failure in understanding there can be between young people and police and vice-versa. It strikes me often as totally unnecessary and purely the product of failing to know each other. These sort of feelings too would help to set the moralising tone of the book which, of course, I regret.

STOW: In the fifties you widened your field more than geographically, and produced a volume in the "Great Stories of Canada" series, entitled *Captain of the Discovery: The Story of Captain George Vancouver* (1956). In 1960

and 1962 you went further into the historical field with *The Farthest Shores* and *Fur and Gold,* originally commissioned as C.B.C. dramas about British Columbia's past. What new problems did the writing and dramatizing of history present to you?

HAIG-BROWN: John Gray, of Macmillan, one of Canada's truly great publishing men, talked me into doing the life of George Vancouver. I forget now just what his grounds of argument were but I would assume it was because I know something of the Pacific Coast. One of the problems with work of this type is the need for intensive research. I had some experience of this in working on matters connected with natural history but this was rather different. One becomes fascinated with historical research and the temptation to probe more and more deeply is so great that the question arises "when does one cut off the research and get to the writing?" My instinct always is to go to original sources and I generally feel that in incidental and contemporaneous things like diaries and journals of the explorers matters are better told than they could ever be re-told. In my first attempt at *Captain of the Discovery,* I tried to write practically the whole thing directly depending on quotes from Vancouver's journals. John Gray was not a bit happy with this and persuaded me that it was best to get away from the direct documentary approach. By shifting, I probably changed the age group for which the book is best suited and it is now usually read by younger children than I had anticipated. I get many reactions from them, nearly all favorable but, for at least a few, where it is required reading in the schools, it is a little too heavy still. I am not sure there is much one can do about this except hope that they will develop themselves, because the book really is not difficult. *The Farthest Shores* and *Fur and Gold* presented a problem in the question of technique. As you say, these books were originally developed as radio plays. I felt that one way of making them available for children would be to leave them in dramatic form and let the teacher assign parts in the classroom. I adopted this method with *The Farthest Shores* and I am not too satisfied that it was successful. At all events, Helen O'Reilly and I decided to change and *Fur and Gold* is written in simply literary narrative, or more nearly so anyway. I had intended to convert *The Farthest Shores* to this form and to continue with one, and possibly two other volumes in the series but have never really had the heart to do this, partly because I have become so very busy in Court in the past ten years. I enjoy history very much, especially local B.C. history but I do find the writing of it is quite confining and I should not care to be limited in this way very much of the time. In fact, one of the things I do search for, more than anything else, is the freedom to let imagination range.

STOW: Your best known historical fiction, and according to many critics your best book, is *The Whale People* (1962) which won the Canadian Association of Children's Librarians Book-of-the-Year Award in 1964 (as *Starbuck Valley Winter* had done in 1947). This story about the Hotsath tribe of coastal B.C. who shaped their lives around the pursuit of the whale tells in gripping detail what it feels like to leap onto a sperm whale's back from the bow-thwart of a canoe, and to thrust at him with a shell-tipped lance. Could you tell us about the research which you did in preparation for this book?

HAIG-BROWN: *The Whale People* is a good example of an effort to get away and free the imagination from all restrictions. I deliberately chose to set the story in a prehistoric time which would force me to exercise my imagination with the restriction of only a limited amount of fact. I used a number of sources for the technical details of whaling equipment and the life of the tribes. Philip Drucker's *Northern and Central Nootkan Tribes* was of great importance to me and so also was Alice Ernst's *Wolf Ritual of the North West Coast.* Curtis' pictures were a help to me and so was John Newett's narrative of his captivity among the Nootkas. I had a good deal of other material including a good account of Makah Indian whaling equipment which is essentially similar to Nootka. I spent some time on the Quinault River with an Indian friend who had one of the last ocean-going canoes and a crew to go along with him in search of sea mammals, though they did not hunt whales. From him I got some of the feeling of the sea hunt. Incidentally, he was a Hoh River man, not a Quinault River man, though we worked the Quinault together. The Hoh River people are close to the Makahs but, he told me, hunted whales only for sport and prestige, not for subsistence.

STOW: What I like best about *The Whale People,* apart from the impressive sensory effect of the fishing scenes in it, is the way in which you immerse the reader in the tribal life so that he feels and understands it from the inside. Atlin's visits to his ancestors' shrine, for example, and his imitation in the nearby pool of the swimming movements of the whale, are described with a seriousness and sympathy which make the reader forget his own world and think only of the symbolic meaning of these actions for the boy. The reader also quickly comes to understand the relationship in this culture between man and the animal world. "I do not despise (the whales)" says Nitgass, chief of the tribe, "I love them as my brothers. That is why they take my harpoon and swim quietly to the beach with it." You mentioned earlier your sense of the unity between man and the land about him. Is this feeling widespread among hunters and fishermen, or do you think it is stronger among our native people, perhaps because it is part of their religious view of life?

HAIG-BROWN: Sense of unity between any primitive people depending upon hunting and fishing and the land and the wild creatures they depend on is very strong indeed. It is, of necessity, strong in any good hunter and any good fisherman. The native Indian concepts of the creatures they hunted and fished for were intimate and very beautiful. They were also quite highly self-centered, as one would expect. There was the idea of return, replenishment, replacement. There was a sense of equality rather than superiority, of a shared humanness rather than two alien natures. All these concepts I find very touching and very beautiful and I imagine, under the circumstances of those early lives, very useful. I feel no difficulty at all identifying with Atlin in his observation of the whale rituals and the other preparation for the hunt. I do not find, and never have found, any great difficulty with the concept of

animals as equal life, even though different. I believe that by cultivating it, we can carry our sense of unity with natural things to a much higher plane than even the Indians were able to achieve. Every good hunter (and in the word "hunter" I of course include fisherman) is or should be acutely aware of the whole environment of his quarry and that includes other animals which may or may not have interdependent lives. These things are sharpened by the intensity of hunting and fishing but, at the same time, it is quite possible to go beyond this and escape the somewhat narrow focus of the hunter and fisherman, extending the intensity to everything. Sophisticated thinking is by no means hostile to emotional concepts, and love of the land and the creatures of the land is by no means hostile to religious concepts. The native Indian people at their best use both concepts to the full, as have all culturally developed people. Neither Indian nor white has any monopoly of these sensitivities and both can learn from each other.

STOW: Structurally *The Whale People* is like *Starbuck Valley Winter* and *Saltwater Summer* in that, because Atlin's father dies when the boy is still young, he is forced to put his early training into practice and make himself into a man and a whale-chief. His rapidly increasing physical skill and his growing maturity in his relationships with his friends and followers is an important aspect of his becoming adult, but the story ends at the point when Atlin resolves a conflict with a neighbouring chief and is about to send a robe of sea-otter skins to him as a token of his desire to marry the chief's daughter. In human life marriage marks the point at which childhood decisively ends; would you say that the discussion of man/woman relationships is inappropriate for a children's book?

HAIG-BROWN: I certainly do not think that discussion of man/woman relationships is inappropriate for a children's book. Such discussion may or may not be necessary to the story one wants to tell and I should assume that today one could be much freer, if it were necessary to be so, in discussing this sort of thing than would have been the case ten years ago. Explicit accounts of sexual activities may be entertaining, but they are not usually important in advancing a story. It was necessary for Atlin to develop his interest in the chief's daughter to enable me to tell my essential story, which is this: after successfully solving the problems of leadership and physical achievement, the next step in his chieftainship was a move into the more difficult and subtle diplomatic fields. These were a real and well understood part of Indian life on this coast before the coming of white people and it seems to me that a book that did not recognise them would be in some way rather hollow. By establishing it, I feel the book is given new and stronger dimension and a more accurate picture of what that kind of life was all about. I have no idea how close I have come to getting inside the mind of a young, high-class Indian boy in pre-contact times. I suspect not very close because there is a vast difference in conditioning between us. George Clutesi read the book and said: "I can tell you are a very sincere man." I take that to mean, "you have tried honestly, but you have really not got inside our thinking." (pp. 12-21)

STOW: As a final question, could you say which of your

children's books you most enjoyed writing, and which you feel is your best work?

HAIG-BROWN: I think I enjoyed writing **The Whale People** most of all because, as I have said, it allowed free range for the imagination and speculation. This background information was at once a control and a stimulation to the imagination and one just had to watch a little closely how one directed it. I also felt very close to Atlin and his father in their thinking and in their hopes and fears.

Starbuck Valley Winter has probably been by far my most popular children's book and both it and **Saltwater Summer** have probably been more widely read than any of the others. I enjoyed writing them, as I have enjoyed writing all my books and, as I have told many people, many times, the best book is always the next book.

Answering these questions has been a most interesting exercise but I say again that I have very grave suspicions about myself as a self-critic. There is a great temptation to make it all sound good. Writing a book is a conscious act—planning and developing story and character are also conscious performances in greater or lesser degree; but there is not much doubt that many things of which the writer is little aware can influence him greatly. (p. 22)

> *Roderick Haig-Brown and Glenys Stow, in an interview in* Canadian Children's Literature, *No. 2, 1975, pp. 9-22.*

Ellen Lew Buell

[**Ki-yu: A Story of Panthers**] is a superbly written biography of a panther, Ki-Yu, the strongest, craftiest and most arrogant of all the vicious blackstreak panthers on Vancouver Island; but it is also a story of the wild life of the northern forests told with the veracity of a man who has known this life for a long time, and who can translate the majesty as well as the cruelty of the eternal struggle for existence among animals into vivid, swinging prose.

Ki-Yu's life was comparatively free of this struggle, for with his splendid physique he could kill with deadly accuracy and speed, but he needed all his cunning and knowledge to outwit the hunter who tracked him again and again over a period of years. It is this long-drawn-out duel between man and beast which is the backbone of the narrative, and it is a fitting conclusion that neither wins, for Ki-Yu, still in his prime, but crippled after a vicious fight with another panther, half-blinded by a shot from an enraged farmer, falls a victim to a pack of desperate wolves.

The conviction of the story is augmented by the author's objective treatment of his subject. With the woodsman's realism he wastes little space in conjecture on animal thought, but relies on his knowledge of habit and instinct to portray the panthers hunting, killing, playing or roaming in that apparently aimless wandering which has such sound instincts to guide it.

The book is, unfortunately, too long. It would have been more effective in condensed form, as much of the detail is repetitious, adding little to the original concept of the tale,

so that the attention slackens at intervals. Nevertheless, it is, on the whole, a fine and vigorous story, which should appeal equally to sportsmen and older young people.

> *Ellen Lew Buell, in a review of "Ki-Yu: A Story of Panthers," in* The New York Times Book Review, *February 24, 1935, p. 10.*

Anne T. Eaton

Roderick Haig-Brown, whose **Return to the River** is remembered with pleasure by lovers of the out-of-doors, now tells of a 16-year-old boy's winter in an unexplored valley. [In **Starbuck Valley Winter,**] Don Morgan had trapping, fishing, hunting and a love for the wilderness in his blood; rather than taking a job in the local fish cannery, his choice was to spend the winter in Starbuck Valley trapping for marten. With any luck he would make enough to buy his own Diesel boat to use for salmon fishing in the spring. The boy was self-reliant and a good shot, but he never trapped marten, and a solitary winter in the wilderness presented probable difficulties, even hardship, to the inexperienced.

He found a partner in Tubby Miller, younger and less experienced than himself, but if Tubby, whose naturally cheerful disposition suffered somewhat from the discomfort and difficulties of life in the open, was at times a responsibility, he was also a trustworthy companion, and there was a genuine friendship between the two boys.

How they made their way into the wilds, using Don's canoe, repaired the cabin in which they were to live and ran the trap lines; how the trapping proceeded, though not too successfully at first; how Don, much against Tubby's will, made friends with their nearest neighbor, Lee Jetson, a mysterious trapper of unsavory reputation, with results that were astonishing in several ways, make a story packed full of the kind of incident and adventure which boys enjoy.

In addition, the book is full of the feeling of out-of-doors; the scent of pine and fir; the motion of swift, dark rivers breaking into "white water"; the life of wild animals that are fierce and cunning and brave and also beautiful. Quietly and without effort the author brings his characters to life. We know Don's Uncle Joe, who was "slow and quiet and happy," who "liked his farm and Starbuck country and the color of maple leaves in the fall, and the black leaf-mold of his new clearings in the alders"; Aunt Maud, who was kinder than she seemed; and Lee Jetson, whose wary reserve fell before Don's straightforward friendliness. Throughout the book the author manages to put before us Don's problems and ambitions, his pride in being independent, his determination, his adventures and his triumphs, from a boy's standpoint. A book that boys from 12 to 15 will enjoy and one that they should not miss.

> *Anne T. Eaton, "Trapper's Winter," in* The New York Times Book Review, *November 14, 1943, p. 6.*

Alice M. Jordan

The boy who is the central figure in **Starbuck Valley Winter** is found in this new book [**Saltwater Summer**] with the summer fishing fleet off British Columbia. Don Morgan had always wanted to get away on his own and fish. In the "Mallard" he had a chance to do this and to buffet the backbreaking swells in the storms on that rugged coast. The story is full of the hazards of the sea, the disappointment of poor fishing, the fortunate breaks which sometimes come. Roderick Haig-Brown writes skillfully and with authority, not only of a fisherman's chances, but of a seventeen-year-old boy, carrying a personal worry, and learning to work with hard-bitten men and to know their characters. Don makes good and his story is well worth reading.

> *Alice M. Jordan, in a review of "Saltwater Summer," in* The Horn Book Magazine, *Vol. XXIV, No. 5, September-October, 1948, p. 376.*

John Birks

It is pleasant to encounter every now and again an author who is strongly in sympathy with adolescents, in their emotional and spiritual difficulties, an author who is clearly sincere in his wish to help these young people in their problems.

Such an author we found in Richard Armstrong whose *Sabotage at the Forge* and *Sea Change* were obviously addressed to youths who have some difficulty in adjusting themselves to the new life into which they have been thrown and in which they must, willy nilly, rub shoulders with other men. Sincerity is the keynote of these two books as it must be in all books addressed to readers of this age.

We find another writer of equal sincerity in Roderick Haig-Brown. He also addresses himself to youths though the problems he handles are somewhat different from those of Richard Armstrong. He is at the same time a more accomplished writer.

We met Haig-Brown first in *Silver: The Life Story of an Atlantic Salmon.* This is a book which is outstanding as a vivid picture of a salmon from birth until, as one of the biggest salmon ever, he is at last hooked by the same fisherman who had first clipped the little identity mark on his fin when, as a very small fish, he had paid the penalty of curiosity and had been well and truly hooked. That 'Good Fisherman' had even then prophesied that Silver would grow to be a great fish and when at last he captured this sixty-pounder he was not entirely happy.

> What the Good Fisherman thought or said as he looked at the battered glory that had been Silver and thought of the wonderful heart of the great fish I do not know. But his hands were very clumsy as he sought to remove the hook from Silver's jaw, and his eyes were rather sad as he turned uphill towards the lodge.

It is more than twenty years since *Silver* was first published, and a second edition did not appear until fifteen years later by which time the author had become known through other books. But in *Silver* we recognise, and critics at the time of publication recognised, an author whose careful, quiet style was well adapted to tell the story of the young salmon in his normal life in the salmon river, his journey to the great ocean feeding grounds, and his return from time to time to the spawning grounds. In Haig-

Brown was found also a man whose knowledge both as naturalist and fisherman was extensive and intimate. *Silver,* though not a manual for the angler, is nevertheless a book whose value anglers will acknowledge, and to young readers it offers knowledge of the subject that will go far towards making them interested in the sport, with an attitude to it similar to that of the 'Good Fisherman'. The author's style has a simplicity through which gleams drama or pathos as occasion demands. In Silver's final struggle when, through lack of sufficient water in the river, he fails to reach the spawning grounds after a desperate struggle to obey an irresistible urge and to surmount all obstacles, is an enthralling piece of descriptive writing. (pp. 95-6)

There have been criticisms of [Haig-Brown's *Panther,*] because in it dogs are killed when hunting panthers with their masters. Because there is much killing in the book one critic described it as "bloody and cruel" and for that reason thought it must be kept from many children. "But," says Haig-Brown, "Ki-Yu (the panther 'hero' of the book) was not cruel, or kind either for that matter . . . The question of cruelty did not enter into the matter at all, simply because only man is cruel." The author is convinced also that nothing in nature, so long as it is honestly observed and honestly described, can harm the mind of a child. "Conceal from children if you will the baseness of man, but let them read and understand the ways of animals and birds, of water and wind and earth; for these things are pure and true and unspoiled."

So in *Panther,* the life of Ki-Yu is closely observed and minutely described. The author is absorbed in his book, and with his very effective literary style and sensitive imagination alive to the wonders of nature he gives us not only the life story of a wild animal but a word picture of the loneliness of the wilds, of the self-reliance of the young hunter whose hunting is done—even as Ki-Yu's is done—so that he may live, and of the relationship between man and the wild animals around him.

Haig-Brown's attitude towards this relationship is in marked contrast to that other fine nature writer, Felix Salten. Whereas to the latter, man is the villain of the piece, Haig-Brown accepts facts as they are. He is completely free from sentimentality so far as wild life is concerned. Man is there; he must get a living, and if certain animals might become a menace to that livelihood or if because of this a living can be got by destroying the menace then it is right that the animals should be destroyed.

There are no 'purple patches' in Haig-Brown's writing but there are many breathtaking pages in *Panther.* We admire the fine beast; we are glad that for so long he eludes his human hunters, and the end, inevitable as it may appear, leaves the reader with a feeling of sadness. It leaves him too with a strong realisation of the hard fact that in the animal world perfect physical fitness is essential to survival. This truth is clearly shown in *Silver.* It is more strongly emphasised in *Panther.* When Ki-Yu has his leg broken in battle with a younger animal we know that his days are numbered, and though he puts up a magnificent fight against the wolves who eventually destroy him, the end is never in doubt and Haig-Brown is too good an artist to avoid it or to permit any modification of the obviously inevitable.

In 1944 appeared *Starbuck Valley Winter.* This book marked a change in the author's work inasmuch as it is fiction. It is nevertheless fiction that is based on the author's long experience of life in and near the forests of his chosen country and this experience is so utilised that the scene is intimately described without effort, unconsciously almost. The book is different too in the fact that humans take the stage and the creatures of the wild seem incidental, as indeed they are, to the story. There emerges a definite purpose though this does not obtrude unduly. Here are two youths, one, the main character, obviously the purpose of the book; the other of note principally in that his presence gives an opportunity for the first to develop.

Don Morgan, at sixteen, does not approve of his Aunt's desire that he should obtain a steady job in the sawmills. "Once give a boy a boat and you could call him a tramp for the rest of his life," said Aunt Maud. Worst of all to Don was the fact that, being only sixteen you couldn't go to the game warden and register a trap-line and take out a trapping licence. To Don the trap-line was the life. Instead of a job in the saw-mills it would mean a winter in the woods; instead of a batch of monthly pay cheques that couldn't possibly add up to the price of the 'Mallard' [a fishing boat that Don dreams of buying] by the time fishing started, it meant any possibility you liked to think of . . . Best of all it meant being free in the Starbuck country instead of tied down to a millyard under a boss.

There is the fundamental essence of the story. It encourages the will to be free to succeed or fail according to luck and your own ability; to be answerable only to your own intelligence, initiative, courage and endurance; to develop determination and the will to work; to learn through your own errors; to be downcast at failures and proud and exultant at success. Above all to adapt yourself to your companions and to judge other men for yourself uninfluenced by gossip. All these qualities are found in *Starbuck Valley Winter.*

Don gets his trap-line licence and proceeds with the job . . . He meets and surmounts great dangers and difficulties and in the end wins through to enjoy the applause of his erstwhile doubting though devoted Aunt. Don is fortunate in his Uncle Joe who, though in most things deferring to Aunt Maud, is of the same mind as Don. We find also in Don that which is not common among sixteen-year-olds—a willingness to listen to and to learn from his more experienced elders. He is ever mindful of the advice his Uncle Joe has given him through the years. Had he not been he could not have survived the dangers of his trip. Of course in the end Don earns enough to buy the treasured 'Mallard' but many readers will share my disappointment that he receives it as a gift from his admiring family and does not purchase it himself. This I think is the author's only lapse into near sentimentality and it comes as an anti-climax.

We are left at the end of the book with a feeling of satisfaction that Don has, by persistence and pluck, attained his end. He has proved himself, not only to his family but,

Haig-Brown with his mother, 1921.

more important, to himself. He has shown that a fellow can, with initiative and determination make his own way in life, can be answerable to himself alone, with only himself to blame if things do not work out as planned.

This, in an age when security is preached on all sides as the most desirable thing in life, is important.

In *Saltwater Summer* we find Don and his friend Tubby putting out to sea in the newly acquired 'Mallard' for a season of salmon fishing. There are private reasons why the season must be a very successful one. Needless to say success is attained but the story's value is in its picture of Don's development in character through his contact with other fishermen. He is at times stupid and foolish but his courage in emergency is abundantly clear; his faults the faults of youth.

The characterisation in this book is unusually good and the reader cannot but share Don and Tubby's admiration for Red Holiday and his friend Tom Moore. Don learns much from these two. They are, in effect, the central figures of the story although the limelight dwells principally on Don. They are there to give the needed helping hand to Don, to encourage him to meet his difficulties as a youth of his calibre should and in due course inevitably will. Like all young people Don resents adverse criticism however much deserved, but he has intelligence enough to see its value when made by a man he respects. Danger brings out the best in Don.

These two stories about Don Morgan . . . are the type of book of which there are too few. They will stir the imagination of any youngster who is not content with a humdrum life. If the reader has initiative and a willingness to take chances, an inclination towards a life that offers some freedom of action and that makes a man depend on his own physical and spiritual resources then he could choose no better books than these two.

When old Mikelson was talking about the mortgage that Don had taken out on the 'Mallard' in order to pay the hospital expenses of a friend of his trapline winter he said, "Sure she was paid for. But now she has to be paid for over again. That's right, ain't it Don? Never you mind though, you'll make it. You're not the kind that loses out."

No, Don is not the kind that loses out and those boys who enjoy these stories and take their cue from them will not lose out either. (pp. 97-102)

> *John Birks, "The Work of Roderick Haig-Brown," in* The Junior Bookshelf, *Vol. 17, No. 3, July, 1953, pp. 95-102.*

The Junior Bookshelf

[In **Mounted Police Patrol**, young] Davie Sloane, born and brought up in the lawless atmosphere that apparently exists in some of the back streets of Toronto, goes to live with an uncle and aunt. This uncle is a patrol officer of the Mounted Police. At first Davie is suspicious of the ways of 'coppers' but various experiences—a murder, a robbery or two, a fine chase in high-powered cars—gradually teach him that there are brave men on the side of the law as well as among crooks, and that there is something to be said for right as opposed to wrong.

Roderick Haig Brown, 'fisherman, hunter, naturalist,' is at heart a sensitive observer of birds and beasts and fishes and the particular beauties of the British Columbian countryside. His earlier books, **A River Never Sleeps** and **Return to the River,** were nature stories of the Henry Williamson variety. After these came two good boys' stories which gave a nice breezy, authentic picture of the hunting, trapping, journeying, outback life. In this new book, 'story' has become the thing, a story not better than any B.O.P. serial; character and setting have stiffened into the obvious lines that have for so long represented the Canadian North-West. A pity, because although this is an adequate tale of the work of the Police in the Canadian Prairie country today, it is a disappointing book from an author who has produced such good ones.

> *A review of "Mounted Police Patrol," in* The Junior Bookshelf, *Vol. 18, No. 5, November, 1954, p. 259.*

Stanley E. Read

Of [Haig-Brown's] three novels written for the adolescent reader I cannot find sufficient words of praise. They all have true, firm plots; they have rapidity of movement and reach dramatic, exciting conclusions; they show an amazing understanding of the developing adolescent mind and

emotions; and at times they are genuinely moving. **Starbuck Valley Winter** (1944) and **Saltwater Summer** (1949) are in reality a closely linked pair of stories, telling the adventures of young Don Morgan, an orphan, and his good friend Tubby Miller, first as trappers and hunters, and then as deepsea fishermen. The setting is the West Coast. **Mounted Police Patrol** (1954), however, has a new set of characters and a fresh setting—Alberta. The title of the work is mildly deceptive. The story actually is about the readjustment of the young hero, Dave Sloane, to a new society. He had been brought up in the slums of Toronto; he had hated the cops and despised the law. Now, on the death of his parents, he finds himself adopted by an aunt and uncle—and the uncle is a constable in the R.C.M. Police. The gradual change that comes over young Dave, resulting in his final acceptance of the values of law, order, and justice is the essence of the book. All three books are didactic (in the best sense of the word), stressing the values to be found in hard work, independent action, respect for social values, and the recognition of the dignity and worth of man. But the didacticism is not of that violent, obvious type found in many an earlier book written for the young. It is subtly incorporated within the narratives themselves, and does not detract in the slightest from the excitement of high adventure. These are great books for young ones and, incidentally, they can excite and move those who are older—granted, of course, that they have not forgotten that they too were once young. (pp. 20-1)

> *Stanley E. Read, "Roderick L. Haig-Brown," in* British Columbia Library Quarterly, *Vol. 22, No. 1, July, 1958, pp. 15-22.*

The Junior Bookshelf

There is a wider tendency nowadays to take the romance out of more than one field of old-fashioned adventure. Here the author takes the old idea of fun and games among the Red Indians and transforms tradition into reality without gilding the pill in any way. Life for the Indian Peoples of the Northern Pacific coast appears as a hard business in which most of the pleasure comes from winning a living, an existence even, from the nature around them. The chief delight and ambition of Atlin, chief elect of the Hotsath tribe, is the killing, and capture of whales, and the way to success is hard and wearisome, spiritually as well as physically. One never feels really warm while reading this new book by the author of **Starbuck Valley Winter,** or really dry either. Nevertheless one thoroughly enjoys the rigours and vigour of the hunting and hardening incidents upon which the story revolves. There are many fine descriptions of fights with whales of various sizes and towards the end a human and even homely tinge to the story in the behaviour of Atlin over the wooing of a daughter of a rival chief. The total effect is at least heroic in tone if not quite epic, and a most successful study of a little known people in fictional guise.

> *A review of "The Whale People," in* The Junior Bookshelf, *Vol. 26, No. 5, November, 1962, p. 261.*

Ruth Osler

In the beginning of **Silver,** his biography of an Atlantic salmon, Roderick Haig-Brown says of the Good Fisherman, "He loved salmon as some men love their wives or their books, and his whole heart was bound up in the delight of gaining knowledge of them." He might as well have been speaking of his own love of nature and the preoccupation with wild life that he has built into a literature on fishing and fishermen, life in the wilderness and wild animals. His books show by inference and direct telling the results of a long, deliberate and intelligent observation of the natural world and a deep respect for its laws and customs. Nor is this just a matter of contemplative enjoyment. He finds in the ways of wild life patterns and attitudes entirely worthy of adaptation to men, so that his books on wild life and men have a certain affinity, and in his masterpiece, *The Whale People,* the two are fused in a subject particularly sympathetic for the author, particularly compatible with his interests and beliefs.

For the subject matter of his work Haig-Brown has been able to draw often on the varied experiences of his own life. He was born and educated in England and first came to the Pacific coast as a boy of seventeen. He worked in logging camps, at trapping, and as a guide for three years, then returned to England to write. He came back to Canada two years later and settled on Vancouver Island. Today he lives on a farm by Campbell River farming, fishing and writing. He is as well a stipendiary magistrate and judge of the juvenile court.

From his interest in nature and his social interests have emerged six books of creative fiction for young people: two animal biographies, three adventure stories for boys and a story of the west coast Indians which has many of the qualities of an epic. The books have in common the detailed development of a central character and exact and accurate background material. Themes which are the springboards of his adult novels: conservation, the encroachment of urban society on the wilderness appear only slightly, or by inference. He writes in a clear, polished prose which is often eloquent but seldom light or humorous. He is most successful where his plots develop from a natural background. It is frequently true that his peripheral characters and sub plots are below the standard of his central material.

His first book for young people, in fact his first book, was written in England in 1931. It is *Silver,* the biography of an Atlantic salmon from the time of its emergence from an egg until it is caught, a huge and glorious fish of sixty pounds. He interrupts the narrative from time to time to deliver small sermons on the fish and the art of fishing, and as a consequence it is far less intense than his later books. It has also a quality of light and freshness not often found in his work: "All the muscles in (Silver's) young body pulled themselves together and said 'Jump for joy' and he jumped head over heels out of the water, five or six times."

Silver is an expression of Haig-Brown's intense delight in fishing. And this is a good deal more than the delight of catching a fish. It is the joy of observing the life cycle of the fish and learning his instincts and habits. This book is a detailed and sensitive reconstruction of the salmon's existence according to the laws of its kind and the exigencies of its natural surroundings. He expresses the honour and

respect of the fisherman for a formidable adversary which is later echoed and enlarged in the Indians' attitude to the whale in *The Whale People.*

In 1946 Haig-Brown produced another natural biography, *Panther,* but one of a vitally different style and character. Like *Silver* this is neither a tale of animal adventure nor an exercise in animal psychology. It is as true and accurate an account of the life cycle of a Vancouver Island panther as the author can state, and as such is a bloody, intense and disturbing *tour de force* of nature writing.

The panther is pure animal. His behaviour is dictated by his needs and instincts, by the weather and the balance of nature around him. In following the pattern of his actions Haig-Brown has built up, often by its very repetitiveness, a description of life in the wilderness that grows in ferocity as the panther grows older. Man is no longer an onlooker or sportsman, he is an intruder in the wilderness who must fight to keep his place. David Milton, who tracks the great panther, does so for the protection of the local farmers.

The book offers a remarkable picture of life in the wilderness. More vivid than the physical descriptions are Haig-Brown's perceptions of the sensory world of the animals. And it is full of memorable scenes of wildlife—a panther who has found her young dead snarls in hopeless rage at a hunter, exposing herself to his weapon; a cunning old buck eludes a pack of wolves; and always, descriptions of the sleek, feline panther in motion.

Haig-Brown found it necessary to write a prologue to this book defending himself against the charges of excessive cruelty and bloodshed. He says in part, "Almost all the ills of the human race may be traced to the fact that it has strayed too far from nature and knows too little of the natural order of things. Conceal if you will the baseness of man. But let children read and understand the ways of (nature) for these things are pure and true and unspoiled."

As this infers he feels that in an urban existence man loses his place and his sense of identity. He is better in a small community in which he is a participator. The good life for Haig-Brown is lived close to nature, learning from it. It is a belief he states strongly in his adult books and it is evident in his three adventure stories for boys. These are in part at least an outgrowth of his experience as a judge of the juvenile court, and while they lean heavily on a natural background their concern is increasingly social.

Starbuck Valley Winter was published in 1944. It is the story of Don Morgan, a boy of sixteen who works a trapline one winter in order to make the money to buy a boat. He is faced not only with the difficulties involved in taking his first independent action but also with the mystery of a trapper of bad reputation who stalks him and his companion. Principally this is a very full study of the development of a hardy, resourceful boy. It is also a satisfying story of action, boys learning and accomplishing.

Its sequel, *Saltwater Summer,* was published in 1949. The two boys are fishing on the coast of British Columbia in the boat their winter work paid for. Don finds that while he likes fishing he has little natural aptitude for it. He meets a strange group of people and tests his values in his new situation and re-evaluates his relationships. And he has no easy success at this. He has to sell a half interest in his boat and reconsider his whole future.

The plot of **Saltwater Summer** is moved by a good deal of violent action. In **Mounted Police Patrol,** the most recent and most socially conscious of his adventure stories, this is also true. Its plot has elements of the stock mystery story: threats, robbery and murder. Basically, however, it is the story of the rehabilitation of a boy from a Toronto slum in a small prairie town. The results of crime both for the criminal and his victim are brought home to him through contact with the small community and he develops positive interests in the surrounding countryside. His change of outlook is influenced by a group of villains whose blackness of character almost puts them in the realm of fantasy.

It is a long stride from these books to the **Whale People,** the story of a young Indian chief's search for the whale spirit, his *tumanos.* In the interim, Haig-Brown produced a biography of Captain George Vancouver, and a dramatized history of the west coast. It may well be that his researches on this material led him to the subject. In **Pool and Rapid** he had already dealt with an Indian theme so he was no doubt already interested in the Nootka, the whale hunters of the Pacific coast on whom the book is based. Haig-Brown has found in this material a theme to capture his imagination and fuse his interests, and he has produced a book noble in style and conception.

The Indian people of the Hotsath tribe honour the whale, and for them whaling is almost a mystical experience. For it is not only the source of their food and their wealth, it is a noble and dangerous adversary. The chief of the tribe harpoons the whale from his longboat. It is believed that the chief must gain a spirit worthy of the whale and pleasing to him. The whale spirit is acquired not by magic but through strength and skill, knowledge of the sea and a mighty confidence that little men in boats can kill mighty whales. His *tumanos* is a symbol from the spirit world that the spirit is with him. With such a spirit the whale consents to receive the chief's harpoon, and in its death agony tows the longboat to the shore and not out to sea.

The story is of the son of a great whaling chief who, when his father is killed must find his *tumanos* and lead his tribe. His training, physical and spiritual, his gradual maturing are told with a great economy of language more formal and rhythmic than Haig-Brown has used before. But then this is a book concerned with the spirit and has a theme that is at once more inspiring and more driving than those of his earlier books. Of all his material it is the most completely imagined work.

All Haig-Brown's books are the result of a thoroughness of thought and approach and a quality of imagination that is both creative and realistic. The strength of his writing is easy to underestimate. It often takes a second reading to grasp the breadth of skill, knowledge and understanding that has gone into them. (pp. 16-19)

> Ruth Osler, "Haig-Brown: Fisherman, Nature Lover, Author," in In Review: Canadian Books for Children, *Vol. 1, No. 1, Winter, 1967, pp. 16-19.*

Adele M. Fasick

[*The following excerpt is from a review of the revised edition of* Captain of the Discovery: The Story of Captain George Vancouver, *published in 1974.*]

This revised edition of Roderick Haig-Brown's 1956 biography of Captain George Vancouver contains striking new black-and-white illustrations by Gordon MacLean. The text, however, seems to be virtually unchanged. Although the book is a competent, straightforward biography which does not require significant revision, it is unfortunate that a few inexcusably patronising remarks about native peoples were not eliminated. To write as Haig-Brown does . . . , "Nearly all the natives they dealt with were natural—and highly skilful—thieves until checked," is to accept 18th century European standards without making allowance for cultural differences. And to say that a group of Indians "behaved well" because they were peaceful and traded willingly is to imply that Indian behaviour can be judged by its convenience for Europeans.

Haig-Brown emphasises the careful, painstaking work of exploration which Vancouver did and the hardships he and his crew endured. Like most biographies for children, the book omits references to the less edifying aspects of Vancouver's life, notably the controversial Camelford Affair in which Vancouver was accused of having a midshipman flogged.

Since the entire book is an account of voyages, clear, detailed maps are important in understanding the action. Unfortunately, the map of the coastline of British Columbia—the most important map in the book—does not differentiate between land and sea by shading or colour and is crowded with difficult-to-read place names. No list of maps is given so that they are almost inaccessible for reference. The lack of an index is also a weakness in a book which could be useful for class projects and reports.

Despite its flaws, this biography is an important one for any children's collection.

> Adele M. Fasick, in a review of "Captain of the Discovery: The Story of Captain George Vancouver," in In Review: Canadian Books for Children, *Vol. 8, No. 4, Autumn, 1974, p. 48.*

Sheila Egoff

The real heir of [Ernest Thompson] Seton in the writing of the realistic animal story is Roderick L. Haig-Brown, one of Canada's foremost writers in many fields. *Silver: The Life of an Atlantic Salmon* was published in 1931 and *Ki-Yu: A Story of Panthers* in 1934. *Silver* describes the life cycle of a salmon from the time he is spawned until he is finally caught in his own stream by the 'Good Fisherman' in true sportsmanlike fashion. Completely authentic in its details of salmon life, it is lightened by an intimate, at times almost lyrical style. Haig-Brown addresses his readers as if he were telling the story in person and is quite explicit when he is 'making things up', such as what Silver might have said or thought. Fishing skills, sportsmanship, and conservation are skilfully woven into a story. It takes a craftsman to make something as narrowly special as salmon interesting to the general reader, but Haig-Brown manages to do it.

Ki-Yu: A Story of Panthers is Seton and [Charles G. D.] Roberts brought to complete realism. Ki-Yu is by no means an attractive character. (Even the most predatory animals of the earlier writers are appealing.) The wilderness is presented in all its starkness and there is little to show 'the kindred of the wild'. Ki-Yu is perhaps more a documentary of wild-animal life than a sympathetic animal biography. Haig-Brown simply prefers to let the facts speak for themselves. The drama of the story appears in the deliberate stalking of Ki-Yu by a professional panther hunter; when his dogs are killed by the panther, the sympathy is with the dogs and the man rather than with the hunted animal. Although man plays no more important a role here than in Seton, we are made to feel much more the depredations of wild animals upon domestic animal life.

Haig-Brown, like Roberts and Seton, also shows the inevitableness of death in the wilderness. In the end, when Ki-Yu is old and wounded and caught between two enemies, man and wolves, it is his own wild kind that tear him apart.

Ki-Yu is over-long and sometimes wearying, particularly in the description of the constant killing and feeding of the wild animals. Even so, all the details in the story are so realistically presented that they have a considerable holding power. Haig-Brown convinces by realism, not by invention. When Ki-Yu's mother, Nassa, is training her cubs—a surprisingly long, slow job—she wants to leave them at times, and the cubs seem to know when not to follow her. Haig-Brown is careful not to indulge in imagination at this point. 'She dropped them now, at the foot of the lake. What she did, how she persuaded them to stay behind instead of following her as they had followed her all the morning, it is difficult to say.' He ascribes feelings to animals, but in this form:

> Ki-Yu, in killing and feeding and sleeping, in roaming by himself and with females, was beginning to find his life. His joys were utterly subconscious joys, utterly joys of the senses. As he turned down from the heather-laden breezes of the Plateau, the damp, earthy scent of the woods was pleasant to him—though he did not know it and would never have turned back from the Plateau to find the scent.

Basically Haig-Brown does not care to engage our sympathies for Ki-Yu; he is concerned to present life in the wilderness—in this case Vancouver Island—and in carrying the realistic animal story to its logical conclusion he has perhaps gained in accuracy and restraint, but at the expense of dramatic emotion. (pp. 140-41)

Haig-Brown's *Starbuck Valley Winter* (1943) and *Saltwater Summer* (1948) were obviously inspired by tremendous feeling for particular places—British Columbia's range lands and the ocean that washes its coastline. However, there is more than feeling in these books. Haig-Brown has looked at what he describes and so feels with his hero not only a 'sudden pride' in his surroundings but

Haig-Brown with tyee he caught on the Nimpkish River near Vancouver Island, Canada, in 1932.

also a 'sense of ownership through knowledge'. He invests his readers with this sense of ownership and can thus impart to them, without ever veering into pedagogy, many unfamiliar activities, like trolling, seining, skinning a buck, making a water-wheel, canoeing up a river, setting traps. He has a Homeric appreciation of the well-done task, the well-made artifact, and an observant eye that is never sentimental. He more than sees: he understands and feels as well. 'He looked at everything, trying to use it and make it his own'—this describes Haig-Brown as well as his hero. Such an intimacy between the hero and what he makes or creates enables Haig-Brown to escape the common pitfall of obtrusive information and explanation. . . . Haig-Brown is always sure-footed in traversing detail. *Starbuck Valley Winter* and *Saltwater Summer* are *real* stories as *Swiss Family Robinson* and *Kidnapped* are real.

Haig-Brown's honesty of description is reflected in his plots, which have drama but no impossible deeds. In *Starbuck Valley Winter,* Don's initial decision to save his friend's life is grandly heroic, but the actual journey he undertakes turns out to be almost devoid of sensational incident. The plots of both books are extremely simple but have implicit moral dimensions. In *Starbuck Valley Winter,* Don Morgan and his friend spend a winter trapping in the woods; in *Saltwater Summer* they spend the summer in commercial fishing. Both are basically chancy enterprises and it is the natural hazards, the inherent violence of outdoor life, rather than artificial 'adventures' that give the tales their impact. The mistakes made, while adding to the suspense, are those that would plausibly be made by anyone of youth and inexperience.

Don Morgan's personality is as believable as his experiences. Haig-Brown presents him as a rather complex person, by no means as straightforwardly 'nice' as his great friend Tubby Miller. He is more moody, more ambitious, and impulsive enough to break the law on one occasion. His path to heroism is a process of development, not a melodramatic change of heart. Perhaps even more remarkably, Haig-Brown knows how to handle adults. In most Canadian children's books the world of youth is quite divorced from the world of adults. The latter are shadowy figures who are almost nameless: simply the Father, the Mother, the Boss, etc. Almost never do we find grown-ups as vivid and as memorable as Alan Breck or Long John Silver. Haig-Brown's adults do not catch the imagination as do Stevenson's great creations, but at least they exist. They have mixed motives, complexity, reality. We understand how they have come to live in isolation on range or coast and what their environment has done to them. (pp. 155-57)

> *Sheila Egoff, "The Realistic Animal Story" and "Realistic Fictions," in her* The Republic of Childhood: A Critical Guide to Canadian Children's Literature in English, *Oxford University Press, Canadian Branch, 1975, pp. 131-52, 153-203.*

W. J. Keith

The relation between an immigrant and his adopted country is a complex one, especially for a writer who has established his literary niche as a detailed and wide-ranging commentator on his new land. One gets the impression when reading through Haig-Brown's work that he has been particularly conscious of a responsibility to justify his change of allegiance by a thorough mastery of all the historical, zoological and sociological aspects of the province in which he lives. [What follows is] a passage in *Starbuck Valley Winter* (1943) in which Don Morgan, following in his creator's footsteps (he is also an immigrant, but in his case from the United States), is about to establish a trapline in the wilds:

> He had names of his own for most of the creeks and swamps he could see, and even for some of the logging roads. Standing there, looking over it, he felt a sudden pride in the country, a sense of ownership through knowledge, through having set his feet upon so much of it in the three years he had lived there.

Similar sentiments recur in Haig-Brown's writing. Here, for example, is the continuation of the account of his Dorset upbringing in *A River Never Sleeps:* "In the years since then I have fished one or two Vancouver rivers [*i.e.,* the Nimpkish and the Campbell] until I know them as well as I know the Frome; I feel at home in them, and everything I see in them or about them has its meaning for me, as the life of the Frome meadows had." Ultimately,

he can observe: "I fish the Campbell with a sense of ownership fully as strong as that of any legitimate owner of fishing rights in the world. . . . The sense of ownership grows simply from knowing the river."

The image of exploration and discovery may be seen as a unifying thread that links his numerous writings. In his historical books for schoolchildren—*Captain of the Discovery* (1956), *The Farthest Shores* (1960) and *Fur and Gold* (1962)—he has brought to life the exploits of the men who first explored both the coast and the interior (Bering, the Spaniards, Vancouver, Mackenzie, Fraser, Thompson, etc.) and in the last-named the administrators and politicians (notably James Douglas) who consolidated the achievements of the explorers and initiated the subsequent development of British Columbia. In *Silver* and *Return to the River* (1941), at first sight books of a very different kind, a comparable interest is to be found, though this time the discovery is scientific; Haig-Brown is fascinated not only with the life-cycle of the salmon but with the efforts of dedicated human beings (the unnamed "Good Fisherman" in the first, Senator Evans and Don Gunner in the second) to discover and reveal the complex secrets of natural processes. In his juvenile adventure stories—especially *Starbuck Valley Winter* and *The Whale People* (1962)—the boy-heroes embark upon personal voyages of discovery, venturing into new places and proving themselves in new accomplishments. Haig-Brown's own role as fact-finder and sympathetic interpreter is less dramatic but no less real; he communicates to his readers a sense of intellectual discovery through painstaking research and a lifetime of practical experience.

His favourite subject is, of course, fishing, and he has written on virtually every aspect of it, from practical handbooks like *A Primer of Fly-Fishing* (1964) to authoritative surveys like *The Western Angler* (1939), though he is at his best in the more personal mode, in such books as the four accounts of the fisherman's year divided according to the seasons, and books of essays on fishing subjects like *A River Never Sleeps.* But he is by no means confined to the literature of angling. His ownership through knowledge extends over many other areas. One of his novels, *Timber* (1942; published in England as *The Tall Trees Fall* [1943]) is based upon his intimate acquaintance with the logging industry, and he made a special study of cougars in order to write *Ki-Yu* (1934; later republished as *Panther*) and another of the traditions of the Indians of the Pacific Coast for *The Whale People.* But the seal on his intellectual ownership of his adopted province was set by his writing of *The Living Land* (1961)—a veritable anatomy of British Columbia, which surveys its natural resources and future prospects on the basis of the studies produced by a series of Resources Conferences.

This whole image of ownership can, however, be carried too far. Haig-Brown is acutely aware of the fact that "any given generation of men can have only a lease, not ownership, of the earth; and one essential term of the lease is that the earth be handed on to the next generation with unimpaired potentialities" [*Measure of the Year*]. He also knows that ownership of any kind, though accompanied with privileges, carries with it duties and responsibilities.

It was not enough for him merely to discover and enjoy the wild life and natural beauty of British Columbia; these constitute a priceless heritage that must be both shared and conserved. The sharing of both his knowledge and his enthusiasm for the natural world has been accomplished by means of his writings. The need for conservation has similarly been urged through the written word, but it has in addition been furthered through his action and example.

Although his preoccupation with wild life had been fostered by his early upbringing and the practice of his father, he is by no means a blind follower of traditional ways. While his father's book reflected, in the son's words [in *A River Never Sleeps*], "a vigorous man's love of shooting and fishing," his own development has been towards protection. During the half-century in which he has known Vancouver Island, the situation of its wild life has changed out of all recognition, and Haig-Brown has recognized and adapted to this change. As he writes in *Measure of the Year* (1950):

> I hunt as often as I can get out, with greater enthusiasm and interest than ever; I shoot less and less, and with an ever-increasing reluctance, because a wholly new factor has come in to destroy all the calculations that once seemed to make my measure of killing reasonable and sane: I am no longer a single hunter among a few others of my kind; I am a part of a vast and always increasing army of hunters that suddenly seems to threaten the future of every wild creature I love.

More recently he has made comparable statements concerning the population explosion among fishermen, and has proposed more stringent legislation and advocated rules of self-discipline to meet the new dangers involved. Although to some outsiders the combination of the roles of hunter, angler and protector of wild life seems contradictory, Haig-Brown is one of our leading conservationists, and he carries special conviction because of his previous, and continuing, experience as a sportsman.

He defines [in *The Living Land*] conservation as "a religious concept—the most universal and fundamental of all such concepts, the worship of fertility to which man has dedicated himself in every civilization since his race began." But his arguments have hardly anything in common with those of urban arm-chair conservationists who all too often have little or no familiarity with the wilderness they profess to defend, and whose opinions are abstract and theoretical. Like Thoreau and Jefferies before him, he is prepared to defend sport because "carrying a gun has taught me a thousand things about animals and country and wind and weather that I should not otherwise have bothered to learn" [*Measure of the Year*]. He knows the differences between hunters and butchers, and insists that genuine sportsmen "are the keenest and most effective of all conservationists," that they can play a powerful and, indeed, essential part in any rational programme of protection.

In recent years, Haig-Brown has devoted a great deal of time and effort to his civic duties as magistrate and judge. This side of his life has found little immediate reflection

in his writings (two amusing essays in *Measure of the Year,* the boys' adventure story, *Mounted Police Patrol* [1954], some uncollected articles in popular magazines), and it seems, indeed, to have interfered substantially with his writing—*The Salmon* is his first book for a decade, and even this is little more than an up-to-date recapitulation of earlier material. We may well regret this, but it is not difficult to see the relation of this work to the overall context of his life. Haig-Brown is very much a humanist, and he knows that the framing of wise laws and the firm but humane enforcement of them are essential to our own survival and also to that of the other species with which we share the earth. His emphasis on ethics and restraint extends from conduct when hunting and fishing to behaviour in day-to-day living. Whether as magistrate, sportsman or writer, he actively upholds the need for human understanding, co-operation and discipline. (pp. 9-12)

> W. J. Keith, "Roderick Haig-Brown," in Canadian Literature, No. 71, Winter, 1976, pp. 7-20.

Alec Lucas

Haig-Brown set the course of his literary career with his first book, *Silver* (1931), the biography of an Atlantic salmon. Like it, all of his other works centre on the natural or rural world and reveal the same concept of writer as teacher. All told, however, only three of his twenty-three books belong to the animal biography genre: *Silver, Panther* (1934, published also as *Ki-Yu* in the same year) and *Return to the River* (1941). Of these he wrote only *Silver* especially for children, though the other two books, he was pleased to note, also found many readers among the young.

Actually the course of Haig-Brown's literary career had been set in England long before *Silver.* He was the son of a field naturalist and angler and, like father like son, also became an ardent angler in the streams of his own county, Sussex, and of Dorset where, as a boy, he came under the tutelage of a sportsman uncle, Decie, and his father's old friend, Major Greenhill, who may well be the model for the Good Fisherman of *Silver.* Moreover, in becoming a "naturalist writer," as he called himself, he was again following in the footsteps of his father, who had pointed the way with two outdoors books, *Sporting Sonnets and Other Verse* (1903) and *My Game-Book* (1913), which he dedicated to his year-old son. Not unexpectedly either, Haig-Brown lists [Charles G. D.] Roberts and [Ernest Thompson] Seton among the authors who "instructed and influenced" him in general [quoted in *Canadian Children's Literature* (Summer 1975)]. Specifically, however, as regards *Silver,* he laments that he was "still too much influenced by writers like Fortescue who wrote *The Story of a Red Deer* and Charles Kingsley's *Water Babies* and so on."

Despite this remark, there is no question that Haig-Brown aimed to make his animal biographies "authentic," to use his own term. He wished to be true to the facts and spirit of the natural world and to instill some appreciation of it in his readers. In this aim, his adult and children's books are one. He wanted "all people to see and understand more because there is both pleasure and fulfillment in seeing and understanding lives about them, whether they are the lives of trees and plants, or lives of animals or lives of fish." In such seeing and understanding lay, he believed, "the only hope of preserving the natural world." These aims motivated all Haig-Brown's animal stories, but *Silver* and *Return to the River* much more obviously than *Panther* which works for the cause of conservation, if at all, almost wholly through the vivid presentation of a magnificent beast.

Haig-Brown is more at home in the animal biography than he ever was in the later boys' adventure stories and his fiction. In the first he avoids for the most part the difficulty he always had in creating living human characters. The Good Fisherman in *Silver* is largely peripheral to the story, however important he may be as a sensitive and reflective angler. Both he and the narrator of the story appear again, as it were, in *Return to the River* as Senator Evans and a biologist, Don Gunner. They enable Haig-Brown to drop the subjective first-person for the more objective (and "scientific") third person point of view and to present much of his natural history as dialogue rather than exposition. Yet they are essentially an animate frame of reference for the full-length biography of a magnificent Oregon salmon, Spring. The cougar hunter Milton in *Panther,* however, called for greater individuation than either Evans or Gunner. Milton shares the story and theme of the book with Ki-yu, representing man in nature's struggle to survive as civilization encroaches on the wilderness. Yet he fills his role simply by being a hunter; his struggle with nature is never psychological, and, as a flat character, he gives his creator much less trouble than the teenagers whom, in his boys' stories, Haig-Brown tries to depict dramatically and dialectically.

In *Silver,* Haig-Brown attempted to achieve three specific goals: to tell an interesting story, to keep to the truth about salmon and to instruct Master Dickie (to whom the narrator tells the story and Haig-Brown dedicates the book) in the ways of true sportsmanship. He adopted a tone and stance he considered suited to a story for a very young child and often tried to involve him by using a cosy "we" as if to ensure the child's identification with *Silver,* a fish lacking somewhat in dramatic appeal. To vitalize the facts of the life cycle of the salmon, he employs a variety of narrative techniques that children like and that range in this story from a short *in media res* opening to a sharp climax and a brief and tranquil denouement, whose sadness reminds one of Seton's "Lobo" and "Redruff." He uses suspense effectively, at times withholding or hinting, and at times providing curtain lines or curtain endings for his chapters. "That gash will kill him long before he feels salt water again," is one of the best of the curtain lines. It creates suspense, sets the stage for Silver's death, and hints at a situation in which the Good Fisherman, in catching Silver, seems, paradoxically, even more like her guardian angel.

Here and there Haig-Brown dramatizes the action. Sometimes the fish talk. Sometimes he introduces human characters who as fishermen, especially poachers, add tension to the story and give it another dimension in which nature is pitted against man. He creates little climaxes in which

Silver is caught or nearly killed, working up to the great struggle with the Good Fisherman that concludes the book. Yet *Silver* is by no means an animal adventure story. The "conflict" of the plot centres largely on the annual cycle and life-death pattern in Silver's development. "It would be a pity to make [Silver] seem impossible," the narrator says, "by inventing stories about him when there are so many true ones waiting to be told."

Looking back years later, Haig-Brown criticized *Silver.* Too much in the English tradition of Kingsley and his kind, he found it cute and anthropomorphic, though [W. J. Keith, in *Canadian Literature* (Winter 1976)] suggests that the book's central image of discovery as a voyage and as quest for knowledge, reveals the influence of the author's experiences in the late 1920's on the West coast of North America. In view of the tender age of Master Dickie, the listener, the problem lies not so much in the anthropomorphism as in the teller of the story. Up to a point one accepts fish talking in a child's story if they speak of fish affairs, but not interpretations of fish behaviour in which, to give but two examples, it is said that Grace, the hen salmon, is "fussy and particular, as all good mothers are" and that Silver, "like many people who are great and important, had an idea he was just a bit greater and more important than he was."

Again as an obtruding and didactic commentator, the story-teller often shifts focus (and unfortunately sometimes point of view). At one point he holds forth on unemployment and the need of the young people of Britain to buckle down, at another on his vermin-based concept of conservation, in which—in addition to preaching fair play among those who catch fish for sport—he damns gulls, which catch fish to live. Poachers fare much better. They are "not bad men; poachers seldom are, for if things were slightly different [i.e. if they had money] they'd mostly be sportsmen." He reverts to nineteenth-century thinking when he notes that the Dog salmon are so numerous in British Columbia that "nothing ever could affect their numbers noticeably." Reasoning of this kind led to the extermination of the passenger pigeon and the great auk. Sometimes he lectures knowledgeably on ichthyology, but his observations are not always demonstrably "authentic," and Master Dickie has to accept as the "truth about salmon," a story in which they learn to jump nets, to take a fly through ill-temper, to migrate to the sea because of a liking for the "bitter taste" of the water, and to make "such terrific efforts" to reach their spawning ground because of "fear [of] exhaustion." Often the story-teller moves from his intimate "we" and such comments as a "silly little fin" to a professional "I" and a heated commentary, surely over poor Master Dickie's head, on the significance of heredity or the causes of migration, another contentious subject. On a different level the story is ambivalent about nature. She is Mother Nature at times and at others Dame Nature, a stern school-mistress, always rational and moral. Yet the narrator makes observations that reveal Nature as only a force manifesting itself in the lives of wild creatures through both heredity and environment and natural and sexual selection. Indeed his attack on gulls stems from the fact that they eat "thousands and thousands of salmon smolts, who might otherwise have lived to become big and valuable salmon." As a result of all these shifts and discrepancies, *Silver* comprises a strange melange of adults' and children's interests and attitudes.

Whatever delight and information Master Dickie got from the story Haig-Brown learned, he disclosed later, that writing of the kind for children put too many restraints on him, as a comparison of *Silver* and *Return to the River,* his next book on salmon, makes clear. With *Silver,* he perhaps simply wished to recreate a situation once his, when a devoted and learned father told him stories of fish and fishermen. At least he wrote no more books like *Silver* and so with it paid his last direct respects to his childhood and the humanized nature he had known then. After it he wrote under the influence of the new world wilderness. Even when working on *Silver* his heart was far away on the Pacific coast, as Chinook's experiences in the book suggest, for he was, he says [in *Maclean's Magazine* (June 1973)], living then in "exile" in England, where "the rivers were tame and tiny" and where there were "no mountains, not even a rock bluff, no mauve and purple twilights with the trolling lines cutting the tide-rippled waters." The criticism Haig-Brown made of *Silver* derived mainly from these circumstances. In it he had tried to combine two views of nature—the English sentimental, romantic one and the Darwinian or realistic one (with a leavening of the old tradition of Walton and his followers)—and he seems to have thought it necessary to compensate for the latter by emphasizing the sentimental view, with the result that he axiomatically stressed the "cuteness" of his story.

As if again to compensate for the sentimentality of *Silver,* Haig-Brown with *Panther* came out firmly for the realistic animal story. In its objectivity it stands at the opposite pole to *Silver* and, in ways, even to *Return to the River.* It has none of the "cuteness" and anthropomorphism that he believed marred his first animal biography. That he did not write *Panther* "especially for children" is a fact significant not only in itself but also as an indication of his approach to his subject. He was free now to be "authentic," to let the facts speak for themselves. If not written as a children's story, however, *Panther* has long been accepted as one by young readers (and librarians and literary critics), though with recent attempts to read Canadian animal stories as expressions of the national psyche, the book may now have secured a place as adult reading as well as children's.

As with *Silver,* Haig-Brown drew on his own experiences for *Panther.* He was once a bounty hunter himself and, in the winter of 1932-33, was in the field with Cecil (Cougar) Smith, a government predator hunter, to whom he dedicated the first edition of his book and to whom he owed, he admits, much of his knowledge of cougars. His research was that of naturalist and hunter rather than mammologist. Yet without the sophisticated methods of modern field work—tranquillizing bullets and electronic tracking—the book marks an important beginning in the study of the ecology and life history of the Pacific coast panther. It describes the mating habits, family relationships, methods of hunting and feeding of the cougar, and even such details as its way of plucking a bird, of purposely opening a carcass to prevent bloating, and (even more challenging to credulity) of swallowing hair to guard against tapeworms.

Panther is, however, more than matters of fact. As is also required of the animal biography, it is a work of fiction, and, in this example, one of considerable imaginative power. A living creature stalks through its pages. Haig-Brown is not trying to tell a story of heroic animal exploits, nor is he using animals as human archetypes, as critics [Joseph] Gold and [Clare] McCulloch now seem to think Roberts did. The book is an animal biography, and Ki-yu is simply a great beast of instinct and primordial reason. Not for him a broken heart like Seton's Lobo, or a clever escape over the backs of a flock of sheep like Roberts' Red Fox. Ki-yu "remembered" his mother, "loathed" wolves and watched his prey with "eyes flaming," but otherwise stays in bestial character throughout. Typical of wild animal biographies, however, Ki-yu is the fittest of his kind, but not because, as often with Roberts' and Seton's animal heroes, of human qualities, but because of his sheer animality and because he embodies the spirit of "places where men did not come to break the pattern." As excessive anthropomorphism mars *Silver* as "science," so a marked anti-anthropomorphism mars *Panther.* The very realism of the protagonist tends to detract from his role. Purely animal, he consequently provides little with which the reader can identify. In trying to avoid humanizing Ki-yu, Haig-Brown has stripped him of much emotional impact.

Although *Panther* recounts Ki-yu's life history directly and chronologically, it is artistically patterned. Its setting balances farm and wilderness; its telling, narration and dramatic episodes; and its plot, hunted and hunter. It, however, avoids themes that are drawn from stories about people and that frequently characterize stories about people and animals. Here no Springfield Fox feeds poisoned bait to her captive cub in the name of liberty or death, no Pacing Mustang plunges from a cliff for the same cause. Though Blackstreak, Ki-yu's father, killed King, Milton's favourite dog, early in the story, Haig-Brown never tries to make anything of the revenge motif. He even concludes the biography as if to make an ironic comment on sentimental "fictional" plots of animal stories. Milton and Ki-yu do not meet at the end in a great moment of drama. Instead the old cougar is torn to pieces and eaten by a pack of wolves.

On one hand the story is a simple one involving Ki-yu and Milton, a bounty hunter, worked out for the most part in terms of crises, hairbreadth yet plausible escapes and acts of derring-do. Ki-yu swims an icy river eight times, or leaps to the safety of tree or bluff to fool Milton's dogs, or fights savagely with a bear or with some rival cougar. Dave Milton escapes from a pack of wolves. (Haig-Brown is careful, however, not to present them as deliberate maneaters.) He crosses a great chasm on a flimsy, fallen tree. He struggles, though injured, through the night-time wilderness to the safety of his home. Yet the sensationalism of these events is never sensationalism for its own sake, for *Panther* is more than an outdoors book of thrilling adven-

Haig-Brown at his desk.

tures. It has a theme of broad implications and tells a story rooted in the old conflict of man and nature.

If Ki-yu embodies the spirit of the animal world, Milton embodies that of man's, and the plot derives from Ki-yu's efforts to live between two worlds—one, nature's, red in tooth and claw, and the other, man's, forever encroaching on the wilderness with ax and plough, and dog and gun, for man, too, must kill to preserve his way of life as he pushes the frontier farther back into the unclaimed lands. (Here, however, Haig-Brown is silent about the inroads the sportsman makes on wildlife.) Settler and cougar become involved automatically in the struggle to survive, and, in this way, Milton and Ki-yu are "kin." To stress the point Haig-Brown places much of the action of the concluding chapters in the settlers' world (as a counterbalance to the wilderness setting of much of the action of the earlier sections) which, ironically, Ki-yu tries to make his refuge. Like the hero caught between big business and big government in a later novel, *On the Highest Hill* (1949), Ki-yu has no place to hide. His story ends movingly, if not tragically, as the once powerful beast, now blinded in one eye—almost eyeless in the Gaza of man's world—and long since lame from a ferocious fight in his own world, dies in a valiant fight for his life against

wolves—an ending all the more ironic since they have hitherto skulked through the book as craven, "slobbering" "villains."

Despite this central tension, *Panther* lacks overall dramatic effect. It tries to be two books in one, an animal biography and the life of a hunter. It lacks the focus that makes Seton's "Krag" so very effective. Despite the fact that hunting is an all-pervasive theme, the stories of Ki-yu and Milton often go their separate ways, except during the hunts and at the end when Ki-yu makes the settlement his stamping ground. In *Panther,* there are no heroes or villains, or perhaps better, the two protagonists are both heroes and villains caught up in a specific conflict that in the end neither wins. Haig-Brown's refusal to take sides, as he says [in *Canadian Children's Literature* (Summer 1975)], with either Ki-yu or Milton comes through almost as indifference. His emotions are scarely ever involved. He never smiles or sheds a tear. Hence the emotions of the reader are scarely ever involved. He is moved, however, by the deaths of Osa and her cubs, by the death of Ki-yu when his animal dignity rises to nobility, and by the faithful dogs who fight for their master's cause even unto death. In fact, the love Milton has for his dogs gives him a much-needed human touch and counteracts somewhat his callous killing of the mountain cougars.

The savage fights, the maiming, and the killing evoke horror but little terror. Although Ki-yu can be cruel and is said to have become "a terror" in the farm country, he is never depicted as a fierce and deadly threat to a human being. On the contrary, sometimes he even shows himself at Hollister's farm as a big, curious, and whimsical cat. By and large, however, he simply lives a life motivated by hunger and sex, pitting animal against animal, frequently disrupted by moments when man would hunt him down or when he, changing roles, is forced to carry the struggle for survival into his enemies' farmlands.

Nature for Haig-Brown may be amoral but it is not monstrous, and in *Panther* he presents it impartially in Darwinian terms and lets the "message" of the book stand at that. By refusing to express sympathy for the victims in the struggle for survival, he avoids the kind of adulterated Darwinism that Seton so frequently indulges in. For Haig-Brown, a squirrel could never be, as it was for Seton, "a red-haired cutthroat" with a "strange perverted thirst for birdling blood." Nor within his Darwinism does he attempt (as Seton and Roberts so often attempted) to demonstrate or prove explicitly the truth of evolution by stressing animal ratiocination and emotionalism. For him even the fittest—"Nurm, a magnificent five-point buck," or Ki-yu—is largely a beast of instinct and habit, "whose joys are utterly subconscious joys, utterly simple joys of the senses."

A story, a study of natural history and Darwinism, *Panther* is also an outdoors book about a hunter and, like most of the genre, incongruous as it may seem, about predator-control. Haig-Brown puts all his nature writing in human context so that here he is not simply following a literary pattern but also considering an extant problem of the time. Although he never reduces Ki-yu to vermin, he apparently speaks as one with the bounty hunter in the dramatized episodes of the story. At least he never speaks against bounty hunting and he obviously tries to make Milton into a kind of folk hero, the successful backwoods hunter. Ki-yu, according to Milton, was a "menace." "Sooner or later he would," Milton continues, "turn down to the farms and begin killing sheep and cattle. To shirk from hunting him would be to shirk the very work for which he was paid, to render all the rest of his hunting stupid and pointless." All this hopefully hides the fact that Milton often kills just for cash without a thought of protecting anything and without compunction. One wants to feel that man is more than animal. The simple comment, "In the past winter David had killed all [Ki-yu's] females save two," reveals the casualness of David's killing. So, too, does the following (with excellent prose that accentuates the fact):

> [The panther] was lying asleep under a log, a little way from the kill and sprang up as she heard them, [The dogs] rushed her as soon as they saw her and forced her into a small hemlock tree. David hurried on when he heard the dogs baying and found her there, half-way up the tree, watching the dogs with a careless curiosity. She turned her head as he came up and snarled when she saw him, but otherwise she made no move.

> David caught the dogs, tied them a little way from the tree, then shot her.

Unfortunately the scene was not presented to reveal its barbarity or to strike a blow for conservation. It would be unfair, however, to count it as a balancing of accounts for dogs killed in cougar fights. In them a gun had had no part.

Given the power of rebuttal, Ki-yu (and almost all the panthers that Milton had deliberately entered the wilderness, the panthers' own domain, to destroy) might easily have pointed to the self-justification of Milton's logic. Milton tries to present a practice aimed at annihilation under the guise of a campaign of control. Years later, in a new introduction to *Panther,* Haig-Brown was to write of cougars, "A few aberrant individuals may become a danger to livestock or even to humans, and these should be hunted down and removed to protect the reputation of the species as a whole." This assessment makes sense, though in the last several words he steps out of Milton's character and, it would seem out of his own at the time when the book had been written.

As regards the place of the predator in the natural order, Haig-Brown is somewhat ambiguous. He does not damn cougars for killing deer, the hunters' usual complaint. Rather he falls back on the old economic argument in their defence. "They are wholly beneficial to man, for they keep the deer from growing too numerous, to be half-starved then decimated by disease." However true the observation may be, it would be equally so without "beneficial to man." Nevertheless Ki-yu's role here is equivocal. As protagonist (and hence strongest) he kills heavy bucks swiftly and cleanly and, moreover, refuses to eat a diseased deer. Wolves, the other major predators in *Panther,* however, always appear in an unfavourable light. They harass the deer herds relentlessly, so keeping them half-starved. Not for the wolves even the heroic fight of individual against individual, but the onset of the many, the gang, against the one. As if to emphasize their "ignobility," Haig-Brown gives them the role of killing the valiant Ki-yu, thus inadvertently placing in a bad light creatures that are merely demonstrating the acceptable function of predators.

Panther combines the objectivity of science with the heartlessness, if not cruelty, of the hunter. It never questions the morality or benefits of bounty hunting and, since it concerns itself so very much with hunting, Haig-Brown later tried to explain his position on the matter, a position that helps give the book its peculiar double focus. "I have personal experience as a hunter," he writes, "and of the hunter's very deep respect for his quarry. . . . The hunter has his function although it may be misconceived by some standards." Perhaps unsatisfied with this effort to defend Milton's role in *Panther*, Haig-Brown returns to the subject again in his new edition of the work. He removes the foreword praising John Cecil Smith, "the greatest of all panther hunters," and the preface vindicating all the blood-letting and replaces them with an introduction that seems at odds with his earlier attitudes and comments, reading in part as follows: "Many of us believed that cougars have a proper and valuable place in the ecology of deer and elk ranges even as long as forty years ago and were arguing, against strong opposition, for the abolition of bounty hunting." Surely *Panther* could not have been a strong part of that argument.

Criticized for all the cruelty and killing in *Panther,* Haig-Brown, despite a disclaimer against violence in children's books, justified his story on his usual grounds of authenticity. The violence was needed "to show something as it really is." "To deny death, which is often beautiful, to children is an offense. To conceal injury and pain is an offense. To exploit either or both is the worst offense of all." Haig-Brown is dealing here, of course, with a problem common to many realistic stories of wild animals, but especially the animal biography and again especially when it is long and based on the life of a large predator.

Paradoxically some of this criticism derives from Haig-Brown's strengths as an author. The chapter on Milton's night alone with his dogs in the woods, a splendid vignette, clearly discloses his ability to write realistic description:

> It was a wretchedly cold night, but David kept the fire piled with bark and managed to sleep a little now and then—facing the fire until his back grew cold enough to wake him, turning away from it until his back grew warm again and his face and chest were freezing. At one time during the night the wolves began to howl on the other side of the lake. Jack whimpered nervously in his sleep and, still asleep, drew a little nearer to the fire. Mona shivered and pressed herself closer to David.
>
> But daylight came at last, a grey, faint daylight, with snow in the northern sky. The valley was still and cold and drab. David piled bark on the fire and set the billy to boil snow-water just once more. He swallowed several cups of hot, strong tea and set out on the trail again.

There is little here or elsewhere in Haig-Brown's work of Roberts' or Grey Owl's purple-prose romanticism, nor of the excessive detail that often spoils realism.

When, however, Haig-Brown presents action in the same vivid manner, he catches it so dramatically that he seems consequently, as some critics argue, to emphasize violence:

> Ki-yu spat and growled and snarled. The bear squealed and roared. Ki-yu's sharp claws ripped through the bear's flesh, tearing muscles to the bone. The bear's long blunt claws raked Ki-yu from shoulder to haunch. Ki-yu's teeth tore at the bear's throat and face, once gripped a forearm and bit until it almost snapped before their grip was broken. The bear's teeth split open Ki-yu's shoulder and cut one of his ears to ribbons. Ki-yu's hindclaws thrust downward mightily and gashed the bear's belly until the entrails showed through the hide.

There are no fewer than five fights such as this and seven hunting scenes described in detail in the book. As a result, some critics have attacked it for its repetitiveness as well as its violence. Yet in all the episodes involved (which one critic likes for their cumulative effect), Haig-Brown tries

to solve the problem of repetition of scene, if not the sameness of violence. Ki-yu plays different tricks to elude his pursuers; he fights different adversaries for different reasons—a bear for food, a rival for a mate, a pack of wolves for life itself. Both flaws—if flaws—however, have a common source in the nature of the genre. *Panther,* even aside from the hunting scenes, again simply demonstrates the violence and repetition that must be part of a full-length realistic biography of a large predatory animal.

Following the long years spent on *The Western Angler* (1939), a study of West Coast salmon and trout and a commentary on fishing, Haig-Brown turned to the animal biography again, with another book on salmon, *Return to the River.* This time, however, he wrote of a Pacific spring salmon (*Oncorhynchus tshawytscha*) as opposed to an Atlantic one (*Salmo salar*), the subject of *Silver,* and the new book was not especially for children, for he wished not to make "concessions to simplicity, concreteness or anything else [he] considered desirable in writing for children." "I would think," he suggests, "that the difference in my own age and stage of maturity made more and greater difference between *Silver* and *Return* than the difference in setting" between Britain and Canada. At the same time he was aware, he admits, that

> the setting of *Return* had a certain grandeur and the fish themselves, in their massive abundance, were an altogether bigger and more impressive story than the smaller run of the smaller river in Great Britain. So [he] would say the mood is substantially different and [he] would suspect that the conclusions left to the reader would be different too since [he] had, in *Return,* a more sophisticated concept of salmon as a massive and important resource.

Unquestionably *Return to the River* was an off-shoot of his work on *The Western Angler.* It contains much the same natural history under the guise of fiction. In using this approach he had several aims. He wished to tell the story of a species in terms of an individual, the common aim of the animal biography, and so reduce his canvas to manageable size. He wished also "to straighten the records about salmon." Most of all, however, he wanted to create a general interest in salmon ichthyology and ecology, and to discuss the problem of electric power dams that were strangling the salmon rivers.

Although Haig-Brown did not intend *Return to the River* particularly for children, he believed the book enabled them, as well as adults, "to reach beyond themselves, into new sympathies, new understandings, bright and livelier imaginings" [as he stated in *Canadian Author and Bookman* (Spring 1959)]. All this aside, children are by nature interested in animals. Again, whereas *Panther* is admirable, *Return to the River* is both admirable and likeable. Moreover, with its vast setting, it provides an attraction lacking in *Panther.* The child, unconcerned with theories of migration and problems of fish management, can travel in imagination with Spring, the fishy "heroine," along great rivers, through forests and farmlands and cities to wander in the mysterious deeps of the ocean, led on by a story full of entertaining events.

For all the grandeur of the setting, however, Haig-Brown does not indulge in picturesque word-painting or the impressionism of the romantic. Neither is he Thoreauvian nor Wordsworthian. He feels for his world without trying to draw it into a poetic vision. For one thing, he is not trying to drive his reader out into some vague abstract world but to make him stand in awe, specifically of Spring and her world, and Haig-Brown has the vision and skill to achieve this aim. The description of the river that opens the book skilfully moves from a dynamic prose to a more static form, a precise expository prose, to depict the spawning bed. Again, the almost rhythmical linking of verbs ending in "ing" and those in the past tense, in the description of Canyon Pool, which Spring will leave and to which she will return, catches superbly the life and death struggle there, and also reinforces the controlling image of the book.

Time, as the long ago, like the spaciousness of the setting, adds an important dimension to the book, for its historical perspective gives it depth and feeling. When the Indian boy who spears Chinook draws its shape on the sandy shore of Salmon River, he expresses an attitude that has its roots in a prehistoric culture. When Spring moves to and from the ocean along the rivers of the Pacific coast, she is following a pattern as ancient as the mountains and valleys through which they flow, a setting that is within and beyond time for it is now, as in the beginning, a world of "fierce competition" and "sudden dangers," a stage on which the protagonists still play out their struggle for survival according to the law of the jungle.

In a neat contrast Haig-Brown brings the past into sharp focus in the present. Senator Evans, remembering his youth, speaks as Old America warning the New of the dangers to its natural resources if it continues to act on values that had effected "the rape of America." Now the salmon pass through valleys where once the "Douglas firs stood tall and straight" and through cities where sewage befouls the river and its very banks. Once free-flowing when "the splashings of Spring and her ancestors whitened the broad river from shore to shore," the Columbia, with the Williamette, Mackenzie, and the Snake, has become a strait-jacket of dams, ditches, and fish ladders. The primitive animistic Indian fisherman with his dip net has given way to seiners, trollers, and canners and to the technocrats who manage the salmon run in the name of science and the annual crop.

The nature of the material in *Return to the River* allowed Haig-Brown greater scope in one way than *Panther* had; yet it posed the old problems of the realistic animal biography, the sameness of chronological pattern, the similarity of event (escaping one predator being much like escaping another, climbing one fish ladder being much like climbing another), and writing fiction that would hold attention without falsifying natural history. With Spring he faced an even greater challenge than normal with the characteristic flatness of the protagonist's character. No salmon could have the "personality" of Ki-yu, nor could its story, since Haig-Brown refused to invent episodes, have the same dramatic possibilities as the cougar's with its terrestrial setting, its exciting scenes of violence, and its cast of hunt-

ers and farmers. Spring was an Everysalmon; Ki-yu was himself alone. *Return to the River* demanded of its author a different approach.

For one thing Haig-Brown emphasizes science more. He sets out the life history of the salmon (often in scientific terminology) in great detail. He describes the construction of the redds, spawning activities (including such matters as scale counts, age-sizes, and colouration), and finally mating and death. He specifically includes information about the oceanic distribution and range of salmon, once thought of as merely "somewhere" out there, tracing Spring's peregrinations along the continental shelf to the waters off Grahame Island, a hundred miles from Alaska. Aside from Don Gunner's patently ironic comments on Eastern experts who challenge the Westerners' (and Haig-Brown's) theories of salmon migration, *Return to the River* is surprisingly much less argumentative than *Silver.* Haig-Brown willingly admits (through Don Gunner) that *Return to the River* is in part conjectural. Nor is he himself afraid of "perhaps," particularly as regards fish movement.

If less openly didactic than *Silver, Return to the River* is far more subjective than *Panther.* Through Senator Evans, Haig-Brown adds an emotional element to his natural history, and he himself occasionally indulges openly in the pathetic fallacy, impressionistic biology, or anthropomorphism, call it what you will. Peregrines (in some doubtful ornithology) chase "the strongest flocks. . . . for the sport of it, because their fierce, quick brains and pulsing muscles craved instant satisfaction of the urge the sight of movement stimulated in them." Spring, too, "exults" in movement, feels pleasure in the drive of her muscles, and is buoyant at "the taste of salt water." She knows "a stronger delight as she nears the spawning grounds," where "an excitement possessed her" as she prepared a redd. The humanizing of animal behaviour here strikes a happy balance between that of *Silver* and *Panther.* The author perhaps reads into Spring's behaviour more than is scientifically justified, but not more than what, lacking contradictory evidence, seems a valid interpretation and a sincere tribute to a vital and splendid creature. *Return to the River* combines something of the old sentimental tradition of his first book with the realistic tradition of *Panther* and so has a quite different tone and imaginative thrust from the latter book. *Return to the River* is of course more mellow anyway because the nature of its protagonist precludes ferocity and gore, and it is more mellow, too, since it concerns itself more with conservation, but it differs most from *Panther* in that it reveals that Haig-Brown has got the feel of the grandeur of North America and has combined it with attitudes rooted in the imaginative sympathies of his childhood and youth.

Return to the River is more unified than *Panther* with its introductory chapters on Blackstreak, Ki-yu's father, and its two protagonists and divided narrative. In *Return to the River,* the story centres on the salmon and has an overall "plot" in as much as Senator Evans, early in the book, marks the fingerling Spring and so sets up a book-length question—will she return and in view of the tremendous odds against a double recapture by the right people, will he recapture her? Moreover, if Senator Evans and Don Gunner are, like Milton in *Panther,* often absent from long stretches of the book, their absence is far less significant, for they are essentially observers, not participants, in the story. Even if Milton is seen as symbolizing the threat of civilization to the natural world, the divided narrative reduces greatly, if it does not deny altogether, his effectiveness as a unifying force in the story. Again, even though Haig-Brown, for the sake of variety, but mainly for the chance to discuss fish management in different areas, breaks the conclusion of *Return to the River* into accounts of Sachem, Chinook, the tagged salmon, and Spring, he does not harm the unity of the narrative in any serious way. All go through the same general experiences. All are salmon, and the reader does not identify so strongly with any one of them as to preclude the four fish, in large part, having a common identity.

Spring lives in two worlds. On one hand there are nets, dams, and pollution, as if all mankind, not one lone hunter, stood against her. Unlike Ki-yu, however, she does have protectors among these enemies, a fact that helps differentiate the tone of *Return to the River* from *Panther.* On the other hand there are nature's predators—gulls, herons, ospreys, and mergansers, sharks, lampreys, squawfish, and sticklebacks, minks, bears, seals, and sea-lions. Each has a part in a drama governed largely by "the laws of hunger," which sets animal against animal and in which Spring is both hunted and huntress. Haig-Brown makes more of her in the former role, however, since it adds variety and some suspense to the story. Spring catching *Euphausia pacifica* and smelt has far less to offer dramatically and thematically than Ki-yu hunting deer or lying in wait for farmyard cattle, for her killings are unlikely to stir the reader's feelings either against the one or for the other.

For all of Spring's brushes with death in *Return to the River,* suspense does not become significant in itself, except perhaps in the remarkable descriptions of a heron fishing, an Indian boy waiting for Sachem, and one or two short episodes involving net or hook. The reader knows that Spring, for the sake of science and the story, bears a charmed life and will live out her days, even in defiance of Seton's dictum that "no wild animal dies of old age." The narrative flows and eddies, now moving through a series of experiences in the protagonist's life, now loitering in peripheral situations to describe a lamprey attacking a salmon, and eagle robbing an osprey, or to explain methods of trolling. Here and there it even stops while scientist and angler comment on problems related to the behaviour and conservation of salmon.

Obviously meant to vitalize these subjects and to give them a human touch, these interludes involving Gunner and Evans seem text-bookish. Their opening discussion on migration reads like a debate, and only with the trollers, Red Gifkin and Charlie Wilson, does the conversation seem natural. They are not burdened with a mission. They are cut from the same cloth as Milton, the kind of men Haig-Brown met and liked when he was a hunter and fisherman. By contrast Evans (who may have been drawn from Senator Charles L. McNary of Oregon) and Gunner

Haig-Brown on the Campbell River, British Columbia. From the National Film Board of Canada documentary A River Never Sleeps.

never appear experiental or real; their *raison d'être* centres on the thematic and didactic.

Senator Evans looks much like an atonement for Milton (and the author of *Panther*). An "incorrigible old sentimentalist," his attitudes toward nature are the very opposite to those expressed or implied in that book, though, since fly fishing is regarded as the sport of gentlemen, he can take a trout with a fly and still remain a nature lover. Remembering the days of his youth when the salmon abounded, he introduces a feeling of nostalgia and remorse that gives the cause of salmon conservation an emotional basis. It fits the story and gives it emotional depth, too, that he, now an old man, at the conclusion should watch Spring in her spawning—on her life-giving death-bed— which he "felt in his heart" was the last natural spawning of the chinooks that belonged to his river. Like the salmon runs, his way of seeing nature faces the danger of being lost in a nation dedicated to industrial and commercial exploitation in the name of Progress, to science and to biologists like Don Gunner, Evans' foil—those "cold-blooded people" who, with their rationalizations and their racks, traps, trucks, fish ladders and hatcheries, would leave no place for a sentimental attachment to nature. Yet the Senator comes to recognize "these white-coated young men" of the State and Federal Agencies as "the symbol of America's salvation." Thanks to them the dam at Bonneville supplied power without hurting fish, thus satisfying his pride in American enterprise and his concern for salmon.

For Haig-Brown, these scientists are only half the problem. He has a place for the Senator Evanses, also, for he has Don Gunner say to Evans when speaking of a salmon pool, "You may not be able to name all the whys and wherefores, but you understand without that. You feel it." As for Haig-Brown himself, he plots his book so that the old man (and Silver) have a moment of triumph at the conclusion when a flood carries away the rack that Evans had tried to demolish and that had denied the fish their freedom to "spawn as they were meant to spawn." His central point, however, as regards the Evanses, is that they are the people who must motivate and direct the work on salmon.

Aside from a naturalist and scientist, the *dramatis personae* of **Return to the River** include an Indian boy who sees salmon as food and as sacred beings and those, like Happy Hammond the troller, who consider them in terms of profit. Once, too, it includes a drowsy angler whom Spring playfully awakens, thus supplying the one touch of humour (never a strong point with Haig-Brown) in all the high seriousness of the book. Unfortunately it omits a canner, a spokesman from the business world, to round out the circle of Spring's observers.

The trollers, however, do come close to being the businessman's representative for, as Charlie Wilson says, their fleet seemed "a perfect symbol of individual effort." It must have seemed so to Haig-Brown too, if the later **Saltwater Summer** (1949) is evidence, for that book celebrates the hard work and self-reliance of the off-shore trollers as the criteria of success. Indeed Senator Evans and Don Gunner could fit easily into Haig-Brown's juvenile fiction. Kindly and wiser older men and resourceful young men are central to it. Evans and Gunner, like the protagonists of the boys' books, have little moral or psychological complexity. Their motivations and reactions are direct responses to things and circumstances rather than to matters of their own personalities. They are as much sounding boards and propagandists as they are human beings. Had they been otherwise, they might easily have drawn attention away from the true subject of the book.

Beyond all these characters is the river itself which, without being personified, is a living presence in the book. Haig-Brown loved rivers and had already written a story of one in **Pool and Rapid** (1932), and in **Return to the River** he has actually written another, for Spring is the embodiment of the spirit of the river. "The salmon [are] the river. . . . they are its yield, growing from it, growing on it, giving themselves back to it. . . . " The ditches, dams, and pollution desecrate it and the salmon die in consequence. Yet in the end the river, in a magnificent gesture of defiance, rises like a champion and sweeps away the rack that keeps the salmon from their home waters. It would be easy to follow this line of thought too far and see it as a comment on nature's ultimate power over man and so on, or as a revelation of a wish fulfillment deriving from Haig-Brown's youthful attitudes to nature or from his fundamental dislike of the commercial world. Whatever its purpose or origin, however, it is more than a *deus ex machina* to supply the story with as happy an ending as possible, given the fact that Spring and all the others returning with her must die.

Return to the River does not, like "The Last Barrier," Roberts' story of a salmon, centre on Darwinism. Haig-Brown's dams are man-made, not accidents of nature as in Roberts' story. His concern over Spring is for a species in an environment that modern entrepreneurial man has refashioned, and not a concern over the killing of individual animals by hunter and fisherman. Haig-Brown's vision here has a different and broader orientation.

While a great salmon may be an object of awe for Evans, the trolling fleet, as earlier indicated, symbolizes for Charlie Wilson the best spirit of private enterprise (though Donald Waterfield in *Continental Waterboy* (1970) questions the observation). The author carries this kind of materialistic argument to its ultimate when he himself is moved to justify the survival of the salmon because of their value to industry:

> If the sum of this efficiency [of nets and boats] was a threat to Spring and her race, it was also a justification for their survival. Year after year the drift gill-nets take their millions of pounds of chinooks in the Columbia and men live by it, fairly and freely—fisherman, packers, cannery workers and the men who supply these people with their daily needs and the men who sell salmon in the cans. . . . a solid block of human life dependent upon the salmon runs. . . .

Even if he can cite the Old Testament as evidence that the creatures of nature are here for man's use, even if his argument is practical—and for business and government unquestionably the most persuasive—the word "justification," as used here, is disturbing, as it would be in any other modern discussion of conservation, and it is a denial of Senator Evans' basic view of nature.

Return to the River supposedly demonstrates the need to recognize, not fundamentally to deny, the view of Senator Evans. Without his way of seeing, there was the danger (as the Grand Coulee dam revealed) that technology would concern itself with fisheries *vis-a-vis* hydro-electric power development only if the value of the first allegedly surpassed the second. Like Senator Evans, Haig-Brown is caught in a dilemma. He, too, leans to the "sentimental" view of nature and yet believes that the one chance salmon have rests with science and engineering. So both author and Evans look with favour on the Bonneville dam. There is the suggestion also that they appreciate the whole programme of damming the rivers inasmuch as it made the "Fisheries guys" wise to all "them haywire" dams and ditches that do the "real harm." Certainly both are impressed by the ingenious way in which salmon are trapped and trucked to their spawning streams, for all these developments hold out hope for the future of the salmon runs. Yet though Evans (and the author) make little of the real difficulties of hydrologic coordination and fish management (the dangers of fish having the "bends" below the dams, of reservoir or so-called lake silting, and of temperature and chemical changes in the waters) the senator (and probably the author) is unsatisfied. The uncertainty enters to the detriment of the book because it superimposes the story of Senator Evans on the life history of Spring, for whatever the flood means as fiction, it takes almost all the emotional force of the argument for conservation away from science and technology, if it does not actually put them in a bad light. Haig-Brown's heart and head are not at one here. As *Panther* lacks focus since the author seems never quite decided whether his subject is Ki-yu or Milton, though the conflict between them is often direct and centre stage, so there is an ambivalence in *Return to the River.* Here Evans and Spring stand against a special manifestation of civilization so that according to the plot the balance favours nature and the old-time values of an old naturalist, though the gist and logic of the argument for conservation in the book would seem to tip it the other way.

Return to the River is an American book. When it appeared, Canada had not yet begun a dam-building programme on the West coast, much less the Bennett Dam on the Peace River. The story of Spring, written to entertain, warn, advise, and reassure the Americans, may well have been intended also for Canadians. Whatever its intent, its message seems to have fallen on deaf ears. B. C. Hydro's plans to dam the Fraser River and probably the Skeena and the Stikine stand witness to the fact. In this perspective the book seems dated. In a foreword to a new edition (1976), Haig-Brown himself becomes a Senator Evans. "Two or three years ago," he writes, "I watched a few spawning chinooks far up the Salmon River in Idaho, a sad little shadow of the runs of old" in the Columbia which, once a "magnificent river," is now little more than a "series of freshwater impoundments." But like the Senator, he is half-hopeful and notes that the oxygen levels of the polluted Willamette, which once led Spring to the sea, now "rarely fall below the minimum requirements of salmon."

On another level *Return to the River* has not dated, for beyond all the matters of fiction, characters, and conservation, it treats with impressive sensitivity the miracle of migration, "the far journey and faithful return," which constitutes the lives of salmon and in which Spring concretizes the dynamic force of nature. The story is more than a dramatized presentation of a natural wonder, however. Its roots are deep in the life of man, for it reflects aspects of his own world, the struggle for freedom against great odds, the questing spirit and the odyssean search for home. By juxtaposing the natural and the human, *Return to the River* puts each in a light that is common to both and that reveals the dangers of the alienation of man from nature.

Haig-Brown wants so much to be an affirmer. If all is "cycles within cycles, freshness and decay," all is also, he writes, "constant change, death and new life." In his animal biographies, this wish seems to put him on all sides at once: as hunter and nature lover, as scientist and sentimentalist, and as one who reveres the spirit of free enterprise, but laments what economic man has done and is doing to America. His ambivalence may derive from his English background. *Panther,* which is truly North American, seems in part to have been an experiment, since *Re-*

turn to the River, with its sentimentality and its interest in the rights of animals in a man-centred world, turns back some distance to the English tradition. Here Haig-Brown differs from his peers Roberts and Seton and gives the Canadian animal biography a new direction in that he openly makes his concern for the species and its environment integral to his theme and art. (pp. 21-37)

> Alec Lucas, *"Haig-Brown's Animal Biographies,"* in Canadian Children's Literature, No. 11, 1978, pp. 21-38.

Carole Gerson

The Whale People was published in London in 1962, in New York in 1963, and in 1964 it was selected as Children's Book of the Year by the Canadian Association of Children's Librarians. In *The Republic of Childhood,* Sheila Egoff describes it as "an outstanding historical novel for children," and in 1980 Joan McGrath, elementary school libraries' consultant for the Toronto Board of Education, listed it first in her series of "Reviews in Retrospect," discussing out of print Canadian children's books in *In Review* [August, 1980]. Hence the current Totem reprint should be warmly welcomed by those who select and promote children's books, as well as by readers between the ages of ten and fourteen.

Two decades do not constitute a vast time span in the realm of literature, and one would expect a book so well received twenty years ago to stand up well today. As an adventure story, *The Whale People* is exciting and eloquent; Haig-Brown's vivid descriptions of pre-technological whaling and his sympathetic account of the physical training and spiritual preparation of a Nootka youth as he is initiated into manhood still ring lively and sincere. In the first few pages, this novel threatens to belong to that class of informative children's literature in which every object is followed by a description of its materials and manner of construction. But the narrative's basic delineation of pre-contact life among the Hotsath Indians of the west coast of Vancouver Island soon modulates into a paean to what the fisherman Roderick Haig-Brown must have seen as the ultimate fishing experience: the successful pursuit of the largest sea creatures with the simplest of mechanical aids.

The story follows several years in the life of Atlin, adolescent son of a whale-chief. As Haig-Brown describes the education of the boy, who must attain both physical prowess and spiritual power in order to take over from his father when the latter dies while hunting a sperm whale, he reveals his detailed research into prehistoric Nootka fishing techniques and his appreciation of the Indians' intimate relationship with nature. Atlin must do more than learn the habits of whales and acquire the stamina to pursue them: he must enter into symbolic communion with their spirits, so that his hunting and the survival of his people will be part of the unity of nature rather than a struggle against it. And he must learn to operate out of a psychological wholeness which will give him the self-confidence and wisdom to work in harmony with the other men of his tribe, and the diplomatic generosity needed to pacify his people's irritable neighbours.

In the details of Atlin's fasts and trials, moments of doubt and triumph, Haig-Brown certainly succeeds in presenting to modern day adolescents a realistic portrait of a youth living in a culture which expected children to grow up quickly and often painfully. Many episodes, such as Atlin's first trip with the whalers, his visit to the Shark Pool, and the potlatch and Shaman's Dance, are written with a masterful control of tension and suspense. However, I personally found the total picture of Atlin's life to be rather sparse. Details of fishing equipment and dramatic accounts of whaling excursions abound, yet we learn almost nothing of Atlin's family life, or his food, clothing, or shelter. While I am in no way suggesting that the author should have produced an anthropological tract, I do feel that his intention to have his reader enter Atlin's skin is somewhat undercut when the reader has to guess what is covering or nourishing that skin.

I have already said that this book has worn well. However, its reprinting in an age of great sensitivity to sexual and racial discrimination gives rise to questions engendered by its new context. In a 1975 interview [in *Canadian Children's Literature*, No. 2], Haig-Brown clearly indicated that he knew he had approached his subject from the outside:

> I have no idea how close I have come to getting inside the mind of a young, high-class Indian boy in pre-contact times. I suspect not very close because there is a vast difference in conditioning between us. George Clutesi read the book and said: "I can tell you are a very sincere man." I take that to mean, "you have tried honestly, but you have really not got inside our thinking."

However, one would be hard-pressed to find particular instances of condescension or detraction. The characters speak simply, without the symbols and metaphors that well-meaning white writers often put into Indian mouths, but also without contractions (in contrast to the colloquial, slangy speech which enlivens Haig-Brown's *Starbuck Valley Winter* and *Saltwater Summer*). Haig-Brown may be guilty of idealizing the spiritual side of Hotsath life, but his romantic tendencies are somewhat balanced by his descriptions of physical and psychological distress. More pertinent, I think, is the matter of sexual bias. This is very much a boys' book, which presents an almost exclusively male society. Atlin's mother makes several fleeting appearances near the beginning, and at the end, Atlin will ensure future peace by marrying the daughter of his enemy. Not only are women excluded from the rituals and work of whaling, but in this novel their activities remain utterly unrecorded—although their day-to-day presence could scarcely have touched Atlin's life as little as the author indicates. I don't particularly approve of faulting a writer for simply reflecting the biases of his age; perhaps in this decade someone will produce the story of Atlin's sister or wife, so that Canadian children will be able to read about Whale People of both sexes. (pp. 113-15)

> *Carole Gerson, in a review of "The Whale People," in* Canadian Children's Literature, *Nos. 31-32, 1983, pp. 113-15.*

Heather Kirk

What, specifically, are the merits of Haig-Brown as a writer for children? In my opinion he was one of the very few Canadians who took his vocation seriously and yet avoided simple-minded moralizing. Furthermore, he was an innovator, applying high standards of technique and subject matter to his work, and being above all thoughtful. Never degenerating into writing sequels, he produced outstanding books in at least three of the four genres he chose to try. At the root of his accomplishments was an unusual vision of life which matured as he attempted over and over again to express it. His was an attempt to find meaning for himself by finding it for others, including children. "My first thought on writing for children," said Haig-Brown in an address to an International Reading Association conference in 1959 [published in *Canadian Author and Bookman* (Spring 1959)], "is that I do not consider it a thing apart."

> It is simply writing to be read by a lively, curious, active and exciting audience. I would not dream of insulting this audience by making things too easy. One of the purposes of writing for them, as in all writing, is to make them reach, cause them to understand something new or something old in a new way, to leave them a little richer in mind and spirit than before.

He challenged children to think hard about life and to feel profoundly by presenting them with a complete view of the world to which they could relate which was exciting yet sobering, and increasingly ripe with spiritual implications and the essence of a fundamental code of ethics. His vision, perhaps best expressed in [Glenys Stow's] phrase "unity with natural things" [Stow, "A Conversation with Roderick Haig-Brown," *Canadian Children's Literature* (Summer 1975)], is wider and deeper in implication than that suggested by W. J. Keith [in *Canadian Literature* (Summer 1981)]—"ownership through knowledge" which evolves through the idea of "responsibility" to the importance of "conservation"—Keith's vision is an important subtext. What Haig-Brown wanted to say to children was that only by fitting into the world as it is—not conforming but rather *per*forming superbly within it—can one find meaning in one's existence. This theme—which evolved in part out of Haig-Brown's early experiences among West Coast loggers where he learned, as he put it [in *Canadian Literature* (Summer 1959)], "the daily truth of hard work and danger"—is reworked again and again until in Haig-Brown's last and best work of fiction for children, *The Whale People,* it receives its most complete and satisfying expression. I would say that in *The Whale People,* as well as to a lesser extent *Starbuck Valley Winter, Saltwater Summer, Panther* and *Silver,* Haig-Brown achieves the ultimate goal of a writer for children, providing for children what Bruno Bettelheim in *The Uses of Enchantment* states a child "ought to gain from the experience of literature: access to a deeper meaning, and that which is meaningful to him at his stage of development."

The world as it is, according to Haig-Brown, must contain nature. Human life must take into account the lives of plants and animals. This implies not only that people must take responsibility for their planet—a now widely disseminated theme of conservationists and ecologist—but also that people must live closely in harmony with nature, and thus with themselves. Throughout Haig-Brown's writing career, what he had to say to and about people was largely based on his observations about the non-human species. In his preface to the 1934 *Panther,* he wrote: "Almost all the ills of the human race may be traced to the fact that it has strayed too much from nature and knows too little of the natural order of things." Forty years later, in the Stow interview, his words were softer and the message had apparently become a polite call for conservation:

> I do, most intensely, want to let people know, whether they are adults or children, something of the way of the life of the world, apart from humans, [that] is. . . . I would like all people to see and understand more because there is both pleasure and fulfillment in seeing and understanding, and because the only hope of preserving the natural world is in the deep understanding of people.

But the later, conventional and acceptable message of the now public man is terribly understated. Haig-Brown is now only able to expose the full implications of his very original feelings and thoughts indirectly, through fiction, where he can with relief "get away and free the imagination from all restrictions." Further on in the Stow interview, when he is discussing *The Whale People,* Haig-Brown expresses himself more clearly, if still in understatement, because he himself is less directly implicated:

> [The] sense of unity between any primitive people depending upon hunting and fishing and the land and the wild creatures they depend on is very strong indeed. It is, of necessity, strong in any good hunter and any good fisherman. The native Indian concepts of the creatures they hunted and fished for were intimate and very beautiful. They were also quite highly self-centred, as one would expect. There was the idea of return, replenishment, replacement. There was a sense of equality rather than superiority, of a shared humanness rather than two alien natures. All these concepts I find very touching and very beautiful and I imagine, under the circumstances of those early lives, very useful. . . . I believe that by cultivating it, we can carry our sense of unity with natural things to a much higher plane than even the Indians were able to achieve. . . . Sophisticated thinking is by no means hostile to emotional concepts, and love of the land and the creatures of the land is by no means hostile to religious concepts. . . .

This is not merely a call for conservation. Nor is this merely a nostalgic longing for an idealized past of another, idealized race—Golden Age escapism. This is a strong statement by a highly civilized man of a radical view: contemporary man, however sophisticated, must recognize that he himself is subject to the laws of nature—if he is to survive *psychologically* as well as physically, if he is to be whole and well.

Haig-Brown's view—which was probably rooted in the pantheism and idealization of childhood that Peter Coveney [in his *The Image of Childhood,* 1967] has identified

Haig-Brown's wife Ann at the dedication of the Roderick Haig-Brown Conservation Area at Adams River, British Columbia, in 1978.

in most late-19th and 20th-century British writers for children as late-Romantic, middle-class revolt against "utilitarian values and the Machine," but developed beyond mere escapism because of Haig-Brown's early and thorough exposure to the raw West Coast wilderness and the men who dealt with it—is expressed in his fiction for children in three stages corresponding to the beginning, middle, and end of his writing career when he wrote respectively his animal stories, his outdoors-adventure fiction, and his historical fiction. At all three stages there is one central metaphor, hunting, which symbolizes meaningful work. For a being to be whole and well, according to Haig-Brown, he must have meaningful work: activity which demands the best of him and which ultimately contributes to the well-being of his species. [Compare this to Bettelheim: "To find deeper meaning, one must be able to transcend the narrow confines of a self-centred existence and believe that one will make a significant contribution to life—if not right now, then at some future time"]. At all three stages there are hunters and hunted, and the hunters themselves are hunted, or at least vulnerable. In the animal stories, the focus is on the hunted animals, while in the outdoors-adventure fiction and the historical fiction the focus is on man the hunter, but at all three stages the main concern is with man's place in the natural cycle and integration and interdependence—the so-called "web of life" extended to people as well as plants and animals—emerges increasingly as the ultimate goal.

In his animal stories, *Silver: An Atlantic Salmon* and *Panther,* Haig-Brown, as Stow comments, makes "the natural cycle so engrossing that we can sense the drama in the life-death pattern of a salmon's journey, for example, or of a panther's struggle for survival." Yet authenticity is never sacrificed for the sake of emotional impact. On the contrary, as [Alec] Lucas points out [in *Canadian Children's Literature* (Summer 1978)], Haig-Brown's worthy successors in the unique Canadian tradition of the realistic animal story begun by Charles G. D. Roberts and Ernest Thompson Seton, offer even greater realism than their predecessors. Haig-Brown, according to Lucas, does not use animals as "human archetypes" like Roberts does; he avoids the "adulterated Darwinism" of Seton and Roberts; and he does not indulge in either the "purple-prose romanticism" of Roberts or Grey Owl or the "excessive detail that often spoils realism." [Sheila] Egoff too mentions [in her *Republic of Childhood,* 1975] that Haig-Brown "emphasizes the truths of wild animal life to an even greater degree than Roberts and Seton."

For the sake of authenticity, both *Silver* and *Panther* are structurally based on the life cycle of the animals concerned. In the opening paragraphs of *Silver,* two nameless salmon are spawning while a nameless man looks on with "tremendous interest." The salmon turn out to be the parents of Silver, who is from birth the "strongest and healthiest" salmon of them all, the one who manages to survive all sorts of danger and deprivation, reach the colossal weight of 60 lbs., and go up river to spawn not just once but four times. (This presumably is authentic, "survival of the fittest" Darwinism.) The man turns out to be the "Good Fisherman," because he is "such a great fisherman and fine sportsman," knowledgeable about the ways of fish and concerned about conservation, but also so emotionally involved in the natural phenomena he observes as to be virtually a worshipper: "for he loved salmon as some men love their books or their wives, and his whole heart was bound up in the delight of gaining new knowledge of them." When he catches Silver before he is full grown, the Good Fisherman marks one of his fins with a "small metal disc," and returns him gently into the water. ["Small trout and salmon parr are delicate little things: if you just throw them back into the river any old how they're almost sure to die"]. When Silver is full grown and, on his fourth journey to spawn, is unable to make the leap up the waterfalls because the water in the river is too low, the Good Fisherman is the only angler wily enough to catch the fish, and the catch is not merely a prize to the man, for he is deeply moved by the sight of the "great fish" with the "wonderful heart," fighting magnificently to the end, until he is simply "the battered glory that had been Silver." The Good Fisherman's entire raison d'être is to observe and care about the salmon; the salmon exists only to struggle and reproduce, and his struggle is admired by—is even the chief inspiration to—the man.

Panther likewise begins with the mating of the parents of the principal character, Ki-yu, who is again the strongest and most aggressive of his siblings, as well as the only

male. It ends with Ki-yu's death. Again the animal's life consists of one long struggle to survive and reproduce. Again there is a human observer of the animal, who hunts him yet who also understands and appreciates him. This time the hunter is named—his name is David Milton—and though his role is similar to that of the Good Fisherman, he is less sentimentalized and more fully developed as a character. That is not to say that his personality is probed in any depth; he has a wife, for example, but this relationship is completely unexplored. Rather his skill is elaborated upon: Haig-Brown carefully explains why he is such a good hunter. Basically, Milton has hunted all his life, and he is made for hunting. He has "confidence and understanding" as well as "experience and endurance." His physical features are made to seem admirable because functional:

> His face was clean-shaven and pleasant, with a fine straight nose and a good-natured mouth and chin; but it was entirely dominated by his dark eyes—clear, keen, tolerant eyes that told of endless patience, of a calm, good-natured acceptance of the queer things his life forced upon him. After his eyes, his body was remarkable; long-armed and long-legged, supple and lightly built as a boy's, yet very sure of itself and carried with an ease that was perfect grace. He walked smoothly with a long, flat, straight-footed stride and an almost imperceptible spring to each step. He carried a rifle in the crook of his left arm and a half-filled packsack on his back—and he was so used to both burdens that they seemed to fit his body perfectly.

Indeed, Milton the hunter is remarkably like Ki-yu the hunted (who is of course also a hunter): a glorious animal different only in that he can think as well as follow instincts.

David Milton's attitude toward the panthers he hunts is not sentimental. At times he can even be shockingly perfunctory. When, for example, Milton shoots Ki-yu's mate, Haig-Brown manages to put pathos in the scene without putting pity in Milton. Ki-yu's mate, Osa, enraged because she has just lost all her young to a wolverine, is threatening one of Milton's dogs when he comes upon her:

> He shouted, but she did not hesitate or look up; her eyes were fixed on Mona [the dog]. Swiftly he raised his rifle and fired. The bullet flew past Mona's head and struck Osa squarely between the eyes, so that she plunged forward and crumpled. Both dogs were upon her in an instant, tearing at her hide while she was still kicking; but the movement of her legs was feeble and uncontrolled and her claws had drawn in at the shock of the bullet.

> David went up and stood looking down at the dogs. He heard Carl coming up the hill, hurrying to learn the reason of the shot, but he bent down and caressed both dogs.

> "It's not the right one, is it, dogs?" he said softly. "But we don't care do we?"

Nor is Milton's attitude toward his dogs sentimentalized, for his feelings are inextricably linked to his working relationship with the animals. When, for example, Milton thinks that both his dogs Jim and Jack have been killed, he is "wretched" mainly because of what the loss will mean to his ability to make a living:

> He had time now to realise what his loss meant: Jim was dead; Jack also must have been killed or he would have returned by now—the only two dogs he had that were fully trained, the two dogs he had been hunting with for years and had learned to trust, which were his livelihood. Three years to train a panther-dog, he told himself bitterly, three years and less than a minute to lose one.

Milton's place in the web of life is not idealized. Milton hunts simply because he is "essentially a professional hunter. He made his living—supported a family and kept up his house at the mouth of Wapiti River—almost entirely by hunting panthers." Nor does Milton have higher motives like conservation—though he does regard it as his duty to kill panthers who are threatening farms and though he never kills wantonly.

If there is a conservation message in *Panther,* the message is subtle and indirect. One becomes so interested in the animal that one admires him—even though he is a killer who does become overconfident and kills wantonly and attacks farm animals, and even though he is never anthropomorphized. One feels that, so long as he kills to survive and does not interfere with legitimate human endeavours, he has as much or more right to roam free in the wild as does the man who hunts to feed himself and his family. Haig-Brown's motive seems to be to ennoble both Ki-yu and David Milton: to ennoble them and to show them as beings fulfilled because they engage themselves utterly in the ultimate life-and-death struggle. Their understanding of and struggle with each other ennobles them. There is here an almost Hemingway-esque code of ethics. This code raises rugged individualism almost to the level of religion, but the code in the final analysis is not quite satisfactory because it ignores questions about interrelationships between man and man. In the final analysis, *Panther* is very much a boys' book in the tradition of Robert Louis Stevenson's *Treasure Island* and Rudyard Kipling's *Jungle Books.* Although the central characters in *Panther* are adult through most of the story, and although the treatment of animals is quite original, as is the theme, the central characters (with whom presumably the child identifies) mainly engage in having great adventures off by themselves away from society; and in doing so they consistently prove themselves clever and able fellows. In other words, *Panther* is an extended coming-of-age story where the protagonists never stop proving themselves until the day they die (inevitably of unnatural causes).

In the outdoors-adventure fiction written almost fifteen years after the animal fiction, *Starbuck Valley Winter* and *Saltwater Summer,* the hunter's side of the man-and-nature connection is still more fully explored. The coming-of-age story is divided into two parts, with the first book being about the individual finding his self, and the second being about the individual finding his place in human society. The central character in both books is Don Morgan, who is sixteen years old, an orphan living with his uncle and aunt on a farm in British Columbia. In the first book, *Starbuck Valley Winter* (1944), one witnesses Don's growth to independent manhood, a growth of mind and spirit that takes him to the threshold of self-confident competence in his chosen profession as a hunter and trapper. In the second book, *Saltwater Summer* (1947), one watches the young man growing into a social being, taking his place as a man among men. The two books together take place over the course of one year; Don's development is far faster than it would be in life; Haig-Brown has learned how to compress. The plots of both books are admirably crafted to highlight Don's step-by-step development without sacrificing suspense. In the first book the developments are task-related; in the second they are decision-related.

In *Starbuck Valley Winter,* the question "Can I be a hunter?" is answered gradually as Don proves his skills initially by killing a deer by himself, then by successfully hunting and trapping for an entire winter, despite many difficulties and obstacles like loneliness, inexperience, his aunt's opposition to the scheme, a hostile neighbour, and his partner's being seriously injured. The minor subplots—Don's inventing, building and testing a waterwheel to pump water to his uncle's house and his cousin Ellen's wanting to marry someone her mother does not approve of—carefully underline the importance of self-reliance and skill, and the need for young people to assert their independence despite parental opposition. Don's discoveries about his eccentric, aggressive hermit neighbour Lee Jetson—that he is a prospector like Don's own father; that he has been treated badly by people and is therefore overly suspicious of them; and that he can be a knowledgeable and helpful friend when he is offered understanding and treated well—underline the paradox that in becoming more confident of himself, Don becomes less rebellious against the adults around him. But it is Don's growing knowledge of himself, rather than of others, that is the most important in this book: others are mainly sketchy father-figures like Uncle Joe and Jetson who teach him hunting skills, or a peer like Tubby who lacks these skills and so suffers by comparison with Don. Like David Milton in *Panther,* Don Morgan is born to hunt. In *Starbuck Valley Winter,* rather than a whole personality developing, one sees a hunter emerging; yet the text is not without psychological subtleties or without wider ramifications—one witnesses also the growth of an inventive, independent mind. This is made clear in the opening paragraphs:

> Young Don Morgan lay with his back against the roots of a big alder tree, looking out at the quick, broken flow of the Starbuck River. A long-handled, four-pronged digging fork was on the ground beside him and just back of where he lay was the dark-soiled clearing in the alders where he had been digging spuds since morning. Watching the river, his mind was busy with sudden inspiration. There it was, all that water going past, right past the farm, twenty-four hours a day, year in, year out, and there was, as they had said a thousand times, no way of getting it up on the land—no way that they could afford, anyhow. But the house was something else again. Now they pumped water by hand

from the well outside the back door. Don's sudden inspiration showed him the river pumping its own water, not enough to irrigate the pastures perhaps, but enough for the house.

The flow of water to turn a wheel and the wheel's movement used to drive the pump—even that old hand pump at the back door. It wasn't clear in his mind yet, but he knew he could work it out; it was a wonder Uncle Joe hadn't thought of it years ago, except Uncle Joe wasn't the mechanical kind.

But even the new thought didn't make Don altogether happy. He wasn't exactly miserable—he hadn't any reason for being miserable and he had several good reasons for being happy—but he had so darn much figuring to do that for the moment the world seemed just too big to cope with.

Everything was going on at once and nothing was happening, and from somewhere in the revolving, oppressive mix-up he had to find what he was going to do during the winter. . . .

Don Morgan is, as Sheila Egoff says, a "believable" teenage boy.

In *Saltwater Summer* as the question "Can I be a fisherman?" is answered—if he is to hunt in the winter, he must fish in the summer when he cannot hunt—Don's psychology is proved far more extensively as he comes to decisions about how to behave on the basis of his observations of the adults around him. Don is seen to be, as Egoff asserts, "a rather complex person" who is "moody," "ambitious" and "impulsive." His "path to heroism," says Egoff, "is a process of development, not a melodramatic change of heart." What's more, the psychology of the adults is also probed—an important innovation on Haig-Brown's part. "Haig-Brown knows how to handle adults," says Egoff:

> In most Canadian children's books the world of youth is quite divorced from the world of adults. . . . Haig-Brown's adults do not catch the imagination as do Stevenson's great creations, but at least they exist. They have mixed motives, complexity, reality.

I cannot recall *any* children's book—British, American or Canadian—where the central, child character wants to and must involve himself with adults to such a degree. Indeed, to my knowledge, virtually all the important works of fiction for children of the last century or so in English have been written according to the unwritten law that children live in a world quite separate from adults. As Don learns to be a man among men, he is not just searching for a role model (although this is certainly a great part of what he is doing), he is also absorbing realities of the adult world to a remarkable degree. As Don sets off with his friend Tubby for the fishing grounds far north of where his uncle and aunt live, he begins to lose the prestige and self-respect that he earned through his hunting prowess the previous winter as he makes one mistake after another in his new situation—mainly because he does not follow the right examples. Some of the other men are lazy or ignorant, or they make excuses for themselves and drink to forget their troubles. One man, "Old Cowbells," is suc-

cessful but strange and eccentric, keeping too much to himself. The partnership that most draws Don is unfathomable because Red Holiday, who seems so competent, puts up with Tom Moore who is strangely silent, whose hands shake, who suddenly attempts suicide and then sobs uncontrollably. Gradually Don learns that Tom has been in the war and is suffering combat fatigue; Red served with him and remembers him as an outstanding leader of men. As Don learns by trial and error to balance confidence and assertiveness with a recognition of the worth of others, Tom (because of Red's faith in him and care) slowly recovers. When the men argue about the rights of the Japanese Canadians to fish and own land on the West Coast, Tom shows himself the clearest thinker. Later in several rescues, he shows himself courageous and strong, a leader again, but always capable of co-operation. By the end of the book, one supposes that Don too will eventually be some sort of leader (an outstanding specimen like Silver and Ki-yu), but he will be very much aware of his limitations, and of the necessity and strengths of others.

Otherness is likewise the crucial concept in *The Whale People,* written nearly fifteen years after *Starbuck Valley Winter* and *Saltwater Summer,* the book which Egoff calls one of Canada's best works of historical fiction for children, and which Stow says many call Haig-Brown's best work—otherness being both other people and other creatures, human society and nature. In *Starbuck Valley Winter* and *Saltwater Summer,* the man-nature, man-man interface is not perfectly realized, with the former book concentrating more on Don's ability to cope with the wilderness and the latter on his ability to cope with people. In both books, man's relationship to nature is somewhat indirectly expressed in particular moments when Don finds himself very moved by his connectedness with the land and living creatures (as in the "ownership through knowledge" passage quoted by Keith) or when Don learns an important lesson about nature like the need for conservation (as when he is goaded by drunken fishermen into killing a deer out of season, is shocked at his own behaviour, and thinks "Wrong to kill deer out of season, but it was more deeply wrong to kill and waste meat.") In *The Whale People* Haig-Brown achieves a remarkable, even poetic vision of perfect integration between self, nature and society. *The Whale People,* says Egoff, has a "simple strength, dignity, and even starkness that are akin to the great northern myths." Haig-Brown's creative imagination, says Egoff, makes us "part of man's long quest, first to find himself and then to find his place in the world around him." *The Whale People* is, Egoff also says, a remarkable example of "dramatic unity." Egoff is quite right. In this coming-of-age story, the action takes place over three years (not two, as Egoff says). During that short span, the central character, Atlin, son of a Hotsath tribe chief, develops from carefree childhood to competent adulthood. He experiences tragedy, triumph, and love; he learns how to earn a livelihood and lead his people; he wins a wife and saves his tribe from war; yet he is not a hero, but rather part of the long traditions of a proud people. That the title of the book is not *Atlin's Quest,* or some such thing, but *The Whale People,* points to the unusual maturity of Haig-Brown's vision here, where he seeks to celebrate a people rather than an individual, a people whose existence depends upon their knowledge of and respect for nature and their ability to co-operate with each other.

Yet Atlin, like all Haig-Brown's protagonists in his fiction for children, is a remarkable being with whom a child would gladly identify. And too, the focus of the narrative is always on the boy, always on doing rather than thinking or feeling, and never blurs into abstract theorizing or moralizing. The book opens, for example, with a description of Atlin and a friend fishing:

> It was a hot day, with a westerly wind, but inside Kashutl Inlet, behind the rock bluffs of the northern shore, the water was still as glass. The two boys, Atlin and Hinak, were letting the canoe drift over the cod-bank that lay a few hundred feet out from the bluffs. The canoe tilted far over as both boys gazed down into the still water. They could not see the bottom, even in the strong sunlight that streamed past them into the water, but the water itself was alive with the drift and movement of millions of tiny creatures and the flash of the eel-like bodies of the needle-fish. The boys gazed past all this, into the deeper invisible depths from which they hoped to draw another movement.

One does not quickly get inside the main character through a dramatic outburst that reveals his emotional state, nor does one quickly get inside the action through a lively scene that arrests one's attention. Yet the boys are not merely part of a static, picturesque scene. They are named, after all, and they are in the act of hunting, blending as perfectly as possible into the surroundings and searching for prey. The reader is looking at the boys, and the boys are looking into the water, and the water is a vision of flux and fecundity, and their quarry is an integral part of the whole pattern of life—to illustrate this is the function of the abstract language in the last sentences of the paragraph. Beyond the "drift" and "flash" are the "deeper invisible depths" from which they hope to draw not, specifically, a salmon or cod, but "another movement."

When one focuses more closely on the boys in the next paragraph, it is again what they are *doing* that is most important:

> Hinak, a tall slender boy of fourteen, was pushing a long pole rather carefully down into the water, hand over hand. Atlin, who was shorter, more heavily built and some two years younger, was holding another pole in a thrusting position, but his eyes were on the distorted length of Hinak's pole as it pushed down into the depths. . . .

Also important, warranting more detailed description than the boys themselves, is the instrument they use to hunt. Atlin's pole is "an old two-headed salmon spear of his father's, with points of bone and horn set in sockets at the tip and secured to the shaft by short lines of nettle fibre." The boys' relationship is defined in terms of roles established by their position in their society, roles from which they cannot deviate:

Although he was the younger of the two, it was Atlin and not Hinak who held the spear and made all the final decisions. He was the chief's son. Hinak was the son of a slave from a distant tribe, taken in war many years earlier.

In the third paragraph, when Atlin spears the cod, the boys work closely together, according to their roles. In the fourth paragraph, when they finally speak, their conversation is strictly about the catch, about Atlin's frustration at merely catching cod, which is "women's work," and about Atlin's desire to be allowed to go seal hunting, a closer step to his ultimate goal, hunting whales. Atlin's identity is being defined strictly in terms of his position in the ancient, Hotsath-tribe society. The action of the story will be subjugated entirely to Atlin's step-by-step development toward taking over his position as chief.

In the first half of the book (Chapters One to Eleven), Atlin is still a child, learning from his father Nit-gass, the chief. In the second half (Chapters Thirteen to Twenty-two), after a transitional chapter in which Atlin dreams about his father, Atlin is chief because Nit-gass is dead but he is not really ready to take on all the responsibilities entailed and is struggling to put to use what his father taught him. Atlin's main lesson from his father is that leadership requires spiritual power, as well as superlative skill and physical strength. The chief must not only lead the whale hunts and do the actual spearing of the whale, but also he must play a ceremonial role in daily life as well as in great festivals, and in doing so must ensure that through ritual real spiritual sustenance is given and received. Much of Nit-gass's teaching is devoted to clarifying the differences between mere superstition and good sense in spiritual matters. At the shrine, for example, Nit-gass lays aside Atlin's naive worries about "the skulls and skeletons and newly dead corpses that whalers were said to use in seeking the favour of the whale spirit" and shows him how to gain self-confidence, knowing it is "the real secret of success in striking and killing whales." Spiritual preparation for the whale hunt consists in purifying oneself and concentrating one's thoughts on the task at hand. This is achieved by fasting, swimming in cold water like a whale, and praying where and when praying seems appropriate. Nit-gass's approach is contrasted to that of a lesser, neighbouring chief, Eskowit, who makes magic by robbing graves "so that dead whales will drift to the beaches." While Nit-gass places great emphasis on exact craftsmanship in the making of hunting tools and painstaking preparations for the hunt, as well as team effort, the objects of worship are mere symbols that can be changed at will according to how one's beliefs grow and change as one observes life. In his rational approach to religion, Nit-gass follows the tradition of his father, also a chief, who in his day halted the tradition of spearing the flesh of Hotsath chiefs at the winter festivities because one of their strongest men had died through this. Tetacus decided that the spearing had become merely a "game" not important enough to warrant its repercussions, and so dropped the ceremony. When Atlin is on the verge of truly being able to fulfill his chiefly duties, he too exhibits such powers of mind, for example dismissing the superstitious fears of the slave Hinak and explaining to him that the currents, rather than magic, bring whales to Eskowit's beaches.

What Atlin learns is that survival depends upon peaceful interaction with other tribes, effective co-operation within his own tribe, and good hunting. To achieve these ends, the chief must employ clear understanding of other people and animals; his efforts at purification and concentration help him totally identify with other people and animals, so that he is self-confident but not over-confident. Nit-gass respectfully listens to the council of his uncle Tokwit, whom he acknowledges as wiser than himself. He has a strong fellow feeling about whales: "I do not despise them," Nit-gass tells Atlin. "I love them as my brothers. That is why they take my harpoon and swim quietly to the beach with it." A chief, Atlin's grandfather Tetacus explains to him, must "be all things to his people;" yet he is "nothing without his people." When at the climax of the novel Atlin kills his first whale, Atlin is a recognizable, proud, normal young man; yet he knows that the triumph is not his alone, although it is also his:

> It was a moment of elation and a memory that would stay with him until he died—the memory of the first time his heart and mind and body, the crew behind him and the gear they used had worked perfectly together to achieve their purpose.

And Atlin's greatest moment comes in the final chapter when, having proven his prowess as a hunter beyond all doubt, he shows magnificent generosity as well as diplomatic sagesse by giving the neighbouring chief his hard-won kill, making peace, assuring all concerned of a future common well-being. Atlin proves himself a master of the necessary struggle for reciprocity and mutual respect. (pp. 29-40)

> Heather Kirk, "Unity with Natural Things: Roderick Haig-Brown as a Writer for Children," in Canadian Children's Literature, No. 51, 1988, pp. 25-42.

Sarah Ellis

During a year that I once spent living in the United States, only two Canadian children's books were ever mentioned spontaneously, each one by an adult remembering childhood favorites. The books were *Anne of Green Gables* and the animal stories of Charles G. D. Roberts. Anne is holding her own nicely, but the nature stories of Roberts, his contemporary Ernest Thompson Seton, and their literary heir Roderick Haig-Brown are largely unavailable and unknown to the modern child. In their time these animal stories, a blend of carefully observed factual information and dramatic narrative described by Sheila Egoff as "animal biographies," constituted a unique Canadian genre, an original response to the question of anthropomorphism in the portrayal of the natural world.

A recent reissue of Roderick L. Haig-Brown's *Silver: The Life Story of an Atlantic Salmon,* first published in 1931, suggests that the time for animal biography may have come around again. In this era of concern for the environment we are having to re-evaluate the fundamental relationship between humankind and the natural world. The questions of our rights and responsibilities with respect to animals and of the ways in which we are both linked and distinct from them form the structure of these stories.

Roderick Haig-Brown, a naturalist best known for his treatises on sport fishing and often compared to Izaak Walton, was born in 1908 and grew up on the stories of Roberts and Seton. *Silver,* his first book, is the biography of a particularly long-lived Atlantic salmon. As Silver goes through the various stages of his life cycle, the narrative is punctuated by encounters with trout, seals, nets, and poachers, and with more contemplative scenes featuring a shadowy, almost emblematic, figure called the "Good Fisherman." One of Silver's venturings, from the Atlantic to the north Pacific and back, strains credulity somewhat, but the tale is otherwise convincing and suspenseful.

Although he was later to describe the books as "a substantial surrender to the anthropomorphic school" and although the reader can feel him pulling toward identification with Silver, Haig-Brown does in fact take care to identify all attributions of loyalty, courage, and joy to Silver as speculative. There is a sprinkling of animal dialogue and one Grahame-like scene where a small bird and a trout named Alderman Speckles comment on the august Silver as he makes his third trip to the spawning grounds. But on the whole Haig-Brown sticks to detailed description, delighting in the technical terms of *fry, parr,* and *kelt,* and trusting to the inherent drama of Silver's life.

Some of the interest of the book is certainly historical. Such devices as direct address to the reader brand the story as old-fashioned, and the tone is conversational and more leisurely than a rigorous modern editor would allow. Debates on the finer points of angling, musings on animal communication, and a bracing speech about the social consequences of unemployment replicate, perhaps, the thoughts of a fisherman at his task and are reminiscent of Victorian children's books, with their wide-ranging comments on the social, political, and scientific issues of the day.

Particularly telling are Haig-Brown's references to Charles Kingsley's *The Water Babies. Silver,* like *The Water Babies,* has a spiritual dimension, particularly in the character of the Good Fisherman. And, like Kingsley, Haig-Brown reveals an interest in the human implications of the doctrine of evolution. Some of his conclusions have an ethically queasy flavor for today's world:

> Nature is far too wise to let her domain be controlled by accident. That clever old lady is always planning and scheming to improve her children and to increase her stock of them. She says to herself, "Handsome, healthy parents mean handsomer, healthier children, and more of 'em," and so she takes jolly good care to bring the handsome couples together, just as she generally prevents deformed or weak and sickly things from having any children at all. Her school is a hard one, but it breeds the right sort, and we human beings can learn a great deal from her methods if we will.

(pp. 640-41)

> Sarah Ellis, "News from the North," in The

Horn Book Magazine, *Vol. LXVI, No. 5, Sep-tember-October, 1990, pp. 640-41.*

Gareth Owen

1936-

English author of poetry, fiction, and drama.

Major works include *Salford Road* (1979), *The Final Test* (1985), *Song of the City* (1985), *The Man with Eyes like Windows* (1987), *Saving Grace* (1989).

Owen is a celebrated author of verse and fiction for primary school readers and young adults. His works for the latter audience are considered among his finest, and are praised for revealing his keen insight into adolescent attitudes and behavior as well as his refreshingly humorous and empathetic perspective. Owen maintains, "My novels and poems aren't children's books but are about childhood. I try to see the world through the mind of the child that once was me but I use the skill and experience of an adult to try to make the vision significant, interesting, or funny." The author is frequently commended for the realistic manner in which he presents experiences common to children; boredom, disappointment, loss of confidence, fear, problems with siblings, and other difficulties are examined objectively to foster reader association and self-discovery. The theme of maturation is also prominent in Owen's writings, as his protagonists struggle with such concerns as friendship, betrayal, and death. Closely linked with this theme is Owen's use of popular sports to offer his characters positive examples of achievement within parameters of sportsmanship based on honor and fair play. As part of their maturation, Owen's characters learn to face the often harsh realities of life by observing sports figures who must continuously overcome failure and disappointment. These themes, common to both Owen's poetry and his fiction, are enhanced by the author's highly regarded style. While Owen's verse is acclaimed for its thoughtful construction, imagery, and wordplay, his fiction is especially praised for its use of first person-narratives that effectively create an atmosphere of confession and authenticity. In discussing Owen's verse Anne Merrick has asserted that its "most outstanding feature . . . is its voice." Merrick continues, "dramatic monologues, dialogues, narratives, reflections—all capture the genuine tunes and tones and wordscapes of the child's own voice." *Times Literary Supplement* reviewer Alan Brownjohn summarizes Owen's achievement by asserting that his "art is in talking simply without patronizing, and in telling a good tale."

Raised in Lancashire, Owen received a certificate in education from the University of Leeds and began teaching in a secondary school in Essex in 1961. This experience prompted the author's first attempts to write poetry. Owen explains, "with the children in my class I began writing snatches of verses to illustrate certain poetic conventions. . . . In the available anthologies there seemed to be a lack of poems concerned with the mundane matters of everyday life with which the children could identify. This was my favoured territory." Some of the poems writ-

ten by Owen during his four years in Essex were anthologized in the poetry collection *Wordscapes,* edited by Barry Maybury and published in 1971. Five years later, Owen's first collection of poetry, *Salford Road,* was privately printed; it was later published by Kestrel Books. Named for the author's birthplace, the volume contains poems which relate many of his childhood experiences in postwar England. Owen describes such familiar occurrences as trips to the dentist, football games, and school plays in straightforward language and with a style that eschews sentimentality. *Song of the City,* the author's second collection of verse for children, similarly focuses on elements common to the lives of urban children. Character and comic dramatic monologue are considered Owen's strengths in this collection, which also includes references to science fiction, western movies, comic books, and other features of postwar popular culture. Of *Song of the City,* Shaun Traynor has written, "Owen's strength as a poet-for-children lies in his understanding of the young and adolescent mind. He is spokesperson for the growing-up, but happily writes of that anguish with a great sense of humour." Colin Mills adds that *Song of the City* is "undoubtedly one of the richest collections of poetry for children to appear in the 1980s." Noted for sharing subjects, themes, and literary characteristics with his poetry, the author's young adult novels, *The Final Test, The Man with Eyes like Windows,* and *Saving Grace,* are books about maturation that focus especially on the relationships between his protagonists and their peers, siblings, and parents. *Saving Grace,* in which a group of young people join forces in an attempt to save a local football field targeted as the site for an urban development project, highlights the more extended maturation process through which a young person becomes socially aware and demonstrates, as Anne Merrick notes, concern "for the whole community, for a way of life, for history itself." Owen has also written books and plays for primary school readers and verse and drama for adults. *Song of the City* won the Signal Award for poetry in 1986.

(See also *Something About the Author Autobiography Series,* Vol. 14.)

AUTHOR'S COMMENTARY

'In addition to reading your poems we'd like you to do a poetry workshop with our third years,' says the teacher at the other end of the line and the thud is the sound of my heart dropping.

It's not that I'm against Creative Writing per se, or whatever term is current, rather that I'm sceptical about how much real understanding of the nature of verse writing can be effectively transmitted. Most of the time now I persuade the schools to let me work on prose with small groups of say five or six children. I ask them questions about their lives and then write out a kind of composite, anecdotal narrative so that they can observe something of what goes into the writing of a story. It's almost impossible to illustrate in any meaningful way what goes on in a writer's head during the imaginative process but at least with this method they can observe something of the journey we make together; what is retained, what jettisoned and what invented. I also try to persuade them to accept the notion that the use of actual people, places and events in a story does not constitute some kind of cheating.

Imagination is much more to do with selective memory than with mere invention. Thus, I try to encourage in them the habit of accurate recall, vigorously restricting them to providing only observable evidence. At the same time I discourage them from attempting to intuit feelings and emotions, which duty is properly the preserve of the putative reader.

Arthur Miller said a marvellous thing concerning this when talking of Ibsen. He said, 'When Ibsen is most concerned with feelings he is most writing about things.'

A writer's concern is with the 'thingness' of the world.

Finally, and this is perhaps most difficult of all, I try to get them to write good, short, simple sentences. A strange sickness grips people when they pick up pen to write imaginatively. They appear constitutionally incapable of writing straightforward, sequential and informative sentences. The language becomes florid; it gestures and flourishes and waves at one so that the matter of it becomes ob-

scured. There seems no cure for this disease. One thirsts for modest information on the lines of: 'He opened the door and walked in.'

There is much good sense in Dr Johnson's advice: 'Read over your compositions, and where ever you meet with a passage which you think is particularly fine, strike it out.'

But poetry. That's another matter.

In the last few years I've been asked to judge a number of competitions and have found the results disappointing. Poem after poem about Spring or Winter or Ghosts or Snow or Fog or Bonfire Night. The language inert and lacking any sense of an individual voice; of any feeling of a real world; false in sentiment and aspiration. Poems like the following which is totally indistinguishable from a hundred, nay a thousand others.

The Castle

Tall jagged towers reaching towards the blue
  sky,
Whistling wind through thin arrow slits.
Rippling of the cold dirty water round the castle.

Voices echoing round cold empty rooms.
Sounds of water dripping from low roofs.
Slimey slippery bridges where no one will walk.
Rooms without roofs open to the sky.

This is a kind of non-poem, which perhaps we elders have encouraged by example; poems where each sentence follows the same form, a kind of shorthand, note form with the articles omitted to lend a spurious portentousness to what is being said; where participles search unsuccessfully for conclusions so that what we end up with is the poem as shopping list, where an image or metaphor gains a house point and where there is a straining after sensitivity and feeling that is false and unachieved.

And yet when one talks to young children their language is often vigorous and amusing and they have a wealth of experiences that they enthusiastically describe for us. It's almost as though they feel that their own experiences provides inappropriate raw material for poetry; that their own speech patterns and nuances of language don't pass some kind of test.

I have to confess that I'm as guilty as the next man and have worked with classes where we've started from a stimulus or where I've prefaced their writing with a talk on metaphors and where, if I'd received the above poem from a child in my class, I'd have been relatively pleased. But, visiting schools now as a writer, I feel that these methods are too coercive and the meagre results don't justify the outlay of hope and energy. Also if I am involved in the writing task I feel more energetic; my attitude is more realistic and enthusiastic and I think the children sense that I'm not playing at it or dispensing desperate praise where none is deserved. And finally, I suppose, somewhere deep down, I believe that one comes to an understanding of poetry (and prose for that matter) only through reading a great deal of both fiction and verse when young; by becoming immersed in various forms of language. There's no real short cut.

Owen (left) at eleven with his best friend, Ian Harnden.

What then do I do when the teachers are so charming and insistent; so convinced of the benefits that a poetry workshop will bring the children, that to refuse seems churlish?

I employ something of the methodology of the prose narrative lesson using, where possible, the words and phrases that the children themselves have offered, thus demonstrating that a poem can be about *them;* their homes, their streets, their experiences. That it can be expressed in *their* language and still come out convincingly as that mysterious thing, poetry. (pp. 23-5)

> Gareth Owen, "On Writing in School," in Books for Keeps, *No. 59, November, 1989, pp. 23-5.*

GENERAL COMMENTARY

Anne Merrick

Gareth Owen first published poems for children in Barry Maybury's collection *Wordscapes* in 1970. Altogether in that collection there were five of his poems. In 1976 his own collection, **Salford Road,** was published privately, and in 1979 it was published by Kestrel Books.

It was a slow start for a writer whose poetry has now entered the canon of work considered eminently suitable for children of primary and early-secondary school age. His published output has not been prolific. It comprises two volumes of poetry, **Salford Road** . . . and **Song of the**

City, plus three novels: **The Final Test, The Man with Eyes like Windows,** and **Saving Grace.** He has also published a number of plays, and there are new books in the pipeline, but as yet none of these is easily or widely available.

Paradoxically Owen is both very well known—in the United Kingdom, at least—as a writer for children and at the same time underpublicized. It is as though the relatively small group of poems by which he is best known has served to obscure the rest of his work. Yet throughout and consistently his writing has real and remarkable qualities. It is those qualities I should like to examine.

Salford Road, the poem which gave its title to the first published volume, is itself a key to the world in which all Gareth Owen's work has its roots:

> Salford Road, Salford Road
> Is this the place where I was born,
> With a green front gate, a red brick wall
> And hydrangeas round a lawn. . . .
>
> The Gardeners lived at fifty five,
> The Lunds with the willow tree,
> Mr. Pool with the flag and the garden pond
> And the Hamdens at fifty three. . . .

Both in time and space it is a firmly circumscribed world. The time is immediately post-Second World War, the place the lower-middle-class suburbs of an English city. From the house and the road it spreads out to embrace the neighborhood of city streets, the school, the whole community of family and friends, local landmarks, and local characters. It is a world keenly remembered and accurately captured. But if that were all it would hardly explain the popularity of the poetry among children of the late eighties. Working within the confines of an apparently narrow world, Owen, like Jane Austen, shows us an infinitely wider one. That he views this world through the child's eyes makes it no less relevant to the adult while at the same time making it readily accessible to the child. Seeing life and ourselves through the lens of the child's eye, gives the view a startling, sometimes a shocking, freshness. From the lightness of:

> Real
> Genuine
> Saturdays
> Like marbles
> Conkers
> Sweet new potatoes
> Have their special seasons
> Are all morning
> With mid-day at five o'clock.

to the darkness of:

> I'd a face like the map of the weather
> Flesh that grew to the bone
> But they tore my story out of my eyes
> And turned my heart to stone.
>
> Let me wind from my source like a river
> Let me grow like wheat from the grain
> Let me hold out my arms like a natural tree
> Let my children love me again.

Owen's work ranges from catching the concreteness and

immediacy of the child's day-to-day experience to pene-trating and powerful examinations of ourselves and our world. Though the angle of vision is often oblique—and all the more revealing for that—the lens is always clear, unclouded—and without a hint of a tint of rose!

Moreover, although throughout both volumes there is a note of sadness for the passing of childhood:

> My friends walked out one summer day,
> Walked singing down the lane,
> My friends walked into a wood called Time.
> And never came out again.

and of regret for the harsh assaults that the twentieth century has made on the land- and cityscape which contained it, the past is never glamorized or sentimentalized. Partly this is because one of the strongest elements in Owen's work is its consistently wry—but warm—humor. Partly it is that the things he chooses to show us of childhood experience in the forties and fifties are precisely those which do not change from generation to generation and which are common to us all.

Throughout the poems—and the novels—children undergo illness, disappointment and frustration, anger, anxiety, and terrorization by adults, by animals, and by other children. They endure boredom, problems with siblings and other relatives, quarrels, loss of confidence, and fear. They enjoy self-dramatization and games of pretend, moments of elation, fun with friends, storytelling, laughter . . .

The list could go on and on and all the categories overlap and intertwine. From simply playing with words:

> Dear Miss Hinson
> I am spitting
> In front of my top ratter
> With the rest of my commercesnail sturdy students
> Triping you this later. . . .

to asking the BIG QUESTIONS:

> And where would the ocean go to
> If there were no gravity?
> And where was I before I lived?
> And where's eternity? . . .

these experiences are handled with a deft, light touch. But there is seriousness at their heart.

Children's own feelings about and reactions to themselves and their world are the basic material of these poems, but other themes recur constantly. Sport of all kinds, but particularly football, is of central importance, and it links up with another recurrent theme in the poetry which is taken up more fully in the novels. The honor, decency, and fairness of the rules of sport at its best are just those qualities by which the growing child strives to measure himself or herself and others. The heroes of sport are heroes to emulate. And to try to *become* a hero is important. In all Owen's work we see children who are acting out little dramas of which they are the heroes:

> . . . Markey in possession here
> Jinking skilfully past the dustbins;
> And a neat flick inside the cat there.
> What a brilliant player this Markey is

And he's still only nine years old!

But Owen's view of the hero is no simple or conventional one. In this same poem, the hero, having kicked the ball into Mr. and Mrs. Spence's back garden (to their and their dog's great displeasure), becomes a runaway:

> . . . He's down the yard and on his way
> And I don't think we're going to see
> Any more of Markey
> Until it's safe to come home.

The "hero" in Owen's work is persistently demytholo-gized. Heroism is important but it is neither morally unambiguous nor easy of achievement. When they look at themselves in the mirror of Owen's poetry, children might see themselves as heroes, but they also see the whites of their own eyes! Indeed the tendency of all Owen's work is to reveal us honestly to ourselves, highlighting our hypocrisies, our self-deceivings.

Using his very sure insight into the world of children's fantasies about themselves and others, Owen skilfully reveals the contrast between the dream and the reality. (Paradoxically he sees the "dream," the ability to imagine, as crucial to the child's spiritual growth, but I want to return to that later in dealing with the novels.) He does not, however, underestimate either the value or the cost of *true* heroism. In the poem **"Arthur the Fat Boy,"** we are shown a most unlikely hero. The unlikeliness is, of course, the point. Heroes do not always look like heroes. Nor do those perceived as heroes always justify the view. In this poem Arthur, fat, discouraged, jeered at, wins the race he sets out to run. He does so through the power of his dream and the sheer tenacity of his practice but it is not an unequivocal victory:

> Then a mocking voice sings high and clear
> It's a voice he's heard all his life
> And the jeering, leering mockery
> Twists in his heart like a knife.
>
> And it's anger that sets him moving
> Anger that lifts him again
> It's anger that pushes his aching legs
> Crawling across the line.

Reading carefully through these two collections of poems one becomes very aware of their informing spirit. It is humane, tolerant, warm, ironic, and above all honest. It operates through an exceptional understanding of the child's worldview. This understanding is based on an unusually clear recollection of what it felt like to be a child during the course of a particular childhood in a particular place but it is reinforced by lifelong contact with—and acute observation of—children from a much wider world. And if there is regret for what is lost in growing up there is also an acknowledgment that the pains, problems, and challenges of growing up are the means by which the civilizing process takes place in us:

> "Mad Billy left one morning
> Crept away without being seen
> Left his body for me
> That fits perfectly
> And a calm where his madness had been.

Owen uses a wide variety of structures and his verse

throughout is original, inventive, and flexible. Three particular qualities, however, distinguish it.

First, it is very carefully crafted. In these poems there is not a word which does not carry its full weight.

Second, its language is plain, direct, and accessible but never patronizing to the child. Its strength lies in the way the language is employed in strong and telling images whereby the "outer" and "inner" worlds are frequently revealed in one fused whole.

In a brief introduction to **Nineteen Fragments,** Owen's very first collection of poems, he says:

> One afternoon I was taken by an impulse to set down a poetic account of a woman's mind under stress. The result was an austere and fairly precise image . . . shortly another image came to the surface . . . the pattern repeated itself.

It is a pattern which has gone on repeating itself throughout his work, gaining in strength and sharpness of focus as he has grown as a poet. (pp. 5-10)

Finally, however, it seems to me that the most outstanding feature of Owen's verse is its "voice." Dramatic monologues, dialogues, narratives, reflections—all capture the genuine tunes and tones and wordscapes of the child's own voice—and a whole variety of other voices, too. Often in the first person, they reveal the speaker: fears, hopes, prejudices, preferences, quirks and quiddities, warts and all. From **"Street Boy"** . . . , to **"Bossy Queen Eileen"** . . . , to the boy experiencing the first stirrings of romantic feeling [in **"Salcombe (1948)"**] . . . , the voices of the poems are many and various, individual yet universally recognizable, as indeed are the experiences captured in their lines.

After publishing two successful collections of poetry, feeling that he was running out of steam, Owen responded to a friend's suggestion that he should try his hand at a novel.

In 1985 Victor Gollancz published **The Final Test.** It shows that whatever else was happening to Owen, as a writer he was certainly not running out of steam.

In both **The Final Test** and **Saving Grace,** there is an acknowledgment to the schools in which Owen worked, reading the stories to the children chapter by chapter as they were written and working on them in the light of the children's reactions. It is, I suppose, a rare privilege for a writer to be able to monitor his work in this way, but the result in each case is a book whose strong roots in Owen's own experience as child *and* adult, as man *and* writer, are strengthened still further by contact and dialogue with the world of today's children.

All the novels share the same world, the same underlying concerns, the same verbal characteristics as the poetry. And in all three, various aspects of popular culture play a central part. **The Final Test,** set in 1947, has, as its title suggests, much to do with cricket. It is the story of a developing friendship between two boys in which both the game itself and the values of the game are crucial.

Told in the first person by Cecil, a schoolboy with modest skills in cricket, the events of the story put him through

a series of "tests" which are in fact rites of passage into growing up. In the manner of a mythic hero he faces each test in turn. So far so commonplace perhaps. But it is the way in which the "life" tests are mirrored metaphorically in the tests of the game, and vice versa, that gives this book its originality and its strength.

The book opens with Cecil passing through a rapid series of miniature tests before he meets Skipper. Skipper's name belies him, for he is an invalid and cannot even walk. About the same age as Cecil, whose name also is significant—and significantly rejected by its owner—he is the other hero of the book.

The friendship which develops between them is paced by their playing a game of miniature cricket based on the Test Matches of the mid-thirties and working up to the Final Test. Parallel with this is the story of Cecil's own involvement with real cricket, which is also to culminate in a final test. But far more serious is the third strand in the story, which follows Cecil's progress through a series of tests of his own courage and honor in relation to his friendship with Skipper. That Cecil fails his own greatest test serves to highlight the complex view of heroism which runs through all Owen's work. It also gives this particular novel great power. For it is a test of major proportions— no game—and his failure is proportionate to that of Winston Smith in *Nineteen Eighty-Four.*

"Everybody wants his father to be a hero, doesn't he?" asks Skipper at one point in the book. But the outcome of the life test here hangs upon the fact that the heroism of Skipper's own father was a lie, a deceit. Moreover Skipper, brave, mature, and remarkable as he is, has maintained and clung to the lie about his father. In the end the *real* final test is that by which, through the medium of their mutual care, healing is brought to the relationship in the recognition and acceptance of a painful truth. By this means, too, Cecil is freed to go on into the next stage of life—and cricket. More important than conventional heroism is the attempt to face honestly the harsh and disappointing realities of life. And being able to do so is an important step in growing up.

In **The Man with Eyes like Windows,** the elements of popular culture which give the book its metaphorical focus are Western films and country-and-western music. It is significant that each of the cultures Owen uses in this way has a wealth of heroes, and in the worlds they inhabit, even the most ordinary of us can aspire—especially in childhood—to become a star. This twentieth-century tendency, touched upon in several of the poems, is much more fully worked out in this novel.

The story has all the marks of the mythical quest: the need for something lost to be recovered; the search which is also a journey; the dangers encountered and overcome; and the dearly bought but successful outcome. Making it much richer, however, is the fact that it is also, like the *Odyssey,* the story of a long journey home after a quest completed. These strong basic patterns give the novel resonance and a wider frame of reference than the small world in which it is set would suggest.

The quest story is that of the boy narrator, Louie. The

name again is important, implying, like "Cecil," a distinctly nonmacho identity. On the verge of adolescence Louie is distressed by his father's constant absence, and jolted into action by what he sees as a danger to his whole family, he sets out to find his father and bring him back. The search puts Louie through a variety of adventures ranging from the comic to the truly dangerous. When they end he has earned, like Cecil in the earlier book, the right to move into the next stage of his growing up.

In the way that Owen's themes typically reflect and echo each other, the *Odyssey* story concerns the father, who although adult has never grown up. A dreamer ("Dad should have been a salesman selling dreams"), he has sought fame through the medium of films. In Hollywood he found parts as an extra in a whole sequence of Westerns. But in no film is he ever seen as a whole man, and those bits of him which are fleetingly visible on screen are the most anonymous: arms, legs, back, and bottom! For his son, seeking him through film after film, this hardly makes him a satisfactory hero. Moreover, in a way which is a mirror image of his situation on the screen, he is also an unsatisfactory father: always missing, invisible when he is most needed. Running reels of film through his own imagination the boy can never see his father's face, and the

consequent distress turns both waking and sleeping dreams to nightmares.

The ability to dream, however, is of supreme importance, and in Owen's world nothing is ever morally simple. Louie's real father may be unsatisfactory because he has allowed his dreams to run away with him and has confused the real and imaginary worlds, but he is much less unsatisfactory than the undreaming, repressed man who is threatening to become Louie's stepfather. All Owen's protagonists act out fantasy situations, which in turn helps them to deal with real ones. By means of their imaginations they are helped to cope with the enormity of the world. Above all, sustained exercise of the imagination enables them to acquire a wider and more complex view of the world and a truer view of self and others.

As in **The Final Test,** it is the caring of one person for another—in this case, father and son—and the restoration of the truth between them which brings the novel to its resolution, a resolution in which Louie's father is offered the chance to harness his dreams creatively but responsibly. He, too, can begin to grow up and in doing so can free his son for his own growing up.

Also, just as he uses cricket as a central, unifying metaphor in **The Final Test,** in this book Owen uses the Western film to bond form and content. "Westerns" are fantasies with fantasy heroes. Our own fantasies unfold in series of images very similar to those of film, and we ourselves are their heroes. To begin with, the boy seeks his father through real and imaginary film sequences, and later many of the real events of his quest have strong filmic qualities. Through this dream world and the allied one of country-and-western music, his father moves as an elusive, illusory hero. In the end, however, it is that world itself which proves illusory, and the real source of Louie's father's own dream is shown to be something different from its seductive glamor: "It's not money. It's not fame. It's leaving something. Something the sea can't wash away"—the ultimate desire perhaps of us all.

Owen's most recent novel, **Saving Grace,** was published . . . in June 1989. All the characteristics and strengths of the earlier books are to be found in this one, too. Primarily concerned with the process of maturation it goes wider and deeper than anything Owen has done before both in the themes it handles and in the skill with which they are integrated with the narrative structure.

Like the book itself the title contains many layers of meaning. On the surface it relates to the literal attempts of a group of children to save the town's old football ground—Grace Park—from the developers. It also retains its common, metaphorical meaning. But there is a deeper implication. Saving the park is a symbolic as well as a real act. The world it represents had a greater grace than our own late-twentieth-century world, where we and our surroundings are at the mercy of a harsh commercial dynamic and where human progress is seen in terms of more and bigger buildings, roads, supermarkets, machines.

Interestingly, for the first time in a Gareth Owen novel, there is a girl—as well as the boy narrator—at the center of the novel's interest. Once more the names of the two

At sixteen, Owen joined the Merchant Navy. This photo shows him, at right, with a fellow cadet on his first sea trip.

main characters are more than mere labels. The narrator's real name is only mentioned once. He is always known as Ben or Benbow, and Benbow was the surname of his maternal grandfather, who was a top player on the town's football team when Grace Park was in its heyday. (History—personal, social, and political—is a central issue in this book). The girl's name is Francesca, but her boyish nickname, Frankie, is as illuminating as were Cecil's and Louie's rather feminine ones. She is not, however, a "boy in girl's clothing." She is a well-imagined and convincing girl, and it is she who is the catalyst for the book's action and for the questions it proposes.

Through the power of her very special imagination Frankie extends the boundaries of her own and Benbow's childhood fantasy world as far as China in one dimension and "forever" in another. More mature and possibly brighter than him she brings Ben up against questions he might never have thought to ask, thus widening his mental horizons. This widening of horizons is important in his own growing up, and important, too, in widening the whole scope of the book's concerns from the personal to the political. Caring for family and friends is extended into caring for the whole community, for a way of life, for history itself.

Frankie, too, is a flawed hero, but when she redeems herself she does so, characteristically, through the medium of imagination intelligently used.

The narrative moves from high comedy through tragedy to catharsis. Over a longer time scale than the previous novels we see Frankie and Ben growing up and eventually outgrowing the friendship, which has been a creative, formative influence upon that growing up. At its conclusion, and in accord with the historical perspective of the book, Ben's younger brother, Sam, is, in developmental terms, where Ben was at the beginning.

In case this whole essay sounds like a hymn of praise, here is one quibble. Weighed against the whole range of qualities in Owen's work it is a very small quibble, particularly as it has to do with those things which (as yet) he has left undone rather than with anything he has done! *Saving Grace,* like the earlier books, is told in the first person. There, as elsewhere, Owen handles the language—and the voice which speaks that language—sensitively, observantly, and even powerfully. But precisely because it is the boy's own voice and rings so true as such, it does limit the vocabulary and the possible syntactical and metaphorical subtleties to that boy's mental, emotional, and experiential level. It would be good to see Owen tackle a novel in the third person, where he could employ the full range of his considerable linguistic skills.

That said, it seems to me that this book marks yet another stage in Gareth Owen's development as a writer. From the start he has shown himself to be a natural storyteller, but in *Saving Grace* we see his increasing skill in weaving together the many and various elements within the novel in such a way that, multifaceted, many-layered, complex, and complicated as it is, it actually reads as though it just fell off the end of his pen! I hope indeed that he no longer

feels he may be running out of steam. For the evidence is all the other way. (pp. 10-15)

Anne Merrick, "From 'Salford Road' to 'Saving Grace': A View of Gareth Owen, Poet and Novelist," in Children's literature in education, Vol. 21, No. 1, March, 1990, p. 5-15.

TITLE COMMENTARY

Salford Road (1979)

[Salford Road *was originally published as a private edition in 1976. The following excerpts are from reviews of the 1979 edition.*]

Gareth Owen's *Salford Road,* a first book of poems written for children, raises in acute form the question of what happens when trying to suit the poem to the reader. One thing that currently can happen is a chorus of praise for "speaking their own language", as if poets writing for the young were somehow misguided in speaking theirs. There is a sharp difference in Owen's absorbing . . . volume between the places where he attempts to speak the words of the young, and the places where he actually succeeds in articulating their experience. **"Our School"** reads like something easily written, calling up all the stock responses; and is ultimately condescending: "There's this playground with lines for rounders, / And cricket stumps chalked on the wall, / And kids with their coats for goalposts / Booting a tennis ball / Around all over the place and shoutin' and arguin' about offside . . . ". Whereas **"Saturdays"** both grips and stretches the imagination:

People passing
Wave over garden walls,
Greengrocers and milkmen are smiled upon

And duly paid.
It is time for the chequered tablecloth

And bowls of soup.

The writer who caters for what he assumes are the expectations of young readers may find that they have moved on and are expecting something else.

Alan Brownjohn, "Favourite Things," in The Times Literary Supplement, No. 4004, December 14, 1979, p. 128.

These poems illuminating a Liverpool childhood are sometimes descriptive at free-verse length—as in **'Going to the Dentist'** or **'Our School'**, in which narrative is stiffened by occasional images; sometimes the particular *shape* of a poem on the page enforces humour, as in **'Boredom'** or **'The Stomach Ache'** or the onomatopoeic **'Ping Pong'**; there are also more formal stanzas in which structure enforces a sardonic note (especially in **'Hymn to the Twentieth Century'**). Rhythm and assonance with repetition are used to good effect in **'This and That'**, in which 'Two cats together in bee-heavy weather' indulge in a placid, sleepy dialogue. Children trying to put their own observations and emotions into verse might think at first, after looking at Gareth Owen's work, that it was an easy task, but I hope that his craftsmanship with words, their sound and and meaning, will not entirely escape them.

Margery Fisher, in a review of "Salford Road," in Growing Point, *Vol. 18, No. 5, January, 1980, p. 3636.*

There are still not nearly enough poems about childhood and the child's response to the world in which he finds a place. It is encouraging to find these particular poems promoted (if that is a suitable word) from the limbo of private publication for a wider audience. Gareth Owen escapes the bog of sentimentality and the quicksand of precociousness to recapture so many of the moments or experiences which had meaning and on which the backward glance dwells happily when innocence is no more. He can be comical, as in **"Jonah and the Whale"** or **"The Cat"**; whimsical, as in **"This and That"**; nostalgic, as in **"Salford Road"**; and catch the enviable boredom of school holidays in **"Sitting on Trev's Back Wall on the Last Day of the Holidays Trying to Think of Something To Do"**.

With these thirty-two poems Owen seems to outdistance all the better known poets who have managed only two or three memorable pieces on similar topics in a lifetime of work.

A. R. Williams, in a review of "Salford Road," in The Junior Bookshelf, *Vol. 44, No. 2, April, 1980, p. 87.*

Salford Road and Other Poems (1987)

[*The following excerpts are from reviews of the 1987 edition of* Salford Road and Other Poems.]

Salford Road is a reissue of Gareth Owen's book of nine years ago, with some new poems. The earlier edition was strongly and evocatively illustrated by John Warwicker with drawings which imposed helpful "intervals" on the poems: Owen tends to length, yet he is so accurate in conjuring up this half-deprived and wholly warm-natured urban atmosphere that the authenticity outweighs the awkwardness. But in the new volume something odd has happened: smaller, coy and curiously antiquated pictures (boys in short trousers) largely fail to catch the spirit of the poems; sometimes even appear to misunderstand them: the defiant black lad in **"Street Boy"**, for example, bumbles along in heavy coat and thick boots. Salford Road is nevertheless a real community, where characters recur and the reader gets to know people and locations, and appreciate the alarms and consolations of life in these backstreets. Owen's art is in talking simply without patronizing, and in telling a good tale.

Alan Brownjohn, "Left Out and Back in: Poetry for Children," in The Times Literary Supplement, *No. 4435, April 1-7, 1988, p. 368.*

[This is] definitely a collection that deserves to be an essential item in every classroom or library, not to mention jacket pocket. This is a selection of 'growing up' experiences that youngsters *can* relate to. The football match on Saturday, with its heroes and villains; visiting the dentist; the playground as battleground and meeting place; the ex-cruciating drama lesson; they are all here. Owen's anthem of the street, with its tribes and rituals, says it all: 'Just you read my name, man, / Writ for all to see / The walls is red with stories / The streets is filled with me.' Of the new ones, **'Dear Examiner'** has a relevant message within the context of the present 'testing' climate, while **'Conversation Piece'** is an ideal model for the teacher wanting to get children writing.

B. B., in a review of "Salford Road and Other Poems," in Books for Keeps, *No. 50, May, 1988, p. 14.*

The Final Test (1985)

Don't be put off by the first paragraph which goes on relentlessly for more than a page and by the first chapter, which is equally taxing. It is all leading up to a remarkably original and perceptive study of a friendship between two boys with very different backgrounds and a common insight. This is Gareth Owen's first book for children, and a notable debut it is.

In the years immediately following the War, Taters is just an ordinary sports-crazy boy, all his efforts directed to getting into the junior County cricket team. By a just plausible chance his path crosses that of Skipper, chronically-ill, son of a War hero, enjoying cricket vicariously through the toy game that he and his father devised. With Taters' help the game can continue, and while they play the boys discover, layer by layer, their strange affinity. The idyll is interrupted by the intrusion of Sawbum, the school bully, a gross creature who attempts to terrorize Skipper as he has all the younger children in the school. Skipper, however, who has two useless legs, has immensely strong arms as compensation, and he routs the bully. The boys are estranged when Taters discovers that his friend's father is no War hero but a deserter. Then, in a terrifying episode, Taters is set upon by Sawbum and his cronies and blurts out the truth. In a strange and moving climax Taters plays the innings of his youth and finds reconciliation with his friend. The story ends with a good old-fashioned death-bed scene.

I have told too much of the plot, but it is the inner working of the boys' relationship that matters more than the external action. The story is told in the first person, always a perilous device, but in this instance it comes off effectively. For all his experiences Taters' voice remains that of a young teenager, not too articulate, fumbling his way through a puzzling world. Through his eyes we are allowed to see Skipper, the clever, sensitive lad, hiding his hurts behind a calm countenance and joking wryly in the face of death. As for Sawbum, Skipper has the last word: 'People like him, they're a waste of good skin'. (pp. 279-80)

M. Crouch, in a review of "The Final Test," in The Junior Bookshelf, *Vol. 49, No. 6, December, 1985, pp. 279-80.*

Gareth Owen's **The Final Test** tackles large themes: friendship, betrayal, death. It does so without becoming ponderous or portentous; there is an understated economy in its best passages that is moving and effective. There are also, however, passages of exaggerated incident or emotion which dull the keenness of the best writing. It is, in other words, a promising first novel.

[The] lean narrative is padded with needless melodrama. The bullies are crudely drawn; suggestions that Skipper and Taters have some sort of telepathic link coarsen rather than strengthen their friendship; there is a scene of daredevil driving out of some other sort of story. The chief technical difficulty is the first-person narration. The book is told by the adult Taters, and veers in viewpoint from retrospect to participation. Making Taters both the subject and the shaper of the story confuses its impact. The overplaying of certain scenes derives largely from the need to turn an elegiac memoir into a pacy children's tale.

The least satisfactory aspect of *The Final Test* is the mystery surrounding Skipper's disgraced and missing father, who lurks menacingly at the brink of the story without ever properly entering it.

> *Neil Philip, "At an Angle to History," in* The Times Literary Supplement, *No. 4318, January 3, 1986, p. 22.*

Gareth Owen catches you at the start of this gripping, poignant story of adolescent friendship and comradeship, and doesn't let go. A sports story in a different class from the rest of the genre, as the reader empathises with the boy 'dribbling along the pavements and crashing in shots against the gates' or flinging the tennis ball so that it 'ricocheted off garden walls to perform miraculous catches in the slips'. The mere act of walking home from school has to be accompanied by impersonations of the 'commentary, complete with crowd noises, in which my skill with the ball was fulsomely praised'. The story builds from the reader's empathy with 'Taters', through his chance meeting with 'Skipper', onto nostalgia and finally sadness at Skipper's untimely death. The sadness, though, is rationalised and reconciled in a realistically factual way within the youngster's mind. 'He couldn't really be dead, because some of him was in me too.'

> *B. B., in a review of "The Final Test," in* Books for Keeps, *No. 48, January, 1988, p. 18.*

Song of the City (1985)

Owen's voice is all his own. I should more accurately say 'voices', since the collection . . . contains verse in various styles. Also, character and comic dramatic monologue are Owen's strong points. If my overall impression was that the light, comic verse published this year contained less facetiousness and more real humour than last year's titles, that was probably largely due to *Song of the City;* on his best form Gareth Owen is very funny indeed. (p. 71)

Song of the City is an intentional mixture of several different types of verse, and thus, inevitably, is itself variable in achievement. The title poem, appearing at the end of the book, indicates that nearly all (though not quite all) the contents are city-based verses on subjects familiar either from children's everyday lives or as the stuff of popular

Owen at twenty-one.

culture: science fiction, comics, horror films, sporting dramas, Westerns, all fields for which Gareth Owen conveys a great relish. I felt he was least successful when writing conventional four-line verses on gentle, almost Stevensonian childhood themes, as in **'Thoughts Like an Ocean'**; more successful in his free verse touching on childhood fantasy—**'The Cisco Kid of Cable Street'** and **'Shed in Space'**, which is also second-childhood fantasy, since it's Grandad Lewis, enjoying a space trip with the child narrator in his garden shed, who

> . . . never won
> That prize for shallots,
> But as the captain
> Of an intergalactic shed
> There was no one to touch him.

There are also a couple of very good bouncy, rhythmic skipping rhymes, nicely fusing the modern and the traditional. Even better are the longer verses where the child's personal fantasy comes to private life as described by himself: invisibility (**'Invisible'**), metamorphosis (**'A Dog's Life'**). I say 'himself' advisedly, because Owen's typical child narrator is a boy, his fantasies fiercely cherished and introvert. The girls are seen from outside: **'Bossy Queen Eileen'** and **'My Sister Betty'** (who is going to be a famous actress, 'unhappy but beautiful', and is obviously just shaping up for soap opera), and they have no inhibitions about expressing their extrovert imaginings.

Best of all, however, are some half a dozen long, comic monologues. I remember reading 'Albert and the Lion' in one of last year's anthologies, enjoying it a lot, but thinking that something depended on being able to hear Stanley Holloway's voice rendering it in the mind's ear. However, with the best dramatic monologues (take Browning), there is no need for a spoken voice, or stage directions, or anything; the writer provides all the voice you need, and Gareth Owen has a real gift in this line. **'The Commentator'** instantly conjures up the hysterically overblown tones of every T.V. sports commentary you ever heard, all projected on the thrilling inner drama of nine-year-old Danny scaling heights of footballing glory in his mind as he evades Mr and Mrs Spence next door, who have had enough of giving his ball back. And anyone who's ever listened to a child telling, at length, the complicated plot of something viewed or read will need no extraneous speaker to convey the tone in which **'Horror Film'** is written:

> . . . And the mad violinist of the vaults sir
> He starts going funny all over the flagstones.
> And like, Algernon sir,
> No not him sir, the other one,
> He can't do nothing about the squid in the bogs
> Because he's turning into this pig with hairy
>   knuckles.
> Anyway before that sir, I should have said,
> There's this huge mummy in the library . . .

(Hereabouts I wondered, briefly, if one was laughing *at* the narrator, from an adult viewpoint, but . . . these monologoues go down well with [children] . . . , so that's all right . . . in fact, it would not be the first time that a humorous work about children, with a strong appeal to adults, has appealed to children themselves as well; Richmal Crompton's William books are a classic example.)

With the sensible nonsense of **'Typewriting Class'** a speaker would be irrelevant anyway; the essence of the verse is that you really need to see it on the page to get the full benefit of the splendid Freudian slips of which it consists:

> Dear Miss Hinson
> I am spitting
> In front of my top ratter
> With the rest of my commercesnail sturdy stu-
>   dents
> Triping you this later . . .
> . . . I am thinking of changing
> To crookery classes.
> I would sooner end up a crook
> Than a shirt hand trappist
> Any die of the wink.

My particular favourite is **'Miss Creedle Teaches Creative Writing'**:

> . . . Are you imagining a time before you were
>   born?
> What does it look like? Is it dark?
> (Embryo is a good word you might use.)
> Does the music carry you away like a river?
> What is the name of the river? Can you smell it?
> Foetid is an exciting adjective . . .
> . . . If there are indescribable monsters
> Tell me what they look like but not now.
> (Your book entitled *Tackle Pre-History This
>   Way*
> Will be of assistance here.)

The reason it is my favourite, I think, is that it turns quite serious towards the end:

> . . . I dream of peaceful ancient days
> In Mr Swindell's class
> When the hours passed like a dream

Filled with order and measuring and tests.
Excitement is not one of the things I come to
    school for.

These comic poems are the great successes of Gareth Owen's book, which aims for and does achieve considerable variety of content. . . . *Song of the City* is a book that has made me look out hopefully for the author's name elsewhere. . . . (pp. 72-4)

What I like about *Song of the City* is that Gareth Owen has clearly been in touch quite recently with children, and although the poems are much more traditional to the eye and ear than, say, McGough's or Rosen's, there is in them no hint of the poet groping to rediscover his own childhood, which is the hallmark of much poetry written by established adult poets and which, to my mind, is as fatal as the merely jokey approach. Gareth Owen's poems are wholly inhabited by their child subjects: rarely a hint of the intervening adult author. . . .

[Many] many of the most successful poems are monologues, for example, **'Typewriting Class'**, which reveals verbal and psychological humour beyond the scope of most pop poets—

> The truce is Miss Hinson
> I am not hippy with my cross.
> Every day on Woundsday
> I sit in my dusk
> With my type rutter
> Trooping without lurking at the lattice.

—or **'Miss Creedle Teaches Creative Writing'**, a beautifully and affectionately targeted poem, though for me slightly spoilt by the pointing-out in the last stanza; . . . I would rather have been left with just Miss Creedle's voice. **'The Commentator'** is a back-garden football international (I eagerly await his darts match). . . .

Then there is 'Bossy Queen Eileen' ('just as bossy upside down / As she is the right way up'); **'Horror Film'**, a poem exquisitely balanced between the foot-hopping eagerness of the child to communicate *everything* and the bizarre, cliché-ridden nature of what he has to communicate: Gareth Owen is excellent on anything just over the top -

> Well sir, first of all there was this monster
> But like he's not really a monster
> 'Cause in real life he's a bank clerk sir
> And sings in this village choir . . .

And **'A Dog's Life'**—'Waking up last Friday and dressing for school / I found I'd turned into a dog'—avoids Kafkaesque cliché in a masterly way.

Successful too are the more rhythmic, foot-tapping and hand-clapping **'Bouncing'**, **'Mandy Likes the Mud'** and **'Skipping Song'**, and there are a number of more reflective poems (**'Half Asleep'**, **'Arthur the Fat Boy'**, **'Sally Won't You Walk with Me'**, **'The Old Man of Wells'**, **'Shed in Space'**) that confirm what we already know from anthologies, that Gareth Owen's poetry has a range of style and subject that is unusually extensive in one writing for the young. The poems are unself-consciously contemporary in theme without taking on an attention-seeking cartoon quality, solidly constructed and traditional in value. They assume our attention and merit it. (pp. 81-3)

One can be confident that Gareth Owen has much more to say on the themes of the title poem and the inhabitants of that city:

> My brain is stiff with concrete
> My limbs are rods of steel
> My belly's stuffed with money
> My soul was bought in a deal . . .
>
> I'd a face like a map of the weather
> Flesh that grew to the bone
> But they tore my story out of my eyes
> And turned my heart to stone.
>
> (p. 83)

> *Anthea Bell and Brian Morse, "The Signal Poetry Award," in* Signal, *No. 50, May, 1986, pp. 71-85*

[This] is a varied collection of poems about life, mainly in a city, so that swimming is not in a river or the sea but in the public baths and cricket is played in the street. There are poems about a building site and a rubbish tip as well as verses about holidays and Christmas, shared by both city and country children. Many of the poems are both amusing and topical. All school children will recognise the experience of being challenged to produce 'creative writing', and the spelling errors lying in wait in the Typing class. Is city life or the life of the countryside to be preferred? The poet's last poem reads thus: 'My brain is still with concrete / My limbs are rods of steel / My belly's stuffed with money / My soul was bought in a deal / . . . Let me wind from my source like a river / Let me grow like wheat from the grain / Let me hold out my arms like a natural tree / Let my children love me again.' (p. 86)

> *E. Colwell, in a review of "Song of the City," in* The Junior Bookshelf, *Vol. 51, No. 2, April, 1987, pp. 86-7.*

[*Song of the City*] is not as urban as it sounds; in fact there are poems in it which are distinctly pastoral but at least it is a book of new, original and possibly lasting poems. Gareth Owen's strength as a poet-for-children lies in his understanding of the young and adolescent mind. He is spokesperson for the growing-up, but happily writes of that anguish with a great sense of humour and I hope he can make his young readers laugh at themselves. **"My sister Betty"** certainly understates the effect 13-year-olds have on other people—

> My sister Betty said "I'm going to be a famous actress," last year she was going to be a missionary. "Famous actresses always look unhappy but beautiful," she says pulling her mouth sideways . . .

So it goes on, exposing relentlessly the foibles of teenage vanity. The funniest poem in the book is about a creative writing class. Some of us can shudder there! This book is highly recommended.

> *Shaun Traynor, in a review of "Song of the City," in* The Times Educational Supplement, *No. 3701, June 5, 1987, p. 57.*

Bright Lights Blaze Out (with Alan Bold and Julie O'Callaghan, 1986)

[In this one volume] the work of three poets for children is represented. . . .

The third poet, Gareth Owen, maintains that he does not write *for* children but *about* them, using his adult skill to interpret them to others. An amusing poem gives a child's idea of what makes a desirable residence: 'Space for two eight-year-olds plus one small dog, / or two cats or six gerbils.' The den would also contain a space capsule and make an effective hiding place when 'in a state of war / with older sisters.' A tender poem describes an older sister watching her young sister practising skating 'like Torvil'. Alas she spins 'like a hippo'.

A collection of modern poetry which might well offer interesting and challenging poems to introduce to children.

> *E. Colwell, in a review of "Bright Lights Blaze Out," in* The Junior Bookshelf, *Vol. 50, No. 6, December, 1986, p. 229.*

The three poets represented here vary in the provision they make for young imaginations. Alan Bold's lines evoke childhood moods of melancholy, speculation and gaiety; he uses space as a subject in a striking 'Ballad of the Flat Earth'. Beside this mixture of regular stanzas and free verse Gareth Owen's looser, unrhymed narrative structures reflect everyday in a most stimulating way, for instance in **'Moving House'** and **'Geriatrics'**. Julie

Owen acting in his one-man play The Confessions of Jon-Jak Crusoe, *1991.*

O'Callaghan's verses are compressed and taut, with an emphasis on the passage of time and the growth of emotion in the young. The precise allocation of words in 'Marathon Man' and 'High Jumper' support a talent for suggesting action, and her ironic use of ballad form in 'Wolf-Cub meets the World' offers a wide dimension of thought to those who can respond to the overtones of poetry. Altogether, much in little, for the forming of taste and the expanding of emotional horizons.

> *Margery Fisher, in a review of "Bright Lights Blaze Out," in* Growing Point, *Vol. 25, No. 6, March, 1987, p. 4774.*

The Man with Eyes like Windows   (1987)

To Louie his Dad is a hero. To Louie's Mum he is all talk and forever chasing after rainbows. He is in many films but only as a shadowy figure in the background. He spoke a line once but it was cut from the final edition. Now he is hoping to make it in the Pop world as a singer, songwriter and guitar player. Louie's Mum swears she will not have him back and Louie sets off to track him down.

He jumps a train ride to Birmingham: takes a lift with a child-molester: escapes in a horse box and eventually catches up with his Dad with Murray Palermo's road show where he discovers that his hero is not in the band but just a driver.

Louie tells his own story so that the reader has privileged access to his thoughts and feelings. We share his embarrassment when he comes face to face with the shapely Sheila Whiteley with whom he has been in love for some time but never spoken to. The real menace of the man in the car slowly dawns upon Louie as he interprets the coded conversation and the inquisitive fingers.

This well-written story set in the contemporary scene of a successful rite of passage through adolescence must surely be a winner. (pp. 287-88)

> *D. A. Young, in a review of "The Man with Eyes like Windows," in* The Junior Bookshelf, *Vol. 51, No. 6, December, 1987, pp. 287-88.*

The Man with Eyes like Windows is essentially a quest-tale. The journey to Birmingham and thence to Stockport is also a journey into experience, as the boy learns to make his own decisions and, indeed, decisions for his father, who has too easily allowed his talent to be exploited. The world of show business is hardly idealised in this story of a relationship which is largely explored through dialogue, beginning in the everyday small change of family life and gradually becoming franker and more exacting as individuals learn to trust one another.

> *Margery Fisher, in a review of "The Man with Eyes like Windows," in* Growing Point, *Vol. 26, No. 5, January, 1988, p. 4904.*

Routine is stultifying—too often a crippling necessity. Thus I have sympathy for Harold Langton, whose dreams give him eyes like windows—full of glimpses of freedom and adventure.

On his current extended leave from his family he is following his latest dream of having his songs recognised and recorded by his one-time singing partner, now an international recording star. . . . [His son,] Louie, sets off alone to find his father and bring him back.

The book makes interesting reading but although lip-service is paid to Harold's philosophies the issues which are raised are never fully developed. The fairytale ending deadens the impact of the book still further. It does have a certain charm and humour, however, and would probably fill a niche in class libraries for competent—and restless—third-year boys.

> *Val Randall, in a review of "The Man with Eyes like Windows," in* Books for Keeps, *No. 56, May, 1989, p. 13.*

Saving Grace   (1989)

This is Gareth Owen's biggest book to date. In fact it might, without serious loss, be appreciably shorter. Mr. Owen tells his excellent story at a leisurely pace, lingering over each episode in a way which may put an undue strain on the patience of some readers. There are many good things to enjoy, however, including a convincing illustration of the different paces by which boys and girls grow towards maturity.

In the beginning Ben and Frankie and their friends are children playing their uncomplicated games, especially an interminable series of World Cup football matches played in Grace Park, scene of great professional football in former days. Grace Park is sold to developers, with the full support of the local council, and the children try in vain to mobilize opinion against the scheme. Demonstrations, petitions and more dubious activities only serve to put Ben deeper into trouble with the authorities. Meanwhile Frankie, that lively and resourceful girl, has put away childish things and is walking out with the enemy. She makes amends by cocking one last audacious, and highly public, snook at the adult powers which disregard youth. By now Ben too has begun to grow up.

Ben tells the story in a convincing manner in an acceptable style which avoids the more dating forms of colloquial speech. It is perhaps consistent with his artlessness that he does not apply professional selectivity to his narrative. Everything goes in, including each tedious repetition of Grandad's reminiscence about his footballing past. The portraits of adults, too, especially those of the appalling headmaster and the hardly less contemptible town clerk may be explained as the caricatures created by a young boy rather than serious attempts at character-drawing. Probability is put under considerable strain at times, more particularly in the final episode. (Would these unpleasant council officials have failed to check on a monument prior to its official unveiling?) WE are entitled to ask such questions because Gareth Owen is an important writer, no maker of routine stories. **Saving Grace** makes an enjoyable read, and every right-minded reader will be captivated by Frankie, a most subtle and three-dimensional portrait. (pp. 299-300)

M. Crouch, in a review of "Saving Grace," in The Junior Bookshelf, Vol. 53, No. 6, December, 1989, pp. 299-300.

This is Gareth Owen's third novel for teenagers and it is extremely good. The plot is full of incident which is more or less plausible—a wasteland and sports ground is built over by a large-scale shopping centre and the school gang feel their protests to be useless. Meanwhile life continues with rivalries, a convincing school play, brutal fights, and parental rows until the denouement which satisfies all criteria, putting down the pompous by a bold stratagem devised by the main female character. The interest is not only in the plot, however, but in the way the main character, Ben, responds to those around him. Gareth Owen communicates the insecurity adolescents feel when they can no longer rely on their usual mates and their former amusements pall. **Saving Grace** has not quite the poignancy of **The final test** . . . but it also avoids the trap of much teenage fiction—saccharin romance. It can therefore be recommended for boys and girls from eleven to fifteen.

Celia Gibbs, in a review of "Saving Grace," in The School Librarian, Vol. 38, No. 1, February, 1990, p. 30.

With teenage novels, there is a tension between writer and audience that is missing from the novel directed at an adult audience. It is that the writer of the teenage novel knows that the working-class audience is potentially more available; there is an army of English teachers and librarians out there who plead, nudge and cajole school students to read something. This has meant that writers sitting down to work on a teenage novel know that working-class life is on the agenda. For some, this has simply meant upping the quota of illicit sex and crime while others, like Bernard Ashley, have delt with passions born out of the restrictions and struggle of working-class life.

Gareth Owen's **Saving Grace** is part of this second tradition. Benbow and his pals play knockabout football on the derelict site of the "Town" football stadium, where Benbow's grandad was a latterday cup hero. They hear that the site is to be developed as a shopping mall and try various half-hearted and abortive ways of stopping the development, until there is a compensatory pay-off on the mall's opening day. This bald summary might suggest that Owen has played about with the third great sop to the proles (after sex and crime), sport. In fact football scarcely figures after the first few pages: the deal here is change. Benbow struggles throughout the book with a complicated set of feelings towards a girl called Frankie. At the same time he has to live with his grandad's death and his own discovery of himself as someone who can act both in the theatrical and existential sense. Meanwhile, the place he lives in has changed too.

There are some fine moments of tension with scrapes with dogs, head-teacher, town clerk, bullies and other obstacles which Owen refuses to resolve into little-guy-beats-bigguy. Benbow himself tells the story and Owen has him doubling back several times to fill in vital phases in the evolution of his character. In other words there are two levels of challenge to a conventional narrative form: the constantly inconclusive nature of events and the rambling

narration of the hero. I'd be in no doubt about wanting to plead, nudge or cajole anyone over 12 into reading this.

Michael Rosen, "Well-Pitched," in The Times Educational Supplement, No. 3842, February 16, 1990, p. 68.

Douglas the Drummer (1989)

Douglas dreams of being a famous drummer, like his grandfather before him, and while the rest of the family dream peacefully in their beds, Douglas sleepwalks downstairs to the set of drums in the front room. He wakes the entire street with his drumming and the police and fire brigade arrive. The following night Douglas cannot sleep and creeps down to the set of drums again, though this time not to play them. He hears crackling coming from Grandad's room and when he is beaten back by the smoke pouring from under the door he raises the alarm by hammering on the drums as loudly as he can.

An entertaining story with a very satisfactory ending. . . .

Margaret Banerjee, in a review of "Douglas the Drummer," in The School Librarian, Vol. 38, No. 2, May, 1990, p. 67.

Ruby and the Dragon (1989)

In **Ruby and the Dragon,** Ruby is the dragon in the school play. She gets lost when her dragon head jams shut over her eyes and she blunders round the empty school looking for the stage. She routs two burglars pinching the school cups and blindly drives them on to the stage. As the police arrive the play dissolves into a triumphant riot. Once again, [illustrator] Bob Wilson's "deceptively naive comic images" win the day.

Raymond Briggs, "In the Frame," in The Times Educational Supplement, No. 3858, June 8, 1990, p. B12.

I got off to a bad start with **Ruby and the dragon;** the front cover is too cluttered for my taste and, never having had comics as a child, I do not feel as comfortable with the format as many people do. *But* . . . I went on to enjoy myself, chortling at the wry humour, and generally being carried along by the triumphs and disasters of the effervescent black heroine, Ruby, as her class prepares for the performance of a play. There is a predictable burglary and the expected happy ending, but the details of how this all comes about provide some entertaining surprises.

Angela Redfern, in a review of "Ruby and the Dragon," in The School Librarian, Vol. 38, No. 3, August, 1990, p. 104.

Omelette: A Chicken in Peril! (1990)

It must be said that **Omelette, A Chicken in Peril!** is basically comedy, but it does not run against the grain. The bantam chick in the egg picked up by the magpie and accidentally dropped on a distant farm, is in luck. The farmer and his wife don't believe in killing and eating animals, and the bantam—named for the omelette that he didn't become—grows up happily, though he has much to learn. How he acquires a friend—the goat; how they escape from the thieves' lorry, are lost for days in a forest, nearly drown in a river, lose track of each other, and have still more dire adventures. The baddies, an extremely nasty human pair, who steal, trap, and set up battery farms (or try to) meet their match in goat and bird: no nonsense here about mildness to your attacker. It's a preposterous story, but with some underlying truths. No one would wish to take the inept thugs as role models.

> *Naomi Lewis, in a review of "Omelette: A Chicken in Peril!" in* The Times Educational Supplement, *No. 3878, October 26, 1990, p. R4.*

If you generally dislike stories with talking animals, this could be the one to change your mind. A bantam chick's egg is stolen by a magpie, but then dropped into a farmyard. He is christened when the vegetarian farmer's wife cracks the egg to make her husband's breakfast! After surviving the ordeal of farmyard teasing, he is befriended by Eric the goat. Their adventures begin when the entire farm's livestock is stolen by rustlers. They escape and end up in a farm where the elderly farmer's greedy sons are planning to kill their disapproving father so that they can install a chicken battery but the timely intervention of Omelette and Eric saves his life, and liberates the chickens in the battery. A skillful blend of thrills, spills and laughs with some serious agricultural issues.

> *W. Kani, in a review of "Omelette: A Chicken in Peril!" in* Books for Your Children, *Vol. 26, No. 1, Spring, 1991, p. 21.*

Zilpha Keatley Snyder

1927-

American author of fiction and poetry.

Major works include *The Egypt Game* (1967), *The Changeling* (1970), *The Headless Cupid* (1971), *The Witches of Worm* (1972), *Below the Root* (1975).

A prolific author who is best known for her fiction for readers in the middle grades through high school, Snyder is respected for the diversity of her works, the beauty of her writing, and her insight into the concerns of young people. Addressing themes of friendship, maturation, and, especially, the power of the imagination, she imbues her works, which range from pure fantasy to realistic fiction and often blend the two, with elements of mystery, suspense, and the supernatural. The author maintains that "if you can give that 'I just couldn't put it down' feeling to children it's worth the sacrifice of at least a little realism." In a prose style that has been lauded for its elegance and clarity, Snyder writes of what she describes as "the kind of world we wake up to every day of our lives—but about a day that somehow turns out to be transformed into something strange and new and magical." She is often praised for her ability to capture the fanciful world of young people and the creative ways in which they combat boredom and attempt to cope with and learn from anxiety and disappointment. Her principal characters—often lonely young girls—are invested with a depth and individuality which has prompted critics to describe several of them as especially memorable. Snyder is also commended for the details comprising her stories, which reflect her careful research on matters ranging from poltergeists to ancient religious ritual. Her studies of the latter inform *The Egypt Game*, a work noted for its insightful depiction of children at play and often acknowledged as Snyder's best novel. *The Headless Cupid*, another of Snyder's works considered among her finest, uses thoroughly researched, detailed settings to effect a realistic portrayal of a child's fascination with the supernatural in attempting to cope with feelings of resentment and frustration over her parents' divorce and subsequent changes in family circumstances. The author has also written a group of science fiction adventures that is referred to as the "Green-sky Trilogy." *Below the Root, And All Between* (1976), and *Until the Celebration* (1977) each share the fictional setting of the planet Green-sky, where the peace-loving "Kindar" populace, refugees from a planet that was destroyed by war, are terrorized by what they perceive to be monsters who live below the ground. The monsters are revealed as exiled Kindars called Erdlings, whose integration into Kindar society is noted for mirroring several contemporary issues. The works examine themes of peace and brotherhood but also abuse of power, questioning the means by which utopian conditions may be effected. Since her "Green-sky" books, Snyder's writings have largely eschewed fantasy and the supernatural to focus more intently on such contemporary childhood problems as abusive

parents, blended families, and peer pressure. Occasionally the author has been criticized for crafting weak conclusions from excessively fortuitous or seemingly contrived circumstances and for creating superficial supporting characters. The critical consensus, however, is largely reflected in the comments of Alethea K. Helbig and Agnes Regan Perkins, who have written of Snyder's work, "Although her conclusions often seem unsatisfying and characters are sometimes types or overdrawn, she builds suspense well, uses literate and vigorous language, and creates interesting, imaginative, intelligent protagonists"; Ilene Cooper adds, "Snyder continues to be one of our best storytellers."

Snyder was born and raised in California, the setting of several of her works. After teaching middle graders in a variety of states, including New York, Washington, and Alaska, she became master teacher and demonstrator for education classes at the University of California at Berkeley. Her fiction, and especially the astute, realistic dialogue for which it is praised, draws on her teaching experiences as well as events from her own family and childhood. Realizing her longtime dream to become a writer, Snyder published her first work, *Season of Ponies,* in 1964. Featuring a storyline used successfully in many of her works, *Season of Ponies* relates the imaginative adventures of lonely ten-year-old Pamela who has been left by her father in the care of his two elderly sisters. The story concludes when Pamela, strengthened by her experience, sings a song in her mind which is "heard" by her father, who then returns to reclaim his daughter. *The Velvet Room* (1965), Snyder's next work, similarly portrays a young female protagonist who seeks escape from the unpleasant realities of life in a family of migrant workers. The young heroine finds solitude, a secret diary, a disappearance mystery, and, ultimately, the value of love and family when she discovers the beautiful library of an old home on the ranch where her father has found work. After the publication of these first two works, Snyder's son, according to the author, complained that he "was tired of sad stories about girls and wished she would write a funny story about a boy." *Black and Blue Magic* (1966) was Snyder's response, relating the tale of a lonely, clumsy boy whose kind assistance of an elderly man is rewarded with a magic potion that enables him to fly. Complete with a happy ending for its young hero, the novel is considered one of Snyder's most humorous.

The author returned to her previous formula—imaginative female protagonist sent to live with her grandmother—in *The Egypt Game,* a novel which features a wealth of creative twists, suspense, and a diverse cast of ethnic characters. This latter detail is considered unique for the period in which Snyder wrote; at the same time, the novel's depiction of a murderer who stalks the protagonist has stirred controversy among those who question the suitability of such a device in a children's book. *The Headless Cupid,* a realistic novel set in a large California country home, introduces the Stanleys, a recently married couple and their five children who must learn to function as a family. Central character Amanda, her mother's only child, seeks attention through her spiritistic paraphernalia and a series of misdeeds which she attributes to the influence of an evil cat. Further adventures of the Stanley family, *The Famous Stanley Kidnapping Case* (1979), *Blair's Nightmare* (1984), and *Janie's Private Eyes* (1989), highlight the resourcefulness of Amanda and her siblings in a variety of mysterious and suspenseful situations. In addition to these and similar works as well as her "Green-sky" trilogy, Snyder has also written verse for middle graders and fiction for adults. *The Egypt Game* was named a Newbery Medal honor book in 1968, and received the Lewis Carroll Shelf Award in 1970 and the George G. Stone Recognition of Merit in 1973. *The Changeling* and *The Headless Cupid* each won the Christopher Award, in 1971 and 1972 respectively, while the latter work was also named a Newbery honor book in 1972 and was placed on the International Board on Books for Young People (IBBY) honour list for Text/USA in 1974. *The Witches of Worm* was a National Book Award finalist in 1973, when it was also named a Newbery honor book.

(See also *Contemporary Literary Criticism,* Vol. 17; *Something about the Author,* Vols. 1, 28; *Something about the Author Autobiography Series,* Vol. 2; *Major Authors and Illustrators for Children and Young Adults; Contemporary*

Authors, Vols. 9-12; and *Contemporary Authors New Revision Series,* Vol. 38.)

AUTHOR'S COMMENTARY

My fascination with a world that seems ordinary and mundane but in which one cannot really be certain about boundaries and possibilities began, I think—as so many things do—in childhood. Growing up in a rather limited, narrow environment, I escaped through books and games into a much wider world. I loved almost any kind of story, any kind of imaginary world, but I loved best the kind that suggested that around any corner, no matter how unpromising, a free and boundless adventure might be waiting.

Rather than choosing to write about a totally diverse world, one set on another planet or in a different time span, I began by writing about a close, familiar world—the kind of world we wake up to every day of our repetitive, predictable lives—but about a day that somehow turns out to be transformed into something strange and new and magical. A reviewer once wrote about me that I was the kind of writer who tended to walk the boundaries between here and otherwhere with a foot on either side. An apt description, I think.

A long time ago Jean Karl told me that what an author must know about her story is like an iceberg—a huge pyramid only the tip of which appears in the written text but which is supported and authenticated by the underlying mass. I've found this to be true—and in the case of an alternate world, terribly true. One must work out every detail of the new society, every aspect of their domestic, social, educational, commercial, agricultural, governmental, and religious lives. It's a large order. I remember that when I was working in Green-sky, I amassed huge amounts of information about my new world—much of which never appeared in the books. I even knew, for instance, what the plumbing was like in Green-sky.

It's such a wonderful feeling to watch a child discover that reading is a marvelous adventure rather than a chore. I know that many writers for children say they do not write specifically with a child audience in mind. They write to please themselves, and what they have to say just happens to be right for children also. This isn't true for me. I am very aware of my audience. Sometimes I can almost see them out there reacting as I write. Sometimes I think, "Oh, you're going to like this part."

So, if I have a credo it is "I write for joy." For if there is no joy, what a book may have to say about significant issues matters very little, because its readers will be very few. (pp. 189-90)

Zilpha Keatley Snyder, "Alternate Worlds," in Innocence & Experience: Essays & Conversations on Children's Literature, *edited by Barbara Harrison and Gregory Maguire, Lothrop, Lee & Shepard Books, 1987, pp. 189-90.*

GENERAL COMMENTARY

Jean Karl

[The following excerpt is from an essay by Jean Karl, Snyder's editor at Atheneum.]

I was introduced to Zilpha Keatley Snyder through a manuscript, **Season of Ponies.** It came to Atheneum in the fall of 1961. . . . The manuscript was twenty-seven pages long and the story dealt with a girl, Pamela, who lived with two strange old aunts on an isolated farm. Left to her own devices for entertainment, with the help of a magic amulet, Pamela encountered Ponyboy and his herd of pastel-colored ponies. Together they developed a circus and also foiled the wicked Pig Woman who wanted to enchant them. The story had an atmosphere that made the reader believe it; but the manuscript needed development. The characters were too hastily sketched in, the actions of the plot too mechanical and sometimes too awkward, the telling not long enough for all the things that happened.

A long correspondence about **Season of Ponies** began early in 1962. On the first revision the manuscript grew from 27 to 63 pages. By the time it was finished, the story was well over 100 pages. Quantity does not always mean quality, but in this case the two went hand in hand. As Zil looked at her story each of the three or four times it went back to her for revision, she had the capacity to see it afresh and to work hard on it again. . . . Zil was honestly wanting help and wanting to be a real writer. And she really looked at her book each time it was returned.

The results were changes that got at the heart of the plotting and character problems, that transformed the story from a brief, casual sequence of events to a novel of depth and strength. For example, on December 18, 1962, she wrote, "Chapter V (A Warning) I rewrote almost completely (it really was too melodramatic). I also changed the sequence so that the Shadow Glen incident, with the foreshadowing of the Pig Woman, now comes before the circus episode.

When the book was finally published in the spring of 1964 it was well received. . . . (p. 785)

But before **Season of Ponies** was even published, Zil was deeply into another book. . . .

The first ten chapters of **The Velvet Room** came in on April 3, 1963. "This time I think I had the story pretty well plotted and the conflicts and the resolutions worked out before I began. It helps," she said. The ten chapters went back on April 10. "Surprise," I said. It must have been, after the months of waiting each time on **Season of Ponies.** And this story was not underplotted, but overplotted. The characters, writing style and general idea seemed good, however, far better than the first draft of the first book. . . .

The finished manuscript of **The Velvet Room** was mailed to me on April 10, 1964 after several revisions, beginning in November 1963. The problems were partly with character, but mostly with getting the plot to mesh properly, to make it all seem believable. The plot was an exciting one, but the events had to seem plausible, and it took time to get everything cast in the right perspective. The book, when it was published, was a Junior Literary Guild selection.

On June 3, 1964, Zil wrote, "I'm working now on another fantasy. When I get a bit further along, I would like you to see it." Then on July 31, she wrote "I'm sending the first 72 pages of my new fantasy, **Black and Blue Magic,** to you for your evaluation and advice." (p. 786)

The first 72 pages of **Black and Blue Magic** went back on August 27 with a note saying, among other things, "Your characters are excellent. Harry is an absolute marvel, and his mother is equally good. And I love the boarders. . . . The greatest problem with the book as it is now is that the fantasy is not wholly convincing. I am sure you can make it so, because you managed so well in **Season of Ponies. . . .** Of course Harry is the type who rushes into things. He doesn't need preparations, but his reading audience does." The story deals with the problems of an awkward boy who, among other things, wanted to play better baseball and wanted to find a husband for his widowed mother. He managed both after a summer of using a magic flying ointment.

On October 7, 1964, Zil wrote, "I have an anecdote about Dougie (my 8 year old) and **Black and Blue Magic.** He more or less ordered the book as he was 'tired of sad stories about girls and wanted a funny one about a boy.' Recently I read him the first 11 chapters. I could see that he was entranced because (like Harry) his mouth hangs open. When I finished, he didn't say a word. He jumped up on his chair, stuck his arms out behind him, leaped off, and flapped out of the room. For a few minutes I heard him running through the house, apparently making occasional leaps from furniture (forbidden). Then he 'flew' back into the room looking delighted, threw his arms around my neck and said 'That's great, Mom. I'll bet it wins the Blueberry Award!' "

The entire manuscript came in early in January of 1965, went back soon after because it was still pretty much a first draft, and came back to me on March 3, 1965. The letter with it said, "Susan just came up with the mail and your letter concerning the reprinting of **Season of Ponies.** I am very pleased and happy." This second version of **Black and Blue Magic** needed a little further work to make the pace more consistent. This was completed by June 11, and by that time good reviews for **The Velvet Room,** published in March, had begun to arrive. A little more work—again on the pace—and on July 23 came a letter and the manuscript, "I've been working on Harry again and I think I've at least partly solved the problem. And I am glad I had this chance to work on it further because I had fun with this rewriting and I like some of the results. I added quite a bit of magic to the first part of the book and did some cutting. In the second half I rewrote mostly in places where my point of view had slipped . . ."

On October 4 she wrote, "I'm returning the galley proofs for **Black and Blue Magic. . . .** It's good to see it so nearly in final form. There were times when I wondered if it would make it. . . . I'm also underway on another 8-12 book, a story of an interracial group of children such as

I taught in Berkeley. No racial issues (just as there seemed to be none in our classroom there) just 5 children (plus a little brother) of various races, who share an adventure. The adventure, at this point, hasn't quite settled on its position somewhere in between magic and science fiction."

Then on January 11, 1966, she wrote, "About *The Egypt Game:* I intended to write a fantasy, but it refused to be one. For some reason this story is particularly headstrong. It keeps leading me into sensitive areas. For instance, I've had the hardest time trying to keep April from swearing." (In 1966 we worried if they did; today, we worry if they don't).

Three chapters of the book came in, in February. They simply whetted my appetite for more. My one bit of advice was: "Don't make it overly dramatic. Keep it underplayed if anything, especially the attack and what follows and the Professor's account of his earlier life. It is so easy and often so much fun to really go all out on these things, but then they tend to take over the book when other things are more important. . . . Keep the balance strong, and let the children and their problems predominate. Don't let it run into melodrama or sentimentality. I don't think you will, but I know how strong the temptation can be."

On April 18, 1966—"Just to keep you posted—It's done!! *Egypt Game* is finished. I can't wait to see what you think, but I do have to do some typing and rewriting. I should have it in shape to send in a week or two. . . . Could you tell me what authorities your copy editors go by in deciding how compound words should be written? (To hyphen, to compound or NOT) I never thought much about it until I started to write, but now it seems every other paragraph has a compounding decision to make and authorities seem to differ. I seem to be getting more and more confused."

The work was done on May 6. "Well, here it is. . . . I tried hard to keep a tight rein on myself in the last few chapters—I do tend to ooze into melodrama. I think I've been at least partly successful."

On May 18, I replied, "You are right, *The Egypt Game* is the best thing you have done. It is a marvelous story and very well worked out. It is wonderfully real and childlike. And yet it is far out and different enough to be continuously fascinating. I am sure kids are going to love it. There is really very little that needs to be done to it before it is ready for the typesetter. All it needs is a little smoothing and polishing here and there. Basically it is just perfect." That smoothing and polishing was done by June 8, and *The Egypt Game* was ready to be a book.

Published in the spring of 1967, *The Egypt Game* was selected as a Newbery Honor Book, and was on the American Library Association's list of Notable Books for 1967. Zilpha Keatley Snyder has arrived as an author, certainly, but not only in recognition and acclaim. She has arrived as a writer who knows how to put a book together.

Snyder (right) with her parents Dessa J. and William S. Keatley and her sister Elisabeth, about 1930.

Writing a book is never easy. There is no really thoughtful, conscientious author who would say it is. . . . Because Zil is an author who constantly moves in new directions and explores new territories, and who makes new discoveries in each book, every new effort brings new problems. Yet the elementary tools of the trade are hers to use. The length, pacing, plotting, development of character, setting of background were no longer major hurdles to overcome each time. These skills had become hers to use. The problems had become the larger ones of making stories express fully her own rich insight into living.

"Sometimes," she said once, "I know right from the start what I am writing about, and sometimes I don't really know what is trying to come out through a story until I get to the end, or nearly to the end. I think the books I don't know about turn out the best. When I'm too conscious of what I'm doing, the point gets too heavy." Strange for an author in control of her medium? No, not at all, but the words of an author who has learned the most important lesson of all, that a story must be allowed to grow and shape itself. The best writing comes from the deep unconscious knowing within an author. Words, phrases, all the patterns of expression, must be the product of a developed skill, but the ideas they carry must lie deep beneath the surface. (pp. 786-88)

When Zil first began to write, her children were small, she was still teaching, and writing filled only a corner of her life, though she had wanted to write since she was a child. (Her mother still has some fine stories and poems she wrote in grade school). Now with her children nearly grown, and after a number of years as a full-time writer, she still finds the challenge and joy in it that she did initially. And this may be the secret of why each new book is fresh and different and full of joy for readers too. (p. 789)

> *Jean Karl, "Zilpha Keatley Snyder," in* Elementary English, *Vol. 51, No. 6, September, 1974, pp. 784-89.*

Margaret P. Esmonde

In her books, ***Below The Root*** and ***And All Between***, Zilpha K. Snyder chooses to examine man's inhumanity to fellow man arising out of the abuse of power. She sets her story on a planet called Green-sky to which, long ago, the people came after "a desperate flight from a far distant planet, which had been totally destroyed by the terrible curse of war." The Kindar, as they called themselves, built their cities in the giant trees of the planet and, through rituals of joy and peace, developed remarkable mental powers of psychokinesis and telepathy. The only shadow in this utopia is the Pash-shan, vicious monsters who dwell below the impenetrable roots of the forest floor waiting to kill Kindar unwise enough to descend from the trees. After rescuing a little Pash-shan girl, three young initiates into the priestly ruling class discover that the Pash-shan are not monsters but only imprisoned Kindar who had disagreed with the Ol-zhaan, the ruling caste. ***Below The Root*** ends with the promise to "rekindle the light of the dream for all Green-sky." In her sequel ***And All Between***, Snyder attempts an interesting literary experiment. The same story told in the first book is now told from the point of view of Teera, the rescued girl. Snyder repeats the iden-

tical dialogue expanding only Teera's part of the story. The first reaction to the technique is "what an easy way to write a second novel," but a fairer assessment of Snyder's attempt to provide a dual point of view must be made. The dual narration is an interesting innovation, but it would have been more effective if the two points of view could have been integrated into one novel to avoid the repetition of so much of the dialogue. In this second book, the plot is carried beyond the conclusion of the first book to a confrontation between the power factions of Green-sky. Snyder poses the age-old question: should one submit to evil, or use evil methods to oppose it? Her thought-provoking portrait of a society seeking to escape the curse of violence and her experiment in narrative technique make these books stimulating reading. (p. 219)

> *Margaret P. Esmonde, "After Armageddon: The Post Cataclysmic Novel for Young Readers," in* Children's Literature: Annual of the Modern Language Association Seminar on Children's Literature and The Children's Literature Association, *Vol. 6, 1977, pp. 211-20.*

TITLE COMMENTARY

Season of Ponies (1964)

The author establishes a tone of realism in the first scene; Pamela's father again drives away, leaving the ten-year-old alone at Oak Farm with his two neurotic spinster sisters. Pamela forgets the familiar emptiness when she hears faraway flute notes and follows the sound. Her summer of sadness transforms into "a season of ponies"—of floating, mystical ponies and of Ponyboy, their young master. It's a singular world of fantasy which the author has constructed of mist, webs, and fresh air. The friendship of Girl (Pamela) and Ponyboy is defined clearly, and the effect of their companionship on Pamela's other, more immediate life seems logical to the reader because of the convincing presentation. Topflight fantasy.

> *A review of "Season of Ponies," in* Kirkus Reviews, *Vol. XXXII, No. 3, February 1, 1964, p. 108.*

Ten-year-old Pamela is very lonely living with her elderly aunts until one night a strange boy becomes her secret playmate, together with his band of lovely horses, her very favorite animals. (p. 20)

An explanation of what actually happens is hinted in terms of dreams, sleep-walking, illness following exposure in a marsh, and Pam's memories of her dead mother who had been a bareback circus rider. But this rationalization is less important than the poetic manner in which the tale is told. This wistful little story, combining elements of magic and practicality with touches of humor, is well illustrated [by Alton Raible] in black-and-white crayon drawings. It should appeal to children who still retain a hope of crossing the border from everyday life to fairyland. (pp. 20, 22)

> *Aileen Pippett, in a review of "Season of Ponies," in* The New York Times Book Review, *May 10, 1964, pp. 20, 22.*

A story that is written on two levels—realistic and fanciful—with a dénouement in which the solution at one level depends on acknowledgment of the other. It doesn't quite come off. . . . Some of the writing in the story is excellent, both in exploring relationships in the real situation and in describing the misty and fanciful events in the imaginary sequences. The two facets do not fully mesh, nor do they quite stand alone.

> *Zena Sutherland, in a review of "Season of Ponies," in* Bulletin of the Center for Children's Books, *Vol. XVIII, No. 1, September, 1964, p. 20.*

The Velvet Room (1965)

The heroine of this story is somewhat less of a dreamer than the girl in the author's **Season of Ponies.** But to get away from some of the realities of life in a sharecropper's family Robin frequently disappears just to be by herself. When at last her father finds a job at the McCurdy ranch Robin finds her own secret place for solitude and reading in the Velvet Room, the library in the beautiful old Palmeras house on the McCurdy property. Kindly old Bridget who still lives in a little cottage on the ranch gave her the key. Robin also finds a friend in Gwen McCurdy and new security in her school life. After she stumbles on the secret of Bridget's true identify and saves Palmeras house from destruction by fire she realizes that belonging to a place isn't as important as belonging to people you love and who also love you. There are several things that seem contrived and unrealistic here; yet somehow the author manages to transform lack of reality into a fairy-tale like quality so skillfully that the combination emerges as a meaningful story of an ordinary little girl who enjoys the fleeting happiness of escapism and emerges a more mature individual.

> *Patricia H. Allen, in a review of "The Velvet Room," in* School Library Journal, *Vol. 12, No. 6, February, 1965, p. 50.*

Robin's character has far more facets than the usual sensitive child of fiction who needs a private place for dreaming. She is normally selfish and has a tough resilience behind her sensitivity. Her brothers and sisters are real children too. The reader, however, remembers not the realism of the rather stark tale of a migratory worker's family, but the magical aura through which an imaginative child sees the world.

> *Ruth Hill Viguers, in a review of "The Velvet Room," in* The Horn Book Magazine, *Vol. XLI, No. 2, April, 1965, p. 173.*

Black and Blue Magic (1966)

Money was always needed for emergencies in the boardinghouse run by twelve-year-old Harry Houdini Marco, and his mother, and this summer was no exception. Their vacation trip had to be canceled, and with all his friends away, Harry anticipated a dull summer. But his kindness to a strange little man, who gave him a bottle of ointment to apply to his shoulders, changed everything. Then

Harry, "probably the clumsiest kid in ten states," had, whenever he wanted them, a tremendous, powerful pair of wings to cope with. Exploring San Francisco on wings by night, through fog and starlight, gave Harry some remarkable adventures, afforded a few citizens some startling experiences, and brought about a wonderful change in the Marcos' fortunes. Magical events, which are always humorous and often downright funny, a good sense of place, and amusing characterizations make a book that can be introduced successfully even to boys who normally scorn fantasy.

> *Ruth Hill Viguers, in a review of "Black and Blue Magic," in* The Horn Book Magazine, *Vol. XLII, No. 3, June, 1966, p. 308.*

A fantasy may be laid in the here-and-now, but in order to soar beyond its everyday setting, it must be written with imagination and better than average prose. Zilpha Keatley Snyder succeeds in humorously portraying the *ordinary* events in the life of Harry Houdini Marco, a 12-year-old with a legacy of magic, because she pays attention to slapstick details. But she fails to lift fumble-footed Harry into the *extraordinary,* which successful fantasy demands. Her language relies too heavily on the colloquial and lacks any touch of the poetic. A workable fantasy plot . . . is fettered by slangy prose; and events and characters that should surprise become predictable. While Harry soars on magic wings over San Francisco, **Black and Blue Magic** remains earthbound.

> *Jane Yolen, in a review of "Black and Blue Magic," in* The New York Times Book Review, *July 24, 1966, p. 22.*

An entirely diverting story that blends realism and fantasy in a most successful way. . . . The book has a happy ending, made believable; Harry's mother marries the man that Harry has been scheming to get for a stepfather. Since the boarding house sequences are realistically concerned with chores, troublesome boarders, and trying to make ends meet, the element of fantasy is quite distinct and admirably set off. Harry, while flying, is seen by a few people and is assumed—to his disgust—to be an angel. (pp. 48-9)

> *Zena Sutherland, in a review of "Black and Blue Magic," in* Bulletin of the Center for Children's Books, *Vol. 20, No. 3, November, 1966, pp. 48-9.*

The Egypt Game (1967)

Offbeat kids, in dialogue, ingenious pretense and attendant complications—all the elements for ten, eleven-year-old enjoyment, and then a problem: a criminally insane killer of children. April, an insecure sophisticate, and Melanie, a sensible Negro girl of compatible imagination, transform a deserted back yard into the land of Egypt, and themselves into votaries of ancient rites. The Egypt Game is not only "a terrific game," but also "a life unknown to grownups and lived by kids alone." At its height, the wanton murder of a child occurs in the vicinity, and the adults refuse to let the children out to play. But surveillance relaxes eventually, the ceremonies resume (with new recruits), and on a late night visit to the lot, April is attacked—something grabs her out of the darkness, fingers close on her mouth and throat. She is saved by the shouts of an elderly antique dealer who had been a suspect; the assailant is identified and sent to an institution. The danger to April and the subsequently revealed life story of the antique dealer motivate the solution of most of everybody's family problems, and Melanie and April (much humanized) plan further imaginative adventures. The heterogeneous composition of a university community in California contributes to the subtle (sometimes suspicious, ultimately enriching) relationships among the children, and their Egyptian absorption is all too real. But objections remain: the antique dealer is the stock suspect-turned-sympathetic-sage, and the demented killer is both tangential to the plot and a questionable component in a book for this age. As Melanie says, this is "the kind of thing parents tell their children when they're alone together." Because the episode is handled with restraint, we can only question, not condemn; the decision is yours. (pp. 200-01)

> *A review of "The Egypt Game," in* Kirkus Service, *Vol. XXXV, No. 4, February 15, 1967, pp. 200-01.*

The story moves with suspense and humor, despite evidence that the ingredients were deliberately assembled. The characters, though delightfully real, appear to have been carefully selected to represent a cross section of middle-class Americans, including a lonely child from Hollywood newly come to stay with her grandmother, a Negro girl and her little brother, a Chinese-American girl, a Japanese-American boy. Incidents are contrived to build a story of contemporary urban life (in this case, a large university town in California), complete with the shadow of a murderer lurking in the community. There is little doubt about the appeal of this lively book with its up-to-the-minute speech and situations, even though it was obviously written to fill current "needs" and will soon be dated. One always hopes, however, for a book of lasting quality from so sensitive and competent a writer as Mrs. Snyder. (pp. 209-10)

> *Ruth Hill Viguers, in a review of "The Egypt Game," in* The Horn Book Magazine, *Vol. XLIII, No. 2, April, 1967, pp. 209-10.*

This may prove to be one of the controversial books of the decade: it is strong in characterization, the dialogue is superb, the plot is original, and the sequences in which the children are engaged in sustained imaginative play are fascinating, and often very funny. On the other hand, the murder scare and the taciturn, gloomy Professor seem grim notes. In this story the fact that the children are white, Negro, and Oriental seems not a device but a natural consequence of grouping in a heterogeneous community. **The Egypt Game** is a distinguished book. (p. 56)

> *Zena Sutherland, in a review of "The Egypt Game," in* The Saturday Review, *New York, Vol. L, No. 19, May 13, 1967, pp. 55-6.*

The realistic mode, which shapes so many great contemporary American adult novels, has only in rare instances been successful when utilized by writers for children. In light of the uniformity of modern American life, this is not really surprising. The frontier is gone, and the contemporary child has little opportunity for strange, unusual, or exciting adventures. His life is generally sheltered and routine. What then is a writer with a bent for realism going to create for the child? A drab story about everyday occurrences? A series of adventures which completely avoid all contact with the familiar? Although the latter may seem more attractive, either choice results in second-rate work. What a story gains in adventure, it often loses in credibility.

Even such well received novels as **The Egypt Game,** *From the Mixed-Up Files of Mrs. Basil E. Frankweiler,* and *Ginger Pye* illustrate the difficulty. Adventure in these stories takes the form of a mystery to be solved. But the role the child must assume is out of keeping with his abilities and experience. What a character is, must determine what he says and does. Given certain types of people in a novel, a reader must then feel that the action taken is inevitable. Plot and character, in other words, are not independent ingredients. The novelist cannot create some ingenious adventure or mystery and hope to let just any set of characters enact it; nor can he conceive of characters and allow them to pursue any line of action. Either approach shatters the illusion of reality. Character is the root out of which the novel grows.

What then makes a novel convincing when it is cast in the

Snyder in about 1947.

realistic mode? First, the hero or heroine is a growing, changing being portrayed so fully that his development is believable. Second, character determines action; everything that an individual does is consistent with, and a reflection of, his age, experience, and personality. In the third place, it follows that each character and his story are unique. Finally, and prerequisite to all of the above, the reader is able to participate fully in the events. He can see and experience from the hero's point of view.

Most novels, of course, neither completely fail nor succeed. Those mentioned above are partial successes, but in each case, the treatment of character reduces credibility and, proportionately, the depth of satisfaction to be gained from the book as a whole.

In *The Egypt Game* by Zilpha K. Snyder, two apartment-dwelling children, April and Melanie, are engrossed in their "imagining" games. As a result of the two highly developed imaginations, a small storage yard surrounded by a high fence springs to life as ancient Egypt, and as long as the novel deals with this game, realism is preserved. But apparently the game led the author to a dead end. A murderer and his eventual attempt on April's life are dragged in to complicate and eventually conclude the story.

The real difficulty is inadequate characterization. April is given a few touches which crystallize her as a child who makes every effort to hide her insecurity. Her outlandish dress, affected speech, and attempts to reveal how much better her earlier life was with her mother, are all evidence that she is homesick and more than a little frightened that she does not belong anywhere. However, that Melanie, the playmate across the hall, should understand this is scarcely convincing. Melanie repeatedly interprets April's behavior as an intelligent adult would. Granting Melanie such insight is convenient. Since she is more tolerant than most children would be, she does not allow April to shut her out, and their friendship is quickly established. But the author uses Melanie to verbalize what she would otherwise have to show. The use of a narrator is, of course, a legitimate device, but Melanie is a child and cannot be expected to understand so much. Moreover, much of the drama (not to mention the reality) of the growth of Melanie's and April's friendship and of its effect on April are lost. Characterization is ignored for the sake of adventure; the details of the game and the children's encounter with a murderer are stressed.

Absorption in the game leads nowhere because the author has not laid the groundwork for a story about people. Melanie understands too much; *what* happens and not *why* is given the major emphasis. (pp. 109-10)

> *Virginia L. Wolf, "The Root and Measure of Realism," in* Wilson Library Bulletin, *Vol. 44, No. 4, December, 1969, pp. 409-15.*

Against a well-realized background, using an imaginative game as a framework, the author has constructed an exciting, unified plot. Episodes in the game arouse interest, provide action, and create suspense. Motivation is provided for the characters' actions so that events move logically and inevitably to the climax. Because of the game, the real-life situation of two of the characters is greatly improved.

In the playing of the game, April has gained good friends, for the first time in her life. She has been searching for her identity and for improved personal relationships as well. Through the game she has gained both. Because of his involvement in the game, the Professor is drawn from his shell back into the world.

The fact that the children are white, black, and Oriental seems not a device but the natural intermingling that exists in the university section of a large western city. Even the murder, though sinister, does not seem out of keeping with this neighborhood. Melanie and Marshall's parents are engaged in occupations that are not stereotyped for blacks: their mother is an elementary school teacher and their father is a graduate student at the university. The dialogue is lively. The illustrations capture both the mood of the Egypt Game and the personalities of the children who play it. (p. 174)

> *Marilyn Leathers Solt, "The Newberry Medal and Honor Books, 1922-1981: 'The Egypt Game'," in* Newbery and Caldecott Medal and Honor Books: An Annotated Bibliography, *by Linda Kauffman Peterson and Marilyn Leathers Solt, G. K. Hall & Co., 1982, pp. 173-74.*

Eyes in the Fishbowl (1968)

To fourteen-year-old Dion James, Alcott-Simpson's Department Store represented life as he wanted to live it. The store was organized, elegant, an enchanted palace—like something on a different planet. He and his father lived in an old dilapidated mansion on a street that had long lost its air of dignified prosperity. Part of the house was leased to students as casual about paying the rent as Dion's father was about collecting payment for the music lessons he gave. Dion could scarcely remember when he was not working to help out the family finances, or when the house was not overflowing with people, conversation, music, and uninvited, needy guests. When he was not at school or busy about his various jobs, he wandered about in Alcott-Simpson's, avoiding floorwalkers and house detectives but getting acquainted with several of the clerks. One day Dion noticed a young girl with amazingly beautiful eyes, who was neither customer nor employee but seemed to be taking surprising liberties with the merchandise. What was her role in the epidemic of small disasters plaguing the store, which detectives and police could not fathom? Dion was drawn deeper and deeper into the mystery and even into danger, unable to resist the power that drew him into the very heart of a supernatural manifestation marking the end of the unreal world of Alcott-Simpson's. Although the events are not gentle, the relationship between Dion and Sara suggests the *Portrait of Jennie*. Strange, unresolved, it will delight some young people, baffle others. Especially interesting is the characterization of Dion. To one of the students who tries to reconcile him to his very likable father, Dion exclaims, "I can't help it if I'm not rebelling in the right direction. Everybody has to rebel against what he has to rebel against." Dion is so real that what happens later must be real too. (pp. 182-83)

Ruth Hill Viguers, in a review of "Eyes in the Fishbowl," in The Horn Book Magazine, *Vol. XLIV, No. 2, April, 1968, pp. 182-83.*

The fantasy is weakened by being drawn out, but it is in essence effective. The department store setting is superbly realistic, and the relationship between Dion and his easy-going father, a theme that runs concurrently with the fantasy, stands out in shining bas-relief.

Zena Sutherland, in a review of "Eyes in the Fishbowl," in The Saturday Review, *New York, Vol. LI, No. 19, May 11, 1968, p. 41.*

To fourteen-year-old Dion James, irritated by the clutter and insecurity of life with his charming, talented, but improvident father, the sumptuous Alcott-Simpson department store has been a symbol of elegance and order since childhood. Intrigued by the rumors of strange events going on in the store, Dion becomes personally involved when he meets the lovely, exotic Sara who, along with invisible child companions she refers to only as "the others," appears to be living in Alcott-Simpson's. Although the puzzling blend of the real and supernatural may be confusing to some young readers, the first-person narrative is an unusual contemporary story enriched with subtle but discerning commentary on human values.

A review of "Eyes in the Fishbowl," in The Booklist and Subscription Books Bulletin, *Vol. 64, No. 18, May 15, 1968, p. 1097.*

Today Is Saturday (1969)

"There's nothing sloppier, slipperier, floppier. / There's nothing slickier, stickier, thickier. / There's nothing quickier to make grown-ups sickier, / Trulier coolier. / Than wonderful mud." The **"Poem to Mud"** is one of the more viable offerings in this collection of short poems, each accompanied by a photo or two [by John Arms] showing just what's supposed to be happening, which leaves no room for individual imagination. Often the images tend to be dreamy and wistful in a way nine- and ten-year-olds don't usually take to "the wrinkling sand is only a skin. / A thin, thin skin. / Between the world and me." On the other hand, **"What a Ride"** and **"What If?"** have dependable rhythms for reading aloud and most will grasp the irony of **"The One Who Holds the Flag."** Poems of varying appeal in a frame that limits reference.

A review of "Today Is Saturday," in Kirkus Reviews, *Vol. XXXVII, No. 3, February 1, 1969, p. 104.*

There is youth in this collection of poems by Mrs. Snyder (who wrote *The Egypt Game*). In her first published poems she has captured much of the zest and the intensity of joy and of sorrow of the young. The photographs which illustrate her poems, while excellent, do not leave room for young poets to add their own poetical vision. Read the poem **"Tree"** or **"The Ghosts of the Galilee"** and see if you agree. You'll want to read them anyway, whether you agree or not.

A review of "Today Is Saturday," in Publish-

ers Weekly, *Vol. 195, No. 12, March 24, 1969, p. 54.*

An attempt via poetry and photographs to capture a child's impressions *Saturday,* really only succeeds when the child orientation isn't leaned on. Of the 24 poems in the book, only eight are distinctly good poetry: e.g., **"What a Ride"** and **"To Dark Eyes Dreaming."** In these, the author expresses personal emotions and not the imagined ones of unreal children. The rest of the poems are satisfactory, but no child will be lured into believing that they are genuinely childlike. The diverse subjects are appealing—animals, chalk painting on the pavement, playing fort, spinning on a playground bar, playing in mud—and John Arms's fine photographs enhance each poem. But altogether, while this is an attractive browsing item that may be admired by teachers and parents, it probably won't speak to children from a place on the library shelf.

Cherie Zarookian, in a review of "Today Is Saturday," in Library Journal, *Vol. 94, No. 12, June 15, 1969, p. 2505.*

The Changeling (1970)

However palpable, Zilpha Snyder's world is always at an intriguing remove from reality; and when, as in *The Egypt Game,* her characters plunge intensely into make-believe, there are few girls who will not plummet after. Although or perhaps because divested of its strange, prickling nimbus, this becomes the transformation of fat, seven-year-old Marty Mouse, the nonentity in a self-assured, preoccupied household, into beautiful blonde Martha Abbott, the Sophomore "who's in all the school plays." Meanwhile Ivy Carson, self-proclaimed changeling, can't escape the family reputation for shiftlessness and worse. Their affinity is most firmly forged in play-acting the Tree People, an evasion for Ivy but a catharsis for Martha who masters the meanest role. Repeatedly the Carsons leave under a cloud only to return, and increasingly. Martha is torn between loyalty to Ivy and the past, and the social pressures / lures of the present. In eighth grade Ivy would pledge them not to grow up to "Know all the Questions, but not the Answers. Look for the Different, instead of the Same. Never Walk when there's room for Running. Don't do anything that can't be a Game." But when she beats out contemptuous Kelly Peters for the lead dancer's role in the school play, the sky falls: Kelly accuses Ivy and Martha of vandalism and only brother Tom Abbott's disclosure that he was in the raid led by a 'respectable' dope-pushing classmate clears them. It is the turning point for Martha, the Abbotts becoming more attentive, less complacent, and the vanishing point for Ivy, a subsequent letter tells that she's in New York studying dancing; it is also the weakest point in the book. But once magicked, the reader is not to be dislodged by a topical intrusion or a Cinderella (re)version.

A review of "The Changeling," in Kirkus Reviews, *Vol. XXXVIII, No. 14, July 15, 1970, p. 744.*

In her seventh story, the author appears to have lost none of her fecundity of imagination, her sensitivity, or her fluency of speech. But neither has she been able to overcome a tendency to dull the edge of her originality with some stereotyped characters and incidents. . . .

As the girls grow into their teens, Martha becomes more relaxed and self-confident, while Ivy's calm nonconformity, creativity, and family background enrage her classmates. But now the author piles on too much, for in attempting to emphasize the girls' defiance of false teen-age standards and conventions, she introduces carefully arranged, but well-worn, contemporary situations and characters. In the end, the impact of the book is diffused.

> *Ethel L. Heins, in a review of "The Changeling," in* The Horn Book Magazine, *Vol. XLVI, No. 5, October, 1970, p. 479.*

It will be comforting to children to hear that they can grow up without necessarily turning into those dull creatures known as "grown-ups. . . ." [Martha and Ivy] create an ebullient and magical world inhabited by a secret sea monster, an aging horse, a baby who casts spells, a race of Tree People and a lady artist. But the question is—can the magic last? Indeed, can it even survive the eighth grade when there are, as there are bound to be, popular and self-centered girls like Kelly Peters around, when there are grown-ups who see only grown-up patterns?

The answer is a triumphant yes—not because the story requires a happy ending, not because this is fantasy (it is not), but simply because Mrs. Snyder is affirming the power of the human imagination. And doing it gloriously. Why wouldn't she? Mrs. Snyder is obviously a changeling, herself, and for that we can be grateful.

> *Jean Fritz, in a review of "The Changeling," in* The New York Times Book Review, *December 13, 1970, p. 26.*

[The] helplessness of a child in the face of adult pressures is a theme to be variously interpreted but though nobody would suggest that a children's writer should deliberately trivialise it, it seems obvious that a reader of nine or ten is likely to be more interested in the child's view of such a situation than in an analysis of the social or emotional motives of the adults in question. So, in *The Changeling,* we are told the reasons why Martha Abbott's lawyer father and snobbish mother discourage her friendship with Ivy Carson, youngest but one of a large, feckless and far from law-abiding family, but the reasons are stated, not explored. It is the relationship between the two girls that is developed. At first the seven-year-old Martha is captivated by dark-haired Ivy's assertion that she is not a Carson at all but a changeling and willingly joins in evolving spells and developing, ostensibly to entertain Ivy's little sister, the game of Tree People. As time goes on the game, in Ivy's hands, becomes a defence against the unpredictable adult world and a consolation to Martha when the Carsons from time to time vanish strategically from the locality; and when the girls have to admit that their plan never to grow up is unworkable, and Ivy goes to New York to fulfil her ambition to become a dancer. Martha realises how far her life has been planned round the other girl's presence. Amusing, perceptive and touching, written with ease and point, this is an almost classic example of the book programmed directly for young readers—none the worse for it, but proving, perhaps, that there *is* such a thing as a "children's book".

> *Margery Fisher, in a review of "The Changeling," in* Growing Point, *Vol. 15, No. 3, September, 1976, p. 2939.*

Mrs. Snyder has some excellent ideas about childhood and adulthood: the precious quality of the child's imagination; the awfulness of phoney conformism; asking questions is more important than knowing answers; etc. She has been a teacher and is obviously well acquainted with Paul Goodman and other radical educationists. The trouble with **The Changeling** is that it is written to present these ideas. The characters don't develop, they have little individuality: they are types and they go through the textbook stages of growing up. Thus, the book is necessarily episodic though fortunately the storytelling is witty and inventive. Martha comes from a typical American middleclass home, with all the usual aspirations and worries; Ivy, her great friend, comes from a socially unacceptable family and is rather strange. The book takes them from seven to fifteen, every so often skipping a couple of years when Ivy is elsewhere. And as episode succeeds episode, the girls discover the theories that the author wants them to discover.

> *M. H. Miller, in a review of "The Changeling," in* Children's Book Review, *Vol. VI, October, 1976, p. 21.*

The Headless Cupid (1971)

[Of the heroine of **The Headless Cupid**] we are told, "Amanda was indeed something else again. A student of the occult, she arrived in her ceremonial costume, complete with her Familiar, a crow named Rolor." After just 40 pages of tedious narrative in which nothing much happened except a lot of talk, I became aware that if Amanda was "indeed something else again" she was also rather a put-on. The author really didn't believe in the uncanny; she had merely dressed her characters up to tell the same old child's story of making friends. (p. 43)

> *Richard Elman, "A Goulash of Ghouls," in* The New York Times Book Review, *November 7, 1971, pp. 42-4.*

[**The Headless Cupid**] pokes fun in a discerning way at the current interest in the occult and its beaded young practitioners, at the same time leaving an avenue open to a belief in ghosts and poltergeists. Twelve-year-old Amanda, replete with ceremonial costume and a familiar (a crow who dislikes her as much as she dislikes him), attempts to initiate her new stepbrother, David, and his young sisters and brother, into the rites of witchcraft and seances, with often hilarious results. But this is more than just a funny book for 9-13 year olds; it is a serious, sometimes sad story of a child, hurt by the divorce of her parents, who is trying to get even with the world, and of her gradual adjustment to her new family. The characterization and writing are among the best of the season; Mrs. Snyder has a fine ear for dialogue and the nuances of family life. (p. 180)

Snyder and her husband Larry on their wedding day, June 18, 1950.

Elizabeth Minot Graves, "The Year of the Witch," in Commonweal, *Vol. XLV, No. 8, November 19, 1971, pp. 179-82.*

This most readable and enjoyable book races along absorbingly. The American author has a keen ear for dialogue; the conversation between the children, and between them and the adults, is slyly accurate. The characters of the five children involved in the story are subtly different and while the hero's father and his stepmother have less important roles to play in the plot, they are refreshingly much more substantial than mere shadows. The central situation is a contemporary one, and will be familiar to many young readers—the combining of two families. A widowed father marries a woman who has divorced her husband. He brings to their new home (a shabby old house very important to the plot) David, a sensitive and practical boy of about twelve who at first rather resents his stepmother, and the fact that his younger brother and sisters so quickly forget their real mother and change their allegiance, when the book begins has overcome his prejudice and become fond of Molly; then there are Janice and Tester, his younger and thoroughly individual sisters, and small Blair, his intriguing brother who 'sees and understands different things from other people'. Molly brings her somewhat eccentric and unco-operative daughter Amanda, who arrives dressed in unorthodox garments which she claims are magic ceremonial robes, with a Centre-of-power sign stuck on her forehead, a case full of

books about magic, and a large ill-tempered crow. The plot thickens fast and is intriguing, but ultimately more interesting, are the subtly changing relationships between the children and the way in which they are finally happily resolved.

Barbara Sherrard-Smith, in a review of "The Headless Cupid," in Children's Book Review, *Vol. III, No. 5, October, 1973, p. 146.*

There is never any doubt about the motive power behind **The headless cupid.** This is a case-history of the most open kind and the extra-human agency, though carefully prepared for throughout the story, seems almost like an afterthought. . . . Every one of Amanda's actions can be traced not to magic but to her laughable but passionate longing for power to offset her own immaturity—every one of *her* actions but not the last mysterious explosion of sound in which the lost head from the carved banisters suddenly reappears. What makes this shock ending credible is the character of Blair, the almost totally silent four-year-old who has his own peculiar contact with a different dimension from the one he lives in from day to day. Blair is created not as a case-history but as an individual and he, if anyone, saves the book from being yet another somewhat portentous study of emotional confusion in the young. (pp. 2287-88)

Margery Fisher, in a review of "The Headless Cupid," in Growing Point, *Vol. 12, No. 6, December, 1973, pp. 2287-88.*

Snyder's **The Headless Cupid,** the first book of what is now a trilogy about the Stanley family, skillfully flirts with the fantastic while working perfectly well as a tale of family dynamics. It concerns the arrival and eventual acceptance of Amanda, the Stanley children's new stepsister— that is, with her acceptance both *of* and *by* the family— after a series of upsetting events Amanda would like everyone to believe were caused by a poltergeist. The author has a perceptive understanding of children's ways of thinking and talking, as well as a robust sense of humor, and she handles the impingement of the supernatural on the family's everyday life with delicacy.

Diana Waggoner, "Supernatural or Not?" in Fantasy Review, *Vol. 8, No. 12, December, 1985, p. 26.*

The Witches of Worm (1972)

Worm, the skinny gray crocodile-eyed cat, must be possessed by a demon; what else, Jessica reasons, could make her do all those nasty things—pushing Brandon's trumpet out the window, throwing her mother's fur trimmed dress in the washing machine and scaring Mrs. Post with that story about a prowler. While everyone else realizes that rejection, not possession, is Jessica's real problem, and Jessica herself has read how Ann and the other girls of Salem learned "how much power they could have by making people believe that nothing they did was their fault." But the solution when it comes begins with an exorcism, not her visit to the psychiatrist, and Jessica's tears, which prove that she's not a witch, are also a form of self therapy.

There's some danger that adults will be as spooked by Jessica as she is by Worm's evil eye, but the cat's bewitchment proves a perfect medium for a sensitive, sympathetic probing of a disturbed child's fears and anger—and for a story that economically, seemingly effortlessly, captures the elusive eeriness of the supernatural.

> *A review of "The Witches of Worm," in* Kirkus Reviews, *Vol. XL, No. 14, July 15, 1972, p. 803.*

[*The Witches of Worm*] describes an angry, belligerent young person, twelve-year-old Jessica for whom family life has not been easy. . . . This is a haunting story of the power of mind and ritual, as well as of misunderstanding, anger, loneliness and friendship. It is written with humor, pace, a sure feeling for conversation and a warm understanding of human nature.

> *Elizabeth Minot Graves, in a review of "The Witches of Worm," in* Commonweal, *Vol. XCVII, No. 7, November 17, 1972, p. 157.*

Although Jessica's overwrought imagination lends a quality of suspense to the book, the resolution is limp and unsatisfying. The author of *The Egypt Game* and *The Headless Cupid,* in both of which suspense is skillfully maintained by the give and take of children brought together, has possibly wandered beyond her depth in an attempt to rationalize witchcraft.

> *Paul Heins, in a review of "The Witches of Worm," in* The Horn Book Magazine, *Vol. XLVIII, No. 6, December, 1972, p. 596.*

In a succession of distinguished books, Zilpha Keatley Snyder has been exploring the nature of magic, not only for the benefit of children, one feels, but to satisfy herself—which is, of course, how all good books are written. Invariably at the center of her magic is an oddball—a highly individual, nonconforming, compelling character, so inventive (like April Hall in *The Egypt Game* and Ivy Carson in *The Changeling*) as to suggest that magic lies within the power of imagination itself.

Ivy and April both had the ability to transform life, as if they had found an octave higher than the normal range of experience. Amanda, in *The Headless Cupid,* pursuing the darker side of imagination, was able to take life to a lower-than-natural octave. With each book, the pattern of Mrs. Snyder's magic becomes clearer, more closely entwined with reality. In one sense, her characters are themselves the magicians. Unlike Alice, who emerges from her rabbit hole ready to take up childhood just where she left off, they are never quite the same after their adventures. And indeed, one asks, how can magic not leave a mark?

The Witches of Worm is one of Mrs. Snyder's most haunting stories and one of her deepest probes. For the first time she speaks from the point of view of the magic maker Jessica, whose anger and loneliness are the driving force behind the plot as they are so often in this author's work. (pp. 8, 10)

Witches, Mrs. Snyder contends, are those who have learned the trick of making people believe that nothing they do is their own fault. Here is the essence of the theme that recurs in her books, always in fresh form but never so well articulated: magic is, on the one hand, the projection of forces that lie in the human psyche, and on the other hand, it is mystery.

Perhaps because she never underestimates the mystery, perhaps because she walks the thin line between real and phantom worlds so knowingly, Mrs. Snyder's brand of fantasy is convincing on many levels. Certainly we are ready to believe that Jessica, having come to terms with the source of black magic, will have no trouble practicing white magic with Brandon—who, happily, is restored to her in the final pages. Indeed, we would like to be around it. (p. 10)

> *Jean Fritz, in a review of "The Witches of Worm," in* The New York Times Book Review, *December 10, 1972, pp. 8, 10.*

[*The Witches of Worm*] is not really fantasy at all. Rather, it's a psychological novel about an unhappy, possibly unstable adolescent girl living in a broken home. . . .

The novel is a solid merger of 70s New Realism and mild horror fiction though not, to my way of thinking, a true classic. Katherine Paterson's *Jacob Have I Loved* is a much more effective study of the alienated adolescent girl.

> *Michael M. Levy, "The Evil That Young Girls Do," in* Fantasy Review, *Vol. 9, No. 6, June, 1986, p. 29.*

The Princess and the Giants   (1973)

"Long ago, when magic was everyday, instead of maybe . . . a princess lived in a huge castle, bigger even than McIver's barn . . ." and only the pictures [by Beatrice Darwin] (black for reality and purple for fantasy in the manner of Anglund's *Little Cowboy* books) indicate that this is really about a freckle faced farm girl who imagines the dangers dire and faithful steed and enchanted bird the text describes. Thus when we read dragon we see a bull, when we read of fierce giants, a lonely midnight flight through strange lands, and rescue by his majesty the King, we see angry parents, a frightened runaway lost in the brush, and a little girl being carried home by her father. The gimmick isn't new but Snyder proficiently sustains the two levels of action and her melodic prose flows along in effortless cadences and unobtrusive internal rhymes.

> *A review of "The Princess and the Giants," in* Kirkus Reviews, *Vol. XLI, No. 13, July 1, 1973, p. 683.*

The author's first tale for younger children recalls the fanciful games invented by the two girls in *The Changeling.* The story is told like a romantic fairy tale: "Long ago, when magic was everyday, instead of maybe, there lived in a small kingdom, a princess, who was as beautiful as a peach orchard in April." . . . Only in the pictures is it apparent that the princess is actually a determined little girl with a head full of fantasy; that the giants are her hardworking parents needing help with the chores; that the courtyard and gardens are farmyard and vegetable patch—while the wolves are the dogs in the kennel, and the dragon is only the rampaging bull in the field. Thus the illustrations carry a heavy burden, for they must reveal all the delicious irony in the book; but they are disappointing. The pictorial device—using color for the imaginary story and black for the actual one—has been used elsewhere with more success; the scraggly, inexpressive drawings lack any real character or substance.

> *Ethel L. Heins, ina review of "The Princess and the Giants," in* The Horn Book Magazine, *Vol. XLIX, No. 5, October, 1973, p. 459.*

There are a few hints in the flowing text that this is not just a fanciful tale about a little princess (e.g., Snyder compares the princess' huge castle to "McIver's barn."). The black-and-white sketches, however, plainly reveal an ordinary child with red and violet overlays illustrating her fantasy world. Reminiscent of Shulevitz's *One Monday Morning* (Scribners, 1967) or *And I Must Hurry for the Sea Is Coming In* by George Mendoza (Prentice-Hall, 1969) in which a child's boundless imagination removes tiresome restrictions of daily existence, Snyder's story contains humor and suspense which the other titles do not.

> *Betty K. Waesche, in a review of "The Princess and the Giants," in* School Library Journal, *Vol. 20, No. 5, January, 1974, p. 44.*

The Truth about Stone Hollow (1974: British edition as The Ghosts of Stone Hollow)

Zilpha Keatley Snyder has proven herself a nimble-fingered craftswoman before, in *The Egypt Game* and *The Velvet Room,* but in *The Truth About Stone Hollow* she never even gets her materials together. There are some wisps and scraps labeled *creepy cottage, new boy at school, crippled father,* and there are some ghosts blowing around the landscape like plastic bags, but there are so many loose ends in this book you could build a bird's nest out of them.

> *Jane Langton, in a review of "The Truth about Stone Hollow," in* The New York Times Book Review, *March 31, 1974, p. 8.*

The sureness with which the author draws her young characters and the deep perception and wisdom of her understanding of peer interplay and conversation will draw the reader into the story with its shadowy overlays of mystery and magic. In 1938, at Taylor Springs, California, Amy Polonski becomes friend and defender of an English boy, Jason Fitzmaurice, who is an odd-man-out in her sixth-grade class. Together they visit the supposedly haunted Stone Hollow, which their classmates slavishly avoid. There they sense the presence of ghostly shapes. " 'At the Stone . . . you can see things that happened in other places.' " Jason sees Indians, and a small piece of stone he gives to Amy enables her to bring something magical to view in her attic at home. But the story consists of more than discoveries and wonderings. A clear picture emerges of the smug little town riddled with religious prejudices and family differences. If not rich in the creation of atmosphere and mood, nor always successful in dealing

with the supernatural, the story is, nevertheless, fresh and readable.

> *Virginia Haviland, in a review of "The Truth about Stone Hollow," in* The Horn Book Magazine, *Vol. L, No. 4, August, 1974, p. 380.*

Somehow Mrs. Snyder's two previous books published in England have passed me by. On the evidence of this third book here is a major writer, one who blends with the most delicate dexterity fantasy with a picture of the everyday world.

The atmospheric scenes in the valley, and Amy's strange vision at home, are beautifully handled. Their effect is strengthened by the effective way in which Mrs. Snyder presents the everyday events of home and school. She captures the authentic cadences of the speech of these appealing and individual children. This is a book whose effect is not immediate. It exerts its authority gradually upon the reader, and is still more impressive at a re-reading. One is left with the most lasting impression of Amy herself, the little girl who discovers that her grandfather was like God—and how terrible to live with God.

> *M. Crouch, in a review of "The Ghosts of Stone Hollow," in* The Junior Bookshelf, *Vol. 42, No. 6, December, 1978, p. 324.*

Below the Root   (1975)

The future-fantasy world of Greensky—where a race called Kindar, clad in winged shubas, practice daily ceremonies of Love, Peace and Joy in their groundtree-top nid-places and children in the Garden exercise the skills of pensing, teleporting and grunspreking—is a long way from Snyder's usual contemporary settings, but the concerns and attitudes expressed here are less remote. Settled by survivors from another world destroyed by war, Greensky is a vegetarian society where the words hate and kill do not exist and the only threat is from the dreaded Pash-shan who live below the root and who capture and enslave babies and occasional adults who fall or venture to the forest floor. Lately however the protective vine is withering, citizens fall ill of the Wasting or overindulge in Berry-dreaming, and thirteen-year-old Raamo D'ok, unusually gifted in spirit-power and newly chosen to join the ruling priestly Ol-zhaan, finds suspicion and subterfuge even in the inner sanctums. But where until recent years the hero might have led a glorious victory over the Pash-shan or at least uncovered a plot between them and certain of the Ol-zhaan, here Raamo, alerted by a suspicious older novice named Neric and aided by his female counterpart Genaa, discovers that the dwellers below the root are not monsters after all but exiled Kindar who had become too curious about the forest floor and the secrets of their guardian priests. Greensky is a bit too ritualized and bloodless for our taste and we miss the stronger personalities of Snyder's previous, less highly evolved characters, but as revisionist fantasy this is worth the trip.

> *A review of "Below the Root," in* Kirkus Reviews, *Vol. XLIII, No. 5, March 1, 1975, p. 239.*

"This rock is my house. You can have that one." Children don't just stare at nature the way adults do. They use it. Puddles, ditches, sticks and stones become the playing pieces in a good game called Let's Pretend.

It is Zilpha Snyder's stock in trade. In ***The Egypt Game*** her young characters play at Egypt, using the miscellany in a back yard. "So that was the way Set started—Set the god of evil and black magic. At first he was just supposed to be a character in that particular game, and that first day he was represented by a picture of a man with an animal's head that Melanie drew on a piece of cardboard. But once he got started, he seemed to grow and develop almost on his own, and all out of control; until he was more than evil, and at times a lot more than Egyptian. For instance, at different times, his wicked tricks included everything from atomic ray guns to sulphur and brimstone."

And in ***The Changeling*** she writes about a pair of children who play in a grove of trees and invent a planet called the Land of Green Sky, where the Tree People could "glide like blowing leaves." At the end of the book, Green Sky is forgotten by the children because they grow up, but not by the author herself, who fortunately doesn't. For Zilpha Snyder the notion obviously developed on its own, all out of control like Set, until it became this book, ***Below the Root,*** in which the once-playful Land of Green Sky is a world presented whole.

Of course the children's invention had to be broadened and surrounded with an ethical framework, until it resembled other alternate societies that exist in books, systems running back and forth in time, settings in which the physical or moral bravery of the characters reflects or is pitted against some good or evil imbedded in the nature of things. The seven cities of this Green-sky are a kind of gentle oligarchy ruled by the wise and kindly Ol-zhaan, who alone can assign roles, who declare certain thoughts forbidden. Because of his gift of spiritual intuition they choose young Raamo to join their number. One is reminded of Ursula Le Guin's *Wizard of Earth-Sea,* in which the boy Ged is valued for his mage-like powers.

Zilpha Snyder's sober style does not quite achieve the sinewy grandeur of Le Guin's, nor does her leafy landscape have the scope of that island-dotted main. But the fact that her structure is reminiscent of other made-up countries is not to be held against her. Writers of science fiction have long since explored all time and space and transformed the remotest frontiers into pious Salt Lake Cities or glittering Las Vegases, and of course most American children have been bussed so often around the slums and suburbs of the galaxy by Capt. James Kirk in the Starship Enterprise and dumped in so many tourist resorts run by hairdressers or blobs of glup that they can't be surprised by anything any more anyway.

After all, the Green-sky arrangement was first recommended by Plato, who dreamed of a republic in which philosophers would be the guiding kings. And it has been found wanting by so august a critic as Thomas Mann in *The Magic Mountain,* when his Hans Castorp has a vision of a beautiful race of men who play like children on the golden sand while their priestesses dismember babies in the secret temple. (You just can't trust those priestesses and philosophers.)

In idyllic Green-sky, one guesses that something is awry and that the Ol-zhaan are lying about the evil nature of the enemy, the Pash-shan, who live down there under the root of the great tree that houses and nourishes them all. And of course there is something ominous about the drug-like berry that keeps the childlike people in a state of happy ignorance officially known as Joy (hints of *1984* and *Brave New World*). The moral is not surprising: that knowledge must be free, that there must be no secrets in lofty places (mild overtones of Watergate).

But it is not the moral or the events that make ***Below the Root*** such a pleasing book. It is the fact that it is a full realization of the game of Let's Pretend. The seven cities are distributed about the branches of a group of enormous trees, and the citizens of Green-sky can swoop down from one branch to another by spreading their gauzy clothes like the sails of flying squirrels.

The sense of this light-dappled green world encloses the reader throughout, and the author has worked out in detail its charming possibilities, the rocking hammocks, the giggling cries of drifting birds, the massive limbs that are the corridors from one city to the next.

This branch is my house, that one yours. It is a lovely game. (pp. 32, 34)

> *Jane Langton, in a review of "Below the Root,"*
> *in* The New York Times Book Review, *May 4, 1975, pp. 32, 34.*

After a slow-moving start Snyder's sci fi fantasy gathers speed and moves along with suspense to a not quite satisfactory end—one which certainly calls for a sequel. . . . There are long passages of description and explanation establishing Green sky as a believable world, and though at times the allegory is a little heavy-handed, this is still an interesting suspenseful fantasy.

> *Matilda Kornfeld, in a review of "Below the Root," in* School Library Journal, *Vol. 22, No. 1, September, 1975, p. 112.*

Snyder and her husband on a camel named Moses, 1985

And All Between   (1976)

Readers of last year's future fantasy **Below the Root** will find this slow to start; approximately the first half covers the same events from a different viewpoint—that of eight-year-old Terra, the little girl from the world below whom novice Raamo D'ok and his two fellow Ol-Zhaan-in-training rescue from the forest floor—but without any of the new perspectives or shattered assumptions that such a doubling back requires to maintain interest. However, Terra's story does fill us in on the starving Erdlings' underground life and, later, on Kindar history and the current machinations of their ruling Ol-Zhaan priests. After that both idea and action—which become one and the same as things fall into place—crackle with revelation, reversal and excitement. In the end the young people are on the way to freeing the populations both above and below the root, and there is no longer any question that the innocence of the Love, Peace and Joy-loving Kindar has depended on enforced ignorance and subtle enslavement. Snyder leaves us with a firm, concrete impression of her created world and some teasing thoughts about our own.

> *A review of "And All Between," in* Kirkus Reviews, *Vol. XLIV, No. 3, February 1, 1976, p. 135.*

And All Between is the self-contained successor to the author's earlier **Below the Root.** (It is so self-contained, in fact, that the first 125 pages are devoted to a recapitulation of previous action from a different point of view.) Once the story proper gets under way, we find that it winds up the tale of the schism between the tree-dwelling Kindar and the subterranean Erdlings, the latter exiled and depicted as monsters because they know or suspect a forbidden truth.

This truth is simply that of the possibility of violence, whether verbal, emotional or actual, as a human character trait. The powerful priestly class of Ol-zhaan have suppressed the fact that all Green-sky's inhabitants are refugees from a planet where it was once conceivable not only to kill but to experience anger, resentment, and jealousy. The strongest possible term for any of these emotions among the Kindar is "unjoyfulness." In such a society, we follow the adventures of two novice Ol-zahhan, Raamo and Genaa, as they seek to liberate the Erdlings and expose the self-sustaining myth structures of the priests.

If you accept Green-sky on its own terms, the tale is lively and the world it depicts is complex and consistent. The deep sense of malaise that assails this reader arises from something that underlies the book's ostensible concern with truth in government. Criticism is directed against falsifying history but not, it seems to me, at falsifying emotions. When Joy is always written with a capital letter, when a child's normal resentment of discipline is considered obscene, then good is transmuted into goody-goody and we have entered the airy-fairy world of Victorian elf-kins flitting from flower to flower. The Kindar really do flit. They also illuminate their houses with creatures like fireflies, and take shelter under mushrooms. And of course they never, never kill anything. Zilpha Snyder writes well, and I have enjoyed many of her previous books. However,

And All Between gave this aspiring pacifist a severe attack of unjoyfulness.

> *Georgess McHargue, in a review of "And All Between," in* The New York Times Book Review, *May 23, 1976, p. 16.*

A brief review such as this does not permit full recounting of the exciting characterizations, marvelous depth and intricate yet most readable plot that Mrs. Snyder has created. Although a sequel to her well received **Below The Root,** this work is an even more powerful story. In this reviewer's opinion **And All Between** ranks as Mrs. Snyder's best book yet! Her presentation of two different societies that evolved from that of our earth somewhere in the future is a compelling and forceful commentary on our actions today. A superior book for grades 5 and up.

> *James A. Norsworthy, in a review of "And All Between," in* Catholic Library World, *Vol. 48, No. 3, October, 1976, p. 138.*

Until the Celebration   (1977)

This third volume in Snyder's admirable Green-sky trilogy continues to mirror contemporary issues in a soundly realized future world. By now Green-sky's priestly Ol-zhaan class has been stripped of its mystique, its gentle Kindar population and those banished Erdlings long imprisoned below the root have been reunited, and all of Green-sky is preparing for the ceremonial celebration of the Rejoining. But suspicions and resentments remain general and there are practical problems in integrating the rougher, money-using, meat-eating Erdlings into the Kindar society and child gardens. More seriously, both the treacherous Ol-zhaan D'ol Regle and the vengeful power-hungry Erdling Axon Befal are plotting separate takeovers. And the trilogy's hero Raamo D'ok, novice Ol-zhaan and now a leading Rejoiner, fears the people's tendency to worship the two children (one from each culture) who inspired the Rejoining by demonstrating their command of ancient powers. But the two little girls essentially effect their own demytholigization by behaving like normal children, and in the end the hope rests as it must with all the children. This is intellectual fantasy in that the ideas are in complete control, but throughout the trilogy they always come embodied in well-paced action. And if personalities fail to materialize (though Raamo himself is sacrificed near the end you won't really grieve, having identified chiefly with his views), character is consistently strong and shaded.

> *A review of "Until the Celebration," in* Kirkus Reviews, *Vol. XLV, No. 3, February 1, 1977, p. 95.*

This is the third book about the land of Green-sky. The first was a pleasing fancy of cities high in the branches of enormous trees. The childlike people speak a dreamy language. *Nids* are hammocks. *Shubas* are the silken garments by which they float from branch to branch. But there is menace too. The *tool-of-violence* is some sort of gun or explosive weapon. . . .

Like Graham Oakley [in *The Church Mice Adrift*], the author attempts an overview of her troubled nation-states. But she doesn't have the zoom lens, or even an intercom. We seem to be reading the minutes of countless meetings, running down the pages of Kindar and Erdling phone books, rather than witnessing events. The air is befogged. We catch only occasional glimpses of stately figures with veiled faces moving from limb to limb before the mist wraps them again in obscurity. One wants to grab the tree and shake it, or pick up the tool-of-violence and leap from branch to branch, firing in the air.

> *Jane Langton, in a review of "Until the Celebration," in* The New York Times Book Review, *May 8, 1977, p. 41.*

Although very slow-starting, unevenly paced, unconvincingly motivated and concluded, gimmicky, and obviously didactic, (not nearly as well crafted as Snyder's realistic novels), this will probably interest those who have read the other two books and wish to learn what finally happened to Raamo and his friends.

> *Alethea K. Helbig, in a review of "Until the Celebration," in* Children's Book Review Service, *Vol. 5, No. 11, June, 1977, p. 112.*

The Famous Stanley Kidnapping Case (1979)

The four Stanley children—David, Janie, Esther, and Blair—and their stepsister Amanda, whose occult dabblings carried the plot of the author's *Headless Cupid,* appear again in this suspenseful mystery that takes the family on a sabbatical year to Italy. A leisurely beginning lingers too long on the technicalities of getting to Europe and on the family's sightseeing jaunts to Venice and Florence. Only after settling in a villa near a small Tuscan village does the tension begin to build. A casual boast about her wealthy father makes Amanda a prime kidnapping target; and when the other four follow her into the night, all are captured and imprisoned in an abandoned basement. The kidnappers have their hands full, however, as Janie gives constant advice, Esther fusses about the food, Blair claims to see visions of a "Blue Lady," and Amanda and David plan an escape. The story, told through David's eyes, has a typical 12-year-old's perceptions; and the imaginative character portrayals texture the narrative where the storyline is thin.

> *Barbara Elleman, in a review of "The Famous Stanley Kidnapping Case," in* Booklist, *Vol. 76, No. 4, October 15, 1979, p. 358.*

What the kidnappers don't bargain for [when they abduct Amanda] is holding five children captive, and Snyder makes the whole affair believable and very funny. The story would be enjoyable in any case for the action, the humor, and the colorful setting, but Snyder gives it substance by good dialogue and characterization, by a fluid narrative style, and by the perceptively seen intricacies of the relationships among the children and the changes in Amanda.

> *Zena Sutherland, in a review of "The Famous Stanley Kidnapping Case," in* Bulletin of the Center for Children's Books, *Vol. 33, No. 4, December, 1979, p. 82.*

The children are the same distinct individuals they were in the previous book, and in scenes that are occasionally frightening but usually funny, they react in characteristic ways to the somewhat inept brutality of their abductors; ultimately they are released in a marvelously slapstick episode. While the novel lacks the depth of *The Headless Cupid,* it is wholly entertaining, a work of zip and polish. Conveying a vivid sense of the Tuscan hill country and its inhabitants, the book reads like a scenario for a first-rate children's film.

> *Ethel L. Heins, in a review of "The Famous Stanley Kidnapping Case," in* The Horn Book Magazine, *Vol. LV, No. 6, December, 1979, p. 666.*

A Fabulous Creature (1981)

One thing should be set straight. The fabulous creature of Zilpha Keatley Snyder's new novel is more than the sleek and taut 12-point stag that appears on the jacket. It's Griffin Donahue, an appealing 13-year-old who is both kooky kid and mystical creature, "pure and free and beautiful." But both Griffin and stag are on the same side in the war in which hero James Archer Fielding finds himself.

Brought not altogether willingly to a Sierras cabin for a vacation just outside the exclusive playground, The Camp, 15-year-old James soon discovers the magnificent stag roaming free in a nearby canyon. This makes him all the more contemptuous of The Camp with its sunken bathtubs, pavilions and chain-link fence. Then he meets camp inhabitant, Diane, a tanned, "hot-pink-bikinied" goddess.

Swimmer, hunter and outrageous flirt, Diane is after trophies, and James nearly becomes one of them. When she greets him with her sensuous "Ka-pow!" the hit is visceral. Under her spell James toys dangerously with his values and, in the end, even the enchanting Griffin cannot save James from sharing the secret of the stag's existence with the trophy-hunting Diane.

It's a good book—not only because it pits the plastic people against the wilderness people and mixes the mythic and real, but because Snyder is true to her own story. She herself does not succumb to the expediencies of plasticity and artifice. In a richly symbolic texture, her settings of camp and wilderness become powerful protagonists. Griffin does indeed become "the fabulous creature," and even lesser characters are fully drawn, from the wise, good-humored Mrs. Fielding to Diane's cruelly indulgent father.

It is not a perfect novel. Sometimes Diane's dialogue rings of stereotype, sometimes the polarity between the two worlds seems strained. Still, it is a novel of flesh, idea and design, a novel that dares approach what a fine juvenile novel can be.

And the ending? At a time when the wilderness is quickly disappearing, there may not be much relief when the question of the stag's survival is solved only for the day. On the final page James says: "What came next was going to take some careful thought." And in that statement there is at least hope—not an extravagant amount, but the right, real amount.

> *Patricia Lee Gauch, in a review of "A Fabulous Creature," in* The New York Times Book Review, *March 15, 1981, p. 31.*

This beautifully developed story has a remarkable integration of theme and plot, it has memorable characters, and it's written in a polished style that comprises some acidly sharp characterization, strong family relationships, an appreciation of nature, and one of the funniest bittersweet depictions of unrequited first love in fiction.

> *Zena Sutherland, in a review of "A Fabulous Creature," in* Bulletin of the Center for Children's Books, *Vol. 34, No. 8, April, 1981, p. 162.*

The author underlines the contrast suggested by the intellectual quality of James's parents and the brash materialism of Diane's family, disclosing at the same time the emotional and physical reactions of the teenagers. Like Ursula Le Guin's *Very Far from Anywhere Else* the book portrays a sensitive, intelligent, but fallible protagonist and transcends the conventional subject matter of the new realism. (p. 314)

> *Paul Heins, in a review of "A Fabulous Creature," in* The Horn Book Magazine, *Vol. LVII, No. 3, June, 1981, pp. 313-14.*

Come On, Patsy (1982)

Elementary irony is the keynote of this very brief rhyming monologue in the seemingly upbeat, brisk and friendly words of a little girl inviting another, named Patsy, to play. Sounding at first like a simpy Dick-and-Jane contrivance—"Hi, Patsy. Do you want to play? / Want to go to the park? / I know a new way"—the words are soon revealed as those of a headlong, insensitive bully who drags poor weeping Patsy through all kinds of hazards with only impatient reprimands ("I told you to hurry. . . . You should have jumped higher. . . . Why didn't you say you don't like to go high") as Patsy falls and scrapes her knee, has her clothes bitten by a bulldog, gets sick from the merry-go-round, and so on. [In her illustrations, Margot] Zemach makes the speaker's obliviousness amusingly obvious and Patsy's distress comically pathetic, though she never goes beyond the requirements of the single-minded, far from catchy text. This is incidental Zemach and incidental Snyder—but it's a sufficiently novel diversion, with the added educational value of a guided reading between the lines.

> *A review of "Come On, Patsy," in* Kirkus Reviews, *Vol. L, No. 18, September 15, 1982, p. 1056.*

Patsy is at first unable to say no to any of her friend's schemes but by the end of this story, the reader sees that Patsy has learned her lesson and will not be exploited again. The subtle humor of the plot is conveyed in a very

simple and short rhyming text; the brilliant watercolor and ink illustrations show two active girls amidst piles of falling leaves. The rich colors are beautifully reproduced and the book as a whole is delightful to look at. The only problem: the assumed misspelling of "climb," printed "clumb."

> *Ellen Fader, in a review of "Come On, Patsy," in* School Library Journal, *Vol. 29, No. 5, January, 1983, p. 68.*

The Birds of Summer (1983)

Whatever happened to yesterday's hippies, to the free spirits who rejected middle-class values and aspirations? Some, like Oriole, became mothers. Oriole now lives in a trailer with her two daughters; and 15-year-old Summer has a lot to worry about: her irresponsible, childlike mother, her 7-year-old sister Sparrow and the mysterious, frightening goings on which seem to be taking place next door. There's a sense of impending disaster in this novel, a feeling that is realized when Oriole's helpless nature thrusts her into an involvement with disreputable characters: she ends up in jail, the children in a shelter. A caring teacher comes to the children's rescue, and the story's conclusion is optimistic. What's presented here is a plausible situation, handled in a striking and unpredictable manner. While there seems to be an underlying indictment of a certain life style, Summer's strong, believable characterization and point of view prevent the story from sounding too didactic. The environment is portrayed vividly, with an undercurrent of electric tension that keeps the story going at a steadily accelerating pace. In the end, Summer has to make a decision regarding her responsibility for her "birds," a decision made possible through her heightened maturity and an ability to survive despite obstacles.

> *Marilyn Kaye, in a review of "The Birds of Summer," in* School Library Journal, *Vol. 29, No. 9, May, 1983, p. 85.*

Zilpha Keatley Snyder's **The Birds of Summer** is an unrelentingly "contemporary" novel for young adults, in which the suspense formulas and the hip northern California scene are predictable and thereby offputting at first glimpse. The plot turns on strange happenings in a secluded house, scary nights, drug busts and thugs named Angelo and Bart. The story is also sprinkled with onetime flower children and the opposing horsy set and with pop allusions galore—to The Berkeley Barb, Buckminster Fuller, Darth Vader. In short, it is an R-rated relative of recent Nancy Drew titles.

Summer McIntyre, 15, appears as rigid and as disgustingly right as Nancy. An exemplary student, she displays sage judgment and is praised by every adult she meets. Summer thinks her way through the complications at the nearby Fisher place, where it looks as if marijuana is the cash crop. She holds Nicky, her suitor, at bay much as Nancy manipulates Ned. She has two whimsical, lightweight companions—her mother, Oriole, and her sister, Sparrow.

The Birds of Summer, surprisingly enough, outgrows these clichés. For one thing, Summer is the result of an af-

Snyder speaking to a group of California schoolchildren, 1993.

fair between Oriole and a medical student who passed through her life one summer. Mrs. Snyder portrays their newfangled mother-daughter relationship with a compelling and truthful ambiguity. In the end, Summer hatches a plan to make her mother more responsible and save 7-year-old Sparrow from a life dependent on foodstamps and the kindness of neighbors. Summer is an anxious and ambitious teen-ager whose circumstances provide little reason for optimism. But Summer's love for her odd family, which surfaces gradually, and her intelligent perserverance give cause for hope. (pp. 29-30)

> *Carol Billman, in a review of "The Birds of Summer," in* The New York Times Book Review, *September 25, 1983, pp. 29-30.*

The appealing cover, showing Summer and Sparrow, implies a girls only book, but there are substantial male characters and plenty of action. Highly intelligent overachiever Summer is almost unbelievable at first, but she is a real personality. Like Sara Crewe in Burnett's *Little Princess* she is both strong-and-high-minded under dire circumstances. What a joy to find a truly heroic heroine in a book whose plot alone will endear it. (pp. 208-09)

> *Eleanor Klopp, in a review of "Birds of Sum-*

mer," in Voice of Youth Advocates, *Vol. 6, No. 4, October, 1983, pp. 208-09.*

Blair's Nightmare (1984)

Don't be misled by the title or the frightening jacket picture of a giant dog's head, red eyes glowing and fangs exposed, dwarfing the image of a wondering child in pajamas—all displayed against what seems to be a blue moon in a jet black sky. There is no terror in Blair's nightmare, and although dreams play a part in the story, they serve mostly to underscore the theme—which is that errors of judgment and erroneous assumptions occur when people are locked into a particular point of view.

For example, David Stanley, the 13-year-old through whose eyes the events take place, knows that his little brother Blair has a highly developed imagination. So he does not take it seriously when Blair tells him about the dog he sees in the yard at night. The animal, David assumes, belongs in never-never land along with Blair's imaginary playmate.

David can figure out why a dog is on his brother's mind. All five children in the household are eager to get a dog, but Mr. Stanley will not allow it. When the children adopt a stray, they keep it a secret from their parents as long as they can.

A dog, imaginary or real, is not David's only problem. He dreads the arguments between his father and his step-mother, believing them to be far more serious than they really are, and he lives in fear of being beaten up by Pete, the class bully, who has sworn revenge against David after a classroom showdown in which David injudiciously stands up to him. Pete's sudden interest in David's home and family only increases David's apprehension. No matter how friendly Pete seems, David is sure he is only waiting to attack.

David's problems are resolved satisfactorily, partly through his own efforts and partly through the help he gets in changing his perspective.

Blair's Nightmare is the third book about the Stanley family, following **The Headless Cupid** and **The Famous Stanley Kidnapping Case.** Skillfully drawn, each member is distinct and has a point of view. There is enough mystery to keep the reader turning the pages and enough realism to illustrate the theme.

> *Felice Buckvar, in a review of "Blair's Nightmare," in* The New York Times Book Review, *July 8, 1984, p. 15.*

There are a multitude of subplots—David's changing relationship with step-sister Amanda, Amanda's attraction to the menacing Pete (and vice-versa), increasing arguments between the parents which lead David to fear a divorce is in the offing—but, surprisingly, these secondary themes do not intrude upon the overall flow of the story. Snyder's characters are well drawn, particularly David, who comes across as sensitive without being wimpy. The author seems to assume that children know the members of the Stanley family, which makes the opening chapters confusing to those who are unfamiliar with the characters. Even so, the Stanley kids are realistic and ultimately recognizable. Eminently readable, this will delight Snyder's fans and earn her new ones. (pp. 77-8)

> *Kathleen Brachmann, in a review of "Blair's Nightmare," in* School Library Journal, *Vol. 30, No. 10, August, 1984, pp. 77-8.*

If this book is any indication of the quality of her past efforts, it is no wonder that Zilpha Snyder has won three Newbery awards for her children's books. **Blair's Nightmare** is a beautiful, compelling adventure story that subtly and gently imparts some important lessons to young adolescents.

Told from the perspective of 13-year-old David, this story is about the discovery of his five-year-old brother Blair's "nightmare," which is actually an enormous Irish wolfhound that appears on the Stanley family's property only at night. As she describes the efforts of the five Stanley children to hide the dog from their parents, the author deftly interweaves revelations about the dynamics of the relationship between stepparents, stepchildren and half brothers and about the nature of imagination—especially in young children. In and through it all, she emphasizes

the importance of the individual; the potentially stereotypical "bully," the little sister with the genius IQ, and even David himself, for example, defy their categorizations with surprising words and actions. This is one of the book's great assets: it shows a reader of about David's age when "fitting in" is so important—that you can be different, fit in a little less than perfectly, and still be happy. That she is able to share such an important insight in such a painless—indeed, pleasurable—way is testimony to the author's skillfulness.

What sets this book apart from other exciting adventure stories is Ms. Snyder's beautiful writing. The language is just sophisticated enough to enhance the vocabulary of the young reader, while the structure of the sentences, paragraphs and chapters will certainly demonstrate to her audience just what good writing is.

> *Eleanor P. Denuel, in a review of "Blair's Nightmare," in* Best Sellers, *Vol. 44, No. 6, September, 1984, p. 237.*

The Changing Maze   (1985)

Soft colors, strong lines, and dramatic composition make [illustrator Charles] Mikolaycak's full-page pictures both eerie and romantic; as both, they are appropriate for a romantic, mysterious story in the Oscar Wilde tradition. The writing is occasionally convoluted (". . . the wizard-king a vigil kept. . . .") or ornate ("The hedge grew thick and wondrous fast. . . .") and there are sporadic rhymings that check the natural flow of the story, but the style is on the whole colorful and the story has good structure and suspense. A shepherd lad and his pet lamb stray into the maze created by the evil wizard-king; in the long years since it was built the maze has changed every person who has stumbled through it, but the boy resists the lure of the gold at the heart of the maze in order to save his lamb. And thus, through love, he saves himself.

> *A review of "The Changing Maze," in* Bulletin of the Center for Children's Books, *Vol. 39, No. 3, November, 1985, p. 52.*

Frequent internal rhymes in the prose narrative help convey the hypnotic sway of the maze and add to the old-tale quality of the telling. In drawings that seem to crowd off the edges of the pages, Mikolaycak suggests the menace of the labyrinth, adding chalky, empty-eyed statues clutching coins or stones, which chase the boy to the iron gates at the climax. The mystery, challenge and threat of a maze lie at the heart of this unobtrusively allegorical adventure.

> *Patricia Dooley, in a review of "The Changing Maze," in* School Library Journal, *Vol. 32, No. 4, December, 1985, p. 83.*

Laden with unexpected rhymes and elaborate images, [Snyder's] prose takes on an element of artificiality; yet the story emerges with considerable strength. The artist's dramatic, baroque style nicely complements the storytelling. Making a handsome picture book for older children, his double-page drawings, rendered in pencil and watercolor, capture the suspense, the emotional quality, and the implications of the tale. Moreover, his judicious use of clean, clear white with gradations of subdued color—predominantly greens, browns, and grays—beautifully counterbalances the author's rhetorical tone.

> *Ethel L. Heins, in a review of "The Changing Maze," in* The Horn Book Magazine, *Vol. LXII, No. 1, January-February, 1986, p. 52.*

And Condors Danced   (1987)

Eleven-year-old Carly's world is circumscribed by a stern, intolerant father and an oblivious, ailing mother. But Carly is filled with resourcefulness, and she knows who loves her: her older siblings, her friend Matt, and especially Great-aunt Mehitabel and her Chinese housekeeper, Woo Ying. It's 1907, and Carly's large family has settled in southern California's citrus-growing country. But an ancient feud and a water-rights dispute keep them from enjoying prosperity. Carly romanticizes, dramatizes, and fantasizes the events in her life, until two terrible things happen: her dog and her mother both die, and Carly's grief is more profoundly felt over the dog. This coming-of-age story, with its vividly realized historical California setting, will be enjoyed by readers of Hunt's *Up a Road Slowly* (Follett, 1966). The one jarring note: the characterization of Woo Ying as a "crazy Chinaman" who speaks in verbless sentences (reminiscent of Peter Sellers' nemesis in the "Pink Panther" movies) seems straight out of Central Casting. The story is an interesting one, though, moving along at a leisurely pace that should appeal to thoughtful readers.

> *Susan H. Patron, in a review of "And Condors Danced," in* School Library Journal, *Vol. 34, No. 3, December, 1987, p. 88.*

Set in rural southern California in 1907, **And Condors Danced** vividly captures the daily life of the farming community of Santa Luisa in Ventura County before the automobile superseded the horse and buggy or indoor plumbing replaced the outhouse. Zilpha Keatley Snyder has written many popular novels for preadolescents, including **The Egypt Game** and **The Headless Cupid.** This memorable narrative has sufficient intellectual substance to reward older readers as well. Deftly written, the story blends a traditional and tightly constructed plot with effective treatment of contemporary issues: Carly's emotional isolation and difficulty in dealing with grief are sensitively handled, and a romantic subplot touches on racial and religious tensions.

> *Wendy Martin, in a review of "And Condors Danced," in* The New York Times Book Review, *December 27, 1987, p. 17.*

This is a meaty book (219 pages; no illustrations) for good readers age 10 years and upwards. . . . There is action and incident aplenty; the story moves swiftly yet with a sense of place and personality. . . .

The author has written a thoroughly absorbing, detailed and intricate novel. Characters come and go in profusion. The Californian landscape is expertly created on the page.

Very much a rich and rewarding read for children wishing to expand their awareness of the world and its inhabitants.

> *W. M., in a review of "And Condors Danced," in* The Junior Bookshelf, *Vol. 54, No. 1, February, 1990, p. 54.*

Squeak Saves the Day and Other Tooley Tales   (1988)

Seven stories center on adventures of tiny folk called Tiddlers, who avoid human STOMPERS except for the rare occasion when a brave Tiddler like Trinket Tooley takes an abandoned doll for her friend Dimity, or when Nipper Tooley and his friend Tuck save a lost baby. Several of these stories poke fun at adults, as in the story of Nipper and Trinket's mother getting fed up with a visiting fairy, or their father's frustrated ambition to become a cowboy. There are some funny bits (In Grumbie language "M-M-M-M-rumph" means something like "fat chance") and word play (one story about chickens prefixes "qu" in front of cock, hen, and chickie to feature quocks, quens, and quickies); but there's an overall precious note and some obvious contrivance. The principal reading appeal will be the secret world of diminutive people.

> *Betsy Hearne, in a review of "Squeak Saves the Day and Other Tooley Tales," in* Bulletin of the Center for Children's Books, *Vol. 41, No. 9, May, 1988, p. 189.*

The episodic chapters in this disappointing fantasy tell the story of one Tiddler family, the Tooleys. Jib is a farmer presiding over his family, raising miniature chickens called quarks and trying to control stubborn jumbies, tiny Tiddler oxen. His wife outwits a pesky, demanding fairy who overstays her welcome. Daughter Trinket finds a discarded human "treasure" and through her discovery learns about sharing. Mischievous Nipper, the youngest Tooley, flirts with danger by invading Stomperdom to bring back live souvenirs, such as his pet mouse Squeak. Snyder's humorous anecdotes and witty dialogue produce an occasional smile, but the short, choppy sentences do little to enhance the mood of lightness needed to sustain such a frothy fantasy. . . . The overall result, . . . is formulatic fiction, peopled with stock characters involved in adventures which are all too familiar. Early middle readers should rediscover Peterson's "The Littles" series, while older fantasy lovers will find Norton's "The Borrowers" a richer literary experience. (pp. 98-9)

> *Martha Rosen, in a review of "Squeak Saves the Day and Other Tooley Tales," in* School Library Journal, *Vol. 34, No. 11, August, 1988, pp. 98-9.*

Janie's Private Eyes   (1989)

In a fourth book about the Stanley family, the protagonist is thirteen-year-old David, whose investigation into the mystery of who is stealing dogs is spurred by his sister (Jane, age eight) who has set up a "detective agency." Precocious Janie manages, entertainingly, to get in and out of trouble along with the six-year-old twins and two Vietnamese refugee children. The solution of the mystery is nicely woven into the problems of the Vietnamese family. The story is softened by the durable affection within the Stanley family, and is lightened by the deft treatment of the love-struck swain of stepsister Amanda. The mystery is credibly solved in a nicely crafted story that has suspense, humor, and natural dialogue.

> *Zena Sutherland, in a review of "Janie's Private Eyes," in* Bulletin of the Center for Children's Books, *Vol. 42, No. 5, January, 1989, p. 135.*

Even though it will be obvious to some from the beginning who the bad guys are, Snyder has put a number of twists, turns, and red herrings into the plot to make it intriguing. The inclusion of the plight of the Trans and their problems as refugees in small-town U.S.A. make an interesting sidelight to the mystery. The characters, particularly precocious detective Janie, are deftly and humorously portrayed. A funny and quick read that fans of the Stanley family will enjoy, but no one has to have read the others to understand this one.

> *Kathryn Havris, in a review of "Janie's Private Eyes," in* School Library Journal, *Vol. 35, No. 6, February, 1989, p. 83.*

Libby on Wednesday (1990)

Five seventh-grade winners of a writing competition are required to form a creative writing workshop where their diversity—which at first makes them unwilling, even hostile, collaborators—eventually draws them together as friends.

For protagonist Libby, who is the granddaughter of a famous local novelist—and who has been taught at home until this year when her remarkable family of five adults has decided that it's time for her to be "socialized"—each of the others is a threat: G. G., whose bullying is paralleled by the violence in his stories; Alex, who can't "write" and goes to a special class, but who proves to be a gifted satirist; obstreperous, punk Tierney, whose hard-boiled detective stories aren't *meant* to be parodies; even cheerleader Wendy, who writes trite romances but whose niceness turns out to be real. As the five learn to give and accept constructive criticism, they also begin to respect each other's gifts; by the time their advisor is hospitalized, the group has become so important that they continue meeting privately, in the fabulous treehouse built by Libby's granddad.

The characters here are pungent and believable, their interaction well-realized. Revealing details—Libby's extensive collections, kept in the servants' quarters of the old family mansion; the stories read at the workshop sessions—meld with a carefully paced story that comes to a climax when the others dramatically rescue G. G. from his abusive father, but that also thoughtfully explores the enriching value of diversity—and demonstrates, along the way, how to use words to reflect it. A grand, multileveled novel.

> *A review of "Libby on Wednesday," in* Kirkus

Reviews, *Vol. LVIII, No. 3, February 1, 1990, p. 185.*

Writing has always been Libby's refuge; through her journal entries and a third-person narrative, her story unfolds. The two styles mesh perfectly; from Libby's voice, readers gain insight into her thoughts and feelings, and from the narrative they see her in her broader surroundings. The classmates with whom Libby interacts, all members of a writers' club that meets on Wednesdays, have serious problems of their own, and yet the group seems neither contrived nor unlikely. Their writing, too, contributes greatly to the development of their characters. Libby's family members may not be the stuff of real life, but they add a touch of levity that keeps the story from becoming a clinical study of the effects of family expectations, child abuse, and physical disabilities. Vivid descriptions and clear portraits of the characters give an honest, forthright picture of these classmates-turned-friends who come to accept their difficulties and to care about each other. It's an absorbing story, filled with real young people and genuine concerns.

> *Trev Jones, in a review of "Libby on Wednesday," in* School Library Journal, *Vol. 36, No. 4, April 1, 1990, p. 124.*

Unfortunately Zilpha Keatley Snyder, a popular writer for young adults, has not delivered a completely satisfying product. There are certainly pleasing moments in the novel—Libby and her family in particular are well drawn—but other characters seem stereotypical. In addition, the dialogue, though colloquial, can be irritating; the inclusion of a case of abuse by an alcoholic father seems gratuitous; and the resolution is a little too pat. This is a novel that tries too hard to please.

> *Susan Perren, in a review of "Libby on Wednesday," in* Quill and Quire, *Vol. 56, No. 6, June, 1990, p. 20.*

Song of the Gargoyle (1991)

Snyder plunges readers into a mercurial, uncertain medieval time as young Tymmon begins a quest to find his father. Although Tymmon's father, Kommus, was born noble, he gave up his station in life to become a court jester. Tymmon has never understood his father's motivation, nor entirely approved of his choice. But when Kommus is kidnapped by a knight who wants Tymmon as well, the young man must hide in the forest sustained only by his vow to rescue his father until Troff comes along. Troff is a gargoyle, although he can be mistaken for a dog if people don't look too closely. Together, the boy and the enchanted creature team up to entertain people in villages and towns, hoping to learn something of Kommus, though the lessons Tymmon learns are, for the most part, about himself. Snyder's long passages of descriptions, though beautifully executed, will deter some who prefer a quicker pace. One part of the story that does reveal itself briskly is Tymmon's discovery of his father, but since the search for Kommus is at the core of the story, it is unfortunate that when the jester is finally found, it is only by chance, not through Tymmon's efforts. Despite some flaws, Snyder continues to be one of our best storytellers. This tale, a mixture of magic and hard-won truths, is deeply layered and affecting.

> *Ilene Cooper, in a review of "Song of the Gargoyle," in* Booklist, *Vol. 87, No. 11, February 1, 1991, p. 1127.*

Drawing on conventions from both fantasy and historical fiction, Snyder takes yet a third path of legendary chronicle, much as Lloyd Alexander did in his Westmark trilogy. Troff, the huge, ugly dog that guides Tymmon on his journey, so resembles a gargoyle that Tymmon believes him to be a fantastical beast, and indeed he seems so; yet nothing he does is totally beyond the capabilities of canine intelligence and strength—not counting the conversations Tymmon believes he has with Troff. Between forest frights, vengeance oaths, and endearing orphans, the action here is nonstop, with solid characterization and practiced style. The adventurous plot more than makes up for occasional slips to cliche (". . . a tingle of nervous excitement raced up his spine. What would Dame Fortune have in store for him today in the great city of Montreff?"). Although the setting is medieval, the viewpoint is modern, with the young hero coming to realize, as his father did, that it is more humane to become a court jester than a knight errant, something for children of any time to consider while pursuing their own quests for survival and glory. (pp. 177-78)

> *Betsy Hearne, in a review of "Song of the Gargoyle," in* Bulletin of the Center for Children's Books, *Vol. 44, No. 7, March, 1991, pp. 177-78.*

Here Snyder weaves another enthralling tale, not as subtle as *The Egypt Game,* but rife with danger and intrigue. . . .

The Middle Ages remain in most people's minds a time of romance and mystery, teeming with brave knights, sprawling castles and haunted forests. But for all the wondrous images, Snyder reminds us that it was also a very harsh time, when punishments could be meted out willy-nilly by whoever had the strength. . . .

Much of *The Song of the Gargoyle*'s success comes from Snyder's ability to engage all the senses. Sounds are moaning wails, deep throbbing cries and sharp high-pitched yelps. There is bloodred sky, a sharp-ribbed animal and a dull-faced countenance. Foods are porridge, pheasant, dried fruit, meat pies and sweet pastries.

She further authenticates the milieu by employing words like paternoster, doublet, jerkin, wattle, jongleur and sabaton. Her towns have names that are great fun to read aloud, like Qweasle, Unterrike, Nighmont, Bondgard, Nordencor and Montreff.

As Tymmon starts to seek answers to his many questions, the mysteries are gradually resolved. The further he follows his uncertain path, the more he learns and the surer he becomes of himself and his future. Kind of like real life now as well as in the Middle Ages.

> *Margaret Camp, "Once More into the Woods," in* Book World—The Washington Post, *May 12, 1991, p. 14.*

Martin Waddell

1941-

(Also writes as Catherine Sefton) Irish author of picture books and fiction, scriptwriter, and editor.

Major works include *Island of the Strangers* (1983), *Starry Night* (1986), *Frankie's Story* (1988), *Can't You Sleep, Little Bear?* (1988), *The Beat of the Drum* (1989), *Farmer Duck* (1991).

A prolific and popular writer whom Liz Weir has called "two authors in one" for his work both as Catherine Sefton and under his own name, Waddell is applauded for his range, variety, skillfulness as a literary stylist, and understanding of children and young people. The creator of picture books, early readers, stories for middle graders, and young adult novels, he characteristically writes his works for preschoolers and primary graders as Martin Waddell and his teenage fiction under his pseudonym. Waddell is acknowledged for investing many of his works with meaningful themes, both in his picture books and stories for older children; he most often addresses the relationship between generations, the continuity of life, the rights of the individual, and the effects of prejudice and injustice. Setting several of his Sefton novels in Northern Ireland, Waddell is acknowledged for presenting young readers with a balanced picture of life in his homeland. Although he clearly shows the effects of the current political and social situation, including injury and death, he uses the backdrop of Northern Ireland to center on the growth and maturation of his young protagonists—both male and female, Protestant and Catholic—who cope with problems while confirming their decisions, often made at personal risk, to reject prejudice and respond positively to those on the other side. Waddell's earliest and most recent stories with an Irish background concentrate on representation of landscape and family and community life rather than on the political situation; in all of his works about Northern Ireland, Waddell is commended for his evocation of setting and atmosphere. As Catherine Sefton, Waddell demonstrates the effect of the past on the present through his inclusion of ghosts, who haunt to aid the living or because they need assistance themselves. Along with mystery, suspense, economical texts, superior characterizations, and a moving, thought-provoking quality, the Sefton novels are noted for their humor, an element that is also important to Waddell's picture books and stories under his own name. These works—which draw on fantasy, realism, and a blend of the two—are written by Waddell as pure entertainment and include rhythm, rhyme, and word repetition to appeal to young children.

Born in Newcastle, County Down, Northern Ireland, Waddell is descended from Scotsmen who came to Ireland in the seventeenth century; "I am neither Protestant nor Catholic, Ulster Loyalist nor Irish Nationalist," he has written, "so it is difficult for me to identify with any of these groups. This difficulty is explored in many of my

books." As a child, he was influenced by the stories told to him by his father and a friend, Terence Pym, as well as by the books read to him by his mother: "When I came to write books for the very small," he says, "I have this period in mind." Waddell attempted to become a professional football player at sixteen, an experience he reflects in his series of "Napper" stories for middle graders about talented young goalie Napper McCann. After being released from the Fulham Football Club in London, Waddell began to write. His first major success was as an adult novelist: his series of humorous thrillers about Gerald Arthur Otley, an antique dealer in Swinging London, caused him to be called, in his own words, "Britain's Youngest Satirist." After moving back to Northern Ireland, Waddell began to write for young adults, crafting the pseudonym Catherine Sefton from his grandmother's maiden name and his affection for the name Catherine. Drawing on his own experiences and those of his children, Waddell began writing shortly thereafter for a younger audience under his own name. In 1972, Waddell was badly injured by a bomb that exploded in a small Catholic church in Donaghadee, the largely Protestant town where he was living at the time. Although he recovered, he suffered writer's block from the incident until 1978; he has since used his experience in *The Ghost Girl* (1985), the story of a young Protestant woman who solves a mystery with the help of a ghost while on holiday in Northern Ireland.

Waddell is celebrated for creating several works under both monikers which are considered classics of their genres. He is perhaps best known as Catherine Sefton for his three related novels about the troubles in Northern Ireland which have been called the "Irish trilogy," although the books share only common themes. In these novels, *Starry Night, Frankie's Story,* and *The Beat of the Drum,* he draws parallels between the worlds of his Protestant and Catholic protagonists to show the effect of the Irish situation on teenagers. Robert Leeson writes, "The author has resolutely completed his aim, to help the teenage reader grasp the reality of North Ireland's tragedy. The trilogy is a real contribution to the understanding which must one day bring that suffering to an end." In addition to his works as Catherine Sefton, Waddell is equally respected for the books he has created under his own name. Many of these books are published as series: among the most popular are the "Harriet" stories about the humorous exploits of a well-meaning but accident-prone small girl; the "Little Dracula" books about a vampire and his family; the "Bertie Boggin" books about a boy who befriends a ghost; and the "Rock River" stories, historical fiction about pioneer life in the American West that are called excellent introductions to the novel for young readers. Waddell is best known as an author of picture books for his "nighttime theme" books *Can't You Sleep, Little Bear?, The Park in the Dark* (1989), and *Let's Go Home, Little Bear* (1991): in the first and third books, Big Bear assures his friend Little Bear about his fears and anxities in a loving and reassuring manner, while the second work describes the closeness and protectiveness of three stuffed animal friends who venture into the night to go to the playground. In addition, Waddell is lauded as the creator of *Farmer Duck,* a picture book that echoes *Animal Farm* and is praised for its wit, precision, and tenderness: in this barnyard story, a duck does all the work for his lazy farmer before the other animals chase the farmer away and prepare to help their friend. Many of Waddell's picture books reflect the love and understanding between old and young: for example, *My Great Grandpa* (1990) underscores the special relationship shared by an elderly man and his young greatgranddaughter as she takes him in his wheelchair to the house where he used to live, and *Grandma's Bill* (1990) stresses the closeness between a grandmother and her young grandson as she shows him photographs of her deceased husband, the boy's namesake. Waddell is also the author of radio plays for children and the editor of a collection of stories by young people from Northern Ireland. He has won several awards both as Martin Waddell and Catherine Sefton. *The Ghost and Bertie Boggin* was named a runner-up for the Federation of Children's Book Club Award in 1982; *Island of the Strangers* was nominated for the Carnegie Medal in 1984; *Can't You Sleep, Little Bear?* won the Smarties Grand Prize in 1988 and Le Prix des Critiques de Livres pour Enfants from Belgium in 1989 as well as the Kate Greenaway Medal for its illustrator, Barbara Firth, in 1988; *The Park in the Dark* won the Kurt Maschler/Emil Award in 1989; *Starry Night* won the Other Award in 1986 and was a run-

ner-up for the Guardian Award in 1987; and *Rosie's Babies* won the Best Book for Babies Award in 1990.

(See also *Something about the Author,* Vol. 43, *Something about the Author Autobiography Series,* Vol. 15, *Contemporary Authors New Revision Series,* Vol. 34, and *Contemporary Authors,* Vol. 113.)

AUTHOR'S COMMENTARY

A picture book tells a story, at least mine do. Storytelling is what interests me, because I am a storyteller.

The working difference between writing a story and writing a picture book is that when I write a story and finish it, it *is* finished. When I write a picture book text I am just at the beginning of a long process, in which the whole structure and meaning of the story will be re-interpreted by someone else, an artist who deals in images.

I once boasted to David Lloyd, my editor at Walker Books, that I wrote 'in images'. 'You do,' he replied, 'But you are very bad at it!' It was a neat put-down, but also true. I am a writer, not an imagemaker. The danger of thinking you write 'in images' is when it leads to the expectation that the artist will faithfully reproduce *those* images . . . will 'illustrate' the story you have written.

This is the way to produce a *bad* picture book, because the images have been imposed on the artist by a non-specialist—someone who writes. I know this to be so from my own experience, but it is still difficult to come to terms with.

A case in point is **The Hidden House**. . . .

I began the story in a bedsit above the Conservative Party Offices in Ladbroke Grove in 1958 (this is not a political statement, I just happened to be camped there). I was in bed with a heavy case of 'flu, and the 'Dollmaker' idea came to me. Out of bed, off with the 'flu, on with the story, back to bed. It was then called 'Dominic'. The manuscript is lost to me, but I suppose it lies within whatever vault holds the rejects from Hutchinson New Authors Ltd, an imprint from which I received great encouragement, short of being published. An old man makes dolls to keep him company, that was roughly the story.

Twenty-five years later, walking up a lane from Tipperary woods towards the Mournes, I discovered the Dollmaker's house, choked with weeds and ivy, grimy windows still intact.

Glorious moment . . . the thing is a picture book text, full of images! White heat stage . . . lovely . . . the story was written in about an hour.

'Good story!' David Lloyd said.

Happy puffs on pipe from cheery author, expecting big . . . well, biggish . . . cheque.

'You got the end wrong,' he added. 'If it isn't the end, it's something else.'

Distressed puffs on pipe, then excitement. We tweaked the

story here and there, working and re-working, until it came right, and it was still *my* story, *my* possession.

'Angela Barrett,' Amelia Edwards, Walker Art Director, said. They showed me *The Snow Queen.*

Two reactions: 'She is good. Very good.'

'What has she got to do with *my* story?' Big Question Mark. (Note the possessive adjective.)

I agreed nervously to go ahead.

Moment of maximum pain. The first pictures laid on the desk, with David and Amelia doing their David-and-Amelia Act, gazing at me gazing at it, and waiting for the pipe to twitch.

Oh God! I have been nearly thirty years getting *my* story right, a story full of ideas about warmth and togetherness and love and renewal, and look-what-this-woman-has-done-to-it! A strange image, an old child-scaring man on a bench with three huge elongated dolls. Help me somebody! What do I say to them?

'Oh-er,' or words to that effect.

Pipe clenched, while over-heating brain clicks. What is this *Angela* doing? This image is something from inside her, not anything to do with me. Get rid of it! I don't want it in *my* book.

David: 'I think it is brilliant.'

Pipe puffed furiously.

Amelia, defiantly, as the smoke ascends: 'It *is* brilliant.'

Crushed Author: 'Y-e-s, it is, but . . .'

Chorus (What a double act): '*Look* at it, Martin!'

And I did.

I looked for a long time.

It is brilliant. It is how the book should be, not as I saw it. As I saw it, it would have been a safe book about cuddly dollies, albeit dealing with life and death, but this book is altogether different; it has a whole new dimension. It *works.*

My story became *our* book . . . a picture book, not just a text. 'A perfect blend,' somebody was nice enough to say, but it wasn't just a blend, because blending conveys intermingling, and there is more to it than that. A picture book grows somewhere in the process. In the end it doesn't belong to either the writer or the artist, but both together, and *them* . . . the people whose names are not on the cover: editor, designer, whoever chose the paper, all the people who add the little bits that make it work.

The writer's sense of possessiveness is the first great danger to a picture book. I am, and always will be, very possessive about my picture book texts, but this can be taken no further than protecting them against the 'wrong' artist. This means the artist who is plain bad, or the artist who is technically good, but brings nothing of his or her self to the story.

The key moment is when you realise that the artist has taken over . . . unfortunately that is usually the moment when the possessive writer feels most hurt. It's a funny mix of feeling, because the hurt is mingled with a feeling of joy and a sense of wonder. '*Look what has happened to it!*' followed by, '*It works!*'

More and more I am writing now without indications to the artist that come from my own sense of image . . . it is an inferior sense, it only gets in the way.

The Park in the Dark is an example of the right way to do it.

'Me and Loopy and Little Gee.'

Editor to Writer: 'What are they?'

Writer to Editor: 'Don't know. Just words.'

Neither of us needed to know, we are wordsmen. The toys in ***The Park in the Dark*** were in Barbara Firth. They came from her own childhood, they belonged to her, and so when she drew them, she felt them, and that feeling comes over in the pictures.

So the writer just writes little stories, and after that it is all up to the artist, and the design department? Not so . . . not 'little' stories; a picture book is often much more than that. A really good picture book is a 'big' story, written in very few words, often layered so that many meanings lie within it.

What does 'big' mean? It can mean 'about-something-that-matters': ideas like the wheel of life, as in ***Once There Were Giants*** (a terribly difficult book for Penny Dale to make work); ideas like fear of the unknown as in ***Can't You Sleep, Little Bear?.*** Those are big 'adult' ideas, we recognise them as big easily, and the craft of the thing is to render them comprehensible to very small children.

How about 'Justice'? Children say, 'It isn't fair!' and they mean it, it *matters* to them.

> There once was a duck
> Who had the bad luck
> To live with a lazy old Farmer
> The duck did the work,
> For the farmer stayed all day in bed.

Justice for the Duck! And the right artist! Helen Oxenbury is doing ***Farmer Duck.***

There are other 'big' ideas, which are big for the very small. How about splashing? The sheer joy of splash-splash-splashing in cool water on a warm day . . . a big celebration of a very small thing that children love.

> One day Neligan went into town.
> It was hot. It was dry.
> The sun shone in the sky.
> Neligan's pig sat by Neligan's pond.

A fat, steamy pig. A duck and goose splashing in the pond, teasing the pig with quacks and honks of pure pleasure then . . .

> SPLAAASH!
> The pig's in the pond!
> The pig's in the pond!
> The pig's in the pond!

The word spread about,
Above and beyond.
At Neligan's farm,
The pig's in the pond.

Pig in the Pond. Jill Barton's pig now.

Noise . . . that's another celebration one. 'Tum-tum-te-tum, diddle-diddle-dum, ratta-tat-tat-boom!' *The Happy Hedgehog Band.* Jill again.

So big ideas can be small from an adult point of view, but then an adult point of view is not very helpful. A 'big' idea is something which instantly interests a child, and if you can shade in some more subtle themes alongside it, so much the better.

I work on the principle that the eventual book will usually be read one-to-one, a shared thing, often at the end of a difficult day. The day may have thrown up barriers between the adult and the child, and the picture book, particularly the old familiar picture book, can bring them together again. It may even open the possibility of airing whatever the matter is.

A picture book text is a script for performance by the reader, performing to a very personally involved audience that wants to stop, ask questions, look, and point things out. There should be words to work on for that performance, lots of rhythm and rhyme and alliteration and fun and jokes and things happening, a story with a beginning, a middle and an end, a story that often says something about loving relationships between 'big' and 'small'.

No problem! You have three to five hundred words to do it in, ideally less.

Finished?

Get it to the *right* artist. (pp. 26-7)

> Martin Waddell, "Writing Texts for Picture Books," *in* Books for Keeps, *No. 68, May, 1991, pp. 26-7.*

GENERAL COMMENTARY

Liz Weir

Newcastle, County Down, is a town set on the edge of Dundrum Bay, some 30 miles south of Belfast. To people in Northern Ireland it's known primarily as a seaside resort, but it is here in a large Victorian house on the seafront where Martin Waddell alias Catherine Sefton lives and works. (p. 12)

Martin is an amazingly prolific author with 54 books published and some 17 due for publication, written under his own name and his pen-name of Catherine Sefton.

The obvious first question which children (and adults) clamour to ask is 'Why the two names?' The reason is quite sensible: the Martin Waddell books are very different from the Catherine Sefton books. Whilst most Martin Waddell titles are simply for fun, featuring, for example, growling budgies or green mice, the Catherine Sefton books are longer and more emotionally based, involving more adult themes such as jealousy or family intrigue.

'Sefton is a family name—my father's mother was a Sefton from Belfast who dyed her hair with tea-leaves and wore big straw hats. Catherine is a clear bright name and I wanted my books to have a clear bright feeling about them. Putting both types of my books under the same name would only confuse people.'

When asked, as he invariably is, about why he chose a woman's name, Martin responds 'Why not? The books came first, the name was invented afterwards. The name had to fit the books and I think that it does.'

Martin lived in Newcastle as a child, growing up in a region rich in legends such as Maggie's Leap and place names like Bloody Bridge, unconsciously collecting material which has reappeared since in his work. The young Martin had ambitions to become a professional footballer and was accepted to play as goalkeeper with Fulham FC's youth team where he spent a year. This real life experience has undoubtedly contributed to the authenticity of the 'Napper' series and Martin's continued interest in soccer is witnessed as he awaits the weekly match results to hear how 'our lads' (Fulham) fared!

The early determination which he showed in pursuing a career in the competitive English Football League was to stand him in good stead for his next challenge, to make it as a writer. Despite early rejections he wrote addictively and the breakthrough came with the acceptance of *Otley,* an amusing adult spy thriller which was made into a feature film. . . . The success of *Otley* meant that Martin could write full-time and today the original cinema poster for the film hangs on the wall above his desk.

The first success in the world of children's books came in 1972 with *In a Blue Velvet Dress,* which was televised on BBC's 'Jackanory'. There followed another Catherine Sefton novel, *Sleepers on the Hill;* in both books Martin draws on *real* places, changing and weaving them into the tale. 'So the *real* places I use are *unreal,* because they get all mixed up in the stories, but I need real places to begin with, if only to give me a map.'

Just when he was getting into his stride as a children's author, disaster struck when he was badly injured in a bomb explosion near his home and for a while Martin wrote nothing at all. Having taken the decision to return to Newcastle, he went on to write a third children's book, *The Back House Ghosts,* set in Ballaghbeg, the Irish name for the town. The house where Martin now lives with his wife Rosaleen and three teenage sons, Tom, David and Peter, closely resembles 'Bon Vista', the guest house in the book, and whilst it doesn't have a backhouse it isn't hard to imagine how it would feel to have to move out when the summer visitors come to town.

Today no ghosts lurk behind the brightly painted blue door, just an 11-month-old retriever called Bessie who delights in gazing at the sea from the first-floor drawing room window! Martin's study doesn't face the shore but it is here where he puts all his energies to work. 'I come to this room each day and I stay in it—by a process of boredom I get to the typewriter!'

But boredom is the last word to associate with Martin

Waddell at nine months.

Waddell and the shelves of books which line the walls are proof of his tremendous creative output. Having all his books in front of him acts as an encouragement for him to write more. 'I have a whole lot of stories and want to get on to the next. The idea of running out of ideas doesn't occur to me.'

Indeed, gazing at the shelf full of manilla folders each containing another book, no-one would disagree! The folders don't just contain what Martin calls the 'stars'—here too are the 'corpses', manuscripts which might not have made it this time around but which could still reappear one day, perhaps as a completely different book. Martin feels strongly about his need to rewrite.

'Sometimes I completely blot out what I have just written and produce something quite different.' He admits to writing 'frenetically', mailing off five or six different things some weeks and because of the speed of his work he feels he owes a great deal to his agent, Gina Pollinger. 'I need an agent creatively. Gina has a feel for a manuscript and can spot something wrong. Because I work very fast some things can be half baked. I am heavily edited and regard the editor as part of the writing process. I spend a lot of time sitting at a desk with an editor writing, and this can sometimes produce a different book!'

Martin finds what he calls his 'bright ideas' all around. In his study are various objects which have prompted him to start work on stories—a painting, a set of plaster teeth, a boat sign—ideas are everywhere. It is this truth which Martin demonstrates to children when he visits primary schools. About three weeks a year are spent out and about meeting young people in many parts of Britain. For these visits he has devised his 'Build a Story' sessions. Children are encouraged to create a story from scratch, building up character, a happening, and adventures which arise from it. The children use their imaginations to the limit, discuss, select and reject elements and the whole process moves at a fast pace with Martin questioning and stimulating until the time limit is up. The excitement of these sessions touches every child in the class and makes great demands upon Martin who throws himself into it body and soul to the point of exhaustion on some occasions! No bland prepared speech with *this* author!

Sessions such as these have often themselves provided a starting point for stories—the tunnels under one local school providing an idea for *Harriet and the Crocodiles.* Children are encouraged to send their own stories to Martin and he makes a point of acknowledging them all. He feels that this contact with children is vital: 'It is very easy to disconnect from the reality of what kids *are*—publishers are even more remote.' This contact with children isn't just local—a recent letter came from a ten-year-old Australian girl and like the others she will receive a photograph and a personal note.

Martin works a five day week during school term to enable him to spend more time with his family. . . . The versatility of these two authors in one is quite breathtaking as he covers a range of themes from liberated princesses to a 'choose your own' type adventure, from Great Gran Gorilla to a little bear who can't get to sleep! Obviously it is impossible to compare them all, as Martin says:

'They are different products, written with different things in mind.' The change from a deeply moving Catherine Sefton to a fast moving slapstick is 'like a mindwash and back again'. A stream of visual ideas can spring from a very short text, perhaps the starting point might even be lost in the finished book.

'I do start with an idea and then create people—every time people don't fit I let them go and do their own thing. The characters take over and lots of ideas go. I believe in giving children exciting stories with a strong read-on hook and often an edge of the supernatural. I believe in writing very carefully for children because they become much more involved in the small details of character than the average adult reader.'

Starry Night, winner of the 1986 Other Award and runner-up for the Children's Fiction Award, formed the first part of a trilogy of Catherine Sefton books for older teenagers set in contemporary Northern Ireland. 'I believe in there being a moral message in children's stories. They show a pattern of family life and how you cope with problems. Irish teenagers don't get on with living their lives, they are interfered with by side issues.'

The trilogy for older readers is intended to show the effects of the political and social situation in Northern Ireland today on young people at crucial moments in the development of their personal lives. Being a teenager is difficult enough, given modern pressures, but in these books Martin hopes to show how being a teenager in his native land can be even harder still. 'I'm aware of the pressures constantly crowding in on my own kids; the necessity of having to hang labels of identity on themselves. I've always tried to teach them to look at the views of the other side and in the books I'm preaching the same philosophy.'

The second part of the trilogy, *Frankie's Story,* tells of a teenage girl trying to cope with the difficulties of a parental break-up, squabbles with her sister and boyfriend trouble—the last thing she needs is for the 'troubles' to intrude further into her already complicated life. The story makes for compulsive reading, made more harrowing by the truthful observation of the contemporary scene. It makes sense that the author of such an emotionally draining book should look in his other writing for lighter relief. Leaving Newcastle the imposing facade of the Slieve Donald Hotel is clearly seen on the sea front—what a glorious idea to imagine it, as in *The Great Green Mouse Disaster,* full of green mice scurrying about. What a world apart from the daily news bulletins. Martin Waddell manages to capture the imagination at both ends of the spectrum. (pp. 12-13)

> Liz Weir, "Authorgraph No. 48: Martin Waddell," in Books for Keeps, *No. 48, January, 1988, pp. 12-13.*

TITLE COMMENTARY

In a Blue Velvet Dress: Almost a Ghost Story (as Catherine Sefton, 1972)

Jane Reid is a bookworm so when she arrives at the Hildreth's house for a holiday and discovers that she has left all her own books at home, that her hosts consider reading a waste of time and that there is no library or book shop in the little town, she is in despair. Then each night a book mysteriously appears beside her bed and vanishes again in the morning. She sees a girl in a blue velvet dress in her room and connecting the girl with the books she eventually solves the mystery of their appearance. Written in a pleasant style, the story may be somewhat fanciful but ghost stories are so popular that although this is described only as 'almost a ghost story', it will be well read in a junior school library.

> Lucinda Fox, in a review of "In a Blue Velvet Dress," in The School Librarian, *Vol. 20, No. 3, September, 1972, p. 275.*

An old, empty, ruinous house with a history attached—this familiar focal point for a youthful adventure is apt to reveal deficiencies in an author's technique if it is not handled with proper care. *In a blue velvet dress* is described as "almost a ghost story" and the mistiness of the gentle spirit that haunts the Hildreth's house seems to have rubbed off on the story, which is lacking in emphasis and individuality. Mary Quinton died of grief when she was only thirteen, after her father had been drowned; a century or so later she appears to a girl of eleven who has been sent to the house while her parents are sailing in Scotland. There is an opportunity here to link Jane's thoughts about her parents with Mary's tragedy, but it is not taken. The ghost, if she may be so termed, visits the house at night to leave books for Jane to read but it is some time before

we see any obvious connection between the curious way old-fashioned volumes appear on her bed-table and the ruined house in the woods whose history is put together piece by piece. Past and present somehow don't mesh as they should, perhaps because Jane's character is not strong enough to bring this about.

> Margery Fisher, in a review of "In a Blue Velvet Dress," in Growing Point, *Vol. 11, No. 5, November, 1972, p. 2036.*

The barriers of time in this charming Irish story are continually dissolving and reforming. . . . [The] imaginative plot is narrated with most endearing and effective humour, whereby the author jumps a stage or two to the amusing results of an action or remark, producing devastating reversals and surprises.

> M. Hobbs, in a review of "In a Blue Velvet Dress," in The Junior Bookshelf, *Vol. 36, No. 6, December, 1972, p. 412.*

The Sleepers on the Hill (as Catherine Sefton, 1973)

Until they find out the truth, Tom and Kathleen think that old Miss Cooney's accident has left the large house on the hill untenanted. And the finding out of the truth is something which keeps you reading from the beginning of the book to the end, as Catherine Sefton lures the reader on with her seemingly disorganised story that nevertheless embraces every point and takes the plot on surely, step by step. With an Irish lilt subauditorily beneath every line, very living words tell of the threat of darkness, of the compulsive evil of the bangle Tom innocently picks up, and of the threat to the people of the village from the tourists and developers. The idea of fantasy, of the sleepers of the hill and their arousal, provides the luxury of a Celtic supernatural frisson on top of what is essentially a story about the flurry of events that most children know as home-life. And these events wind up to a tense climax in the mysterious house, with thieves, a wasps' nest, fire and rescue, everything indeed to compensate for the unappealing jacket. Approachable, clear, concise, interest age eight to ten years. (pp. 179-80)

> C. S. Hannabuss, in a review of "The Sleepers on the Hill," in Children's Book Review, *Vol. III, No. 6, December, 1973, pp. 179-80.*

The story is set in a remote part of Ireland where the presence of a prehistoric site can still influence the thinking of the inhabitants. The plot revolves round the appearance of a gold bangle from this site and its suggestion to local rogues that it could lead to the easy recovery of more of the same. The varied characters are well drawn and in particular the narrator is the sort of boy the reader can identify with. The language and sentence construction are just different enough to suggest the Irish scene. The plot develops at the right pace to keep the reader's interest and there are some excellent surprises and dangerous moments.

> Harold A. Jester, in a review of "The Sleepers on the Hill," in The School Librarian, *Vol. 22, No. 1, March, 1974, p. 99.*

[The] echo of rural superstition doesn't quite mesh with the community's problems of a housing plan in which they would all lose their homes and the more pervasive problem of losing the young people who are either bored by rural life or cannot find employment.

While such considerations make the setting more interesting, they do tend to obscure the story of the children, the artifact, and the source from which the metal ring came, the "Sleepers'" Hill. The writing style is adequate, but neither style nor construction is impressive. (pp. 162-63)

> *Zena Sutherland, in a review of "The Sleepers on the Hill," in* Bulletin of the Center for Children's Books, *Vol. 32, No. 9, May, 1979, pp. 162-63.*

The Back House Ghosts (as Catherine Sefton, 1974; U.S. edition as *The Haunting of Ellen: A Story of Suspense*)

The contrast between the busy seaside resort, the Bailey's boarding house and the glimpses of the ghostly family who once lived in the 'back house' has produced a story that is full of excitement and humour, whilst the varying characters of the children involved must strike a sympathetic chord with even the most down-to-earth reader.

Practical Bella and dreamy Ellen move into the cottage at the end of the garden (known as the back house) with their mother, when suddenly faced with thirteen Mooneys instead of the four they had expected. A sudden vacancy means that Mrs. Bailey can move back into the main house, but the two girls remain. Ellen finds that sometimes the view from the window is different, that her pen suddenly begins to write in another hand and with words which are not her own. She also sees people in oldfashioned dresses and, eventually, finds a duelling pistol in the chimney. While Ellen is absorbed in her mystery, the Mooneys are trying to trace their mini-bus which has been stolen, together with all their belongings.

Ellen, and Violet Mooney become friends and together gather information about the family who once lived in the cottage, while Bella and the eldest Mooney, Paul, set out after the mini-bus which Paul has spotted weaving its way through the traffic. The separate investigations bring them all together on the night of the firework display when much is solved: the mini-bus is recovered and Ellen comes close to laying the troubled ghost of the back house. As well as being a ghost story without terror, this is also a family tale, which, being set in Northern Ireland, gives a kindly view of that country, without reference to the troubles. The author holds the reader's interest whilst the clues are gathered which lead to a romantic conclusion, to make a book especially appealing to girls of eleven to thirteen years.

> *Sylvia Mogg, in a review of "The Back House Ghosts," in* Children's Book Review, *Vol. V, No. 1, Spring, 1975, pp. 22-3.*

A combination of ghost story and the everyday adventures of several young people. . . .

Ellen is a lively character, and her insatiable curiosity involves her in amusing situations. Amongst the family of thirteen there is an obnoxious small boy who is always at the centre of every disaster.

The reason for the ghost's unrest provides an intriguing mystery, and the ghostly visitations are not really frightening. Margaret communicates by automatic writing, not treated too seriously here, for when one of the girls tries to abandon her will to the ghost, she can only produce the words "Tottenham Hotspurs"! The end of the story, however, leaves the reader wondering *why* Ellen's discovery should bring peace to the ghost, for the people to whom it mattered are long since dead, and Ellen is not free to tell the story to any living person.

The story moves quickly and introduces a variety of interests and excitement. It is enlivened by a feeling of spontaneous gaiety.

> *E. Colwell, in a review of "The Back House Ghosts," in* The Junior Bookshelf, *Vol. 39, No. 2, April, 1975, p. 131.*

Dependent on plot rather than on depth of characterization or evocation of setting and mood, the story of Ellen's brush with the occult succeeds primarily as an uncomplicated suspense story—with just a soupcon of love added for good measure. Light entertainment for preadolescents. (pp. 383-84)

> *Mary M. Burns, in a review of "The Haunting of Ellen," in* The Horn Book Magazine, *Vol. LI, No. 4, August, 1975, pp. 383-84.*

The Ghost and Bertie Boggin (as Catherine Sefton, 1980)

Such a comfort to Bertie is this particular ghost. He is rather a Dickensian character who lives in the coalshed. He is somewhat particular about his appearance and very conscientious about the hours he spends haunting the Spectre's Arms. Bertie is the youngest of the Boggin family and rather put upon, so it is very satisfying to see how the Ghost can turn events Bertie's way and they have lots of merry times. As each chapter can stand on its own the book is a good one for story-telling and children will come back for more, for who wouldn't want such a ghost as one's Best Friend. Catherine Sefton uses comfortable rhythmic sentences and her dialogue is up to date and witty.

> *Eileen A. Archer, in a review of "The Ghost and Bertie Boggin," in* Book Window, *Vol. 7, No. 3, Summer, 1980, p. 14.*

Bertie is the youngest of three and finds he has no one to play with, until he discovers the ghost who has taken up residence in their coalshed. This ghost enlivens his life and they become 'best friends', even to the extent of getting measles together. Mr Boggin is sceptical to the last but Mrs Boggin gradually comes round to the idea. There are some delightful moments in this story, which is full of humour and has some sharply drawn pictures of family life, particularly in Bertie's struggles to keep up with his older brother and sister. The ghost talks of the Battle of Inkerman and Florence Nightingale, and takes his coal scuttle to the beach in order to build a bigger sandcastle.

A gem of a story for the seven to nines. . . .

> *Janet Fisher, in a review of "The Ghost and Bertie Boggin," in* The School Librarian, *Vol. 28, No. 3, September, 1980, p. 268.*

This episodic story is very British both in language and tone, but the warm and identifiable content should spill over geographic boundaries. Sefton shows keen insight into family dynamics, while the supernatural element is handled in so down-to-earth a way that readers will be well prepared when Mrs. Boggin eventually spies the apparition herself. Problematic, though, is Bertie's age. He appears to be six or seven, perhaps too young a protagonist for children with the skills to read the book.

> *Ilene Cooper, in a review of "The Ghost and Bertie Boggin," in* Booklist, *Vol. 78, No. 18, May 15, 1982, p. 1261.*

Emer's Ghost   (as Catherine Sefton, 1981)

[A] story whose effect depends on its setting—a lough-side village in Northern Ireland on the border with the Republic, where a girl of twelve or so and her siblings, living with their widowed mother, find the past vividly brought before their eyes. The catalyst is an old doll, picked up in the hedge by Emer, who is of the right age and temperament to realise that the sad little ghost who begins to show herself is looking for her old plaything and suggesting the possibility of reward. The riddle of the ghostly child is explained, finally, in a way which the reader should be able to accept because Emer's narrative, youthfully sympathetic and light-hearted, makes her own belief so clear. A treasure is found, an ancient wrong righted, and a plot often used before is refreshed by the lilting idiom and the lucid manner of the book. (pp. 3945-46)

> *Margery Fisher, in a review of "Emer's Ghost," in* Growing Point, *Vol. 20, No. 3, September, 1981, pp. 3945-46.*

Emer's Ghost is set in the author's own country—the borders of Eire and Northern Ireland, beneath the blue shadow of the Mountains of Mourne—and the story focusses on a small village community with its legend of a lost chalice, hidden from Cromwell's marauders and never recovered. To Emer, living in the present-day village with her mother and sisters, comes the ghost of the long dead girl and the realization that she, Emer, and she alone, can lay bare the mystery of the chalice. Her final ordeal, in which her own life and that of her closest sister are at risk, is a true test of her courage and selflessness; it is also a piece of writing which for sheer economy of style and intensity of drama would be hard to equal. There is about the whole of this beautifully wrought story a timeless quality, reminiscent of *The Stone Book Quartet*, Catherine Sefton shares with Alan Garner a gift for rooting a plot so deeply in its setting that even the supernatural is a totally acceptable extension of reality, rather than some clever, superimposed trick. Add to this an uncanny insight into the workings of a child's mind, an acute ear for dialogue and an eye

for the odd idiosyncrasy which stamps a character indelibly on the reader's mind, and you have a writer of a rare order. This latest book may not make box office history but it should be remembered for its sheer quality.

> *Ann Evans, "Extensions of Reality," in* The Times Literary Supplement, *No. 4103, November 20, 1981, p. 1359.*

For all its meatiness . . . , this is a very funny book. The characters are well-observed. The dialogue of the Irish villagers is reproduced in all its charming inconsequentiality and cunning, and the convent school scenes are beautifully true to life as the girls prepare for a historical pageant for the Bishop's visit, and Emer, with her mind on other things, falls foul of Sister Consuelo's caustic tongue, while Breige determines to become a nun in South America. Skilfully the pageant provides by degrees the historical clues which link the present with the past, the lost St. Aidan's chalice hidden from the Cromwellians, the monks' settlement, and the strange construction mapped by the ghost on the window and by the fortune-teller. It is a lively and realistic narrative, with food for thought.

> *M. Hobbs, in a review of "Emer's Ghost," in* The Junior Bookshelf, *Vol. 46, No. 1, February, 1982, p. 32.*

Napper Goes for Goal   (1981)

Between quality fiction for children and the commercially produced formula material lies the useful range of ordinary reading. Its ordinariness often belies its usefulness—much of it is accessible to many children of average reading ability, and much too is sensibly directed at the eight-to-eleven age group where reading is at its most avid. **Napper Goes for Goal** is a football story for this very group: it is full of excitement as a primary school sets up a team, the Red Row Stars, and proves its mettle in a hard-fought victory over a rival school. Simple language, wholly authentic as a vehicle to establish character and entirely accessible to the reading age of the book, adds to a thorough insider's knowledge of football and some well-designed illustrations [by Barrie Mitchell] to make this book a sure success, especially for private reading. It will lure readers on from comics and lead them to other football writers like Glanville and Hardcastle. (pp. 21-2)

> *C. Stuart Hannabuss, in a review of "Napper Goes for Goal," in* British Book News, *Children's Supplement, Autumn, 1981, pp. 21-2.*

In rivalry with the 'Stringypants' team from the local big school, Napper and his friend Terence are prime movers in the formation of a team at the Red Row Primary School. In a five-a-side match with their rivals Napper disputes a saved goal till the argument is stopped by a spectator of a rather surprising kind. It is not easy to describe games to the uninitiated; with humour, sharp character touches and a firm, direct prose, Martin Waddell has brought the teams, their Irish neighbourhood and the matches themselves vigorously to life.

> *Margery Fisher, in a review of "Napper Goes*

for Goal," in Growing Point, *Vol. 26, No. 5, January, 1988, p. 4928.*

This is one of a series called 'Blackie Sports Fiction'; as such it is a formula novel with a purposely narrow focus. The subject is boys' football and the characters, centring on 'Napper' McGann who is telling the story, never step outside the small, impersonal world of the sport. Characterisation is two-dimensional and action is predictable—it is the equivalent of a boys' comic. Once these limitations are accepted, however, it can be regarded as a competent piece of work. A group of boys at Red Row Primary School form a football team. At first they are unskilled, disorganised and quarrelsome; and they lose matches; but doggedly they prepare for the big match against a neighbouring school. The final two chapters of the book describe this match in detail, illustrated by sketches and diagrams, and this is a sustained piece of descriptive prose which football enthusiasts will find exciting and convincing. Martin Waddell has written far better than this in his guise as Catherine Sefton, but it would be wrong to regret that the book is no more than it set out to be. Fine for the football enthusiast, then, but beyond that it has little appeal.

> *Richard Brown, in a review of "Napper Goes for Goal," in* The School Librarian, *Vol. 36, No. 1, February, 1988, p. 22.*

The Great Green Mouse Disaster (1981)

The mice in the **Great Green Mouse Disaster** . . . are a troupe let loose in a hotel and, in the course of 11 double spreads [by illustrator Philippe Dupasquier], the consequences are pictured. There are no words: you have to work out the sequences of events for yourself, minutely examining cutaway views of all seven hotel floors where everything from burglary to wallpapering is going on. It's a clever idea, and the execution is a triumph of detailing and continuity. But the effort required to keep dozens of incidents in mind at a time is considerable: best given, perhaps, to precocious Rubik's-cubists.

> *William Feaver, in a review of "Great Green Mouse Disaster," in* The Observer, *December 6, 1981, p. 28.*

[A] magnificent wordless saga. . . . Eleven double spread expanses of detailed illustration depict the progressive disintegration of a hotel invaded by the Mouseman's performing hordes. The cross-sectional design exposes the effects of the catastrophe unfolding in different rooms; you can focus on one room at a time and trace the mounting mayhem within it from page to page, or you can feast your eyes on the sprawling intricacies of the whole panorama.

Children in both reception and upper junior classes found this book a treat, and I have had occasional difficulties in wresting my copy from the various adults who have picked it up for a browse. Highly recommended for everybody.

> *George Hunt, in a review of "The Great Green Mouse Disaster," in* Books for Keeps, *No. 58, September, 1989, p. 9.*

Waddell (left) with Terence Pym and a friend, Hubert Bailey, in 1949. An actor who lived near Waddell, Pym read to him and told him stories; Waddell writes, "He was part of the stories, he was the characters, and I am sure that some of my love of story comes from those long days living stories in the woods . . . "

The Finn Gang (as Catherine Sefton, 1981)

Dodger Finn and his domineering sister Mary constitute the Finn gang. Crisis confronts them when the bogie shed containing the gang's equipment disappears and the gate leading to their terrain, the quarry, is padlocked.

As Chief Special Investigator of the gang Mary determines to discover what is happening. Unfortunately the down and out living near the quarry proves too alarming to interrogate, and a bird watching teacher warns the Finn gang to keep away from the area. Suddenly it becomes apparent that an actual crime has been committed. Somewhat improbably, the activities of Dodger and Mary culminate in a dramatic rescue, recovery of the loot, and capture of the criminals.

The Finns have distinctive, credible personalities, and this story moves briskly. However, the Antelope series is offered to readers just capable of reading complete books on their own, and for such a market Catherine Sefton's plot seems involved and confusing.

R. Baines, in a review of "The Finn Gang," in The Junior Bookshelf, Vol. 46, No. 4, August, 1982, p. 146.

Napper Strikes Again (1981)

Sporting stories have a long and honourable pedigree, serving as they do the double purpose of enhancing the imaginary world of the reader and enabling writers to get their athletic rocks off without risk of injury.

Behind the Edwardian title of Martin Waddell's book there is a thoroughly up-to-date football tale about Red Row School Team. Miss Fellows, in charge of football has, it seems, failed to enter her team in the primary schools' friendly circuit and in any case likes a bit more competition, so she has put them in for the local youth league instead. What the head-teacher thinks of this is not in the story, but the ensuing events will not have made him feel any more comfortable. Through the lively and often funny narration of one of the team members, we hear of Red Row's progress through the competition.

Gerald Haigh, in a review of "Napper Strikes Again," in The Times Educational Supplement, No. 3766, September 2, 1988, p. 25.

The Emma Dilemma (as Catherine Sefton, 1982)

Writers for the young can only hope that they will rouse certain associations through their stories. For example, children of ten or so reading **The Emma Dilemma** may have met dopplegangers in folk tales; some might also think of the mysterious changes that come upon Alice, as they follow the perplexities of a child of nine who, in a long dream-hallucination after a fall, believes she has become two identical selves, one sensible and the other anarchic. Since only one Emma can be seen at a time (except by the cat Dracula), there is no way in which the unfortunate girl can explain who wrecked the classroom, brought wet seaweed into her bedroom and disturbed her dentist father in his surgery. With a satisfying logic, Emma returns to her normal state after being hit by a stone while she is getting her brother's watch back from a bully, thus escaping retribution because of her courage. The situation is worked out in a spirit of comedy sharpened by touches of personality in Emma, her friends and her family, and the story moves along the edge of reality with enough prosaic details of dirty clothes, school discipline, meals and so on to prevent the fantasy from taking off completely into a realm of psychological terror.

Margery Fisher, in a review "The Emma Dilemma," in Growing Point, Vol. 21, No. 1, May, 1982, p. 3895.

[This] is both a fantasy and an entertaining family story in which Emma is catapulted in and out of an odd situation by a blow on her head. What emerges in between is another, identical Emma—only this one, who claims she's the real Emma, is transparent. Nobody else can see her,

although the family cat is aware that there's an Emma who smells right but is invisible. The two Emmas squabble much of the time, but the Other Emma proves to be very useful: she plays pranks on the real Emma's least favorite people—and some of the time that includes her siblings. Nobody can quite understand what's going on (except the real Emma) and it is all very amusing (if one-track) and filled with well-paced action. A nice blend of fantasy and realism, in a story written with vitality.

Zena Sutherland, in a review of "The Emma Dilemma," in Bulletin of the Center for Children's Books, Vol. 37, No. 2, October, 1983, p. 37.

Harriet and the Crocodiles (1982)

This light-hearted romp of a book will spend little time on the library shelf because the Dandy and Beano style of farcical humour will appeal to young readers. Harriet, the scourge of Slow Street Primary, belongs to the Pansy Potter family of terrifying females. Good at heart she may be, but she sends one teacher shrieking to lock herself in the toilet and swallow the key, and the results of her zoo visit make the headmistress hit the medicinal brandy bottle and really show the Slow Street spirit. Harriet steals a baby crocodile from the zoo and brings it back to school, and all the other crocodiles in the zoo follow through the town drains. It is broad comedy of the simplest kind, and it made me laugh. There is one jarring note: 'Harriet was an adopted child, which is why she was so big and the Smiths were so small. Nobody knew who her real parents were.' This I find insensitive and offensive, but I enjoyed the rest. (pp. 40-1)

Peter Kennerley, in a review of "Harriet and the Crocodiles," in The School Librarian, Vol. 31, No. 1, March, 1983, pp. 40-1.

Harriet is the school terror, in fact the town terror: the bus company displays a "Warning Notice with Big Red Letters" along with Harriet's picture. She adopts a crocodile as her new bodyguard (his predecessor was a snail) and pandemonium ensues as the crocodile (and later, lots of crocodiles) eats everything, and scares everybody. The story has relentless humor, both broad and arch, but the uniformly hysterical pitch rapidly becomes monotonous.

Zena Sutherland, in a review of "Harriet and the Crocodiles," in Bulletin of the Center for Children's Books, Vol. 37, No. 10, June, 1984, p. 195.

This outrageously funny tale is of British origin, and its humor is therefore of the dryly understated, not thigh-slapping, variety. The wild irreverence is akin to that of Davies' Marmalade and Rufus; here, teachers and other grown-ups are made to look ridiculous while Harriet matter-of-factly goes about the business of locating her wayward crocodile. A rollicking eight-chapter read-aloud—not for the fainthearted—and a bang-up addition to the humor shelves, complete with enticing cover paintings that will propel **Harriet** into instant circulation. (pp. 1630-31)

Karen Stang Hanley, in a review of "Harriet and the Crocodiles," in Booklist, *Vol. 80, No. 22, August, 1984, pp. 1630-31.*

Island of the Strangers   (as Catherine Sefton, 1983)

Prejudice and violence are fashionable topics, but by their very nature are hard to bring home to the young reader. The prejudiced, by definition, do not realise their own blindness, and violence is always apparently someone else's fault. To show the stupidity of the 'They started it' mentality takes great skill in a writer.

This book is set in a remote village on the coast of Northern Ireland. A coachload of tough Belfast kids—the Gobbers—invade it, and a war ensues. Among the local children, only Nora is reluctant to participate. Already socially isolated because her mother is dead and her father away, she becomes morally isolated from her Gobber-baiting friends, and then physically isolated on the 'enemy' island. Nora is a convincing heroine: self-doubting, misunderstood, unheroic, crying with fear in the violent, dramatic climax. Loyalty, responsibility, hatred and acceptance are all explored in this Ulster in miniature. It is done in powerful prose too: simple, spare, and sinewy. And if readers need any more inducement, there is also a slight supernatural element which might sell it to those who care for such things. (pp. 272, 275)

Pauline Thomas, in a review of "Island of the Strangers," in The School Librarian, *Vol. 31, No. 3, September, 1983, pp. 272-75.*

Although other characters are not particularly well developed, Nora comes across as a strong individual: rejecting the parochial attitudes of friends and neighbours, she demonstrates the need to be true to oneself. At one level this is a book about gang warfare; on another, about intolerance and, perhaps, the whole Northern Ireland conflict. The powerful themes are accentuated by the brisk, unemotional style of an author whose versatility has been evident over a number of years.

A review of "Island of the Strangers," in The Signal Review of Children's Books, 2, *1983, p. 38.*

Sefton's taut story gets under the skins of its characters, and, despite the isolated setting, there is a gripping universality about these young people's feelings and emotions. To add to the story's appeal, Sefton includes a dash of mystery revolving around the haunted island. A strong, sure-handed effort.

Ilene Cooper, in a review of "Island of the Strangers," in Booklist, *Vol. 82, No. 9, January 1, 1986, p. 687.*

The story centers around Nora, a girl whose father is away and is cared for by Stella, a distant relative who doesn't take the place of Nora's mother. These two have a personal battle that reflects the gang war outside. The scene in which their relationship is finally resolved into a warm understanding is very real. The element of mystery in the story is in full force in the wild and frightening climax. If

the Briticisms are glossed over, this is a short, accessible suspense novel that could be used as a springboard to a serious discussion on the nature of conflict and its resolutions.

J. Alison Illsley, in a review of "Island of the Strangers," in School Library Journal, *Vol. 32, No. 5, January, 1986, p. 70.*

Going West   (1983)

This is Kate's story of her family in Mr Crowe's wagon train, "going West to look for better land". It is a story of high adventure—a swollen river, a buffalo stampede, an Indian attack; yet the least romantic and most conscientious wagon train story imaginable. Martin Waddell has deliberately made Kate the representative witness of a whole social history. What she experiences is danger, loss and death, but also new gains and achievements, signified by relics and gifts passed on by people who are themselves passing on. She sets everything down carefully. "Louisa and Mrs Sullivan drank bad water. They got sick. I didn't get sick." The language is elementary, appropriate to a little girl's diary (and to an early reading book); but also elemental, bare, summoning the reader's own emotional responses.

Going West is a picture book and Philippe Dupasquier's illustrations hold up the same balance. Panoramas of generalized but authentic beauty demonstrate the perilous nature of the trek by the sheer scale of landscape; while close scenes show people working together, pulling a wagon out of mud or praying around the campfire. . . . A tiny figure on top of a bluff is the Indian scout whose people will ambush and destroy most of the train seven pages later. ("Big Chokey says we stole the Indians' land. They don't like us. That is why they killed Mr Crowe.") While Big Chokey shows Kate the things he keeps in his hollow wooden leg, there is Louisa in the background pointing out the fatal waterhole to Mrs Sullivan. Nearby skulls mutely signal the disaster to come.

Of some twenty wagonloads only Kate's family gets through to the fertile valley, with Mrs Sullivan and the redoubtable Big Chokey. "Big Chokey gave me his leg. He made himself a new one. Then he went on." This is a book to be read with an enquiring child, who will want a good deal of commentary: on the American frontier, wilderness survival, Indian burial customs, deserts and blizzards, and the facts of death.

Colin Greenland, "Rites of Passage," in The Times Literary Supplement, *No. 4219, February 10, 1984, p. 150.*

Children's books about the frontier era typically skip over certain grisly truths. After describing the long drive up the Chisholm Trail, for instance, most books will not spell out what becomes of the dogies when, having survived rattlesnakes and rustlers, they are shipped east "to market."

Going West is of a very different spirit. . . .

The illustrations, by the French artist Philippe Dupasquier, are the book's great strength. They manage to seem cartoonishly lighthearted in the face of grim happenings, while simultaneously being realistic. Mr. Dupasquier's human figures recall those of the Tintin series, and his vistas of the Great Plains and Rockies resemble the works of Alfred Jacob Miller, the young artist whose paintings from the 1830's constitute the main historical record of what the frontier looked like. The illustrations also contain the small clues that children love to discover: On close inspection, the fatal waterhole proves to be surrounded by the bones of animals that drank there and died.

The harsh naturalism of the text, however, seems more suited to an adult sensibility than to most children's. It is very brief—a sentence or two per page—and contains no direct explanation about the frontier of the pioneers. Its main literary payoff is the contrast between Kate's deadpan narrative and the wrenching events. The last words in the book, accompanying a picture of a cabin standing in utter wilderness, are, "Pa says we will by happy here." There is also an undertone of Kate's growing fear: Whenever someone points out that her dying sister can't be saved because she is so little, Kate notes, "I am smaller than Louisa."

Nearly every line in the book rings with the apprehensive stoicism that adults recognize in children. I am not sure that children, as readers, recognize or value it so highly. *Going West* may be an accurate portrayal of frontier life, but my 7-year-old craved more information about what the pioneers did, apart from dying on the trail.

> *James Fallows, in a review of "Going West,"* in The New York Times Book Review, *March 25, 1984, p. 31.*

At first glance this extraordinary book appears to be a mix of rather overdrawn cartoon pictures of an American family's adventures 'going west' in their covered wagon and a text with a limited vocabulary: 'We crossed the river. There was a lot of water.' But look at Dupasquier's pictures of wagons fording a torrential river, horses rearing, a boy washed away (and then saved), and you realize with a shock that dramatic illustration and deadpan prose are carefully counterpointed to produce a deep emotional involvement in a story that is unique in this medium. For in the story little Louisa becomes very ill. 'There was a blizzard. The snow stopped. Louisa died . . . Louisa was bigger than me.' A book that helps us to see history and human life from the emotional perspective of a young child. (pp. 44-5)

> *Elaine Moss, in a review of "Going West,"* in Picture Books for Young People, *revised edition, The Thimble Press, 1985, pp. 44-5.*

My Gang (as Catherine Sefton, 1984)

What defence does a small boy have against his older sister and her gang of girls if they intend to keep him in his place and are on the lookout for any excuse to beat him up? Noel's crafty plan to set his tormentors against each other works perhaps a little too well to be credible. He gets rid of them one by one with the facility of a fairy tale, but the reader is too much on his side to quibble greatly and the

unexpected way in which he turns the tables in the last chapter demands applause.

> *Rodie Sudbery, in a review of "My Gang,"* in The School Librarian, *Vol. 32, No. 2, June, 1984, p. 138.*

A funny and imaginative story from a writer who is always interesting. Noel wants to get into his big sister's gang. He tries to take it over; the girls put up a spirited fight. It gave rise to a great deal of talk, with a class of first-year juniors, as to what boys and girls could and couldn't do. It got them, and me, thinking.

The girls here are rounded and sparky characters. The dialogue is crisp: "Couldn't we play Little Houses instead?" suggested Lisa. "We could make Noel his tea." "No we can't," said Rosamund. "We'll be space ladies who have conquered the Universe, and he can make us our tea."

> *Colin Mills, in a review of "My Gang,"* in Books for Keeps, *No. 45, July, 1987, p. 15.*

Small matters vividly described with the central point of gender-rivalry. . . . Playground, library and garden provide the setting for skirmishes, physical and psychological, which have a definite reality because of a brisk prose style and a sharp definition of personalities in the age-old battle for supremacy.

> *Margery Fisher, in a review of "My Gang,"* in Growing Point, *Vol. 26, No. 3, September, 1987, p. 4864.*

Harriet and the Haunted School (1984)

Harriet is a very determined little girl. Unfortunately, more often than not, when she determines to do something she leaves a trail of disaster. Finding a horse for her friend Anthea presents no great difficulty for Harriet, but where does one keep a horse? She discards various possibilities such as their fathers' garages, Anthea's parents' greenhouse, and so on. Then Harriet finds the perfect solution—the games cupboard at school. Being one of Harriet's projects, this can only lead to complications, not least the rumour that the old phantom of Slow Street walks again. Substance is added to this when hoofbeats are heard pounding up and down the school corridors at night. A rollicking story with plenty of incidents to hold attention until the end of the book, making it ideal for children launching out into the enjoyment of reading a book right through for themselves. (pp. 242, 245)

> *Lucinda Fox, in a review of "Harriet and the Haunted School,"* in The School Librarian, *Vol. 32, No. 3, September, 1984, pp. 242, 245.*

Martin Waddell has captured all the appealing ingredients for a book that should have readers from eight to eighty laughing and smiling from beginning to end, for I suspect that he had more than youngsters in mind when writing.

Featuring once again the redoubtable Harriet, ably supported by an array of acutely observed quirky characters, she temporarily obtains a horse on behalf of her friend Anthea and accommodates it in a cupboard within the school.

Perceptively, the author has blended a range of features such as schools, gangs, ghosts and horses, as well as the inevitable teachers who as characters in fiction never cease to intrigue children and has created a lively and very humorous story. This is aided by page after page of free-flowing dialogue that allows the thespian plenty of scope to perform when reading aloud or to themselves.

> *Ron Morton, in a review of "Harriet and the Haunted School," in* Books for Your Children, *Vol. 19, No. 3, Autumn-Winter, 1984, p. 128.*

This refreshing adventure of bungling elementary school staff and students will entertain readers and become a popular addition to library collections. Most of the teachers, as well as the Anti-Harriet League (a group of kids who bond together against her because individually they feel they have no chance), choose to ignore or avoid Harriet, a girl who uses unconventional methods to attain her goals. In this second book about her, Harriet decides to "borrow" a horse and store it in the school broom closet so that her friend, Anthea, can practice "falling off." But the school cleaning lady, after a drop or two of tonic wine, assumes that the Slow Street Phantom has returned and sends the school into panic. [Mark] Burgess' illustrations, many full page, capture the impish nature of the story, and the large print and open format add to the appeal. Although Harriet's goals are somewhat predictable, her methods will intrigue and motivate children to read on.

> *Ellen S. Wilcox, in a review of "Harriet and the Haunted School," in* School Library Journal, *Vol. 32, No. 1, September, 1985, p. 140.*

Big Bad Bertie   (1984)

Martin Waddell's work has always shown his understanding of just what makes young children tick. Whether the emotional response is to laugh or cry he can evoke it with consummate ease.

The story follows the life of Big Bad Bertie from birth to death. Beginning as a card playing, beer drinking baby (don't be too alarmed, but he does actually get worse!). Bertie grows up to forsake his way of life when at the pinnacle of his achievements his poor mum dies. Sad? Well don't worry because despite his own demise (flattened by a steamroller) Bertie meets up with her in heaven and enjoys eternal happiness.

Children in the 6-8 age range loved the story, were fascinated by each page of brightly coloured illustrations [by Glenys Ambrus] filled with humorous characters in a variety of activities. This delightful picture-story book is guaranteed not to be left on any shelf.

> *Ron Morton, in a review of "Big Bad Bertie," in* Books for Your Children, *Vol. 20, No. 1, Spring, 1985, p. 15.*

Napper's Golden Goals   (1984)

All young football fans will definitely enjoy this lively sports fiction story told in the first person by Napper McCann, demon goalscorer and skipper of Red Row Stars First Team Squad. All the tense action and excitement on the field is conveyed very much in the nature of a running commentary. Fans / readers will be transported on the instant; they will be *there* where it's all happening, detail by detail. [Barrie Mitchell's copious] black and white drawings, diagrams and stratagems produce this immediacy of spectator effect. The six Bulletins of the Primary Schools League report on each round and its strategies and players. Results of each team are also tabulated in the League Table, giving a print media effect and underscoring the 'reality' of everything taking place. The pace, action, touches of humour, and no 'unnecessary' intrusions of irrelevant details keeps the focus squarely on the game—it is everything, with Napper, its super star. The very book for sports-minded children who may be reluctant readers.

> *Cynthia Anthony, in a review of "Napper's Golden Goals," in* Magpies, *Vol. 5, No. 1, March, 1990, p. 29.*

The Ghost Girl   (as Catherine Sefton, 1985)

The twentieth-century figure who tells the story of the ghost girl goes in for a confiding, breezy narrative: "My name is Clare Campbell and I'm the one who saw the ghost"; "Other people don't go red. I must be the reddingestgoing person in the whole world", and so on. In this manner, Clare explores both her ambiguous position and the history of the ghost with whom she finds it hard not to identify. She herself is an uncommitted creature, caught between well-defined camps to none of which she fully belongs.

At the edge of adolescence, she is old enough to resent the tiresome company of her small brother, but young enough to be impatient with the consuming mysteries her elder sister makes of her boyfriends. Her home is in Northern

Waddell playing soccer, 1961.

Ireland. But the book is set in Donegal, where the three children are on holiday after their parents' shop is burnt out by bombers. They go through the book therefore in the classic fictional state of being free of parents. "I'm Irish, *and* a Brit", thinks Clare. "I. R. A. PROVO RULE", say the local graffiti: "DEATH TO INFORMERS".

The informers who obsess Clare are 200 years old. In 1744, on the eve of the Jacobite Rebellion, the guest house where Clare is staying was the English soldiers' garrison at the time when a Catholic priest was hanged as a spy and a local islander acquired the tag "Soraghan the Betrayer". With the relics of a violent history all around, she becomes educated in the ancestral divisions and hasty judgments being handed on: a past tale of bitterness weighs on the present, evident in inherited names, traditions and opinions. Clare's present-day equivalent of the hanged priest is a sympathetic elderly Canon. A historian himself, he helps her with a mixture of information and scepticism (the find-me-one-shred-of-evidence style of challenge) to piece together the story of her ghost girl. Detective work on the past forms the action of the book.

Although Clare puts up a token resistance to supernatural manifestations ("Obviously I was having a nervous breakdown"), she is in tune with the idea of another girl caught in the middle of troubled times, and colludes in the elision of the 200-year time gap:

> I closed my eyes, and I could feel the room about me. I'd touched it in some way, and its past was oozing out of the crooked walls, right through the rose and petal wallpaper and the religious pictures and the plastic flowerpots on the mantelpiece.

Catherine Sefton has set up an illuminating device for writing about contemporary Northern Ireland. The book is both serious and gentle. Indeed, almost too gentle. Strangely, Clare's world, notwithstanding references to the Troubles, contains no real sense of menace. Though she has experienced the one and only imagined the other, the IRA bombs in the north seem less immediate than the era of the hanged priest. The theoretical personal solution that the Canon offers Clare across the division of their respective denominations is that she must stay in Ireland "because someone's got to see both sides" and profit from an understanding of the past. But the sympathies of both Clare and the author seem more attuned to the past than to the present, and Catherine Sefton finds herself unable to give due weight to one period or the other. The contemporary details which ought to lend conviction to the modern story are often slightly uncomfortable—especially when they approach adolescentiana ("If she was padding her bra I would have a good laugh at her!"). And in the context of a children's book, simply told, the explication that has to be gone through in conversation between Clare and the Canon is a little too dogged to be properly exciting.

> *Joanna Motion, "Ancient Informers," in* The Times Literary Supplement, *No. 4280, April 12, 1985, p. 418.*

The romantic tragedy which Clare is able to unravel with the help of the ghost girl is not easy to follow, but it does in a small way put events in Ireland into historical perspective.

The main characters in this book are not very credible. Clare discovers too much too easily. The book is too short. It skips over too much to be convincing. The story is one for older girls and yet the format of the book will encourage younger girls to choose it. (pp. 359-60)

> *Sheila Allan, in a review of "The Ghost Girl," in* The School Librarian, *Vol. 33, No. 4, December, 1985, pp. 359-60.*

Some years ago Irish writer Martin Waddell (alias Catherine Sefton) was injured by an I. R. A. bomb. That experience is echoed and explored in his new book ***The Ghost Girl.*** After her home has been bombed by the I. R. A. Clare is sent with her brother and sister to a remote part of Ireland. A sensitive pre-adolescent she soon finds that the ghost which haunts the house she lodges in tries desperately to communicate with her. From that moment on she becomes gradually involved with a brutal and bitter part of Irish history. A brave book which tries, quite successfully, to give young readers some insight into the historical background behind the current Irish 'troubles'.

> *George English, in a review of "The Ghost Girl," in* Books for Your Children, *Vol. 20, No. 3, Autumn-Winter, 1985, p. 21.*

The Blue Misty Monsters **(as Catherine Sefton, 1985)**

Ma, Pa, Odle and Mo descend to Earth from their distant planet to satisfy their curiosity; having acquired solid shapes as a disguise, they seem unable to do anything about their blue faces, but young Spud cheerfully takes them for granted when the two youngsters descend on his garden by mistake, and he is glad to make use of their oddity to scare the Petter-Bullies in his street when they set off his Guy Fawkes fireworks prematurely. An element of mild satire is achieved when the 'Monsters' comment critically on the 'Two-Leggers' and their incomprehensible behaviour: from the point of view of Earth-dwellers the antics of the visitors are equally surprising. The two angles of vision are expertly alternated in a brisk, entertaining comedy of an alien visit.

> *Margery Fisher, in a review of "The Blue Misty Monsters," in* Growing Point, *Vol. 24, No. 4, November, 1985, p. 4539.*

A fast-paced, science-fiction comedy that fizzles with life and fun. The Misty family (large, cloud-like creatures) come to earth for a holiday. Their daughter Mo is inadvertently separated from them. She meets Spud, a bespectacled boy who spends most of his time alternately guarding his hoard of fireworks and devising stratagems to avoid the dreaded Peppers gang. Spud first disbelieves in Mo's existence, then thinks her a ghost, but finally feeds her and quarrels with her. Her family meanwhile, dressed up to look like guys for Guy Fawkes Night, roam the streets searching for food and for Mo, and become the butt of much public amusement. The story moves to a splendidly anarchic finale in which the Peppers get their comeuppance and the Mistys save the day. The position of aliens in an alien society could give rise to some interesting discussion, but this is not Catherine Sefton's purpose: she is out to entertain.

> *Richard Brown, in a review of "The Blue Misty Monsters," in* The School Librarian, *Vol. 33, No. 4, December, 1985, p. 339.*

A friendly book this, and one which cleverly offers younger readers a different perspective on life. . . . Throughout the reader is given the monster's viewpoint; humans are seen as 'unclever', ungainly, uncouth individuals. However, they are generously tolerated by the Misty Monsters which saves us from becoming totally alienated from ourselves as we read. . . .

Another excellent read for Middle Juniors from a writer whose style and good humour are, in my experience, much enjoyed by this age group.

> *Nigel Spencer, in a review of "Blue Misty Monsters," in* Books for Keeps, *No. 41, November, 1986, p. 15.*

Harriet and the Robot   (1985)

Harriet is a comic-strip character in words. She first appears stuck in a dustbin, terrifying her friend Anthea who sees only a Bin-Thing shrieking 'Wouch!' and 'Get we wout!' Harriet is looking for a body for her robot, which she succeeds in making at the expense of her home. Her parents remark, 'We'll be able to replace the whole house!' and take refuge in the garden. Next morning the robot is ready. Harriet treats it with scientific detachment, controlling it with whistles, but Anthea calls it Big Dolly. The basketball teacher's whistle confuses Big Dolly and her computer brain gets stuck on Copy Mode. Into the net goes the gym teacher and into the rosebush goes the headmistress. Mayhem ceases only when Anthea approaches Big Dolly and calms her with kindness. This is a cheerful romp of a book, short and lively. . . . It would suit six- to nine-year-olds who are on to proper books, but might be daunted by anything too long and heavy.

> *Jocelyn Hanson, in a review of "Harriet and the Robot," in* The School Librarian, *Vol. 34, No. 2, June, 1986, p. 156.*

Another hilarious episode in the extraordinary life of the antiheroine of *Harriet and the Crocodiles* and *Harriet and the Haunted School*. . . .

This is slapstick made funnier by a satirical perspective on the Slow Street School, which has matter-of-factly mobilized as best it can to defend itself against the frequent depredations of Harriet, whose innocent inventions invariably lead to explosions and other mayhem. Interestingly, Waddell is a native of Belfast; these misadventures can be seen as the comic side of a tragic conflict—what better balm than laughter?

> *A review of "Harriet and the Robot," in* Kirkus Reviews, *Vol. LV, No. 8, May 1, 1987, p. 727.*

Starry Night   (as Catherine Sefton, 1986)

Fifteen-year-old Kathleen lives in Kiltarragh just inside the Province. Across the road lies the Republic and down the road run the Brits in their armoured cars. It is a small place, a farming community, with Belfast and Dublin a world away, and it lies, also, on the borders of past and present.

And Kathleen lives on the borders between childhood and womanhood, between innocence and a painful awareness of outside realities and of hidden complexities amid the certainties and beliefs she has held about life, about people in Kiltarragh and the world beyond.

Kathleen, in the holidays, is busy about the farm, run by Mammie, who runs everything and everyone. She is exasperated when left to mind Imelda, daughter of Carmel, married to much loved Frank. Mammie does not admire Carmel who is modern, pushing and opportunistic—and has disturbed the Family. So Kathleen is not that keen on Carmel, either.

It is part of the strength of this short, but full-to-bursting novel that Catherine Sefton (Martin Waddell) allows us to see Kathleen, over the course of a few days, slowly change her ideas about people (the Family's ideas in fact), as she probes the secret the Family is hiding from her.

Is it about the future of the farm? Is one of the boys involved with the IRA? Kathleen forms her theories, tests them, discards them, while she argues with a more sophisticated school friend from Belfast about sex, politics, about Ireland (There's a neat passage in which her friend goes into raptures over a visit to Tara, seat of kings, while Kathleen, her head full of old tales and legends takes Tara for granted).

As the pace of the story quickens and finally bursts into the violence of a family dispute, Kathleen learns the truth about the much loved, but feckless "sister" Rose (the "Kiltarragh bicycle"), and also about herself (a truth everyone but she has known all along). It is Carmel who brings it home to her, throwing light on Mammie, Frank, Mike, all those people she knows so well, and so little.

Over-ambitiously the author has attempted to mirror in Kathleen's young view of the world, a wider romantic Republican outlook, and the parallels do not always meet. (The brutal realities of Protestant politics recently made all too clear find almost no reflection in the novel's background). To portray a young person at a turning point in their lives and see them as a microcosm of larger, changing social and political realities, needs I think a larger canvas than this small book. But it succeeds memorably in showing through such a young life a whole rural way of life now slipping into the past.

> *Robert Leeson, "Irish Anguish," in* The Times Educational Supplement, *No. 3649, June 6, 1986, p. 55.*

Fifteen-year-old Kathleen lives near to the border between Northern Ireland and the Republic, as confused in her thinking and loyalties as many children must be by the political situation. (pp. 158-59)

Kathleen remains centre stage in a shifting scenario of family and friends, a fusion of personalities who show both understanding and harshness, sympathy and physical violence. The dreams of starry nights are elbowed out by Kathleen's growing awareness of differing attitudes towards the grim struggle just over the border. It is a story that has its share of humour but its thrust is a sensitive exploration of a young girl coming to terms with truth and adult values on several levels. (p. 159)

> *G. Bott, in a review of "Starry Night," in* The Junior Bookshelf, *Vol. 50, No. 4, August, 1986, pp. 158-59.*

Fifteen-year-old Kathleen Fay, the central character in Catherine Sefton's new novel, is given to dreaming. She dreams of marriage, of a new bungalow to replace the ramshackle family farmhouse and of the day when a united country will see the end of the British soldiers who patrol her native Kiltarragh, precariously placed on the northern side of the border separating Northern Ireland from the Republic. When, however, it becomes clear that her family and acquaintances are party to secrets which, apparently, she is not to share, she is forced to re-examine these aspirations. So *Starry night,* like much teenage fiction, is primarily about growth, about identity, about the need to relate dreams to reality; and, like much well-intentioned 'Ulster' teenage fiction, it is about the need to abandon prejudices to allow for the experiences and perceptions of others. In terms of theme, therefore, it has few claims to originality, though its heroine's optimistic sense of humour and its author's ear for the colourful idiosyncrasies of Ulster speech give it some measure of individuality, contrasting with its general blandness and predictability. Readers who enjoyed earlier Sefton titles such as *Emer's ghost, Island of the strangers,* and *The ghost girl* will, I regret to say, be slightly disappointed here.

> *Robert Dunbar, in a review of "Starry Night," in* The School Librarian, *Vol. 34, No. 3, September, 1986, p. 274.*

Owl and Billy (1986)

Owl and Billy tells of a boy voicing his fears and trepidations at the approach of his first day at school, through his best friend, a homemade toy owl. When there is a new arrival at the houses for old folk, Billy mistakes an elderly motor cyclist for a spaceman. The obliging gentleman plays along with him and Billy makes a real friend. This amusing tale shows a good understanding of the fears and fantasies of a four-year-old, but not of the attention span of that age-group, who would find it overlong.

> *Maisie Roberts, in a review of "Owl and Billy," in* British Book News Children's Books, *September, 1986, p. 35.*

Billy is a week too young to start school on the first day of term and the wait is a boring prospect until the arrival of the 'Spaceman' to live in his street. The book contains seven episodes leading up to Billy's first day at school, told

in a simple straightforward way most appropriate for reading aloud to those of around Billy's age (four to five) rather than for older solo readers who may well find Billy's adventures and the manner of telling, too young to hold their interest.

> *Jill Bennett, in a review of "Owl and Billy," in* Books for Keeps, *No. 53, November, 1988, p. 7.*

Little Dracula's Christmas; Little Dracula's First Bite (1986)

[*Little Dracula's Christmas*] is basically *Mad* magazine without its wit or art. Baby Millicent has blood in her baby bottle, and Igor happily finds a chopped off human leg in his Christmas stocking. The book never gets any better. The cartoon illustrations [by Joseph Wright] are cluttered and crass. There is a pre-pubescent age that may find this mildly humorous, but that doesn't make the book good. To try to sell this as a Christmas story is a new low in the commercialization of the season.

> *A review of "Little Dracula's Christmas," in* School Library Journal, *Vol. 33, No. 2, October, 1986, p. 113.*

Two pieces of enjoyable nonsense which will attract many a new young reader and many an older reader with a taste for the comic fantastic. A whole Dracula family is here born out of the conventions of horror movies (and the Addams family?) with Little Dracula centre stage.

In *First Bite* Little D. wants to 'fright 'em and bite 'em' just like Dad. He fails miserably and loses two milk teeth in the process. Only at the dentist's does he manage to succeed (or suck blood, rather . . .).

The Dracula family Christmas is all it should be with paper chains, lots of presents and a man-trap for Santa. The family fails to capture him but Little D. insists, as Mum tucks him up in his coffin bed, that they'll get him next year.

The text, however, is only half the book, probably less in strict proportions. Joseph Wright's illustrations carry on their own stories while developing that of the text. Castle Dracula is peopled by tiny weirdos who ride around in the family's carpet slippers; Big D. wears red Y-fronts; the servant doubles as a yard broom, guinea-pig for Igor and coach-horse; the disembodied hand, known as Handy, gets a fingerless glove for Christmas and so on. Splendid! The book needs poring over by small groups who can ooooh! and eurrgh! in delighted horror at such as the Christmas dinner of fingers, ears and a variety of viscera.

Some may see such sadistic/masochistic goings-on as objectionable. For this reader the overall impression was of good-humoured nonsense. Children were keen for them to go on longer and commented only on things nearest to their own experience—food, going to the dentist, Christmas presents. Just as *Fungus the Bogeyman* turns the world upside down, these books leave it a bit bent—but not, I think, twisted.

> *Bob Jay, in a review of "Little Dracula's First*

Bite" and "Little Dracula's Christmas," in Books for Keeps, *No. 41, November, 1986, p. 16.*

The latest intruder on the under-fives' regulation world of pop-up snowmen, peripatetic postmen, complacent cats and arty reworkings of well-worn fairy tales is a vampire. Hard on the heels of Ted Hughes' verse saga of Ffangs the Vampire comes Little Dracula, making his debut in *Little Dracula's First Bite* and *Little Dracula's Christmas*. . . .

There's a whole new family at Castle Dracula obviously bursting to begin a fresh literary career: Big Dracula and Mrs, Baby Millicent, Igor, Batty and Little Dracula himself, whose attempted first bite lands him in the dentist's chair and whose pursuit of Santa Christmas works up a good appetite for Christmas dinner. The pictures are packed with witty detail, the stories vivid and economical; but what makes the two adventures so welcome is the arrival of a new character who isn't just a replica of one of the money-spinning formats in recent children's books.

> *Andrew Clements, in a review of "Little Dracula's First Bite" and "Little Dracula's Christmas," in* New Statesman, *Vol. 112, No. 2906, December 5, 1986, p. 27.*

Our Wild Weekend (1986)

Fifty years ago our parents would have thought Mr. Waddell's teenagers smutty and in some of their conversation it is still a little difficult to decide where precocity ends and prurience begins though charitable—or liberal—minds will recognise it all as a form of healthy irreverence. Whatever it is there is no doubt that it is sharply observed and amusing to a degree. The Albert Memorial School field trip develops into a romp over which the author never loses control. Consequently the adults concerned do not lapse into caricature and the serious sides of life are remembered; in grudging consideration for Mr. Fisher's hopes for one last successful nature walk and in James Espie's discovery of the pleasure of calf-love. There also emerges in Martin Waddell's general attitude a thread of sympathy for the unfairness of life for certain youngsters at certain times and in some inescapable relationships.

> *A. R. Williams, in a review of "Our Wild Weekend," in* The Junior Bookshelf, *Vol. 50, No. 5, October, 1986, p. 194.*

A wicked and, I suspect, perceptive look at what really goes on in the minds and off-duty moments of the children we take on residential visits. Having many times twittered lyrically about the delights of Roman remains and inspirational architecture, I now wonder what the private thoughts were behind the wide, brown eyes and dutifully scratching pencils.

James and his friends are real in their irrepressible youth and vulnerabilities. For older readers this is a must; well-written enough to keep 'us' happy and with romance and rebellion enough to satisfy 'them'.

> *Pam Harwood, in a review of "Our Wild*

Weekend," *in* Books for Keeps, *No. 65, November, 1990, p. 11.*

The Tough Princess (1986)

A handsomely designed book, this nonsexist spoof of the traditional fairy tale has pages that spaciously and artistically accommodate the blocks of clean type and sprightly, colorful pictures [by Patrick Benson] that have wit and vitality—and just occasionally, for contrast, a bit of the macabre. When Princess Rosamund is born to her impoverished parents, they agree to annoy a bad fairy so that their child will go through the usual rescue-by-handsome-prince routine. Alas, our heroine grows up to be very tall, very thin, and very courageous, but not very beautiful or very pitiable. She also slays dragons, knocks the glasses off the Bad Fairy, rescues princes, and bicycles around the kingdom being valiant. When at long last she finds a beautiful prince, fast asleep, she kisses him, he awakens, and they fall in love and live happily ever after.

> *Zena Sutherland, in a review of "The Tough Princess," in* Bulletin of the Center for Children's Books, *Vol. 40, No. 4, December, 1986, p. 78.*

Another modern fairy tale about an assertive female achiever, in this case leavened with the sort of ebullient good humor that sensibly whisks problems away as fast as they arise.

The king and queen, an inept pair whose mismanagement has landed them in a leaky caravan home, are disappointed when their child turns out to be a girl, but " 'Never mind,' said the King, '. . . I will annoy a bad fairy and get the Princess into trouble. Then a handsome prince will rescue her . . .' " But competent bad fairies are rare, and after cheerfully swatting the worst he can find, Rosamund sets off on her bicycle for a brief series of adventures, concluding with waking an enchanted prince with whom she lives happily ever after.

So tongue-in-cheek as to be a parody of its genre, this is satisfactorily amusing, although the outcome is somewhat at odds with the feminist repartee. . . . A jolly romp, this should be useful either as picture book or young reader. (pp. 1863-64)

> *A review of "The Tough Princess," in* Kirkus Reviews, *Vol. LIV, No. 24, December 15, 1986, pp. 1863-64.*

In a now-familiar twist on fairy tales, this describes how Princess Rosamund, a rock 'em, sock 'em gal, resists her parents' plans for her future. When Rosamund is a baby, her father decides to pull a common fairy-tale ploy: he will insult a fairy, who will put a curse on his daughter, and in time a prince will rescue and marry her. The king indeed insults the Bad Fairy, but when she curses Rosamund, the princess decks her. Then Rosamund hops on a bike and takes off on an adventure where she slays dragons, outsmarts a few goblins, and finally finds her own sleeping prince to awaken and marry. The book's one difficulty is all the smashing and bashing that goes on; Rosamund takes on some of the worst characteristics of macho

Waddell with his sons David (left), Peter, Tom, and their dog Fred, 1987.

men. This problem is balanced by the story's humor and a heroine who obviously knows her own mind.

> *Ilene Cooper, in a review of "The Tough Princess," in* Booklist, *Vol. 83, No. 12, February 15, 1987, p. 906.*

Shadows on the Lake (as Catherine Sefton, 1987)

This new adventure story from Catherine Sefton has a convincing, tough and realistic setting in rural Northern Ireland. The teenage first-person narrator, Annie, spends much of the story under a misapprehension and the denouement showing that her older brother is a hero rather than a thief will surprise the reader. The position of the motherless family, working for their landlord, with the oldest son unemployed and moonlighting is well conveyed and many readers will find it oppressive and sad. The absence of hope is marked but this may strike a chord for teenage readers encountering for the first time intractable human problems in their own lives. (pp. 33-4)

> *Celia Gibbs, in a review of "Shadows on the Lake," in* British Book News Children's Books, *March, 1987, pp. 33-4.*

Annie is a robust girl who takes a poor view of capitalists, exploiters, would-be stepmothers, flouncing flirts, bad company of any sort for her brother Baxter: people, however, who fall into these categories may well not be as black as she (the narrator) paints them. She is, after all, an adolescent disturbed by her mother's untimely death, and resentful of the fact that this impending event was kept from her for as long as possible.

Annie's state of mind is crucial to the plot, and so is the failure of everyone in the know in other areas to say what is going on. This is one of those books in which a lot of trouble could have been avoided if various questions had been asked and answered at suitable moments—a "had-I-but-known" adventure transferred from detective to children's fiction. Annie is a girl of good heart, and brave and resourceful to boot. This story by "Catherine Sefton" . . . makes agreeable, undemanding reading.

> *Pat Raine, "Had We But Known," in* The Times Literary Supplement, *No. 4385, April 17, 1987, p. 421.*

I enjoyed this novel set in Northern Ireland. The narrator is thirteen-year-old Annie Orr, practical and organised, holding her family together after the death of her mother.

Annie has some reason to believe her elder brother, Baxter, is a petty thief. . . . Clues that Baxter is not a thief are scattered throughout the story, but Annie in her protective anxiety wilfully ignores them. It all leads to a splendidly exciting climax.

The Northern Ireland background is important in that the reader is shown how people have adjusted to the violent politics they live with and are essentially untouched because these troubles are the stuff of their ordinary lives. So, the tourist cabins by the lake are no longer in demand because visitors are scared. The local RUC sergeant wears a flak jacket as he makes his routine calls. Annie explains that police road blocks are not 'unusual round here, because of the I.R.A.'. There is a map of the locations at the front of the book—a lake and the scattered buildings around its shore. I can never resist a map. I liked checking out the routes of the boat journeys and the scenes of the action. I expect twelve- to fourteen-year-olds will too.

> *Sandra Hann, in a review of "Shadows on the Lake," in* The School Librarian, *Vol. 35, No. 2, May, 1987, p. 159.*

Harriet and the Flying Teachers (1987)

This is the fourth story about Harriet, a well-meaning but accident-prone schoolgirl, so feared by her teachers that they have declared a Harriet-Free Zone around the staffroom, complete with sandbags and barbed wire, and so disliked by her fellow pupils that they have formed an Anti-Harriet League. This time round, the Anti-Harriet League has tricked her into making a special fruit salad for the teachers, and tricked them into eating the salad, in the hope of disposing of them all in one fell swoop. Instead, her alcoholic concoction causes the teachers to fly and the rest of the town of Mitford to behave very oddly indeed. This is a highly entertaining, well-paced story with a most endearing main character. Harriet's adventures should appeal to most eight to eleven year olds with a taste for absurd and comic adventures.

> *Maureen Porter, in a review of "Harriet and the Flying Teachers," in* British Book News Children's Books, *December, 1987, p. 30.*

What Martin Waddell is after with **Harriet and the Flying Teachers** is signalled at once on the first page: "The two girls were standing in the main corridor of Slow Street primary school up against the fence and barbed wire and sandbags that marked the Harriet Free Zone. The zone extended 20 metres on either side of the staff-room, and had been installed by Miss Granston, the headmistress, as a Teacher Protection Measure".

Devotees of the Leavisite approach to literature need read no further. Here we're in the world of *The Beano* and *The Dandy*—of Desperate Dan and Keyhole Kate. Mark Burgess' illustrations catch just the right spirit of frenetic, free-wheeling anarchy as Harriet's contribution to the end-of-term feast gives the teachers a lift—into orbit, pretty nearly. It's all as daft, and endearing, as a favourite comic-strip.

> *Chris Powling, "Adult-Free Zones," in* The

Times Educational Supplement, *No. 3736, February 5, 1988, p. 54.*

Little Dracula at the Seaside (U.S. edition as *Little Dracula at the Seashore*); *Little Dracula Goes to School* (1987)

Waddell and [illustrator Joseph] Wright take youngsters on two wacky excursions into the world of the green-faced, fanged Dracula family. Bats fly freely around Castle Dracula, where Igor bowls with a skeleton head, the children sleep in miniature coffins after downing a comforting bedtime glass of blood and the pet dog is—literally—all bones. In the first volume, this macabre clan visits the seashore, where they cavort underwater and sample such amusements as the house of horrors and the ghost train. The second book describes Little Dracula's first night at school—the Academy for Boys and Ghouls—where his classmates are monsters of all shapes and colors, and lunch consists of eyeballs and slimy green creatures. Though the concept here is one with intrinsic kid appeal, it is Wright's outlandish, detail-packed cartoons that make these titles a monstrous success. Too silly to be truly spooky, this is all good, ghoulish fun.

> *A review of "Little Dracula at the Seashore" and "Little Dracula Goes to School," in* Publishers Weekly, *Vol. 238, No. 54, December 13, 1991, p. 56.*

[**Little Dracula Goes to School**] is essentially a book that attempts to amuse kids by turning their lives upside down to reflect a vampire's similar experiences—he sleeps during the day, goes to school at night, drinks blood instead of water to help him sleep, and is really happy with such gross stuff as eyeballs in the school lunches. The cartoons have lots of silly details, and the humor is about on the level of early *Mad* magazine (well, not quite that good). The only obvious female in the story (aside from the cowering peasants who live around the castle) is Mom Dracula, who wears an apron and carries the baby. Is this bit of fluff worth purchasing? No way!

> *JoAnn Rees, in a review of "Little Dracula Goes to School," in* School Library Journal, *Vol. 38, No. 3, March, 1992, p. 225.*

[In **Little Dracula at the Seashore** the] story line is slight and any humor lies in the busy, cartoon illustrations, which are not for the squeamish; severed lady fingers are topped with "blood clot" ketchup, and Mrs. Dracula empties the brain from a decapitated head into a frying pan for the morning meal. Little Dracula aspires to grow up just as "horrible and nasty and disgusting" as his parents; using this book as a primer will get him started on the right path.

> *Anna DeWind, in a review of "Little Dracula at the Seashore," in* School Library Journal, *Vol. 38, No. 4, April, 1992, p. 101.*

Frankie's Story (as Catherine Sefton, 1988)

Violence erupts like lava through the surface of the everyday in both these books. In Catherine Sefton (Martin Waddell)'s book, it is the familiar violence of Northern Ireland. Familiar from news bulletins, but what do we really know of life for these beleaguered people? Martin Waddell is out to show us teenagers caught in a web of small town malice, sectarian hatred and thwarted Republican politics. It's a tall order to portray flesh and blood people and desperately complex politics in a short, fast-paced novel. In his first of three novels on this theme, *Starry Night,* the politics were off-stage. In *Frankie's Story,* they are centre stage.

Sometimes the explanations, in long soliloquys by Frankie the heroine, don't quite succeed in clarifying the issues, but Martin Waddell makes the reader *feel* the rights and wrongs of the case. We follow her, generous, impulsive, out to save the Protestant boy she has just ditched (no Romeo and Juliet) through clashes with vicious kids, police, Provo block leaders, until branded wrongly as an informer her young life is nearly destroyed by a fire bomb.

All Waddell's skill at character drawing is deployed—lovable unreliable Dad, running from exasperating, understandable Mum, Gerry the sister who nearly became a friend, Kelly the brave Republican, Con the sinister Provo—the town, the book are packed with real people.

> *Robert Leeson, in a review of "Frankie's Story," in* The Times Educational Supplement, *No. 3739, February 26, 1988, p. 25.*

Frankie's story is also Northern Ireland's story. Catherine Sefton bestows on her some of the staple traumas of the teenage novel: an absconding dad, dependent mother and temperamental younger sister. But, from the beginning of the novel, it is clear that these events are only part of a far wider pattern of distress, which inexorably constrains Frankie's life. A realistic mixture of chance happenings, with others deriving directly from Frankie's own fiercely-individualistic character, brand her as a Protestant sympathizer. And, in her own blunt phrase, a tag like this in her tightly-knit Catholic community can lead to '. . . a knee-cap job.' The novel charts a terrifying escalation of violence, from ugly rumours and taunts to actual attack on Frankie, interwoven with the killing of two Provisional IRA men.

The entire story is a forceful demonstration of the power of prejudice to fuel fanaticism and divide a community, a nation. It dramatizes the closed logic which demands a continual spiral of revenge attacks, drawing the reader with Frankie into a world of traps and checks. *Frankie's Story,* told in her own jaunty, disaffected voice, gives life to what is too often a disregarded news story. It will make it harder for any teenage reader to forget the 'war in Britain's backyard.'

> *Caroline Heaton, in a review of "Frankie's Story," in* British Book News Children's Books, *March, 1988, p. 32.*

This powerful story of Northern Ireland is a sequel to *Starry Night,* published in 1986, although it can be read on its own without serious loss.

Frankie is a teenager living on a Catholic estate with the

notorious Hagens for near neighbours and Con, who is not to be trifled with, not far enough away for comfort. Frankie sticks out in this community, not just because she has, rather half-heartedly, a Protestant boy-friend and a father who has broken the pattern by taking up with the lady from the cheese-counter, but because she has a mind of her own. Moreover she has the crippling disadvantage of being able to see all sides of a problem in a community in which blinkers are the order of the day. She fears Con, not simply because his word can decree life or death, but because she understands what makes him tick. Then she has this dangerous habit of social responsibility; when she finds a man apparently dying she calls the police. Such behaviour merits spitting, knee-capping or petrol-bombs. So Frankie makes her bullheaded way through a dangerous world and pays the price of her honesty.

Catherine Sefton (a man, we are told) has the same kind of honesty. In fact, if there is to be a criticism of his novel, author and heroine are too much alike. Frankie may often seem to be the writer's mouthpiece, seeing adult problems in an adult way. But I am not inclined to look for flaws in this book. The subject, and the writer's integrity, are too important for quibbling. *Frankie's Story* is an important reminder of one of the major issues of the day, and it matters that young readers on both sides of the Irish Sea should, like Frankie, see both sides of the problem. Catherine Sefton tells the story briskly, in terse unadorned sentences, building up tension and rising to a disturbing climax. But it is the matter, rather than the manner, of this book which leaves its indelible impression on the reader.

> *M. Crouch, in a review of "Frankie's Story," in* The Junior Bookshelf, *Vol. 52, No. 2, April, 1988, p. 109.*

Alice the Artist (1988)

Alice the Artist is told in the tradition of the mild cautionary tale. The story begins in a cool, spacious studio where Alice is painting a picture. One of her friends arrives with an elephant and suggests that Alice's picture would look better with an elephant in it. And so the story continues with Alice adding something to her painting as each new friend arrives. The ensuing chaos ends with a tiger eating the picture and Alice starting again.

Jonathan Langley's clear, clean illustrations build up the tension and rhythm of the story as Alice's room fills up and the reader wonders what will happen as the next page is turned. A simple, entertaining and funny book for three- to six-year-olds.

> *Helen Cook, in a review of "Alice the Artist," in* British Book News Children's Books, *June, 1988, p. 14.*

When Alice steps back to look with satisfaction at her completed painting, her friends come along offering suggestions for improvement. Alice willingly obliges each of them until her painting is literally eaten by one of the suggestions, a tiger who pronounces it "rotten." Everyone leaves, and Alice once again is inspired to paint, this time resolving to do it her own way. Waddell's clean and simple text is brought to life in Langley's illustrations. . . . The strong tie between the text and the illustrations will guarantee the popularity of this book with young readers. Especially attentive children will notice that Alice's window will clue them in to the next zany addition to come, making **Alice the Artist** all the more fun.

> *Laura McCutcheon, in a review of "Alice the Artist," in* School Library Journal, *Vol. 35, No. 1, September, 1988, p. 175.*

This book hits the nail on the head! Alice, like so many children, has a wonderful idea for a painting but is swayed by her friends to change it and include all their ideas with bizarre results. We travel with her into fantasy as she learns to trust her own judgement and finally returns to paint her original idea. The story works well, touching a chord of self awareness in many. . . .

> *Judith Sharman, in a review of "Alice the Artist," in* Books for Keeps, *No. 59, November, 1989, p. 7.*

Bertie Boggin and the Ghost Again! (as Catherine Sefton, 1988)

Five-year-old Bertie lives in Belfast and enjoys the occasional company of the ghost domiciled in the family coalshed. Pleasant though their friendship is, it puts a certain strain on the boy who, in this second instalment of their adventures together, has to release his invisible friend from a large book in the library and to console it for a cough induced by Mrs. Cafferty's impetuosity with the Hoover. When Bertie's small sister is born the ghost threatens to seek a more peaceful home but he is mollified when he is told (erroneously) that the baby has been christened after his heroine, Florence Nightingale. Told largely in spontaneous, clattering dialogue loosely linked by narrative . . . , the absurd tale goes with a swing.

> *Margery Fisher, in a review of "Bertie Boggin and the Ghost Again!" in* Growing Point, *Vol. 27, No. 4, November, 1988, p. 5078.*

Tales from the Shop That Never Shuts (1988)

The shop is a survival of the past among a clutch of seven houses known as End Cottages in a dead-end round the corner from Dunoon and Killateer on an Irish lough. It is enough of a place to have a football pitch, a pier and a caravan-site—and the village shop run by McGlone's Mammy. McGlone (Mary by baptism) leads a gang comprising wee Biddy O'Hare and Flash and Buster Cook. Mary (McGlone) invents things for them all to do without which, it has to be faced, they might be pretty bored with the holidays and all. The bases of the five incidents or episodes are quite everyday; a treasure hunt based on mistaken data; the search for a monster (misidentified as a result of McGlone's defective eyesight—is there a moral here?); the minding of the shop which arises out of an accident to Wheezy Roberts while mending the roof of same while officially on the sick; and wee Biddy gets lost, but has an unexpectedly exciting birthday. No one is rich here. Per-

haps in their quiet way these are cautionary tales, too, suggesting that even in a settled pattern of living the need for vigilance is always there.

> *A. R. Williams, in a review of "Tales from the Shop That Never Shuts," in* The Junior Bookshelf, *Vol. 52, No. 6, December, 1988, p. 296.*

Five stories depicting the humble delights and tribulations of childhood are told through the gang's conversations and through illustrations [by Maureen Bradley] which snuggle into the warm flow of the narrative.

Although the author succeeds perhaps a little too well in conveying the atmosphere of a quiet place where little changes, this book should provide urban readers with a poignant glimpse of a different and more tranquil world.

> *George Hunt, in a review of "Tales from the Shop That Never Shuts," in* Books for Keeps, *No. 62, May, 1990, p. 13.*

Class Three and the Beanstalk (1988)

The rousing parody in **Class Three and the Beanstalk** is enough to keep a newly fledged reader turning the pages. The class teacher provides Gro-bags for everyone's seeds, but who was it who bought 'Jackson's Giant Beans' which blacked out the room and swept everyone into the sky, where a benevolent giant and his wife gave them eggs stamped 'Laid in Giant Land' and conducted a tour of the wonders of the place before lowering them safely to earth in a bucket? Lively, bizarre drawings confirm the amusing details of an extraordinary episode in an otherwise orderly and ordinary classroom; exaggeration is cleverly controlled in a brief and entertaining book.

> *Margery Fisher, in a review of "Class Three and the Beanstalk," in* Growing Point, *Vol. 27, No. 5, January, 1989, p. 5096.*

Can't You Sleep, Little Bear? (1988)

Martin Waddell and Barbara Firth have created a classic picture book. . . . A familiar situation to many parents is perfectly captured as Little Bear fails to get to sleep because he is afraid of the dark. Each time Big Bear produces a larger lantern until the only solution is to take Little Bear out to look at the moon. The delightful repetition of Big Bear stumbling through his book is yet another felicitous touch in this altogether perfect piece of storytelling.

> *Keith Barker, in a review of "Can't You Sleep, Little Bear?" in* The School Librarian, *Vol. 37, No. 2, May, 1989, p. 56.*

Move over, *Goodnight Moon*. Margaret Wise Brown's enduring bedtime classic may have found a worthy successor in this collaboration by Waddell and Firth. Their gentle story is, in fact, highly reminiscent of Brown at her snug and cozy best. Set in a forest in winter, the tale features a winning bear duo—a great tender-hearted fellow named Big Bear and an exuberant toddler named Little Bear.

Waddell's tranquil tale is perfectly attuned to a child's

need for security and bedtime ritual; combined with Firth's serene watercolors, it's a triumph of genuine affection. Young readers will delight in the text's repetition and revel in the illustrations' warm details—as Big Bear reads in the aptly named Bear Chair (complete with claws and paws), for example, Little Bear can be glimpsed frolicking on his bed. These memorable bruins—worthy companions of Pooh and Paddington—inhabit a sweet, reassuring world that children (and adults) will want to enter again and again.

> *A review of "Can't You Sleep, Little Bear?" in* Publishers Weekly, *Vol. 238, No. 53, December 6, 1991, p. 73.*

This warm, charming look at a small bear's fear of the dark is right on target for the preschool set. . . . Big Bear's compassion for his small charge is most evident in his loving facial expressions and in the warmth of the full-page watercolor and soft pencil illustrations. Blue arched borders around pages showing indoor scenes give the impression of looking into the cave from the dark outside; they provide a clear contrast to the wide-open snowy woodland settings at the book's beginning and end. Little Bear is the epitome of everychild, persistently (but endearingly) pestering for a little more attention and one last hug. The soft banter between the two characters, combined with a touch of repetitive phrasing, add to the book's strong child appeal. It's bound to become a beloved bedtime ritual in many households.

> *Susan Scheps, in a review of "Can't You Sleep, Little Bear?" in* School Library Journal, *Vol. 38, No. 1, January, 1992, p. 100.*

In this comforting story about a big bear trying to help a little bear overcome his fear of the dark, both the affectionate humor and the beguiling variations on a repetitive theme are reminiscent of Minarik's classic *Little Bear* (1957); but this British team gives a fresh flavor to the old formula. For one thing, these bears live in a cave, comfortably furnished but just the site for lurking shadows. Big Bear (who looks like an informally updated version of one of L. Leslie Brooke's amiable Three Bears) is trying to read, but willingly fetches first one and then another and another ever-larger lantern to dispel the dark that troubles the restless little bear; finally, they go into the real dark outside to admire the full moon and Little Bear drifts off to sleep, safe at last in Big Bear's encompassing arms.

Waddell's charming narration has the grace and economy of old nursery tales. Using frames of mellow slate blue, Firth sets her pencil and watercolor illustrations beneath gentle arches that suggest the cave's interior, comfortably accommodating the text among vignettes and larger spreads. As in Brooke's illustrations, there are delightful domestic details to explore, but the bears are best of all. Perfect for bedtime, or anytime.

> *A review of "Can't You Sleep, Little Bear?" in* Kirkus Reviews, *Vol. LX, No. 1, January 1, 1992, p. 58.*

The storytelling is repetitive in a way that seems meant to be cozy but comes across as coy and a bit patronizing. While this pair isn't as engaging as, say, Gabrielle Vincent's Ernest and Celestine (and Little Bear is no *Little Bear*), their sleepytime patter might make for satisfactorily soothing fare. Firth's crayon-and-wash illustrations have a gently lined warmth that nestles dark and light together for a lulling effect.

> *Roger Sutton, in a review of "Can't You Sleep, Little Bear?" in* Bulletin of the Center for Children's Books, *Vol. 45, No. 8, April, 1992, p. 224.*

Great Gran Gorilla and the Robbers   (1988)

These Grans are hilarious. The story opens in the park with the Gran Gang of four getting up to all the antics (mostly forbidden) enjoyed by children of all ages and on motorbikes too! Then the Grans, summoned by "hearing aid", race off on a terrifyingly outrageous motor cycle combination to apprehend some bank robbers. Crash! Yug! Ug! Splatt! The "fierce" miscreants are no match for our battling Grannies led by great Gran Gorilla. The gang reluctantly surrender to this load of old ladies who even at rest in their granny flat are still unconventional and dip their crumpets in beer! Our boys especially loved all the improvised gadgets and laughed at every page. You will all enjoy this story but don't lend it to your Gran, you wouldn't like her getting ideas, or would you? We are all waiting for their next adventure. Excellent for promoting reading confidence!

> *J. C. Haydn-Jones, in a review of "Great Gran Gorilla and the Robbers," in* Books for Your Children, *Vol. 24, No. 2, Summer, 1989, p. 11.*

Owl and Billy and the Space Days   (1988)

A highly amusing and enchantingly written foray back into a world filled with the sunlit innocence of childhood. Billy's half-term stretches out in front of him, seven whole days to play with his friends Owl, Woggly man, Mum and Mr Bennett from the old folks home. It is a big secret between these few friends that Mr Bennett is really a spaceman who receives space messages giving them ideas about what to do each day. Together they, and we, enjoy seven splendid adventures on Moonday, Chooseday, Weddingsday, Fairsday, Pie-day, Sat-on-day and Funday.

A book full of fun which had my six-year-old visitor enthralled and was enormous fun for me as the reader too. The sheer delight in playing with words and the strong repetition made for good reading and very loud joining in!

> *Pam Harwood, in a review of "Owl and Billy and the Space Days," in* Books for Keeps, *No. 59, November, 1989, p. 10.*

The Park in the Dark   (1989)

"Me and Loopy and Little Gee," are the stuffed animals (a monkey, an elephant and a puppy) who make their way to the park each night after their young owner has gone to sleep. Out the window, through alleys, across light-swept streets they travel, and only Little Gee is afraid.

Waddell with illustrator Barbara Firth, who provided the pictures for the "Little Bear" books, at the ceremony for the Children's Book Award, 1989.

And then, the "Thing" comes—a train passing the park—and the three scamper home before first light. The graceful mood of the text contrasts aptly with the playful postures of the toys, who take care of each other like three siblings—the bigger one carries the smaller, and they buck up each other's courage. [Barbara] Firth washes her pictures with soft blues and other dusty colors, rendering each dark corner safe. The abrupt ending feels forced, but that's easily forgiven. These three friends make the nighttime world a welcome place.

> *A review of "The Park in the Dark," in* Publishers Weekly, *Vol. 235, No. 6, February 10, 1989, p. 69.*

A stuffed monkey, a knitted elephant and a toy dog sneak away from their sleeping child for an adventure on the playground. "When the sun goes down / and the moon comes up / and the old swing creaks / in the dark, / that's when we go / to the park, / me and Loopy / and Little Gee, / we three." The streets and trees are full of terrors, all graphically reflected in gray-blue watercolor illustrations with faces in surprising places. Yet there's a safe balance between the scary and the secure. Youngsters will love the glorious swoosh of the friends as they swing up into the night sky and the wild run home as they flee from the THING (a passing train). Rhythmic in verse and art, this has a dream quality with plenty of clearcut action that addresses the fears and fantasies of the very young. (pp. 183-84)

> *Betsy Hearne, in a review of "The Park in the Dark," in* Bulletin of the Center for Children's Books, *Vol. 42, No. 7, March, 1989, pp. 183-84.*

Here is a picture of childhood which is beautiful and true and also accessible. . . . The text has been crafted with much skill, and its repetitions will appeal to the child listener. The softly coloured pictures, very well drawn by Barbara Firth, take the story into a different dimension, expanding the simple narrative with a mass of amusing and appropriate detail. Miss Firth has given the three characters memorable form. 'Me and Loopy and Little Gee' are clearly made of fabric but are still full of life. A lovely book and a sure winner with any child lucky enough to encounter it. (pp. 64-5)

> *M. Crouch, in a review of "The Park in the Dark," in* The Junior Bookshelf, *Vol. 53, No. 2, April, 1989, pp. 64-5.*

A picture book told in rhyme about the adventures of three stuffed animals. . . . The language, while evocative and poetic, could be confusing to children who may not understand ruined mills and "withers that wobble." Children will recognize the depth of the friendship shared by the toy animals, and the protective stance of the largest creature for the smallest. The book succeeds primarily because of its illustrations. It offers a chance to share in the shadows cast in the city by bright moonlight. It's a good choice to share with a fair-sized group of kindergartners or first graders, and a nice addition to nighttime theme books such as Rice's *Goodnight, Goodnight* (Greenwillow, 1980) and Memling's *What's in the Dark?* (Parents, 1971; o.p.)

> *Reva Pitch Margolis, in a review of "The Park in the Dark," in* School Library Journal, *Vol. 35, No. 11, July, 1989, p. 77.*

The Beat of the Drum   (as Catherine Sefton, 1989)

With *The Beat of the Drum,* Martin Waddell . . . completes his trilogy set in divided Northern Ireland. . . .

In this third novel, Brian Hanna, in his wheelchair, crippled and orphaned by an IRA bomb, must make his way through the very heart of the violence.

Immobilized but not helpless, brought up by Auntie Mae, to hate not his attackers but the very senseless hatred that grips both his friends and their enemies, Brian lives a whole life in a matter of hours and days.

We see around him the network of Protestant militancy, the local tear-aways of the Temperance Young Defenders, marching behind the drums, Pastor Martin, thundering God's love from the pulpit, with illegal arms hidden in his mission hall, Val his wide-eyed daughter, pushing Brian in his wheelchair to her secret trysts with forbidden boy friends.

We see the block leaders, other side of the medal to the Provos across the "Divide", cynically organizing a bomb scare to drive out one more Catholic family, leading police and army a devilish dance, while they shift their arms cache. And Hicky, Brian's rootless friend, with his mysterious wads of money, who ends up a corpse in a sack in one of the derelict houses he played in as a kid.

No light read this; the very force with which the author's words strike home, makes the reader feel inside the courage of Brian's final decision to stay on that blighted estate with Auntie Mae and hapless, bigoted Uncle Billy.

As a personal tale, this does not have the subtleties of relationship of the first and second volumes. There is too much to tell, too great an urgency of purpose, for lingering on such matters. The book is a declaration of outrage.

It is full of telling sentences: "It is the beat of fear, but the fear is in the drummer", or "the people who did that to Hicky were probably out in the sunshine with us, licking their ice creams or bouncing their babies".

The author has resolutely completed his aim, to help the teenage reader grasp the reality of Northern Ireland's tragedy. The trilogy is a real contribution to the understanding which must one day bring that suffering to an end.

> *Robert Leeson, in a review of "The Beat of the Drum," in* The Times Educational Supplement, *No, 3801, May 5, 1989, p. B7.*

It is no secret that Catherine Sefton is the serious side of that cheerful writer Martin Waddell. **The Beat of the Drum** is the third of his/her novels about the Troubles in Belfast. (To describe them as a trilogy may be a little misleading; they have a common theme but no common characters.) In this latest book the scene is the Protestant side. The narrator is Brian, a young teenager. Brian's parents were killed in an IRA bomb attack and he was crippled for life. He is perforce a spectator, and this has given him a broader view than is possible for his contemporaries caught up in events. Brian sees all, thinks much, says as little as possible. He has much in common with his Auntie Mae. Uncle Billy long ago surrendered independent thought. 'He's happy with his little house, and our street, and Northern Ireland. He gets very angry with the IRA for trying to blow it all up.'

Situations like that of Belfast produce stereotypes. Most of the characters act as if operated by strings. Even Val, the big clumsy teenage girl who pushes Brian's chair, partly out of the goodness of her simple heart, partly because it gives her the freedom to see her boy-friend, talks like a parrot or an echo of her parson father—'All God-is-Love one minute, and black bitter Protestantism the next.' The one maverick in this community is Hicky, the wild boy who goes his own way and ends up horribly dead. Brian, who has longed to escape from Belfast, gives up this dream. Auntie Mae may tell him 'You don't owe anybody anything', but she is wrong. Brian is responsible, and he is doomed.

There is little comfort in reading **The Beat of the Drum,** except that there are people like Brian. I don't think that mainland children will read it in search of comfort, but to clear their minds. The story is told with relentless power. It portrays no heroes, few villains, many people bound to the wheel of traditional hatreds. It is not easily put out of the mind.

> *M. Crouch, in a review of "The Beat of the Drum," in* The Junior Bookshelf, *Vol. 53, No. 4, August, 1989, p. 193.*

Unlike most teenage fiction dealing with the 'troubles' in Northern Ireland, this splendid novel highlights the divisions and fears within one particular community, here an almost exclusively extreme-Protestant enclave. . . . The book's strength—other than its strong sense of place and atmosphere—lies in its depiction of Brian's maturing process. His initial response is to seek escape from the constraints of Ulster life, but the loss of his girl and the murder of his best friend in a punishment shooting force him to realise that his country, despite the evil being perpetrated there, has given him love and an identity: we leave him accepting that he has a duty to stay and attempt to dilute the hatred and fear so vividly represented in the beat of the Orange drum.

Carole Redford, in a review of "The Beat of the Drum," in The School Librarian, *Vol. 37, No. 3, August, 1989, p. 117.*

Fred the Angel (1989)

A cheerful lightweight frolic. Fred is an apprentice angel. Passing his exams is not too hard, but the practical tests really stretch him—which is what it is all about. Wortsley, Chief Inspector, really puts him through it. Fred's life is not made easier by Basil, the bad brother, whose advice is always persuasively attractive. His help and encouragement come not only from such as Hermoine, 'the loveliest angel of all', but from Sarah, a little girl on earth in whom Fred acquires a guardian role. In the event, all tests passed, it is with Sarah that Fred shares his slice of that special Christmas Birthday cake.

The five chapters are told with quiet good humour. Fred's disasters may have their farcical side, but this is not knockabout comedy, rather character comedy.

M. Crouch, in a review of "Fred the Angel," in The Junior Bookshelf, *Vol. 53, No. 4, August, 1989, p. 182.*

Once There Were Giants (1989)

Giants? No, not really; only adults that seem like giants to a young child growing up in a huge family. This story reads like a reminiscence: a narrator suggests how it might have felt as a small child to always be looking up—or to be the odd one out, usually in some kind of fix. Memories begin with infancy and cover the breadth of childhood and adolescence all the way through to adulthood. Each episode is told economically, while the accompanying pen-and-wash drawings [by Penny Dale] depict the occurrence. The art is relaxed and affectionate; Dale has a good eye for casual family surroundings in which babies and children are loved. A warm recollection that may prompt similar exchanges between readers and their caretakers.

Denise Wilms, in a review of "Once There Were Giants," in Booklist, *Vol. 86, No. 5, November 1, 1989, p. 560.*

Martin Waddell has a fine idea. The baby describes life as she sees it, with her family as giants. As she grows the scale changes. In time she is 'taller than Mum'. Before long she too is a mum, and to her baby she is a giant. The story is told, in a series of family snapshots, with fine economy and with a deceptively simple eloquence, and Penny Dale's lovely watercolours provide just the right support. I would hail the book as an outstanding success but for the nagging doubt about who it is for. The answer, I fancy, must be for parents who will find in its tenderness and gentle humour a confirmation of their own aspirations if not their own experience.

M. Crouch, in a review of "Once There Were Giants," in The Junior Bookshelf, *Vol. 54, No. 2, April, 1990, p. 71.*

Like Martin Waddell's Smarties prizewinner *Can't you* *sleep little bear?* and his Emil winner *The park in the dark,* this has a beguiling lilt. It is also beautifully designed, with a tall narrow picture on the left complementing the full-page one on the right. Penny Dale's illustrations are warm and realistic, and delightfully evocative of family life, whether this is a fight in the kitchen with brother Tom or a run in the park for them all. My only reservation about the book is that the text seems slightly forced into a mould, with no real surprise in the final line on each page. This may however be an adult reaction. There is plenty of interest for reading aloud and sharing with a young child, while the simplicity of the text with its repeated words but underlying sophistication makes it a suitable picture-book reader. What a glimpse of thrilling horizons it provides! (pp. 60-1)

Jennifer Taylor, in a review of "Once There Were Giants," in The School Librarian, *Vol. 38, No. 2, May, 1990, pp. 60-1.*

Judy the Bad Fairy (1989)

Judy is a bone-idle drop-out of a fairy who prefers vegetating in a hammock to meddling in the real world. The Fairy Queen's attempts to start her on a career are greeted with reluctance, and then a crafty enthusiasm which unleashes all manner of strife and carnage, guaranteeing her an early retirement.

The storyline of this book is slight, but entertaining. The vigorous illustrations [by Dom Mansell] provide splendid panoramas of the anarchy created by a very resourceful heroine.

George Hunt, in a review of "Judy the Bad Fairy," in Books for Keeps, *No. 68, May, 1991, p. 11.*

My Great Grandpa (1990)

Whimsical British touches in [Dom] Mansell's scratchy, double-page color illustrations support and broaden this warm intergenerational story. In irregular rhythm, a little girl tells (in rhyme) about her great-grandpa, who "knows things that no one else knows." The youngster takes him for outings in a wheelchair—blue umbrella attached—sometimes when her granny doesn't know. Their favorite destination is his old house, now dilapidated with an overgrown, rubbish-strewn garden. Through this charming story, even children who don't know grandparents and great-grandparents will gain an insight into familial love. The pleasure the old man and the child take in one another is evident throughout. The obvious rhyme can be distracting; however, children involved with the story and the expansive, detailed pictures won't mind.

Virginia Opocensky, in a review of "My Great Grandpa," in School Library Journal, *Vol. 36, No. 3, March, 1990, p. 202.*

Dom Mansell's sympathetic, but unsentimental, illustrations complement Martin Waddell's joyful yet uncompromisingly truthful portrayal of old age. There's a magic here. The special relationship between the old man and his great-granddaughter is delicately drawn, allowing us to share in the clarity of her wisdom. She values him, accepting him as he is and recognising that the quality of his life should not be dismissed because he has moved onto a different phase. From the mouths of babes and Martin Waddell. . . .

> *Judith Sharman, in a review of "My Great Grandpa," in* Books for Keeps, *No. 68, May, 1991, p. 11.*

> My great grandpa is slow . . .
> His eyes are weak and his legs don't go.
> But he knows things that
> no one else knows.

And he shares his secrets with his great granddaughter. She understands him better than anyone else does and going out with him is fun.

Through simple rhythmic text and detailed illustrations, we enter into a small girl's special friendship with her great grandfather. Sad, funny and touching, this story can be enjoyed at many levels. It's the best picture book I've read for a long time.

> *L. Bennett, in a review of "My Great Granpa," in* Books for Your Children, *Vol. 26, No. 2, Summer, 1991, p. 7.*

We Love Them   (1990)

This deceptively simple story possesses a distinctive warmth all its own. A small boy tells of the bond that forms between Ben, the family dog, and Zoe, a lost rabbit that the boy and his sister Becky adopt. Each animal thinks the other is one of its own species: "They didn't know they'd got it wrong. Becky said we wouldn't tell them." One day old Ben dies; the children and their rabbit grieve. A puppy is found in the hay, however, and becomes a loving friend to the threesome—and Zoe thinks the new dog, Little Ben, is a rabbit also. Filled with affectionate details of country life, [Barbara] Firth's pastel-colored washes and Waddell's theme—new bonds forming even in the aftermath of loss—will be a source of comfort. (pp. 60-1)

> *A review of "We Love Them," in* Publishers Weekly, *Vol. 237, No. 13, March 30, 1990, pp. 60-1.*

Author Martin Waddell and illustrator Barbara Firth have produced one of the most delightful picture books I have seen in the last twelve months.

The plot is beautifully simple and easy to read. The text is easy to follow even by the least competent beginner reader. It begs to be read aloud by adult or youngster. The story can be told through the wonderful illustrations without use of the text at all. . . .

It is suitable for the preschool reader beginning to read alone or to have read aloud to them. It would be a worthy addition to library picture book collections.

> *S. D., in a review of "We Love Them," in* Magpies, *Vol. 6, No. 1, March, 1991, p. 25.*

Amy Said   (1990)

A young boy (the narrator) and his older sister, Amy, are having fun at grandmother's house. And why not? When the boy wants to bounce on the bed, Amy tells him to go ahead. She also encourages him to swing on Gran's curtains and write on the walls. As they barrel through the house, wreaking havoc wherever they go, Gran is nowhere to be seen. But when she finally spots them, sweet old Gran lets loose with "That's enough! NO MORE! . . . Please try to be good!" And Amy and her brother do—now that the day is over and it's time for bed. Small watercolors [by Charlotte Voake], outlined in ink, dance across the pages—a fine device for a story with so much action. Though the story goes on a bit long, there's nothing here that listeners won't recognize. Devilish, down-to-earth fun.

> *Ilene Cooper, in a review of "Amy Said," in* Booklist, *Vol. 86, No. 16, April 15, 1990, p. 1640.*

Two preschoolers get into horrendous but perfectly realistic mischief, including swinging on Gran's curtains, drawing on the walls, and picking *all* Gran's flowers—until Gran (whose patience is more than exemplary) finally says, "NO MORE! *Please*," and the kids go peacefully to bed. Voake sketches the miscreants with a delicate innocence that comically belies their antics—a gentle reminder that little children, however naughty, are indeed innocent at heart. Less irrepressible children will regard the many pranks with delighted disapproval, glorying in their own rectitude. A funny and (one hopes) effective lesson by negative example. (pp. 586-87)

> *A review of "Amy Said," in* Kirkus Reviews, *Vol. LVIII, No. 8, April 15, 1990, pp. 586-87.*

A deliciously sly sense of fun pervades the story of an overnight visit to Gran's by a young boy and his older sister, Amy. . . . Half the fun in his book is wondering whether Gran will ever catch on to the children's mischief;

Waddell at an integrated public school in Ballymena, County Antrim, 1990.

the other half is in Voake's understated watercolors, which splendidly convey the exuberance with which young children unwittingly destroy the established sense of order in a household. A book for every child who has said, "I didn't mean to . . . I couldn't help it . . . She said I could!" (pp. 330-31)

> *Ellen Fader, in a review of "Amy Said," in* The Horn Book Magazine, *Vol. LXVI, No. 3, May-June, 1990, pp. 330-31.*

The Hidden House   (1990)

An old man living in a cottage fashions three large wooden dolls to keep him company. One day Bruno leaves and doesn't return. Slowly everything changes. The dolls are mute but interested observers as spiders spin webs and mice scurry around. After many years a man and his family rediscover the hidden house and work to revive it. The man's little girl finds the dolls and carefully repairs them. [Angela] Barrett's watercolors give the book a soft, sweet, almost Victorian look, in keeping with Waddell's simple and charming story. A wry attitude throughout balances realism and fantasy; the print is large and, without compromising the integrity of the story, the vocabulary is simple enough for second graders to handle. In outline it seems like an extremely simple story, but it is handled with wit and delicacy by both the writer and the artist to create a very satisfying whole.

> *Judith Gloyer, in a review of "The Hidden House," in* School Library Journal, *Vol. 36, No. 7, July, 1990, p. 65.*

Here in the words of Martin Waddell is a familiar storyteller's voice, lapsing comfortably into the first person to deliver opinions, shuttling between past and present tenses, directing our eye to elements in the artwork with gentle superiority. Even before we consider the story, we are pleased with the sound of how it's told. Bravo, Martin Waddell. . . .

In a restrained palette of fern, gray, rose, and sepia, Angela Barrett has presented nearly two dozen watercolors of unusual power, all the more striking for the immobility of the central characters. Meticulous endpapers featuring bug and flower initiate the motif of natural growth, the sinuous motion of which provides the story's primary visual movement. The picture of the dolls sitting before the cobwebbed window, one leaning slightly forward with his forehead against the glass, is as moving an individual illustration as we have had for some years. **The Hidden House** is a quiet book, but it will not, I wager, allow itself to be lost or abandoned.

> *Gregory Maguire, in a review of "The Hidden House," in* The Five Owls, *Vol. IV, No. 6, July-August, 1990, p. 105.*

Firstly I feel obliged to say that **The Hidden House** is a beautifully executed picture book. I was seduced by Angela Barrett's sometimes haunting and sometimes extravagant illustrations before I had time to read the text. In this tale of life and death, decay and regeneration, much is inferred. (p. 27)

Dealing as it does with themes of death and regeneration **The Hidden House** is a story rich in symbol, and also richly illustrated. It is indeed a fine picture book with appeal to the aesthetic and the intellect. Highly recommended. (p. 28)

> *Scott Johnston, in a review of "The Hidden House," in* Magpies, *Vol. 6, No. 2, May, 1991, pp. 27-8.*

Rosie's Babies   (1990)

In this picture-story of a little girl, her mother and her toys, Martin Waddell teeters on the brink of banal sentimentality but never falls in. It is an example of controlled brinkmanship which invites admiration. Mother and child talk together. Mother is caring for her baby, and Rosie explains how she too looks after her babies, her Teddy and her Rabbit. All the time the little girl is in fact asserting her own right to a share of mother's attention. The words are few and chosen with a skill which conceals itself. . . . I am not sure for whom the book is intended. Mums will like it. Elder sisters of babies may like to see themselves so accurately portrayed, or they may regard it as an intrusion on their privacy. One can but experiment.

> *M. Crouch, in a review of "Rosie's Babies," in* The Junior Bookshelf, *Vol. 54, No. 4, August, 1990, p. 172.*

Martin Waddell has come up with another strong idea, and, collaborating this time with Penny Dale, produced another classic picture book. Aimed at older toddlers, it shows Rosie claiming her mother's attention with her fantasy world; and while encouraging Rosie with questions her mother is dealing with the practical details of getting baby ready for bed. It has to be said that this is the traditional comfortable middle-class family but that does not detract from the imagination of the illustrations. The format contrasts reality on the left-hand page with fantasy in the full-page illustrations on the righthand side. Rosie's babies are a bear and a rabbit who live in a tree-house, drive cars, like stories and are scared of dogs. (A lively touch is Rosie scaring away a dog larger than herself—a child's-eye view?). Naturally once baby is in bed, Rosie's babies are sleeping too and she wants her mother's attention for herself.

> *Janet Sumner, in a review of "Rosie's Babies," in* The School Librarian, *Vol. 38, No. 4, November, 1990, p. 145.*

Daisy's Christmas   (1990)

An imaginative little girl chooses a different dream each night in the week before Christmas. Sometimes Daisy dreams of going on a journey to Egypt or to outer space; other times she is Noah, a circus performer, or a pirate. But on Christmas Eve, she dreams of Santa arriving with a giant stuffed bear, and that dream comes true. Full-color paint and line illustrations [by Jonathan Langley] show Daisy in her bedroom, which becomes more densely decorated with Christmas trappings as the calendar ticks off the seven days before Christmas. While the story can be complimented for ignoring the hype of the holiday, it lacks sparkle.

Susan Hepler, in a review of "Daisy's Christmas," in School Library Journal, *Vol. 36, No. 10, October, 1990, p. 40.*

Grandma's Bill   (1990)

Martin Waddell has devised a most moving book from the relationship between young and old: I must confess I found tears in my eyes at the end. In response to small Bill's question about her husband's photograph, Grandma goes through her album with him, bringing alive the generations, his grandfather Bill (whom he never knew), their son, young Bill's father, and early pictures of Bill himself, a most natural child who reacts authentically: his incredulity at seeing younger versions of adults, his amusement at old-fashioned clothes and his inability (in Jane Johnson's illustrations) to keep still. Her facial expressions are particularly truthful, especially at the end, when Bill snuggles up uncertainly to his grandmother after learning that big Bill "went away", with "It's all right, isn't it?" and she reassures him.

M. Hobbs, in a review of "Grandma's Bill," in The Junior Bookshelf, *Vol. 55, No. 1, February, 1991, p. 18.*

The subject of this book is safe and familiar: children grow up, marry, have children, become grandparents—the continuity of life, a straightforward picture-story book for the young. So why this lump in the throat? Why this prickling behind the eyes of an experienced, dispassionate book reviewer? Why this urge to share the book with relatives, with children and with colleagues? There is repetition in abundance. Of the ninety-five lines of simple text, thirty-eight end with 'Bill', thirty-six end with 'Grandma', and incidentally, two end with 'wrinkles'. The word 'said' seems to occur in three-quarters of the lines. But such boldness works emphatically and the ordinary and everyday become wonderful as we peer over the sofa and join in Grandma's sharing of her photo album with Bill. Even the simple title could as well refer to the price that's paid as to a person Bill. The clear pictures convey many messages by devices such as the use or absence of firm edges and by unmentioned revelations of the development of characters. The whole book, with its inviting layout, displays consummate artistry, ageless in a life of its own as well as in appeal. It is more than it seems.

Chris Brown, in a review of "Grandma's Bill," in The School Librarian, *Vol. 39, No. 1, February, 1991, p. 21.*

While the sadness is clear, it is dealt with sparingly and as a natural part of the rhythm of life. The elder Bill's participation in a war and his resulting disability is dealt with in equally tactful prose. The role of photographs in preserving precious memories to be passed on to future generations is salient here, as is the familial love. The English setting is often in the foreground, but Johnson's finely detailed watercolors make the characters appear real, al-

though occasionally awkward, mirroring the look of old, posed photographs. The family resemblance carries well through the years, and the overall effect is quaint and warm.

Ruth K. MacDonald, in a review of "Grandma's Bill," in School Library Journal, *Vol. 37, No. 5, May, 1991, p. 85.*

Little Obie and the Flood   (1991)

Don't be misled by large type and the seemingly simple vocabulary. The theme of these four tales involves the larger things of life. A flood sweeps away most of Bailey's Ford. Marty Hansen's Pa is drowned which is why Marty comes to live with Little Obie and his grandparents. She quietly grieves until a pig bites Grandma's ankle and she took to her bed. Marty comes alive and busies herself about the house. When a tree falls on Gerd Weber and crushes his leg Little Obie has to ride the horse to get help. Despite the fact that neither Marty nor Little Obie has any money they manage to make presents for Grandma's birthday.

Life in Cold Creek on the Rock River in the American West is tough and primitive. Scraping a living is hard enough without such disasters as floods and falling trees. Martin Waddell has a magical way with words and it is easy to see what a successful read aloud this little book will provide. The illustrations [by Elsie Lennox] are in pencil with an accuracy and sensitivity to match the text. A gem of a book.

D. A. Young, in a review of "Little Obie and the Flood," in The Junior Bookshelf, *Vol. 55, No. 3, June, 1991, p. 105.*

Life on the generic American frontier, as imagined by a capable, prolific British picture-book author, is dominated by calamities. . . . Pleasant open format and soft pencil drawings signal Wilder territory; but though the relationships are wholesome and the events certainly exciting, there is virtually no sense of real historical time or place here; and, while Waddell is fairly skillful in sprinkling his text with down-homey names and turns of phrase, the American accent is not quite convincing. At best, adequate supplementary reading.

A review of "Little Obie and the Flood," in Kirkus Reviews, *Vol. LX, No. 13, July 1, 1992, p. 856.*

This is a story of quiet, undemonstrative people who work hard and have few possessions, but always have enough to share. In four chapters, the taciturn grandparents, the grief-numbed girl, and the doughty boy become real people whom the reader admires. Elsie Lennox's pen-and-ink sketches are both straightforward and complex, just like the characters Waddell presents. This is an excellent introduction-to-the-novel book for young readers, and the illustrations, large print, and action-filled chapters may attract reluctant older readers too.

Sheilamae O'Hara, in a review of "Little Obie and the Flood," in Booklist, *Vol. 89, No. 1, September 1, 1992, p. 62.*

Squeak-a-Lot (1991)

A bored, lonely little mouse goes out in search of friends, but a bee wants to play "Buzz-a-lot," the dog wants to play "Woof-a-lot," the chicken wants to play "Cluck-a-lot," and the cat wants to play "WHAM! BAM! SCRAM!" The harrassed mouse goes off by himself to play "Squeak-a-lot," and the familiar sound attracts a group of (mice) playmates. After the furry friends exhaust themselves imitating the games the mouse has observed, they engage in "Sleep-a-lot." Although far from a literary masterpiece, this will be high on the child-appeal scale. Youngsters will certainly relate to the idea of searching for compatible friends, and will delight in the animal noises, word play, and visual humor. The simple, understated text borders on the mundane, but is suitable for beginning readers. . . . Not a necessary purchase, but a fun romp.

> *Heide Piehler, in a review of "Squeak-a-Lot," in* School Library Journal, *Vol. 37, No. 6, June, 1991, p. 92.*

A small, small mouse comes out of a small, small house in search of a friend to play with. Mouse doesn't like the suggestions of a bee, a dog, a chicken, not to mention a cat, but they do provide the rodent with some useful ideas for games to play with fellow mice. I can guarantee there will be much squeaking, buzzing, woofing and clucking as young readers join in the games. Variations in the scale of [Virginia Miller's] illustrations and the words are used for dramatic effect and also show how to read the tale. The repeated patterned language of the main text is highlighted against a brown background, and the irresistible animal sounds make this an ideal book for shared reading.

> *Jill Bennett, in a review of "Squeak-a-Lot," in* The School Librarian, *Vol. 39, No. 3, August, 1991, p. 103.*

Let's Go Home, Little Bear (1991)

This is a wonderful picture book with Martin Waddell working his own particular style of magic. The story is simply constructed around two bears walking home through the woods, with the younger one hearing all kinds of worrying sounds that he takes to be mysterious followers. Big bear is sensitive to his fears and eventually carries him back to their warm and safe home. Martin Waddell is a master of the picture book form, knowing when an idea needs repeating, knowing when to push the narrative along, and how to resolve the tensions of the story in a satisfying climax.

> *G. English, in a review of "Let's Go Home, Little Bear," in* Books for Your Children, *Vol. 26, No. 2, Summer, 1991, p. 11.*

This strong yet simple story, beautifully illustrated, is a worthy sequel to the award-winning *Can't you sleep, Little Bear?* . . . Author and artist are in perfect harmony here and both adults and children must surely respond to the enormous overall appeal of this book, from the spoken sound of the 'Plodders and Drippers' to the animals' engaging facial expressions. Highly recommended.

> *Hazel Townson, in a review of "Let's Go Home, Little Bear," in* The School Librarian, *Vol. 39, No. 3, August, 1991, p. 103.*

The Little Bear's fears about sounds and happenings in the snow reflect a young child's fears and imaginings about his surroundings. Likewise his confidence in Big Bear would reflect a child's own feelings about his parents.

The language is simple and repetitive, but this has a resonance which is almost poetic, and timeless. The illustrations contribute greatly to the book's impact; they are in restful pastel shades but full of expression: the starkness of the snow scenes contrasts with the warmth of the pictures of their cave home.

> *S. M. Ashburner, in a review of "Let's go Home, Little Bear," in* The Junior Bookshelf, *Vol. 55, No. 5, October, 1991, p. 210.*

The Toymaker (1991)

Two linked short stories make up this touching picture book. In the first a masterly toymaker makes for his invalid daughter dolls which are models of the children she watches at play through the toyshop window. In the second an old lady takes her little granddaughter for a last visit to the now disused toy-shop, and finds . . . These are gentle stories, lovingly told, appropriately illustrated [by Terry Milne]; they are fairy stories, with a touch of magic. All the elements combine to make this a lovely book to share. Highly recommended.

> *Jo Goodman, in a review of "The Toymaker," in* Magpies, *Vol. 6, No. 5, November, 1991, p. 25.*

The Toymaker has an emotional depth far beyond the smooth coloured toys and the artistically planned shop where they are disposed, not only for customers but also for the entertainment of the owner's daughter Mary, who is too ill to go outside but who can continue a pretence life with dolls made to simulate her old playmates until she is finally allowed to meet them in the street. In the second part of the book the dolls are found in a cupboard by the toymaker's great-grand-daughter and her grandmother; reunited with her former friends, the old lady finds a happy solution to a story which relates past to present and one generation to another subtly, in gentle, rhythmic prose and in finely conceived backgrounds for sharply individualised dolls.

> *Margery Fisher, in a review of "The Toymaker," in* Growing Point, *Vol. 30, No. 5, January, 1992, p. 5625.*

An offbeat and appealing book. . . . Through both words and pictures, the book suggests tender, caring relationships between Mary and her father, her friends, and her granddaughter. The sadness and happiness of the past are intermingled in this quiet, pleasant, but nonessential story. (pp. 86-7)

> *Judy Constantinides, in a review of "The Toymaker," in* School Library Journal, *Vol. 39, No. 1, January, 1993, pp. 86-7.*

Farmer Duck (1991)

Martin Waddell has read *Animal Farm* to some purpose. **Farmer Duck** is no cosy tale of talking animals but a story with a sharp edge to its wit. The farmer stays in bed all day, while the duck does the work, in doors and out. He toils away, bringing sheep from the hills (a distressing sight), chopping logs, washing up and ironing spurred on by a shout of 'How goes the work?' from the bedroom. Karl Marx had a word for this duck. He would have worked himself to death, but the rest of the farmyard had a better idea. After that there is the same amount of work, but the labour is shared. A really good story is told with great precision. For once there is more to a picture-book than the pictures, but these are by Helen Oxenbury who makes a perfect partner for Mr. Waddell—fine drawing, good design, the right blend of drama and humour. It couldn't be better.

> *M. Crouch, in a review of "Farmer Duck," in* The Junior Bookshelf, *Vol. 55, No. 6, December, 1991, p. 246.*

Waddell's uncomplicated story gently encourages readers to recognize and fight injustice. Boldface animal sounds—Quack! Moo! Baa!—pepper the text, infusing it with the energy so appealing to young listeners. The amiable animals in Oxenbury's airy watercolors depict an enormous range of emotion—the duck's droopy feathers and haggard face (complete with bags under his eyes) truly tug at the heartstrings. By book's end, young readers will flap for joy right along with the endearing web-footed hero.

> *A review of "Farmer Duck," in* Publishers Weekly, *Vol. 239, No. 4, January 20, 1992, p. 64.*

The sanctimonious moral of "The Little Red Hen" gets a salutary restructuring here, with the focus on the duck's uncomplaining toil and the other animals' generosity. Waddell's narration is a marvel of simplicity and compact grace; Oxenbury's soft pencil and watercolor illustrations have the comic impact of masterly cartoons, while her sweeping color and light are gloriously evocative of the English farm scene. Like Waddell's *Can't You Sleep, Little Bear?* a book with all the marks of a nursery classic.

> *A review of "Farmer Duck," in* Kirkus Reviews, *Vol. LX, No. 6, March 15, 1992, p. 401.*

The Happy Hedgehog Band (1991)

Young children love sounds and noises and Martin Waddell has capitalised on that in this charming story about a hedgehog percussion band. Each hedgehog's drum makes a different noise, from tum-tum-te-tum to diddle, diddle, dum, and these alliterative phrases are repeated often to give young listeners ample opportunity to join in. Other animals in the wood also want to play in the band, and each is given a task to perform such as hooting, whistling and clapping, so that the story ends in a cacophony of sounds and rhythms. There are lots of opportunities for participation and even for drama, as the theme lends itself well to being acted.

> *Teresa Scragg, in a review of "The Happy Hedgehog Band," in* The School Librarian, *Vol. 40, No. 1, February, 1992, p. 18.*

The theme of the joys of making your own music is secondary to [Jill] Barton's watercolors of the winsome, jubilant musicians. While teachers may find this a good jumping-off point for making music with children, the story lacks rhythm and zing. Bill Staines's *All God's Critters Got a Place in the Choir* (Dutton, 1989) does a better job with the same idea.

> *Susan Hepler, in a review of "The Happy Hedgehog Band," in* School Library Journal, *Vol. 38, No. 6, June, 1992, p. 104.*

Man Mountain (1991)

Oscar and Rose share a common malaise: they are both very lonely. Oscar was the last of the giants back in the era of dinosaurs. His loneliness drove him to lay down and sleep. Over time geological and climatic changes took over and transformed Oscar into a hill and forested part of the landscape; the settlers to the area called the area Man Mountain.

Rose and her grandfather moved into the area, she became bored and lonely and explored the country, particularly the mountain. To her absolute surprise she discovered that the mountain was in fact Oscar who had feelings and a desperate need for companionship.

Simply told and beautifully illustrated by Claudio Muñoz, this picture book will appeal to young readers and evoke discussion about loneliness and, that often things are not what they seem. If we search and reach out we are often surprised by what we discover, often on our own doorsteps.

> *Neil Mackenzie, in a review of "Man Mountain," in* Magpies, *Vol. 7, No. 1, March, 1992, p. 28.*

This has to be another future classic of children's literature for Martin Waddell. It's stunning both visually and in terms of the storyline. To try to describe it would not do it justice. It's one of those books that will be part of anyone who reads it, so that never again will they look at the world around them in quite the same way.

> *Judith Sharman, in a review of "Man Mountain," in* Books for Keeps, *No. 75, July, 1992, p. 9.*

Spotting shapes in the landscape is a favourite game with my children. The shapes on Man Mountain and its amusing place-names—Mouth Cave, Moustache Bushes—are at first the only clues to the fact that the mountain used to be Oscar, the last of the giants, who went to sleep because he was lonely. . . .

This is a delightful book in which each reading reveals something new. Children will have great fun picking out all the bits of Oscar from the landscape. The lively text and sensitive, funny illustrations, provide endless scope for the imagination and offer small children a way of cop-

Waddell at his desk.

ing with the fearsomeness of vast landscapes and the forces of nature.

> *J. A. Tweedie, in a review of "Man Mountain," in* Books for Your Children, *Vol. 27, No. 3, Autumn-Winter, 1992, p. 21.*

Coming Home (1991)

This is a very moving and evocative story about an old man's journey from the United States to Ireland, the land of his birth. He is accompanied by his grandson, Patrick, from whose viewpoint the story is told. Although the account is matter-of-fact, the underlying sadness and homesickness of the old man is vividly conveyed. Initially his grandson sees the holiday merely as adventurous fun, but he comes to understand and appreciate his grandfather's deeper feelings.

The text is simple and the book is in the picture book format. The illustrations [by Neil Reed] form a major part of the book being very realistic, full of relevant detail and showing clearly the contrast between the more opulent American home and its surroundings, and the less affluent Irish homes and their surroundings.

As well as being suitable for pre-school and infant school children to share with a parent, this would be an appropriate book for adult literacy schemes because of the emotional depth of the story.

> *S. M. Ashburner, in a review of "Coming Home," in* The Junior Bookshelf, *Vol. 56, No. 2, April, 1992, p. 58.*

Little Obie and the Kidnap (1991)

In the second of his collections of 'Rock River' stories, Martin Waddell fills in some more of the history of a remote community of the American West. This time the focus is on Mrs. Jumping Joseph, a formidable bear-like woman who lives rough and has no great regard either for her neighbours or for social conventions. Even she has her weakness. When the Cutler children are rescued after the death of their parents, and nobody can think what to do with them, Mrs. Jumping Joseph makes a quick decision. ' "Ain't never had no children . . . Looks like I got some now." ' Ham and Ezekiel do not go short of love, but not everyone is happy about this solution to a social problem. Mrs. Jumping Joseph is loving all right but can she feed the children and teach them manners? Grandad and Effie conspire to steal the Cutlers and civilize them forcibly. It is not an ideal solution, but it serves.

Mr. Waddell handles these four episodes with all his usual assurance. The rough eloquence of Western speech seems to come naturally to him, and he wastes no words. The direct, vigorous narrative, as much as the large print, makes the stories good reading practice. The rough-hewn philosophy behind the simplicity puts this little book well above the 'easy reader' category. (pp. 148-49)

> *M. Crouch, in a review of "Little Obie and the Kidnap," in* The Junior Bookshelf, *Vol. 56, No. 4, August, 1992, pp. 148-49.*

Along a Lonely Road (as Catherine Sefton, 1992)

Here is the antidote to the children's adventure story. 'No nice Uncle Bill to rescue everybody, and no parrot, and no clues on parchments or secret tunnels.' Just bleak terror and helplessness. Catherine Sefton . . . has written powerfully about the IRA, and *Along a lonely road* seems at first to be another of the kind. Before long Ruth, the resourceful fourteen-year-old who tells the story, realises that the action is not developing to type. When she and her family are held as hostages by the unlovely Gettigans on their lonely farm, 'they just didn't *feel* like the IRA . . . the IRA are *ordinary* ones, and the Gettigans were . . . *flash,* him with his yellow shoes and his leather jacket, and her with her made-up face you could leave footprints on if you were a fly.' Not the IRA then, but dangerous, and there are moments of blind fear as well as frustration before the siege of Dooney Farm comes to its dramatic and satisfactory end.

Sefton is highly successful in capturing both the thought and speech of a bright young adolescent and the atmosphere of a promontary at the end of nowhere in Northern Ireland. The setting is vital to the working of the action, which is presented in precise detail (a sketch plan helps) without description ever being allowed to hold up the story. So also with the psychology; we get to know these baddies and goodies, but there is no analysis of character at the expense of action. The writing is crisp and urgent; short sentences and paragraphs mark the moments of greatest crisis. A great adventure story then, though in no way a stereotype one. At the end the reader is left with much to ponder, about human greed, courage and truth to oneself. It is not a story easily forgotten.

> *Marcus Crouch, in a review of "Along a Lonely Road," in* The School Librarian, *Vol. 40, No. 1, February, 1992, p. 33.*

Earlier books by the same author have tended to draw upon the IRA/Loyalist confrontation to salt the story line but *Along a Lonely Road* proves that skilful writing is more than enough to produce a masterpiece of suspense.

Ruth never steps out of her rôle as the 14 year old narrator who shares with the reader her unravelling of the strange events. The arrival of the police and the army are expertly handled and the climax of the attempt by Mrs. Gettigan

to escape with the two young children with a gun held at the head of the youngest is wholly credible.

There are some books that have to be read through at a sitting. *Along the Lonely Road* is just such a one.

> *D. A. Young, in a review of "Along a Lonely Road," in* The Junior Bookshelf, *Vol. 56, No. 2, April, 1992, p. 79.*

Sailor Bear (1992)

With unerring simplicity and grace, the prolific Waddell fashions yet another Distinctive tale for the very young.

The little bear is lost, but he knows what to do: since he's wearing a sailor suit, he'll go to sea. The boats look too big, so he finds himself a piece of a barrel; the sea is enormous, so he scouts out a peaceful stream, but even that grows unexpectedly rough and he capsizes. Wondering what to do next but still unperturbed, he's spotted by a little girl who takes him home. Now he's "found," and again he knows what to do: "he cuddled up . . . and he stayed." The self-reliance and childlike logic of this gentle toy character are truly appealing. [Virginia] Austin's understated rough pencil sketches, enhanced with watercolor, strike just the right note, depicting a storybook world broad enough for an imaginary adventure and cozy enough to come home to. A charming choice for lap or group. (pp. 545-46)

> *A review of "Sailor Bear," in* Kirkus Reviews, *Vol. LX, No. 8, April 15, 1992, pp. 545-46.*

This is a wonderful book to read aloud. Martin Waddell recounts the adventures of Small Bear, who decides to go to sea, in words as rhythmical and satisfying as a poem.

The 5 to 6's at our local school especially loved Virginia Austin's gentle illustrations which capture the mystery and vastness of the world Small Bear discovers, and the comfort of the story's end. A very special and beautifully produced book.

> *H. Trotter, in a review of "Sailor Bear," in* Books for Your Children, *Vol. 27, No. 3, Autumn-Winter, 1992, p. 15.*

Owl Babies (1992)

This simple story pales in comparison to the exceptionally well-crafted illustrations [by Patrick Benson]. Rendered in black ink and watercolor with an abundance of cross-hatching used to show background, shadow, texture, and depth, each stunning woodcutlike panorama fills a double-page spread. Benson has chosen shades of turquoise, pale yellow, and light green for the large-type text in order to avoid detracting from the blue-and-green dominated paintings. Realistic as they appear, the three, fluffy, white baby owls and their mother are infused with distinct personalities. The owlets awaken one night to find their mother gone. Sarah, the largest, reasons that she is out hunting for food. Mid-sized Percy tends to agree, while tiny Bill will only repeat, "I want my mommy!" Mom, just out for a night flight, does return, of course, and her fledglings are delighted to see her. The repetition just doesn't work. The plot is too meager, the text too unexciting. Hutchins's *Good Night Owl* (Macmillan, 1991), Thaler's *Owly* (HarperCollins, 1982), and Yolen's *Owl Moon* (Philomel, 1987) are all better stories for preschoolers. Simple, well-written books about mother love and reassurance for this age group are abundant.

> *Susan Scheps, in a review of "Owl Babies," in* School Library Journal, *Vol. 38, No. 12, December, 1992, p. 93.*

Sam Vole and His Brothers (1992)

This book is noteworthy not only for its elegant little narrative and its superb illustrations [by Barbara Firth] but also for the coining of the verb 'to vole' which will always have for me an exact connotation. It means to explore, search and acquire in ways peculiar to voles but applicable to all other species including humans. Young Sam Vole becomes tired of voling with his brothers so goes voling by himself. He likes it at first: then he wishes his brothers were with him. Finally he meets them and they all go home. That's all. But Martin Waddell's sure touch, with its sensitive rhythms and repetitions, make this a reverberating story; and Barbara Firth's illustrations, in which the individualistic voles inhabit a world of extraordinary plenitude, complement it entirely satisfyingly.

> *Dennis Hamley, in a review of "Sam Vole and His Brothers," in* The School Librarian, *Vol. 40, No. 4, November, 1992, p. 143.*

Many picture books focus on the problem of older children who must put up with tagalong younger siblings. This one tells of a young fieldmouse who would like to do things without older brothers hovering about, doing everything better than he does and diminishing his sense of accomplishment. Early one morning he slips out to the meadow alone and has a terrific time. But, little by little, he begins to miss them. Sharp-eyed youngsters will spot them lingering nearby in the foliage. They have a joyous reunion and take home a rich bounty of nuts and fruits and a special feather for their mother. Waddell's story pleasantly presents the subtle shades of emotions among siblings.

> *Judith Gloyer, in a review of "Sam Vole and His Brothers," in* School Library Journal, *Vol. 39, No. 1, January, 1993, p. 86.*

Children's
Literature
Review

CUMULATIVE INDEX TO AUTHORS

This index lists all author entries in *Children's Literature Review* and includes cross-references to them in other Gale sources. References in the index are identified as follows:

AAYA: *Authors & Artists for Young Adults* Volumes 1-9
CA: *Contemporary Authors* (original series), Volumes 1-138
CAAS: *Contemporary Authors Autobiography Series*, Volumes 1-16
CABS: *Contemporary Authors Bibliographical Series*, Volumes 1-3
CANR: *Contemporary Authors New Revision Series*, Volumes 1-39
CAP: *Contemporary Authors Permanent Series*, Volumes 1-2
CA-R: *Contemporary Authors* (first revision), Volumes 1-44
CDALB: *Concise Dictionary of American Literary Biography*, Volumes 1-6
CLC: *Contemporary Literary Criticism*, Volumes 1-76
CLR: *Children's Literature Review*, Volumes 1-31
CMLC: *Classical and Medieval Literature Criticism*, Volumes 1-10
DC: *Drama Criticism*, Volumes 1-3
DLB: *Dictionary of Literary Biography*, Volumes 1-121
DLB-DS: *Dictionary of Literary Biography Documentary Series*, Volumes 1-9
DLB-Y: *Dictionary of Literary Biography Yearbook*, Volumes 1980-1991
LC: *Literature Criticism from 1400 to 1800*, Volumes 1-22
NCLC: *Nineteenth-Century Literature Criticism*, Volumes 1-39
PC: *Poetry Criticism*, Volumes 1-6
SAAS: *Something about the Author Autobiography Series*, Volumes 1-14
SATA: *Something about the Author*, Volumes 1-71
SSC: *Short Story Criticism*, Volumes 1-11
TCLC: *Twentieth-Century Literary Criticism*, Volumes 1-49
YABC: *Yesterday's Authors of Books for Children*, Volumes 1-2

Author Index

CUMULATIVE INDEX TO NATIONALITIES

Nationality Index

Seredy, Kate　**10**

INDIAN
Mukerji, Dhan Gopal　**10**

IRISH
Bunting, Eve　**28**
Dillon, Eilis　**26**
Lewis, C. S.　**3, 27**
O'Shea, Pat　**18**
Waddell, Martin　**31**

ISRAELI
Ofek, Uriel　**28**
Orlev, Uri　**30**
Shulevitz, Uri　**5**

ITALIAN
Collodi, Carlo　**5**
Munari, Bruno　**9**
Rodari, Gianni　**24**
Ventura, Piero　**16**

JAMAICAN
Berry, James　**22**

JAPANESE
Anno, Mitsumasa　**2, 14**
Iwasaki, Chihiro　**18**
Maruki, Toshi　**19**
Nakatani, Chiyoko　**30**
Say, Allen　**22**
Tejima　**20**
Watanabe, Shigeo　**8**
Yashima, Taro　**4**

NEW ZEALAND
Mahy, Margaret　**7**

NIGERIAN
Achebe, Chinua　**20**

NORWEGIAN
d'Aulaire, Ingri　**21**
Proysen, Alf　**24**

POLISH
Hautzig, Esther R.　**22**
Janosch　**26**
Orlev, Uri　**30**
Pienkowski, Jan　**6**
Shulevitz, Uri　**5**
Singer, Isaac Bashevis　**1**
Suhl, Yuri　**2**
Wojciechowska, Maia　**1**

RUSSIAN
Korinetz, Yuri　**4**

SCOTTISH
Bannerman, Helen　**21**
Barrie, J. M.　**16**
Burnford, Sheila　**2**
Hunter, Mollie　**25**
Stevenson, Robert Louis　**10, 11**

SOUTH AFRICAN
Gordon, Sheila　**27**
Lewin, Hugh　**9**
Naiddoo, Beverley　**29**

SOUTH AMERICAN
Breinburg, Petronella　**31**

SPANISH
Sanchez-Silva, Jose Maria　**12**

SWEDISH
Beckman, Gunnel　**25**
Beskow, Elsa　**17**
Bjork, Christina　**22**
Gripe, Maria　**5**
Lagerlof, Selma　**7**
Lindgren, Astrid　**1**
Lindgren, Barbro　**20**

SWISS
d'Aulaire, Edgar Parin　**21**
Duvoisin, Roger　**23**
Spyri, Johanna　**13**

THAI
Ho, Minfong　**28**

WELSH
Dahl, Roald　**1, 7**

WEST INDIAN
Guy, Rosa　**13**

Nationality Index

CUMULATIVE INDEX TO TITLES

Title Index

Title Index

Title Index

How Droofus the Dragon Lost His Head (Peet) **12**:201

How God Fix Jonah (Graham) **10**:104

How Green You Are! (Doherty) **21**:55

How Heredity Works: Why Living Things Are as They Are (Bendick) **5**:47

How, Hippo! (Brown) **12**:104

How I Came to Be a Writer (Naylor) **17**:53

How Insects Communicate (Patent) **19**:149

How It Feels When a Parent Dies (Krementz) **5**:155

How Lazy Can You Get? (Naylor) **17**:54

How Life Began (Adler) **27**:8

How Life Began: Creation versus Evolution (Gallant) **30**:92

How Many Days to America? A Thanksgiving Story (Bunting) **28**:62

How Many Miles to Babylon? (Fox) **1**:77

How Many Teeth? (Showers) **6**:242

How Much and How Many: The Story of Weights and Measures (Bendick) **5**:35

How Pizza Came to Queens (Khalsa) **30**:149

How Pizza Come to Our Town (Khalsa) **30**:149

How Puppies Grow (Selsam) **1**:163

How Rabbit Tricked His Friends (Tresselt) **30**:211

How Santa Claus Had a Long and Difficult Journey Delivering His Presents (Krahn) **3**:104

How Summer Came to Canada (Cleaver) **13**:65

How the Doctor Knows You're Fine (Cobb) **2**:65

How the Grinch Stole Christmas (Seuss) **1**:86; **9**:184

How the Leopard Got His Skin (Achebe) **20**:8

How the Reindeer Saved Santa (Haywood) **22**:105

How the Whale Became (Hughes) **3**:92

How to Be a Hero (Weiss) **4**:225

How to Be a Space Scientist in Your Own Home (Simon) **9**:218

How to Be an Inventor (Weiss) **4**:230

How to Behave and Why (Leaf) **25**:129

How to Eat Fried Worms (Rockwell) **6**:236

How to Eat Fried Worms and Other Plays (Rockwell) **6**:239

How to Make a Cloud (Bendick) **5**:44

How to Make Your Own Books (Weiss) **4**:227

How to Make Your Own Movies: An Introduction to Filmmaking (Weiss) **4**:227

How to Read a Rabbit (Fritz) **14**:112

How to Run a Railroad: Everything You Need to Know about Model Trains (Weiss) **4**:228

How Tom Beat Captain Najork and His Hired Sportsmen (Blake) **31**:19

How Tom Beat Captain Najork and His Hired Sportsmen (Hoban) **3**:78

How We Found Out about Vitamins (Asimov) **12**:51

How We Got Our First Cat (Tobias) **4**:218

How You Talk (Showers) **6**:242

How Your Mother and Father Met, and What Happened After (Tobias) **4**:217

Howard (Stevenson) **17**:156

Howliday Inn (Howe) **9**:58

Howl's Moving Castle (Jones) **23**:195

Hubert's Hair-Raising Adventure (Peet) **12**:193

Hug Me (Stren) **5**:230

Huge Harold (Peet) **12**:194

Hugo (Gripe) **5**:142

Hugo and Josephine (Gripe) **5**:143

Hugo och Josefin (Gripe) **5**:143

The Hullabaloo ABC (Cleary) **2**:47

The Human Body: Its Structure and Operation (Asimov) **12**:37

Human Nature-Animal Nature: The Biology of Human Behavior (Cohen) **3**:40

The Human Rights Book (Meltzer) **13**:140

Humbert, Mister Firkin, and the Lord Mayor of London (Burningham) **9**:40

Humbug Mountain (Fleischman) **15**:109

Humphrey: One Hundred Years along the Wayside with a Box Turtle (Flack) **28**:123

Hunches in Bunches (Seuss) **9**:194

Der Hund Herr Mumueller (Heine) **18**:145

The Hundred Islands (Clark) **30**:61

A Hundred Million Francs (Berna) **19**:33

The Hundred Penny Box (Mathis) **3**:149

The Hundredth Dove and Other Tales (Yolen) **4**:264

Hungarian Folk-Tales (Biro) **28**:34

Hunted in Their Own Land (Chauncy) **6**:92

Hunted Like a Wolf: The Story of the Seminole War (Meltzer) **13**:129

Hunted Mammals of the Sea (McClung) **11**:191

The Hunter and the Animals: A Wordless Picture Book (dePaola) **24**:89

Hunter in the Dark (Hughes) **9**:74

Hunters and the Hunted: Surviving in the Animal World (Patent) **19**:156

The Hunting of the Snark: An Agony in Eight Fits (Carroll) **2**:34

The Hurdy-Gurdy Man (Bianco) **19**:53

Hurrah, We're Outward Bound! (Spier) **5**:219

Hurricane Guest (Epstein and Epstein) **26**:59

Hurricane Watch (Branley) **13**:51

Hurricanes and Twisters (Adler) **27**:6

Hurry Home, Candy (DeJong) **1**:58

I, Adam (Fritz) **2**:81

I Am a Clown (Bruna) **7**:52

I Am a Hunter (Mayer) **11**:165

I Am a Man: Ode to Martin Luther King, Jr. (Merriam) **14**:197

I Am Papa Snap and These Are My Favorite No Such Stories (Ungerer) **3**:201

I Am Phoenix: Poems for Two Voices (Fleischman) **20**:67

I Am the Cheese (Cormier) **12**:139

I Am the Running Girl (Adoff) **7**:35

I Can (Oxenbury) **22**:147

I Can Build a House! (Watanabe) **8**:217

I Can--Can You? (Parish) **22**:165

I Can Count More (Bruna) **7**:51

I Can Do It! (Watanabe) **8**:217

I Can Read (Bruna) **7**:50

I Can Ride It! Setting Goals (Watanabe) **8**:217

I Can Take a Walk! (Watanabe) **8**:217

I Can't Stand Losing You (Kemp) **29**:123

I Don't Live Here! (Conrad) **18**:86

I Feel the Same Way (Moore) **15**:141

I Go by Sea, I Go by Land (Travers) **2**:178

I grandi pittori (Ventura) **16**:197

I Had Trouble in Getting to Solla Sollew (Seuss) **9**:189

I Hate You, I Hate You (Leaf) **25**:135

I Have Four Names for My Grandfather (Lasky) **11**:114

I Have to Go! (Munsch) **19**:145

I Hear (Oxenbury) **22**:147

I, Houdini: The Autobiography of a Self-Educated Hamster (Reid Banks) **24**:193

I Klockornas Tid (Gripe) **5**:145

I Know What You Did Last Summer (Duncan) **29**:70

I Like Old Clothes (Hoberman) **22**:112

I Like Winter (Lenski) **26**:115

I Love My Mother (Zindel) **3**:248

I Love You, Stupid! (Mazer) **16**:131

I Met a Man (Ciardi) **19**:76

I, Momolu (Graham) **10**:106

I Need a Lunch Box (Caines) **24**:64

I Never Asked You to Understand Me (DeClements) **23**:36

I Never Loved Your Mind (Zindel) **3**:248

I Own the Racecourse! (Wrightson) **4**:242

I Read Signs (Hoban) **13**:107

I Read Symbols (Hoban) **13**:107

I Saw the Sea Come In (Tresselt) **30**:205

I See (Oxenbury) **22**:147

I See a Song (Carle) **10**:76

I See What I See! (Selden) **8**:197

I Sing the Song of Myself: An Anthology of Autobiographical Poems (Kherdian) **24**:109

I Stay Near You: One Story in Three (Kerr) **29**:155

I Thought I Heard the City (Moore) **15**:142

I Touch (Oxenbury) **22**:147

I, Trissy (Mazer) **23**:221

I Walk and Read (Hoban) **13**:108

I Want a Dog (Khalsa) **30**:146

I Want to Go Home! (Korman) **25**:106

I Want to Stay Here! I Want to Go There! A Flea Story (Lionni) **7**:137

I Was Born in a Tree and Raised by Bees (Arnosky) **15**:2

I Was There (Richter) **21**:189

I Wear the Morning Star (Highwater) **17**:32

I Went for a Walk (Lenski) **26**:120

I Wish That I Had Duck Feet (Seuss) **1**:87; **9**:189

I Would Rather Be a Turnip (Cleaver and Cleaver) **6**:106

The Ice Ghosts Mystery (Curry) **31**:77

The Ice Is Coming (Wrightson) **4**:245

If All the Swords in England (Willard) **2**:219

If Dragon Flies Made Honey: Poems (Kherdian) **24**:108

If I Asked You, Would You Stay? (Bunting) **28**:56

If I Had... (Mayer) **11**:164

If I Had My Way (Klein) **2**:98

If I Love You, Am I Trapped Forever? (Kerr) **29**:144

If I Owned a Candy Factory (Stevenson) **17**:152

If I Ran the Circus (Seuss) **1**:87; **9**:181

If I Ran the Zoo (Seuss) **1**:87; **9**:178

If It Weren't for You (Zolotow) **2**:234

If Only I Could Tell You: Poems for Young Lovers and Dreamers (Merriam) **14**:201

If the Earth Falls In (Clark) **30**:61

If This Is Love, I'll Take Spaghetti (Conford) **10**:98

If Wishes Were Horses and Other Rhymes from Mother Goose (Jeffers) **30**:133

If You Say So, Claude (Nixon) **24**:141

If You Were a Writer (Nixon) **24**:151

Iggie's House (Blume) **2**:17

Ik ben een clown (Bruna) **7**:52

Ik kan lezen (Bruna) **7**:50

Title Index

Title Index

Title Index

Title Index

ISBN 0-8103-5704-6